Healthy Helpings

Healthy Helpings

800 FAST AND FABULOUS RECIPES
FOR THE KOSHER (OR NOT) COOK

Norene Gilletz

whitecap

Food Photography:	Perry Beaton
Author Photograph:	Soly Zamir
Cover Design:	Blue Mammoth Design
Tableware and Accessories:	Genin Trudeau USA
	Amyot & Watt Ltd.
	La Mesa
Selected Pottery:	The late Marilyn Levitt

Library and Archives Canada Cataloguing in Publication

Gilletz, Norene
    Healthy helpings / Norene Gilletz.

Includes index.
Previous versions of this book published in Canada under title:
    MealLeaniYumm!
ISBN 1-55285-788-3

    1. Cookery. 2. Nutrition. 3. Low-calorie diet—Recipes.
4. Cookery, Jewish. I. Gilletz, Norene MealLeaniYumm! II. Title.

RM237.7.G544 2006   641.5'63   C2005-906774-8

The publisher acknowledges the support of the Canada Council for
the Arts and the Cultural Services Branch of the Government of British
Columbia for our publishing program. We acknowledge the financial
support of the Government of Canada through the Book Publishing
Industry Development Program for our publishing activities.

Printed in Canada

Dedication

Healthy Helpings is dedicated to my first granddaughter, Alexandra Lauren Sprackman, who helped me test carrot soup when she was just four days old. When I tried to explain to Lauren what light cooking is all about, she just blinked as if to say "The only problem with all this 'light' in the kitchen is that it makes it hard for me to keep my eyes open!"

Healthy Helpings is also dedicated to the memory of my grandmothers, Doba Rykiss and Masha Winer, who gave me many of my first taste memories. And this book is for my mother, Belle Rykiss, who taught me that food is not only for survival, it's a special way to show love and caring for your family. You taught me well, Mom!

To my children, Jodi, Steven and Douglas, their families and all their future generations, I wish them all light years ahead!

Contents

Foreword

I was delighted when Norene Gilletz asked me to write the foreword for her cookbook *Healthy Helpings*. Her three previous books have been the mainstays of my cookbook collection. When I got married, I received *Second Helpings Please!* Dog-eared and food-stained, it still sits with dignity on my cookbook shelf, along with *The Pleasures of Your Food Processor* and *MicroWays*.

Both originally from Winnipeg, Norene and I met some twenty years ago in Montreal. Even back then, Norene's cooking classes displayed her enormous creativity and flexibility. Anyone who turns on an oven, flips a food processor switch, or presses a button on the microwave can benefit from Norene's practical, lighthearted approach to food.

Although Norene and I have been acquainted for a long time, our relationship has really grown during the past few years. Her newest cookbook was usually the topic of our conversation. Painstakingly, she researched, checked, double-checked and triple-checked all of the recipes and information included in this book. We talked extensively about nutrition because Norene wanted her book to be as precise as possible. I know that she worked through many a night verifying the food analyses, using the latest and most accurate nutritional data.

As someone who has had the opportunity to read through *Healthy Helpings* and try a number of recipes, I have something to tell you—you're about to be introduced to a wonderful culinary experience! Norene's recipes are delicious, easy to follow and appeal to both the eye and palate. She has bridged the gap between good taste and good health. Norene has cleverly adapted her recipes to reflect current nutritional recommendations, increasing the fiber and lowering the fat and sodium content. That's a winning combination!

Norene's personality shines through in her warm and easy writing style. She shares her excitement and love of good food with her readers, inspiring them to explore new, healthier cooking techniques and food styles. You'll feel as if Norene is standing right beside you as you cook, answering your questions and leading the way to new and flavorful food adventures.

As a dietitian, and more important, as a friend, I commend Norene Gilletz on her wonderful new achievement, *Healthy Helpings*—a cookbook for now and for the future.

Ilene Gilbert
Professional Dietitian

Acknowledgments

Healthy Helpings is a collection of recipes, tricks and techniques from so many people that it is virtually impossible to name them all. Thank you to everyone who helped in any way, from sharing recipes, testing, tasting, proofreading, or just being there when I needed someone to listen. These very special people were outstanding in their support. I couldn't have done this book without them.

A big thank you goes to my devoted friend and assistant, Doris Fink. She was always there when I needed her, as only a true friend could be! She shopped, schlepped, tested and proofread. Doris also assisted with props and food styling for the food photography. She encouraged me to go for long walks with her when my body and brain were in conflict. If it weren't for Doris' friendship, support and nagging (even long distance!) this cookbook might never have been written!

Next, special thanks go to my dear friend Cathy Ternan, my exercise buddy and sounding board, for her research, proofreading, organizing and sensible suggestions. She made sure that Marten Ternan woke me up early to exercise! Most important of all, she encouraged me by saying "Go for it!"

There is no way I can ever thank Gloria Schachter, who started off as my student, volunteered to be a proofreader, but became so much more. Gloria was so focused on helping me complete this book that she became my "Miss Picky." She checked (and rechecked!) even the smallest detail. Many times when I couldn't find the necessary word or phrase, Gloria knew exactly what I wanted to say and magically provided the words I needed. Her caring, encouragement and dedication were beyond all expectations. She is a very special person and friend.

When I moved to Toronto, Nancy Gordon provided many creative ideas and willingly tested recipes. Her skills were a great asset. Elaine Kaplan was like a gift from heaven. She jumped right in to help complete and edit the final manuscript. Her positive attitude, organization and suggestions were just what I needed to reach the finish line! Dedicated Devah Wine completed our "dream team" as a proofreader. We all bonded quickly, working together as if we had been doing it for years!

Thanks go to Margie Feder, Christine Balit, Marty Lesser and Alexia Ryan for proofreading. Carly Gordon helped with data input. Liane Segal kept me "well-balanced." Rosie and Howard Krakower upgraded my word processing skills.

My longtime and creative friend, Roslyn Brown, shared many wonderful recipes with me. She's been beside me through thick and thin (literally!) and was a source of encouragement and ideas.

The residents of Manoir Montefiore, a Kosher senior residence in Montreal where I was the food and menu consultant, shared many taste memories with me. Special thanks to the cooks and staff for their creative, innovative ideas. My colleague, Hershel Schecter, Kashrut supervisor, answered my Kosher culinary queries. He expanded my knowledge of Jewish food traditions so I could update them into nutritious dishes for today's health conscious eaters plus future generations to enjoy.

Ilene Gilbert, my friendly dietician, was invaluable in providing expert nutritional information and advice. Ilene taught me that the most important thing of all in weight management is to get right back on track (and on the track!) after my little "vacations" from food sanity. Exercise is a necessary "ingredient" for my weight control because I have to balance all the tasting that's required in my work with physical activity.

The support staff at ESHA Research in Salem, Oregon was most helpful in providing nutritional information for the analysis of my recipes. They always did their best to find the answers for missing or complicated data and were supportive through very difficult periods.

How can I ever thank my fabulous family? My dear sister Rhonda listened when I needed a sounding board or logical advice. She encouraged me when I became frustrated and her love, support and caring (plus a few lectures) got me through many difficult moments. Thanks, Sis, you're the best!

My Mom, Belle Rykiss, an outstanding, creative cook (and my first cooking teacher), shared her recipes, techniques and low-fat culinary discoveries with me (long distance)! She helped shape this cookbook in so many ways, as only a mother can. There's no one like my Mom!

My children, Jodi and Paul Sprackman, Steven and Cheryl Gilletz, Douglas and Ariane Gilletz, are a constant source of encouragement, advice and support. They were always there whenever I needed them, and I am very proud of them all. Each one of them is "my favorite" in their own special way. Cook well, eat well, be well!

A big "thank you" to Soly Zamir, who was an integral part of my team in producing this book. He solved computer problems, entered data for nutritional analysis, screened phone calls, schlepped groceries and tested recipes. He encouraged me to continue when I was "fed up" with the workload and had unbelievable patience when I was cranky and exhausted. Soly kept everyone's coffee cup filled throughout the editing and proofreading of the book. *Todah Rabah.*

My assistant Shirley Millett worked tirelessly by my side, keeping me organized and focused. Her commitment, dedication and friendship are invaluable and her attention to details helps keep me on my toes!

And last but not least, a big thanks goes to my wonderful students! Their questions and comments kept me focused on what people want and need to know in today's kitchen. I hope this collection of recipes inspires them to establish new traditions and taste memories for future generations to come. Enjoy in good health!

About the Nutritional Analysis

The nutritional analysis was done using The Food Processor Plus® (Version 6.20) from ESHA Research, Salem, Oregon. The analysis was based on the following guidelines:

- The smaller number of servings was analyzed when there was a range (e.g., "4 to 6 servings" was analyzed for 4 servings).
- The analysis of ingredients was based on Imperial weights and measures (e.g., 1 cup, 1 pound).
- The first ingredient listed was analyzed when there was a choice of ingredients: (e.g., "1 cup of non-fat or low-fat yogurt" was analyzed for non-fat yogurt; 1 cup of skim milk or orange juice was analyzed for skim milk).
- The smaller measure of an ingredient was analyzed when a range was given ("1/4 to 1/3 cup" was analyzed for 1/4 cup).
- When analysing the serving size, 1 tablespoon was analyzed as 15 grams and 1/4 cup as 60 grams.
- Canola and olive oils were my oils of choice. Fleischmann's unsalted pareve tub margarine, which contains no dairy products, was the margarine of choice because of dairy-free, vegetarian and Kosher considerations. There are also excellent brands of dairy margarine available (e.g. Becel).
- Skim milk, non-fat yogurt and cottage cheese were the products of choice throughout, unless otherwise indicated. However, if feeding young children, be flexible. They eat small amounts, but need their calories to develop and grow, so use whole, 2% (or 1%) milk products for them. Ask your pediatrician or dietician for guidance.
- When chicken or vegetable broth is called for, the analysis was done with fat-free canned chicken or vegetable broth. Homemade broth is a better choice because it is lower in sodium, but it's not always handy. Instant chicken-flavored soup mix (pareve) plus water can be substituted.
- When cream cheese is called for, the analysis was done using low-fat (light) cream cheese. You can substitute firm Yogurt Cheese (p. 53) or non-fat pressed (dry) cottage cheese.
- Specific measurements of salt (e.g., 1/2 teaspoon salt) were included in the analysis, but "salt to taste" was not. Use the minimum amount of salt suitable for your palate and specific health concerns, or use a salt substitute if you prefer.
- Optional ingredients and garnishes in unspecified amounts were not calculated.
- Variations of a recipe were not always analyzed for nutrients due to space constraints. I like to offer variations of a recipe to allow for different tastes and availability of ingredients.
- With the exception of fat, all other nutrient values have been rounded off to the nearest whole number (e.g., 2.6 grams protein was rounded off to 3 grams, 2.4 grams was rounded off to 2 grams).
- With the exception of fat, all other nutrient values less than 0.5 are shown as "trace" (e.g., 0.4 grams fiber is shown as "trace fiber").
- Non-zero values higher than 0.5 but less than 1 gram are shown as <1 (e.g., 0.6 grams carbohydrate is shown as <1 gram carbohydrate).
- For fat, nutrient values have not been rounded off.
- When cooked dried legumes, pasta and/or rice were called for, the analysis was done as if they were not prepared with salt.
- A serving of at least 2 grams of fiber is considered a moderate source. A serving of 4 grams of fiber is a high source, and 6 grams of dietary fiber is considered a very high source.

Introduction

You don't have to be Jewish to enjoy the 800 fast, fabulous and healthy recipes in *Healthy Helpings*. You'll discover low-fat, high flavor dishes that are great for anyone with health and weight concerns, or those who couldn't care less but just love good food!

Even with today's busy lifestyle, it's easy to serve healthy, "heart-y" helpings to family and friends. You'll learn how to prepare simply irresistible meals that appeal to both the eye and the palate. There are dairy-free and vegetarian options for those who are lactose intolerant, as well as simple, yummy dishes that even kids will love. *Healthy Helpings* is an excellent resource for cardiac patients, weight-watchers, diabetics, or anyone who wants to eat healthy, delicious meals.

Tradition . . . Tradition! Old-world foods, readily available ingredients and new flavors have been blended together to help you prepare lean and luscious meals that are sure to please. Holiday feasts are still filled with flavor, but I've slashed the fat and calories. Now you can enjoy the taste of yesterday in today's . . . and tomorrow's, kitchen.

No time to shop? No time to cook? No problem! *Healthy Helpings* will "show you the weigh" to choose heart-healthy, lower-fat foods. You'll learn what to keep on hand for a well-stocked pantry and freezer. Your microwave and food processor can help you prepare luscious, low-fat dishes without fuss or muss. Zip it, zap it, eat it. Now that's cooking with the speed of light!

Mastering successful, low-fat cooking techniques is an ongoing process. *Healthy Helpings* is a compendium of my learning experiences. I've had my share of culinary disasters along the way. Even my dog, Tootsie, turned her little nose up at some of my offerings when I tried to pretend that my flops were fabulous! But I kept experimenting in order to create recipes that satisfied several basic requirements. They had to be 1) high in flavor and nutrients 2) lower in fat and calories 3) quick to prepare and 4) a source of guilt-free pleasure (except for a few indulgences, which we all need once in a while)!

As I developed these recipes, I could almost hear your questions and concerns. "What's the best oil to use? Can I reduce the sugar (or fat)? I need recipes that are high in fiber, but don't taste like sawdust! Beans give my husband "gastric distress"—oy, what should I do? Can this dish be frozen? Two vegetarians are coming for our Passover Seder and I don't know what to serve them!"

I've tried to anticipate and answer your questions in *Healthy Helpings*. I have included a variety of recipes from various ethnic cuisines, but have adapted them to follow Kosher dietary guidelines. Availability of products may vary from area to area, but most can be found on supermarket shelves or at your local health food store.

My recipes are all quick and easy to prepare. I usually cook from scratch, but there are days when I need shortcuts because I'm short on time due to my busy schedule. I hope my book gives you the knowledge and confidence you need to feed your friends and family nutritious, delicious meals without spending a lot of time in the kitchen.

So turn the pages and let's get cooking! Eat in good health!

SECTION 1

Things You Want to Know

Things You Want to Know

Good Foods, Bad Foods?

- There's no such thing as the perfect, magical food. High consumption of even the most nutrition-packed food won't guarantee good health.
- Eat a wide variety of foods every day and focus mainly on The Big Four: Vegetables, Fruits, Grains and Legumes. Then you'll be on your way to a healthier "weigh" of living.
- Eat smart and go "4-ward" into the future! Choose foods that are: 1) low in fat 2) low in sugar 3) high in fiber, vitamins and minerals and 4) varied and well-balanced.
- If you follow these four principles, you'll automatically make healthier choices and also increase your diet's nutrient content.
- You'll also be able to eat more. For example, you can have two oranges instead of one glass of juice. Oranges are full of fiber, but the juice contains almost as much sugar as a soft drink. If you choose a chicken wing with the skin, you get 7 grams of fat. Instead, eat a roasted chicken breast without skin. That's a better deal and a more filling meal!
- Don't get mad at yourself if you goof. You're human and we're all tempted by those old favorites, those fatty comfort foods! Just do your best and try, try again. The only failure in life is failing to try! Make up for indulging one day by cutting back the next.
- Eating small portions of higher-fat foods and doing a little more exercise are two good examples of how to live in a world full of temptation without feeling guilty or deprived!

Ship-Shape Shopping!

- It all starts out in the shopping cart! If it's not in the cart, it's not in your kitchen. If it's not in your kitchen, it's not going to be in your tummy! So don't be a dummy and shop smart.
- Don't grocery shop when you're hungry! You'll buy too much junk food. (I speak from experience!)
- Make a list and stick to it. Group the items according to the areas where they are found in the supermarket. Try not to give in to temptation. Don't buy the "trigger foods" that set off a binge!
- Shop the perimeter of the store. This is where fruits, veggies, meats, dairy products and breads are generally found.
- Try not to buy large amounts of processed and/or packaged foods. For maximum nutrition, buy mainly fresh fruits, vegetables, whole grains and legumes. Frozen or canned fruits and veggies are also nutritious, as well as convenient.
- The nutritional information should be based on standard (and realistic) serving sizes. After all, who can eat just a seventh of a package of potato chips, even if they're low-fat!
- Low-fat products contain less than 3 grams of fat per serving. Avoid products that contain saturated fats (e.g. palm, palm kernel or coconut oil) and trans fats, which are used to extend the shelf life of processed foods. Trans fats are found in fried foods (e.g., french fries), margarines and commercially baked goods.
- Light margarines are not recommended for baking or sautéeing because part of the fat has been replaced by water, but they are fine as spreads for breads or to flavor vegetables.
- The butterfat in milk, sour cream, yogurt, cream cheese and cottage cheese is saturated. Choose skim or 1 percent dairy products if possible. Flavorful, low-fat Kosher cheeses are a little more difficult to find. Try to find "light" brands. They should have at least 25 percent less fat than the regular version.

- Limited time to shop? The following pages contain a list of staples that are great to have on hand. They have an excellent shelf life, so you'll have to go shopping less often. I've also included a list of perishables that are used as ingredients in many of my recipes. Timesaving tips are given throughout this book on how to minimize waste, ways to use up leftovers and what can be frozen.

Be Able to Figure Out the Label!

- Are you confused by the information on food labels? Invest a little time and you'll soon be an expert at interpreting the information so you can make wise choices when shopping.
- Some brands of processed foods are higher in fat than others. Wherever possible, substitute lower-fat, lower-calorie versions.
- Compare similar products to make the wisest, healthiest choice. Bran flakes and corn flakes are both low in fat, but their fiber content differs.
- Check the label for nutritional information. Avoid products which contain hydrogenated fats or oils. Choose products low in saturated fats and that do not contain trans fats.
- A food label should show the serving size, the number of servings in a package and the calories per serving. The label may list major vitamins and minerals as well as other nutritional data.
- Ingredients are listed in descending order by weight. The ingredient with the largest amount is listed first.
- The nutrient content is usually listed for one serving. If you eat more than the serving size indicated, this will affect the calories, fat, carbohydrates, etc. that you are consuming.
- Serving sizes should be realistic, as well as uniform. For example, one manufacturer may claim that 2 teaspoons of oil contain 9.2 grams of fat. Another may declare that 1 tablespoon of oil contains 14 grams of fat. However, tablespoon for tablespoon, all oils contain the same amount of fat.
- Labels don't always tell the whole story! Nutritional information on labels may not be complete. If a label makes a claim such as "light," it only has to list the nutrients it's making a claim about. For example, tomato sauce may be "light" but it could be very high in sodium, which may not be listed on the label because the manufacturer did not make any claims about sodium.
- Watch out for misleading claims. A product may claim to be "cholesterol-free" but that doesn't mean it's fat-free. (Free can become very expensive, necessitating the price of a new, larger wardrobe!)
- If a product claims to be "light" or "lite," that doesn't mean you are going to be lighter in weight just because you bought it! "Light" can refer to flavor, color or texture.
- Don't be too carefree with foods labeled "fat-free." They can contain up to $1/2$ gram of fat (0.5 g) per serving and still be labelled fat-free. If you have several servings a day of these so-called fat-free products, you can manage to eat a significant amount of fat (and calories).
- A low-fat label doesn't always mean that a food is a good choice. Some low-fat foods are high in sugar, salt and/or calories. Many people are tempted to eat more because a food is labelled "low-fat," taking it as a license to eat as much as they want. Portions are the problem!
- Check out the expiration date (especially on economy-sized packages) before making your way to the checkout counter! Also refer to storage information to minimize waste.
- Follow these guidelines and it won't take very long to learn which products are best to buy.
- So, shop . . . and cook in good health!

Staples

Oils/Vinegars:
Canola oil (for sautéeing, salads, marinades or baking)
Extra-virgin olive oil, preferably first cold pressing (for salads, marinades)
Olive oil (for sautéeing, salads, marinades)
Oriental sesame oil (for marinades, sauces)
Non-stick cooking sprays (use for greasing pans and casseroles, for pan-frying and sautéeing)
Vinegars (rice, red wine, balsamic, raspberry, cider, distilled white vinegar)

Mayonnaise/Salad Dressings:
Non-fat mayonnaise (add a dash of lemon juice and mustard to boost the flavor)
Low-fat/light/calorie-reduced mayonnaise
Mayonnaise-type salad dressing (e.g. Miracle Whip Light)
Salad dressings (fat-free and low-fat)

Dried Legumes:
Dried beans (black, navy, kidney, lima, black eyed peas, pinto beans, chickpeas/garbanzos, soybeans)
Dried lentils (brown, green, red)
Dried split peas (yellow, green)

Tomato Products/Sauces/Condiments/Spreads:
Canned tomatoes (whole or ground)
Stewed tomatoes
Sun-dried tomatoes (dehydrated, not oil-packed)
Tomato juice
Tomato paste, tomato sauce
Vegetarian/marinara spaghetti sauce (I prefer those sold in a jar—read labels to select low-fat variety, or use homemade)
Salsa (mild, medium, chunky, or homemade)
BBQ sauce, steak sauce, horseradish

Definitions of Terms on Labels

- Calorie-free: Less than 5 calories per serving.
- Sugar-free: Less than 1/2 gram of sugar per serving.
- Fat-free: Less than 1/2 gram of fat per serving.
- Low-fat: 3 grams or less fat per serving.
- Low-saturated fat: 1 gram or less saturated fat per serving.
- Low-sodium: 140 mg or less sodium per serving.
- Very low sodium: 35 mg or less per serving.
- Low-cholesterol: 20 mg or less and 2 grams or less of saturated fat.
- Low-calorie: 40 calories or less per serving.
- Lean (refers to fat content of poultry, meat and seafood): Less than 10 grams fat, 4.5 grams or less saturated fat, and less than 95 mg cholesterol per serving and per 100 grams.
- Extra-lean: Less than 5 grams fat, less than 2 grams saturated fat, and less than 95 mg cholesterol per serving and per 100 grams.

Ketchup/chili sauce
Hoisin sauce
Soy sauce (lite/low-sodium–regular soy sauce can be diluted with water)
Tabasco (hot pepper sauce)
Tamari (wheat-free soy sauce)
Teriyaki sauce
Worcestershire sauce
Capers
Mustard (Dijon, honey-style, prepared)
Peanut butter (refrigerate after opening to prevent rancidity)
Low-sugar jams, preserves, marmalade (apricot, orange, strawberry, cherry, raspberry, blueberry)

Canned Vegetables/Legumes/Fruits/Fish/Soups:
Canned vegetables (artichokes, corn niblets/

creamed corn, mushrooms, peas, bamboo shoots, water chestnuts)

Canned beans/lentils (garbanzo/chick peas, kidney beans, pinto beans, lentils, vegetarian baked beans)

Canned fish (salmon, tuna packed in water or vegetable broth, sardines)

Canned fruits in natural juice (pineapple tidbits/crushed, mandarin oranges)

Soups (canned, dehydrated—choose reduced-sodium, low-fat brands)

Powdered soup mix (I use Kosher pareve "chicken-flavored" instant soup mix for convenience, but use only ½ teaspoon powder for each cup of water to reduce sodium.)

Pastas/Grains/Cereals:

Pasta, enriched: (soup noodles, vermicelli, angel hair, spaghetti, linguini, fettucine, lasagna, spirals, ruffles, shells, elbow macaroni, bowties, orzo, soba noodles); whole-wheat pastas are excellent or experiment with those made from less common grains (e.g. quinoa, buckwheat)

Barley (pot barley, pearl barley)

Bulgur

Cornmeal (white or yellow—fine or medium)

Couscous (fine or medium, whole wheat)

Kasha/buckwheat (fine, medium, coarse)

Millet

Quinoa

Rice (brown or white basmati), long grain, short grain, arborio (instant rice has no taste or texture, little nutritional value)

Wheat berries

Wild rice

All-Bran cereal, 100% natural wheat bran

Cream of wheat/cream of rice

Granola cereal (low-fat)

Multi-grain, shredded wheat, puffed wheat, puffed rice, Cheerios, Special K, corn flakes, rice krispies

Oat bran/oatmeal

Whole grain/high fiber cereals (preferably with at least 4 grams of fiber per serving)

Snack Foods/Cookies/Crackers:

Almonds with raisins (small portions)

Baked potato chips and/or tortilla chips

Graham crackers, social tea biscuits

Low-fat cookies (check labels)

Low-fat crackers, animal crackers, arrowroot biscuits

Matzo, matzo crackers

Nuts and seeds (walnuts, almonds, pistachios, sunflower seeds), small portions

Popcorn (air-popped/low-fat microwave)

Pretzels (low-sodium, if available)

Rice cakes, flatbreads, melba toast

Sherbet/gelato/yogurt (low-fat)

Breads/Bread Crumbs, etc. (stone-ground breads are excellent):

Bagels (plain, whole-wheat, multi-grain, cinnamon raisin, etc.)

Baguette, Ficelle, French, Italian

Challah (commercially baked challah is usually high in eggs and fat)

Focaccia bread

Multi-grain, country-style

Pitas (regular or whole wheat)

Rolls (whole wheat, French, Italian, etc.)

Rye, kimmel, pumpernickel, black, corn

Sourdough bread (white or whole wheat)

Tortillas (flour/corn)

Whole wheat, oatmeal

Bread or cornflake crumbs (packaged or make your own)

Cornstarch

Matzo meal, potato starch, cake meal, matzo farfel

Beverages/Juices/Miscellaneous:

Cocoa (unsweetened)

Coffee/decaffeinated

Diet soft drinks (contain sodium)

What's in a Serving?

- ¼ cup - The size of a golf ball.
- ½ cup - The size of a tennis ball.
- 1 cup - The size of a baseball.
- The way we used to eat? The size of a football!

Are You On the Ball?

Juices—unsweetened (tomato, vegetable, orange, apple, pineapple, cranberry)

Orange, lemon and lime juice (bottled/fresh)

Teas (green/herbal/decaffeinated)

Water (mineral/soda water, Perrier, seltzer)

Wine (white or red—if you can drink it, then it's fine for cooking!)

Rum/brandy/liqueurs (coffee, chocolate, orange, almond-flavored—use instead of vanilla extract in baking!)

Dried Herbs & Spices:

Allspice
Basil
Bay leaves
Cayenne
Cajun seasoning
Celery seed
Chili powder
Cinnamon
Cloves
Cumin
Curry powder
Dried dill weed
Garlic powder
Ground ginger
Italian seasoning
Liquid smoke
Dry mustard
Nutmeg

Onion flakes
Oregano
Paprika (preferably Hungarian)
Pepper (black, white, pink peppercorns)
Poppy seeds
Red pepper flakes
Rosemary
Saffron
Sage
Savory
Sesame seeds
Salt, salt substitute (e.g. Mrs. Dash)
Tarragon
Thyme

Baking Supplies:

Almond extract, pure vanilla extract
Applesauce (unsweetened)
Baking powder
Baking soda
Cocoa (unsweetened)
Chocolate chips (small packages, so you won't be tempted to nibble!)
Cream of tartar
Dried prunes, apricots, dates
Flax seed (store in refrigerator)
Flour (all-purpose, unbleached, stone ground, whole wheat)
Graham cracker crumbs/corn flake crumbs
Honey/maple syrup/corn syrup
Molasses
Nuts (small amounts—store in the fridge or freezer to prevent rancidity)
Raisins, craisins (dried cranberries)
Sugar (granulated, brown, powdered sugar)
Sweetened condensed milk (low-fat)
Wheat germ (toasted, untoasted)
Yeast (regular, rapid-rise or bread machine)

Perishables

Eggs/Dairy/Cheeses/Margarine:
Egg whites, egg substitutes (in refrigerator or freezer section—¼ cup = 1 egg)
Eggs (to reduce cholesterol and fat, substitute 2 whites for 1 whole egg)
Milk (skim, 1%, lactose-free, buttermilk)
Sour cream (non-fat or low-fat)
Yogurt (many brands offer non-fat or low-fat choices; some are flavored with fruit, sugar or sweetener)
Cottage cheese/Quark cheese
Feta cheese
Goat cheese
Ricotta cheese (low-fat)
Low-fat/light cream cheese (contains about half the fat of regular cream cheese)
Fat-free/non-fat cream cheese
Low-fat hard cheeses (Swiss, Havarti, part-skim mozzarella, grated Parmesan, cheddar). Some very low-fat cheeses are rubbery; look for varieties with 20% or less fat.
Butter (use in limited amounts)
Margarine (soft tub)—avoid hydrogenated margarines or those containing trans fats

Frozen Foods:
Frozen vegetables (without butter or sauce):
  Asparagus
  Broccoli
  Brussel sprouts
  Baby carrots
  Corn kernels
  Green beans
  Green peas
  Mixed vegetables (e.g. California mix)
  Oriental mixed vegetables
  Snow peas
  Spinach
Frozen bread dough/pizza crust (whole grain)

Frozen fruits/juices:
  Berries (blueberries, strawberries, raspberries, cranberries)
  Bananas (freeze bananas that are turning black!)
  Grapes (great right from the freezer!)
  Orange/apple juice concentrate
Frozen desserts: sherbet, frozen yogurt, gelato, low-fat ice cream
Phyllo dough (frozen is handy, fresh is preferable)

Poultry/Meat/Fish (Fresh/Frozen):
Chicken parts/breasts/tenders/cubes/scaloppine/stir-fry (boneless, skinless)
Chicken or turkey bones (for soup stocks)
Turkey breast, turkey cutlets, cubes, stir-fry
Minced chicken/turkey (have butcher grind without adding fat)
Extra-lean ground beef/veal
Lean veal cubes/chops/roast
Lean beef (for stir-fries)
Lean beef brisket (first cut—for occasional use)
Fish (sole, whitefish, snapper, pickerel/doré, bass, salmon, salmon trout, halibut, tuna, trout, haddock, orange roughy)

Vegetarian Ingredients & Alternatives:
Kombu (for cooking beans)
Textured vegetable protein (TVP), meat substitute/veggie ground round
Nori (seaweed) & other sea vegetables
Tofu (extra-firm, firm, silken, 1% fat)
Seitan (store-bought or homemade)
Tempeh
Vegetarian burgers/deli products
Soy milk, rice milk, soy cheese, soy yogurt, etc. (check your local health food store for more offerings!)

Fresh Vegetables/Herbs (buy what's in season):
Asparagus
Beans (green, yellow, haricot/fine beans, Chinese long beans)

Beets, beet greens
Bok choy
Broccoli/broccoflower
Brussel sprouts
Cabbage (green, red, Savoy/crinkly, Nappa/
  Chinese)
Carrots, baby carrots
Cauliflower
Celery, celery root
Collards
Coriander/cilantro/Chinese parsley
Corn
Cucumbers
Eggplant (Italian, baby, Oriental, regular)
Endives
Fennel
Fiddleheads

Garlic
Ginger root
Herbs (basil, dill, oregano, thyme, tarragon, rose-
  mary, marjoram, sage)
Jicama
Kale
Leeks
Lettuce (romaine, iceberg, Boston, Bibb,
  hydroponic, radicchio, mesclun/mixed field greens,
  arugula/rocket, Chinese, mâche/lamb's lettuce)
Mushrooms (shiitake, porcini, oyster, chanterelle,
  enoki, portobello, white cultivated)
Onions (red, yellow, green onions/scallions, chives,
  sweet, Spanish, Bermuda, Vidalia)
Parsley (Italian/flat leaf, curly)
Parsnips (sometimes called white carrots)
Peas, snow peas

Wrap It Right, "Mike" It Right

- To reduce your exposure to questionable chemicals (e.g., phthalates and bisphenol A), don't microwave food in disposable plastic containers from the supermarket, plastic bags or plastic wrap. When subjected to heat, chemicals can leach and migrate into foods, particularly fatty foods. It is not known which plastics contain hormone-disrupting chemicals. Better be safe than sorry!
- Don't store hot foods in disposable plastic containers. Instead, use heat-resistant glass (e.g. Pyrex, Corning Ware, glass jars), ceramic dishes and casseroles.
- Plastic cling wrap: Minimize or eliminate its direct contact with food, particularly hot food. Reduce consumption of fatty foods prepackaged in plastic and heat-sealed containers.
- When microwaving, use the casserole cover or a microsafe plate if food requires covering.
- Cooking parchment makes an excellent covering for containers which don't have a cover. To make parch-

ment more flexible, place it under running water. You can then mold it easily around the dish or casserole! Parchment is available in kitchenware shops, or ask your local bakery if they will sell you individual sheets. (It's used for non-stick baking of baked goods.)
- The Microsafe Dish Test: Measure $\frac{1}{2}$ cup of cold water into a Pyrex measuring cup. Place it in your microwave. Place the empty dish you want to test next to the cup, but not touching it. Microwave on HIGH for 1 minute. If your dish is cool and the water in the measuring cup is hot, the dish is microsafe. If the dish is hot, don't use it for microwaving. (P.S. Your dish may be microsafe when you test it, but it will get hot from the heat transferred from the food you are heating or cooking!)
- One cup of water (250 ml) boils in 2–2$\frac{1}{2}$ minutes on HIGH. Two cups (500 ml) boil in 4–5 minutes in a 650-700 watt microwave oven.

Peppers (red, green, yellow, orange)

Chili peppers (the smaller, the hotter! Green, yellow, orange, red, jalapeños, serranos, finger, cherry)

Okra

Potatoes (Idaho/Russet, Yukon Gold, red, new potatoes)

Radishes (Chinese, black, red)

Shallots

Sorrel (sourgrass)

Spinach, baby spinach

Sprouts (alfalfa, bean, radish)

Summer squash (chayote, pattypan, yellow, baby zucchini)

Sweet potatoes, yams

Swiss chard

Tomatoes, cherry/grape tomatoes

Turnips

Watercress

Winter squash (acorn, butternut, hubbard, pumpkin, spaghetti, zucchini)

Fresh Fruits (buy what's in season):

Apples

Apricots

Avocados

Bananas

Berries (strawberries, raspberries, blackberries, blueberries, cranberries)

Cherries

Figs

Grapefruits

Grapes

Kiwis

Kumquats

Lemons/limes

Mangoes

Melons (cantaloupe, honeydew, crenshaw)

Nectarines

Oranges (tangerines, mandarins, clementines)

Papayas

Passion fruit

Peaches

Pears (bosc, anjou, bartlett)

Persimmons

Pineapples

Plums

Pomegranates

Prickly pears/cactus pears

Rhubarb (A vegetable that is used as a fruit. Leaves are poisonous—don't eat them!)

Star fruit (makes a great garnish)

Watermelon (red, yellow, seedless)

Hooray for Herbs!

Herbs are a wonderful way to enhance the flavor of food, especially when cutting back on fat! Herbs are generally the fragrant leaves of plants, and spices are usually grown for their seeds, berries, bark or roots. Choose fresh herbs with a clean, fresh scent, without any sign of wilting, browning or rust. Purchase in small amounts to maintain peak flavor and quality. As a general rule, substitute 1 teaspoon dried (or ¼ teaspoon of powdered or ground) for 1 to 2 tablespoons of fresh herbs.

How to Store Herbs: Wrap fresh herbs in damp paper towels, place in a plastic bag and refrigerate. They'll keep about 4 or 5 days. For longer storage, usually 7 to 10 days, place the bouquet of fresh herbs stem end down in a tall glass or jar. Add cold water until ends are covered by 1 inch. Cover tops of leaves with a plastic bag and secure it to the jar with a rubber band. Change the water every 2 days. Fresh herbs can also be washed, thoroughly dried, chopped and stored in the freezer in airtight containers for a month or two. Don't thaw before using. Frozen herbs are best in cooked dishes.

Dried herbs are available year-round. Their flavor is stronger and more concentrated than fresh. Store in a tightly sealed, airtight container in a cool, dark, dry place away from sunlight or heat. They will keep about 6 months. If using fresh herbs in a long-cooking dish, add towards the end of cooking to maintain delicate flavor. Add dried herbs at the beginning of cooking. Rub them between your fingertips to release their flavor before adding them to a dish. To reconstitute dried herbs for salads and other uncoooked dishes, soak herbs for 20 minutes in some of the liquid which is being used in the recipe (e.g. lemon juice, olive oil).

Chef's Secret: If fresh herbs are not available, chop together equal parts of fresh parsley with the dried herb. For example, for 1 tablespoon fresh basil, chop together 1/2 tablespoon dried basil with 1/2 tablespoon fresh parsley. The parsley will take on the flavor of the dried herb, and the herb will also taste fresher. The flavor of fresh herbs diminishes during long cooking, so add a little extra just before serving.

Rainbow Tabbouleh Salad (p. 283) is an excellent example of using fresh herbs in a salad. Herb Roasted Chicken (p. 156) can be made with either fresh or dried herbs. Chocolate Mint Leaves (p. 348) can be eaten completely. Use the herbs you like best. Experiment, enjoy!

Basil: A member of the mint family, it's great with tomatoes, garlic, vegetables, mixed salad greens, dressings, dips, herb breads, soups, stews, casseroles, spaghetti and tomato sauces. Excellent with beef, veal, lamb, chicken, turkey, fish, omelets, stuffings, pasta, rice, couscous, millet, bulgur, kasha and polenta. Perfect on pizza, used in Italian recipes, compatible with cheese dishes. It's an essential ingredient in pesto. The best way to chop basil is to stack the leaves in a pile, roll them into a cylinder and cut into narrow strips (chiffonade). Basil has a calming effect, so take a little sniff and feel good!

Bay Leaf: Add to sauces and stews at beginning of cooking to release its flavor. Remove before serving. Use with beef, veal, chicken, turkey, poached fish, in vegetable soups, tomato or spaghetti sauce, with lentils, beets, carrots, potatoes and tomatoes. Good in marinades and pickling brines. If using powdered bay leaf, use only a pinch. If using the whole leaf, half of a leaf is usually enough.

Bouquet Garni: Combine three or four sprigs of parsley, two sprigs fresh thyme and one-third to one-half of a bay leaf in a cheesecloth bag, or inside several celery ribs tied together with white string. Remove after cooking. Compatible with soups, stews, meats, fish, poultry and vegetables.

Chervil: This delicately flavored herb is a member of the parsley family and tastes slightly like licorice. It's excellent with fish, cottage or cream cheese, in omelets, soups, pasta, rice, bulgur and couscous. Use with chicken, fish, green salads, dips, or to flavor cooked vegetables (asparagus, beets, carrots, peas, green beans, squash or tomatoes). Available dried, but its flavor is best when fresh.

Chives: Excellent with cream cheese, in omelets, sauces, salads, salad dressings, dips, spreads, mild-flavored fish, poultry, veal and potatoes. Use as a garnish, or to replace green onions/scallions. Snip with scissors; add at the end of cooking time to retain delicate flavor. To freeze, blanch chives in boiling water for 10 seconds. Plunge them into ice water for 1 minute, then dry thoroughly.

Coriander (Cilantro/Chinese Parsley): Often mistaken for Italian parsley, it is easily distinguished by its strong-smelling, pungent fragrance. (It's an acquired taste!) Mix with equal parts of chopped parsley for a milder flavor. Add to salsa, Oriental stir-fries, cooked rice and lentils. Great over grilled chicken or fish. It's often used in Middle-Eastern, Indian, Mexican and Oriental dishes.

Dill: Add dill weed towards end of cooking to preserve flavor. Use in salads, salad dressings, vegetables, soups (epecially chicken soup), meats, poultry, fish and omelets. Great in sauces, dips and spreads.Try it in tuna, egg or salmon salad, cottage cheese, cream cheese, yogurt, or with cucumber, carrots, or cabbage. Add to potato salad, pasta, rice, stuffings or herb breads. Store fresh dill in a tightly sealed glass jar. Do not add water. It will keep for a few weeks. Dill seed is the dried fruit of the herb. Use in the brine for dill pickles and marinades. Dill seed's flavor is stronger than that of dill weed.

Fines Herbes: A French herb blend of finely chopped herbs, usually chervil, chives, parsley and tarragon. Add to cooked dishes shortly before serving. Compatible with mild-flavored fish, eggs, cheese, salad dressings, cream or wine sauces, poultry and veal dishes.

Herbes de Provence: A blend of dried herbs most commonly used in Southern France. Contains basil, fennel seed, lavender, marjoram, rosemary, sage, summer savory and thyme. Used to season meat, poultry and vegetable dishes.

Lemon Balm: Lemon-scented, mintlike leaves are often used to brew tisane, an aromatic herbal tea. Lemon Balm is also used in salads, jellies and jams.

Marjoram (Sweet): Related to oregano, with a more delicate flavor. Compatible with lamb, veal, poultry, fish, omelets, vegetable dishes, tomato sauce and other tomato-based dishes. Try with grains, salad dressings, dips, spreads, cooked beans, lentils, potatoes, brussel sprouts, cabbage, carrots, celery, corn, green beans, eggplant, onions, peas, spinach and zucchini.

Mint: Over thirty species are available. Fresh leaves add flavor to fresh fruit cup, melon, berries, jellies, ices, sherbets, teas, and chilled fruit drinks. Allow $1/4$ to $1/2$ teaspoon fresh mint leaves per serving. Crush just before using. Lovely with cooked carrots, peas, cucumber, green beans, squash, tomatoes, cooked rice, bulgur, yogurt, cottage or cream cheese. Ideal in salads, cole slaw or with lamb. Popular in Middle Eastern cuisine. The leaves can be steeped in hot water to make mint tea.

Oregano (Wild Marjoram): Similar to marjoram, but with a strong flavor, so use with restraint. Used in Italian, Greek and Mexican cuisine. Goes well with tomato-based dishes. Season meats, poultry, fish, dried beans, omelets, cheeses, cabbage, mushrooms, eggplant, peppers, onions, zucchini, salad dressings, dips, spreads, soups, herb breads, pizza, spaghetti sauce, chili or stews.

Parsley: Comes in milder, curly-leaf form, or more strongly flavored, Italian flat-leaf parsley. Adds flavor and freshness to cooked foods. Add to soups, stews, pasta sauces or omelets. Sprinkle over grilled, poached or roasted meat, chicken, fish, or most vegetables, from artichokes to zucchini. Use in salads and salad dressings to add color, folic acid and vitamins A and C. Dried parsley bears little resemblance in flavor to fresh. Chew on fresh parsley to freshen your breath after eating onions or garlic. Curly parsley is ideal for garnishing platters.

Rosemary: Delicious with grilled or roasted lamb or chicken, flavorful fish such as salmon or tuna, herbed breads (focaccia), tomato sauces, roasted potatoes, mushrooms, tomatoes, peas and rice. When using fresh or dried rosemary, chop or crumble thoroughly, since its needle-like leaves are hard.

Sage: Best known as a seasoning for poultry stuffing. Use just a touch to season poultry, veal, legumes or rice dishes. Try a pinch in vegetable soups, or to season lima beans, Brussels sprouts, mushrooms, peas, tomatoes or eggplant.

Savory: Summer savory is more delicate in flavor than winter, but both varieties are very strong, so use with care. Compatible with lima and other dried beans, lentils, vegetables (green beans, peas, cabbage, cauliflower, potatoes, tomatoes and onions). Use just a touch with poultry, lamb, meatloaf, meatballs, burgers, fish, lentil soup or vegetarian paté.

Tarragon: Use with discretion. It is compatible with broiled, baked or poached fish or chicken, with veal, in sauces or salad dressings such as vinaigrettes, with peas, asparagus, carrots, mushrooms or tomatoes. Well known in classic French cooking.

Thyme: Many varieties are available, including lemon thyme. Whatever the variety, it enhances the flavor of beef, veal, poultry, fish and cooked vegetable dishes like mushrooms or green beans. Use in vegetable soups, sauces and stuffings. Essential in Creole dishes and French cuisine.

Fat Facts

Doctors and dieticians will agree that small amounts of fats in the diet are essential for good health. Fats are a major source of energy. They supply the essential fatty acids that the body needs for many chemical activities. Fats transport the fat-soluble vitamins (A, D, E and K) in the body. They are also important for the normal growth and development of our children. Fats add flavor, aroma and texture to foods, making eating more enjoyable. Because fats take longer than proteins and carbohydrates to digest, we feel full longer.

Unfortunately, the typical North American diet is too high in fat, causing weight gain and related health problems. Saturated fat has been associated with elevated cholesterol, a higher risk of heart disease, stroke, diabetes, obesity and some types of cancer. The Heart and Stroke Foundation recommends that adults restrict their total fat intake to not more than 30 percent of each day's calories. Some health professionals believe that we should strive for 20 percent, or even lower. Some health professionals believe that we should strive for 20 percent, or even lower. Others believe we should focus on choosing the right kind of fats instead of worrying about the percentage of fats in our diet.

The type of fats that we consume may be more important than the total amount we consume. Highly saturated, hydrogenated and trans fats raise blood cholesterol and should be avoided. Saturated fats (except for palm, palm kernel and coconut oils) are solid at room temperature. Monounsaturated fats (e.g. olive, peanut and canola oil) and polyunsaturated fats (e.g. corn oil) are liquid at room temperature.

Fat can be visible, like the fat that you see on meat or poultry, or the butter you spread on your bread. It can also be invisible, like the fat used in the processing or preparation of foods (e.g., potato chips, cakes, cookies, muffins). We can cut back on visible fats, but the invisible fats (found in two-thirds of processed foods) can't be removed. There are 9 calories in each gram of fat, compared to 4 calories in each gram of carbohydrate or protein. A little fat goes a long "weigh"!

Unsaturated fats are a healthier choice than saturated fats. Good sources are found in avocados, olives, soy products and nuts (almonds, peanuts, walnuts, hazelnuts, pistachios, peanut butter, almond butter). Choose healthy oils—olive, canola, sesame, walnut and soybean (used in commercial salad dressings). Eat fatty fish (salmon, mackerel, herring, rainbow trout) twice a week. They contain Omega-3 fats, which provide excellent protection for your heart, reduce inflammation and may play a role in fighting cancer.

Nuts are heart-healthy, although they are high in fat and calories. Several major health studies have shown that people who eat nuts regularly are less likely to have heart attacks or die from heart disease than those who rarely eat nuts. One ounce (about ¼ cup) of almonds, walnuts, peanuts or pistachios provides about 8 grams of protein and makes a healthy snack. It's okay to go nuts! Just watch those portions if you're watching your weight. A serving of nuts (a small handful) five times a week is a healthier choice than potato chips or candy. Nuts and seeds (sunflower, sesame, flax) are a healthy alternative to red meats and full-fat cheeses, which are high in saturated fats.

Enjoy old favorites but cut back on the portion size. Compensate with larger servings of low-fat foods (nutrient-dense whole grains, veggies, fruits). If your food intake is more than your energy output, the body converts excess calories to fat and you will gain weight.

Do you suffer from fat phobia? Fat-free foods (especially processed foods) are not magical. They still contain calories and often are full of additives (e.g., diet salad dressings, cookies). A fat-free label does not give you a license to eat without restraint! Don't go to extremes and worry about every drop of fat you eat. It's okay to indulge once in a while. Just cut back on your portions the day before and the day after, and increase your physical activity. (I know your parents taught you it's important to save, but they were referring to money. You have to spend your fat deposits!)

It's confusing to read the newspapers or magazines with this month's latest medical "breakthrough" or discovery. There is so much conflicting information, making it difficult for us to make wise choices. Use your common sense. Aim for a balanced diet which is lower in fat and calories and includes dark green leafy vegetables, legumes (beans, peas, lentils and soybean products), whole grains and fruits. A healthy diet should satisfy all (or hopefully most!) of the members of your family.

If you have young children who are still growing, it's important to be more flexible in terms of their fat intake. Don't eliminate nutritious, higher-fat foods such as whole or 2 percent milk, regular cheeses and peanut butter from their diets. Offer them a variety of foods and don't make a fuss if they refuse to try new, healthful dishes. Also, don't let them fill up on juices. Little kids have little tummies and they get full quickly. Speak to your pediatrician or a professional dietician for guidance.

Since science is always evolving, dietary recommendations from the experts are sure to change. There isn't one perfect diet or food that's right for everyone. We each have personal tastes, set habits, food traditions and health concerns.

The information included throughout this book is meant as a guide. It is not meant to replace medical advice. Any medical questions should be addressed to your physician. The key to healthy, happy eating is finding the balance between good food, good health and good taste!

"Wise Weighs" to Fight Fat and Eat Better!

• **Current dietary recommendations are flexible.** Different individuals have different nutritional needs, medical histories and lifestyles. For general good health, 50% to 60% of calories should come from carbohydrates, 30% or less from fat and 10% to 20% from protein. Keep saturated fat to a minimum. Strive for ¹/₂ to 1 hour of physical activity throughout the day.

- **The foods that are healthiest** for us are the same foods that will help us lose (or maintain) our weight. For optimum health and a leaner body, eat a wide variety of foods based on whole-grain products (breads, cereals, rice, pasta), legumes (beans, peas, lentils), vegetables and fruits.
- **Choose lean meats** and skim or low-fat dairy products. Use small amounts of vegetable oils (e.g., canola and first-pressed olive oil).
- **Strive for five a day!** That means three servings of vegetables and two servings of fruit, according to the National Cancer Institute. One serving means: ¹/₂ cup of cooked or raw fruit or vegetables, 1 cup of raw leafy green vegetables, 1 medium piece of fruit or 6 ounces of fruit or vegetable juice. Some groups advocate even more daily servings of vegetables and fruits to reduce the risk of cancer, heart disease and stroke.
- **A good rule to follow** is to eat either some fruit or veggies with each meal or snack. Add tomatoes to a sandwich, slice fresh fruit into yogurt, munch on baby carrots or red pepper strips!
- **Vegetables and fruits** are excellent sources of vitamins, as well as "phytomins" (phytochemicals) which fight serious diseases like cancer. They have the added benefit of fiber, which is good for both your heart and your digestion. Fruits and vegetables are a good source of potassium.
- **Green cuisine is lean (excluding mint chocolates)!** Dark green leafy vegetables (cabbage, kale, collard greens, romaine, spinach) are concentrated sources of the vitamins and minerals most people should eat more often for optimum health, plus they're virtually free of fat and calories.
- **Watch out for the calories,** sugars and fat lurking in many salad dressings! Use low-fat or non-fat versions of salad dressings and mayonnaise. Lemon juice, balsamic vinegar, non-fat or low-fat yogurt, herbs and spices are also great in salads and can be enjoyed freely. Portion control is important. Don't drown your salad in dressing.
- **A cup of whole (3.5 percent) milk** has over 50 percent of its 170 calories from fat. Forget about that!
- **A cup of 2 percent milk** has 35 percent of its calories from fat. It contains 121 calories, 18 mg cholesterol and 4.7 g fat (2.9 saturated).
- **A cup of 1 percent milk** has 23 percent of its calories from fat. It contains 102 calories, 10 mg cholesterol and 2.6 g fat (1.6 g saturated).
- **A cup of skim milk** gets 5 percent of its calories from fat. It contains 86 calories, 4 mg cholesterol and 0.4 g fat (0.3 saturated).
- **Compare these fat facts:** One tablespoon regular cream cheese contains 51 calories and 5.1 gram fat (2 grams saturated). One tablespoon low-fat cream cheese contains 35 calories and 2.6 grams fat (1.7 grams saturated).
- **Choose lower-fat cheeses** which contain 20 percent or less fat. Use small amounts of strong rather than mild cheeses (e.g., Parmesan, strong cheddar) for maximum flavor, minimum calories.
- **Get hooked on fish!** It's lower in calories and saturated fat than meat, and recent research indicates that eating at least two fish meals a week protects your heart and may lower the risk of many diseases.
- **Choose the leanest cuts** of beef, veal and poultry. Remove all visible fat before cooking.
- **Bake, roast, grill or broil** more often instead of frying. Watch out for high-fat sauces.
- **Cook meat or poultry** on a rack so that the fat can drain off during cooking.
- **An average 3 pound (1.4 kg) roasted chicken** has 2¹/₄ pounds of meat containing 880 calories, and ³/₄ pound of skin containing 1,745 calories!

Remove the skin, trim the fat; you'll get thin, you'll like that!

- **Eat high-fat, processed delicatessen meats less often,** in small amounts. Add a food which contains good sources of vitamin C (e.g. tomato or orange juice, sliced tomato) to reduce the formation of nitrosamines, according to Joseph A. Schwarcz, Ph.D. "Dr. Joe" is the consultant for the excellent book *Foods That Harm, Foods That Heal* (Reader's Digest).

- **Eat meatless meals more often** (but be sure not to load them up with fat)! For example, instead of topping pasta with high-fat, creamy sauces, substitute tomato sauce and add some herbs and lots of vegetables to boost the flavor. Or make spaghetti sauce using ground meat substitute instead of ground beef, or add some canned beans, chickpeas or cubes of tofu. Moving towards a plant-based diet helps reduce disease risks and improves well-being.

- **Experiment with tofu.** There are many delicious ways to include it in meal planning, such as stir-fries, spreads and vegetarian stew. (See Index for recipes and ideas.)

- **Beans and legumes** are a nutritional powerhouse. They are low in fat, contain B vitamins, potassium and protein, and are a good source of calcium. High in soluble fiber, they are digested slowly, making them a good choice for diabetics and those who are insulin-resistant because they can help regulate blood sugar. Half a cup of cooked beans daily may help reduce cholesterol levels.

- **Canned beans and legumes** are higher in sodium than those cooked from scratch, but they save time. Drain and rinse well under cold running water to cut the amount of sodium in half.

- **If legumes are used** as a meat substitute, 1/2 to 1 cup of cooked dry beans, peas or lentils is equivalent to one serving. For diabetics, 1/3 cup cooked beans = 1 starchy/bread choice.

Recommended Daily Fat Consumption Goal

If You Eat		Your Daily Fat Goal Will Be . . .	
	30%	25%	20%
1,200 calories	40 grams	34 grams	27 grams
1,500 calories	50 grams	42 grams	33 grams
1,800 calories	60 grams	50 grams	40 grams
2,000 calories	67 grams	56 grams	44 grams
2,500 calories	83 grams	69 grams	56 grams
3,000 calories	100 grams	83 grams	67 grams

- **One gram of protein or carbohydrate** contains 4 calories. One gram of fat packs more than double the wallop with 9 calories. One gram of alcohol contains 7 calories.

- **Beware of snack attacks!** Watch out for high-salt and/or high-fat foods like packaged popcorn, chips, crackers, etc. If you are in the mood for salty and/or crunchy munchies, make your own pita, tortilla, potato or wonton chips. (See Index for recipes).

- **Limit your intake of sweet,** fatty baked goods. When you bake something yourself, it's easier to control the fat (and sugar) content.

- **Instead of higher-fat ice cream,** eat low-fat frozen yogurt or tofu, sherbet, gelato or frozen fruit desserts. Portion control is important. Eat very slowly and enjoy!

- **For a luscious, long-lasting** snack, freeze individual containers of fat-free yogurt. (Lemon is my favorite!) Insert a wooden stick before freezing and wrap well. (Thanks to Nancy Gordon for the great idea!)

How to Calculate Your Daily Fat Consumption Goal

- **There are differing opinions,** but most diet experts generally agree that fat levels (mainly unsaturated) should make up 30 percent of a healthy diet. Wherever possible, limit your intake of saturated fats and avoid trans fats, which are found in hard stick margarine, vegetable shortening, commercially baked goods like crackers, cookies, cakes and muffins, and fried foods prepared in restaurants.
- **Not all fats are bad.** Unsaturated fats protect against heart disease and other chronic conditions.
- **An intake of 30 percent fa**t is enough to maintain your ideal weight, but is probably not low enough to lose weight.
- **Lower levels of fat intake** are recommended if there is a risk of diabetes, heart disease, stroke, high cholesterol, cancer or obesity in your family.
- **If you eat less fat,** you can eat more food for the same number of calories!
- **If you need to watch** your fat intake for medical reasons, counting fat grams is important for you. However, don't become obsessed with the numbers game and become fat phobic! Just use common sense and eat a well-balanced diet composed mainly of vegetables, fruits, legumes, breads, cereals and whole grains. Eat small to moderate amounts of lean meat, fish and poultry. Include low-fat dairy products to help build up your calcium reserves against osteoporosis.
- **Counting fat grams should NOT** be your only focus. Think of it as a way to become aware of where the fat is found in the foods you eat!
- **Speak to your dietician** or physician for guidance on how many calories you require daily, based on your age, sex, height, present weight, body frame and level of physical activity.
- **If your physician recommends** that your daily total fat intake should be 10 percent of calories for medical reasons, refer to the chart in the sidebar "Recommended Daily Fat Consumption Goal" and divide the 20 percent column in half. (e.g. If you eat 1,800 calories, your daily fat goal will be 20 grams.)
- **Think of keeping track** of your fat grams as an educational process. It's annoying at first, but before long, you'll instinctively know when you've eaten too much fat in a day. Instead of counting fat grams, you can count on being healthier and feeling better!
- **Here's a riddle for you.** What weighs more, muscle or fat? Surprise! Muscle does not weigh more than fat. A pound of muscle and a pound of fat each weigh 1 pound. However, pound for pound, muscle takes up less space than fat. You may notice a favorable change in your body shape rather than a change in your body weight and the numbers on the scale when you start to exercise!

Balance the Fat Budget!

- **Butter or margarine?** Both can fit into a healthy lifestyle, but use them sparingly. Butter contains the kind of saturated fat which raises levels of LDL (bad) cholesterol. Some of the newer margarines are low in saturated fat, high in unsaturated fat and don't contain trans fats. Whenever possible, think about substituting olive or canola oil in your cooking and baking.
- **Butter and margarine contain** almost the same number of calories, but tub margarine is lower in saturated fat. One tablespoon of butter has 102 calories and 11.5 g fat (7.2 g saturated), whereas 1 tablespoon of margarine has 101 calories and 11.4 g fat (2.2 g saturated). See Better Than Butter Spread (p. 125).

- **Choose soft, spreadable** tub margarine. Softer margarines that are nonhydrogenated are a better choice as they don't contain trans fatty acids. Avoid stick margarines; they contain trans fats. "Trans free" varieties of margarine are now available.
- **Check margarine labels carefully.** Look for liquid oil as the first ingredient (canola, safflower, soybean, sunflower or corn oil). Add up the grams of unsaturated fats (polyunsaturated plus monounsaturated). Base your choice on the total of these two numbers. Ten grams (2 teaspoons) of margarine should contain a total of 6 grams (or more) of unsaturated fat.
- **When buying light margarine,** choose a brand with a total of 3 grams or more of unsaturated fat for a 10 gram (2 teaspoons) serving. Light margarine is used mainly as a reduced-fat spread.
- **Light margarine may contain gelatin.** It can replace regular margarine or butter in streusel toppings and is fine in many "formerly fatty" baking recipes, but not all. You need to experiment!
- **The recommended oils** today are monounsaturated oils like canola and olive oils. Canola oil is ideal for baking, cooking or salads, whereas olive oil is best used for cooking and salads.
- **Extra-virgin olive oil** is ideal for salads because of its intense flavor, so a little goes a long way. For sautéeing, use canola or pure olive oils, which are less expensive than extra-virgin olive oil.
- **One tablespoon of vegetable oil** provides enough linoleic acid and fat to transport all the fat-soluble vitamins necessary for a day! No more than 10 percent of your total fat intake should be saturated.
- **Half a cup of sugar** contains nearly 400 calories, 1/2 cup flour has more than 200 calories, but 1/2 cup of oil (even recommended oils like olive or canola) contains almost 1,000 calories! Make smart choices and you'll be "oil" right!

Calling All Cholesterol!

- **Dietary cholesterol is different** from blood cholesterol. Dietary cholesterol is found in animal foods (meat, poultry, fish, dairy products, egg yolks). Plant foods don't contain cholesterol.
- **Health experts recommend** limiting dietary cholesterol intake to less than 300 mg daily.
- **For some people,** the amount of cholesterol in their diet has little effect on the amount of cholesterol in their bloodstream, while for others, there is a direct effect.
- **Bottom line:** Eggs can be a regular part of a healthy diet for most individuals, so get cracking! Omega-3 eggs are an excellent choice.
- **Eat small servings of meat,** fish and poultry, about 3 ounces, the size of a deck of cards. Trim away excess fat before cooking. Use lower-fat cooking methods (baking, broiling, steaming).
- **When blood cholesterol is too high**, it settles on the inside walls of blood vessels. Eventually, blood vessels become clogged and blood cannot flow properly to the heart and brain, increasing the chances of having a heart attack or stroke.
- **Soluble fiber may help** lower blood cholesterol levels. It can be found in oats, peas, beans and barley (just like the song we sang as kids!), as well as carrots, apples and grapefruit.
- **The Heart and Stroke Foundation** suggests keeping your diet low in fat, especially saturated and trans fats. (Trans fats aren't always listed on labels! They are believed to act like saturated fats.) Monounsaturated, polyunsaturated and omega-3 fats are better for heart health, but they're still fats, so eat small amounts. if you are watching your weight They're found in vegetable oils and in fatty fish such as salmon.

Calci-Yummy—Very Dairy Good!

- **Enjoy a daily well-balanced diet** including foods rich in calcium for healthy bones. Vitamin D is essential for calcium absorption. Milk, cheese and other dairy products are super sources of calcium, but only milk contains vitamin D. Dee-licious!
- **Aim for at least 1,000 mg of calcium** a day if you're 19 to 50, 1,200 to 1,500 mg if you're 50 plus.
- **To reduce fat intake,** choose 1 percent or skim milk. The calcium content is the same as in whole milk. Substitute 2 percent milk for cream. Use milk and milk products in soups, sauces and desserts.
- **One cup of milk** contains about 300 mg of calcium. Calcium-enriched milk is available in some supermarkets in skim and low-fat varieties. One cup contains about 425 mg calcium. Some people are lactose intolerant (i.e., cannot digest milk sugar). For them, lactose-free milk is a good choice. There are also lactase drops or pills which digest the lactose in your system.
- **Yogurt with live cultures** is usually tolerated by those who are lactose intolerant. One cup of yogurt contains 450 mg of calcium (most of the calcium is found in the whey)!
- **In the U.S., milk and margarine** are fortified with Vitamin D. One cup of milk contains 100 IU. One tablespoon of margarine contains 80 IU. Other food sources of Vitamin D are salmon, tuna, sardines, herring, mackerel, egg yolks and fortified breakfast cereals.
- **Vitamin D is manufactured** by our bodies if our skin is exposed to sunlight without sunscreen. The amount of sunlight you need depends on the time of day, the season, where you live and how easily you burn. Aim for 10 to 15 minutes a day several times a week between 8 a.m. and 4 p.m. So take a walk in the sunshine, strengthen your bones and burn calories!

Chef's Secrets: Eggs!

- Eggs are nutritious and economical, containing many important nutrients. However, because each egg yolk contains over 200 mg of cholesterol ($2/3$ of the recommended daily intake), eggs got a bad reputation and were considered unhealthy. Recent research based on health studies of nearly 120,000 men and women showed that there was no evidence of a significant overall link between egg consumption and the risk of heart disease or stroke in healthy adults. However, for those with diabetes, higher egg consumption may be linked to a higher risk of development of heart disease.
- One egg yolk contains 213 mg dietary cholesterol and 5 grams of fat. Lower-cholesterol eggs are now being developed. If your blood cholesterol levels are high, limit egg yolks to 3 or 4 per week. Egg whites don't contain cholesterol, so substitute two whites for for one whole egg in recipes. Alternatively, replace each egg with $1/4$ cup egg substitute. When baking, don't replace more than half the eggs in your recipe with just whites or the texture could be affected.

- **In northern climates,** there is not enough sun from October to March. Plan a winter vacation for some fun in the sun! Consider a multi-vitamin supplement with Vitamin D. Ask your doctor or dietitian for guidance. Too much vitamin D from supplements, not sun, can be toxic.
- **The Osteoporosis Society recommends** adults receive 400 IU of vitamin D a day, and older adults or those with osteoporosis need 400 to 800 IU a day.
- **Milk protein may trigger** an allergic reaction in some people. For non-dairy alternatives to increase the calcium in your diet, read "Calcium Without Bothering the Cow" in this section.

- **Calcium Without Bothering the Cow!** Calcium is found in leafy dark green vegetables (cooked broccoli, collards, kale, bok choy, baked beans, dried beans, chickpeas, soybeans, tofu (processed with calcium), peanuts, walnuts, hazelnuts, almonds, sesame and sunflower seeds, soy flour, blackstrap molasses, figs, raisins, oranges, orange juice (fortified in the U.S.A.) and seaweed. Eat canned salmon and sardines with the bones. You may also want to consider taking a calcium supplement.
- **Soy, what's new?** Non-dairy beverages such as soy milk can be fortified with calcium, vitamins A, B-12, D, riboflavin and zinc. Other nutrients may also be added. Great for vegans!
- **Many foods bind with calcium,** reducing the amount actually absorbed by the body. Large quantities of oxalic acid, phytic acid and fat can prevent proper calcium absorption.
- **Oxalic acid is found** in chocolate, cocoa, spinach, Swiss chard, parsley, beet greens and rhubarb.
- **Phytic acid is found** in legumes, as well as in the bran of whole-grain cereals.
- **Choose lean protein** sources as listed in Smart Meal Planning on p. 41.
- **Excess alcohol, caffeine** and sodium raise your risk of osteoporosis. Avoid soft drinks. Caffeine is found in cola, coffee, tea and cocoa. Go for cappuccino!
- **Vitamin C enhances calcium** absorption, so add red peppers to your bulgur pilaf or bean salad!
- **The National Osteoporosis Foundation** is an excellent resource. Phone: (202) 223-2226.

How Sweet It Is!

- **Eat sugars and sweets in moderation.** They supply calories, but little else nutritionally.
- **Jujubes and jelly beans** may be fat-free, but they contain empty calories. Four jelly beans are equivalent to eating 2 teaspoons of sugar! If you can't resist sweets, buy the smallest package you can. Chew very slowly. Savor the flavor, and if possible, share with a friend.
- **Words ending in "ose"** on a food label usually refer to sugars. Examples are fructose, lactose, maltose, glucose (dextrose).
- **Added sugars are found** in candies, soft drinks, jams, jellies, table sugar, canned fruits, ice cream, cookies, cakes, pies and diet foods. For information on substitutes, see Sweet Delights (p. 365).
- **The American Diabetes Association** recommends that individuals with diabetes eat the majority of carbohydrate in their diets in the form of complex carbohydrate, fiber-rich foods rather than as simple sugars. Check out their excellent website at www.diabetes.org for healthy lifestyle guidelines and management of diabetes. Their phone number is 800-DIABETES (800-342-2383).
- **Sugar can be eaten in moderation** by diabetics. However, sugars should be substituted for other carbohydrates, not added to the meal. Spread sugars throughout the day as part of slowly digested meals (meals that include starch, protein and fats). Balance with extra exercise.
- **It is essential to consult** with a registered dietician or your diabetes health team to help you integrate sweets into your meal plan and learn how to substitute them occasionally for other food choices. Within the context of a healthy diet, diabetics can substitute sugars for other choices without any adverse effects on blood sugar control.

Shaking the Salt Habit!

- **Health experts recommend 2,400 mg of sodium** (about 1 teaspoon) daily. Foods high in hidden salt include deli meats, many cheeses, most canned soups and vegetables, soy sauce, pickles, tomato sauce, tomato juice, but mostly snack foods (crackers, chips) and sweet desserts.

· **Look for low-sodium or sodium-free** products (e.g. tomato juice, canned tomatoes, cottage cheese, bread crumbs). Use lite soy sauce, or dilute regular soy with equal amounts of water.

· **To reduce salt** in cooking, use herbs, spices and lemon juice. Combine basil and/or dill with lemon or lime juice; use basil, oregano and bay leaf for excellent flavor. Add salt at the table, if necessary.

· **Prepare homemade sauces,** soups, bread crumbs, etc. instead of using processed products.

· **To remove most of the salt** from Koshered chickens, soak them in cold water plus a little lemon juice for at least $1/2$ hour before cooking. Rinse and drain thoroughly.

· **If you have a tendency** to retain sodium, cut back on salty foods and eat plenty of fresh fruits, vegetables, whole-grain cereals and legumes for potassium. Go for the gold . . . and green, red, yellow and orange (potatoes, beans, peppers, tomatoes, bananas, melons and oranges)!

Healthy Habits

· **You are what you eat!** Change those old "fattitudes" and develop new, healthy attitudes.

· **Don't set unrealistic goal weights.** It's the amount of body fat, not total body weight, that should be your focus in weight management. (Even thin people can have excess body fat!)

· **Avoid starvation diets!** Your body will try to protect its weight by slowing down its metabolism.

· **Eat at least three balanced meals a day.** This helps supply your body with fuel to maintain your basal metabolic rate. Plan menus in advance and stick to them. You are responsible for what you eat!

· **Try not to skip meals.** The calories you save by skipping breakfast and/or lunch will probably show up at four o'clock in the form of a binge!

· **Consume most of your calories** early in the day. Supper should be your lightest meal. Many people consume most of their calories between supper and bedtime (often eating in bed!) Many experts recommend that you shouldn't eat three hours before going to sleep.

· **Be aware of what,** when, where and why you are putting food in your mouth. A daily food diary helps prevent "food amnesia." (But be honest about what you ate!)

· **Drink lots of ice cold water**, at least eight large glasses a day. Most of hunger is thirst.

· **Social eating can be an excuse to indulge . . . and bulge!** Never go to a party hungry. Keep your back to the buffet table. (No, I didn't say to go back to the buffet table!)

· **Don't try to lose more than 1 to 2 pounds** per week, or you may start to burn lean muscle tissue. Then if you regain your weight, you will gain more than you lost originally, and it will be harder next time for you to lose the accumulated fat. (This is the voice of experience speaking!)

· **Make small changes gradually.** Don't try to change all your eating habits in one day or even one week. Old habits helped you put on excess fat. It takes new habits to lose fat and keep it off.

· **Focus on one day at a time.** Steady, determined persistence and commitment will help you achieve your goals for a healthier, happier lifestyle and a leaner body.

· **Everybody slips once in a while.** Just pick yourself up, dust yourself off and start all over again!

High-Low and A-Weigh We Go!

- **Regular exercise increases metabolism,** gives you a healthier heart, reduces high blood pressure, builds muscle, gives you a general feeling of well-being, builds stronger bones, improves diabetes, helps prevent or improve arthritis and burns calories! Now that's a bargain. Regular exercise and good nutrition go hand in hand.

- **Walking is probably the easiest exercise** (and the least expensive)! It is an aerobic (fat burning) activity that can be done by almost everybody. The only equipment you need is a pair of good walking shoes. Walk in the sunshine for your daily dose of vitamin D!

- **If you have difficulty walking long distances** or are short on time, even a short walk is beneficial. Just take a five minute walk before and after each meal and you've got thirty minutes of walking under your belt. (And use your wok for low-fat stir-fries to help you tighten your belt!)

- **If you want to avoid** gaining weight, or lose it if you need to, stop making excuses and get up off your "buts"! Physical activity burns calories that would otherwise end up stored as fat. It also builds muscle, which is essential for weight control. Your muscles constantly use energy. The more active you are, the more calories your muscles burn. Aim for 30 to 60 minutes of physical activity each day. Exercise helps keep you healthy and protects you from chronic diseases (e.g. heart disease, high blood pressure, high cholesterol, adult-onset diabetes, some cancers, depression, osteoporosis and obesity).

- **You didn't gain all of your excess weight** in just a few days, so don't expect it to disappear instantaneously just because you worked out for thirty minutes at the gym and ate diet cabbage soup and bananas! There are no shortcuts to success.

- **One hundred calories** a day translates into a 10 pound weight-loss or gain per year! One hour of walking (10,000 steps) burns about 300 calories. Each 20 minutes of brisk walking burns about 100 calories, so walk your "weigh" to success—one step at a time!

- **Be more active than you already are.** Increase your daily physical activity level. Use the stairs instead of the elevator, park your car a little further away from your destination . . . and most important of all, push yourself away from the table!

Simple Secrets for Success

- **The secrets for successful weight control** are to decrease your intake of total fat, eat satisfying foods which are nutrient-dense, and increase your physical activity. Strive for balance.

- **Plan healthy meals and snacks** that have variety so you don't get bored. Keep low-fat, nutrient-dense foods on hand. Keep high-fat, low-nutrient foods out of the house. Store tempting foods in inconvenient places, or have someone else in the family hide them from you!

- **Change your cooking techniques** and recipes to low-fat. Don't get in a rut with your menus. Experiment and try new recipes (but not on a day that you're expecting company)!

- **Measuring can help limit portion sizes** of higher-fat foods. Instead of putting out bowls of food so everyone can help themselves at the table, help yourself by filling plates at the counter!

- **You don't have to finish all the food** on your plate. It won't help starving children elsewhere in the world! Leave the table immediately if you can't resist "one more lovin' spoonful."

- **If you are tempted by second helpings,** prepare only the amount of food you need. If there are any leftovers, ask your family to help clear the table and put leftovers away quickly.

- **Choose only one or two locations** in the house for eating. (In front of the T.V. is not a good place!)
- **There are no "musts"** and there are no "no's". Everything in small portions is acceptable. Moderation is the key. Focus on the positive, eliminate the negative.
- **Try to make wise choices** most of the time and forget the guilt trip if you indulge occasionally. Just get back on the highway to the low weigh!
- **There are no good or bad foods.** It's difficult to establish new, healthy ways. In the long run, it's your pattern of eating over a period of time that counts. Your brain has been programmed to reach for certain comfort foods in times of stress. It's difficult to change the message that's been on automatic pilot for many years. Keep trying and you will establish healthier habits.
- **There are no magical foods.** The media often makes big headlines about a "new" or "important" discovery, then retracts their claims, confusing the consumer. Magazines at the check-out counter of your grocery store feature the lastest "miracle" or fad diet. The only thing that is sure to get leaner will be your pocketbook!
- **A multiple vitamin-mineral supplement** will not replace good eating habits. A supplement is just an addition to your diet, not the sole source of nutrients. Try to get most of the nutrients your body needs by choosing a wide variety of foods from all four food groups and "other foods." (See Smart Meal Planning, p. 41).
- **However, some people require** certain supplements, especially if they have a busy lifestyle and can't always eat properly. Pregnant women may need extra iron and folacin. People with lactose intolerance or osteoporosis may need extra calcium. Ask your physician about supplements.
- **Different people need different** amounts of particular types of food. The revised RDAs (now called the DRIs) provide an adequate guide to what your overall food intake should be comprised of. Visit the website of the Food and Nutrition Information Center (part of the USDA) for more specific information: www.nal.usda.gov/fnic/etext/000105.html.

More Nutri-Tips & Strategies

- **Mental visualization is a terrific tool** that can help you become Slenderella (or fella)! It's used by many atheletes who know the importance of being physically fit and lean.
- **Create a mental picture** of how you would like to see yourself. Visualize yourself succeeding. Relax, breathing slowly and deeply. Picture each part of your body being lean, strong and fit.
- **Relaxation and visualization** are two excellent tools for stress reduction. Try tai chi or yoga!
- **Divide your goals into mini goals.** Otherwise, they may be too overwhelming. For example, if you have 30 pounds to lose, visualize yourself 10 pounds thinner. Imagine how you will look, how your old clothes will feel, and how great you'll feel wearing your new, smaller clothes!
- **Think positive!** Eliminate that "failure feeling." Stop negative self-talk before it stops you. When you have negative thoughts, think of them as if they were clouds and visualize blowing them away.
- **Learn from your past mistakes.** History doesn't have to repeat itself. Only you can determine your destiny. Take positive action, focus on your goals and you'll surely succeed. Imagine that!
- **Expect the unexpected.** It's almost impossible to follow set plans all the time, so don't have unrealistic expectations.
- **Failure is a decision not to try again.** Work towards a lifestyle change. No matter what happens, don't give up. If you do slip, get back on track as soon as possible and move forward.

- **There is no such thing as cheating, only wandering.** It's not easy to change old habits. Don't pass judgment on yourself for wandering. It's normal.
- **If you want less fat** on you, put less calories and fat in you!
- **Instead of two to three large meals daily,** try to eat several smaller meals. The individual fat cells may actually adapt to a pattern of large, infrequent meals by becoming more efficient at storing fat.
- **Eating frequent light,** nutritious meals and snacks helps keep the body's metabolic systems churning away, making fat loss and weight management easier.
- **Stretch small portions of higher calorie,** higher fat foods with hearty helpings of fat-free, fiber-full veggies. (For example, combine macaroni and cheese with lots of steamed mixed veggies.)
- **The wider the variety** of nutritious foods you eat, the greater exposure you'll have to a variety of beneficial substances found in food.
- **Restaurants usually serve portions** that are too large. This is one of the main reasons so many people are overweight today! Make friends with your waiter and ask which are the heart-healthy choices on the menu. Share your meal with a friend, or ask for a doggy bag for leftovers.
- **Resign from the Clean Plate Club!** (That means your plate and your kids' plates too!)
- **It's not only what you eat,** it's how much you eat. Sometimes we lose track of appropriate portion sizes. Many of us have "Sometimers." (Sometimes we forget what or how much we ate!) A food diary can help make you aware of what and how much you're eating.
- **Food and mood.** Keep a food diary or journal for at least a week or two. Mark down everything you eat, no matter if it's good or bad for you. Don't feel guilty. Mark down how much you ate, your mood, the time you ate. Where were you, what were you doing, who was with you? These notes will help you know your automatic triggers.
- **Exercise and proper eating habits** go hand in hand in weight control. Diet alone is not enough to create a lean, toned body. Much of the weight lost by dieting is muscle and water, not fat.
- **Take a walkman,** take a friend, take a walk! With the buddy system, you motivate each other to keep that body moving. (And it's difficult to cancel on a friend who depends on you!)
- **Aerobic exercise burns the most fat.** It uses the body's major muscles in a continuous rhythmic manner for extended periods of time (e.g., walking, jogging, cycling, swimming, dancing). Do what you enjoy and what is most convenient. Most behavior is based on the pleasure principle. If you don't like it, you won't do it! (P.S. Laughter is an aerobic activity!)
- **Exercise as early as possible in the day.** It gives your metabolism a big boost for the whole day, and also increases your energy levels. (I speak from experience!) Also, if you write your exercise down in your Food/Mood Diary, you'll feel motivated and more positive about yourself.
- **Try to exercise most days** for 30 to 60 minutes per session for optimum fat-burning benefits and overall good health. Exercising on a consistent basis promotes fat loss and builds muscle. Start slowly. Do 20 minutes two or three days a week, then increase gradually to longer and more frequent workouts.
- **To maximize fat loss,** exercise at a low to moderate intensity. You should be able to walk and talk at the same time. If you can't catch your breath, you're probably burning carbohydrates, not fat. A burning sensation in your muscles is another indication you aren't burning fat.
- **Exercise is non-negotiable!** It's the secret ingredient to a healthy weight.
- **Once you decide to make lifestyle changes,** the hardest part is over. There is no time or age limit. Just keep focused on your goal and you'll succeed.
- **My way or the high weigh!** No way! Listening to

others who are "experts" on how you should live your life is not the best idea. Remember, you have the power of choice, those simple choices that make life right (and light) for you. The only person you have to answer to is yourself.

- **Feeling good is the secret to looking good.** Try not to worry about the numbers on the scale and don't allow losing weight to become an obsession. (Losing implies that you may find it again!) Try to do your best . . . just for today! I do not diet. I eat almost everything, but try to eat more of the foods that are good for me, with little tastes occasionally of my old favorites that I can't resist.
- **You can lose 25 pounds in a year** ($\frac{1}{2}$ pound a week) just by cutting back 250 to 300 calories a day, or burning them through exercise. After you lose some of your weight, your body requires fewer calories. If you reach a plateau, you probably need to take in less calories or do more exercise.
- **Never go below 1,200 calories a day** without consulting your physician! If you starve your body, it will go into a protective mode and slow down its metabolism. You'll also lose lean muscle mass, which affects metabolism. Muscles use carbohydrates as the main source of energy.
- **Weight gain is less likely** in those people who eat lots of vegetables or who exercise regularly. So stop "vegging out" on your sofa and start "vegging in" your fridge!
- **Potassium, along with sodium,** helps to maintain fluid balance, promotes proper metabolism and muscle function, and also helps to maintain normal blood pressure. Potassium is found in bananas, citrus fruits, tomatoes, potatoes, sweet potatoes, avocados, green vegetables, legumes, whole grains and nuts. The recommended daily intake for potassium is about 3,500 mg a day.
- **Folate (folic acid/folacin)** is one of the B vitamins. Deficiency may cause birth defects. For food sources, think green, like foliage. Leafy fresh green vegetables are a rich source of folacin (and antioxidants too!) It's also in liver, legumes, oranges, sunflower seeds, broccoli and whole grains.
- **Antioxidants help protect against** the effects of disease and aging. Among the major antioxidants are vitamins C and E, beta carotene (which the body converts into vitamin A) and selenium. Rich sources of antioxidants are fresh fruits and veggies, fatty fish, nuts, legumes and vegetable oils.
- **Selenium (found in poultry, seafood, whole grains, onions, garlic, mushrooms)** is an antioxidant that works together with vitamin E to protect cell membranes from the damage of oxidation.
- **So lower your fat intake** and enjoy the benefits of more fruit and vegetables for better health!

A "Handy Weigh" to Measure!

- **A thumb-tip equals 1 teaspoon.** Three thumb-tips (or half of a thumb!) equal 1 tablespoon.
- **A whole thumb equals 1 ounce/25 grams.** (Two thumbs equal a 50 gram serving of cheese.)
- **The palm of your hand** (without the fingers and thumb!) equals a serving of meat, fish or poultry.
- **Your fist equals 1 cup (a serving of salad).** Strive for five to ten servings of vegetables and fruit a day. (It's okay to count them on your fingers. Now that's two thumbs up!)

Smart Meal Planning

A healthy, well-balanced meal should be high in fiber, vitamins, minerals and other nutrients, and low in saturated and trans fats. Different foods offer different nutrients that are essential for good health, so when planning meals, concentrate on color and variety. Remember, food that's good for you should taste good and look good!

Do your best to include at least one serving from each of the following categories of fruits and vegetables each day, focusing on variety and color for optimal health:

- Dark green leafy vegetables (spinach, Swiss chard, bok choy, cabbage, broccoli)
- Yellow/orange fruits and vegetables (cantaloupe, squash, sweet potato, carrots, apricots)
- Red fruits and vegetables (strawberries, watermelon, tomatoes [preferably cooked in a little olive oil])
- Legumes (kidney beans, black beans, chickpeas, lentils)
- Citrus fruits (oranges, lemons, limes)

The quality of the food you eat is just as important as the quantity. Use the following guide to help you with daily meal planning. Select healthy choices within each food group to stay on target with health promotion and disease prevention.

Finally, avoid those "thighs of regret" and exercise each day. (Note: the "forklift" is *not* aerobic exercise.)

GRAINS (5–12 servings):
Choose high-fiber grains (e.g., cereals, whole-grain breads, brown rice, pasta, kasha, etc.) Cut back on processed grains and "fluffy" white foods (e.g., pastries, cookies, white flour, white bread).

VEGETABLES (3–5 servings):
Choose a variety of fresh, colorful vegetables each day, and include plenty of dark green leafy vegetables and legumes each week. Cut back on fried and processed vegetables. One serving is about half a cup cooked and 1 cup raw.

FRUIT (2–4 servings):
Choose a variety of fresh, frozen (without sugar), canned (water-packed) and dried fruit each day. Cut back on fruit in syrup.

MILK PRODUCTS (2–3 servings):
Choose low-fat dairy foods (e.g., low-fat and skim milk, plain yogurt, low-fat cheeses). Cut back on dairy products with added sugar and those that are high in saturated fat.

MEAT, POULTRY, FISH, TOFU, BEANS, EGGS & NUTS (2–3 servings):
Choose lean meats. Be sure to watch your portion sizes. (One serving is the size of a deck of cards.) Cut back on processed and high-fat meats. One serving of nuts is 1 ounce, a quarter cup or a small handful.

FATS, OILS & SWEETS (CHOOSE WISELY):
Choose vegetable oils that are liquid at room temperature (e.g., olive, canola, safflower and grapeseed oils.). Avoid saturated and trans fats, found in full-fat dairy foods, meats, margarine and highly processed foods. Cut back on added sugar to reduce caloric intake.

LOW-CARB DIETS AND THE GLYCEMIC INDEX:
For years, nutrition experts have told us that a low-fat, high-carbohydrate diet should be the basis of a healthy eating plan to lose weight. Now, many weight-loss gurus are recommending that we should limit our intake of carbohydrates to help us lose those unwanted pounds quickly and easily.

On low-carbohydrate diets, one reason that people lose weight quickly (especially at the beginning) is because water is lost when fewer carbohydrates are consumed. This is caused by ketosis, a metabolic shift that takes place in the body when carbs are reduced to a very low level and fats are burned instead of carbs as a fuel source. Another reason many people who follow low-carb diets lose weight is because they consume fewer calories than they previously did.

A sensible, safe approach to following a low-carb weight-loss program is to cut back on (but don't totally eliminate) carbohydrates. Choose "good" or complex carbs, those that are found in high-fiber vegetables, fruits, whole grains and legumes. Choose "good" proteins, those that are low in saturated fats. And choose "good" fats (e.g., monounsaturated fats such as olive oil and canola oil). Balance is the key.

The Glycemic Index (GI) has become a popular diet tool. It is a system that ranks carbohydrate foods on a scale from 0 to 100 according to the extent to which they affect blood sugar levels after eating.

Foods with a high GI (more than 70) are rapidly absorbed, resulting in rapid rises in blood sugar and insulin levels. Low GI foods (less than 55) are more slowly digested and absorbed, producing gradual rises in blood sugar and insulin levels. Foods between 55 and 70 are considered medium GI foods.

Choosing foods with a low GI appears to reduce the risk of heart disease and prevent type 2 diabetes. Low GI foods can also help curb your appetite so you lose weight.

Many of the rapidly digested carbohydrates we eat have a high GI (e.g., white bread, bagels, potatoes, sweet cereals, sugary foods, soft drinks). They trigger rapid spikes in blood sugar and insulin levels, leading to a rapid drop in blood sugar, resulting in rebound hunger. Meals and snacks with a low GI can help control appetite and delay hunger.

Whole grains, beans, most fruits and vegetables have a low to medium GI, generating smaller, slower increases in blood glucose levels. If grains are eaten whole or cracked into large pieces, they are converted slowly into glucose. If grains are stripped of the fibrous bran coating and pulverized into flour, the fine starch particles are easily digested and rapidly converted into glucose. Beans are high in fiber, which slows down the digestion of the starch.

Low GI foods include pasta, oats, beans, barley and some varieties of rice. Some higher GI foods such as bran flakes, carrots and watermelon are low-calorie and very nutritious, so don't avoid them completely. Some low or medium GI foods such as candy bars are high in empty calories. Don't eat too much of them or you'll crowd out essential nutrients and gain weight.

Oranges and strawberries have a lower GI than ripe bananas and watermelon. Instead of tropical fruits (bananas, mango, papaya, pineapple, etc.) you can choose temperate climate fruits like apples, peaches and nectarines, which have a lower GI.

Instant oatmeal has a lower GI than steel-cut oats. Multi-grain bread has a lower GI than white bread. Whole wheat pasta has a lower GI than pasta made from white flour. If pasta is cooked al dente, its GI is even lower. Brown rice has a lower GI than white rice. Basmati rice or converted rice has a lower GI than short-grain rice (used for sushi and risotto). Sweet potatoes and new potatoes have a lower GI than white potatoes.

Low GI diets have been shown to improve both glucose and lipid levels in diabetics. They also lower insulin levels and insulin resistance. Several large studies have demonstrated that eating foods with a high GI appears to be a risk factor for type 2 diabetes.

Choosing the right type of carbohydrates in your diet, preferably whole grains that are as unprocessed as possible instead of refined carbohydrates, can protect you from many chronic diseases. They will also offer new, delicious taste adventures.

Traditional Mediterranean diets, which include plenty of fruits, vegetables and beans, are higher in good fats and are fairly low in easily digested carbohydrates. They also have a relatively low impact on blood glucose levels.

While the Glycemic Index is a useful tool for deciding what to eat, don't judge a food only by its GI value. Effective and long-term weight management evolves out of a healthy change in lifestyle, not a brief commitment to eating only certain foods because of where they rank on a chart. Although the Glycemic Index can be helpful, it does have some shortcomings.

The GI does not consider calories or portion size, which are essential factors in weight control. Also, diets that exclude vegetables and fruits for long periods of time are lacking in essential nutrients. Vegetables, fruits and grains offer valuable vitamins, minerals, fiber and phytochemicals and should be included as part of a healthy lifestyle.

The GI does not take into account that people usually don't eat individual foods; they eat meals comprised of various nutrients. To lower the GI of a meal, eat carbohydrate-rich foods with a little protein and/or fat. For example, sprinkle a little olive oil on a baked potato, or add some diced tofu or chicken to rice pilaf. This will slow digestion and prevent blood sugar from rising too quickly.

Try to include at least one low GI food at each meal or snack. If you add legumes (beans, peas, lentils) to carbs like pasta or rice, their high soluble fiber content will lower the glycemic effect. Whenever possible, eat fruits, vegetables and grains in their whole form rather than refined, processed or juiced foods. Whole foods contain more fiber, slowing down digestion.

Use rolled oats instead of bread crumbs in meatloaf and meatball recipes. Instead of a vegetable and a starch with your main dish, choose two vegetables. If drinking a cocktail or juice, mix it with diet soda or sparkling water. In baking, substitute up to half of the flour with whole or cracked grains.

For a delicious, low-carb alternative to mashed potatoes, boil cauliflower florets until tender, then drain and mash well. Add a little olive oil, some chicken broth and season with salt and pepper to taste. Voila, mashed faux-tatoes!

There is concern that the Glycemic Index and low-carb diets may be sending out the message that if you want to lose weight, you should eat more meat and fat. However, diets high in meat are usually high in saturated fat. They may increase the risk of heart disease and possibly breast, colon and prostate cancer.

Remember, all fats are not considered equal. Instead of choosing a high-fat steak, a smarter choice would be a fiber-packed salad drizzled with extra-virgin olive oil and lemon juice, topped with sliced turkey breast and slivered toasted almonds.

Diets based on the elimination of carbohydrates are not recommended by most experts for long-term use. Carbohydrates are easily digested sources of energy for the body. Since carbohydrates are the main source of energy for our muscles, it can become more difficult to exercise on a low-carb diet. Exercise is non-negotiable if you want to control your weight. Exercise also makes you less insulin resistant.

Remember, it is the total calories that count when it comes to weight loss, regardless of their source. A low-fat, high-carb diet won't help you lose weight if total calories are not limited; neither will a low-carb, high-fat diet. For a filling, nutritious and balanced meal, your plate should contain 2/3 of vegetables, fruits, whole grains and beans, and 1/3 of protein (e.g., meat, poultry, tofu, eggs or cheese).

Different individuals have different risk factors for disease. For people at risk for diabetes or those with high triglycerides, it is important to follow a reduced-carbohydrate diet (40 to 50% carbohydrates). Athletes need to consume a higher-carbohydrate diet (60 to 65% carbohydrates). People with high cholesterol levels need to limit the amount of saturated and trans fats in their diet.

What's the bottom line? Again, balance is the key. Don't eliminate a food group or consume one food group in excess. Total calories consumed and regular exercise are the keys to losing and maintaining weight. The types of foods you choose each day play an important role in disease prevention. Follow the advice of a registered dietitian, who will recommend a nutritious, delicious diet based on your health and lifestyle requirements.

SECTION 2

Appetizers & Starters

Party Pleasures

- So you're going to a party and you're worried that you might eat all the wrong things. Why not call your host or hostess in advance and say you have trouble digesting fatty foods? An excellent excuse is to say that you're allergic. Certain foods make you break out in fat!
- A super idea is to buy a copy of this book as a gift for your host or hostess, but give it to him or her before the party! That way, everyone will be "de-lited."
- Eat a lite bite at home before you go. When you arrive, watch out for the danger foods: cheesy, doughy appetizers (e.g. traditional quiche) or deep-fried foods (e.g. egg rolls). Did you know that one little chicken wing contains nearly 7 grams of fat?
- Choose vegetable-based appetizers, but go easy on the dip. Don't go nuts over that bowl of nuts. Half a cup of peanuts contains 35 grams of fat! Pretzels and air-popped popcorn are better choices than packaged potato or tortilla chips. Keep away from the cheese tray. A 2-inch cube of regular Cheddar cheese contains 15 grams of fat! Choose low-fat cheeses when possible.
- Many crackers contain hydrogenated oils such as palm kernel oil or coconut oil. (This is another way of saying that they contain saturated fat!) Some brands of crackers are high in salt.
- Watch out for those little party sandwiches. They're so easy to pop into your mouth and they slide down much too quickly! Also, they're usually loaded with mayonnaise.
- Make pretty pinwheel sandwiches with flour tortillas. Spread with lighter versions of tuna, salmon or egg salad. Other spreads are: Healthier Hummus (p. 57), Dill-Icious Lox & Cheese Spread (p. 55), Creamy Salmon Paté (p. 125). Roll up like a jelly roll, cover with plastic wrap and chill. To serve, trim off ends and slice rolls on an angle into pinwheels.
- Cucumber rounds can be piped with Dill-Icious Lox & Cheese Spread (p. 55) or Herbed Cheese Spread (p. 54), Yogurt Cheese Spread (p. 54) or Gravlax (p. 68).
- Cherry tomatoes can be hollowed out and stuffed with Creamy Salmon Paté (p. 125), Smoked Whitefish Spread (p. 64) or lighter versions of tuna, salmon, egg, chicken or turkey salad.
- For beautiful bright green broccoli florets for your crudité tray, dip them for a second or two into boiling water. So pretty! The leftover stems can be saved to use for soups or stir-fries.
- Tortellini Pesto Kabobs: Combine cooked cheese tortellini with a little Best-O Pesto (p. 195). Arrange on small wooden skewers alternating with pieces of red, green &/or yellow peppers. (Red or yellow cherry tomatoes are also pretty.) Serve at room temperature.
- Best-O Cheese or Tofu Kabobs: Marinate small cubes of low-fat mozzarella cheese (preferably fresh unripened mozzarella) or tofu in Best-O Pesto or Sun-Dried Tomato Pesto (p. 195). Arrange on 4-inch wooden skewers alternately with bite-sized pieces of colored peppers and cherry tomatoes (or Sun-Dried Tomatoes, p. 264).
- The following crunchy munchies are perfect as party fare: Wonton Chips or Crisp Lasagna Chips (p. 71), Homemade Potato Chips or Sweet Potato Chips (p. 71), Pita or Tortilla Chips (p. 72) and Bagel Chips (p. 72).
- Remember, indulging on special occasions doesn't have to be a disaster. It's unrealistic to go to a party and eat only crudités and drink Perrier water with a twist of lemon! It's better to lighten up the day before and the day following a party. Do a little extra exercise. Forget the guilt—it's counter-productive. If you feel deprived, you'll eat twice as much, probably right after you arrive home after the party! Life is short and pleasure is an important part of life, so choose wisely and enjoy. Live it up!

Crudités & Dips—The Garden of Eatin'!

For maximum eye appeal, include a variety of shapes and colors. Use a mixture of raw and blanched vegetables in your presentation. These are a few of my favorite greens . . . and yellows and reds and oranges and whites! Many of them are also great garnishes. Remember, we eat first with our eyes!

Asparagus, lightly steamed
Belgian Endive Cups (below)
Broccoli florets, raw or lightly steamed
Broccoflower florets, raw or lightly steamed
Cauliflower florets, raw or lightly steamed
Carrot Sticks or Coins (p. 49)
Baby carrots
Celery Curls or Sticks (p. 49)
Cherry or grape tomatoes (red or yellow)
Cucumber Wheels (p. 49)
Green beans, trimmed & lightly steamed
Mushrooms (read "Be a Mushroom Maven" on p. 255)
Pepper Strips (p. 49)
Radish Roses or Fans (p. 49)
Scallion Brushes (p. 49)
Sugar snap peas, raw or lightly steamed
Snow peas, raw or lightly steamed
Zucchini sticks or slices (or miniatures)

The Basket Case: Create an attractive arrangement by placing a bed of greens in an attractive shallow basket, flat container or tray. (Lettuce, spinach, red cabbage, kale, radicchio and parsley all look pretty.) Line the container with aluminum foil or plastic wrap to protect it.

How Does Your Garden Grow? Arrange the vegetables in bunches among the greens. Allow ¹/₂ pound (250 grams) of vegetables per person. Cut the larger vegetables into slices or strips so they can be picked up easily. Tuck some fresh herbs (e.g. dill, rosemary, basil, chives) in between the vegetables to give a gardenlike appearance. Why not tuck in a few fresh flowers as well?

Containers: Place your favorite "skinny" dip in a bowl. Attractive containers can also be made from various vegetables. Slice off tops from any of the following: tomatoes, peppers, round squash, cabbage, eggplant, etc. Hollow out and fill with dip. Serve with Pita or Tortilla Chips (p. 72).

Pumpernickel Bowl: Cut 1 inch off the top of a pumpernickel bread. Hollow out the inside, leaving a wall of bread about ¹/₂-inch thick. Cut bread you've removed into bite-sized cubes. Fill hollowed-out bread with your favorite dip. Serve with cubes of bread and assorted veggies.

Leftovers? Use the leftover veggies to make a big pot of vegetable soup. Add a little skim milk or yogurt to leftover dip and use as a low-fat salad dressing.

Belgian Endive Cups

Choose yellow and/or red endives with tight heads. (Green endives have been exposed to light and are bitter.) Cut ends off the endive and pull apart the leaves. Wash and dry well. Place the desired filling, dip or spread in the center of a round platter. Fan the leaves around the outside edge like the petals of a flower. (For a large party, fill the endive cups in the kitchen for convenience in serving.)

Carrot Sticks or Coins

Carrot Coins: Peel and trim medium-size carrots. Slice on the diagonal $1/2$-inch thick. (A wavy-edged cutter, available in kitchenware shops, is a terrific tool.)

Carrot Sticks: Cut carrots into 4-inch lengths. Cut into sticks. Chill in ice water.

Celery Curls or Sticks

Celery Curls: Cut strips of peeled celery into 4-inch lengths. Cut several slits at both ends. Chill in ice water for an hour or two so they'll open up and curl.

Celery Sticks: Cut strips of peeled celery into 4-inch lengths. Cut into sticks. Chill in ice water.

Cucumber Wheels or Boats

Cucumber Wheels: Pull the tines of a fork down the length of a firm cucumber. (English cucumber doesn't need peeling.) Slice $1/4$-inch thick with a sharp knife or wavy-edged cutter. Roll edges in paprika.

Cucumber Boats: Cut away a thin slice along the length of a small cucumber to form a stable base. On the opposite side, cut away a thick slice about one-fourth of the way down. Hollow out the seeds and part of the pulp with a spoon or melon baller. Fill with tuna salad, chicken salad, carrot sticks, green beans or asparagus. Garnish with minced red pepper.

Pepper Strips, Flowers or Baskets

Red, green, orange and yellow peppers are all excellent sources of vitamin C.

Pepper Strips: Slice off the top and bottom of each pepper. Remove seeds. Cut peppers into strips. (Save tops and bottoms to dice and sprinkle over a salad, or mince finely and add to the dip.)

Red Chili Pepper Flower: Trim $3/4$-inch from the tip of a red chili pepper. Make long, narrow cuts from the cut tip almost to the stem end. Soak in ice water for about an hour, or until petals open.

Pepper Baskets: Cut off the tops, making a zigzag design with a sharp knife. Remove the ribs and seeds. Use peppers as a container for dips or salads.

Radish Roses or Fans

Radish Roses: Trim stems from radishes with a thin, sharp knife. Start from the top end of the radish and peel the red skin away in five or six thin petals, leaving the petals attached to the base. Cut a second layer of petals if you wish. Place in ice water and refrigerate for an hour, until petals open.

Radish Fans: Trim stems from oval-shaped radishes with a sharp knife. Cut crosswise five or six times, but don't slice all the way through. Chill in ice water for several hours so they'll fan out.

Scallion Brushes

Choose scallions (green onions) which are at least $1/2$-inch thick at the bulb end. Cut off most of the green part. Trim off the roots, leaving the white bulb intact. They will be about 4-inch long after trimming. At both ends, make several cuts about 1-inch long with a sharp knife. Place in cold water to "blossom" for one-half hour. Dip ends in paprika, pressing down gently so "brushes" will open up.

Tomato Roses (or Citrus Roses)

Choose a firm tomato (or orange, lemon or lime). Starting at the bottom, use a sharp paring knife to remove the skin in one long, continuous strip about ³/₄-inch wide. Cut with a slight zigzag motion, so the edges of the strip will be wavy. Be careful not to tear the skin. Rewind the skin in a fairly tight coil until you have a rose shape. Start with a fairly tight turn to form the center of the rose, then let each successive turn open outward a bit more. Try to keep the base of the rose a little tighter than the upper part. Place on serving platter and use fresh basil, mint or other fresh herbs to make the leaves. These make great garnishes!

Smoked Salmon Roses

Use long, narrow strips of smoked salmon. Wind up in a coil to make a rose shape. Start with a fairly tight turn to form the center of the rose, then let each turn open outwards a bit more, keeping the base a little tighter than the upper part. Use as a garnish for fish platters. Use dill sprigs for the leaves.

Citrus Cartwheels or Twists

Citrus Cartwheels: Use a lemon stripper to cut lengthwise grooves about ½-inch apart in lemons, limes or oranges. (Use thick-skinned fruit for best results.) Slice thinly. Each slice will have a notched edge. Use to garnish the edges of platters or bowls, or float them on top of a fruit punch.

Citrus Twists: Cut oranges, lemons or limes crosswise into thin slices; discard ends. Make a cut from the center of each slice to the outer edge. Twist half of the slice forward and half of the slice backward. Use lemons or limes with fish, vegetables or salads. Use oranges with poultry, fish or vegetables.

Tomato Baskets

Trim the top and bottom of large, firm tomatoes to form a stable base at both ends. Mark an imaginary or pencil line around the middle. Cut in half with a V-shaped knife, available in kitchen boutiques. (If you don't have a V-shaped knife, make uniform zigzag cuts with a sharp knife.) Be sure to cut all the way through to the center. Adjust the last cut to meet the first cut. Separate the halves.

Remove pulp with a sharp paring knife or serrated grapefruit spoon. Tomato baskets can be filled with your favorite dip, tuna, egg, chicken, pasta or bean salad. Cooked vegetables like peas, broccoli or cauliflower florets are also attractive served in tomato baskets. Serve on a bed of leafy greens.

Basic Skinny Dip

Use fresh dill for a simply dill-icious dip! Your processor will help you prepare this in a flash.

1/2 c. smooth non-fat cottage cheese
1/2 c. non-fat yogurt
1/4 c. green onions, minced
1/4 c. minced green pepper
2   tbsp. grated carrots, optional
2   tbsp. fresh dill, minced (or 1/2 tsp. dried)
1   tsp. lemon or lime juice
Salt & pepper, to taste

1. Combine all ingredients and mix well. Chill until serving time. Serve with assorted vegetables.

Yield: about 1 1/4 cups. Keeps about 3 or 4 days in the refrigerator.

8 calories per tbsp., 0 g fat (0 g saturated), <1 g cholesterol, 1 g protein, <1 g carbohydrate, 22 mg sodium, 25 mg potassium, 0 mg iron, trace fiber, 15 mg calcium.

- **If using creamed cottage cheese,** drain off excess liquid. Process cottage cheese until completely smooth, about 2 to 3 minutes in the processor. Add remaining ingredients. Blend in with quick on/offs.
- **Skinny Variations:** Use basil instead of dill. Add 1 clove minced garlic, if desired. Substitute 1/4 cup minced red pepper or Roasted Red Pepper (p. 57) instead of green pepper. Use minced red onion instead of green onions.

Garden Vegetable Dip or Dressing

Add a little skim milk to leftovers for a "deliteful" salad dressing.

1   clove garlic, minced
2   tbsp. minced green onions
1   tbsp. fresh dill, minced
2   tbsp. red pepper, minced
2   tbsp. finely minced carrot
1/2 c. non-fat yogurt
1/2 c. fat-free or light mayonnaise
Salt & pepper, to taste
Dried basil & oregano, to taste

1. Combine vegetables with yogurt, mayonnaise and seasonings. (If you have a processor, first mince the veggies, then quickly blend in remaining ingredients.) Season to taste. Serve chilled with veggies.

Yield: about 1 1/4 cups. Keeps for 3 or 4 days tightly covered in the refrigerator.

9 calories per tbsp., 0 g fat (0 g saturated), trace cholesterol, trace protein, 2 g carbohydrate, 47 mg sodium, 24 mg potassium, 0 mg iron, trace fiber, 13 mg calcium.

- **Some non-fat yogurts** tend to be watery, making the dip too thin. If this happens, place the dip in a strainer lined with a paper coffee filter. Place strainer over a bowl. Let drip about 30 minutes.
- **Instead of yogurt and mayonnaise,** you can substitute 1 cup of Creamy Yogurt Cheese (p. 53).

Best-O Pesto Dip

1/2   c. non-fat yogurt
1/2   c. fat-free or light mayonnaise
2   to 3 tbsp. Best-O Pesto (p. 195)

1. Combine all ingredients and mix until blended. Chill before serving. Serve with crudités.

Yield: about 1 cup. Keeps for 3 to 4 days in the refrigerator.

11 calories per tbsp., 0.3 g fat (0.1 g saturated), trace cholesterol, <1 g protein, 2 g carbohydrate, 53 mg sodium, 25 mg potassium, trace iron, 0 g fiber, 16 mg calcium.

• **If you don't have any Best-O Pesto,** substitute 2 tablespoons grated Parmesan cheese and 1 tablespoon minced fresh basil (or 1/2 teaspoon dried).

Spinach & Herb Dip

A favorite in my cooking classes!

2   c. non-fat natural yogurt (or
1 1/4 c. Creamy Yogurt Cheese, p. 53)
1/2   of a 10 oz. (300 g) pkg. frozen spinach, thawed &
    squeezed dry
2   cloves garlic, minced
4   green onions, minced
1   medium carrot, minced
1/4   c. fresh parsley, minced
2   tbsp. minced fresh dill (or 1 tsp. dried)
1   tbsp. minced fresh basil (or 1 tsp. dried)
1/3   c. fat-free or light mayonnaise
Salt & pepper, to taste
1   tsp. lemon juice
1   round pumpernickel bread (optional)

1. Place yogurt in a strainer lined with a paper coffee filter or cheesecloth. Place over a bowl and let drain in the fridge for 2 to 3 hours. Combine drained yogurt with remaining ingredients and blend well. (If using a processor, first mince the veggies, then blend in remaining ingredients with quick on/off turns.) Chill dip before serving to blend flavors.

2. If using bread as a container, cut 1 inch off the top. Hollow out inside, leaving a wall of bread about 1/2-inch thick. Cut bread you've removed into bite-sized cubes. Fill hollowed-out bread with dip. Serve with veggies and bread cubes.

Yield: about 2 1/2 cups of dip. Dip keeps for 3 or 4 days in the refrigerator.

9 calories per tbsp., 0 g fat (0 g saturated), trace cholesterol, <1 g protein, 2 g carbohydrate, 22 mg sodium, 38 mg potassium, trace iron, trace fiber, 19 mg calcium.

• **Read the notes** following Yogurt Cheese (p. 53).
• **No time to drain the yogurt?** Use 3/4 cup undrained yogurt and increase mayonnaise to 3/4 cup.
• **Use a sharp knife to cut** frozen package of spinach in half. Wrap and freeze the unused portion.

Easy Spinach Dip

An enlightened version of an old favorite. This dip is usually served in a hollowed-out round pumpernickel or country bread. See Pumpernickel Bowl (p. 48).

10   oz. pkg. (300 g) frozen chopped spinach, thawed &
    squeezed dry
1   8 oz. can (227 ml) water chestnuts, drained &

    chopped
4   green onions, chopped
1/2 pkg. dehydrated vegetable soup mix
1 1/2 c. non-fat yogurt
1/2 c. fat-free or light mayonnaise

1. Combine all ingredients and mix well. Serve chilled with assorted crudités and cubes of bread.

Yield: about 3 1/2 cups. Dip keeps about 3 or 4 days in the refrigerator.

7 calories per tbsp., 0.1 g fat (0 g saturated), trace cholesterol, <1 g protein, 1 g carbohydrate, 25 mg sodium, 33 mg potassium, trace iron, trace fiber, 16 mg calcium.

Tzadziki

Great as a dip, or use it as a spread with crusty bread! I love Tzadziki with lots of garlic, but you can add the amount you like. Non-fat yogurt can be used, but the flavor is superior using 2% yogurt.

4   c. non-fat or low-fat natural yogurt
1   English cucumber, peeled & grated
3–4 cloves garlic, crushed (to taste)
1   tbsp. fresh lemon juice
1–2 tbsp. fresh oregano or dill, minced
    (or 1 tsp. dried)
Freshly ground pepper
Salt, to taste
1   tsp. olive oil

1. Place yogurt in a strainer lined with a paper coffee filter or cheesecloth. Place over a bowl and let drain in the refrigerator for 3 hours, or overnight.

2. Place grated cucumber in a colander in the sink.

Sprinkle generously with salt and let drain for about 1 hour. Rinse well; pat dry. Combine drained yogurt with remaining ingredients. Adjust seasonings to taste.

Yield: about 2 3/4 cups. Tzadziki keeps for 2 or 3 days in the refrigerator.

9 calories per tbsp., 0.1 g fat (0 g saturated), trace cholesterol, <1 g protein, 1 g carbohydrate, 7 mg sodium, 32 mg potassium, 0 mg iron, trace fiber, 19 mg calcium.

- **Tzadziki makes a delicious dip** for veggies or pita chips, or a super spread on slices of grilled crusty bread. Try Tzadziki as a topping for baked potatoes or grilled fish. Very, dairy good!
- **Leftover tzadziki** can be thinned down with a little milk and used as a luscious salad dressing. It also makes an excellent alternative to mayonnaise for egg, tuna or salmon salad.

Yogurt Cheese

A truly guilt-free dip or spread! Use yogurt without added gelatin, starch or stabilizers.

1. Line a strainer with either cheesecloth, paper toweling or a paper coffee filter. Place strainer over a bowl. Spoon 2 cups of non-fat yogurt into strainer. Cover, refrigerate and let drain.

Creamy Yogurt Cheese: In 3 to 4 hours, you will have creamy-textured Yogurt Cheese, an excellent substitute for mayonnaise, sour cream or whipped cream.
Firm Yogurt Cheese: After 12 to 24 hours, you will have firm-textured Yogurt Cheese, a smooth and creamy alternative to cream cheese or cottage

cheese.

Yield: about 1 cup. Keeps approximately one week in the refrigerator.

11 calories per tbsp., 0 g fat (0 g saturated), trace cholesterol, 1 g protein, 2 g carbohydrate, 11 mg sodium, 38 mg potassium, 0 mg iron, 0 g fiber, 30 mg calcium.

- **Don't throw away the whey!** The watery liquid (whey) that drains off contains about ⅓ of the calcium and potassium found in whole milk. Whey keeps about a week in the fridge. Use whey instead of buttermilk or yogurt in muffins, coffee cakes, yeast breads and soups. (Add some yogurt or skim milk if you don't have enough whey.) No waste, no increase in your waistline!
- **Homemade Cottage Cheese** (Buttermilk Cheese) is easy to make. See recipes (p. 145).
- **Yogurt is an ancient wonder food** which boosts immunity and is antibacterial. It is believed that yogurt with acidophilus prevents yeast infections in women.
- **Several manufacturers make Yogurt Strainers.** Donvier makes a compact unit (Wave Yogurt Strainer) which comes with a cover, plus a receptacle to catch the drained whey—so practical.

Yogurt Cheese Spread (or Dip)

Fat-free, flavorful and creamy smooth. What more could you ask for? For a nutritious and tasty dip, thin the mixture with a few drops of yogurt or skim milk. Dip to your heart's delight!

1	c. Firm Yogurt Cheese (see preceding recipe)
¼	c. minced green onions
1	clove garlic, minced
¼	c. red pepper, minced
2	tbsp. minced sun-dried tomatoes, optional
1	tbsp. fresh basil, minced (or 1 tsp. dried)
1	tbsp. fresh dill, minced (or 1 tsp. dried)
½	tsp. honey

1. Prepare Yogurt Cheese as directed. Combine with remaining ingredients and blend well. (If using the processor, first mince vegetables, then mix all ingredients together with quick on/offs. Do not overprocess or yogurt will get watery.) Serve chilled with pumpernickel bread, crackers or bagels.

Yield: about 1¼ cups. Mixture will keep for 2 or 3 days in the refrigerator.

10 calories per tbsp., 0 g fat (0 g saturated), trace cholesterol, 1 g protein, 2 g carbohydrate, 9 mg sodium, 37 mg potassium, 0 mg iron, trace fiber, 24 mg calcium.

Herbed Cheese Spread

½	lb. (250 g) non-fat cottage cheese (low-fat or non-fat cream cheese can be substituted)
1	clove garlic, minced
¼	c. green onions, minced
¼	c. red or green pepper, minced
¼	tsp. each of dried basil & oregano
1	tsp. lemon juice

1. Combine all ingredients and blend well. (Can be done in the processor.) Serve chilled with assorted crackers or breads. It also makes a great spread for bagels. Mixture keeps for 2 or 3 days in the refrigerator.

Yield: about 1¼ cups. Can be frozen.

9 calories per tbsp., 0 g fat (0 g saturated), <1 mg cholesterol, 2 g protein, <1 g carbohydrate, 35 mg sodium, 16 mg potassium, 0 mg iron, trace fiber, 8 mg calcium.

- **If using dry cottage cheese,** add a little skim milk or yogurt. It will make the spread more creamy. If using curd-style cottage cheese, drain excess liquid. Then process cheese until very smooth and lump-free (about 3 minutes) before adding remaining ingredients.
- **Other delicious herbs** which work well in this recipe are dill, parsley and thyme. Fresh herbs add wonderful flavor, but dry herbs can be used successfully.

Dill-icious Lox & Cheese Spread

½ lb. (250 g) non-fat cottage cheese (low-fat or non-fat cream cheese can be substituted)
2 tbsp. fresh dill, minced
2 tbsp. green onions, minced
1 tbsp. honey-style mustard
2–4 tbsp. skim milk or yogurt (as needed)
3 oz. (85 g) lox (smoked salmon), minced
Freshly ground pepper

1. Combine cheese, dill, green onions and mustard; mix well. (The food processor does it all in less than a minute.) Add just enough milk to make mixture creamy and spreadable. Gently stir in lox by hand, or let processor run to make the cheese mixture a pale salmon color. Serve chilled as a tasty spread for bagels, pumpernickel bread or assorted crackers.

Yield: about 1¼ cups. Mixture keeps about 3 days in the refrigerator. Can be frozen.

12 calories per tbsp., 0.2 g fat (0 g saturated), 2 mg cholesterol, 2 g protein, <1 g carbohydrate, 104 mg sodium, 16 mg potassium, 0 mg iron, 0 g fiber, 7 mg calcium.

- **If using curd-style cottage cheese,** process until very smooth and lump-free, about 2 to 3 minutes. Then combine with remaining ingredients. The amount of milk needed will vary, depending on moisture content of the cheese. Firm Yogurt Cheese (p. 53) can be substituted, but do not freeze.

Creamy Salsa Dip

1¼ c. Creamy Yogurt Cheese (p. 53) (non-fat or low-fat sour cream can be substituted)
2 tbsp. minced green onions
¼ c. bottled or homemade salsa (ketchup or chili sauce can be substituted)
Pinch of sugar, optional

1. Combine all ingredients, adding a pinch of sugar if mixture is too tangy. Chill before serving.

Yield: about 1½ cups. Leftovers can be used as a delicious salad dressing. Do not freeze.

10 calories per tbsp., 0 g fat (0 g saturated), trace cholesterol, <1 g protein, 1 g carbohydrate, 24 mg sodium, 32 mg potassium, 0 mg iron, trace fiber, 24 mg calcium.

Mexican 7-Layer Dip

You'll love this de-liteful version of a formerly fat-laden dip. Did you know that avocado is a fruit? Buy two avocados when making this recipe. Mash one to use as a facial. Use the other one for this recipe. You'll look great and so will the dip!

1   19 oz. can (540 ml) black beans
3/4   c. fat-free or light mayonnaise
3/4   c. Creamy Yogurt Cheese (p. 53) (or low-fat sour cream)
1   tsp. chili powder
1/2   tsp. each of cumin & dried oregano
6   green onions, chopped
1/2   c. sliced black olives
2   tomatoes, diced & drained
1   medium avocado, diced
1   tbsp. fresh lemon juice
3/4   c. grated low-fat cheddar cheese

1. Drain beans; rinse well. Mash beans and spread evenly in a 10-inch pie plate or quiche dish. In a small bowl, mix mayonnaise, yogurt cheese and spices. Spread over beans. Arrange green onions, olives and tomatoes in layers. Mix avocado with lemon juice and spread over tomatoes. Sprinkle with cheese. Cover tightly with plastic wrap and chill. Serve with Pita or Tortilla Chips (p. 72).

Yield: about 6 cups (18 to 24 servings). Do not freeze.

13 calories per tbsp., 0.5 g fat (0.2 g saturated), <1 mg cholesterol, <1 g protein, 2 g carbohydrate, 42 mg sodium, 19 mg potassium, trace iron, <1 g fiber, 13 mg calcium.

Chef's Secrets: Avocados!

Buy avocados several days ahead of time. Store ripe avocados in the refrigerator for about a week. Put unripe avocados in a perforated brown paper bag to ripen. I prefer Hass avocados, with their dark skin and lovely, buttery taste.

To dice an avocado, cut it in half lengthwise. Gently twist the 2 halves back and forth until you can separate them. Stick the tip of a sharp knife into the pit and move it back and forth until it loosens. Hold the avocado half in your hand and dice the flesh without cutting through the skin. Scoop out diced avocado.

Roasted Red Pepper Dip or Spread

This is delicious as a dip with veggies, or makes a super spread for toasted bagels, especially when topped with sliced ripe tomatoes! Thanks to my assistant Gloria Schachter for the great idea!

1   Roasted Red Pepper (see following recipe)
1   clove garlic, crushed
2   green onions, cut up
1   tsp. fresh lemon juice
1/2   c. Firm Yogurt Cheese (p. 53), low-fat cream cheese or cottage cheese

1. Process roasted pepper, garlic and green onions in the processor until finely minced. Add cheese and process with quick on/offs, just until blended. Transfer to a serving bowl and chill until needed.

Yield: about 1 cup. Do not freeze. Serve with assorted crudités, Pita or Tortilla Chips (p. 72) or Bagel Chips (p. 72). Fabulous as a filling for party sandwiches or loaves!

8 calories per tbsp., 0 g fat (0 g saturated), trace cholesterol, <1 g protein, 1 g carbohydrate, 6 mg sodium, 34 mg potassium, trace iron, trace fiber, 18 mg calcium.

• **A small jar of roasted red peppers** can be substituted. However, $3^{1}/_{2}$ oz. (100 grams) of roasted red bell peppers contain 364 mg sodium. To remove excess sodium, rinse peppers well. Drain thoroughly and pat dry with paper towels.

Roasted Red Peppers

Roasted yellow and orange peppers also taste great! Very delicious, very versatile!

1. Preheat the broiler or grill. Broil or grill peppers until their skin is blackened and blistered. Keep turning them until they are uniformly charred. Immediately put them into a brown paper bag or covered bowl and let cool. Scrape off the skin using a paring knife. Rinse quickly under cold water to remove any bits of charred skin. Pat dry. Cut in half and discard stem, core and seeds. If desired, cut peppers into strips. These freeze beautifully.

20 calories per pepper, 0.1 g fat (0 g saturated), 0 mg cholesterol, <1 g protein, 5 g carbohydrate, 2 mg sodium, 121 mg potassium, trace iron, <1 g fiber, 7 mg calcium.

• **If you have a gas stove,** roast one pepper at a time over a high flame using a long-handled fork. Buy peppers in the fall when prices are cheap. Broil or barbecue a large bunch of them at one time, then cool and peel. Discard the stem, core and seeds. Freeze in small containers.

• **An easy way to freeze** these is to place roasted pepper halves or pieces in a single layer on a foil-lined baking sheet. When frozen, transfer them to freezer bags and store in the freezer until needed. Defrost as many as you need at one time.
• **Roasted pepper strips** are absolutely wonderful in sandwiches. They're also yummy when mixed Simply Basic Vinaigrette (p. 293), bottled low-cal Italian dressing or balsamic vinegar.
• **Puréed roasted red peppers** add a smoky taste to salad dressings, soups, sauces, dips and spreads.

Healthier Hummus

My original recipe called for $^{2}/_{3}$ cup of olive oil and $^{1}/_{2}$ cup of tahini. I reduced the fat considerably and used some of the chickpea liquid to provide moistness. As a shortcut, use canned chickpeas.

2	c. cooked chickpeas or 19 oz. (540 ml) can chickpeas
$^{1}/_{4}$	c. fresh parsley
3	cloves garlic (or see "hummus with roasted garlic" later in recipe)
1	tbsp. olive oil
2	tbsp. tahini (sesame paste)
3	tbsp. fresh lemon juice
	Salt & pepper, to taste
$^{1}/_{2}$	tsp. ground cumin
	Dash of cayenne pepper or Tabasco sauce

1. Drain chickpeas, reserving about $^{1}/_{2}$ cup of the liquid. (If using canned chickpeas, rinse under cold running water to remove excess sodium; drain well.)

2. Process parsley and garlic until finely minced, about 15 seconds. Add chickpeas and process until puréed. Add remaining ingredients and process until very smooth, adding enough of reserved chickpea liquid for a creamy texture. Processing time will be about 3 minutes. Chill before serving. Serve as a dip with raw or steamed vegetables, crackers or toasted pita wedges. Great as a spread on grilled pita bread, focaccia or bagels.

Yield: about 2 cups. Hummus keeps about 1 week in the refrigerator. Do not freeze.

23 calories per tbsp., 1.1 g fat (0.1 g saturated), 0 mg cholesterol, 1 g protein, 3 g carbohydrate, 1 mg sodium, 34 mg potassium, trace iron, <1 g fiber, 7 mg calcium.

- **If desired, omit oil** and increase tahini to 3 tablespoons. Although tahini is fairly high in fat, it contains important nutrients such as zinc, iron and calcium, and also provides flavor. Tahini can be found in supermarkets, Middle Eastern groceries or health food stores.
- **To lower the fat** in tahini, discard oil that comes to the top of the jar. Less fat, same flavor!
- **Skinnier Hummus:** Omit oil and tahini; add 1 green onion, minced. One serving contains 65 calories and 1 gram of fat.
- **Hummus with Roasted Garlic:** Use 1 head of Roasted Garlic (p. 252) in above recipe.
- **Hummus with Roasted Red Peppers:** Add ½ cup roasted red peppers (homemade or from the jar) to chickpeas. Process until fine. Blend in remaining ingredients until smooth.
- **White or Black Bean Spread:** Instead of chickpeas, substitute white kidney beans or black beans. Instead of the bean liquid, thin the mixture with a couple of spoonfuls of non-fat yogurt.
- **For a "handy" light and nutritious meal,** spread pita or bagel with any of the variations of Healthier Hummus. Top with sliced tomatoes and cucumber, red onion, red pepper (or roasted pepper strips) and sprouts. Great for the lunch box along with some fresh fruit and a thermos of soup!

Ethel Cherry's Smoky Eggplant Dip

This recipe is a winner! The peppers and onions are baked, not fried, in this tasty dish.

2	medium eggplants (about 2 lb/1 kg)
2	green peppers
1	large onion, peeled & sliced
1	clove garlic
1–2	tbsp. olive oil
1	tbsp. vinegar
½	tsp. sugar
1	tsp. cumin, or to taste
¼	c. chopped coriander (cilantro) or parsley
4	drops liquid smoke (available in health food or gourmet stores)

Salt & pepper, to taste

1. Preheat oven to 400°F. Place eggplants, peppers and onions on a sprayed baking sheet and bake until soft. Peppers and onions will take 30 minutes; eggplants will take 45 to 50 minutes.

2. Cut eggplants in half and scoop out flesh. Drain well; discard the skin. Cut peppers in half and discard seeds. Combine all ingredients except eggplant in the processor; chop coarsely. Add eggplant; process with quick on/offs. Transfer to a serving bowl and refrigerate.

Yield: about 4 cups. Serve with toasted pita chips or crackers. Mixture keeps 4 or 5 days in the fridge.

6 calories per tbsp., 0.2 g fat (0 g saturated), 0 mg cholesterol, trace protein, 1 g carbohydrate, <1 mg sodium, 34 mg potassium, trace iron, trace fiber, 2 mg calcium.

Babaganouj (Mediterranean Eggplant)

Tasty and colorful! The eggplant is broiled in this recipe, but it can be microwaved (see below).

1   large eggplant (about 1½ lb/750 g)
1   clove garlic, crushed
1   small tomato, chopped
½   of a green pepper, chopped
2   to 3 tbsp. tahini (sesame paste)
3   tbsp. fresh lemon juice
Salt & pepper, to taste
¼   tsp. cumin, or to taste
2   tbsp. non-fat yogurt, optional
2   tbsp. chopped fresh parsley, to garnish

1. Preheat broiler. Cut eggplant in half. Pierce skin in several places with a fork. Place cut-side down on a broiler rack. Broil 4 inches from the heat for about 20 minutes. Do not turn eggplant over during cooking. Remove from oven and let cool. Squeeze gently to press out excess moisture. Scoop out pulp and mash well. Mix together with remaining ingredients except parsley. Place in a serving bowl; garnish with parsley. Served chilled with pita and/or crudités. Keeps 3 or 4 days in the fridge.

Yield: about 3 cups. If freezing, add tahini and yogurt after defrosting eggplant.

7 calories per tbsp., 0.3 g fat (0.1 g saturated), 0 mg cholesterol, trace protein, 1 g carbohydrate, <1 mg sodium, 37 mg potassium, trace iron, trace fiber, 2 mg calcium.

• **How to Microwave Eggplant:** Wash eggplant and dry well. Pierce skin in several places with a fork. An average eggplant weighs about 1½ pounds and takes 7 to 8 minutes to cook. Place on a microwave-safe rack. Microwave uncovered on HIGH, allowing 5 to 6 minutes per pound. Halfway through cooking, turn eggplant over. At

Eggplant Etcetera!

- There are many varieties of eggplant, ranging from 2 to 12 inches in length, from oblong to round in shape. The most common variety is pear-shaped, with a dark purple skin. Japanese (Oriental) eggplant is straight and narrow in shape, with a tender, slightly sweet flesh. Baby (Italian) eggplant is similar in appearance to the common variety, but its skin and flesh are more delicate. White eggplant has a tougher skin, but its flesh is firmer and smoother. Sicilian eggplant is like a round purple ball. It is excellent for Easy Eggplant Parmesan (p. 251).
- Eggplant is perishable and becomes bitter with age. It keeps about a week in a plastic bag in the fridge. The skin of an older, tougher eggplant can be peeled for recipes when it is cut up and simmered with other ingredients. However, if the skin is tender, don't bother to peel it.
- Salting eggplant draws out bitter juices and excess moisture. Smaller varieties usually don't need to be salted before cooking. They also cook more quickly.
- Sprinkle eggplant pulp with lemon juice immediately after cooking to keep it from discoloring.
- Some cooks discard the seeds after cooking; they feel it makes the eggplant taste bitter. (I don't.)
- Cooked eggplant freezes beautifully, but if you add raw onion, the flavor may become too strong. I freeze cooked eggplant without anything added, then add the other ingredients after defrosting.

the end of cooking, it will be tender when pierced with a fork and will collapse slightly. Remove from microwave and let stand for 10 minutes. Cut in half and scoop out pulp. Sprinkle with a little lemon juice to keep the color light.

Grilled Eggplant Roumanian-Style

2 medium eggplants (about 2½ lb/1.2 kg)
1 tbsp. olive or canola oil
3 tbsp. lemon juice or balsamic vinegar
2 cloves garlic, crushed
Salt & pepper, to taste
2 tbsp. chopped parsley
¼ c. each chopped red & green pepper
¼ c. chopped green onions

1. Preheat broiler or grill. Broil eggplants about 4 inches from the heat on a sprayed baking sheet, or grill them, turning them every 5 minutes, until charred and tender. When cool, peel off skin. Gently squeeze out liquid. Combine all ingredients and beat or process until smooth and light. Chill to blend flavors. Serve with crackers or pita chips, or on salad greens.

Yield: about 4 cups. Keeps about 3 or 4 days in the refrigerator.

6 calories per tbsp., 0.2 g fat (0 g saturated), 0 mg cholesterol, trace protein, 1 g carbohydrate, <1 mg sodium, 36 mg potassium, trace iron, trace fiber, 1 mg calcium.

Tuna & Black Bean Antipasto

My sister (and best friend!) Rhonda Matias helped me create this delicious new way to prepare an old Winnipeg classic. The ingredient list is long, but it's quick to make. It's worth it!

1 medium onion
1 stalk celery
2 carrots
1 red pepper, cored & seeded
1 c. cauliflower florets
2 6½ oz. (184 g) cans solid white tuna
10 oz. (300 ml) can sliced mushrooms
½ c. sliced green stuffed olives
½ c. sliced black olives
1 c. sweet mixed pickles
19 oz. can (540 ml) black beans
1½ c. ketchup
1½ c. bottled chili sauce
1 c. salsa (bottled or homemade)
½ tsp. each of chili & garlic powder
¼ tsp. each of rosemary & oregano
2 tbsp. lemon juice
1 tbsp. Worcestershire sauce
1 tsp. sugar

1. Cut onion, celery, carrots and red pepper into ½-inch pieces. Break up cauliflower into bite-sized pieces. Blanch vegetables in boiling water for 1 to 2 minutes. They should still be somewhat crunchy. (Or sprinkle them with 2 tablespoons water and microwave covered on HIGH for 3 to 4 minutes.) Rinse under cold running water. Drain well. Drain tuna, mushrooms, olives, pickles and beans.

2. Combine all ingredients together in a large bowl and mix well. (Don't mash the tuna. It should be somewhat chunky in texture.) Adjust seasonings to taste. Serve chilled with crackers or in a mound on a bed of assorted salad greens.

Yield: about 12 cups. This keeps approximately 2 weeks in the refrigerator, or freezes beautifully.

12 calories per tbsp., 0.2 g fat (0 g saturated), <1 mg cholesterol, <1 g protein, 2 g carbohydrate, 96 mg sodium, 28 mg potassium, trace iron, trace fiber, 4 mg calcium.

- **To reduce sodium,** rinse black beans, olives and sweet mixed pickles under cold running water for at least 1 minute, then pat dry. You can also use low-sodium ketchup, make your own salsa and omit Worcestershire sauce.

Super Salsa (Uncooked)

See photo (P-17). This fresh salsa makes a delicious dip for crudités or Pita or Tortilla Chips (p. 72). It's also a terrific topping for Bruschetta (p. 73) or is great with grilled fish, chicken or burgers.

4–5	large, ripe tomatoes (or 8 Italian plum tomatoes), finely chopped
2	cloves garlic, crushed
1/2	c. coriander/cilantro or parsley, minced
1	jalapeno pepper, seeded & minced
2	tbsp. fresh basil, minced (or 1 tsp. dried)
1/4	c. green onions, chopped
2	tsp. olive oil, to taste
2	tbsp. fresh lemon juice, to taste
	Salt & pepper, to taste
	Dash of cayenne or Tabasco sauce
1	tbsp. tomato paste, optional

1. Combine all ingredients except tomato paste and mix well. (The processor does a quick job of chopping the vegetables.) If mixture seems watery, add tomato paste. Season to taste.

Yield: about 3 cups. Serve with Pita or Tortilla Chips. Salsa keeps for 2 to 3 days in the refrigerator in a tightly closed container. Do not freeze.

5 calories per tbsp., 0.2 g fat (0 g saturated), 0 mg cholesterol, trace protein, <1 g carbohydrate, 1 mg sodium, 32 mg potassium, trace iron, trace fiber, 2 mg calcium.

- **Italian plum tomatoes** make a thicker salsa than regular tomatoes because they're firmer, with less seeds and juice.
- **Don't rub your eyes** after handling hot peppers. It's a smart idea to wear rubber gloves. Don't forget to remove the gloves before touching your eyes . . . or you'll be yelling "eye, eye, eye!"
- **Mediterranean Salsa:** Follow recipe for Super Salsa, but add 6 pitted and chopped black olives and 3 tablespoons drained capers. Use 1 tablespoon each of lemon juice and balsamic vinegar.
- **Black Bean Salsa:** Add a pinch of cumin and 1 cup of canned black beans, rinsed and drained, to Super Salsa.
- **Salsa Salad Dressing:** Combine leftover salsa with a little tomato juice or V8 vegetable cocktail in the food processor. Process with six or eight on/off turns.
- **Speedy Salsa Gazpacho:** Combine 1/2 cup of chopped cucumber, 1/2 cup chopped green pepper, 1 1/2 cups tomato juice and 2 cups of salsa. Add crushed garlic, salt and freshly ground pepper. Serve chilled.
- **Salsa Supper in a Snap:** Cut several large squares of cooking parchment or aluminum foil. Place a boneless chicken breast or fish fillet on each square. Top each one with a spoonful of salsa. Seal packets tightly. Arrange on a baking sheet and place in a preheated 400°F oven. Fish cooks in 10 to 12 minutes and chicken breasts take 20 to 25 minutes. Easy and good!

Simple Salsa

This makes an excellent alternative to bottled salsa. It's convenient to make any time of the year because the recipe uses canned tomatoes. Simmer it for a few minutes to use as a pasta sauce.

28 oz. can (796 ml) canned tomatoes, drained
6 green onions (³/₄ c. chopped)
3 cloves garlic, crushed (to taste)
4 oz. can diced green chilis, drained
¹/₂ tsp. cumin
¹/₂ tsp. dried basil
Salt & pepper, to taste
2 tbsp. fresh coriander/cilantro (or 1 tsp. dried cilantro), if desired

1. Combine all ingredients in the processor. Process with quick on/offs, until coarsely chopped.

Yield: about 3 cups. Simple Salsa can be refrigerated for 3 or 4 days or may be frozen.

4 calories per tbsp., 0 g fat (0 g saturated), 0 mg cholesterol, trace protein, <1 g carbohydrate, 42 mg sodium, 8 mg potassium, trace iron, trace fiber, 4 mg calcium.

• **If green chilis are not available,** substitute 5 or 6 drops of Tabasco plus half of a green pepper.

Belle's Chunky Salsa (Cooked)

Another treasured recipe from my Mom. What a great way to use up those ripe tomatoes!

1 medium onion, chopped
2 stalks celery (about 1 c. chopped)
1 green pepper, chopped

2 cloves garlic, crushed
1 tsp. canola oil
3 medium tomatoes, chopped
¹/₂ c. canned or bottled tomato sauce
1 tsp. sugar
1 tbsp. balsamic or red wine vinegar
¹/₂ tsp. dried basil
Dash each of cumin, red pepper flakes & cayenne pepper
Dash of allspice, if desired
3–4 tbsp. water, as needed

1. Chop vegetables. Heat oil in a non-stick skillet on medium heat. Sauté onion, celery, peppers and garlic in oil for 3 or 4 minutes, until soft. If needed, add a little water to prevent sticking.

2. Add remaining ingredients. Simmer uncovered on low for 20 minutes, stirring occasionally. If mixture becomes too thick, add a little more water.

Yield: about 2 cups. This keeps a week in the fridge or can be frozen.

6 calories per tbsp., 0.2 g fat (0 g saturated), 0 mg cholesterol, trace protein, 1 g carbohydrate, 21 mg sodium, 39 mg potassium, trace iron, trace fiber, 3 mg calcium.

Avocado Guacamole

Although avocados are high in fat (¹/₂ cup mashed avocado contains 185 calories and 17.6 g fat), the main fat is monounsaturated oleic acid, which is also concentrated in olive oil. Take heart! Avocados benefit arteries, dilate blood vessels and lower LDL (bad-type) cholesterol. It is believed that they also block many carcinogens. Read Chef's Secrets (p. 56).

2 medium-size ripe avocados (preferably Hass avocados)
2 tbsp. fresh lime or lemon juice
2 cloves garlic, crushed
1 medium-size ripe tomato, chopped
4 green onions, chopped
1/2 of a red pepper, chopped
5–6 drops Tabasco sauce
Salt & pepper, to taste

1. Coarsely mash avocado. (A potato masher works well, or use quick on/offs in your processor.) Immediately sprinkle with lime or lemon juice. Combine with remaining ingredients and mix lightly. Transfer to a serving dish. Place plastic wrap directly on food to prevent discoloration. Serve chilled as a dip with Pita or Tortilla Chips (p. 72). A scoop of Guacamole can also be served as a salad over assorted greens, or as a vegetarian sandwich spread for corn tortillas or pita pockets.

Yield: about 2 cups. Mixture keeps for a day or two in the refrigerator. Do not freeze.

17 calories per tbsp., 1.4 g fat (0.2 g saturated), 0 mg cholesterol, trace protein, 1 g carbohydrate, 2 mg sodium, 68 mg potassium, trace iron, <1 g fiber, 2 mg calcium.

Green Pea Guacamole

With this recipe, you won't have to worry about finding ripe avocados. Frozen green peas will be ready when you are, and they won't turn brown when mashed. One cup of green peas contains 111 calories and only half a gram of fat!

1 c. frozen green peas
1 clove garlic

2–3 tsp. fresh lime juice (to taste)
3 tbsp. mild or medium salsa
3 tbsp. non-fat yogurt or sour cream
1/2 tsp. extra-virgin olive oil, optional
Salt & pepper, optional
Pinch of cumin

1. Microwave peas on HIGH for 2 minutes, just until defrosted. In the food processor, drop garlic through the feed tube and process until minced. Add lime juice and peas. Process until minced, about 1 minute, scraping down sides of bowl several times. Blend in salsa, yogurt and oil, if using. Season to taste. Transfer mixture to a bowl, cover and refrigerate until ready to serve. (Can be made up to one day in advance.)

Yield: about 1 cup. Do not freeze. Delicious as a dip with Pita or Tortilla Chips (p. 72).

9 calories per tbsp., 0 g fat (0 g saturated), 0 mg cholesterol, <1 g protein, 2 g carbohydrate, 19 mg sodium, 27 mg potassium, trace iron, <1 g fiber, 9 mg calcium.

Stuffed Snow Peas

Snow peas are completely edible. They are most tender in the spring.

Herbed Cheese Spread (p. 54)
3 dozen snow peas
2 quarts of boiling water
Cherry tomatoes, to garnish the platter

1. Prepare herbed cheese filling as directed. Trim ends from snow peas; remove strings. Drop in boiling water for 10 seconds. Rinse immediately under cold running water. Place on a towel and pat dry.

2. Use a sharp knife to slit pea pods open along one side. Use a cake decorating bag and star tube to pipe about ½ tablespoon cheese mixture into each pea pod. Arrange on a serving platter like the spokes of a wheel. Place cherry tomatoes between the pea pods. Serve chilled.

Yield: 3 dozen. Do not freeze.

7 calories per snow pea, 0.1 g fat (0 g saturated), trace cholesterol, 1 g protein, <1 g carbohydrate, 29 mg sodium, 16 mg potassium, trace iron, trace fiber, 6 mg calcium.

• **Dill-icious Lox & Cheese Spread** (p. 55) or Smoked Whitefish Spread (below) also make great fillings for snow peas.

Smoked Whitefish Spread

Guaranteed to please! Use tweezers to remove any tiny bones from the smoked whitefish fillets.

2	tbsp. fresh dill
4	green onions
1	stalk celery
½	each of a green & red pepper
2	slices rye bread, torn into chunks
1	medium-size smoked whitefish (about 1½ c. after skinning & filleting)
3	hard-cooked eggs (discard 2 yolks)
2	tsp. lemon juice
⅓	c. fat-free or light mayonnaise

1. In a food processor, process dill and vegetables, using quick on/offs, until finely chopped. Add bread and process until ground. Add whitefish fillets, eggs, lemon juice and mayonnaise. Process with several on/off turns, until mixed. (You may need a little extra mayonnaise, depending on the size of fish.) Chill before serving. Can be served as a spread with crackers or pumpernickel bread, or serve a scoop on a bed of lettuce and garnish with sliced tomatoes, cucumbers, radishes, etc.

Yield: about 3 cups. Do not freeze.

55 calories per ¼ cup, 0.9 g fat (0.2 g saturated), 26 mg cholesterol, 6 g protein, 5 g carbohydrate, 319 mg sodium, 145 mg potassium, trace iron, <1 g fiber, 16 mg calcium.

Mock Chopped Herring (Sardine Spread)

Sardine bones are an excellent source of calcium, so be sure to include them!

2	cans (3¾ oz/106 g) sardines, packed in spring water
1	slice of whole-wheat bread
1	medium onion
1	apple, peeled & cored
3	tbsp. white vinegar (to taste)
3	hard-boiled eggs (discard 2 yolks)
1	tsp. sugar

1. Drain sardines thoroughly, but do not remove bones. Moisten bread with cold water and squeeze out excess moisture. Chop onion, apple and sardines until fine. (So quick in the processor!) Add remaining ingredients and mix together until blended. Use as a spread with crackers or thinly sliced pumpernickel, or serve on a bed of lettuce and garnish with sliced tomatoes, cucumbers and onions.

Yield: about 2½ cups. This keeps for several weeks in the refrigerator. Do not freeze.

73 calories per ¼ cup, 3.1 g fat (0.7 g saturated), 36 mg cholesterol, 7 g protein, 4 g carbohydrate, 228 mg sodium, 139 mg potassium, <1 mg iron, <1 g fiber, 24 mg calcium.

Mushroom Mock Chopped Liver

Most recipes for mock liver are based on beans, peas or lentils. Sylvia Pleet of Ottawa gave me this gem, which is great for Passover or all year-round! I reduced the fat slightly to lighten it up.

    2   tsp. soft tub margarine or oil
    2   large onions, sliced
    2–3 tbsp. water or vegetable broth
    1   pint mushrooms, sliced
    2   hard-boiled eggs (or 1 hard-boiled egg plus 2 hard-
        boiled whites)
    2   tbsp. finely chopped walnuts or almonds
    Salt & pepper, to taste

1. Melt margarine in a skillet over medium heat. Add onions; sauté until nicely browned, about 5 minutes. If onions begin to stick, add water or broth as needed. Add mushrooms and sauté until well browned. When cool, combine with remaining ingredients in the processor. Process with quick on/offs.

Yield: about 2 cups. Serve chilled. Do not freeze.

49 calories per ¼ cup, 2.8 g fat (0.5 g saturated), 40 mg cholesterol, 2 g protein, 5 g carbohydrate, 19 mg sodium, 129 mg potassium, <1 mg iron, <1 g fiber, 14 mg calcium.

• **Microwave Magic!** Break 2 eggs into individual custard cups (or break 1 egg into a custard cup and the egg whites into another cup). Pierce yolk(s) with a fork to make an "x." (It doesn't matter if the yolks run.) Cut 2 pieces of parchment paper and place them under running water. You'll then be able to mold the parchment paper around the custard cups! Microwave covered on MEDIUM (50%) for 2 to 2½ minutes, until firm. Let stand 1 minute. How "egg-citing"—hard-boiled eggs!

Molly Naimer's Green Pea Mock Liver

Molly Naimer lived at Manoir Montefiore, a Montreal senior residence where I was the food consultant. If you make her recipe, perhaps you'll also live into your 90s! When I asked Molly if this dish could be frozen, she replied "I don't know. I never had leftovers. It was always eaten up!"

    1   large onion, finely diced
    1   tbsp. canola oil (approximately)
    19 oz. (540 ml) can green peas, drained and mashed
    4   hard-boiled eggs, peeled & grated
    8   walnut halves, chopped (not ground!)
    Salt & pepper, to taste

1. In a non-stick skillet, brown onion in oil until crispy. Combine with remaining ingredients and mix well. Season to taste. Refrigerate to blend flavors. Use as a vegetarian alternative to chopped liver.

Yield: about 3 cups. Mixture keeps for 3 or 4 days in the fridge.

71 calories per ¼ cup, 4 g fat (0.7 g saturated), 73 mg cholesterol, 4 g protein, 5 g carbohydrate, 95 mg sodium, 98 mg potassium, <1 mg iron, 1 g fiber, 18 mg calcium.

- **If you discard 2 of the yolks,** ¼ cup of the above spread will contain 64 calories, 38 mg cholesterol and 3.2 g fat (0.5 g saturated).
- **Compare the difference!** An equal amount of chopped chicken livers with egg and onion has 132 calories, 212 mg cholesterol and 10.4 g fat (3.2 g saturated).

Chickpea Mock Chopped Liver

Canned lentils can be substituted for chickpeas.

3 medium onions
1½ c. cooked or canned chickpeas, rinsed & drained
2 tbsp. almonds or walnuts, optional
2 hard-boiled eggs (or 1 hard-boiled egg plus 2 hard-boiled whites)
Salt & pepper, to taste
1 tsp. honey

1. Preheat oven to 400°F. Place unpeeled onions on a baking sheet and bake for 40 minutes, until soft. (Or pierce onions in 3 or 4 places with a sharp knife; place on a plate and microwave on HIGH for 6 to 8 minutes.) Cool slightly; remove peel. Combine all ingredients in processor. Process 30 seconds, until finely chopped. If mixture seems dry, blend in a little water. Chill before serving.

Yield: about 2¾ cups. Mixture keeps for 3 or 4 days in the refrigerator. It can be frozen, but season mixture lightly because the pepper's flavor will become stronger.

74 calories per ¼ cup, 2.4 g fat (0.4 saturated), 39 mg cholesterol, 4 g protein, 10 g carbohydrate, 14 mg sodium, 132 mg potassium, <1 mg iron, 2 g fiber, 25 mg calcium.

Smoked Salmon Tortilla Pinwheels

Instead of tortillas, substitute thin pitas which have been split in half crosswise. Recipe can be doubled for a crowd. You can use other fillings such as salmon, tuna or chopped egg. Let color be your guide!

Dill-icious Lox & Cheese Spread (p. 55)
3 whole-wheat or flour tortillas

1. Prepare lox and cheese filling as directed; spread in a thin layer on tortillas. (Leave a ½-inch border around the bottom edge of each tortilla so that cheese will not ooze out when rolled up.)

2. Roll up tightly, cover and refrigerate until needed. (These can be eaten like a roll-up, if you wish.) When needed, trim off ends. (They're for nibbling!) Slice each roll on a slight angle into 8 slices. Arrange on a large platter lined with lettuce or spinach leaves. Serve chilled.

Yield: about 24 pinwheels or 3 roll-ups. Do not freeze if Yogurt Cheese was used in the spread.

22 calories per pinwheel, 0.2 g fat (0.1 g saturated), 2 mg cholesterol, 2 g protein, 3 g carbohydrate, 130 mg sodium, 27 mg potassium, trace iron, trace fiber, 9 mg calcium.

- **Variation:** Place a narrow band of roasted red peppers (jarred or homemade) along one edge of tortillas before rolling up. So pretty!

Sun-Dried Tomato & Olive Pinwheels

*Use dry pack sun-dried tomatoes, or make them
yourself. (See recipe on p. 264.)*

1	c. Firm Yogurt Cheese (p. 53), light cream cheese or quark cheese
¼	c. sun-dried tomatoes
¼	c. green onions, minced
1	clove garlic, minced
2	tbsp. pitted black olives, finely chopped
3	whole-wheat or flour tortillas (or very thin pitas, split in half crosswise)

1. If using Yogurt Cheese, drain yogurt the day
before. Cover sun-dried tomatoes with boiling
water and let stand for 10 minutes. Drain well; pat
dry. Cut into small pieces with scissors or a sharp
knife.

2. Place cheese in a bowl with remaining ingredients except tortillas; mix lightly to blend. (Do not
use a processor or the mixture will become too
thin.) Assemble as directed for Smoked Salmon
Tortilla Pinwheels in recipe above.

Yield: about 24 pinwheels or 3 roll-ups. Do not
freeze if using Yogurt Cheese.

**19 calories per pinwheel, 0.2 g fat (0 g saturat-
ed), trace cholesterol, 1 g protein, 4 g carbohydrate, 47 mg sodium, 57 mg potassium, trace
iron, <1 g fiber, 22 mg calcium.**

• **Roasted Red Pepper Pinwheels:** Substitute a
double recipe of Roasted Red Pepper Dip or
Spread (p. 56) as the filling in the above recipe.
You will have enough to fill 4 or 5 tortillas.

Bev's Smoked Salmon Spirals

*This is another variation of party sandwiches using
tortillas or pitas. My friend Bev Binder of Winnipeg
wrote me the day I was working on this section of
my cookbook. "This is a great recipe! Excellent to
have on hand for guests! Steamed asparagus or
strips of red, green or orange peppers can replace
the smoked salmon."*

8	oz. (250 g) cream cheese (low-fat or fat-free)
2	tbsp. Russian or honey-style mustard
1	tbsp. fat-free or light mayonnaise or sour cream
4	10" flour tortillas (whole wheat or flavored tortillas work well)
4	Romaine lettuce leaves (optional)
8	oz. (250 g) smoked salmon (lox)
2	tbsp. finely minced fresh dill
2	tbsp. finely minced green onions

1. Mix cream cheese, mustard and mayonnaise
together. Spread evenly on tortillas. Cover with lettuce. (Leave ½-inch border around the bottom
edge of each tortilla so that it will stick together
when rolled up.) Top with lox. Sprinkle with dill
and green onions.

2. Roll up tightly and wrap in plastic wrap. Twist
ends to seal, then refrigerate. When needed, slice
each roll on the diagonal into 8 slices. (The ends
are for you to nibble on!) Serve as an hors d'oeuvre. Place 3 spirals on a lettuce leaf. Garnish each
plate with a Radish Rose (p. 49).

Yield: about 32 spirals. Can be frozen if you eliminate the lettuce.

**51 calories per spiral, 2.1 g fat (0.9 g saturated),
6 mg cholesterol, 3 g protein, 5 g carbohydrate,
126 mg sodium, 36 mg potassium, trace iron,
trace fiber, 19 mg calcium.**

Chef's Secrets: Gravlax!

- Unsliced, ready-to-eat Gravlax can be stored in the fridge for up to a week, or frozen for about a month. When needed, it can be sliced a few hours in advance. If frozen, defrost for 10 minutes at room temperature. Use an electric knife to slice it off the skin.
- Spread a thin layer of Firm Yogurt Cheese (p. 53) or low-fat cream cheese on crackers. Top with sliced Gravlax and finely minced red onion and dill. Light and easy!
- Serve slices of Gravlax on English cucumber slices (pat them dry first); garnish with dill.
- Mango Salsa (p. 109) complements the flavor of Gravlax or smoked salmon beautifully!
- I once attended an elegant party where a large platter of Gravlax was served with tiny capers and thinly sliced red onions, surrounded with pumpernickel triangles and cream cheese. "Iced Vodka" was served with it. Fabulous!
- Iced Vodka: Several days before your party, place a 26 oz. bottle (750 ml) of vodka under cold running water, but don't dry it. Place the bottle inside a large, empty juice carton and lay it down horizontally on a baking sheet. Place 2 or 3 peach-colored roses and some baby's breath on top of the bottle. Carefully fill carton partially with water, adding as much as you can without the water spilling out. Freeze until roses adhere to the bottle. Repeat the process several times until you have filled and frozen the entire carton. (You can place the carton upright once the flowers stick to the vodka bottle.) To unmold, run carton under hot water briefly to loosen it. Cut away the carton. To serve, place Iced Vodka in a pretty bowl to hold the melting ice. So cool! (Vodka will not freeze because of its alcohol content.)

Smoked Salmon & Pumpernickel Hors D'Oeuvres

An easy appetizer from student Gloria Schachter, a great proofreader and friend!

6   slices of square pumpernickel bread
5   tsp. honey-style mustard
½   tsp. each of Dijon & prepared mustard
6   oz. smoked salmon (lox)
Fresh dill sprigs, to garnish

1. Spread each slice of bread with combined mustards. Cover with a layer of smoked salmon. Trim off crusts. Cut each slice into 4 squares or triangles. (Can be made several hours ahead, covered tightly and refrigerated until 10 to 15 minutes before serving time.) Garnish with dill.

Yield: 24 pieces. Can be frozen if very well wrapped.

28 calories per piece, 0.6 g fat (0.1 g saturated), 2 mg cholesterol, 2 g protein, 4 g carbohydrate, 116 mg sodium, 28 mg potassium, trace iron, trace fiber, 6 mg calcium.

- **Sliced Gravlax (p. 68)** can replace lox. Garnish with Tzadziki (p. 53) and dill.

Gravlax (Homemade Lox/ Smoked Salmon)

So delicious, so easy. My Mom makes her own lox all the time. If you are salt-sensitive, be aware that Gravlax and store-bought lox (smoked salmon) are very high in sodium.

2 lb. (1 kg) salmon fillet, skin on
3 tbsp. sugar (or maple syrup)
2 tbsp. Kosher (coarse) salt
1 tbsp. coarsely cracked black pepper
1 large bunch fresh dill, chopped
¼ c. vodka, optional (but terrific!)

1. Line a casserole with plastic wrap. Cut salmon into 2 equal pieces. Rub flesh-side with sugar, salt and pepper. Place one piece of salmon skin side down in casserole; cover with dill. Place the other piece of salmon on top, skin side up. Pour vodka over fish. Wrap salmon, leaving ends open so that juices which are released can drain out. Place a rack under salmon. Weigh down with a dish topped with heavy cans. Refrigerate for 3 days, turning salmon over every day.

2. Unwrap salmon and scrape off dill and seasonings. Put salmon on a plate and let it air dry in refrigerator for 8 hours. Then cover it with plastic wrap. To serve, slice paper thin on an angle with a sharp knife.

Yield: 16 servings. Freezes well.

91 calories per serving, 3.6 g fat (0.6 g saturated), 31 mg cholesterol, 11 g protein, 3 g carbohydrate, 897 mg sodium, 285 mg potassium, <1 mg iron, trace fiber, 10 mg calcium.

Hot Potato Kisses

An upscale version of mini potato knishes. Everybody needs a little kiss from time to time!

2 onions, chopped
2 tsp. canola oil
4 potatoes, peeled & cut into chunks

Boiling water
Salt & pepper, to taste
1 egg, separated
6 sheets phyllo dough
3 tbsp. canola oil

1. Heat 2 teaspoons of oil in a nonstick skillet. Sauté onions until golden, about 6 to 8 minutes. If necessary, add a little water to prevent them from burning. Meanwhile, cook potatoes in boiling salted water until tender, about 20 minutes. Drain well. Return potatoes to heat for a minute or two to evaporate excess moisture. Mash potatoes. Add onions, egg yolk and seasonings; mix well.

2. In a small bowl, blend egg white with 3 tablespoons of oil. Working quickly, place one sheet of phyllo on the counter and brush lightly with oil/egg white mixture. (Cover remaining dough with plastic wrap to prevent it from drying out.) Cover with a second sheet of phyllo. Brush once again with oil mixture. Use a small sharp knife to cut dough into 20 squares (4 rows of 5 squares).

3. Place a spoonful of potato filling in the center of each square. Gather corners together and twist to form a small kiss. Place on a lightly greased, foil-lined cookie sheet. Repeat twice more with remaining dough and filling. Brush tops lightly with oil mixture. Bake at 350°F for 10 to 12 minutes.

Yield: 60 kisses. These freeze and/or reheat well.

23 calories per kiss, 1 g fat (0.1 g saturated), 4 mg cholesterol, trace protein, 3 g carbohydrate, 11 mg sodium, 37 mg potassium, trace iron, trace fiber, 2 mg calcium.

• **Sweet Potato & Spinach Kisses:** Prepare Potato Kisses as directed, using 1 potato and 2 sweet potatoes. Defrost half a package frozen chopped spinach; squeeze dry. In Step 1, combine spinach with potato/onion mixture. Add 1 tablespoon minced fresh dill. Assemble as directed above.

Quicky Rumaki

Rinse and drain a can of whole water chestnuts. Cut each one in half. Wrap each piece with a strip of thinly sliced deli chicken or turkey breast (low-fat or light). Fasten with a toothpick. Roll lightly in brown sugar. Broil for a few minutes, until hot. Serve immediately.

Smoked Turkey Breast Wrapped in Snow Peas

Cut smoked turkey breast into 3/4-inch cubes. Trim ends from snow peas, removing strings. Drop snow peas in boiling water for 30 seconds. Rinse under cold running water. Place on a towel and pat dry. Lightly brush cubed turkey with either honey-style mustard, Peanut Butter Sauce (p. 108) or Spicy Dipping Sauce (p. 109). Wrap each cube with a snow pea and fasten with a toothpick. Serve chilled.

Homemade Potato Chips

Packaged chips are full of fat, calories and sodium. One package supposedly contains seven servings. Certainly not for any seven people that I know! These crunchy munchies are easy and guilt-free.

1, 2, 3 or 4 medium Idaho potatoes
Salt, to taste
Basil, oregano, garlic powder &/or cayenne, if desired

1. Scrub potatoes thoroughly; dry well. Slice paper thin, either in the processor or by hand. You should get about 24 slices from each potato. Cook in the microwave or conventional oven (below).

• **Microwave Method:** Place 12 slices at a time on a microsafe rack. Sprinkle lightly with desired seasonings. Microwave on HIGH for 4 minutes, or until dry and crunchy. Watch carefully because cooking time depends on moisture content of potatoes. If necessary, microwave 30 seconds longer and check again. Repeat until crispy. Repeat with remaining potato slices.

• **Conventional Method (for a Large Batch):** Preheat oven to 450°F. Spray a baking sheet lightly with non-stick spray. Place potato slices in a single layer on pan. Sprinkle lightly with seasonings. Bake at 450°F about 15 to 20 minutes, until crispy and golden.

Yield: Calculate 1/2 potato (about 12 chips) as 1 serving. Do not freeze.

67 calories per serving, 0.1 g fat (0 g saturated), 0 mg cholesterol, 1 g protein, 15 g carbohydrate, 5 mg sodium, 256 mg potassium, <1 mg iron, 2 g fiber, 6 mg calcium.

• **These are best eaten within a few days.** The fresher, the better! (They never last very long at my house!)
• **Next time you have a snack attack,** just remember that 15 potato chips (1 oz.) contain 10 grams of fat and 150 calories! Homemade chips are "cheaper by the dozen" in more ways than one!

Sweet Potato Chips

Substitute peeled, thinly sliced, sweet potatoes for Idaho potatoes. (Nutrients are calculated for 1 medium sweet potato, without skin.)

59 calories per serving, 0.1 g fat (0 g saturated), 0 mg cholesterol, 1 g protein, 14 g carbohydrate, 6 mg sodium, 198 mg potassium, trace iron, 2 g fiber, 16 mg calcium.

Crisp Lasagna Chips

You'll flip over these chips! They're perfect party fare. Whenever you make lasagna, cook up some extra noodles for this super snack. Pass-ta chips, please!

    8   oz. (250 g) lasagna noodles (half of a 1-lb pkg.)
    1½ tbsp. olive or canola oil
    3   tbsp. water
    ¼   c. seasoned bread crumbs
    Dash of paprika, if desired
    3   tbsp. grated Parmesan cheese, if desired

1. Cook lasagna noodles according to package directions. Drain well. Carefully separate the noodles and place them on clean towels in a single layer. Pat lightly to absorb extra moisture. Preheat oven to 400°F. Spray two baking sheets with non-stick spray.

2. Combine oil and water in a small bowl. Brush both sides of noodles lightly with oil mixture. Cut into 1-inch strips. Arrange a single layer of noodles on baking sheets. (You will have to make several batches.) Combine bread crumbs, paprika and cheese. Sprinkle noodles lightly with crumb mixture.

3. Bake uncovered at 400°F for 15 to 20 minutes, until crisp and golden. Shake pan once or twice during baking and watch carefully to prevent burning. When cool, store in an airtight container for a week or two, if you can resist them!

Yield: about 12 dozen (12 servings). Calculate 12 chips as 1 serving. If desired, reheat for 4 or 5 minutes at 350°F before serving.

90 calories per serving, 2.2 g fat (0.3 g saturated), 0 mg cholesterol, 3 g protein, 15 g carbohydrate, 84 mg sodium, 14 mg potassium, <1 mg iron, <1 g fiber, 10 mg calcium.

Wonton Chips

These crisp, homemade chips are quick and easy to make, and are a great snack. They're also nice topped with sesame seeds. Wonton wrappers are found in the freezer section of your supermarket.

    24 wonton wrappers (defrost if frozen)
    Salt (or your favorite spices), optional

1. Preheat oven to 350°F. Spray 1 or 2 baking sheets with non-stick spray. Cut each wonton wrapper to make 4 triangles. Place in a single layer on baking sheet. Sprinkle with salt to taste. Bake for 5 to 7 minutes, or until crisp and golden.

Yield: 96 chips (8 servings). Calculate 12 chips as 1 serving. These will keep for a week or two in an airtight container. If desired, reheat for 4 or 5 minutes at 350°F before serving.

70 calories per serving, 0.4 g fat (0.1 g saturated), 2 mg cholesterol, 2 g protein, 14 g carbohydrate, 137 mg sodium, 20 mg potassium, <1 mg iron, trace fiber, 11 mg calcium.

Bagel Chips

3   bagels
1   egg white, lightly beaten
Salt, to taste
1   tbsp. Italian seasoning (basil, dill, oregano &/or
    thyme)
2–3 tbsp. sesame seeds, optional

1. Preheat oven to 350°F. Spray 1 or 2 baking sheets with non-stick spray. Cut bagels in half, so that each half is shaped like the letter "C." Slice each "C" vertically into ¼-inch thick coins. (You should get about 3 dozen round "chips" from each bagel.) Arrange in a single layer on a baking sheet. Brush with egg white; sprinkle lightly with seasonings and sesame seeds. Bake uncovered for 12 to 15 minutes, until golden and crispy. Store in an air-tight container.

Yield: about 9 dozen (8 servings). Allow 14 "chips" as 1 serving. Can be frozen.

77 calories per serving, 0.5 g fat (0.1 g saturated), 0 mg cholesterol, 3 g protein, 15 g carbohydrate, 149 mg sodium, 47 mg potassium, 1 mg iron, <1 g fiber, 29 mg calcium.

Pita or Tortilla Chips

These are addictive! I used to brush them with oil, but was "de-lited" to find out that egg white worked perfectly! If making tortilla chips, try to buy tortillas with no added fat.

6   medium-size pitas or 12 thin tortillas (corn, whole-
    wheat or flour)
1–2 egg whites
Salt, to taste
1–2 cloves garlic, crushed
Dash of basil, oregano &/or thyme

1. Preheat oven to 400°F. If using pitas, split each one into 2 rounds. Use a pastry brush to paint a light coating of egg white on one side. Sprinkle lightly with seasonings. Pile in a stack and use a sharp knife or pizza wheel to cut the stack into wedges. Arrange in a single layer on non-stick or sprayed baking sheet(s).

2. Bake at 400°F for 8 to 10 minutes, until crisp and golden. (Watch carefully to prevent burning.) Serve warm or at room temperature.

Yield: 12 servings. (Allow half a pita or 1 tortilla per serving.) These freeze well.

77 calories per serving, 0.5 g fat (0 g saturated), 0 mg cholesterol, 2 g protein, 15 g carbohydrate, 150 mg sodium, 5 mg potassium, <1 mg iron, 1 g fiber, 21 mg calcium.

- **Pita or Tortilla Ribbons:** Follow directions above, but cut pitas or tortillas into long narrow strips instead of wedges. (You can also sprinkle them with grated Parmesan cheese. For a spicy version, omit salt and spices; sprinkle with Cajun seasoning.)
- **Make & Break Chips:** Follow directions above, but don't cut pitas or tortillas before baking. Bake at 400°F for 8 to 10 minutes. Break roughly into large pieces.

Tomato & Basil Bruschetta

An easy company appetizer from Nancy Gordon and Hart Peikoff.

3   large tomatoes, diced (2 c.)
¼   c. chopped fresh basil (or 1 tsp. dried)
1   clove garlic, crushed
Salt & pepper, to taste
½   loaf of French or Italian bread
1   large clove garlic, halved
1   tbsp. olive oil (preferably extra-virgin)

1. Combine tomatoes, basil, garlic, salt and pepper; refrigerate. Cut bread into 12 slices about 1-inch thick. Broil until lightly browned on each side. Rub the cut side of a garlic clove on one side of bread. Dip pastry brush in water, then in olive oil. Lightly brush oil on bread. (Can be prepared in advance.) Top with tomato mixture and sprinkle with grated cheese. If desired, broil briefly. Serve immediately.

Yield: 12 appetizers. Do not freeze.

98 calories per piece, 2.1 g fat (0.4 g saturated), 0 mg cholesterol, 3 g protein, 17 g carbohydrate, 177 mg sodium, 139 mg potassium, 1 mg iron, 1 g fiber, 26 mg calcium.

• **Variations:** Add ¼ cup of chopped black olives and 1 diced Roasted Red Pepper (p. 57) to tomato mixture. Two cups of Super Salsa (p. 61) can be substituted for tomato mixture. Top with ½ cup of grated low-fat mozzarella cheese or 2 tablespoons Parmesan cheese.

Bruschetta Greek-Style

This recipe was inspired by a "let's do lunch" meeting with my friend Barbara Sotolov in Winnipeg.

8   slices crusty bread (e.g. French, sourdough or country bread), about 1" thick
4   tsp. olive oil
2   cloves garlic, crushed
3   or 4 firm, ripe tomatoes, chopped
1   medium onion, chopped
Salt, pepper & oregano, to taste
¾–1 c. feta cheese, grated or chopped
8   tsp. grated Parmesan cheese, optional

1. Broil bread or grill it until lightly toasted outside but soft inside. Dip a brush in water, then in olive oil. Lightly brush bread with oil, then top it with garlic. Arrange on a foil-lined baking sheet sprayed with non-stick spray. Combine tomatoes, onion and seasonings. (Can be prepared in advance.)

2. Preheat broiler. Spoon tomato mixture onto grilled bread. Sprinkle with cheese. Broil 4 inches from heat until cheese is melted and golden. Cut each piece in half and serve immediately.

Yield: 16 appetizers. Do not freeze. Recipe can be halved or doubled.

73 calories per piece, 3.1 g fat (1.3 g saturated), 6 mg cholesterol, 3 g protein, 9 g carbohydrate, 158 mg sodium, 107 mg potassium, <1 mg iron, <1 g fiber, 48 mg calcium.

Quicky Bruschetta

Spoon chunky salsa (bottled or homemade) on slices of broiled or grilled crusty bread. Sprinkle lightly with low-fat grated mozzarella or Monterey Jack cheese. Broil briefly.

Polenta Triangles

3/4 c. cornmeal (fine or medium)
3 c. water
1/2 tsp. salt (to taste)
1/4 tsp. pepper
1 tbsp. minced fresh basil (or 1/2 tsp. dried)
1 tbsp. olive oil
2 tbsp. grated Parmesan cheese
1/4 c. skim milk

1. Combine cornmeal, water and salt in a very large microsafe bowl. Microwave covered on HIGH for 10 minutes, stirring at half time. Let stand covered for 3 or 4 minutes. (To cook conventionally, combine water and salt in a large saucepan and bring to a boil. Add cornmeal in a thin stream, stirring constantly. Cook uncovered on low heat for 20 minutes, stirring occasionally.) Add seasonings, olive oil, cheese and milk. Adjust seasonings to taste.

2. Line a 9-inch square baking pan with foil. Spray lightly with non-stick spray. Spread cornmeal evenly in a smooth layer. Chill for 2 hours, until firm. Unmold and peel off foil. Cut polenta into 9 squares, then cut each square in half diagonally to make 18 triangles. Arrange on a sprayed foil-lined baking pan. (Can be prepared up to 2 days in advance and refrigerated.) Preheat broiler or grill. Broil polenta for 2 or 3 minutes, until hot.

Yield: about 18 triangles. Do not freeze.

32 calories per triangle, 1.1 g fat (0.3 g saturated), <1 mg cholesterol, <1 g protein, 5 g carbohydrate, 81 mg sodium, 17 mg potassium, trace iron, trace fiber, 15 mg calcium.

- **If desired, add** 1/2 **cup** each of chopped red pepper and zucchini at the end of Step 1.
- **For an appetizer,** spread a thin layer of warm Roasted Red Pepper Coulis (p. 110) on each plate. (Homemade salsa or tomato sauce could also be used.) Top with 3 wedges of grilled polenta. If desired, garnish with fresh basil.
- **Cut chilled polenta in squares.** Add your favorite pizza toppings. Bake at 400°F for 15 minutes.

Spinach Stuffed Mushrooms

These easy "appeteasers" can be prepared in advance and refrigerated. Pop them into the oven right before your guests arrive!

10 oz. (300 g) pkg. frozen chopped spinach
3 dozen medium-size mushrooms
1 tbsp. olive oil
4 green onions, chopped
2 cloves garlic, minced
1/4 c. red pepper, chopped
2 tbsp. fresh basil &/or dill, minced
1 c. soft fine bread crumbs
1/2 c. grated Parmesan or low-fat Swiss cheese
Salt & pepper, to taste
Sesame seeds, if desired

1. Defrost spinach and squeeze dry. Rinse mushrooms quickly and drain well. Pat dry. Remove stems and set mushroom caps aside. Chop stems finely. Heat oil in a non-stick skillet.

2. Sauté green onions for 4 or 5 minutes. Add garlic, chopped mushroom stems and red pepper. Sauté 5 minutes longer. Remove from heat. Combine vegetables with basil, bread crumbs, cheese and spinach; mix well. Season to taste. Fill mushroom caps and sprinkle them with sesame seeds. Place on a sprayed foil-lined baking sheet. (Can be prepared in advance and refrigerated covered for several hours or overnight.)

3. Bake uncovered in a preheated oven at 350°F for 15 minutes, until piping hot. (Alternately, microwave 1 dozen at a time uncovered on a paper towel-lined plate for 3 minutes on HIGH.)

Yield: 3 dozen mushrooms. These reheat well. To freeze, see instructions below.

20 calories per mushroom, 0.9 g fat (0.3 g saturated), 1 mg cholesterol, 1 g protein, 2 g carbohydrate, 42 mg sodium, 69 mg potassium, trace iron, <1 g fiber, 30 mg calcium.

- **Make delicious, wholesome bread crumbs** from rye, kimmel, whole-wheat, multi-grain or challah bread in your food processor. Two slices of bread yield 1 cup crumbs. Gloria Schachter, one of my excellent proofreaders, always stores leftover homemade bread crumbs in a glass jar in the refrigerator. The crumbs keep for several weeks!
- **To prepare and freeze** stuffed mushrooms in advance: In Step 3, bake mushrooms for 10 minutes at 350°F. Cool and freeze. Bake frozen mushrooms covered at 350°F for 15 minutes; uncover and broil until golden.
- **Spinach & Feta Stuffed Mushrooms:** Refer to recipe (p. 148).
- **Spanakopita Triangles:** Refer to recipe (p. 147).

Stuffed Mushrooms with Pesto & Sun-Dried Tomatoes

Your processor will help you make the bread crumbs as well as the easy, tasty filling in minutes.

3	dozen medium-size mushrooms
4–5	sun-dried tomatoes
	Boiling water
2	tsp. olive oil
1	small onion, chopped
1	clove garlic, minced
½	c. red pepper, finely chopped
3	tbsp. Best-O Pesto (p. 195)
1	c. dry or fresh bread crumbs (fresh rye bread crumbs are delicious!)
	Salt & pepper, to taste
½	c. grated Parmesan cheese

1. Rinse mushrooms quickly and drain well. Pat dry. Remove stems and chop finely. Soak sun-dried tomatoes in boiling water to cover for 10 minutes. (Or cover with cold water and microwave on HIGH for 1 minute; let soak for 5 minutes to rehydrate.) Drain well and cut into small pieces with scissors.

2. Heat oil in a non-stick skillet. Sauté onions on medium heat for 3 or 4 minutes. Add garlic, red pepper and mushroom stems. Sauté 5 minutes longer, until mixture is fairly dry. Remove from heat and combine with pesto, bread crumbs, sun-dried tomatoes and seasonings. Mix well. Fill mushroom caps, mounding tops slightly. Sprinkle lightly with cheese. (These can be prepared in advance and refrigerated for several hours or overnight on a sprayed foil-lined baking sheet.)

3. At serving time, bake uncovered in a preheated oven at 350°F for 15 minutes, until piping hot.

(Alternately, microwave 1 dozen at a time uncovered on a paper towel-lined plate for 3 minutes on HIGH.)

Yield: 3 dozen. These reheat well. To freeze, see directions for Spinach Stuffed Mushrooms (p. 74).

29 calories per mushroom, 1.1 g fat (0.4 g saturated), 1 mg cholesterol, 2 g protein, 4 g carbohydrate, 60 mg sodium, 87 mg potassium, <1 mg iron, <1 g fiber, 30 mg calcium.

Soups, Sauces & Beverages

Super Soups—Tops In Taste, Low In Fat!

- Nutrient-packed soups are a delicious way to incorporate more plant-based foods into your diet. If you eat hearty, low-fat soups more often, you'll have less room for high-calorie, high-fat foods!
- Soups can be prepared ahead of time and are a great way to use up leftovers. Save leftover cooked noodles, rice and/or other grains and add them to soups.
- Most of hunger is actually thirst. If you start off your meal with a big bowl of soup, you won't feel as hungry and will be less likely to overindulge (and bulge)!
- It takes 20 minutes for your brain to know that your stomach is full, so sipping a bowl of hot soup at the start of your meal will help you slow down your eating and "lighten your weigh!"
- When you have a hearty, homemade soup simmering on the stove, all you need is a luscious salad and some crusty bread to create a healthy, high-energy meal.
- Worried you're not getting enough protein? No problem. Include a legume (e.g. beans, peas, lentils) and a grain (e.g. rice, pasta, bulgur) in either the soup or salad for a well-balanced meal.
- Homemade soups are generally full of vitamins and minerals and are a great nutritional bargain. If they are prepared properly, they will contain very little fat.
- Beware of rich, creamy soups and chowders. They can be caloric suicide, especially when made with butter or cream.
- To thicken soups and make them creamy, forget the cream! Purée part or all of the vegetables in a food processor or blender, or use an immersion (handheld) blender.
- The best "creamers" for creamless soups are puréed cooked starchy vegetables (e.g. potatoes, carrots, sweet potatoes, cauliflower) as well as puréed cooked beans or lentils. You'll also add vitamins and minerals! Approximately 1 cup of puréed vegetables or legumes will thicken 3 to 4 cups of broth.
- Substitute low-fat alternatives when preparing your favorite fattening cream soups. Use skim or 1 percent milk instead of whole milk, or non-fat yogurt or sour cream instead of regular sour cream.
- To reduce the fat in your favorite soups, 1 tablespoon of oil (or less) is usually enough to sauté 3 to 4 cups of vegetables. Another way to reduce the fat is to use non-stick pans, or spray the bottom of your soup pot with non-stick spray before you brown your veggies. You can also brown onions and other veggies in a little bit of broth or water and omit the oil completely.
- For maximum flavor when making homemade chicken soup, skin the chicken after cooking, not before. Remove cooked chicken from the bones and trim off excess fat. Cooked chicken is great in salads, soups, casseroles or sandwiches. Boiled chicken can be frozen for 1 to 2 months if well wrapped. (Cooked chicken in the freezer is like money in the bank!)
- Be sure to chill chicken broth overnight, then lift off and discard hardened fat from surface.
- Chicken or turkey bones and wings make delicious soup. Sometimes I add the skin as well. After cooking, discard skin and bones. Chill soup overnight; then discard hardened fat. Ask your butcher to sell you bones from deboned chicken breasts. (Poultry bones freeze well.)
- Don't bother peeling the onions when making homemade stock. The skins will add a rich, dark color and flavor to your soup. It's acceptable to be lazy, but be sure to rinse those onions first!
- The tops of green onions or leeks will add flavor to chicken or vegetable broth. Discard them after cooking. The white part of green onions is ideal for salads or as a garnish.
- The soaking water from dried mushrooms adds flavor to soups and stews. Mushrooms contain natural

MSG, providing flavor without the side effects. Soaking water can be frozen.

- Soaking water from sun-dried tomatoes also adds flavor to soups and stews.
- Homemade chicken, beef, veal and vegetable broths are generally low in sodium, unless you add salt. If you are on a low-sodium diet, make broth without additional salt.
- Instead of adding salt to give flavor to your soups, add onions, celery or garlic. Herbs also add flavor, especially dill, basil and parsley. Add fresh herbs at the end of cooking for maximum flavor.
- If you don't have homemade chicken or vegetable broth on hand, use canned soup or instant powdered soup mix. However, canned and packaged soups are generally very high in sodium. Some brands are also high in fat. Be sure to check the label first!
- An easy trick to reduce the sodium in canned and powdered broths is to add double the amount of water. (e.g. If you need 2 cups of chicken broth for a recipe, use 1 teaspoon of powdered soup mix and 2 cups of water.)
- If the label indicates that a canned or packaged soup mix contains hydrolyzed protein, this is another way of saying that it contains monosodium glutamate (MSG). If you have a sensitivity to MSG, avoid products that contain hydrolyzed protein.
- Spoon off the fat from the surface of canned soups. If you place the opened can of soup in the freezer for one-half hour, you can easily lift off and discard the fat which congeals on the surface.
- Canned soups can be used as a quick starter for your own "homemade" soups. Add your own vegetables (e.g. broccoli, carrots, onions, potatoes, zucchini), or throw in some frozen mixed veggies if you're short on time. Drained canned beans also make a good addition. Instant gourmet!
- Soups made with dried beans take time to make, unless you use some of my timesaving secrets! Canned beans can be substituted in many recipes. Rinse them well to remove excess sodium. Read "Using Your Bean" (p. 222).
- Oats, peas, beans and barley are high in soluble fiber, which may help lower blood cholesterol.
- Most soups require little attention once you get them in the pot and they are simmering. Why not make a large batch and freeze several containers for busy days?
- Make sure soups (or any cooked foods) are completely cold before you transfer them to freezer containers. Refrigerate the soup overnight before transferring the contents to containers. Store soup in 1 or 2 cup containers (e.g. freezerproof bowls) in your freezer for future use.
- Fill containers to within 2 inches from the top. Place uncovered containers in freezer. Cover after soup has frozen.
- Freeze homemade chicken or vegetable broth in ice cube trays. One cube equals 2 tablespoons of broth.
- It's so simple to defrost soup in the microwave. Microwave frozen soup on HIGH, stirring occasionally. One cup of broth takes 4 minutes to defrost. It takes another 3 minutes to heat the soup once it has defrosted.
- To reheat soup in the microwave, allow 2 to 3 minutes per cup. Stir once or twice during heating to avoid "hot spots."
- Gazpacho Pronto! Don't throw away leftover garden salad, especially if it was made with Italian or vinaigrette dressing. Process veggies in the processor. Add tomato or vegetable juice to taste. Chill thoroughly. At serving time, garnish with finely diced tomatoes, peppers and green onions.
- Garnish soups with chopped fresh herbs, thinly sliced green onions, chives, red peppers, or a sprinkling of low-fat grated cheese. Parmesan has a strong flavor, so a little goes a long way.

Vegetable Broth ("Almost Chicken Soup")

This recipe and the one that follows are two different versions of vegetarian "chicken" soup.

2 large onions (or 1 onion & 1 leek, including about 2" of green top)
7–8 carrots
4 stalks celery
1 red pepper
1 c. mushrooms, optional
9 c. cold water
Salt, optional
Pepper, to taste
3 cloves garlic, peeled
½ c. fresh dill sprigs (do not chop)

1. Clean vegetables and cut them into large chunks. Place all ingredients except garlic and dill into a large soup pot. Water should cover vegetables by no more than 1 inch. Bring to a boil. Reduce heat, cover partially and simmer for 30 minutes.

2. Add garlic and dill and cook 10 minutes longer. Strain and serve with rice, noodles, orzo (rice-shaped noodles), matzo balls, etc., or use in recipes calling for vegetable broth.

Yield: about 8 cups. Clear broth contains negligible nutrients. Broth can be frozen for 3 or 4 months.

About 20 calories per cup, 1 g fat (0 g saturated), 0 mg cholesterol, 2 g protein, 3 g carbohydrate, 65 mg sodium, trace calcium.

Vegetarian "Chicken" Broth

See photo (P-19). A great soup to serve to your vegetarian guests for Passover or any time. This version makes a larger quantity than the preceding recipe and also includes parsnips and turnips.

8–9 carrots
3 large onions
2 leeks
6 stalks celery
2–3 parsnips
½ of a medium turnip, optional
1 red pepper, optional
½ c. parsley stems
12 c. cold water
2–3 cloves garlic, optional
½ c. fresh dill sprigs (do not chop)
Salt & pepper, to taste

1. Peel vegetables and cut them into chunks. Combine them in a large pot with parsley stems (but no parsley leaves) and water. Water should cover vegetables by about an inch. Bring to a boil. Reduce heat and simmer partially covered for 45 minutes. Add garlic and dill. Simmer 10 to 15 minutes longer. Season broth with salt and pepper to taste.

2. Strain through a fine strainer. Serve with Matzo Balls (p. 394), Herbed Passover Noodles (p. 404) or matzo farfel.

Yield: 8 to 10 servings. Reheats and or freezes well. Clear broth contains negligible nutrients if you discard the vegetables after cooking.

About 20 calories per cup, 1 g fat (0 g saturated), 0 mg cholesterol, 2 g protein, 3 g carbohydrate, 65 mg sodium, trace calcium.

Chef's Secrets—Stocks and Broths!

- Sodi-Yumm? Nutrients are calculated without salt. A teaspoon of salt provides 2,326 mg sodium. The sodium content of sea salt is similar. The recommended daily intake for a healthy person who doesn't need to be on a salt-restricted diet should not exceed 2,400 mg, about 1 teaspoon.
- A cup of canned vegetable broth contains about 1,000 mg sodium.
- Many chefs leave broth unsalted until they are ready to use it. Add salt and pepper if serving this as a vegetarian broth. Salt may not be needed if you are using the broth as an ingredient in a dish containing salty ingredients such as soy sauce or canned beans.
- All or part of the vegetables can be processed in the processor or a blender, then stirred back into the broth.
- The quickest way to cool broth or soups quickly is in an ice bath. Fill your kitchen sink with 5 or 6 inches of cold water. Add a few handfuls of ice cubes and place the pot of soup in the ice water. Replace ice cubes and water as necessary. Stir the soup occasionally to help it cool faster.
- Never store hot soups (or any hot foods) in plastic containers! The plasticisers can melt into the food. Instead, store foods in heat-resistant glass or ceramic containers.
- Pretend Vegetable Broth: Save the cooking water from vegetables and refrigerate or freeze it until needed. I use the cooking water from veggies like carrots, peas, frozen mixed vegetables, spinach or Swiss chard. (Don't use the water from starchy vegetables such as potatoes.) I also like to save the soaking water from dried mushrooms. Any or all of these can be used when vegetable broth is called for in a recipe. They'll add flavor without adding fat!
- While parsley stems add flavor to the soup, the leaves can make your soup bitter! Cut off the leafy end of the parsley, use the stems for soup and save the parsley leaves for another recipe such as Rainbow Tabbouleh Salad (p. 283).
- A handful or two of any of the following can be added to the broth: eggplant, tomatoes, Swiss chard, spinach leaves or any odds and ends of veggies.
- Dried mushrooms such as shiitake, morels or Chinese mushrooms add flavor to any broth. Soak them first in hot water for 20 to 30 minutes to rehydrate, then add both mushrooms and soaking liquid to broth and cook as directed.
- Many chefs freeze the trimmings from vegetables to make broth (e.g. onions, leeks, carrots, celery, mushrooms). When they have enough, they place them in a pot (no need to defrost them), cover with water, add a couple of cloves of garlic, some herbs and a bay leaf. Simmer everything for 45 minutes and voilà, almost instant broth!

Homemade Beef or Veal Broth

This easy, tasty broth can be used in the same way as chicken broth. Homemade broth is lower in sodium than those prepared from powder or cubes. Roasting the bones gives the broth a richer taste.

4–5 lb. (2 kg) beef or veal bones
2   large onions (rinsed; peeling is not necessary)
3–4 stalks celery
4–6 large carrots
1   bay leaf
12 c. water (approximately)
2–3 cloves garlic
1/2 c. fresh dill sprigs (do not chop)
Salt & pepper, optional

1. Place bones in a roasting pan and roast uncovered at 400°F for about an hour, until nicely browned. Transfer bones to a large pot. Add onions, celery, carrots and bay leaf. Add enough water to completely cover the bones and vegetables. Bring to a boil and skim well. Reduce heat and simmer partially covered, adding hot water as needed to keep ingredients covered. Simmer broth for 2 to 3 hours. Add garlic and dill; simmer 10 to 15 minutes longer. If desired, season with salt and pepper.

2. Cool broth slightly. Strain, discarding bones and vegetables. Refrigerate broth overnight. Lift off and discard any hardened fat. Ladle the broth into 1 or 2 cup freezer containers, discarding the layer of cloudy broth at the bottom of the soup.

Yield: about 9 cups. Broth can be frozen for 3 or 4 months.

About 20 calories per cup, 1 g fat (0 g saturated), 1 mg cholesterol, 2 g protein, 3 g carbohydrate, 65 mg sodium, 14 mg calcium.

The Best Chicken Soup (Jewish Penicillin!)

I make my chicken soup with lots of carrots because they add wonderful flavor. Also, I love carrots! When I had pneumonia, my friend Doris Fink nursed me back to health by adding a red pepper to the soup. Since I did recover, I now use her trick when making chicken soup. I also add garlic and lots of dill. Chicken soup really is a marvelous cure for colds and flu, and it tastes terrific!

3   lb. chicken (1.4 kg), cut up
8   c. water (approximately)

Salt, to taste
½   tsp. pepper
7–8 carrots
4   stalks celery
2   onions (or 1 onion & 1 leek)
1   red pepper, cored, seeded & cut up
2   cloves garlic
½   c. fresh dill sprigs (do not chop)

1. Trim excess fat from chicken. To remove excess salt from Kosher chicken, soak it in cold water for ½ hour. Rinse and drain well. Place chicken in a narrow, deep soup pot. Add water. (It should cover the chicken completely.) Add salt and pepper. Bring to a boil. Remove scum completely. Add carrots, celery, onions and red pepper. Cover partially and simmer gently for 1 to 1½ hours. Add garlic and dill. Simmer soup 10 to 15 minutes longer. Adjust seasonings to taste.

2. Cool completely. Strain soup. Discard skin and fat from chicken. Discard all veggies except the carrots. Refrigerate soup overnight. Discard hardened fat from surface of soup.

Yield: 6 to 8 servings. Reheats and/or freezes well.

About 20 calories per cup of clear broth (without chicken), 1 g fat (0 g saturated), 1 mg cholesterol, 2 g protein, 3 g carbohydrate, 65 mg sodium, 20 mg calcium. (Note: clear, skimmed soup contains negligible calories.)

- **Serve soup with noodles,** rice, orzo, kasha, Kreplach (p. 269), mandlen (soup nuts), matzo farfel or Matzo Balls (p. 394). Add a piece of carrot to each bowl, garnish with fresh dill.
- **Serve boiled chicken** as a main dish, or add pieces of cut-up chicken to the soup. Cooked chicken can be used for chicken salad, casseroles, sandwiches or crêpes.

Chefs Secrets: More Soups!

- When cooking soup, should you keep a lid on it? If the soup is completely covered, it may boil over and make a mess! If you cook it completely uncovered, too much evaporation may take place. Hearty soups such as bean and barley or minestrone can become thick and stick to the bottom of the pot. My solution is to cover the pot partially. This makes it easier to control the amount of evaporation that takes place, and still produce a flavorful soup.

- Meat-based broths can be used to make a variety of quick and easy soups. Add whatever fresh or frozen veggies you have on hand (e.g., chopped celery, carrots, potatoes, parsnips, corn niblets, cabbage, zucchini, canned tomatoes). Beans or legumes can be added. Refer to Beans on Demand! (p. 91). Cook until tender. Season to taste.

- Clear broth is delicious served with noodles, rice or matzo balls. Choose your favorite herbs (e.g. thyme, basil, dill). If using dried herbs, add them at the beginning of cooking. If using fresh herbs, add near the end of cooking and let soup simmer a few minutes to release the flavor. Enjoy!

- For convenience, freeze homemade broth in small quantities in ice cube trays. Once frozen, wrap well (or transfer to an airtight storage container). Use to flavor sauces, vegetables and casseroles.

- **Some cooks add** a piece of turnip, celery root, a few parsnips and/or parsley to the soup. It depends on what your mother added when she made her soup (or maybe not)!
- **Jewish chicken soup** is traditionally flavored with dill and the veggies are cooked in large chunks. French chefs add thyme and bay leaf to their soup, and they dice the vegetables neatly. (Who has the time?) That is very good chicken soup, but it's not Jewish chicken soup!

- **Soup Dumplings:** Blend 2 egg whites, ½ cup water, 1 cup flour, ½ teaspoon salt and ½ teaspoon baking powder. Drop from a spoon into simmering soup. Cover and simmer 5 minutes.
- **Turkey Broth:** Follow recipe for Chicken Soup, but use 4 to 5 pounds turkey bones, wings and backs.

Quicky Chicky Noodle & Vegetable Soup

4   c. chicken broth (preferably homemade)
2   boneless, skinless chicken breasts, finely diced (or 1 c. diced cooked chicken)
1   c. cooked fine noodles
1   c. frozen mixed vegetables
Pepper, to taste
1   tbsp. minced fresh dill (or 1 tsp. dried)
2   green onions, finely chopped

1. Place broth in a large saucepan and bring to a boil. Add chicken, noodles and vegetables. Simmer 7 to 8 minutes, or until chicken is cooked. Add pepper to taste. Garnish with dill and green onions.

Yield: 4 servings. Reheats and/or freezes well. Recipe can be doubled easily.

161 calories per serving, 2 g fat (0.5 g saturated), 44 mg cholesterol, 22 g protein, 12 g carbohydrate, 220 mg sodium, 212 mg potassium, 3 mg iron, 2 g fiber, 45 mg calcium.

Caribbean Chicken & Vegetable Soup

Not too spicy, yet full of flavor!

2   tsp. canola oil
2   onions, diced
2–3 stalks celery, diced
1   red or green pepper, diced
8   c. water
4   skinless, boneless chicken breasts
3   carrots, diced
1/2   c. uncooked white rice, rinsed & drained
1 1/2 tsp. salt (or to taste)
1/2   tsp. pepper
1/2   tsp. curry powder
1/2   tsp. chili powder
1/2   tsp. thyme
1   bay leaf
Freshly minced parsley & green onions, to garnish

1. In a large nonstick skillet, heat oil. Add onions and celery. Cook over medium-high heat for 3 minutes. Add green or red pepper and cook 5 minutes longer, until golden.

2. Meanwhile, combine water and chicken breasts in a large pot. Bring to a boil; skim well. Add sautéed vegetables, carrots, rice and seasonings. Bring to a boil. Reduce heat and simmer covered for 20 minutes, or until chicken is cooked. Remove chicken from pot and let cool briefly. Cut chicken into bite-sized pieces. Return chicken to the pot and simmer 5 minutes longer. Discard bay leaf. Adjust seasonings to taste. Garnish with parsley and green onions.

Yield: 8 servings. Reheats and/or freezes well.

155 calories per serving, 2.9 g fat (0.6 g saturated), 37 mg cholesterol, 15 g protein, 16 g carbohydrate, 504 mg sodium, 272 mg potassium, 1 mg iron, 2 g fiber, 36 mg calcium.

• **Variation:** Add a 14 oz. (398 ml) can of black beans, rinsed and drained, with chicken in Step 2.

Chinese Chicken & Corn Soup

Cream-style corn doesn't contain any cream. It's dairy-free!

4   c. chicken broth (canned or homemade)
2   14 oz. (398 ml) cans cream-style corn
2   boneless, skinless chicken breasts, diced (or 1 c. diced cooked chicken)
2   tbsp. cornstarch
2   tbsp. cold water
1–2 tbsp. soy sauce
2   egg whites, lightly beaten
3/4   tsp. Oriental sesame oil
1/4   tsp. Oriental chili oil or red pepper flakes
Salt & pepper, to taste
2   green onions, chopped

1. Skim broth, discarding any fat. In a large saucepan, combine broth with creamed corn and bring to a boil. Add chicken and simmer covered for 6 to 8 minutes, until chicken is cooked. Dissolve cornstarch in cold water. Stir into boiling broth. Add soy sauce and simmer uncovered for 3 or 4 minutes, until thickened, stirring occasionally. Add egg whites in a thin stream, stirring gently to break into shreds. Stir in sesame and chili oils. Season with salt and pepper. Stir in green onions.

Yield: 6 servings. Do not freeze.

200 calories per serving, 2.4 g fat (0.5 g saturated), 24 mg cholesterol, 17 g protein, 30 g carbohydrate, 749 mg sodium, 306 mg potassium, 2 mg iron, 3 g fiber, 26 mg calcium.

- **Homemade broth is best.** Canned broth is higher in sodium and some brands contain MSG. Place the open can in freezer for one-half hour so fat will congeal and can be discarded easily.
- **Vegetarian Version:** Use vegetable broth and tofu instead of chicken broth and chicken.

Quicky Chinese Chicken Soup

4   c. chicken broth (preferably homemade)
2   boneless, skinless chicken breasts, finely diced (or 1 c. diced cooked chicken)
3   c. frozen Oriental vegetables
2   tsp. light soy sauce
1   tsp. minced garlic
1   tsp. minced ginger root
1/4 tsp. pepper
1   c. bean sprouts
1   c. cooked noodles or rice
1   tsp. Oriental sesame oil
1/4 c. green onions, thinly sliced

1. Place broth in a large saucepan and bring to a boil. Add chicken, frozen vegetables, soy sauce, garlic and ginger. Cook partially covered until chicken and vegetables are done, about 6 to 8 minutes. Add remaining ingredients and simmer 2 to 3 minutes longer, until heated through. Adjust seasonings to taste.

Yield: 6 servings. Reheats well. Vegetables will change in texture if soup is frozen.

119 calories per serving, 2.1 g fat (0.5 g saturated), 29 mg cholesterol, 15 g protein, 9 g carbohydrate, 205 mg sodium, 157 mg potassium, 2 mg iron, 2 g fiber, 33 mg calcium.

Avgolemono Soup

A delicious Greek-style chicken soup made with egg, lemon and rice.

4   c. chicken broth (preferably homemade)
1/3 c. uncooked rice, rinsed & drained
2   carrots, diced
1   c. frozen green peas
1/2 c. diced cooked chicken
2   tbsp. fresh lemon juice
1   egg, lightly beaten (at room temperature)
1   tbsp. chopped fresh dill
Salt & pepper, to taste

1. Place broth in a large saucepan and bring to a boil. Add rice and carrots. Cover and simmer on low heat for 15 minutes. Add peas and chicken; simmer 5 minutes longer.

2. Combine lemon juice and egg in a mixing bowl and mix well. Slowly add about 3/4 cup of the hot soup in a thin stream, whisking constantly. (This prevents the egg from curdling.) Slowly whisk the egg mixture back into the simmering soup. Add dill. Season to taste.

Yield: 4 servings. Do not freeze.

211 calories per serving, 3.8 g fat (1 g saturated), 68 mg cholesterol, 17 g protein, 25 g carbohydrate, 268 mg sodium, 242 mg potassium, 4 mg iron, 4 g fiber, 57 mg calcium.

Hot & Sour Soup

½ c. dried Chinese mushrooms
1 c. boiling water
4 c. chicken broth
½ c. canned bamboo shoots, rinsed
1 single boneless, skinless chicken breast
½ lb. tofu (firm, silken or low-fat)
2 tbsp. soy sauce
4 tbsp. white vinegar
1 tsp. balsamic vinegar
½ tsp. pepper
1 tsp. sugar
3 tbsp. cornstarch dissolved in ¼ c. cold water
2 tsp. Oriental sesame oil
1 tsp. Oriental chili oil
1 egg, lightly beaten
2 green onions, finely sliced

1. Rinse mushrooms. Soak in boiling water for 15 minutes. Remove from liquid and set aside. Strain liquid from mushrooms and combine it with chicken broth in a large saucepan.

2. Meanwhile, cut off and discard tough stems from mushrooms. Cut mushrooms, bamboo shoots and chicken into julienne strips. Combine together in a bowl. Cut tofu into julienne strips and place it in another bowl. Combine soy sauce, vinegar, pepper and sugar in a third bowl.

3. Bring broth to a boil. Reduce heat and add mushrooms, bamboo shoots and chicken. Simmer just until chicken turns white, about 2 to 3 minutes. Add tofu and soy sauce mixture. Simmer 1 or 2 minutes longer. (Can be prepared in advance up to this point and refrigerated. At serving time, reheat soup until simmering and continue with the recipe.)

4. Slowly stir in cornstarch mixture. Cook until thick-ened, stirring gently. Add sesame oil and chili oil. Slowly add beaten egg in a thin stream, stirring gently to break it into shreds. Adjust seasonings to taste. Garnish with green onions and serve immediately.

Soup Savvy!

- Skim the fat, keep the flavor! If you don't have time to refrigerate soup overnight to remove the fat, a quick trick is to wrap ice cubes in a clean cloth and pass the cloth over the top of the soup.
- Another option is to place the soup in several small containers and place them in the freezer for a short time. The fat will congeal and can then be lifted off and discarded.
- Use a ladle to skim off the top fatty layer from hot soup. If necessary, blot the top of the soup with paper towels to absorb any remaining surface fat.
- If your soup is too salty, add a piece of raw potato and simmer it in the soup to absorb excess salt.
- Some soups become very thick upon standing, particularly those made with barley, beans or lentils. Just add a little broth or water to bring it to the desired consistency.
- If a vegetable-based soup is too watery, purée part of the vegetables. If you don't have enough veggies, microwave a potato and some carrots. Mash and add them to the soup. Season to taste.
- Rinse barley to remove some of the starch before adding it to soup. Use a heavy-bottomed soup pot to prevent thick soups from sticking to the pot.
- Turkey Vegetable Soup: Use the carcass from a roasted or smoked turkey. Place in a pot and add water to cover. Add a couple of chopped onions, celery, carrots and 2 pounds (1 kg) of frozen mixed vegetables. Cook until veggies are tender. Discard carcass. Season soup with a little salt, pepper and a bit of thyme. (Another great idea inspired by my smart friend Gloria Schachter!)

Yield: 6 servings. If reheating soup, do not boil. Freezing is not recommended.

164 calories per serving, 5 g fat (0.8 g saturated), 12 mg cholesterol, 16 g protein, 13 g carbohydrate, 454 mg sodium, 123 mg potassium, 6 mg iron, 2 g fiber, 67 mg calcium.

- **If you are sodium-sensitive,** use low-sodium soy sauce, or dilute regular soy sauce with water.
- **If available, add 8 tiger lily buds** (golden needles) and 1 tablespoon dried tree ears (Cloud ears) to your soup. (They are usually sold in Oriental groceries.) Soak them first in cold water until soft, about half an hour. Rinse and drain. (Add the soaking water to your plants!) Cut off the hard end from tiger lily buds. Shred the tree ears.
- **Vegetarian Hot & Sour Soup:** Prepare soup as directed above, but use vegetable broth instead of chicken broth and omit chicken breast.

Rozie's Chicken, Lima Bean & Barley Soup

Roz Brown and I have been best friends for more years than we both care to count. This is one of her recipe treasures. Her daughter Stephanie asks for this soup whenever she visits from England! She calls this fiber-full soup "a meal in a bowl."

2	c. dried lima beans
6	c. cold water (for soaking the beans)
1	chicken, cut up (about 3 lb/1.4 kg)
12	c. water (approximately)
2	onions
4	stalks celery
4–5	large carrots
3	parsnips
½	turnip, if desired
2	tsp. salt (to taste)
½	tsp. pepper
¾	c. pearl barley, rinsed & drained
3	or 4 potatoes, peeled & cut in small chunks
¼	c. fresh dill, chopped

1. Rinse beans and place them in a bowl. Cover with cold water and let them soak.

2. Remove skin and excess fat from chicken. Place chicken in a large soup pot. Add 12 cups water and bring to a boil. Remove scum. Add onions, celery, carrots, parsnips and turnip (no need to chop them). Season with salt and pepper. Simmer partly covered for 1½ hours, until chicken is tender. Remove chicken and vegetables from pot and let them cool.

3. Rinse and drain the soaked beans. Add beans and barley to broth. Bring to a boil, reduce heat and simmer covered for about 1 hour. Add potatoes and cook 10 to 15 minutes longer, until tender.

4. Meanwhile, remove chicken from bones. Cut into bite-sized pieces. Slice the cooked carrots. (Roz discards the celery, turnips and parsnips, but they can be added to the soup.) Add chicken and carrots (and remaining cooked veggies, if desired) to pot. Add dill and simmer 10 to 15 minutes longer. Adjust seasonings to taste.

Yield: 12 generous servings. Freezes and/or reheats well. Leftover soup will get very thick and will need to be thinned with a little chicken broth or water when reheated.

263 calories per serving, 4.9 g fat (1.3 g saturated), 30 mg cholesterol, 19 g protein, 36 g carbohydrate, 442 mg sodium, 693 mg potassium, 3 mg iron, 9 g fiber, 39 mg calcium.

Bean, Barley & Sweet Potato Soup

1 c. dried white beans (navy or pea)
3 c. cold water
2 tsp. canola or olive oil
2 large onions, peeled & chopped
4 stalks celery, trimmed & chopped
2 zucchini, chopped (optional)
1 red pepper, chopped (optional)
8 c. chicken broth or hot water
4 carrots, sliced
1 sweet potato, peeled & chopped
1/2 c. pearl barley, rinsed & drained
1/2 tsp. pepper
1 tsp. dried basil
Salt, to taste

1. Soak beans in water overnight. Drain and rinse well. Discard soaking water. Heat oil on medium heat in a large heavy-bottomed soup pot. Sauté onions and celery for 5 minutes, until golden. Add zucchini and red pepper and cook 5 minutes longer. Add a little water if needed to prevent burning. Add remaining ingredients except salt. Bring to a boil. Reduce heat, cover partially and simmer for 2 hours, stirring occasionally. If soup is too thick, add a little water. Add salt; season to taste.

Yield: 10 to 12 servings. Reheats and/or freezes well.

173 calories per serving, 1.3 g fat (0.2 g saturated), 0 mg cholesterol, 12 g protein, 29 g carbohydrate, 175 mg sodium, 498 mg potassium, 4 mg iron, 7 g fiber, 90 mg calcium.

Israeli Bean Soup

2 c. small white beans (e.g. navy beans)
6 c. cold water (for soaking the beans)
1 tbsp. olive oil
3 onions, chopped
3 stalks celery, chopped
3–4 cloves garlic, minced
3 carrots, chopped
6 1/2 c. water
2 potatoes, peeled & cut in small chunks
1–2 bay leaves
1 tsp. dried thyme (to taste)
1–2 tsp. cumin (to taste)
28 oz. can (796 ml) crushed tomatoes
2 tbsp. tomato paste
Salt & pepper, to taste
1/4–1/2 c. fresh coriander/cilantro, minced

1. Soak beans in cold water overnight. Drain and rinse well. Discard soaking water. Heat oil on medium heat in a large heavy-bottomed soup pot. Add onions and celery. Sauté for 5 minutes, until golden. Add garlic and carrots and sauté 5 minutes longer. Add a little water if needed to prevent burning. Add water, beans, potatoes, bay leaves, thyme and cumin. Bring to a boil, reduce heat and simmer partly covered for 1 hour. Add tomatoes, tomato paste, salt and pepper. Cook half an hour longer, until beans are tender. Stir in coriander. If too thick, thin with a little water.

Yield: 12 servings. Reheats and/or freezes well.

181 calories per serving, 1.7 g fat (0.3 g saturated), 0 mg cholesterol, 10 g protein, 33 g carbohydrate, 147 mg sodium, 668 mg potassium, 4 mg iron, 8 g fiber, 114 mg calcium.

Black Bean Soup

Excellent, easy and full of fiber! Impress your guests with its wonderful South American flavor.

2	c. dried black beans, rinsed & drained
6	c. cold water (for soaking the beans)
2	onions, coarsely chopped
4	cloves garlic, minced
4	stalks celery, coarsely chopped
1	tbsp. olive oil
4	large carrots, coarsely chopped
1	tsp. dried basil
1/2	tsp. dried red pepper flakes
1	tsp. cumin (to taste)
8	c. chicken or vegetable broth (about)

Salt & pepper, to taste

1. Soak beans overnight in cold water. Drain and rinse well. Discard soaking water.

2. Prepare vegetables. (This can be done in the processor.) Heat oil in a large soup pot. Add onions, garlic and celery. Sauté for 5 or 6 minutes on medium heat, until golden. If necessary, add a little water or broth to prevent sticking.

3. Add drained beans, carrots, seasonings and broth. Do not add salt and pepper until beans are cooked. Cover partially and simmer until beans are tender, about 2 hours, stirring occasionally. Purée part or all of the soup, if desired. If too thick, thin with water or broth. Add salt and pepper to taste.

Yield: 10 servings. Freezes well.

188 calories per serving, 2.1 g fat (0.3 g saturated), 0 mg cholesterol, 14 g protein, 29 g carbohydrate, 171 mg sodium, 495 mg potassium, 4 mg iron, 10 g fiber, 69 mg calcium.

• **Soak and drain beans** as directed in Step 1. Place soaked beans in a storage container and pop them in the freezer for up to 2 months. When you want to make soup, just add the frozen beans to the pot. No need to defrost them first. (You can use this trick with any kind of beans!)

• **If you have time,** presoak a batch of black beans, then cook them for 1 1/2 to 2 hours, until tender. Drain, cool and freeze. When you want soup, add 3 to 4 cups of frozen cooked beans to the soup pot without thawing. Your soup will be ready in just half an hour!

• **If you're really in a rush,** substitute two 14 oz. (398 ml) cans of black beans, drained and rinsed, instead of soaking dried beans overnight. Cooking time with canned beans is also half an hour.

• **Are you afraid to eat beans** because you're worried about possible embarrassing moments? If you presoak beans, then discard the soaking water, you'll also eliminate the problem of gas! As an extra precaution, rinse the beans again thoroughly after presoaking them.

• **Serving Tip:** For an elegant touch, garnish each serving with a swirl of non-fat yogurt. If necessary, thin yogurt with a little milk. Use a plastic squeeze bottle to squeeze a design with the yogurt. Top with a spoonful of bottled or homemade salsa or chopped Roasted Red Peppers (p. 57).

White Bean Soup

High in potassium, iron, calcium and fiber. A bowl filled with nutrition!

2	c. dried white beans (navy, pea or kidney), picked over, rinsed & drained
6	c. cold water (for soaking the beans)

1 tbsp. olive oil
2 onions, chopped
4 cloves garlic, crushed
8 c. water, vegetable or chicken stock
2 potatoes, peeled & chopped
½ c. grated carrot
¼ c. fresh dill, minced
½ tsp. dried thyme
½ tsp. dried basil
   Salt & pepper, to taste
¼ c. minced fresh parsley

1. Soak beans in water overnight. Drain and rinse well. Discard soaking water. Heat oil in a large, heavy-bottomed soup pot. Add onions and garlic and sauté on medium-low heat until tender and golden. If necessary, add a bit of water to prevent sticking.

2. Add remaining ingredients except salt, pepper and parsley. Bring to a boil, reduce heat and simmer partially covered for 1 hour, or until beans are tender. Season to taste.

3. Purée all or part of the soup, depending on the texture you want. If necessary, thin with additional stock or water. Garnish with minced parsley.

Yield: 10 servings. Soup keeps 4 to 5 days in the refrigerator or freezes well.

189 calories per serving, 2.1 g fat (0.4 g saturated), 0 mg cholesterol, 10 g protein, 34 g carbohydrate, 13 mg sodium, 612 mg potassium, 3 mg iron, 11 g fiber, 91 mg calcium.

• **Time saving secret:** Substitute two 19 oz. (540 ml) cans white kidney beans, drained and rinsed, instead of soaking the dried beans overnight. Cooking time will be 20 to 25 minutes.
• **Sweet Potato & Bean Soup:** Sweet potatoes can be used instead of regular potatoes. Your soup will be a beautiful color, with additional beta carotene and flavor.
• **Beans & Greens Soup:** Just before your soup is done, add 2 cups of the following greens, washed and finely chopped: Swiss chard, spinach or beet greens. Simmer soup 3 or 4 minutes longer. Adjust seasonings to taste.
• **Beans On Demand!** Soak navy, kidney or lima beans (or any beans you like) overnight in lots of cold water. Rinse and drain them well. Pack in 1 or 2 cup containers and pop them into the freezer. When making soup, just add the frozen beans and cook them until tender. (P.S. Don't add salt to your soup until navy or kidney beans are almost done. Otherwise, they'll never get soft! However, if using lima beans, you can add salt at the beginning of cooking without any problem.)

Red Lentil, Zucchini & Couscous Soup

1 large onion, chopped
1 stalk celery, chopped
2 tsp. olive oil
3–4 carrots, grated
2 medium zucchini, grated
1 c. red lentils, picked over, rinsed & drained
6 c. water or vegetable broth (about)
2 tsp. salt (or to taste)
½ tsp. pepper
½ tsp. dried basil
⅓ c. couscous

1. Onions and celery can be chopped in the processor, using quick on/off turns. Heat oil in a 5-quart soup pot. Add onions and celery. Sauté on medium-high heat for 5 to 7 minutes, or until golden. If veg-

etables begin to stick, add a tablespoon or two of water.

2. Meanwhile, grate carrots and zucchini. Add all ingredients except couscous to pot. Bring to a boil. Reduce heat and simmer partially covered for 45 minutes, stirring occasionally. Add couscous and simmer 10 minutes longer. If soup is too thick, thin with a little water. Adjust seasonings to taste.

Yield: 8 servings. Freezes well.

134 calories per serving, 1.5 g fat (0.2 g saturated), 0 mg cholesterol, 8 g protein, 24 g carbohydrate, 612 mg sodium, 430 mg potassium, 3 mg iron, 8 g fiber, 39 mg calcium.

Red Lentil, Vegetable & Barley Soup

1	tbsp. olive or canola oil
3	large onions, chopped
4	cloves garlic, minced
¼	c. fresh parsley, minced
4	stalks celery, chopped
6	carrots, coarsely chopped
1	large sweet potato, peeled & chopped
2	zucchini, ends trimmed, chopped
10	c. water, chicken or vegetable broth
1½	c. red lentils, rinsed & drained
½	c. pearl barley, rinsed & drained
1	tbsp. salt (or to taste)
½	tsp. pepper
1	tsp. dried basil (or 1 tbsp. fresh)
2	tbsp. fresh dill, minced

1. Heat oil in a large soup pot. Add garlic and onions. Sauté on medium heat until golden, about 5 to 7 minutes. Add a little water if vegetables begin to stick. Add remaining ingredients. Bring to a boil, reduce heat and simmer partly covered for 1 hour, or until barley is tender. Stir occasionally. Thin with a little water if soup is too thick. Adjust seasonings to taste.

Yield: 12 servings. Soup freezes and/or reheats well.

169 calories per serving, 1.7 g fat (0.3 g saturated), 0 mg cholesterol, 8 g protein, 32 g carbohydrate, 629 mg sodium, 530 mg potassium, 3 mg iron, 10 g fiber, 55 mg calcium.

Lentil Squash Soup with Rice & Noodles

This recipe was created when I was developing two different soups, but felt something was missing. Feeling frustrated, I spontaneously combined everything in one pot and this terrific, hearty soup was created! (The testing crew was shocked, but delighted with their lunch.) Thanks to Manny and Danielle Glick for suggesting the ingredients that inspired this wonderful soup!

2	large onions, chopped
2	tsp. canola oil
2–3	tbsp. water, if needed
3–4	cloves garlic, crushed
2	carrots, peeled & chopped
1	butternut squash (about 1½ lb./750 g), peeled & diced
8	c. boiling water (approximately)
1	c. brown lentils, picked over, rinsed & drained (red lentils can be substituted)
⅓	c. rice, rinsed & drained
½	c. fine dry noodles
1	tsp. dried basil

½ tsp. dried thyme
Salt & pepper, to taste

1. In a large pot, sauté onions in oil on medium heat for 6 to 8 minutes, until golden. If necessary, add a little water as needed to prevent onions from sticking or burning. Add garlic, carrots and squash and cook 2 to 3 minutes longer, stirring occasionally. Add boiling water and lentils. Bring to a boil; reduce heat and simmer partially covered for 50 to 60 minutes, until lentils are tender. Use a potato masher or immersion blender and partially purée the soup.

2. Add rice to soup and simmer covered for 10 minutes. Add noodles, basil and thyme; simmer covered 10 minutes longer. If soup gets too thick, thin it with a little boiling water. Season with salt and pepper to taste. A meal in a bowl!

Yield: 10 hearty servings. Soup reheats and/or freezes well.

134 calories per serving, 1.3 g fat (0.1 g saturated), 2 mg cholesterol, 7 g protein, 26 g carbohydrate, 20 mg sodium, 488 mg potassium, 3 mg iron, 7 g fiber, 46 mg calcium.

- **Chef's Secret!** To peel and dice squash easily, first microwave it to soften the skin. Pierce squash in several places with a knife. Place it on a microsafe rack and microwave on HIGH for 8 to 10 minutes, turning squash over halfway through cooking. Squash will be partially cooked. Cut away the peel with a sharp knife. Cut squash in half and scoop out seeds. Cut flesh into chunks and add to the pot along with garlic and carrots. Continue as directed above.
- **Variations:** If desired, substitute vegetable or chicken broth for water. You can also substitute 1 pound (500 g) cut-up broccoli for the squash.

Luscious Lentil Soup

Easy and healthy! Although it takes about the same amount of time to microwave this soup as to cook it on top of the stove, it never sticks to the bottom of the pot when you microwave it. Your food processor will chop the vegetables 1-2-3.

  1 large onion, chopped
  4 cloves garlic, minced
  1 tbsp. olive or canola oil
  1 c. brown or red lentils, rinsed & drained
  1 stalk celery, chopped
 28 oz. (796 ml) can tomatoes (or 5 to 6 fresh ripe tomatoes, chopped)
  5 c. water (approximately)
  1 bay leaf
1½ tsp. salt (to taste)
  ½ tsp. pepper
  1 tsp. dried basil or dill (or 1 tbsp. fresh)
     Juice of half a lemon (1½ tbsp.)
  ¼ c. parsley, minced

- **Microwave Method:** In a 3-quart microsafe pot, combine onion, garlic and oil. Microwave uncovered on HIGH for 4 minutes. Add remaining ingredients except lemon juice and parsley; mix well. Microwave covered on HIGH for 1 hour, until lentils are tender. Stir once or twice during cooking. If boiling too much, reduce power to MEDIUM (50%). If too thick, add some boiling water. Add lemon juice. Adjust seasonings to taste. Let stand at least 10 minutes to allow flavors to blend. Discard bay leaf. Garnish with parsley.

- **Conventional Method:** Heat oil in a large soup pot. Add onions; sauté on medium heat until golden, about 4 or 5 minutes. Add garlic and sauté 2 or 3 minutes longer. Add 2 or 3 tablespoons of water if vegetables begin to stick. Add remaining ingredients except lemon juice and parsley. Bring to a boil, reduce heat and simmer 1 hour, until lentils are tender, stirring occasionally. Thin with a little hot water if too thick. Add lemon juice. Adjust seasonings to taste. Discard bay leaf. Garnish with parsley.

Yield: 8 to 10 servings. Tastes even better the next day! Freezes well.

120 calories per serving, 2.1 g fat (0.3 g saturated), 0 mg cholesterol, 7 g protein, 20 g carbohydrate, 603 mg sodium, 533 mg potassium, 3 mg iron, 7 g fiber, 63 mg calcium.

- **Variations:** For more fiber, add 2 or 3 carrots, coarsely chopped, to the sautéed onions. Proceed as directed. Add 1 cup of cooked pasta or rice to the cooked soup, or sprinkle with a little grated Parmesan cheese. For a Middle Eastern flavor, substitute coriander (cilantro) for basil or dill.
- **Lentil, Vegetable & Barley Soup:** Prepare Luscious Lentil Soup as directed above, but add 3 potatoes, 3 carrots and 1 zucchini, coarsely chopped, to the sautéed vegetables. Also add ⅓ cup barley which has been rinsed and drained. Then continue as directed. If cooked soup is too thick, add a little water or vegetable stock.

Cabbage & Lentil Borscht

Although the ingredient list is long, this soup is quite simple to make. Best of all, it makes a lot, so you can freeze some for another day. It's packed with fiber, flavor and nutrients!

1　tbsp. canola or olive oil
2　large onions, chopped
3　lb. (1.4 kg) cabbage, grated
2　carrots, grated
1　c. brown lentils, rinsed & drained
2　parsnips, diced
2　stalks celery, diced
2　cloves garlic, crushed
2　bay leaves
10　c. chicken or vegetable broth (or 10 c. water plus 5 tsp. instant soup mix)
2　5½ oz. (156 ml) cans tomato paste
2　tbsp. chopped fresh dill (or 1 tsp. dried)
⅓　c. brown sugar, packed (to taste)
3　tbsp. lemon juice
Salt & pepper, to taste

1. In a large pot, heat oil on medium heat. Add onions, cabbage and carrots. Sauté for 15 to 20 minutes, until tender, stirring often. Add a little water as needed to prevent burning.

2. Add lentils, parsnips, celery, garlic, bay leaves and broth. Bring to a boil and simmer partially covered for 1 hour. Stir in tomato paste, dill, brown sugar, lemon juice, salt and pepper. Simmer about 30 minutes longer. Adjust seasonings to taste. If soup is too thick, add a little water. Discard bay leaf.

Yield: 15 servings. Freezes and/or reheats well.

152 calories per serving, 1.6 g fat (0.2 g saturated), 0 mg cholesterol, 9 g protein, 27 g carbohydrate, 327 mg sodium, 586 mg potassium, 3 mg iron, 7 g fiber, 73 mg calcium.

- **Red Lentil & Cabbage Borscht:** Substitute red lentils and use only 1 can of tomato paste. Red lentils will become soft and disappear into the soup. Brown lentils will retain their shape.
- **Tomato paste, lemon juice** and salt are added near the end of cooking or lentils will not get soft.

Mushroom Barley Soup

An old-fashioned soup which is warm and satisfying. Full of flavor and nutrition, yet very low in fat! Barley is a good source of soluble fiber.

1 tbsp. canola or olive oil
2 large onions, peeled & chopped
3 stalks celery, trimmed & chopped
2–3 tbsp. water (approximately)
3 cloves garlic, minced
8 c. hot water, chicken or vegetable broth
2–3 potatoes, peeled & chopped
3 carrots, peeled & chopped
2 c. mushrooms, trimmed & sliced
1/2 c. pearl barley, rinsed & drained
Freshly ground pepper
1/2 tsp. dried thyme
1 tsp. dried basil
2 tsp. salt, or to taste
2 tbsp. fresh parsley, minced
1/4 c. dill sprigs

1. Heat oil on medium heat in a large heavy-bottomed soup pot. Add onions and celery. Sauté for 5 to 7 minutes, until golden. Add a little water once onions start to brown to prevent them from burning or sticking to the pot. Stir in garlic and sauté 2 to 3 minutes longer. Add remaining ingredients except salt, parsley and dill.

2. Bring to a boil. Reduce heat, cover partially and simmer for about an hour, stirring occasionally, until barley is tender. If soup is too thick, thin with a little additional water. Add salt, parsley and dill. Season to taste.

Yield: 10 servings. Reheats and/or freezes well.

98 calories per serving, 1.7 g fat (0.2 g saturated), 0 mg cholesterol, 3 g protein, 19 g carbohydrate, 501 mg sodium, 295 mg potassium, 1 mg iron, 4 g fiber, 36 mg calcium.

- **Mushroom, Bean & Barley Soup:** Combine 1/2 cup white beans with 3 cups of cold water in a large bowl. Soak overnight. Drain and rinse well. Discard loose or floating skins. Prepare above soup as directed, adding soaked beans along with barley at the end of Step 1. Simmer for 1 1/2 hours. If cooked soup is too thick, thin with a little water.
- **Lots of Vegetables & Barley Soup:** Prepare Mushroom Barley Soup as directed, adding 1 cup of chopped broccoli and 1 medium chopped zucchini along with barley at the end of Step 1. If desired, substitute 1 leek, trimmed and sliced, for one of the onions.

Green Split Pea & Barley Soup

For a delicious smoky flavor, add the cut-up carcass of a smoked turkey along with the barley!

2 c. green split peas, rinsed & drained
3 carrots, chopped
3–4 stalks celery, chopped
1 medium onion, chopped
12 c. water, chicken or vegetable broth
1/2 c. pearl barley, rinsed & drained
1 bay leaf
Salt & pepper, to taste
2 cloves crushed garlic, if desired
2 tsp. canola oil
2 medium onions, chopped
1/4 c. chopped fresh dill

1. In a large soup pot, combine split peas, carrots, celery and 1 onion with water. Bring to a boil. Stir in barley, bay leaf and garlic, if using. Reduce heat and simmer partly covered for 1½ to 2 hours. Stir occasionally. Add salt and pepper to taste. In a nonstick skillet, heat oil. Sauté the remaining two onions on medium heat until well-browned, about 6 to 8 minutes. Add onions to soup along with dill. Simmer soup 5 to 10 minutes longer. Discard bay leaf (and turkey carcass, if using).

Yield: 12 servings. Reheats and/or freezes well. If soup gets thick, add a little water or broth.

152 calories per serving, 1.3 g fat (0.1 g saturated), 0 mg cholesterol, 8 g protein, 28 g carbohydrate, 31 mg sodium, 427 mg potassium, 2 mg iron, 9 g fiber, 34 mg calcium.

Nancy Gordon's Split Pea Soup

3	c. dried green or yellow split peas, picked over, rinsed & drained
12	c. water
2	bay leaves
½	c. fresh dill
3	stalks celery
2	carrots
1	large potato, peeled
1	large onion
3	cloves garlic
1	tbsp. olive oil
Salt & pepper, to taste	

1. Combine peas and water in a large pot. Cover and bring to a boil. Skim off foam. Add bay leaves and half of the dill. Reduce heat and simmer partially covered until peas are tender, about an hour.

2. Meanwhile, chop celery, carrots, potato, onion and garlic into bite-sized pieces. In a large skillet, heat oil over medium high heat. Cook veggies for 5 to 7 minutes, until soft. Add to soup and simmer covered for 20 to 30 minutes, until veggies are tender. Remove bay leaf. Add remaining dill. Add salt and pepper to taste. Soup can also be puréed. If too thick, thin it with a little water.

Yield: 12 servings. Reheats and/or freezes well.

176 calories per serving, 1.7 g fat (0.2 g saturated), 0 mg cholesterol, 11 g protein, 31 g carbohydrate, 28 mg sodium, 558 mg potassium, 2 mg iron, 11 g fiber, 35 mg calcium.

Broccoli & Sweet Potato Soup

Carrots, broccoli and sweet potatoes are all great sources of beta carotene.

2	large onions, chopped
2	stalks celery, chopped
1	tbsp. canola oil
3	carrots, chopped
1	bunch broccoli (about 4 cups, cut up)
2	medium potatoes, peeled & cut up
2	medium sweet potatoes, peeled & cut up
7	c. vegetable broth
½	c. chopped parsley
2	tbsp. fresh basil or dill, chopped
1	c. skim milk, soy milk or water
1	tsp. tub margarine or butter
Salt & pepper, to taste	

1. In a large soup pot, sauté onions and celery in oil for 5 to 7 minutes, until softened. If necessary, add a little water to prevent burning. Add carrots. Cook 3 to 4 minutes longer, stirring occasionally.

Add broccoli, potatoes, sweet potatoes and broth. Bring to a boil, reduce heat and simmer for 20 to 25 minutes. Add parsley and basil. Purée part or all of the soup. Add milk and margarine. Season to taste.

Yield: 10 servings. Reheats and/or freezes well.

126 calories per serving, 2.9 g fat (0.3 g saturated), trace cholesterol, 5 g protein, 23 g carbohydrate, 753 mg sodium, 416 mg potassium, 1 mg iron, 4 g fiber, 75 mg calcium.

Easy Carrot Soup

This recipe is dedicated to my granddaughter Lauren, who helped test it when she was 4 days old!

1	tbsp. canola oil
2	medium onions, coarsely chopped
1	red pepper, chopped
2	cloves garlic, crushed
8–9	large carrots, cut into chunks
1	large potato, peeled & cut into chunks
4	c. vegetable broth
2	tbsp. fresh dill, minced
	Salt & pepper, to taste
1–1¼	c. skim milk (or water)
¼–½	tsp. ground ginger (to taste)

1. In a saucepan, heat oil on medium heat. Add onions and red pepper. Sauté until golden. Add garlic and sauté 2 to 3 minutes longer. If necessary, add a little water to prevent burning. Add carrots, potato and broth. Bring to a boil, reduce heat and simmer covered for 25 to 30 minutes, stirring occasionally. Purée soup. Add dill, salt and pepper to taste. Blend in milk and ground ginger.

Yield: 6 servings. Freezes and/or reheats well. Do not boil. Serve hot or cold.

133 calories per serving, 3.3 g fat (0.3 g saturated), <1 mg cholesterol, 5 g protein, 24 g carbohydrate, 759 mg sodium, 458 mg potassium, 1 mg iron, 5 g fiber, 96 mg calcium.

• **Creamy Squash Soup:** Instead of carrots and dill, substitute 1½ pounds (750 g) winter squash, peeled, cleaned and cut into chunks. Add ¼ cup orange juice to puréed soup.

Cauliflower Carrot Soup

1	large onion, chopped
1	stalk celery, chopped
½	of a red pepper, chopped
2	cloves garlic, crushed
2	tsp. canola oil or margarine
4	c. cauliflower, cut up (half of a cauliflower)
2	potatoes, peeled & chopped
3	large carrots, chopped
5	c. vegetable broth
1	c. skim milk
2	tbsp. chopped fresh dill
½	tsp. dried thyme
	Salt & pepper, to taste

1. Prepare vegetables. In a large saucepan, heat oil. Add onions, celery and red pepper. Sauté on medium-low heat about 5 minutes, stirring occasionally. If necessary, add a little water to prevent sticking. Add garlic and cook 2 or 3 minutes longer.

2. Add cauliflower, potatoes, carrots and broth to sautéed vegetables. Bring to a boil and reduce heat. Cover partially and simmer 20 to 25 minutes, or until vegetables are tender. Purée part of the soup (or use a potato masher to break up the vegetables). Add milk, dill and thyme. Heat until piping hot. Add salt and pepper to taste.

Yield: 7 to 8 servings. Reheats and/or freezes well.

101 calories per serving, 2.1 g fat (0.3 g saturated), <1 mg cholesterol, 4 g protein, 18 g carbohydrate, 480 mg sodium, 397 mg potassium, <1 mg iron, 4 g fiber, 80 mg calcium.

- **Analysis was done using** canned vegetable broth. If you are sodium-sensitive, use homemade vegetable broth made without salt.
- **Yogurt can be used** instead of milk, but do not boil soup or it will curdle. Do not freeze.
- **If desired, sprinkle each serving** with a little Parmesan cheese and top with a few croutons.
- **Broccoli Carrot Soup:** Substitute broccoli for cauliflower in the above recipe.

Lazy Day Corn Soup

14 oz. can (398 ml) creamed corn
1³/₄ c. of skim milk
Salt & pepper, to taste
¹/₄ tsp. dried basil or thyme

1. Combine corn and milk in a saucepan or large microsafe bowl. Bring to a simmer but do not boil. (It will take about 7 to 8 minutes on HIGH in the microwave). Season to taste. Serve immediately.

Yield: 3 servings.

158 calories per serving, 0.9 g fat (0.3 g saturated), 3 mg cholesterol, 8 g protein, 34 g carbohydrate, 499 mg sodium, 442 mg potassium, <1 mg iron, 3 g fiber, 183 mg calcium.

Corn & Vegetable Chowder

1   tbsp. canola oil
2   large onions, chopped
3   stalks celery, chopped
3–4 carrots, chopped
2   tbsp. flour
6   c. vegetable broth (or 1 tbsp. instant pareve soup mix plus 6 c. water)
3   potatoes, peeled & diced
6   c. frozen corn kernels (1 kg/2 lb)
1¹/₂ c. frozen green peas
1   bay leaf
¹/₂ tsp. dried basil &/or thyme
Salt & pepper, to taste
1¹/₂ c. skim or 1% milk (approximately)
3   ripe tomatoes, peeled, seeded & diced
3–4 tbsp. chopped fresh dill
3   green onions, chopped

1. In a large saucepan, heat oil over medium heat. Add onions, celery and carrots. Sauté on medium heat, stirring occasionally, until onions are tender, about 6 to 8 minutes. (If necessary, add a little water to prevent sticking.) Stir in flour and cook 1 minute longer.

2. Slowly add broth and stir until smooth. Add potatoes, corn, peas, bay leaf, basil and/or thyme. Add salt and pepper to taste. Bring to a boil. Cover, reduce heat and simmer for 20 minutes, until potatoes are tender. Discard bay leaf.

3. Remove about 3 cups of vegetables from the pot with a slotted spoon and place them in the processor. Process until coarsely puréed. Return mixture to the saucepan and stir in milk. If soup is too thick, add a little more milk. If soup is too thin, purée some more of the veggies. Add tomatoes and simmer for 4 to 5 minutes, until heated through. Do not boil. Add dill and green onions. Adjust seasonings to taste.

Yield: about 12 servings. Reheats and/or freezes well. Do not boil.

203 calories per serving, 3.1 g fat (0.3 g saturated), <1 mg cholesterol, 8 g protein, 42 g carbohydrate, 580 mg sodium, 627 mg potassium, 2 mg iron, 6 g fiber, 69 mg calcium.

- **The color of this soup** will be nicer with 1% milk, but the fat content is lower if you use skim milk. Evaporated skim milk can be substituted.
- **To peel and seed fresh tomatoes:** Cut out the stem end using the point of a sharp knife. Plunge tomatoes into a pot of boiling water. Cook for 20 seconds. Pour off water and add cold water immediately to tomatoes to cover completely. Skins will slip off easily. Cut in half and squeeze gently to remove seeds.

No-Cook Lazy Day Beet Borscht

This light and refreshing soup tastes exactly like the dairy borscht my late Aunt Adele was famous for, but with none of the work. The color is incredible. Don't dare tell anyone how easy it is!

2	19 oz. (540 ml) cans beets
48	oz. (1.36 liters) can tomato juice (preferably low-sodium)
1	liter (4½ c.) buttermilk
½	c. sugar (artificial sweetener can be used)
1–2	tbsp. lemon juice, to taste

1. Drain beet juice into a very large mixing bowl. Process drained beets in the processor using the Steel Knife, until fine. Combine all ingredients with beet juice in mixing bowl and mix well. Store in glass jars in the refrigerator. Keeps about 10 days. Serve chilled.

Yield: 10 to 12 servings (about 14 cups). To freeze, pour borscht into storage containers, leaving at least 1 inch at the top of each container.

138 calories per serving, 1.1 g fat (0.6 g saturated), 4 mg cholesterol, 6 g protein, 29 g carbohydrate, 418 mg sodium, 634 mg potassium, 2 mg iron, 3 g fiber, 149 mg calcium.

- **Esther's Easy Vegetable Borscht:** Refrigerate a 32-ounce jar of commercial borscht. At serving time, add some chopped boiled potatoes, cucumber, green onions and fresh minced dill. Great for summer!

New-Wave Gazpacho (Salad Soup)

Now you can sip your salad! So refreshing, so healthy, so tasty.

1	green & 1 red pepper
1	English cucumber, peeled
2	stalks celery
5–6	large, firm, ripe tomatoes
4	green onions
4	cloves garlic, crushed
2	tbsp. each fresh dill and basil, minced
19	oz. can (540 ml) tomato juice
2	c. vegetable broth
1	tbsp. olive oil (extra-virgin is best)
3	tbsp. fresh lemon juice (juice of a lemon)
	Salt & freshly ground pepper, to taste
6–8	drops Tabasco sauce

1. Chop the peppers, cucumber, celery, tomatoes and green onions. Combine together in a large bowl with garlic, dill and basil. Add remaining ingredients and mix well. Chill before serving.

Yield: 7 to 8 servings (about 10 cups). Soup will keep 2 or 3 days in the refrigerator.

84 calories per serving, 2.8 g fat (0.4 g saturated), 0 mg cholesterol, 3 g protein, 15 g carbohydrate, 610 mg sodium, 646 mg potassium, 2 mg iron, 3 g fiber, 37 mg calcium.

• **Gazpacho Rosa:** Stir ⅓ cup non-fat yogurt or sour cream into each cup of soup.

Zucchini, Bean & Potato Soup

2   c. dried lima beans, rinsed & drained
6   c. cold water
1   zucchini, chopped
1   large carrot, chopped
2   large onions, chopped
3   cloves garlic, crushed
4   potatoes, peeled & cut up
7–8 c. water (about)
Salt & pepper, to taste
2   tbsp. minced fresh dill
1   tsp. butter, margarine or olive oil

1. Soak beans overnight in cold water. Drain and rinse well. Discard soaking water and any beans that are floating. In a large saucepan, combine beans, zucchini, carrots, onions, garlic and potatoes. Add enough water to cover the other ingredients by 1 inch. Season with salt and pepper. Bring to a boil, reduce heat and simmer partially covered for 1½ hours, until beans are tender. Mash or purée part of the soup. Add dill and butter.

Yield: 8 hearty servings. Soup reheats and/or freezes well.

157 calories per serving, 0.8 g fat (0.4 g saturated), 1 mg cholesterol, 6 g protein, 32 g carbohydrate, 32 mg sodium, 677 mg potassium, 2 mg iron, 5 g fiber, 43 mg calcium.

Sweet Potato & Zucchini Soup

I developed this quick and easy recipe one day from ingredients on hand. The onions are "sautéed" in water and the olive oil is added at the end of cooking for maximum flavor, minimum fat.

2   onions, chopped
¼   c. water
2   sweet potatoes, peeled & cut into chunks
3   potatoes, peeled & cut into chunks
2   zucchini, cut into chunks (do not peel)
4   c. water or vegetable broth
Salt & pepper, to taste
1   tsp. olive oil
1   tbsp. minced fresh dill (or 1 tsp. dried)

1. Combine chopped onions with water in a large saucepan. Cook on high heat until water has mostly evaporated and onions are soft, about 5 minutes. Add remaining vegetables, water, salt and pepper. Bring to a boil, reduce heat and simmer partially covered for 20 to 25 minutes, until vegetables are soft, stirring occasionally. Stir in olive oil and dill; simmer 3 or 4 minutes longer.

2. Purée soup to desired texture (or mash the vegetables right in the pot with a potato masher to make a somewhat smooth mixture with a few small chunks.) If necessary, thin with a little extra water. (Skim milk is also good.) Adjust seasonings to taste.

Yield: 6 servings. Reheats or freezes well.

165 calories per serving, 1.2 g fat (0.2 g saturated), 0 mg cholesterol, 3 g protein, 37 g carbohydrate, 20 mg sodium, 525 mg potassium, <1 mg iron, 4 g fiber, 38 mg calcium.

Leek & Sweet Potato Soup

A variation of Vichyssoise.

2   large leeks (about 3 c. sliced)
1   tbsp. canola oil
2   cloves garlic, crushed
2   tbsp. flour
6   c. water
2   sweet potatoes, peeled & cut into chunks
2   potatoes, peeled & cut into chunks
1–2 tsp. salt, to taste
1/4 tsp. pepper, to taste
1/4 tsp. dried thyme
2   tbsp. fresh dill, minced

1. Clean leeks. (See Chef's Secrets, below.) Slice thinly, discarding the root end. Heat oil in a large soup pot. Add leeks, cover pot and cook over low heat for 5 minutes, until softened but not browned. If necessary, add a little water as needed to prevent burning. Add garlic and cook covered 2 to 3 minutes longer. Stir in flour and cook uncovered 1 minute longer.

2. Gradually blend in water. Add potatoes, sweet potatoes, salt, pepper and thyme. Bring to a boil, reduce heat and simmer partially covered for 1/2 hour. Purée part or all of the soup. (I usually mash it with a potato masher.) Add dill. Adjust seasonings to taste. If too thick, add a little milk or water.

Yield: 8 servings. Reheats and/or freezes well.

132 calories per serving, 2 g fat (0.2 g saturated), 0 mg cholesterol, 2 g protein, 27 g carbohydrate, 312 mg sodium, 279 mg potassium, 1 mg iron, 3 g fiber, 39 mg calcium.

- **To clean leeks:** Cut off most of the dark green part, leaving the white and light green part. (The dark green part can be added when you make chicken or vegetable broth.) Split the leek in half lengthwise from the top end to within 1/2 inch of the root end. Make a second lengthwise cut. The leek will open up like a broom. Swish in cold water to remove all traces of sand and dirt.
- **If you are short on leeks,** you can substitute 3 cups of sliced onions in the above recipe.
- **One bunch of green onions,** trimmed, is the equivalent of one onion. Two or three bunches (depending on size) are the equivalent of one leek.
- **Passover version:** Substitute 1 tablespoon potato starch for flour.
- **For a dairy version of this soup,** blend in 1 cup of skim or 1% milk and 3 tablespoons grated Parmesan cheese at serving time. Calci-yummy!

Country Vegetable Soup

The microwaved version of this low-calorie soup is made without fat.

1   large onion, chopped
1   stalk celery, chopped
1   large leek, thinly sliced
1   tbsp. oil, optional
1   tbsp. water
2   medium potatoes, peeled & chopped
2   large carrots, peeled & chopped
1   medium zucchini, chopped
1   c. broccoli or cauliflower, cut up

28 oz. (796 ml) can tomatoes (low-sodium)
4 c. hot water
2 tsp. salt
Freshly ground pepper, to taste
1/2 tsp. dried thyme
1/2 tsp. dried basil
2 tbsp. fresh parsley, minced

• **Microwave Method:** Place onion, celery, leeks and water in a 3-quart microsafe casserole. Microwave covered on HIGH until tender, about 6 to 7 minutes, stirring once. Add remaining ingredients except parsley. Microwave covered on HIGH for 20 to 25 minutes, until veggies are tender. Adjust seasonings to taste. Garnish with parsley.

• **Stovetop Method:** Heat 1 tablespoon oil in a large soup pot. Add onion, celery and leeks. Sauté for 7 to 8 minutes, until golden. Add water as needed to prevent sticking. Add remaining ingredients except parsley. Bring to a boil and simmer covered until veggies are tender, about 35 to 40 minutes. Adjust seasonings to taste. Garnish with parsley.

Yield: 7 to 8 servings. Reheats and/or freezes well.

86 calories per serving, 0.4 g fat (0.1 g saturated), 0 mg cholesterol, 3 g protein, 20 g carbohydrate, 707 mg sodium, 599 mg potassium, 2 mg iron, 4 g fiber, 74 mg calcium.

• **If desired,** sprinkle each serving with 1 teaspoon grated Parmesan cheese.
• **If made with oil,** one serving contains 103 calories and contains 2.3 g fat (0.2 g saturated).
• **Country Vegetable Soup with Chickpeas & Barley:** Add 1/4 cup pearl barley and 1 cup canned chickpeas, rinsed and drained, to sautéed vegetables. Add remaining ingredients, bring to boil and simmer covered for 1 hour. Adjust seasonings to taste.

• **Oh My Minestrone!** Make Country Vegetable Soup as directed, but add 1/2 teaspoon oregano along with the dried herbs. A handful of green beans, peas and/or mushrooms and 2 cloves of crushed garlic make tasty additions. Ten minutes before the end of cooking, stir in 1 1/2 cups of canned red kidney beans, drained and rinsed. Add 1 cup of cooked small pasta shells or spirals.

Get Skinny Cabbage Soup

This is a version of the famous "miracle cabbage soup" that people eat in hopes of getting slim quickly. If you want to follow the diet that accompanies the soup, please consult your doctor first!

2 green peppers
1 bunch of celery
1 bunch of green onions
1 medium head of cabbage
28 oz. can (796 ml) canned crushed tomatoes
19 oz. (540 ml) V-8 vegetable juice
1 pkg. dry onion soup mix (4 serving size)

1. Chop vegetables. Combine all ingredients in a large pot, adding water to cover veggies. Bring to a boil; cook for 10 minutes. Reduce heat and simmer partially covered for 25 minutes.

Yield: 12 servings. Reheats and/or freezes well.

61 calories per serving, 0.8 g fat (0.1 g saturated), 0 mg cholesterol, 3 g protein, 13 g carbohydrate, 547 mg sodium, 468 mg potassium, 1 mg iron, 5 g fiber, 76 mg calcium.

• **Add a handful of chopped mushrooms** to the pot along with the chopped vegetables and cook as directed. The soaking water from dried mushrooms can also be added.

· **For a sweet and sour taste,** add a squeeze of lemon juice and a little sweetener.
· **If desired, add a splash** of low-cal cranberry juice to the cooked soup.
· **Just before the soup** is done, add 2 cups of washed, chopped spinach or Swiss chard.

Mock Shaav (Spinach & Rhubarb Soup)

Miriam Bercovitz shared this great recipe! Shaav is usually made with sorrel, which can be expensive.

10	oz. pkg. (300 g) frozen chopped spinach
½	lb. (250 g/2 cups) frozen rhubarb (or 1 lb. fresh rhubarb)
6½	c. water
2	tsp. salt, or to taste
1	egg, lightly beaten
½	c. non-fat yogurt or sour cream

1. Combine spinach, rhubarb, 6 cups water and salt in a large saucepan. Cook on high heat, breaking up spinach and rhubarb with a spoon. Once soup boils, cook uncovered on medium for 5 minutes. Combine egg and ½ cup cold water in a bowl. Gradually add hot soup a spoonful at a time to egg mixture (1½ cups soup in total). Stir egg mixture back into soup. Chill before serving. Serve cold with a dollop of yogurt or sour cream. Garnish with cucumbers, green onions and radishes.

Yield: 6 to 8 servings. Store in jars in the fridge for up to 10 days (without garnishes).

46 calories per serving, 1.1 g fat (0.3 g saturated), 36 mg cholesterol, 4 g protein, 6 g carbohydrate, 850 mg sodium, 244 mg potassium, 1 mg iron, 3 g fiber, 192 mg calcium.

· **Optional garnishes:** chopped cucumbers, green onions and radishes

Florida Water à la Doris

Doris Fink, my Montreal assistant, always prepared a pitcher of this refreshing water for my students!

1. Place 2 sliced oranges, 2 sliced lemons and/or limes in a large pitcher. Fill with ice cold water (preferably spring water). Serve chilled. Simply refreshing! (Contains negligible nutrients.)

Mimosa à la Doris

Doris says that this drink is fat-free and guarantees you a very happy day! It's great for brunch.

1. Add 2 parts orange juice (e.g., Tropicana without pulp) to 1 part sparkling champagne. Mix together in a pitcher. Add sliced oranges, lemons and limes. Serve over ice. So refreshing! (Nutrient data is based on using medium white wine. No data available for champagne.)

91 calories per 6 oz. serving, 0 g fat (0 g saturated), 0 mg cholesterol, trace protein, 13 g carbohydrate, 3 mg sodium, 47 mg potassium, trace iron, 0 g fiber, 5 mg calcium.

Hot Chocolate (Cocoa)

Whenever I have a craving for chocolate or need to lower my stress levels, I have a cup of cocoa and it feels like a warm hug! It also helps you sleep better if you have a cup before bedtime. Calci-yummy!

1   tsp. unsweetened cocoa
1   c. skim milk
Sugar or sweetener to taste (2 tsp. sugar or the
    equivalent in artificial sweetener)

1. Measure cocoa in a microwave-safe mug. Add a little milk and stir to make a smooth paste. Gradually stir in remaining milk. Microwave on HIGH for 2 minutes, until steaming hot, stirring once or twice. Stir in sweetener. Makes 1 cup.

122 calories per serving (with sugar), 0.7 g fat (0.4 g saturated), 4 mg cholesterol, 9 g protein, 21 g carbohydrate, 127 mg sodium, 434 mg potassium, trace iron, <1 g fiber, 304 mg calcium.

• **With artificial sweetener,** one serving has 97 calories and 15 g carbohydrate.

Chunky Monkey

Packed with potassium and fiber, plus 232 mg of calcium, what a yummy breakfast or snack!

³/₄ c. skim milk
¹/₂ of a frozen banana
1   tsp. cocoa
2–3 ice cubes
Sugar or sweetener to taste (2 tsp. sugar or the
    equivalent in artificial sweetener)

1. In a blender or processor, blend the first 4 ingre-

dients together until smooth. Add sweetener to taste. Makes 1 serving.

155 calories per serving (with sugar), 0.9 g fat (0.5 g saturated), 3 mg cholesterol, 7 g protein, 32 g carbohydrate, 96 mg sodium, 566 mg potassium, <1 mg iron, 2 g fiber, 232 mg calcium.

Orange Creamy Dream

Packed with potassium!

¹/₂ c. frozen concentrated orange juice
2¹/₂ c. skim milk
1   c. non-fat yogurt
1   tsp. vanilla extract
2–3 ice cubes
Sweetener to taste (artificial sweetener to equal 2 tsp.
    sugar)

1. Blend all ingredients together until smooth. Makes 5 servings.

119 calories per serving, 0.4 g fat (0.2 g saturated), 3 mg cholesterol, 8 g protein, 21 g carbohydrate, 102 mg sodium, 521 mg potassium, trace iron, 2 g fiber, 257 mg calcium.

Fruit Smoothies

Lush slush!

¹/₂ c. skim milk or yogurt
¹/₂ c. sliced fruit (e.g. strawberries, peaches)
¹/₄ tsp. vanilla extract
2–3 ice cubes
Sugar or sweetener to taste (1 to 2 tsp. sugar or the
    equivalent in artificial sweetener)

The Wonders of Water!

- Water is the ultimate fat-free beverage! Bottled spring water, distilled water, mineral and seltzer water taste better than tap water.
- Water is essential to life. It regulates body temperature, carries nutrients and oxygen to cells, removes waste, protects organs and tissues, and cushions your joints.
- If you have dry skin, just drink more water and the problem will usually resolve itself.
- Water aids in preventing constipation and decreases the risk of developing kidney stones.
- Did you know that water comprises up to 70 percent of the body weight of an average adult?
- Health experts recommend drinking at least 6 to 8 glasses a day, distributed throughout the day.
- Drink more water during hot weather, when exercising, or if you have a cold or fever, even if you don't feel thirsty. By the time you experience thirst, you may already be somewhat dehydrated.
- Drink a big glass of water before meals and snacks to take the edge off your appetite. (Just make sure a bathroom is handy!) Hot water with a slice of lemon is a good alternative.
- Use the cold water tap for all cooking and drinking water. If you haven't turned on the water tap for several hours, let it run for a few minutes until it's cold. Filtered water is an even better choice.
- Fruit juices are often just sugared water, containing little fiber or fruit. Limit your intake since juices are often high in calories. You're better off with the whole fruit! Vegetable and tomato juices (low-sodium) make good beverage or snack choices.
- Fruits and vegetables are 70 to 95 percent water, whereas fish contains about 75 percent water.
- Soup is an excellent way to increase your fluid intake and obtain additional nutrients. It also makes you feel full! Add some skim milk to soup for additional calcium (see Calci-Yummy, p. 35).
- Salty foods increase the body's requirement for extra water to maintain a proper fluid balance.
- Many diet drinks are high in sodium and may contain caffeine. Also, you may feel more thirsty after drinking soft drinks. Large quantities of tea or coffee have a diuretic effect.
- When you increase your intake of high-fiber foods, be sure to increase your intake of liquids.
- Most of hunger is thirst, and water is a wonderful way to keep you full, and healthy too. So raise your glass and say "L'Chaim—To Life!"

1. In a blender or processor, blend the first 4 ingredients together until smooth. Add sweetener to taste. Makes about 1 cup.

87 calories per serving (with sugar), 0.5 g fat (0.2 g saturated), 2 mg cholesterol, 5 g protein, 16 g carbohydrate, 64 mg sodium, 343 mg potassium, trace iron, 2 g fiber, 163 mg calcium.

- **With artificial sweetener,** one serving has 74 calories and 13 g carbohydrate.
- **Banana Smoothie:** Combine ½ banana, ½ cup skim milk, ½ teaspoon vanilla and 1 teaspoon sugar. Blend until smooth. Makes 1 serving containing about 100 calories.
- **Banana Yogurt Smoothie:** Combine 1 ripe banana, ¾ cup non-fat yogurt or buttermilk, ⅓ cup skim milk, 1 teaspoon honey (to taste) and 3 or 4 ice cubes. Blend until smooth. For a thicker smoothie, use a frozen banana and omit ice. Makes 2 servings.
- **Banana Strawberry Smoothie:** Combine 1 ripe banana, ½ cup sliced strawberries, ¾ cup orange or pineapple juice (or skim milk), 1 to 2 tea-

spoons honey and 3 or 4 ice cubes. Blend until smooth. Omit ice cubes if using frozen banana or strawberries. Makes 2 servings.

• **Cantaloupe with a Banana Smoothie:** Combine the flesh of a canteloupe, 1 banana and 3 or 4 ice cubes. Blend until smooth. Makes 2 servings. Full of fiber and vitamins!

Skinny Cappuccino

Caffeine is hard on your bones, so have at least 2 to 3 tablespoons of milk for each cup of coffee. A better guideline is to drink a cup of milk for each cup of coffee, so go for café au lait! Enjoy in moderation.

1. Prepare espresso coffee as usual. Measure ¼ cup skim or 1 percent milk for each serving. Microwave uncovered on HIGH until hot (¼ cup milk takes 45 seconds, 1 cup takes 2 minutes). Process hot milk in the processor for 30 seconds, until foamy. Fill cups or heatproof-handled glasses half full with coffee, then top with steamed milk. Spoon extra foam on top. Sprinkle lightly with cinnamon and/or sweetened cocoa.

37 calories per serving (without sugar), 0.4 g fat (0.2 g saturated), 1 mg cholesterol, 2 g protein, 6 g carbohydrate, 56 mg sodium, 306 mg potassium, trace iron, 0 g fiber, 79 mg calcium.

• **Mochaccino:** Add 1 teaspoon cocoa to hot espresso; top with ½ cup hot foamed milk.
• **Café au Lait:** Combine equal portions of hot skim milk and brewed coffee. Sweeten to taste.
• **Café Latte:** Like café au lait, but milk is foamed. (Remember, one teaspoon sugar contains 16 calories.)

• **Macchiatto:** Omit espresso. Combine hot foamed milk with almond or hazelnut flavoring to taste. Sprinkle with sweetened cocoa.

Dijon Mustard Sauce

Delicious with fish, or use as a zesty spread for your favorite sandwich.

2 tbsp. Dijon mustard
2 tbsp. fat-free or light mayonnaise
1 clove garlic, crushed
¼ tsp. Worcestershire sauce
3–4 drops of lemon juice

1. Combine all ingredients and mix to blend.

Yield: about ¼ cup. Serve chilled. Do not freeze.

14 calories per tbsp., 0.6 g fat (0 g saturated), 0 mg cholesterol, <1 g protein, 2 g carbohydrate, 216 mg sodium, 20 mg potassium, trace iron, trace fiber, 11 mg calcium.

Yogurt Dill Sauce

Delicious with fish, or use it as a creamy-style salad dressing.

½ c. fat-free or light mayonnaise
½ c. non-fat yogurt or sour cream
1 tbsp. fresh lemon or lime juice
2 tbsp. fresh dill, minced
2 tbsp. green onion, minced
Salt & pepper, to taste

Chef's Secrets: Super Sauces!

- Fat-laden sauces and gravies are a source of calories and saturated fat. These recipes and others throughout the book (see Index) are my low-fat alternatives for your eating pleasure.
- Fat-Free Gravy: You need 1 cup of skimmed chicken or turkey broth. Combine ¼ cup of broth with 2 tbsp. flour in a jar. Cover and shake well to prevent lumps. Transfer to a saucepan and blend in the remaining ¾ cup of broth. Heat over medium heat, whisking constantly, until bubbling and thickened. Season with salt, pepper, a dash of thyme and paprika. If desired, add a handful of sliced mushrooms and simmer 3 or 4 minutes longer.

---

1. Combine mayonnaise, yogurt, lemon or lime juice, dill and green onion. Season to taste with salt and pepper. Chill before serving.

Yield: about 1 cup sauce.

8 calories per tbsp., 0 g fat (0 g saturated), trace cholesterol, trace protein, 2 g carbohydrate, 50 mg sodium, 22 mg potassium, 0 mg iron, 0 g fiber, 14 mg calcium.

Quick'n Easy Tomato Sauce (Vegetarian Spaghetti Sauce)

See recipe (p. 191). This is an excellent, versatile, low-fat sauce that can be used in any recipe calling for tomato sauce (store-bought or homemade), marinara or pasta sauce. It's wonderful with chicken, fish, beans, stews or as an ingredient in casseroles.

- **Chef's Secret:** When buying commercial sauces, be sure to read the label. They are often loaded with salt and/or fat!

Tangy Apricot Sauce or Glaze

Perfect for poultry. This also makes a delicious glaze for grilled salmon.

½   c. apricot preserves
¼   c. orange marmalade
3   tbsp. chili sauce or ketchup
2   tsp. Dijon mustard (to taste)
1   tbsp. fresh lime juice
¼   tsp. dried basil
6   drops Tabasco sauce (or ¼ tsp. cayenne)

1. Heat apricot preserves together with marmalade until melted (about 45 seconds in the microwave on HIGH). Combine with remaining ingredients and mix well. If you use this as a glaze for grilled salmon or roasted chicken, don't brush it on until the last few minutes of cooking to prevent burning.

Yield: about 1 cup. Sauce keeps about 1 month in the refrigerator.

32 calories per tbsp., 0.1 g fat (0 g saturated), 0 mg cholesterol, trace protein, 8 g carbohydrate, 50 mg sodium, 22 mg potassium, 0 mg iron, trace fiber, 3 mg calcium.

Peanut Butter Sauce

Use as a marinade and dipping sauce for Satay Chicken (p. 164) or Chinese Dumplings (p. 268).

2   cloves garlic, minced
1/2 c. smooth peanut butter
3   tbsp. soy sauce
1/4 c. sugar (white or brown)
2   tbsp. rice vinegar (or red wine vinegar)
1   tsp. minced ginger, if desired
6   drops Tabasco sauce (or 1/2 tsp. chili oil)
2   tsp. Oriental sesame oil
1/4 c. cold water

1. Combine all ingredients and blend until smooth. If sauce is too thick, thin it with a few drops of water.

Yield: about 1 cup. Sauce will keep up to 2 months in the refrigerator in a tightly closed container.

49 calories per tbsp., 3.4 g fat (0.7 g saturated), 0 mg cholesterol, 2 g protein, 4 g carbohydrate, 152 mg sodium, 44 mg potassium, trace iron, trace fiber, 3 mg calcium.

• **Satay Salad Dressing:** Add 1/4 to 1/3 cup unsweetened pineapple juice to sauce to make a luscious salad dressing! One tablespoon dressing will contain 43 calories, 2.8 g fat (0.6 g saturated) and 3 g carbohydrate.

Garlic "Sparerib" Sauce

This is my version of a very popular bottled Chinese sauce sold in Canada that is used for spareribs and chicken. It's easy, inexpensive and delicious. Recipe can be doubled easily.

1/4 c. soy sauce
1/2 c. water
1/2 c. brown sugar, firmly packed
2   tbsp. molasses
3   cloves garlic, crushed

1. Combine all ingredients and mix well. Store in a covered container in the refrigerator. Use for chicken, meatballs, fish, tofu or vegetables. It's perfect for Quicky Rumaki, (p. 70).

Yield: about 1 cup. Sauce keeps about a month in the refrigerator.

25 calories per tbsp., 0 g fat (0 g saturated), 0 mg cholesterol, trace protein, 6 g carbohydrate, 163 mg sodium, 50 mg potassium, trace iron, 0 g fiber, 9 mg calcium.

• **To thicken sauce,** bring it to a boil. Dissolve 1 tablespoon cornstarch in 2 tablespoons cold water or orange juice. Add to sauce and simmer for 2 or 3 minutes, until thick, stirring often. If desired, add a dash of red pepper flakes to spice up the sauce.
• **Honey Garlic Sauce:** Prepare above sauce, but use only 1/4 cup brown sugar and add 2 tablespoons honey. (Nutrient values are almost identical to Garlic "Sparerib" Sauce.)

Teriyaki Marinade

Excellent with meat, chicken or fish.

1   tbsp. minced fresh ginger
2   cloves garlic, minced
1/4 c. minced green onions
3–4 tbsp. light soy sauce
3   tbsp. rice vinegar, white wine or sherry

2 tbsp. honey, maple syrup or brown sugar
2 tsp. Oriental sesame oil
$1/8$ tsp. red pepper flakes

1. Combine all ingredients in a bowl and mix well. Marinate poultry or meat for 30 minutes at room temperature, or overnight in the refrigerator. Marinate fish for up to an hour.

Yield: about $3/4$ cup marinade, enough for 2 pounds (1 kg) meat, fish or chicken.

24 calories per tbsp., 0.7 g fat (0.1 g saturated), 0 mg cholesterol, trace protein, 4 g carbohydrate, 122 mg sodium, 12 mg potassium, trace iron, trace fiber, 4 mg calcium.

• **Orange Hoisin Marinade:** Decrease soy sauce to 2 tablespoons Add $1/4$ cup orange juice, $1/4$ cup hoisin sauce and 1 teaspoon finely grated orange zest. One tablespoon of marinade contains 23 calories and 0.6 g fat (0.1 g saturated).

Spicy Dipping Sauce

Use as a dipping sauce for Chinese Dumplings (p. 268), or serve with steamed fish or vegetables.

2 tbsp. light soy sauce
3 tbsp. rice vinegar (or red wine vinegar)
2 tsp. minced fresh ginger
2 tsp. minced garlic (about 4 cloves)
$1/2$ tsp. sugar
$1/2$ tsp. Oriental sesame oil
$1/4$ tsp. red pepper flakes

1. Combine ingredients in a bowl or jar and blend thoroughly.

Yield: about $1/3$ cup. Store sauce in a covered jar in the refrigerator. It will keep about a month.

12 calories per tbsp., 0.4 g fat (0 g saturated), 0 mg cholesterol, <1 g protein, 2 g carbohydrate, 148 mg sodium, 10 mg potassium, trace iron, trace fiber, 4 mg calcium.

Mango Salsa

So refreshing! Perfect with grilled fish, chicken, smoked salmon or Gravlax (p. 68).

1 large or 2 small ripe mangoes, peeled & diced (about 1–$1/2$ cups)
$1/4$ c. red onion, finely chopped
$1/4$ c. minced fresh coriander (cilantro)
$1/4$ c. red pepper, chopped
1 jalapeño pepper, seeded & finely minced
3 tbsp. freshly squeezed lime juice
1–2 tsp. brown sugar or honey
Dash of salt & pepper (to taste)

1. Combine all ingredients and mix well. May be prepared up to a day in advance, covered and refrigerated until needed. Bring to room temperature before serving.

Yield: about $1 1/2$ cups.

8 calories per tbsp., 0 g fat (0 g saturated), 0 mg cholesterol, trace protein, 2 g carbohydrate, trace sodium, 21 mg potassium, 0 mg iron, trace fiber, 2 mg calcium.

• **A mango has a large,** oval-shaped pit which clings to the flesh, making it difficult to cut. Using a sharp knife, cut down one side of the flesh, feeling for the pit with your knife. Repeat on the other side. You will have 2 large pieces. Dice mango flesh, but don't cut right through to the skin. Carefully cut mango flesh away from the skin.

- **To know if a mango is ripe,** smell it. It should have a luscious, tropical aroma.
- **Pineapple or Melon Salsa:** Substitute fresh pineapple, cantaloupe or honeydew for mangoes.
- **Papaya Salsa:** Substitute papaya, peeled, seeded and coarsely chopped, for mangoes.
- **Mango Purée is a terrific** fat-free sauce for fresh berries, bananas, pineapple or frozen yogurt! Peel, slice and chop a ripe mango, then push the fruit through a sieve with a wooden spoon. If necessary, add a few drops of honey and a squeeze of lemon or lime juice.

Roasted Red Pepper Coulis

Serve this vitamin-packed, fat-free sauce with fish, chicken, vegetables or Polenta Triangles (p. 74).

> 2–3 large roasted red peppers (homemade or from a jar), chopped
> 1   clove garlic, crushed
> 1   medium onion, chopped
> 1½ c. vegetable or chicken broth
> 2–3 drops Tabasco sauce, optional
> Salt & pepper, to taste
> 1   tbsp. fresh basil, minced (or ½ tsp. dried)

1. In a medium saucepan, combine roasted peppers, garlic, onion and broth. Bring to a boil, reduce heat and simmer for 5 minutes. Cool slightly. Purée sauce. Add remaining ingredients and mix well. If sauce is too thick, add a little more broth or water. Serve warm.

Yield: about 1 cup sauce (4 servings). Sauce will keep for a day or two in the refrigerator.

27 calories per ¼ cup serving, 0.4 g fat (0 g saturated), 0 mg cholesterol, 1 g protein, 6 g carbohydrate, 252 sodium, 106 mg potassium, trace iron, <1 g fiber, 11 mg calcium.

- **See recipe for Roasted Red Peppers** (p. 57). If using roasted peppers from a jar, you'll need about 1½ cups. However, they are higher in sodium.

Homemade Cranberry Sauce

Perfect with roast chicken or turkey.

> 12 oz. fresh or frozen cranberries (1 bag)
> ½ c. granulated sugar
> ½ c. brown sugar, firmly packed
> ¾ c. orange or cranberry juice
> 2   tsp. minced fresh ginger
> 1   tsp. grated orange zest

1. Rinse and drain cranberries. Combine all ingredients in a large saucepan and mix well. Bring to a boil. Reduce heat to medium and simmer uncovered until cranberries pop open, about 10 minutes, stirring occasionally. (To cook sauce in the microwave, use a 3-quart microwave-safe dish. Cover and microwave on HIGH for 10 minutes, stirring once or twice.) When cool, transfer to a serving dish and refrigerate.

Yield: about 2 cups sauce. Sauce keeps for 3 or 4 days in the refrigerator.

21 calories per tbsp., 0 g fat (0 g saturated), 0 mg cholesterol, trace protein, 6 g carbohydrate, 1 mg sodium, 21 mg potassium, trace iron, trace fiber, 3 mg calcium.

• **Chef's Shortcut:** If you have canned whole cranberry sauce on hand, add 1 teaspoon of grated orange rind for a pretend "homemade" taste. (Thanks to Doris Fink for the great tip!)

Sandwiches & Fillings

Sandwiches Make Great Light Meals!

- Sandwiches come in all shapes and sizes, from mini-party sandwiches to multi-footers. The largest I ever prepared was an edible centerpiece for 125 guests at a Sweet Sixteen party. Loaves of bread spelled out the guest of honor's name. They were arranged on a long wooden plank covered with greens. Each loaf contained layers of different fillings and the plank was beautifully garnished. Dagwood would have been impressed. Debra and her guests certainly were!

- Although sandwiches can be a nutritional disaster, they can also fit into a healthy eating plan. Minis make great appetizers, "heart-y" ones become a meal when you add soup and/or salad.

- Many dieters think bread is fattening, but most breads contain only one gram of fat per slice. No need to feel guilty! There's a wide variety of beautiful, crusty breads and rolls to use as the outer covering for your culinary combinations, so feel free to experiment.

- Try multi-grain, sourdough, rye, pumpernickel, kimmel, whole-wheat, gluten-free or crusty country loaves, French baguettes, Italian, onion, corn, sun-dried tomato, olive or herb breads, focaccia, bagels, pita, tortillas—the list goes on and on. If you have the time and inclination, you can bake your own breads.

- Lots of healthy "stuff" can fit between two slices of bread, or you can make wonderful open-faced sandwiches! Use cookie cutters to make attractive shapes.

- Sandwich fillings can be made into roll-ups or wraps using pita or soft flour tortillas.

- Sandwiches can be served cold or hot. Veggie sandwiches can be held together with a little melted low-fat cheese.

- Serve Bruschetta (p. 73) or Mushroom Crostini (p. 242) with a salad for a luscious "lite bite."

- Whole-grain breads are the best choice for maximum nutrition. Look for "whole wheat flour" on the label.

- Hold the mayo! Use fat-free or light mayonnaise. To reduce the fat even further, combine equal parts of fat-free mayo with non-fat yogurt. Blend in a little Dijon or honey-style mustard. Use as a bread spread or to bind sandwich fillings.

- Other low-fat spreads for bread are specialty mustards or salsa. I like to add a touch of maple syrup or honey to Yogurt Cheese (p. 53) for a guilt-free dairy spread.

- For lighter, healthier sandwich fillings, here are several suggestions. Use water-packed tuna; discard half the yolks when making chopped egg; mash in the bones when making salmon filling; use skim-milk cheeses. See lighter versions of these recipes (p. 123, 124–25).

- Sandwich Loaves: Use lighter versions of tuna, salmon or chopped egg salad to fill loaves. Another terrific filling is Roasted Red Pepper Dip or Spread (p. 56).

- Use Creamy Yogurt Cheese (p. 53) instead of cream cheese as a "frosting" for sandwich loaves. Flavor cheese with minced green onions, dill and/or basil and a bit of honey or maple syrup. Another fabulous "frosting" is low-fat curd cottage cheese processed for 3 minutes in your processor, until no curds remain and cheese becomes smooth and velvety.

- The National Cancer Institute recommends that we should 5 to 10 servings of fruits and veggies a day. Veggies are low in fat and high in nutrients, so pack some into your sandwich and enjoy a guilt-free trip to a healthier future. You can handle that!

- Add vitamins, minerals, color, texture and crunch to sandwich spreads by adding finely grated carrots,

- celery, peppers, minced green or red onions, basil, parsley or dill.
- To provide moisture to sandwiches, add lettuce, tomato, cucumber and/or sprouts. To prevent sandwiches from becoming soggy, dry the veggies first with paper towels. For a flavorful filling, add some strips of bottled or homemade Roasted Red Peppers (p. 57). So good!
- Fill pita pockets with your favorite garden salad or Israeli Salad (p. 280). Pita bread makes a perfect holder for the crunchy filling!
- Vegetarian sandwiches are wonderful. Try Tofu Spread (p. 123), Red Lentil Paté (p. 227), Lentil Spinach Paté (p. 227) or one of the vegetarian versions of Mock Chopped Liver (p. 55). Enjoy Healthier Hummous (p. 57), Avocado Guacamole (p. 62) or Yogurt Cheese Spread (p. 54). Top with sprouts, thin-ly sliced red onions and a sprinkling of sunflower seeds.
- Veggie burgers make a "handy" meal. Refer to Fake 'n Bake Burgers (p. 228) and the variations.
- Choose lower-fat versions of traditional meat fillings. I like to cook extra chicken or turkey breasts, chill them, then slice them thinly across the grain to use in sandwiches and salads.
- Watch out for sodium, saturated fats and nitrites in smoked deli products. If you like deli meats, eat them in moderation. A diet high in pickled or salt-cured foods has been linked to an increased risk of certain cancers. Eating ample amounts of fresh fruits and veggies may counteract the risk from pickled foods. So drink a glass of orange or tomato juice with your meal or add some tomato slices to your deli sandwich!

Good for You Kangaroo Pita Pockets!

Minis make great appetizers; regular-sized pitas make a healthy lunch box choice!

6	medium pitas or 24 mini pitas
1	c. Healthier Hummus (p. 57)
1/2	c. chopped red pepper
1/2	c. chopped green pepper
3	tomatoes, cored, halved & thinly sliced
1/2	c. thinly sliced Spanish or red onion
1	English cucumber, thinly sliced
1/2	c. alfalfa sprouts

1. Cut medium-size pitas in half to make 12 pockets (or slit mini pitas open along one edge). Spread insides with Hummous. Fill with peppers, tomatoes, onions, cucumbers; top with sprouts.

Yield: 12 medium pockets or 24 minis. One medium or 2 minis make 1 serving. Do not freeze.

135 calories per serving, 2.2 g fat (0.3 g saturated), 0 mg cholesterol, 5 g protein, 25 g carbohydrate, 166 mg sodium, 227 mg potassium, 2 mg iron, 2 g fiber, 44 mg calcium.

- **Use miniature pitas** for hors d'oeuvres. Fill with your favorite filling.
- **Spread insides of pitas** with low-fat cream cheese, Yogurt Cheese (p. 53) or Tzadziki (p. 53). Add roasted red pepper strips (homemade or from a jar), tomatoes and chopped red onions.
- **Lentil Burgers** (p. 227) make a terrific vegetarian appetizer when served in mini pitas. Top with salsa, sliced onions, roasted red peppers, chutney, etc.
- **Fill pita pockets** with any of the vegetarian variations of Mock Chopped Liver (p. 66).

- **Seafood Salad (p. 124) or Lighter Chicken** or Turkey Salad (p. 292) are a nice change from chicken or tuna fillings.
- **Thinly sliced roast turkey** or chicken breast (homemade or deli-style) make easy, tasty fillings. Mix fat-free mayonnaise with Dijon or honey-style mustard to moisten the inside of pitas.
- **Stir-fry vegetables** make an excellent filling for pita pockets. Add strips of chicken, turkey or tofu.

Vegetarian Harvest Roll-Ups (Fajitas)

Wrap it up! So colorful, so healthy.

2	c. eggplant, unpeeled, cut into strips
1	red & 1 yellow pepper, cut into strips
1	red onion, halved & cut into strips
1	zucchini, unpeeled, cut into strips
2	c. sliced mushrooms
3–4	cloves garlic, crushed
1	tbsp. olive oil
2	tbsp. balsamic vinegar or lemon juice
	Salt and pepper, to taste
2	tbsp. minced fresh basil (or 2 tsp. dried)
3	soft flour tortillas or very thin pitas (preferably whole-wheat)
$\frac{1}{2}$	c. grated low-fat Mozzarella cheese, if desired

1. Either preheat broiler, or preheat oven to 425°F. Mix all ingredients together in a large bowl. (May be prepared in advance up to this point, covered and refrigerated for 3 or 4 hours.) Spread in a thin layer on a sprayed foil-lined baking sheet. Place pan on top rack of oven. Either broil for 10 to 12 minutes, or bake uncovered for 25 to 30 minutes, until tender-crisp and golden, stirring once or twice.

2. Spread hot vegetables in a thin layer on tortillas, leaving about 1 inch at the bottom. Sprinkle with cheese. Fold bottom of tortilla up about 1 inch, then roll around filling in a cone shape. Fasten with a toothpick and serve. (To serve these piping hot, heat at 425°F for 3 or 4 minutes.)

Yield: 3 servings. These also reheat well in the microwave. One roll-up takes 45 seconds on HIGH.

289 calories per serving, 8.3 g fat (1.2 g saturated), 0 mg cholesterol, 8 g protein, 49 g carbohydrate, 350 mg sodium, 776 mg potassium, 3 mg iron, 5 g fiber, 47 mg calcium.

- **With cheese,** 1 serving contains 337 calories, 11.3 g fat (3.1 g saturated) and 169 mg calcium.
- **Vegetarian Focacci-Yumms!** Instead of tortillas, use Focaccia (p. 305). Split in half, fill with veggies and sprinkle with cheese. Return sandwiches to hot oven for 5 minutes.

Hummus Wraps

	Healthier Hummus (p. 57)
6	flour tortillas or very thin pitas (preferably whole-wheat)
$\frac{1}{2}$	c. each of chopped tomato & cucumber
$\frac{1}{2}$	c. chopped onions (red or green)
$\frac{1}{2}$	c. roasted red peppers, in strips
$\frac{1}{2}$	c. alfalfa or bean sprouts

1. Spread $\frac{1}{3}$ cup of hummus over each tortilla. Sprinkle tomato, cucumber and onions over Hummous; top with roasted pepper strips and sprouts. Fold bottom of tortilla up about 1 inch, then roll it around filling. Serve immediately, or wrap in plastic wrap and chill overnight.

Yield: 6 servings. (These can be sliced ½-inch thick into pinwheels for the kids' lunch boxes!)

247 calories per serving, 8.8 g fat (0.9 g saturated), 0 mg cholesterol, 9 g protein, 36 g carbohydrate, 239 mg sodium, 313 mg potassium, 3 mg iron, 5 g fiber, 60 mg calcium.

Uli's Falafel Enlightened

Uli Zamir makes fabulous falafel! He uses the family recipe handed down from his father Shlomo, who sold falafel for 20 years from his kiosk in Kiryat Tiv'on.

1	lb. (454 g) dried chickpeas (2¼ cups)
8	c. cold water
2	slices bread
½	bunch fresh parsley (½ c. minced)
1	bunch (½ c. minced) coriander/cilantro
1	onion, chopped
5–6	cloves garlic, minced
1	tsp. salt
½	tsp. pepper, to taste
¾	tsp. dried cumin
1	tsp. baking soda
4	tsp. canola or olive oil

1. Pick over chickpeas and discard any stones or debris. Place in a strainer and rinse thoroughly. Soak in cold water for 24 hours at room temperature (or in the refrigerator if your kitchen is very warm). Drain chickpeas and set aside.

2. Soak bread in a little water but don't squeeze it completely dry. Use a processor or grinder to finely grind chickpeas. (If using the processor, do it in 2 or 3 batches.) Transfer mixture to a large bowl. Grind parsley, coriander, onion, garlic and bread together until fine. Combine with chickpeas and mix well. Add seasonings, baking soda and 2 teaspoons of oil. (See note below.) Mixture will be thick. Add a little water (about ⅓ to ½ cup) so that mixture is moist but still holds together.

3. Place oven rack in the lowest position in your oven. Preheat oven to 450°F. Line 2 baking sheets with aluminum foil. Spray lightly with non-stick spray, then brush each one lightly with remaining oil. Shape mixture into 1-inch balls and arrange on baking sheets. Bake uncovered at 450°F for 10 minutes, until bottoms are brown. Carefully turn falafel over. Bake 8 to 10 minutes longer.

Yield: about 6 dozen, depending on size. These reheat well or can be frozen.

27 calories per falafel ball, 0.6 g fat (0.1 g saturated), 0 mg cholesterol, 1 g protein, 4 g carbohydrate, 56 mg sodium, 46 mg potassium, <1 mg iron, 1 g fiber, 9 mg calcium.

• **Uli does not** add oil to the chickpea mixture. Instead, he prefers to deep-fry his falafel in hot oil until crisp and golden. They will float to the surface when done. Drain very well on paper towels.

Stuffed Pita Pockets with Falafel & Tahini

Make Uli's Falafel (p. 118). Prepare Tahini Sauce (below). Make the following accompaniments: shredded lettuce, sliced tomatoes, cucumbers, onions, pickled hot peppers and pickles. Serve falafel balls in warmed pita pockets. (You need 6 falafel balls for each pita, depending on the size of pitas.) Add desired accompaniments. Drizzle lightly with Tahini Sauce.

319 calories per serving, 6.2 g fat ((0.8 g saturated), trace cholesterol, 12 g protein, 56 g carbohydrate, 1069 mg sodium, 517 mg potassium, 4 mg iron, 6 g fiber, 109 mg calcium.

- **One tablespoon of Tahini Sauce** provides 3.3 g fat in the above analysis. If you are watching your fat intake, use Tahini Yogurt Sauce (p. 119).
- **The pickled hot peppers** and pickles provide most of the sodium, so choose your toppings wisely!
- **An average pita bread** weighs about 2 oz. and contains 165 calories, 33 grams of carbohydrate, 0.7 grams of fat and 1 gram of fiber.
- **If you deep-fry** the falafel balls instead of baking them, you'll add the equivalent of 1 to 2 teaspoons fat to your falafel sandwich. Just take a long walk after you indulge so you won't bulge!

Tahini Sauce

Although tahini is fairly high in calories, it's necessary for authentic Israeli-style falafel!

$^1/_2$ c. tahini (sesame paste, available in Middle Eastern and health food stores)
$^3/_4$ c. water
1 clove garlic, crushed
$^1/_2$ tbsp. fresh lemon juice (or to taste)
Salt, to taste

1. Place tahini in a jar. Add water and mix well. Add remaining ingredients and shake until blended.

Yield: about 1$^1/_4$ cups. Keeps about 2 weeks in the refrigerator. Do not freeze.

36 calories per tbsp., 3.3 g fat (0.5 g saturated), 0 mg cholesterol, 1 g protein, 1 g carbohydrate, trace sodium, 28 mg potassium, trace iron, <1 g fiber, 9 mg calcium.

- **Fat-Saving Secret!** Instead of stirring tahini before you measure it, pour off the oil which has risen to the top of the jar and discard it.
- **Tahini Yogurt Sauce:** Combine Tahini Sauce with equal amounts of non-fat yogurt.
- **Baked Fish Middle Eastern Style:** Sprinkle halibut steaks (or any thick, firm fish fillets) with salt and pepper. Spread top side of fish with Tahini Sauce (or Tahini Yogurt Sauce). Place on a sprayed foil-lined pan and bake in a preheated 450°F oven for 12 to 15 minutes.

Sloppy "Toes"

A calci-yummy vegetarian version of Sloppy Joes, made with spicy tofu cut into toe-shaped strips! This makes a delicious filling for pitas or crêpes, or can be served over rice or polenta as a main dish.

1 lb. (500 g) firm tofu
1 large onion, diced
1 red & 1 green pepper, diced
1$^1/_2$ c. zucchini, diced
4–6 cloves garlic, sliced
2 tsp. olive oil
1 tsp. Cajun seasoning
$^1/_2$ tsp. each dried basil & paprika
1 c. medium salsa (bottled or homemade)
4 hamburger buns (or whole-wheat rolls), halved

1. Place tofu between 2 large plates and weigh it down with a heavy weight (e.g. several large cans). Let stand for 15 minutes to release extra liquid. Drain well. Cut into strips ³/₄-inch wide by 2-inch long. Preheat oven to 400°F. Spray a 9 x 13-inch casserole with non-stick spray. Combine tofu, onions, peppers, zucchini and garlic in casserole. Drizzle with olive oil and sprinkle with seasonings. Mix well. Bake uncovered at 400°F for 15 minutes. Turn tofu over and bake 10 minutes longer.

2. Pour salsa over tofu and mix well. Bake 10 minutes longer, until heated through. Heat the buns. Spoon hot mixture over bun halves.

Yield: 8 servings. Reheats well. Do not freeze.

180 calories per serving, 7.4 g fat (1.2 g saturated), 0 mg cholesterol, 12 g protein, 19 g carbohydrate, 273 mg sodium, 351 mg potassium, 7 mg iron, 3 g fiber, 174 mg calcium.

Pita Empanadas

10 oz. pkg. frozen chopped spinach
4 green onions
1 lb. pressed non-fat cottage cheese (or 1 lb. 1% low-fat firm tofu)
¹/₄ c. grated Parmesan cheese (or soy cheese)
¹/₄ c. skim milk (or soy milk)
1 tsp. dried basil
³/₄ c. tomato/marinara sauce (bottled or homemade)
Salt & pepper, to taste
6 pita breads (preferably whole-wheat)

1. Pierce spinach package in several places with a sharp knife. Place on a plate and microwave on HIGH for 5 minutes. When cool, squeeze spinach dry. In the processor, mince onions. Add spinach, cheese, milk and seasonings; process for 20 seconds, until mixed. Preheat oven to 375°F. Split one end of each pita open. Spoon some spinach filling into the open end of each pita, then spoon about 2 tablespoons sauce into each pita. Wrap each pita in foil. Bake at 375°F for 20 minutes, until piping hot.

Yield: 6 servings. Do not freeze.

272 calories per serving, 3.3 g fat (1.1 g saturated), 10 mg cholesterol, 19 g protein, 42 g carbohydrate, 826 mg sodium, 406 mg potassium, 3 mg iron, 3 g fiber, 223 mg calcium.

Cajun Chicken Breast Sandwiches

So satisfying. Truly a healthy handful!

4 cooked Cajun Chicken Breasts (p. 170)
8 slices black Russian or pumpernickel bread (or 4 crusty rolls)
2 tbsp. Dijon or honey mustard (to taste)
Lettuce, tomatoes, cucumber & sliced red onion

1. Chill cooked chicken until firm. Slice thinly on an angle against the grain. Spread bread with mustard. Fill with sliced chicken and veggies. Cut in half. Serve chilled.

Yield: 4 sandwiches.

339 calories per sandwich, 7.2 g fat (1.4 g saturated), 73 mg cholesterol, 33 g protein, 37 g carbohydrate, 520 mg sodium, 626 mg potassium, 3 mg iron, 5 g fiber, 79 mg calcium.

• **You can make these** sandwiches with leftover Lemon Dill Chicken (p. 172), or any cooked chicken. For a special touch, add strips of Roasted Red Peppers (p. 57). For variety, stuff pita bread with sliced chicken and veggies.

- **Chicken or Turkey Salad Sandwiches:** Prepare Lighter Chicken Salad (p. 292), Lighter Turkey Salad (p. 292) or any of the variations. Lightly spread the bread with fat-free or low-fat mayonnaise mixed with a little Dijon or honey mustard. Fill with chicken or turkey mixture. Add some roasted red pepper strips (jarred or homemade). Top with lettuce, sliced tomatoes, onions and cucumbers.

Rozie's Portobello Mushroom Burgers

Scrumptious! Even non-vegetarians will love these at your next barbecue!

3   tbsp. balsamic vinegar
1   tbsp. olive oil
Salt & pepper, to taste
4   portobello mushroom caps, 4" in diameter
4   slices of Spanish onion
1   c. roasted red peppers (from a jar or homemade), cut in strips
1/2 c. low-fat grated Mozzarella cheese
1/4 c. fresh basil leaves, shredded
4   hamburger buns (or whole-wheat rolls), lightly toasted or grilled

1. Mix together balsamic vinegar, oil, salt and pepper. Pour over mushroom caps and marinate for 20 to 30 minutes. Preheat grill or broiler. Grill or broil mushroom caps and onion slices about 3 to 5 minutes per side, until nicely browned. Separate onions into rings.

2. To assemble, place a mushroom cap on the bottom of each bun. Arrange onion rings and roasted pepper strips on top of mushrooms. Sprinkle with cheese and basil. Cover with the top of the bun. Wrap in foil and heat on the grill or in a 400°F oven for 5 minutes, until hot.

Yield: 4 servings. Can be made in advance and wrapped in foil. Reheat at serving time.

267 calories per sandwich, 9.2 g fat (3.2 g saturated), 8 mg cholesterol, 12 g protein, 36 g carbohydrate, 517 mg sodium, 374 mg potassium, 4 mg iron, 4 g fiber, 167 mg calcium.

Que Será Quesadillas!

Quesadillas are the Mexican version of a grilled cheese sandwich!

4   8" or 9" flour (or whole-wheat) tortillas
2   c. grated low-fat mozzarella cheese (or cheddar or Monterey Jack)
2   Roasted Red Peppers (p. 57), diced
1/2 c. mild green chiles, diced
1   jalapeño pepper, seeded & finely minced
2   green onions, minced
2   tbsp. fresh basil, minced (or 1 tsp. dried)

1. Place tortillas in a single layer on the counter. In a mixing bowl, combine cheese with remaining ingredients. Spread 1/4 of the cheese mixture over the bottom half of each tortilla. Fold in half to enclose filling; press down gently.

2. Spray a non-stick skillet lightly with no-stick spray. Heat over medium-high heat. Cook tortillas on each side for 2 or 3 minutes, until cheese has melted and tortillas are lightly browned. Transfer to a baking sheet and keep warm in a 250°F oven while you cook the rest. Cool slightly, then cut each quesadilla into 4 wedges with a pizza wheel or sharp knife. Serve immediately.

Yield: 16 wedges. Do not freeze.

67 calories per wedge, 3 g fat (1.5 g saturated), 8 mg cholesterol, 5 g protein, 5 g carbohydrate, 114 mg sodium, 58 mg potassium, trace iron, trace fiber, 109 mg calcium.

- **These make a great light bite.** Arrange 3 or 4 wedges overlapping in a fan design on a plate. Serve these with Creamy 1,000 Island Cole Slaw (p. 278) and sliced tomatoes. These also make excellent hors d'oeuvres.
- **Chef's Secret!** For convenience, purchase roasted red peppers in a jar at your supermarket. If roasting your own peppers, roast several at once, then freeze the extras for another time!
- **Some people like to add** chopped coriander (cilantro) to the cheese filling. You could also place a spoonful of salsa on top of cheese mixture before folding tortillas in half.

Chef's Secrets: Tortilla Talk!

- Corn tortillas are generally used for nachos, enchiladas, tacos and tortilla chips. Flour tortillas are used to make tortilla chips, quesadillas, fajitas, rolled party sandwiches or as a quick pizza base.
- Corn tortillas usually don't contain added fat. However, when you check the label, it will probably show that they aren't fat-free because corn naturally contains a small amount of fat.
- Flour tortillas are available in a variety of colors, flavors and sizes. Whole-wheat tortillas are always an excellent choice. Some manufacturers add flax seeds for added nutrition.
- Flour tortillas usually contain added fat. The amount will vary, depending on the manufacturer. Check the label and choose a low-fat brand.
- To cut tortillas easily, use scissors or a pizza wheel.
- To heat tortillas, stack and wrap them in aluminum foil. Heat at 350°F for 10 minutes, until hot. (To microwave, wrap in damp paper towels. Allow about 10 seconds for each tortilla.)
- Tortillas become stale quickly. Store them in a ziploc plastic bag in the refrigerator, or freeze.
- Hot Tacos: Heat tortillas (see above for method). Heat fat-free canned refried beans. (See Note below.) Sauté onions and peppers in a little oil, vegetable broth or water. Sprinkle with chili powder to taste. Spread each tortilla with 3 tablespoons beans. Top with sautéed onions and peppers. Fold tortillas in half. Put out bowls of desired toppings: salsa (store-bought or homemade), shredded lettuce, grated carrots, Guacamole (p. 63), grated low-fat mozzarella or Monterey Jack cheese, nonfat yogurt or sour cream. Enjoy!
- Quicky Nachos: Prepare your own Tortilla Chips (p. 72), or buy oven-baked, nonfat tortilla chips or nachos. Spread chips in a single layer on a microsafe plate. Drizzle salsa (store-bought or home-made) over chips. Sprinkle lightly with a little low-fat grated cheddar or Monterey Jack cheese. Microwave uncovered on HIGH for 2 to 3 minutes, or until cheese melts. (If you don't have a microwave, bake them in a preheated 400°F oven for 4 to 5 minutes.)
- Note: Fat-free canned refried beans can be found in many health food stores. You can substitute cooked or canned black beans. (If using canned black beans, rinse and drain thoroughly.) Mash with a fork or potato masher.

- **Calories vary depending** on size and type of tortillas used. Flour tortillas can contain 2 to 5 grams of fat, so look for low-fat or fat-free flour tortillas in your grocery or health food store.
- **Wear rubber or disposable gloves** when handling hot peppers! If handling chilis without gloves, wash your hands thoroughly with soap and water immediately afterwards. (And don't dare rub your eyes!)
- **Oven-Baked Quesadillas:** In Step 2, bake them on a non-stick baking sheet at 400°F for 10 minutes, until cheese has melted.
- **Grilled Quesadillas:** Preheat grill. Just before serving, assemble quesadillas. Grill for 2 or 3 minutes, turning them once or twice.

Lighter Chopped Egg Salad

Boil a few extra eggs and throw away half of the yolks. Limit your intake of egg yolks to 4 per week.

4   hard-boiled eggs
3   tbsp. fat-free or light mayonnaise
1   stalk celery, minced
2   green onions, minced
1   tbsp. minced dill, optional
Salt & pepper, to taste

1. Cut cooked eggs in half and discard two of the yolks (or feed them to your dog). Mash remaining eggs. Mix with remaining ingredients and season to taste.

Yield: about 1 cup. Do not freeze.

49 calories per ¼ cup, 2.2 g fat (0.7 g saturated), 91 mg cholesterol, 4 g protein, 2 g carbohydrate, 181 mg sodium, 90 mg potassium, trace iron, trace fiber, 19 mg calcium.

Tofu Spread (Mock Egg Salad)

Don't tell them it's tofu! This tasty spread has fooled many guests who insist they detest tofu.

1   stalk celery
2   green onions
1   small carrot (about ¼ c. grated)
1   tbsp. fresh dill and/or parsley, optional
½   lb. (250 g) tofu
3   tbsp. fat-free or light mayonnaise
Salt & pepper, to taste
2   tsp. Dijon mustard

1. Mince vegetables very fine. Mash tofu. Combine all ingredients and mix until blended. (Can be done in the processor.) Chill. Serve with crackers or assorted breads, or use as a sandwich filling.

Yield: about 1¼ cups. Mixture will keep in the refrigerator for 2 or 3 days. Do not freeze.

63 calories per ¼ cup, 3.3 g fat (0.5 g saturated), 0 mg cholesterol, 6 g protein, 4 g carbohydrate, 103 mg sodium, 134 mg potassium, 4 mg iron, 1 g fiber, 83 mg calcium.

- **Different brands** of tofu vary in moisture content, so you may need a bit more mayonnaise to hold the mixture together.
- **Nonfat yogurt** can replace part of the mayonnaise, if desired. See Tofu Info! (p. 236).

Mock Seafood Salad

1   lb. (500 g) imitation crab (pollock), flaked
4   green onions, chopped
2   stalks celery, chopped
1/2   of a red or green pepper, chopped
2   tbsp. fresh dill, minced (or 1 tsp. dried)
3   tbsp. fat-free or light mayonnaise
3   tbsp. nonfat yogurt
1   tbsp. fresh lemon juice
Freshly ground pepper

1. Combine ingredients and mix well. Serve chilled.

Yield: about 3 cups. Do not freeze. Leftovers will keep for a day or two in the refrigerator.

46 calories per 1/4 cup, 0.5 g fat (0.1 g saturated), 8 mg cholesterol, 5 g protein, 5 g carbohydrate, 348 mg sodium, 82 mg potassium, trace iron, trace fiber, 19 mg calcium.

- **As a main course,** serve a generous scoop on a bed of salad greens. Top with sliced tomatoes, red onions and cucumbers. Garnish with thinly sliced lemon. To round out your meal (but not your hips), start out with a hearty bowl of Luscious Lentil Soup (p. 93).
- **This mixture makes a great** stuffing for cherry tomatoes or mini pitas for your next party! It is also delicious as a sandwich filling for crusty whole-wheat rolls, baguette or black bread.

Lighter Tuna Salad

Half a cup of tuna salad made with regular mayo contains nearly 200 calories and almost 10 grams of fat! Try it my way, with minced veggies added for crunch and fiber. You won't miss the fat!

6 1/2 oz. can (184 g) water-packed tuna
3–4 tbsp. fat-free or light mayonnaise
1   stalk celery, finely chopped
2   green onions, minced (or 1/4 c. red onion)
1/4   c. finely grated carrot
1   tbsp. dill or basil, minced (or 1/2 tsp. dried)
Freshly ground pepper, to taste
1   tbsp. fresh lemon juice

1. Drain tuna thoroughly. Combine all ingredients and mix well. (The processor can be used to mince the vegetables. Add tuna and mayonnaise and process with quick on/offs, just until mixed. Do not overprocess.) Use as a sandwich filling or serve as a spread with crackers. Alternately, serve a scoop of tuna salad on a bed of salad greens.

Yield: about 1 1/4 cups. Do not freeze.

48 calories per 1/4 cup, 0.3 g fat (0.1 g saturated), 10 mg cholesterol, 8 g protein, 2 g carbohydrate, 172 mg sodium, 132 mg potassium, <1 mg iron, trace fiber, 11 mg calcium.

- **Substitute 2 tablespoons nonfat yogurt** for half the mayonnaise. Add 1/4 cup minced red pepper and 1 teaspoon Dijon mustard. Parsley can replace dill or basil; 1/4 cup minced radishes add great texture.
- **Add 1 hard-boiled egg** plus 2 hard-boiled egg whites to tuna mixture for a tasty mixture.
- **Omit dill or basil.** Add half of an 8-ounce can of water chestnuts, well-drained and finely minced, to tuna mixture. Add 1 teaspoon soy sauce and 1/2 teaspoon curry powder.

Lighter Salmon Salad

Yogurt Cheese and salmon bones add calcium.

7½ oz. can (213 g) salmon, well-drained (or 1 c. cooked, flaked fresh salmon)
2–3 tbsp. Creamy Yogurt Cheese (p. 53) or fat-free or light mayonnaise
2 green onions, finely chopped
1 stalk celery, finely chopped
1 tbsp. minced fresh dill (or ½ tsp. dried)
2 tbsp. minced fresh parsley
1 tsp. lemon juice

1. Remove and discard skin from salmon. Mash bones with a fork. Combine all ingredients and mix well. Use as a sandwich filling, as a spread with crackers or serve on a bed of salad greens.

Yield: about 1¼ cups. Do not freeze.

67 calories per ¼ cup, 2.8 g fat (0.6 g saturated), 17 mg cholesterol, 9 g protein, 2 g carbohydrate, 218 mg sodium, 207 mg potassium, <1 mg iron, trace fiber, 112 mg calcium.

Creamy Salmon Paté (Mock Salmon Mousse)

This easy, tasty spread is a good source of calcium, but be sure to add the mashed salmon bones.

4 green onions, minced
2 tbsp. fresh dill, minced
½ lb. (250 g) smooth cottage cheese or low-fat cream cheese
¼ c. nonfat yogurt or sour cream
7½ oz. can (213 g) salmon, drained

1 tsp. lemon juice (preferably fresh)
Freshly ground pepper

1. Combine all ingredients and mix until blended. (If using the processor, first mince green onions and dill, then add remaining ingredients and process just until blended.) Chill before serving. Serve as a spread with crackers, pumpernickel wedges or bagel, or use as a sandwich filling. If desired, garnish with finely minced red onion, thinly sliced cucumber and/or dill.

Yield: about 1½ cups. Mixture will keep about 3 days in the refrigerator. Do not freeze.

55 calories per ¼ cup, 1.6 g fat (0.4 g saturated), 11 mg cholesterol, 8 g protein, 2 g carbohydrate, 197 mg sodium, 128 mg potassium, trace iron, trace fiber, 80 mg calcium.

- **You can substitute** 1¼ cups of Yogurt Cheese (p. 53) for cottage cheese and yogurt.
- **Smoked Salmon Paté:** Add 1 teaspoon liquid smoke and 1 teaspoon Worcestershire sauce.
- **Tuna Paté:** Instead of salmon, use water-packed tuna in the above recipe.

Better Than Butter Spread

Thanks to food writer Marcy Goldman for inspiring this recipe. Although this spread is lower in fat and cholesterol than butter, it's still high in fat. Use as a topping for baked potatoes, steamed veggies or as a spread for toast or sandwiches. Don't use it for frying because it contains yogurt.

⅓ c. lightly salted butter
⅓ c. canola oil
⅓ c. nonfat yogurt

1. Combine all ingredients and blend until smooth. (It takes just moments in the food processor.)

Yield: 1 cup. Mixture keeps about a week in the refrigerator.

80 calories per tbsp., 8.8 g fat (2.8 g saturated), 11 mg cholesterol, trace protein, trace carbohydrate, 45 mg sodium, 15 mg potassium, 0 mg iron, 0 g fiber, 12 mg calcium.

- **This spread works** perfectly to make The New "Cream Cheese" Pastry (p. 374).
- **Butter or margarine?** The debate continues! The fat in butter is mostly saturated. Saturated fats are presumed to raise blood cholesterol levels more than other types of fat. Stick margarines are hydrogenated. Hydrogenation creates high levels of trans fatty acids. Soft nonhydrogenated margarines are a better choice because they contain no trans fatty acids. Both butter and margarine can be incorporated into a healthy diet, but use them sparingly. Moderation is the key!
- **Instead of using butter or margarine** as a spread for your bread, you can dip it in olive oil to which you've added coarse salt, freshly ground pepper, minced garlic, basil, oregano and thyme. Dip lightly, or your hips will spread!

Fish & Dairy Dishes

Fishful Thinking!

- Fishing for compliments? Experiment with salmon, Arctic char, tuna, trout, halibut, pickerel (doré), orange roughy, sole or grouper. Use various seasonings, sauces and cooking techniques.
- Baking, steaming, poaching, broiling, grilling and microwaving are low-fat cooking methods.
- Healthy helpings! Eating fish 2 or 3 times a week is believed to be good for heart health.
- How much is a serving? One lb/500 g fillets yields 3 to 4 servings (depending who's eating)!
- Various species of fish vary in fat content. Salmon is a higher fat fish but contains omega-3 fats. Sardines and herring are also sources of omega-3 fats.
- Fresh fish should have the clean smell of the ocean. If it has a strong fishy or ammonia odor, it's either old or may have been mishandled. The ammonia smell usually occurs when frozen fish is thawed and refrozen. It could also indicate that bacteria are present.
- If small particles of flesh come off when you rub your hand across the fish, it's a sign that it's old. White-fleshed fish should have a bright, white color. Yellow tones indicate that the fish is old.
- To check if a fish steak is fresh, wiggle the center bone. If the flesh pulls away, the fish is old.
- Cook fish within 24 to 48 hours of purchase. Keep it cold as long as possible, preferably just until ready to cook. Store fish in the coldest part of the refrigerator.
- A good way to keep fish cold is to cover it completely with ice. Whole fish with the skin on can be covered directly with ice. If using skinned fillets, don't let ice come in contact with the flesh. Cover fish with a layer of plastic wrap or aluminum foil to prevent ice from damaging the flesh.
- If cooking fish in the microwave, it must be defrosted completely before cooking. Either thaw it overnight in the refrigerator or defrost it quickly in the microwave. You can also place it in a sinkful of cold water to defrost. Don't defrost it at room temperature.
- To defrost fish in the microwave, remove fish from package and place on paper towels on a microsafe plate. Allow 4 to 6 minutes per pound on DEFROST (30%). Turn fish over during defrosting. A few ice crystals should still remain. Then place in ice water for a few minutes, just until ice disappears. Cook as soon as possible. Never refreeze fish after defrosting!
- To cook fish in the microwave, 6 to 8 ounces of fish (1 large or 2 small servings) will take $2\frac{1}{2}$ to 3 minutes to cook. Allow 4 to 5 minutes for 1 pound/500 g.
- The big fish secret! Does your fish pop or explode during microwave cooking? Cook it between layers of lettuce leaves and you'll stop the pop!
- For fish that's full of flavor with a fraction of the fat and calories, simply season it with a squeeze of fresh lemon, orange or lime juice, plus a little salt and fresh (or dried) herbs. However, don't do this more than an hour in advance; otherwise fish will start to "cook."
- It's all in the timing! Overcooking will toughen fish and dry it out. Allow 10 minutes per inch of thickness, or 5 minutes for each $\frac{1}{2}$ inch of thickness. Fish will turn from translucent to opaque during cooking. Check in the thickest area with a fork; the flesh should still be moist.
- Fish can be baked while it is still frozen! Bake uncovered at 450°F and add 4 to 5 minutes to the cooking time. If frozen, a 1-inch thick piece will take about 15 minutes instead of 10 minutes.
- To sauté fish without using a lot of fat, use a non-stick skillet. You'll only need to add a drop of oil to provide a crispy coating.
- Grilling is one of the easiest ways to cook fish, especially firm-fleshed varieties like grouper, tuna and halibut. Serve with Super Salsa (p. 61), Mango Salsa (p. 109), Roasted Red Pepper Coulis (p. 110) or Spicy Dipping Sauce (p. 109). An excellent marinade is Teriyaki Marinade (p. 108).

A (Gefilte) Fish Story— Old and New Traditions

In our grandmothers' time, B.C. (Before Cuisinarts), it was not unusual to find a live carp splashing around in the bathtub, flipping its tail back and forth! The fish would be killed, skinned, filleted, then chopped by hand in a large wooden bowl with a "hackmesser" (chopping knife). Oy, so much work! The minced fish would be mixed with eggs, onions and matzo meal or ground almonds. It was shaped into balls, placed in a pot and simmered in a stock made with fish heads and bones, carrots and onions. The fish bones would cause the cooking liquid to become jelly-like when chilled.

Seasonings would vary, depending on a person's origins. Litvaks used salt and lots of pepper, while Jews of Polish origin added sugar to the fish mixture. Roumanians and Litvaks stuffed the fish skin and then cooked it, which is how it got its name: Gefilte fish means stuffed fish.

The fish mixture would also vary, depending on what was available in different parts of the country. In Winnipeg, where I grew up, my mother, Belle Rykiss, insisted on using whitefish, pike and pickerel (doré). She would never use carp! It was too dark in color and too strong in flavor for her tastes. She also insisted that gefilte fish had to be cooked for at least two hours to be thoroughly cooked. The fish would absorb the cooking juices and become light and fluffy, like matzo balls. So delicious! I remember when I was a young child she once tried to save time by cooking it in her pressure cooker. We had gefilte fish all over the kitchen ceiling!

When I moved to Montreal in 1960, I lived with my father's cousin, Clara Tobin. Auntie Clara shaped the fish mixture into patties, then browned them in oil with onions. She would add water and let the fish steam for about an hour in an electric frypan. I still have wonderful "taste memories" of her fish!

Shula Zamir prepares her gefilte fish Lithuanian-style. She buys light-colored carp and has the fishmonger cut it in slices. The fish is ground, mixed with eggs, onions, carrots, salt and pepper. Then the slices are restuffed and simmered with the head, cut-up onions and carrots for two-and-a-half hours. A piece of cooked carrot or beet is used for the eye of the fish when serving. The adults love it, but the children prefer their fish made into small "kneidlach" (dumplings) without the skin.

Micky Liederman, a Montreal caterer for many years, was famous for his snowy white gefilte fish. He insisted that the mixture had to be beaten at high speed in an electric mixer for at least twenty minutes, until smooth and silky. He formed the mixture into long logs, wrapped them in cooking parchment, then simmered them gently in the cooking broth for an hour and a half. The chilled logs would be sliced and served with "chrain" (horseradish). Micky trained many a chef to make gefilte fish his way!

Both the food processor and microwave oven revolutionized gefilte fish. Instead of a "hackmesser", the fish mixture is prepared in the processor in two or three minutes! The fish balls are dropped into simmering liquid and microwaved covered on 50 percent power. Two pounds of fish take fifteen to eighteen minutes. Let stand covered for another fifteen minutes, then remove fish balls from broth and refrigerate. Gefilte fish can also be cooked in a bundt pan in the oven or microwave. Excellent! See recipe for Gefilte Fish Ring (p. 131). A terrific alternative to horseradish is Super Salsa (p. 61) with a dash of horseradish.

Gefilte Fish Ring

Soryl Ashenmil gave me this great company dish. We developed the microwave method by phone! You can bake it in your oven, but there's no smell in the house when you microwave it, plus it cooks in a fraction of the time! For a nice twist, squeeze a little fresh lime juice into the horseradish at serving time.

3	carrots
2	tbsp. fresh dill, optional
2	medium Spanish onions, chopped
3	lb. (1.4 kg) minced fish (a combination of whitefish, pike & doré)
4	eggs (or 2 eggs plus 4 egg whites)
1½	c. cold water
6	tbsp. matzo meal
3–4	tsp. salt (to taste)
2	tsp. pepper
3	tbsp. sugar

1. Preheat oven to 325°F. Finely mince carrots and dill in the processor, using the Steel Knife. Set aside in small bowl. Chop onions; transfer them to the large bowl of an electric mixer. Add ground fish, eggs, water, matzo meal and seasonings to onions. Mix on medium speed for 15 to 20 minutes. Fold in carrot mixture at the end to avoid changing the color of the fish.

2. Spread mixture in a sprayed 10-inch Bundt pan; it will be almost full. Place in a pan of hot water so water comes 1 inch up the sides of Bundt pan. Bake uncovered at 325°F for 1 hour. Cover loosely with foil and bake 1½ hours longer, until fish tests done. (See below.) Let cool for 20 minutes. Carefully unmold onto a serving plate. Wipe up any juices that collect on the plate. When completely cool, cover and refrigerate. (Can be prepared up to 2 days in advance.) Garnish with tomato and cucumber slices. Serve with horseradish. Super Salsa (p. 61) is great with the Tex-Mex version (below)!

Yield: 24 slices. Do not freeze. Leftovers keep for 3 or 4 days in the refrigerator.

113 calories per slice, 4.4 g fat (0.8 g saturated), 70 mg cholesterol, 13 g protein, 5 g carbohydrate, 337 mg sodium, 244 mg potassium, <1 mg iron, <1 g fiber, 26 mg calcium.

- **Microwave Method:** Prepare fish mixture as directed. Place in a microsafe 10-inch Bundt pan or ring mold sprayed with non-stick spray. Cover pan with a large microsafe dinner plate, waxed paper or moistened cooking parchment. Microwave on MEDIUM (50%) for 18 to 22 minutes. Rotate pan (¼ turn) every 6 minutes. Let stand covered for 15 minutes. Drain off excess liquid. Unmold as directed below.
- **How to Test for Doneness & Unmold:** Top of fish should be firm to the touch and edges should pull away from sides of pan. Insert a wooden skewer into the fish halfway between the centre and the outside edge. Skewer should come out clean. Cool for 20 minutes. Loosen fish with a long, narrow spatula. Cover pan with a serving plate. Invert and shake gently to unmold.
- **Tex-Mex Gefilte Fish:** Use 3 pounds (1.4 kg) minced red snapper fillets. Omit dill. Add ¼ cup chopped coriander (cilantro), 1 jalapeño pepper and 1 red pepper, seeded and diced, plus ½ teaspoon cumin to fish. Serve with horseradish to which you've added a squeeze of fresh lime juice.

New Wave Gefilte Fish

A West Coast innovation, using salmon fillets.
Thanks to Jenny Fried for the great idea!

2   onions, sliced
2   carrots, sliced
6   c. water
1   tsp. salt
1   tsp. sugar
2   onions, finely minced
1   carrot, finely minced
2   tbsp. fresh dill, minced
2   lb. (1 kg) minced fish (use equal amounts of white-
    fish & salmon
3   eggs (or 1 egg plus 4 egg whites)
½   c. cold water
¼   c. matzo meal or ground almonds
2   tsp. salt (to taste)
1   tsp. pepper (to taste)
1   tbsp. sugar (to taste)

1. Fish Stock: Combine 2 onions, 2 carrots, 6 cups of water, 1 teaspoon salt and 1 teaspoon sugar in a large pot and bring to a boil. Simmer partly covered for 15 to 20 minutes.

2. Fish Mixture: Meanwhile, combine remaining ingredients in the large bowl of an electric mixer. Beat on medium speed until smooth and silky, about 20 minutes. (If mixing fish in the processor, divide mixture into 2 batches. Process each batch for 3 to 4 minutes, until smooth and silky.)

3. Moisten your hands and shape mixture into plum-sized balls. Drop carefully into simmering liquid. Simmer partially covered for 1½ to 2 hours. When cool, carefully remove fish balls from broth with a slotted spoon. Garnish each piece with a carrot slice. Serve with horseradish. This dish is terrific hot or cold.

Yield: 15 pieces. Can be frozen, but fish may become watery. If you simmer the defrosted fish for 10 minutes in boiling water to cover, it will taste freshly cooked!

128 calories per piece, 5.3 g fat (1 g saturated), 79 mg cholesterol, 14 g protein, 6 g carbohydrate, 362 mg sodium, 265 mg potassium, <1 mg iron, <1 g fiber, 25 mg calcium.

- **On Passover,** ground almonds can be substituted for matzo meal. Some religious Jews do not eat "gebrocks" (foods where matzo, or its derivatives such as matzo meal, are moistened in water).
- **A caterer's trick** is to shape the fish mixture into logs and wrap them in cooking parchment. Each pound of fish makes one log. (Can be frozen at this point. No need to defrost fish before cooking!) Place parchment-wrapped logs in a deep pan. Add boiling water to cover fish completely. Cover and cook at 350°F for 1½ hours (2 hours if frozen). When cool, remove from liquid and chill.
- **Variation:** Omit onions and carrots from fish mixture. Add ½ cup minced red pepper, ½ cup minced green onions, 2 tablespoons minced parsley, 1 teaspoon basil and ½ teaspoon thyme to fish mixture.
- **Miniatures:** Shape fish mixture into tiny balls.(You should get 4 to 5 dozen, depending on size.) Simmer for 1 hour. These make terrific hors d'oeuvres for a party.
- **Chicken Gefilte Fish:** Substitute 2 lbs. (1 kg) minced boneless, skinless chicken breasts for fish. Turkey breast can also be substituted.
- **Gefilte Tofu:** Marinate cubes of tofu in the liquid from bottled gefilte fish. Refrigerate overnight.

Easy Salsa Fish Fillets

This recipe works with any firm-fleshed fish fillets.
It's perfect when you're rushed for time.

4	sole or whitefish fillets (1½ lb/750 g)

Salt & pepper, to taste
½ c. bottled salsa (mild or medium)
½ c. grated low-fat mozzarella or cheddar cheese (or
    ¼ c. grated Parmesan)

1. Preheat oven to 425°F. Arrange fish in a single layer on a sprayed foil-lined baking pan. Sprinkle with salt and pepper. Top each fillet with 2 tablespoons of salsa; sprinkle with cheese. Bake uncovered at 425°F for 10 to 12 minutes, until golden. Fish should flake easily when tested with a fork.

Yield: 4 servings. Do not freeze.

184 calories per serving, 4.3 g fat (2 g saturated), 87 mg cholesterol, 33 g protein, 2 g carbohydrate, 282 mg sodium, 477 mg potassium, <1 mg iron, <1 g fiber, 139 mg calcium.

- **Serve with basmati rice** and lightly steamed green and/or yellow beans.
- **Salsa Fillets in a Snap:** Cut several large squares of cooking parchment or aluminum foil. Place a fish fillet on each square. Top each one with a spoonful of Super Salsa (p. 61). Seal packets tightly. Arrange on a baking sheet and place in a preheated 400°F oven for 10 to 12 minutes.

Pizza Fish Fillets

6   sole fillets (1½ lb./750 g)
Salt & pepper, to taste
½ c. pizza or tomato sauce
2   tbsp. chopped mushrooms
3   tbsp. minced green pepper or zucchini
½ c. grated low-fat mozzarella cheese

1. Preheat oven to 425°F. Spray a foil-lined baking sheet with non-stick spray. Arrange fish in a single layer. Sprinkle lightly with salt and pepper. Spread sauce evenly over fish. Sprinkle with vegetables; top with cheese. Bake uncovered at 425°F for 10 to 12 minutes, or until golden. Fish should flake easily when tested with a fork. Serve immediately.

Yield: 6 servings. Do not freeze.

169 calories per serving, 3.4 g fat (1.5 g saturated), 82 mg cholesterol, 30 g protein, 3 g carbohydrate, 176 mg sodium, 410 mg potassium, <1 mg iron, trace fiber, 90 mg calcium.

- **Any firm fish** can be used (e.g., whitefish, doré or snapper fillets). Halibut steaks can be used, but increase cooking time to 15 minutes.
- **Serve with Creamy Polenta** (p. 210) and a mixed garden salad.

Crusty Baked Garlic Sole Fillets

An excellent alternative to pan-fried fish fillets.

4   sole fillets (1½ lb/750 g)
Salt & pepper, to taste
2   tsp. olive or canola oil
1   clove garlic, minced
1   tbsp. minced fresh dill (or 1 tsp. dried)
1   tbsp. minced fresh parsley (optional)
⅓ c. seasoned bread crumbs (or cornflake crumbs)

1. Preheat oven to 425°F. Arrange fish in a single layer on a sprayed foil-lined pan. Sprinkle with salt and pepper. Brush with oil; rub with garlic, dill and parsley. Coat both sides of fish with crumbs. Bake uncovered for 10 to 12 minutes, until golden. (No need to turn over the fish.)

Yield: 4 servings. Do not freeze.

206 calories per serving, 4.7 g fat (0.8 g saturated), 80 mg cholesterol, 30 g protein, 9 g carbohydrate, 457 mg sodium, 408 mg potassium, 1 mg iron, <1 g fiber, 51 mg calcium.

• **Serve with No-Fry Fries** (p. 259) and green peas.
• **Quick & Crusty Honey Mustard Fillets:** Dip fish fillets in low-fat bottled honey mustard salad dressing, then in cornflake crumbs. Bake uncovered at 425°F for 10 to 12 minutes.

Baked Herbed Fish Fillets

Light, easy and versatile! If you don't have fresh herbs, sprinkle dried herbs over fish. Dried oregano, rosemary and/or thyme are all excellent choices. Balsamic vinegar can be used instead of citrus juice.

4   sole, doré or orange roughy fillets (1½ lb/750 g)
2   tsp. olive or canola oil
2   cloves garlic, minced
2   tbsp. fresh orange, lemon or lime juice
Salt, pepper & paprika, to taste
2   tbsp. each fresh dill & basil, minced

1. Preheat oven to 425°F. Arrange fish in a single layer on a non-stick or sprayed pan. Brush both sides of fish lightly with oil. Sprinkle evenly with garlic, citrus juice and seasonings. Bake uncovered for 10 to 12 minutes. Fish should flake easily when tested with a fork.

Yield: 4 servings. Do not freeze.

163 calories per serving, 4.1 g fat (0.8 g saturated), 80 mg cholesterol, 29 g protein, 1 g carbohydrate, 124 mg sodium, 433 mg potassium, <1 mg iron, trace fiber, 27 mg calcium.

• **Herbed Halibut or Salmon Trout:** Substitute halibut steaks or salmon trout fillets. Bake 12 to 15 minutes, depending on thickness of fish.
• **Serve with Mango Salsa** (p. 109). and Potato & Carrot Purée (p. 258).

Cornmeal Coated Fish Fillets

4   sole, red snapper or grouper fillets (about 1½ lb/750 g)
Juice of half a lemon
Salt & pepper, to taste
¼   c. buttermilk or nonfat yogurt
4   tbsp. fine cornmeal
2   tbsp. grated Parmesan cheese, optional
1   tsp. dried basil
¼   tsp. cayenne
Paprika, to taste

1. Preheat oven to 425°F. Rinse fish and pat dry. Arrange on a non-stick or sprayed baking sheet. Sprinkle fish with lemon juice, salt and pepper. Brush evenly with buttermilk or yogurt. Combine cornmeal with cheese, basil and cayenne. Sprinkle crumb mixture over fish. Sprinkle lightly with paprika. Bake on top rack of oven for 12 to 15 minutes, until golden and crispy. Serve immediately.

Yield: 4 servings. Do not freeze.

151 calories per serving, 2 g fat (0.5 g saturated), 43 mg cholesterol, 25 g protein, 7 g carbohydrate, 70 mg sodium, 534 mg potassium, <1 mg iron, <1 g fiber, 63 mg calcium.

• **Serve with Simple & Good Ratatouille** (p. 230) and steamed rice.

Yogurt & Dill Fish Fillets

4	sole, red snapper or grouper fillets (about 1¹/₂ lb/750 g)

Juice of half a lemon
Salt & pepper, to taste

¹/₂	c. nonfat or low-fat plain yogurt
4	tbsp. breadcrumbs or cornflake crumbs
2	tbsp. grated Parmesan cheese
1	tbsp. fresh dill, minced (or 1 tsp. dried)
1	tbsp. fresh basil, minced (or 1 tsp. dried)

Paprika, to taste

1. Preheat oven to 425°F. Rinse fish and pat dry. Arrange on a non-stick or sprayed baking sheet. Sprinkle fish with lemon juice, salt and pepper. Spread evenly with yogurt. Combine breadcrumbs with Parmesan, dill and basil. Sprinkle crumb mixture over fish. Sprinkle lightly with paprika. Bake on top rack of oven at 425°F for 12 to 15 minutes, until golden and crispy. Serve immediately.

Yield: 4 servings. Do not freeze.

174 calories per serving, 2.9 g fat (1.1 g saturated), 45 mg cholesterol, 28 g protein, 8 g carbohydrate, 191 mg sodium, 574 mg potassium, <1 mg iron, trace fiber, 157 mg calcium.

• **Baked Halibut Steaks:** Substitute halibut steaks for fish fillets. Cooking time is about 15 minutes.

• **Serve with mashed** or baked potatoes and Mandarin Asparagus (p. 247).

Easy Pesto Fish Fillets

4	sole or whitefish fillets (1¹/₂ lb/750 g)

Salt & pepper, to taste

4	tsp. Best-O Pesto (p. 195)
2	tbsp. grated low-fat mozzarella or Parmesan cheese

1. Preheat oven to 425°F. Line a baking sheet with aluminum foil. Spray lightly with non-stick spray. Arrange fish fillets in a single layer and sprinkle lightly with salt and pepper. Spread pesto evenly over fish fillets. Top with grated cheese. Bake on top rack of oven at 425°F about 10 to 12 minutes, or until cheese is melted and golden. Fish should flake when lightly pressed. (Cooking time may vary slightly, depending on thickness of fish.) Serve immediately.

Yield: 4 servings. Do not freeze.

157 calories per serving, 3.2 g fat (1 g saturated), 82 mg cholesterol, 30 g protein, trace carbohydrate, 152 mg sodium, 425 mg potassium, <1 mg iron, trace fiber, 55 mg calcium.

• **Sun-Dried Tomato Pesto Fillets:** Substitute Sun-Dried Tomato Pesto (p. 195).
• **Serve with Company Stuffed Spuds** (p. 261) and steamed carrots.

Baked Halibut Parmesan

4   halibut steaks (1½ lb./750 g)
Salt, pepper & dried basil, to taste
2   cloves garlic, crushed (or ½ tsp. garlic powder)
2–3 tbsp. fat-free or light mayonnaise (or yogurt)
4   tsp. grated Parmesan cheese
Paprika, to garnish

1. Preheat oven to 450°F. Arrange fish in a single layer on a non-stick or sprayed baking sheet. Sprinkle lightly with seasonings. Brush the top side of fish with mayonnaise. Sprinkle with cheese and paprika. Bake uncovered at 450°F for 10 to 12 minutes, until golden. Serve immediately.

Yield: 4 servings. Do not freeze.

185 calories per serving, 4.2 g fat (0.9 g saturated), 51 mg cholesterol, 33 g protein, 2 g carbohydrate, 174 mg sodium, 702 mg potassium, 1 mg iron, 0 g fiber, 103 mg calcium.

- **Also excellent** with sea bass, salmon, rainbow trout, salmon trout, sole or orange roughy fillets. Bake uncovered at 450°F, allowing 10 minutes per inch of thickness for fish.
- **Rosy Halibut:** Add 1 tablespoon Sun-Dried Tomato Pesto (p. 195) to mayonnaise or yogurt; use to coat fish. You could also use a mixture of equal parts of puréed roasted red peppers and yogurt.
- **Baked Fish with Tahini:** Combine 4 tablespoons tahini, 6 tablespoons water, 2 cloves garlic and a dash of fresh lemon juice. Sprinkle fish with salt and pepper. Coat fish on both sides with tahini mixture; sprinkle with paprika. Bake at 450°F for 10 to 12 minutes, until golden.
- **Serve with Mushroom Risotto with Sun-Dried Tomatoes** (p. 216) and salad.

Grilled Tuna with Mango Salsa

Grilling is a perfect way to cook fresh tuna. Salsa adds a refreshing touch. Great for a summer barbecue!

Mango Salsa (p. 109)
6   tuna steaks (2 lb/1 kg)
2   tsp. olive oil
Salt & freshly ground black pepper, to taste

1. Prepare salsa as directed. (Salsa can be prepared up to a day ahead and refrigerated. Serve it at room temperature.) Prepare grill or preheat broiler. Brush fish lightly with oil. Season with salt and pepper. Quickly grill tuna over hot coals (or under the broiler) about 3 to 5 minutes per side, until just barely cooked through. Tuna should be served rare or it will be dry. Serve with Mango Salsa.

Yield: 6 servings. Do not freeze.

252 calories per serving, 3.4 g fat (0.7 g saturated), 88 mg cholesterol, 46 g protein, 7 g carbohydrate, 73 mg sodium, 936 mg potassium, 2 mg iron, <1 g fiber, 38 mg calcium.

- **Variations:** Substitute salmon or halibut steaks for tuna. Grill 10 minutes per inch of thickness. (That means 5 minutes per side for a piece of fish 1-inch thick.) Fish will be dry if overcooked.
- **Serve with Millet Pilaf** (p. 209) and grilled vegetables.
- **To reduce exposure** to mercury, eat fresh tuna once a week maximum. Women of childbearing age shouldn't eat fresh tuna more than once a month, or more than 8 ounces of canned tuna weekly.
- **The average tuna sandwich** served in restaurants contains double the filling of a sandwich made at home and is usually loaded with mayonnaise,

sodium and calories. So pack your lunch at home!

Gloria's Sea Bass with Honey Mustard

4   sea bass steaks (about 1½ lb/750 g)
2   tsp. olive oil
2   tbsp. prepared honey-style mustard
2   cloves garlic, minced
2   tbsp. fresh lemon juice
2   tbsp. chopped parsley
Salt & pepper, to taste

1. Preheat oven to 450°F. Rinse fish; pat dry. In a small bowl, combine oil, mustard, garlic, lemon juice and parsley. Season fish with salt and pepper; coat with mustard mixture. Place on a sprayed foil-lined pan. Bake at 450°F, allowing 10 minutes cooking time per inch of thickness, about 10 to 12 minutes. If overcooked, fish will be dry. Serve with mashed potatoes and broccoli.

Yield: 4 servings. Serve flaked leftover fish over mixed salad greens.

187 calories per serving, 5.5 g fat (1.1 g saturated), 61 mg cholesterol, 27 g protein, 6 g carbohydrate, 196 mg sodium, 411 mg potassium, <1 mg iron, trace fiber, 26 mg calcium.

• **Quick Sea Bass with Balsamic Marinade:** Coat fish with Orange Vinaigrette (p. 293) or bottled low-fat balsamic salad dressing. Bake uncovered at 450°F for 10 to 12 minutes.

Sea Bass Thai Style

You'll be hooked on this fish dish!
Delicate and delectable.

4   portions of sea bass (1½ lb/750 g)
2   green onions
2   tbsp. coriander (cilantro) &/or basil leaves
1   slice ginger (1 to 2 tsp. minced)
2   cloves garlic
Salt & pepper, to taste
¼   tsp. cayenne
1   tsp. Oriental sesame oil

1. Spray a foil-lined baking sheet with non-stick spray. Place fish on baking sheet. Mince green onions, coriander, ginger and garlic. (I use the processor.) Rub mixture on both sides of fish. Season with salt, pepper and cayenne; brush with sesame oil. Let stand at room temperature for 20 minutes, or cover and refrigerate for up to 2 hours. Preheat oven to 450°F. Bake fish uncovered for 10 to 12 minutes, until golden. Fish should flake when lightly pressed. Serve immediately.

Yield: 4 servings. Leftover fish can be broken into chunks and served on chilled salad greens.

157 calories per serving, 4 g fat (1 g saturated), 61 mg cholesterol, 27 g protein, 1 g carbohydrate, 101 mg sodium, 405 mg potassium, <1 mg iron, trace fiber, 23 mg calcium.

• **Serve with Oriental Rice** (p. 214) and Teriyaki Asparagus (p. 246).

Salmon Balsamico

Tuna steaks are also delicious prepared this way.

4   pieces salmon fillets (1¹/₂ lb/750 g)
Salt & freshly ground pepper, to taste
¹/₄ c. balsamic vinegar
2   tsp. brown sugar
2   cloves garlic, crushed
2   Italian (Roma) tomatoes, chopped
1–2 tbsp. chopped fresh basil or 1 tsp. dried (1 tsp. thyme can be substituted)

1. Arrange fish in a single layer in a sprayed baking dish. Sprinkle lightly with salt and pepper. Combine vinegar with brown sugar, garlic, tomatoes and basil; pour over fish. Marinate for 30 minutes. Preheat oven to 450°F. Bake uncovered for 10 to 12 minutes. (To microwave fish, cover with a layer of lettuce leaves or a piece of cooking parchment. Cook on HIGH for 6 to 8 minutes, or until fish flakes with a fork. If you wet the parchment, you can mold it around the dish.)

Yield: 4 servings. Delicious hot or cold.

285 calories per serving, 13 g fat (2.3 g saturated), 102 mg cholesterol, 33 g protein, 7 g carbohydrate, 85 mg sodium, 535 mg potassium, 1 mg iron, <1 g fiber, 25 mg calcium.

- **Sea Bass or Tuna Balsamico:** Substitute sea bass or tuna steaks for salmon. One serving of bass contains 205 calories, 4.3 g fat (1 g saturated), 144 mg cholesterol and 553 mg potassium.
- **Serve with pasta and vegetables**, e.g., Penne al Pesto Jardinière, (p. 196).

Grilled Teriyaki Salmon (or Halibut)

4   salmon or halibut steaks (1¹/₂ lb/750 g)
Teriyaki Marinade (p. 108)

1. Marinate fish at room temperature for 30 minutes to 1 hour. Prepare grill or preheat broiler. Remove fish from marinade and wipe dry. If using a grill, place fish in a lightly greased grill basket. (Otherwise, spray broiler rack with non-stick spray.) Grill fish over hot coals (or under the broiler) about 3 to 4 minutes per side. Do not overcook or it will be dry. Serve immediately.

Yield: 4 servings. Do not freeze. Delicious with steamed rice and Sesame Broccoli (p. 250).

327 calories per serving of salmon, 15.2 g fat (2.6 g saturated), 102 mg cholesterol, 33 g protein, 12 g carbohydrate, 459 mg sodium, 476 mg potassium, <1 mg iron, trace fiber, 15 mg calcium.

Oriental Salmon

Microwave it in the winter, grill it in the summer. Ah, so good!

6   salmon fillets or steaks (2 lb/1 kg)
2   tbsp. bottled teriyaki sauce
1   tbsp. lemon juice
1   tbsp. brown sugar or honey
1   tsp. minced fresh ginger
1   clove garlic, crushed
¹/₂ tsp. Dijon mustard
2   green onions, thinly sliced

1. Place salmon in an ungreased 2-quart microsafe casserole. Arrange the thicker pieces towards the

outside. Combine remaining ingredients except green onions. Mix well. Spread over salmon. Cover with waxed paper or cooking parchment. Marinate at room temperature for half an hour, or refrigerate up to 24 hours.

2. Microwave salmon covered on HIGH for 8 to 9 minutes. Halfway through cooking, turn salmon over with a wide spatula. When done, fish will flake when lightly pressed and it will be even in color. Let fish stand covered for 4 minutes before serving. Garnish with green onions. Serve immediately.

Yield: 6 servings. Do not freeze.

242 calories per serving, 11.5 g fat (2 g saturated), 91 mg cholesterol, 29 g protein, 4 g carbohydrate, 311 mg sodium, 431 mg potassium, <1 mg iron, trace fiber, 16 mg calcium.

- **Delicious with rice** and Mandarin Asparagus or Snow Peas (p. 247).
- **To cook salmon conventionally,** bake uncovered at 425°F for 12 to 15 minutes. Fish is done if it flakes when gently pressed.
- **Salmon can also be grilled.** Use a lightly greased grill basket for easier handling. Cooking time depends on thickness of fish. Allow 10 minutes per inch of thickness (about 5 minutes per side).
- **Leftovers?** Don't worry! They can be served cold the next day on a bed of mixed salad greens. Add some cherry tomatoes, thinly sliced cucumbers and red onions.

Micropoached Salmon Fillets

A winner in my cooking classes! Other fish fillets (sole, roughy, snapper) can be used. Salmon is a fatty fish, but very high in omega-3 fatty acids, which may help fight heart disease. This recipe is so quick and scrumptious, it's no problem to cook fish two or three times a week!

Iceberg or Romaine lettuce leaves
4   salmon fillets, skinned (1.5 lb/750 g)
Salt & pepper, to taste
1   tbsp. fresh lemon or lime juice
1   tbsp. fresh dill, minced (or 1 tsp. dried)
Additional dill and lemon slices, to garnish

1. Wash lettuce; shake off excess water. Arrange a layer of lettuce leaves in the bottom of a glass pie plate. Arrange fish in a single layer, with thicker edges of fish toward the outside edge of the dish. Season with salt, pepper and lemon juice; top with dill. Cover with another layer of lettuce.

2. Microwave fish on HIGH for 3 minutes. Rotate the plate ¼-turn and cook fish 3 minutes longer. Fish should be even in color. Let fish stand covered for 3 to 4 minutes. It should flake when lightly pressed. If undercooked, microwave 1 or 2 minutes more. Discard lettuce. Garnish salmon with fresh dill and thinly sliced lemon. Delicious hot or cold.

Yield: 4 servings. Leftovers keep 2 or 3 days, or can be frozen to use in casseroles, crêpes, etc.

246 calories per serving, 11 g fat (1.7 g saturated), 96 mg cholesterol, 34 g protein, trace carbohydrate, 76 mg sodium, 851 mg potassium, 1 mg iron, 0 g fiber, 21 mg calcium.

- **Even though salmon** is considered to be a light choice, portion size is the key! A 3½-ounce portion (100 grams) of salmon contains 177 calories and 7.9 grams of fat. However, most people eat at least double that amount, with double the fat and calories!

- **If you don't have a microwave,** bake salmon uncovered on a non-stick baking sheet at 450°F for 10 to 12 minutes, or until fish flakes when lightly pressed. (Eliminate lettuce and brush fish lightly with either olive or canola oil or light mayonnaise before cooking to keep it moist.)
- **Instead of dill,** vary the herbs used to season the fish. Some suggestions are tarragon, parsley, basil, thyme or oregano. If using dried herbs, use one-third the amount.
- **Serve salmon with** Rainbow Rice Pilaf (p. 213) and steamed broccoli. Delicious accompanied by Yogurt Dill Sauce (p. 106), Dijon Mustard Sauce (p. 96) or Mango Salsa (p. 109).
- **Salmon Leftovers:** Add chunks of poached salmon to Pesto Pasta Salad (p. 288) to turn it into a main dish. Leftover salmon is also delicious mixed with light mayonnaise or Creamy Yogurt Cheese (p. 53), minced green onions and celery. Use as a sandwich filling, or serve with mixed greens and garnish with sliced cucumber, tomatoes, minced dill and chives or green onions.

1	tbsp. grated ginger
	Paprika
1	tbsp. sesame seeds

1. Place salmon in a baking dish which has been sprayed with non-stick spray. Sprinkle salmon with lemon juice. Combine remaining ingredients except sesame seeds and rub over salmon. Let marinate for 20 to 30 minutes. Meanwhile, preheat oven to 425°F. Sprinkle salmon lightly with sesame seeds. Bake uncovered for 12 to 15 minutes (or microwave covered on HIGH for 6 to 8 minutes), until fish flakes when lightly pressed.

Yield: 4 servings. Leftovers can be broken into chunks and added to salad greens or pasta.

284 calories per serving, 13.2 g fat (1.9 g saturated), 94 mg cholesterol, 34 g protein, 4 g carbohydrate, 529 mg sodium, 856 mg potassium, 2 mg iron, trace fiber, 32 mg calcium.

- **Chef's Secret:** When microwaving fish, place it between wet lettuce leaves; this prevents fish from popping during cooking. Parchment paper also makes an excellent cover. Place parchment under running water. It will become flexible so you can mold it around the baking dish easily!

Sesame Salmon

Open the "weigh" to a healthy heart! Serve with basmati rice and steamed green and yellow beans

4	pieces salmon fillets (about 1¹/₂ lb/750 g)
	Juice of ¹/₂ a lemon (or 1 tbsp. rice vinegar)
2	tbsp. lite soy sauce
1	tbsp. maple syrup or honey
1	tsp. Oriental sesame oil
2	cloves garlic, crushed

Grilled Moroccan Salmon

If broiling fish in your oven, spray broiler rack with non-stick spray to prevent fish from sticking.

4	salmon fillets or steaks (1.5 lb/750 g)
1	tsp. ground cumin
¹/₂	tsp. paprika
1	tsp. thyme

Salt & pepper, to taste
$^1/_2$ tbsp. olive oil
1 tbsp. fresh lemon juice
1 lemon, sliced

1. Preheat grill or broiler. Sprinkle both sides of salmon with seasonings. Drizzle lightly with olive oil and lemon juice. If using the grill, place fish in a lightly greased grill basket. Grill over hot coals (or under the broiler) 3 to 4 minutes per side. Grill lemon slices quickly. Use as a garnish for salmon.

Yield: 4 servings.

333 calories per serving, 15.7 g fat (2.4 g saturated), 121 mg cholesterol, 44 g protein, 2 g carbohydrate, 97 mg sodium, 1109 mg potassium, 2 mg iron, <1 g fiber, 38 mg calcium.

• **Serve with** Couscous Middle-Eastern Style (p. 205) and Roasted Peppers (p. 57).

Quick Pickled Salmon

Ready to eat the same day, instead of 4 days! Pat Brody of Winnipeg shared her recipe with my Mom.

2 lb. (1 kg) sockeye or cohoe salmon, cut into slices (any fresh salmon can be used)
$^3/_4$ c. sweet mixed pickles
$^3/_4$ c. pickle juice
$^3/_4$ c. ketchup (low-sodium, if available)
1 tbsp. mustard seed (or more, to taste)
1 tbsp. celery seed (or more, to taste)
2 tbsp. sugar
2 tbsp. white vinegar
1 onion, chopped
2 carrots, sliced
1 Spanish onion, sliced

1. Rinse fish; drain well. Combine remaining ingredients except Spanish onion and fish in a large pot; bring to a boil. Add fish to hot brine, reduce heat and simmer covered for 7 to 8 minutes. Turn fish over gently and simmer 5 minutes longer.

2. Cool fish slightly, then transfer to a cutting board. Carefully remove skin and center bone. Place Spanish onion slices in an oblong casserole. Put fish on top and cover with brine. When completely cool, cover and refrigerate.

Yield: 6 servings. Delicious hot or cold. Fish keeps a week in the refrigerator or may be frozen.

354 calories per serving, 12.7 g fat (2.2 g saturated), 91 mg cholesterol, 31 g protein, 29 g carbohydrate, 463 mg sodium, 747 mg potassium, 2 mg iron, 3 g fiber, 87 mg calcium.

• **Pickles, pickle juice** and ketchup are high in sodium. Pickle juice is not included in the nutritional analysis; it is used just for marinating the salmon but is not eaten.

Gingered Pickled Salmon or Halibut

2 lb. (1 kg) Atlantic salmon fillets or halibut steaks
$1^1/_2$ c. water
$1^1/_2$ c. vinegar (or rice vinegar)
$^1/_2$ c. brown sugar, packed
$^1/_2$ c. ketchup (or salsa)
1 bay leaf
$^1/_2$ tsp. thyme
6 thin slices of ginger
1 large Spanish onion, sliced

1. Cut fish in serving size pieces. In a large pot, bring water, vinegar, brown sugar, ketchup, bay leaf and thyme to a boil. Add fish, reduce heat and simmer covered for 10 minutes. Gently turn fish over and cook 5 minutes longer. Remove pot from heat. Add ginger and onion. When cool, carefully transfer to a casserole, cover and refrigerate. Let fish marinate for 3 to 4 days before serving.

Yield: 6 servings. Fish will keep 7 to 10 days in the refrigerator once it has marinated.

345 calories per serving, 12.4 g fat (1.9 g saturated), 107 mg cholesterol, 39 g protein, 15 g carbohydrate, 212 mg sodium, 1113 mg potassium, 2 mg iron, <1 g fiber, 44 mg calcium.

Salmon Patties

A lighter version of a family favorite!
Leftover cooked fish can be used.

1   small onion
$1/2$ stalk celery
1   tbsp. fresh dill (or $1/2$ tsp. dried)
2   slices whole-wheat or Challah bread
$71/2$ oz. can (213 g) salmon, drained (use bones—they contain calcium!)
1   egg plus 2 egg whites (or 2 eggs)
1   tsp. Worcestershire sauce
1   tsp. lemon juice
Freshly ground pepper, to taste
1   tbsp. canola oil (for frying)

1. In the processor, mince onion, celery and dill. Moisten bread under cold running water; squeeze out excess moisture. Add bread to processor; process until finely ground. Add remaining ingredients except oil. Process with quick on/offs, until mixed. Mixture will be quite moist but will hold together. In a large non-stick skillet, heat oil on medium-high heat. Drop mixture by tablespoons into skillet. Flatten slightly with the back of the spoon. Cook on medium heat until brown, about 3 or 4 minutes per side.

Yield: 8 patties. Reheats and/or freezes well. Serve with Dijon Mustard Sauce (p. 106) or Mango Salsa (p. 109).

88 calories per patty, 4.1 g fat (0.8 g saturated), 37 mg cholesterol, 8 g protein, 4 g carbohydrate, 210 mg sodium, 145 mg potassium, <1 mg iron, <1 g fiber, 79 mg calcium.

- **Tuna Patties:** Substitute a $61/2$ oz. can (184 g) water-packed tuna, drained. Each patty contains 77 calories, 2.9 g fat (0.49 saturated), 33 mg cholesterol, 159 mg sodium and 120 mg potassium.
- **Salmon or Tuna Muffins:** Prepare mixture. Bake in sprayed muffin tins 25 minutes, until golden.
- **Leftovers?** Patties are great in sandwiches the next day. Tuck into a pita pocket, or serve on rye, kimmel or black bread. Top with lettuce, tomatoes and cucumber slices. Garnish with sprouts.
- **Salmon or Tuna Loaf:** Prepare mixture for Salmon Patties, but triple the recipe, using only 1 egg (or 2 whites) for each can of salmon or tuna. Omit oil. Spray a 9 x 5-inch loaf pan with non-stick spray. Sprinkle with corn flake crumbs. Pour in fish mixture. Bake at 350°F for about 1 hour. Makes 6 to 8 servings. Leftovers are great cold the next day in sandwiches.
- **Serve with salad,** Minted Peas with Red Peppers (p. 262) and Garlic Mashed Potatoes (p. 257).

Creamy Salmon Filling in Toast Cups

This tasty filling can also be used for crêpes.

Toast Cups (see following recipe)
10 oz. pkg. (300 g) frozen mixed vegetables
2 tsp. butter, margarine or oil
2 green onions, chopped
1 tbsp. flour
1½ c. skim milk or vegetable broth
1 bay leaf
½ c. grated Parmesan cheese
2 tbsp. minced fresh basil (or 1 tsp. dried)
Salt & pepper, to taste
2 7½ oz. cans salmon, drained & flaked

1. Prepare Toast Cups. Cook vegetables according to package directions; set aside. In a 4-cup glass measuring cup, microwave butter on HIGH for 30 seconds. Add green onions and microwave for 2 minutes. Stir in flour. Slowly stir in milk (or broth); add bay leaf. Microwave on HIGH for 4 to 4½ minutes, until bubbling. Stir twice during cooking. Add cheese and seasonings.

2. Combine sauce with salmon and vegetables. (Can be prepared in advance and refrigerated.) Microwave on HIGH for 5 minutes (or 10 minutes if refrigerated), until hot. Adjust seasonings to taste. Serve in Toast Cups.

Yield: 12 pieces (6 large or 12 small servings).

176 calories per piece, 5.8 g fat (2.1 g saturated), 21 mg cholesterol, 14 g protein, 18 g carbohydrate, 450 mg sodium, 307 mg potassium, 2 mg iron, 3 g fiber, 210 mg calcium.

• **Serve with a large garden salad.** Start off your meal with a big bowl of White Bean Soup (p. 90). Fiber-full, flavor-full!

• **Tuna Filling:** Instead of salmon, use 2 cans of water-packed tuna, drained and flaked.

Toast Cups

A great low-fat replacement for fatty patty shells! Use very fresh bread for best results.

12 slices whole-wheat or white sandwich bread
Non-stick spray (olive oil flavor is good)

1. Preheat oven to 350°F. Trim crusts from bread. Spray both sides lightly with non-stick spray. Press each slice into a muffin cup. Bake at 350°F for 12 to 15 minutes, or until golden and crisp.

Yield: 12 toast cups. These can be frozen, but be sure to wrap them airtight to prevent freezer burn!

69 calories per whole-wheat toast cup, 1.2 g fat (0.3 g saturated), 0 mg cholesterol, 3 g protein, 13 g carbohydrate, 148 mg sodium, 71 mg potassium, 1 mg iron, 2 g fiber, 20 mg calcium.

• **Suggested Fillings:** Creamy Salmon or Tuna Filling (p. 143), Black Bean & Corn Casserole (p. 226), Easy Vegetarian Chili (p. 225), Simple & Good Ratatouille (p. 230) or filling for Mushroom Crostini (p. 242).

Tuna, Rice & Broccoli Kugel

Excellent for family or friends. It's perfect for a buffet and wonderful for brunch. Cheese and milk are excellent sources of calcium. Broccoli is a good source of calcium and contains beta carotene.

2   c. water
Salt, to taste
1   c. long-grain rice
3   c. broccoli, coarsely chopped
1   onion, chopped
6½ oz. can (184 g) tuna, drained & flaked
2   tomatoes, diced
3   eggs plus 2 egg whites
1   c. skim milk
1   c. non-fat or low-fat yogurt
¼   tsp. each of basil & oregano
1   c. grated low-fat mozzarella or Swiss cheese
3   tbsp. grated Parmesan cheese

1. In a medium saucepan, bring water and a dash of salt to a boil. Add rice, cover and simmer for 20 minutes. (Alternately, microwave rice, water and salt covered on HIGH for 6 to 7 minutes. Reduce power to 50% (MEDIUM); microwave 10 to 12 minutes longer, until water is absorbed.) Let rice stand covered for 10 minutes using either cooking method.

2. Microwave broccoli and onion covered on HIGH for 4 minutes. Let stand covered for 2 minutes. Broccoli should be tender-crisp. Combine with remaining ingredients except Parmesan cheese and mix well. Spread evenly in a lightly greased or sprayed 7 x 11-inch Pyrex casserole. Sprinkle with Parmesan cheese. (Can be prepared in advance up to this point, covered and refrigerated for several hours or overnight.) Bake in a preheated 350°F for 45 minutes, until golden brown.

Yield: 8 servings. Reheats well and/or may be frozen.

212 calories per serving, 3.4 g fat (1.3 g saturated), 89 mg cholesterol, 16 g protein, 29 g carbohydrate, 222 mg sodium, 427 mg potassium, 2 mg iron, 2 g fiber, 171 mg calcium.

- **Use water-packed tuna,** not oil-packed. You can use 2 cans of tuna for more protein.
- **Egg substitute** can be used instead of eggs for those with cholesterol problems.
- **Serve with Easy Carrot Soup** (p. 97), a large tossed salad and crusty rolls.
- **Salmon, Rice & Broccoli Casserole:** Substitute salmon for tuna. (Green beans can replace the broccoli if you like, but then you have to change the name of the recipe!)

Tuna Caponata

This is similar to ratatouille, but includes tuna, capers and raisins. Vinegar and brown sugar give this versatile vegetarian dish a lovely sweet and sour flavor.

2   lb. (1 kg) eggplant, unpeeled
Salt, to taste
1   tbsp. olive oil
2   medium onions, chopped
2   stalks celery, chopped
1   red pepper, chopped
3   cloves garlic, minced
3   c. mild salsa or tomato sauce
3   tbsp. balsamic or red wine vinegar
1   tbsp. brown sugar or maple syrup
Freshly ground pepper, to taste
1   bay leaf
¼   c. raisins
3   tbsp. capers
½   c. pitted sliced black olives
6½ oz. can (184 g) water-packed tuna, drained & flaked

1. Cut eggplant into 1-inch pieces. Put into a colander and sprinkle with salt. Place a plate on top of eggplant and top with several cans. Let stand for 30 minutes. Rinse thoroughly. Pat dry with towels.

2. Spray a large, heavy-bottomed pot with non-stick spray. Add oil and heat on medium-high heat. Sauté onions, celery and red pepper for 5 minutes. Add garlic and eggplant. Sauté a few minutes longer, stirring occasionally. If necessary, add a little water to prevent sticking.

3. Add remaining ingredients except olives and tuna. Bring to a boil, reduce heat and simmer covered for 25 to 30 minutes, stirring occasionally. Remove from heat and let cool. Stir in olives and tuna. Adjust seasonings to taste. Discard bay leaf. Refrigerate overnight to allow flavors to blend.

Yield: 8 to 10 servings. Keeps about 10 days in the refrigerator, or can be frozen if you omit tuna. Add tuna after Caponata has defrosted.

143 calories per serving, 3.3 g fat (0.5 g saturated), 7 mg cholesterol, 9 g protein, 22 g carbohydrate, 531 mg sodium, 615 mg potassium, 2 mg iron, 6 g fiber, 80 mg calcium.

- **Chef's Serving Suggestions!** Serve chilled in Toast Cups (p. 143), or place a scoop on a large, fresh leaf of Boston lettuce. Garnish with tomato and cucumber slices. Perfect with Honey Mustard Carrot Salad (p. 285).
- **Stuffed Pasta Shells:** Use Caponata as a stuffing for cooked jumbo pasta shells. Top with tomato sauce and sprinkle lightly with grated low-fat mozzarella cheese. Bake uncovered at 350°F for 20 minutes, until bubbling hot.
- **Serve with Black Bean Soup** (p. 90).
- **Caponata makes an excellent** vegetable side dish if you omit the tuna. It can also be served as a dip or spread with Pita or Tortilla Chips (p. 72), crackers, or assorted breads.

Homemade Cottage Cheese

My cousin Wendy Harrison of England taught me how to make this. It's simply delicious!

1. In a large pot, heat 2 liters (quarts) of milk until simmering (use 1% or skim). Sprinkle in lemon juice (about 4 to 6 tablespoons) until mixture begins to separate into curds and whey. Remove from heat.

2. Pour warm liquid into a cheesecloth-lined colander. Tie ends of cheesecloth and let drain for several hours. (Hang it over the faucet of the sink; put a bowl underneath to catch the whey.) For a firmer cheese, squeeze out most of the liquid. Wrap well and refrigerate.

Yield: about 2 cups. This keeps at least a week in the refrigerator.

41 calories per ¼ cup, 0.6 g fat (0.4 g saturated), 2 mg cholesterol, 7 g protein, 2 g carbohydrate, 7 mg sodium, 48 mg potassium, trace iron, 0 g fiber, 34 mg calcium.

- **Buttermilk Cheese (Tvarog):** (Marina Tagger of Winnipeg shared this guilt-free, creamy cottage cheese, which is an old Russian recipe.) Place 2 liters (quarts) of buttermilk in a large covered ovenproof casserole. Place in a preheated 375°F oven for 15 to 20 minutes. It will separate into curds and whey. Drain as directed in Step 2 above. Calci-yummy!
- **Use the whey** which drains off to replace buttermilk when baking muffins, cakes and quickbreads.

Crustless Spinach & Mushroom Quiche

The processor makes quick work of this healthy, flavor-packed quiche!

10 oz. (300 g) pkg. frozen spinach
1   large onion
1/2 c. red pepper
2   tsp. canola oil
1/2 lb. mushrooms
2   cloves garlic, minced
2   slices whole-wheat bread
1   egg plus 2 egg whites
3/4 c. skim milk
1/2 c. grated low-fat Swiss or cheddar cheese
1   c. low-fat ricotta or cottage cheese
2   tbsp. grated Parmesan cheese
Salt & pepper, to taste
1   tbsp. minced fresh dill

1. Preheat oven to 350°F. Spray a 10-inch ceramic quiche dish with non-stick spray (or spray miniature muffin pans very well). Pierce package of spinach with a sharp knife in several places. Place on a microsafe plate and microwave on HIGH for 3 to 4 minutes, until defrosted. When cool, remove from package and squeeze dry.

2. In the processor, chop onion and red pepper with quick on/offs. In a large nonstick skillet, heat oil on medium-high. Sauté onion and pepper until soft, about 5 minutes. Chop mushrooms with quick on/offs. Add to skillet along with garlic. Sauté 5 minutes longer. Remove from heat; cool slightly.

3. Process bread to make soft crumbs. Add spinach and process until fine. Add egg, egg whites, milk and cheeses; mix well. Add sautéed vegetables and mix with quick on/offs. Add seasonings and dill. Spoon mixture into prepared pan(s) and bake at 350°F until golden. Bake minis 18 to 20 minutes or a large quiche for 40 to 45 minutes.

Yield: 10 wedges or 3 dozen miniatures. Reheats and/or freezes well.

115 calories per wedge, 5.3 g fat (3.6 g saturated), 37 mg cholesterol, 9 g protein, 9 g carbohydrate, 220 mg sodium, 230 mg potassium, 1 mg iron, 2 g fiber, 240 mg calcium.

- **Garden Vegetable Quiche:** Omit spinach and mushrooms. Substitute a 10-ounce (300 g) package frozen mixed vegetables (e.g. broccoli, cauliflower, carrots). Cook frozen vegetables as per package directions. Add to quiche mixture along with sautéed vegetables in Step 3.
- **Each miniature quiche** contains 32 calories, 1.5 g fat (1 g saturated) and 10 mg cholesterol.
- **Chef's Serving Secrets!** Instead of using mini-muffin tins, pour quiche mixture into a sprayed 7 x 11-inch casserole. Bake at 350°F about 40 minutes. Cut into small squares.
- **For a crowd,** double the recipe and bake it in a sprayed 10 x 15-inch jelly roll pan. (Sometimes I sprinkle the bottom of the pan lightly with seasoned bread crumbs before adding quiche mixture.) Cut in large squares as a main dish or small squares as hors d'oeuvres.

Spanakopita

Serve this as a de"light"ful dairy main dish. Triangles or rolls are great as hors d'oeuvres.

4   green onions
2   tbsp. fresh dill &/or basil

10 oz. pkg. (300 g) fresh or frozen spinach, cooked & squeezed dry
½ c. sun-dried tomatoes, soaked & drained
1 lb. (500 g) non-fat pressed cottage cheese (or low-fat ricotta cheese)
½ c. feta cheese, crumbled
¼ c. grated Parmesan cheese
2 eggs
Freshly ground pepper, to taste
1 tbsp. canola oil
3 egg whites
8 sheets of phyllo dough

1. In the processor, mince green onions, dill and/or basil. Add spinach; process until minced. Add sun-dried tomatoes, cheeses, eggs and pepper; mix well. In a small bowl, mix oil and egg whites.

2. Spray a 9 x 13-inch casserole with non-stick spray. Line casserole with 4 sheets of phyllo, brushing each sheet lightly with egg white mixture as you layer it in the pan. Let edges of dough hang over pan. Spread filling evenly over dough. Quickly cover with remaining 4 sheets of phyllo, brushing each layer with egg white mixture. Fold overhanging edges over the top and brush with egg white mixture once again. Bake at 350°F for 30 minutes, until golden.

Yield: 12 servings. Reheats well or can be frozen. Serve with Israeli Salad (p. 280).

127 calories per serving, 4.9 g fat (1.8 g saturated), 46 mg cholesterol, 10 g protein, 11 g carbohydrate, 369 mg sodium, 235 mg potassium, 2 mg iron, 1 g fiber, 115 mg calcium.

• **Spanakopita Triangles:** Place a sheet of phyllo dough on a dry surface. Brush with egg white mixture. Top with another sheet of dough; brush again with egg white. Cut dough into 8 strips. Place a

Say Cheese Please!

• Cheese may be high in fat, but is also high in calcium. One ounce of cheddar (1 slice or ¼ cup grated) contains 110 calories and 9 g fat, with 75 percent of its calories from fat. Swiss cheese gets 65 percent of its calories from fat. Select skim or low-fat cheese if possible. Compare labels for fat content.
• Some low-fat cheeses are rubbery; some melt better. Experiment until you find what you like.
• Use small quantities of strong-flavored cheeses (e.g. strong cheddar) for maxi flavor, mini calories. One tablespoon of grated Parmesan contains just 20 calories, so a little goes a long "weigh."
• When you grate cheese yourself, it weighs less than packaged grated cheese. The lower weight costs you less and contains less calories and fat.
• Grate cheese and freeze it in a heavy-duty plastic bag for two to three months. Press out excess air to prevent ice crystals from forming. No need to defrost before using it in recipes. If cheese is frozen in a clump, just give it a few bangs on the counter to break it up!
• Dairy foods are the best source of absorbable calcium (e.g., yogurt, milk, cheeses). Vitamin D is required for calcium absorption. See Calci-Yummy—Very Dairy Good (p. 35). A non-dairy dish which is high in calcium is Terrific Tofu Stir-Fry (p. 237).
• If you're lactose-intolerant, dairy-free soy cheeses are an excellent alternative.
• Yogurt Cheese (p. 53) and Homemade Cottage Cheese or Buttermilk Cheese (p. 145) are low-fat cream cheese alternatives. Flavor with herbs as a spread, or use in cheesecakes and blintzes.

spoonful of filling 1 inch from the bottom of each strip. Fold dough upwards to cover filling. Fold the right bottom corner of dough upwards diagonally to meet the left edge. Continue folding upwards and from side to side to make a triangle. Repeat with remaining dough and filling. Place triangles seam-side-down on a sprayed foil-lined pan. Brush with egg white mixture. Bake at 375°F for 15 to 18 minutes, until golden. (If baked from frozen state, add 2 or 3 minutes to baking time. No need to thaw first.) Makes 32 triangles. Each triangle contains 48 calories and 1.8 g fat (0.7 g saturated).

- **Popeye Pick-Me-Ups!** Brush dough with egg white mixture. Place a narrow band of filling along one edge, leaving a 1-inch border on 3 sides. Roll up into long rolls. Place seam-side down on prepared baking sheet. Brush with egg white mixture. Bake at 375°F for 20 to 25 minutes, until golden. Slice in 1-inch pieces and serve. (These reheat well, but slice rolls after reheating.)
- **Spinach & Feta Stuffed Mushrooms:** Filling can also be rolled into balls and frozen. When unexpected company drops in, drop the frozen balls into mushroom caps and sprinkle lightly with grated Parmesan cheese or sesame seeds. Bake at 350°F for 15 minutes, until piping hot. (Or microwave 1 dozen at a time on a paper towel-lined plate for 3 minutes on HIGH.)

Cottage Cheese Yogurt Latkas (Pancakes)

These light and tender pancakes are fat-free!

2   c. nonfat or low-fat cottage cheese
½   c. nonfat yogurt
2   egg whites (or 1 egg)

½   c. flour
¼   tsp. baking soda
2   tbsp. sugar
1   tsp. finely grated lemon rind, optional
1   tbsp. fresh lemon juice

1. Combine all ingredients in the processor and blend until very smooth. Spray a large non-stick skillet with non-stick spray. Heat over medium-high heat for 2 minutes, or until a drop of water skips on its surface. Spoon the batter by rounded tablespoons onto the pan. Cook pancakes for 2 to 3 minutes per side, or until brown. Turn them over carefully as they are delicate. Repeat with remaining batter. Serve with yogurt and fresh peaches or berries (strawberries, blueberries, raspberries).

Yield: About 20 latkas. These can be reheated in the microwave. They can be frozen.

38 calories per latka, 0 g fat (0 g saturated), 2 mg cholesterol, 4 g protein, 5 g carbohydrate, 105 mg sodium, 40 mg potassium, 0 mg iron, trace fiber, 25 mg calcium.

Cottage Cheese Pancakes

So delicious, so easy. This version is made with milk rather than yogurt.

1   egg plus 1 egg white
1   c. 1% cottage cheese (curd-style)
1   c. flour
1   tsp. baking powder
1   tbsp. sugar
½   c. skim milk

1. In a food processor, process egg, egg white and cottage cheese until smooth and lump-free. Add flour, baking powder, sugar and milk; process a few seconds longer, until smooth.

2. Spray a large skillet with non-stick spray. Heat on medium heat. Spoon the batter by rounded tablespoons onto the hot pan. Fry until bottoms of pancakes are lightly browned. Small bubbles will appear on the surface of the pancakes. Flip them over and brown them on the other side. Serve with yogurt, maple syrup, or your favorite jam. For company, serve with Strawberry or Raspberry Purée (p. 359) or Quick Fruit Compote (p. 349).

Yield: about 16 pancakes. These freeze well. They can also be reheated in the microwave.

50 calories per pancake, 0.6 g fat (0.2 g saturated), 14 mg cholesterol, 3 g protein, 8 g carbohydrate, 86 mg sodium, 48 mg potassium, trace iron, trace fiber, 21 mg calcium.

Homemade Fruit Pancakes

This simple recipe is quick to mix up for a quick breakfast or light lunch.

1³/₄ c. flour (whole-wheat or all-purpose)
1   tsp. baking powder
¹/₂ tsp. baking soda
2   egg whites (or 1 egg)
³/₄ c. skim milk
1   c. nonfat yogurt
2   tbsp. honey or maple syrup
1   tbsp. canola oil
1   c. blueberries, cranberries or grated apple

1. Combine all ingredients except fruit in a bowl or processor and blend until smooth. Stir in fruit.

Spray a large non-stick skillet with non-stick spray. Heat over medium-high heat for 2 minutes, or until a drop of water skips on its surface. Drop the batter by rounded spoonfuls onto the hot pan. Cook pancakes about 2 to 3 minutes on each side, or until brown. Repeat with remaining batter. Serve plain or top with warm maple syrup, applesauce or a dollop of yogurt with fresh berries.

Yield: 16 to 18 pancakes. Refrigerate leftovers. These can be reheated briefly in the microwave.

85 calories per pancake, 1.1 g fat (0.1 g saturated), <1 mg cholesterol, 3 g protein, 16 g carbohydrate, 86 mg sodium, 96 mg potassium, <1 mg iron, <1 g fiber, 48 mg calcium.

Crêpes

So versatile, and inexpensive too! As a main course, fill them with cooked vegetables, chicken or fish. As a dessert, fill crêpes with frozen yogurt and top with fresh fruit.

2   eggs plus 2 egg whites (or 3 eggs)
1   tbsp. canola oil
1   c. plus 2 tbsp. flour
1   c. water (skim milk can be used for dairy crêpes)
¹/₄ tsp. salt

1. Combine all ingredients in the processor or a mixing bowl and blend until smooth. Refrigerate batter covered for at least 1 hour or overnight.

2. Lightly grease a 9-inch non-stick skillet with a few drops of oil, or spray lightly with non-stick spray. Heat pan on medium-high heat for 2 to 3 minutes. Quickly pour about 3 to 4 tablespoons batter into pan. Tilt pan in all directions to coat

bottom evenly with batter. Pour out excess. Cook crêpe about 1 minute on the first side, until the edges brown. Flip crêpe over with a spatula and cook for 30 seconds on the other side. (The first side will look nicer than the second side.) Repeat with remaining batter. Place waxed paper between crêpes to prevent sticking. Fill as desired.

Yield: 12 crêpes. These can be made in advance and refrigerated or frozen. Wrap well to prevent them from drying out. They'll keep about a month in the freezer.

68 calories per crêpe, 2.1 g fat (0.4 g saturated), 35 mg cholesterol, 3 g protein, 9 g carbohydrate, 77 mg sodium, 31 mg potassium, <1 mg iron, trace fiber, 7 mg calcium.

Cheese Blintzes

12 crêpes (p. 149)
1½ lb. (750 g) pressed cottage cheese (nonfat or low-fat)
1 egg white
1 tbsp. fresh lemon juice
1 tsp. grated lemon rind
2–3 tbsp. sugar
2 tbsp. nonfat or low-fat yogurt

1. Prepare crêpes. Combine cottage cheese with remaining ingredients and blend until smooth. Place 3 to 4 tablespoons of cheese mixture on the lower part of each crêpe. Roll up, folding in sides, to seal like an envelope. (May be made in advance, covered and refrigerated overnight.)

2. Spray a large non-stick skillet with non-stick spray, or oil it lightly. Heat pan over medium-high heat for 2 to 3 minutes, or until a drop of water

skips on its surface. Place blintzes seam-side down in skillet and cook on all sides until golden.

Yield: 12 blintzes. Serve with nonfat or low-fat yogurt (fruit flavored yogurt is lovely). Garnish with fresh berries, if desired.

117 calories per blintz, 2.1 g fat (0.4 g saturated), 40 mg cholesterol, 10 g protein, 13 g carbohydrate, 260 mg sodium, 78 mg potassium, <1 mg iron, trace fiber, 40 mg calcium.

Potato, Mushroom & Onion Blintzes

12 crêpes (p. 149)
3 potatoes, peeled & cut into chunks (or 2 potatoes plus 1 sweet potato)
2 onions, chopped
1 tbsp. canola oil
1 c. mushrooms, sliced
2 egg whites (or 1 egg)
Salt & pepper, to taste

1. Prepare crêpes. Boil potatoes in salted water to cover until tender, about 20 minutes. Drain most of water from saucepan, leaving a little to moisten the potatoes. Mash potatoes and set aside. Sauté onions in oil on medium-high for 5 minutes, until golden. Add mushrooms and sauté until well-browned. If necessary, add a little water to prevent burning or sticking. Cool slightly. Combine with mashed potatoes and egg whites; mix well. Season to taste.

2. Place 3 to 4 tablespoons of potato mixture on the lower part of each crêpe. Roll up, folding in sides to seal like an envelope. (May be made in advance, covered and refrigerated overnight.) Cook as directed in Step 2 of Cheese Blintzes (above).

Yield: 12 blintzes. Serve as a vegetarian main dish with reduced-fat sour cream, or as a side dish.

121 calories per blintz, 3.4 g fat (0.5 g saturated), 35 mg cholesterol, 4 g protein, 18 g carbohydrate, 98 mg sodium, 206 mg potassium, <1 mg iron, 1 g fiber, 15 mg calcium.

Vegetarian Crêpes

12 crêpes (p. 149)
Oven Roasted Vegetables, Ratatouille-Style (p. 266)
1½ c. tomato sauce
1   c. grated low-fat mozzarella cheese

1. Prepare crêpes and vegetables as directed. To assemble, place ¼ cup of vegetables at the lower end of each crêpe. Roll up into a cylinder, leaving ends open. Spread half of tomato sauce in a sprayed 9 x 13-inch casserole. Arrange crêpes seam-side down in casserole. Top with remaining sauce. Sprinkle with cheese. (Can be prepared in advance and refrigerated for a day or two.)

2. Preheat oven to 375°F. Bake uncovered for 25 to 30 minutes, until bubbling and golden. Serve with a large garden salad and crusty rolls.

Yield: 12 crêpes. If frozen, vegetables may become soggy.

163 calories per crêpe, 6.3 g fat (1.7 g saturated), 41 mg cholesterol, 7 g protein, 21 g carbohydrate, 447 mg sodium, 489 mg potassium, 2 mg iron, 3 g fiber, 92 mg calcium.

• **Variations:** Fill with Creamy Salmon or Tuna Filling (p. 143), or mushroom mixture for Mushroom Crostini (p. 242).

• **Spinach & Cheese Manicotti:** See Passover version, (p. 405) but substitute regular crêpes.

Cottage Cheese Muffins

These are like individual cheese puffs. Serve them with a salad as a main dish, or use as a side dish with fish or vegetarian dishes. They're perfect for breakfast, brunch or lunch. So good!

3   tbsp. tub margarine (or ¼ c. light tub margarine), at room temperature
1¼ c. nonfat cottage cheese (small curd)
½ c. nonfat yogurt
1   egg & 2 egg whites (or 2 eggs)
1   c. flour
2   tsp. baking powder
¼ c. sugar

1. Spray a muffin pan (or several miniature muffin pans) with non-stick spray. Preheat oven to 400°F. Combine all ingredients in a mixing bowl or processor. Blend until fairly smooth. The mixture will be a little lumpy, but that's okay. Divide mixture evenly among muffin compartments. Bake at 400°F until golden. Regular-sized muffins take about 25 minutes, miniatures take about 18 to 20 minutes. Cool slightly and remove gently from pan. So luscious with yogurt and sliced strawberries.

Yield: 12 muffins or 40 miniatures. These freeze well.

112 calories per serving, 3.4 g fat (0.7 g saturated), 20 mg cholesterol, 6 g protein, 14 g carbohydrate, 171 mg sodium, 88 mg potassium, <1 mg iron, trace fiber, 38 mg calcium.

Johnny Cake

This recipe is based on one shared with me by Nettie Bernofsky of Montreal. I used a combination of Yogurt Cheese and cottage cheese with excellent results, but you can make it with 2 cups of dry cottage cheese and add a few drops of skim milk to make a creamier filling.

Batter:
1/4 c. tub margarine or butter
1/2 c. minus 1 tbsp. sugar
1 egg (or 2 egg whites)
1/2 c. flour
1/2 c. cornmeal
1 tsp. baking powder
Pinch of salt
1/2 c. skim milk

Filling:
1 c. dry cottage cheese
1 c. Firm Yogurt Cheese (p. 53)
1 egg
1 tbsp. sugar
Pinch of salt

1. Preheat oven to 350°F. Spray an 8-inch square baking dish with non-stick spray. To make the batter, combine margarine and sugar in the processor or a mixing bowl and beat until light. Blend in egg. Combine dry ingredients and add them to the creamed mixture alternately with milk.

2. Combine filling ingredients in a small mixing bowl. Mix well. Pour half of the batter into the prepared pan to make a thin layer. Carefully spread filling evenly over base. Drop remaining batter in blobs over the cheese mixture. Spread evenly with a rubber spatula. Bake at 350°F for 45 to 50 minutes. Cut into squares and serve hot with nonfat or low-fat yogurt and berries.

Yield: 9 servings. Freezes well.

201 calories per serving, 6.5 g fat (1.3 g saturated), 50 mg cholesterol, 9 g protein, 27 g carbohydrate, 256 mg sodium, 153 mg potassium, <1 mg iron, <1 g fiber, 89 mg calcium.

Poultry & Meat

Slim Chick-Information

- Go for the white and you'll be light! Discard the skin and you'll be thin!
- Compare the white meat from a quarter of a chicken (skinless breast, without the wing) to the dark meat (skinless drumstick and thigh). White meat has 3.1 g fat, dark meat has 8.2 g fat.
- One roasted single chicken breast, with skin, has 193 calories, 7.6 g fat (2.2 g saturated) and 82 mg cholesterol. Remove the skin and it will have 142 calories, 3.1 g fat (0.9 g saturated) and 73 mg cholesterol.
- One roasted drumstick, with skin, has 112 calories, 5.8 g fat (1.6 saturated) and 47 mg cholesterol. Without skin, it has 76 calories, 2.5 g fat (0.6 saturated) and 41 mg cholesterol.
- One roasted thigh, with skin, has 154 calories, 9.6 g fat (2.7 g saturated) and 58 mg cholesterol. Without skin, it has 109 calories, 5.7 g fat (1.6 g saturated) and 50 mg cholesterol.
- Did you know that one roasted chicken wing (that little thing!) with skin has 99 calories, 6.6 g fat (1.9 g saturated) and 29 mg cholesterol? It's difficult to remove the skin, so use wings in soup.
- A 3-pound (1.4 kg) chicken (with skin) contains 1,547 calories, 88 g fat (25 g saturated) and 570 mg cholesterol. Remove the skin and the calories will fly away!
- Lighten up with turkey! A 3 oz. serving of roasted skinless turkey breast has 115 calories, 0.6 g fat (0.2 saturated) and 71 mg cholesterol. The same amount of skinless dark meat has 159 calories, 6.1 g fat (2.1 g saturated) and 72 mg cholesterol.
- Ground chicken and turkey are often loaded with fat and contain dark meat, increasing the fat content. Know what you're eating! Ask your butcher to grind just the skinless breast meat for you, or grind it yourself quickly in the processor. Remove and discard the skin, bone and excess fat. Cut poultry breast into 1-inch chunks. Process for 15 to 20 seconds, until minced.
- Raw poultry can be frozen for about 6 months at 0°F if properly wrapped.
- Once raw poultry has thawed, it cannot be refrozen unless you cook it first. For example, if your freezer breaks down and your chicken has thawed, cook it. Then you can freeze it again.
- Never defrost poultry at room temperature. Either defrost it in the refrigerator overnight or use the microwave. It takes 5 to 6 minutes per pound (10 to 12 minutes per kg) on DEFROST. Boneless breasts take 4 to 5 minutes per pound (3 or 4 single boneless breasts weigh about 1 pound.) Arrange thicker pieces outward and thinner pieces inward. Remember, thin is in!
- After defrosting poultry in the microwave, it should still be cold to the touch. The ice crystals in the thicker parts will dissolve shortly. Rinse in cold water and let stand 5 to 10 minutes before cooking. Cook immediately, or refrigerate once it is completely defrosted.
- Poultry, whether cooked or raw, should not be left on the counter for more than an hour during the summer, or for more than 2 hours during the winter, to prevent food poisoning.
- To prevent salmonella and cross-contamination, everything that touches raw poultry should be washed with a sanitizing solution of 1 tablespoon bleach dissolved in 1 gallon (4 liters/quarts) of warm (not hot) water. Let surfaces air dry; do not rinse. Discard leftover solution.
- Koshered chickens have already been salted, so don't sprinkle them with salt before cooking. Adjust seasonings at the end of cooking. To remove excess salt from Koshered chickens, soak them in several changes of cold water before cooking.
- Skin or no skin? If roasting poultry without a sauce, leave skin on during cooking to keep it moist; remove skin after cooking. If cooking poultry in sauce, remove skin before cooking. Otherwise, fat from the skin melts and drains into the sauce.

Roast Brisket

See recipes for Coke Brisket and Sweet & Sour BBQ Brisket (p. 398). Although brisket is higher in both fat and cholesterol, it makes a special treat for festive holiday meals!

Herb Roasted Chicken

See photo (P-7). So flavorful, so moist! This recipe will become part of your regular repertoire.

3 lb. (1.4 kg) chicken, cut into pieces
2–3 cloves garlic, crushed
$\frac{1}{2}$ tsp. each of dried basil, oregano & rosemary
$\frac{1}{4}$ tsp. dried thyme
1 tsp. Hungarian paprika
Freshly ground pepper
1 tbsp. olive oil

1. Wash chicken well and pat dry. Loosen chicken skin but don't remove it. Rub flesh of chicken with garlic, seasonings and olive oil. Cover chicken and marinate at least an hour (or preferably overnight) in the refrigerator to allow the flavor of the herbs to penetrate.

2. Preheat oven to 400°F. Place chicken pieces skinside down on a rack in a foil-lined pan. Roast chicken uncovered for 15 minutes. Reduce heat to 350°F. Roast chicken skin-side up for 1 hour, or until golden and juices run clear. Baste occasionally. Remove skin before serving.

Yield: 6 servings. Recipe may be doubled or tripled, if desired. Freezes well.

183 calories per serving, 8.7 g fat (2.1 g saturated), 72 mg cholesterol, 24 g protein, trace carbohydrate, 72 mg sodium, 228 mg potassium, 1 mg iron, trace fiber, 17 mg calcium.

- **Chef's Fat-Saving Secrets!** Loosen the skin from breasts, legs and thighs of chicken. Rub garlic, seasonings and oil over chicken under the skin. Cook as directed; remove skin before serving. Skin keeps chicken moist and bastes it without adding extra fat. Discard fatty drippings before serving.
- **Shortcut BBQ Chicken:** Prepare chicken as directed in Step 1. Preheat the BBQ or grill. Place chicken in a Pyrex casserole and microwave covered on HIGH for 8 to 9 minutes. Turn chicken pieces over, moving small pieces to the center. Microwave 7 to 8 minutes longer. Transfer partly-cooked chicken to hot grill immediately. Cook 15 to 20 minutes longer, until crispy and golden. Remove skin before serving.
- **Chef's BBQ Secrets!** Chicken will be very juicy if microwaved before grilling. To prevent flare-ups, grill chicken over heat, not flame.
- **Chicken is high in protein** and an excellent source of phosphorus and nicacin. It is also a good source of iron, zinc and riboflavin.

Gloria's Limelight Roast Chicken

Gloria Schachter gave me this moist and luscious chicken recipe, which I've adapted. Yummy!

$3\frac{1}{2}$ lb. (1.6 kg) whole chicken
Salt & freshly ground pepper, to taste
1 tsp. dried basil
3 limes
1–2 stalks celery, cut into chunks
$\frac{1}{4}$ c. chopped parsley or coriander (cilantro)

1. Rinse chicken and dry well. Loosen skin; rub seasonings inside the cavity and under skin of chicken. Squeeze juice of one lime over chicken. Marinate for 1 hour at room temperature or cover and marinate in the fridge overnight. Pierce limes with a fork. Place limes, celery and parsley inside the chicken. Close up openings with metal skewers. Place chicken on its side in a roasting pan.

2. Preheat oven to 425°F. Roast uncovered for 20 minutes. Turn chicken onto its other side and roast 20 minutes more. Reduce heat to 350°F and roast breast side up 20 minutes longer, until golden and crisp. Remove chicken from oven. Strain fat from pan juices. Place pan juices in a gravy boat. Cut up chicken; remove skin, limes, celery and parsley. Garnish with additional lime slices.

Yield: 6 servings. Reheats and/or freezes well. Recipe can be doubled for company.

191 calories per serving, 7.4 g fat (2 g saturated), 84 mg cholesterol, 28 g protein, 1 g carbohydrate, 92 mg sodium, 308 mg potassium, 2 mg iron, trace fiber, 26 mg calcium.

• Serve with **Roasted Garlic Mashed Potatoes** (p. 257) and Mandarin Asparagus (p. 247).

Jamaican Jerk Chicken

Chili peppers are very hot, so use rubber gloves when handling!

3½ lb. chicken (1.6 kg), cut up
2   onions, cut in chunks
3   cloves garlic
2   tbsp. ginger
1   hot chili pepper, cored & seeded
½   tsp. ground allspice
1   tsp. pepper
1   tsp. dried thyme (or 1 tbsp. fresh)
3   tbsp. red or white wine vinegar
3   tbsp. soy sauce

1. Rinse chicken; trim fat. Grind onions, garlic, ginger and chili pepper in the processor. Mix in remaining ingredients except chicken. Coat chicken with sauce. Cover and marinate overnight in the fridge. Place chicken on a rack in a foil-lined broiling pan. Place a pan of water in the bottom of the oven. Roast chicken uncovered at 375°F for 45 minutes, basting often. Preheat broiler or grill. Grill or broil chicken until crusty, about 15 minutes. Remove skin before serving. Serve with rice.

Yield: 6 servings. Reheats and/or freezes well.

221 calories per serving, 7.6 g fat (2.1 g saturated), 84 mg cholesterol, 29 g protein, 7 g carbohydrate, 544 mg sodium, 376 mg potassium, 2 mg iron, 1 g fiber, 34 mg calcium.

Chicken with Bulgur & Mushrooms

Easy, tasty and nutritious! Rice can be substituted for the bulgur.

3   lb. (1.4 kg) chicken, cut in pieces
3   onions, sliced
2   c. mushrooms, sliced
1   c. bulgur, rinsed & well-drained
2   cloves garlic, minced
Salt (optional)
Freshly ground pepper, to taste
1   tsp. dried basil
2   c. vegetarian tomato sauce
¾   c. water

1. Wash chicken and remove skin. Trim off excess visible fat. Place onions, mushrooms and bulgur in the bottom of a lightly greased casserole. Arrange chicken pieces on top. Rub chicken with garlic and seasonings. Combine sauce and water; pour over chicken and bulgur. Bake covered at 350°F for 1¼ hours, or until chicken is tender and most of liquid is absorbed. Adjust seasonings to taste.

Yield: 6 servings. Reheats and/or freezes well.

330 calories per serving, 10 g fat (2.3 g saturated), 72 mg cholesterol, 29 g protein, 33 g carbohydrate, 516 mg sodium, 851 mg potassium, 3 mg iron, 7 g fiber, 60 mg calcium.

• **If desired,** chicken wings can be set aside and frozen. When you have enough saved up, make chicken soup!
• **Serve with steamed zucchini** and carrots seasoned with salt, pepper and dill.

Saucy Szechuan Pineapple Chicken

My friend Roz Brown got rave reviews when she prepared this dish for a Passover dinner party.

3   onions, sliced
2   chickens, cut up
Pepper & paprika, to taste
1½ c. Szechuan-style duck sauce
19 oz. can (540 ml) pineapple chunks, drained
    (reserve liquid)

1. Place onions in the bottom of a large sprayed roasting pan. Remove and discard fat from chickens but do not remove skin. Place chicken pieces on top of onions. Sprinkle lightly with seasonings. Pour duck sauce and pineapple chunks over chick-

en, along with half of the reserved liquid. Bake covered at 400°F for ½ hour. Reduce heat to 350°F and bake 1 hour longer, basting occasionally.

2. When cool, refrigerate for several hours or overnight. Discard chicken skin and congealed fat from pan juices. Reheat covered at 350°F for 25 minutes.

Yield: 12 servings. Reheats and/or freezes well.

264 calories per serving, 7.5 g fat (2 g saturated), 84 mg cholesterol, 29 g protein, 19 g carbohydrate, 188 mg sodium, 366 mg potassium, 2 mg iron, <1 g fiber, 27 mg calcium.

• **Serve over Passover yolk-free noodles** along with steamed asparagus.

Dracula Chicken

Spicy and luscious, this simple dish was a hit at our Rosh Hashonah dinner!

2   chickens (about 3 lb./1.4 kg each)
2–3 tbsp. coarse steak spices
1   tbsp. paprika
1   tbsp. dried basil
3   onions, sliced
¾–1 c. water

1. Trim fat from chicken. Rub chicken under the skin with seasonings. Arrange a bed of onions in the bottom of a sprayed roasting pan. Place chicken on top of onions. Cover and refrigerate overnight.

2. Preheat oven to 350°F. Add water to chicken. Cook covered 1½ hours, until tender. Uncover and

cook ½ hour longer, until golden and crispy, basting occasionally. If necessary, add a little extra water to the pan. Let stand for 20 minutes. Cut up into serving-sized pieces, removing the skin to reduce fat. Strain fat from pan juices with a fat separator. Place pan juices in a gravy boat to serve.

Yield: 12 servings. Reheats and/or freezes well.

182 calories per serving, 6.7 g fat (1.8 g saturated), 72 mg cholesterol, 25 g protein, 5 g carbohydrate, 269 mg sodium, 320 mg potassium, 2 mg iron, 1 g fiber, 39 mg calcium.

• **Perfect with Honey-Glazed Carrots** (p. 403) and Broccoli Noodle Kugel (p. 273).

Ilene's Honey Mustard Chicken

My dietician, Ilene Gilbert, shared this terrific chicken recipe with me. Enjoy without guilt!

6	single chicken breasts (with bone)
⅓	c. Dijon mustard
2	tbsp. honey
1	tsp. olive oil
1	tsp. dried tarragon (or 1 tbsp. fresh tarragon leaves, minced)

1. Spray a foil-lined baking sheet with non-stick spray. Remove skin from chicken; trim off fat. In a bowl, combine mustard, honey, oil and tarragon. Rub chicken with glaze, reserving leftover glaze. Arrange chicken bone side down on baking sheet. (Can be prepared in advance and refrigerated covered for up to 24 hours.)

2. Preheat oven to 350°F. Bake chicken uncovered for 45 minutes, brushing with reserved glaze during the last 15 minutes. When done, juices will run clear and chicken will be glazed and golden.

Yield: 6 servings. Freezes and/or reheats well. Recipe can be multiplied for a large crowd.

188 calories per serving, 5 g fat (1 g saturated), 73 mg cholesterol, 28 g protein, 8 g carbohydrate, 401 mg sodium, 249 mg potassium, 1 mg iron, trace fiber, 35 mg calcium.

• **Delicious with Turkish Bulgur Pilaf** (p. 208) and steamed cauliflower.

Ellen Sabin's Honey-Glazed Grilled Chicken

Serve this lightly sweetened chicken dish with additional marinade and hot cooked rice. Be sure to boil the marinade for at least a minute or two before serving it to help prevent salmonella.

4	single chicken breasts (with bone)
¼	c. minced green onions
2	cloves garlic, crushed
2	tsp. grated fresh ginger
1	tbsp. honey
2	tbsp. dry sherry
½	c. soy sauce (preferably low-sodium)

1. Remove skin and excess fat from chicken. In a bowl, combine green onions, garlic, ginger, honey, sherry and soy sauce. Dip chicken breasts in sauce, then place them in a heavy-duty plastic bag and pour in remaining sauce. Seal bag tightly. Let marinate at room temperature for 30 to 60 minutes, or refrigerate immediately and marinate for up to 24 hours.

2. Preheat grill. Place sprayed grill 4 inches above the hot coals. Remove chicken from marinade and drain well. Place chicken on the hot grill. Cook until done, about 25 minutes, brushing chicken with sauce several times during cooking to keep it moist. Turn pieces as needed to prevent them from burning. When done, chicken will be tender and juices will run clear. Boil remaining marinade for 2 minutes. Serve as a sauce with the chicken.

Yield: 4 servings. Can be frozen.

185 calories per serving, 3.1 g fat (0.9 g saturated), 73 mg cholesterol, 29 g protein, 8 g carbohydrate, 1132 mg sodium, 315 mg potassium, 2 mg iron, trace fiber, 27 mg calcium.

• **Great with corn on the cob** and Rozie's Vegetable Medley (p. 266).

Marilyn Goodman's Honey Crumb Chicken

This crumb-coated chicken is yummy, yet easy to prepare! Serve with Potato Wedgies (p. 260).

6 boneless, skinless chicken breasts
1/3 c. honey
1 tbsp. Dijon mustard
Salt & pepper, to taste
1/2 tsp. each of garlic powder & paprika
1/2–3/4 c. cornflake or bread crumbs

1. Preheat oven to 375°F. Spray an oblong casserole with non-stick spray. Rinse chicken; remove excess fat. Coat chicken with honey and mustard. Sprinkle on both sides with seasonings and crumbs. Arrange chicken in a single layer in casserole. Bake uncovered at 375°F for 30 to 35 minutes,

until golden, turning chicken over partway through cooking.

Yield: 6 servings. Reheats well.

237 calories per serving, 3.3 g fat (0.9 g saturated), 73 mg cholesterol, 28 g protein, 24 g carbohydrate, 224 mg sodium, 259 mg potassium, 2 mg iron, <1 g fiber, 18 mg calcium.

Glazed Apricot-Mustard Chicken Breasts with Rosemary

See photo (P-8). Mouth-watering! Dijon mustard is high in sodium, so no additional salt is needed.

6 single chicken breasts (with bone)
1/4 c. Dijon mustard
1/4 c. apricot jam
1 tbsp. honey
1 tsp. olive oil
2 tsp. fresh rosemary (or 1 tsp. dried)
Freshly ground pepper & paprika, to taste
Fresh rosemary, to garnish
14 oz. can (398 ml) water-packed apricots, drained

1. Line a 10 x 15-inch baking sheet with foil; spray with non-stick spray. Remove skin from chicken. Trim off excess fat. In a small bowl, combine mustard, jam, honey, oil and 2 teaspoons rosemary. Mix well. Rub chicken with mustard glaze, reserving any leftover glaze. Arrange chicken bone-side down on baking sheet. Sprinkle lightly with pepper and paprika. (Can be prepared in advance up to this point, covered and refrigerated for up to 24 hours.)

2. Preheat oven to 350°F. Bake chicken uncovered on middle rack for 45 minutes, brushing it with

reserved glaze during last 15 minutes of cooking. When done, juices will run clear and chicken will be glazed and golden. Do not overcook or chicken will be dry. Arrange chicken on a serving platter. Garnish with rosemary. Arrange drained apricots attractively around chicken.

Yield: 6 servings. Freezes and/or reheats well. Recipe can be multiplied for a large crowd.

246 calories per serving, 4.9 g fat (1 g saturated), 73 mg cholesterol, 28 g protein, 23 g carbohydrate, 331 mg sodium, 437 mg potassium, 2 mg iron, 2 g fiber, 50 mg calcium.

- **Variations:** Chicken legs and thighs can be used instead of breasts with the bone. Remove skin and fat; prepare as directed above. If using boneless breasts, bake 20 to 25 minutes at 400°F.
- **Pineapple jam** or orange marmalade can replace apricot jam. Dill or thyme can replace rosemary.
- **Serve with Rainbow Rice Pilaf** (p. 213) and steamed asparagus.

Dip & Flip Chicken Strips

4   boneless, skinless chicken breasts
$1/2$ c. non-fat bottled honey mustard dressing
$3/4$ c. cornflake crumbs
Pepper & paprika, to taste

1. Preheat oven to 400°F. Rinse chicken; pat dry. Cut in long strips about 2 inches wide. Dip in salad dressing, then in crumbs. Sprinkle lightly with seasonings. Place on a sprayed baking sheet. Bake uncovered for 10 minutes. Flip chicken over and bake 5 to 7 minutes longer, until crisp and golden.

Yield: 4 servings. Can be frozen. If reheating chicken, don't heat it too long or it may be dry.

267 calories per serving, 3.1 g fat (0.9 g saturated), 73 mg cholesterol, 29 g protein, 29 g carbohydrate, 611 mg sodium, 296 mg potassium, 3 mg iron, 2 g fiber, 14 mg calcium.

Chicken Fingers

For kids of all ages! These can be used as a main dish or for hors d'oeuvres.

4   boneless, skinless chicken breasts, trimmed of fat ($1^1/2$ lb./750 g)
1   c. cornflake or bread crumbs
$1/4$ c. sesame seeds
Salt, pepper & paprika, to taste
$1/4$ c. honey
2   tsp. orange juice
$1/4$ c. ketchup or chili sauce

1. Rinse chicken; pat dry. Cut into strips about 1-inch wide. In a plastic bag, combine crumbs, sesame seeds and seasonings. In a bowl, blend honey, orange juice and ketchup. Dip chicken in honey mixture, then drop a few pieces at a time into the crumb mixture. Shake to coat chicken well, then arrange in a single layer on a sprayed foil-lined baking sheet.

2. Preheat oven to 400°F. Bake chicken for 7 to 8 minutes. Turn over and bake 7 to 8 minutes longer, until crisp and golden. (If overcooked, chicken will be dry.) Use any of the following as a dipping sauce: honey, chili sauce, ketchup, plum sauce or cherry sauce.

Yield: 24 chicken fingers. These reheat and/or freeze well. Reheat at 350°F for 8 to 10 minutes.

64 calories per chicken finger, 1.3 g fat (0.1 g saturated), 12 mg cholesterol, 5 g protein, 8 g carbohydrate, 91 mg sodium, 57 mg potassium, <1 mg iron, trace fiber, 6 mg calcium.

- **Crunch & Munch Chicken:** Use only ³/₄ cup crumbs and ¹/₄ cup wheat germ. Wheat germ and sesame seeds contain Vitamin E.
- **Shake It Up Coating Mix:** Combine ³/₄ cup cornmeal, ³/₄ cup seasoned bread crumbs, ¹/₃ cup wheat germ (optional) and ¹/₂ cup sesame seeds. Season with a little salt, pepper, dried basil, garlic powder and paprika. Store in a tightly closed container in the refrigerator. It will keep for a couple of months. Use mixture as a replacement for packaged coating mix for chicken. You will have enough coating for 12 pieces of chicken.
- **Slim Chicks!** Rinse 6 chicken breasts (with or without bone). Remove skin and fat. Dip in fat-free or low-calorie salad dressing (e.g. Italian, French), then in Shake It Up Coating Mix or seasoned corn flake crumbs. Bake at 400°F. Chicken on the bone will take about 40 minutes, boneless breasts take about 20 minutes.
- **Nancy's Quicky Chicky!** Rinse boneless, skinless chicken breasts under cold running water but do not dry. Coat with corn flake crumbs seasoned with pepper, garlic powder and paprika. If desired, sprinkle lightly with lemon juice. Bake uncovered at 400°F for 20 to 25 minutes, until golden. Chicken fingers take about 15 minutes.
- **Tofu Fingers:** Instead of chicken, use 1 pound (500 g) of firm tofu. Slice in ³/₄-inch slices, then cut each slice into strips to make 24 pieces. Pat dry with paper towels. Prepare and bake as directed for Chicken Fingers. (Instead of baking, you can fry them in a non-stick skillet in a little oil for 4 or 5 minutes per side, until golden.)

Each tofu finger contains 61 calories, 2.1 g fat (0.3 g saturated), 0 mg cholesterol, 2 mg iron and 50 mg calcium.
- **Serve with No-Fry Fries** (p. 259) and Red Cabbage Cole Slaw (p. 278).

Chinese Chicken Fingers

Allison Schachter, who describes herself as the "Chicken Finger Queen," declares these are the best! Her mother, Gloria, made some from chicken and some from tofu for a Science Fair experiment at son Ryan's school. Both were winners! Use this yummy marinade for chicken breasts on the grill!

Marinade & Chicken:
- 2 cloves garlic, peeled & minced
- 1 tbsp. fresh ginger, peeled & minced
- 2 tbsp. soy sauce
- 2 tbsp. orange juice
- 1 tbsp. lemon juice
- 1 tbsp. honey
- 2 tbsp. hoisin sauce
- 4 boneless, skinless chicken breasts, trimmed of fat (about 1¹/₂ lb/750 g)

Coating Mixture:
- 1 egg plus 1 egg white
- 1 tbsp. water
- ³/₄ c. flour
- 1 tsp. garlic powder (or to taste)
- Salt & pepper, to taste
- ³/₄ c. breadcrumbs
- ¹/₂ tsp. paprika
- 2 tbsp. sesame seeds
- 1–2 tbsp. oil (to cook the chicken)

1. In a shallow bowl, combine marinade ingredients. Rinse chicken and pat dry. Cut each piece of chicken into 6 strips about 1-inch wide. Marinate chicken for an hour at room temperature, or cover and marinate overnight in the refrigerator, basting occasionally.

2. In a pie plate, blend egg, egg white and water. In a medium bowl, combine flour with ½ teaspoon garlic powder, salt and pepper. In another bowl, combine crumbs, salt, pepper, paprika, sesame seeds and remaining ½ teaspoon garlic powder. Remove chicken from marinade. Dip in flour mixture, then in egg, then in crumbs. (Can be prepared in advance and refrigerated for several hours.)

3. Heat 1 tablespoon oil in a large nonstick skillet. Add chicken fingers and sauté for 4 or 5 minutes per side, until golden and cooked through. Add a little more oil if needed. Drain well on paper towels. Delicious served with Chinese plum sauce (or hoisin sauce mixed with a few drops of orange juice and soy sauce).

Yield: 24 pieces. These reheat and/or freeze well. Reheat uncovered at 350°F for 10 minutes.

73 calories per piece, 2 g fat (0.3 g saturated), 21 mg cholesterol, 6 g protein, 7 g carbohydrate, 145 mg sodium, 63 mg potassium, <1 mg iron, trace fiber, 14 mg calcium.

- **These are great** with steamed rice and stir-fried veggies.
- **Chinese Tofu Fingers:** Use 1 pound (500 g) firm tofu instead of chicken. Slice tofu into ¾-inch slices, then cut each slice into strips. Pat dry with paper towels. Marinate and cook as directed above. Each "finger" contains 77 calories, 3.1 g fat (0.4 saturated) and 9 mg cholesterol.

Piquant Apricot Chicken Tid-Bites

4   boneless, skinless chicken breasts, trimmed of fat (1.5 lb/750 g)
⅔ c. apricot preserves
3   tbsp. chili sauce or ketchup
2   tsp. Dijon mustard
¼ tsp. dried basil
5–6 drops Tabasco sauce
¾ c. cornflake crumbs or bread crumbs
Salt & pepper, to taste

1. Spray a foil-lined baking sheet with non-stick spray. Rinse chicken and pat dry. Cut into 1-inch pieces. Each breast will yield about 8 pieces. Heat apricot preserves until melted (microwave for 45 seconds on HIGH). Combine with chili sauce, mustard, basil and Tabasco; mix well. Divide mixture into 2 separate bowls. Use one bowl as a sauce for the baked chicken. Use remaining sauce to coat the uncooked chicken. Season crumbs with salt and pepper to taste.

2. Dip chicken first in sauce, then in seasoned crumbs. Arrange in a single layer on baking sheet. (Chicken and sauce can be prepared in advance and refrigerated. Discard any leftover sauce or crumbs which were used to coat the raw chicken.)

3. Preheat oven to 400°F. Bake chicken for 6 to 8 minutes. Turn pieces over and bake 6 to 8 minutes longer, until crisp and golden. Serve with reserved sauce (or mix chicken with sauce).

Yield: 4 servings. These reheat and/or freeze well. Reheat at 350°F for 8 to 10 minutes, or until hot. Do not overheat or they will dry out.

367 calories per serving, 3.3 g fat (0.9 g saturated), 73 mg cholesterol, 29 g protein, 56 g carbohydrate, 543 mg sodium, 368 mg potassium, 3 mg iron, 1 g fiber, 22 mg calcium.

- **Serve as a main dish** with basmati rice and steamed snow peas.
- **Hors d'oeuvres:** Arrange chicken on a platter and place reserved dipping sauce in a small bowl in the center. Use toothpicks to serve. You should have about 32 pieces.

Mini Satay Chicken Kabobs

A favorite of my catering clients and cooking students! Mini kabobs make great appetizers. To serve as a main dish, prepare Grilled Satay Chicken Kabobs (below).

4   boneless, skinless chicken breasts, trimmed of fat (about 1½ lb./750 g)
1   red & 1 green pepper, cut into ½" chunks
½   c. Peanut Butter Sauce (p. 108)
32 4" wooden skewers (soak in cold water for 20 minutes)

1. Rinse chicken and cut it into 1-inch pieces. Pat dry with paper towels. (You should get about 8 to 10 pieces from each chicken breast.) Marinate in Peanut Butter Sauce for at least ½ hour.

2. Line a baking sheet with foil; spray with non-stick spray. Place a piece of chicken on each skewer. Put a piece of red pepper on one end and green pepper on the other end. (Kabobs can be assembled in advance. Refrigerate kabobs and any leftover sauce.) At serving time, bake at 400°F for 10 to 12 minutes, basting occasionally with sauce. (Kabobs can also be broiled or grilled for 3 or 4 minutes per side. Do not overcook.)

Yield: 32 to 40 miniature kabobs. Reheat at 350°F for 8 to 10 minutes. Do not freeze.

31 calories per miniature kabob, 1.2 g fat (0.3 g saturated), 9 mg cholesterol, 4 g protein, 1 g carbohydrate, 46 mg sodium, 46 mg potassium, trace iron, trace fiber, 3 mg calcium.

- **If you serve the kabobs** with additional sauce, remember that 1 tablespoon of sauce contains 49 calories and 3.4 grams of fat, so don't go nuts and indulge (or you will bulge)!
- **Do not use the sauce** that was used to marinate the raw chicken as your dipping sauce!
- **Tofu can be substituted for chicken.** Cut tofu into 1-inch cubes. Marinate and cook as directed.

Grilled Satay Chicken Kabobs

These make a marvelous main dish for family or friends. Serve them at your next barbecue!

1. Prepare chicken and peppers as directed in the recipe for mini kabobs, but cut them into 2-inch chunks. (You should get 6 pieces from each breast.) Also cut 1 red onion into chunks. Alternately thread chicken, peppers and onions onto 8-inch presoaked wooden skewers. Brush with some of the marinade.

2. Preheat grill or broiler. Grill or broil kabobs about 5 inches from the heat for about 8 to 10 minutes, turning skewers so chicken and vegetables will cook evenly. Brush with marinade occasionally during cooking. Do not overcook or chicken will be dry. Serve with Indonesian Brown Rice Salad (p. 289).

Yield: 8 kabobs (4 servings). Do not freeze. Recipe can be doubled or tripled for a crowd.

130 calories per kabob, 5 g fat (1.2 g saturated), 37 mg cholesterol, 15 g protein, 6 g carbohydrate, 184 mg sodium, 206 mg potassium, <1 mg iron, <1g fiber, 14 mg calcium.

Chinese Chicken Mini Kabobs

Garlic "Sparerib" Sauce (p. 108)
1   tbsp. corn starch
2   tbsp. orange juice
¼   tsp. red pepper flakes
1   tsp. Oriental sesame oil
2   red & 2 green peppers, cut in small chunks
6   boneless, skinless chicken breasts
4   dozen 4″ wooden skewers

1. Prepare sauce as directed. Bring to a boil. Dissolve corn starch in orange juice. Stir into boiling sauce and cook until thickened, stirring continuously. Stir in red pepper flakes and sesame oil. Cool completely.

2. Rinse chicken; trim off any fat. Cut chicken into 1-inch pieces; pat dry with paper towels. (You should get about 6 pieces from each chicken breast.) Marinate chicken in sauce for 20 to 30 minutes. Soak wooden skewers in cold water for 20 minutes.

3. Line a baking sheet with foil; spray with nonstick spray. Place a piece of chicken on each skewer. Put a piece of red pepper on one end and green pepper on the other end. (Can be made in advance and refrigerated.) At serving time, bake at 400°F for 10 to 12 minutes (or grill for 7 to 8 minutes), brushing with sauce occasionally. (Cooking time will depend on the thickness of the chicken.)

Yield: 36 kabobs. To reheat, bake at 350°F for 8 to 10 minutes, just until hot. Do not freeze.

32 calories per mini kabob, 0.7 g fat (0.2 g saturated), 12 mg cholesterol, 5 g protein, 2 g carbohydrate, 32 mg sodium, 58 mg potassium, trace iron, trace fiber, 4 mg calcium.

• **Chinese Chicken Maxi Kabobs:** Cut chicken and peppers into 2-inch chunks. Arrange on twelve 8-inch skewers. Brush with some of the marinade. Preheat grill or broiler. Grill or broil kabobs about 5 inches from the heat for about 10 to 12 minutes, turning skewers so chicken and vegetables will cook evenly. Brush with sauce occasionally during cooking. Do not overcook or chicken will be dry.
• **Mini Kabobs** make great appetizers, Maxi Kabobs can be used as a main dish. Serve with rice and Oriental Cole Slaw (p. 278).

Grilled Orange Teriyaki Chicken

4   boneless, skinless chicken breasts, trimmed of fat (about 1 lb/500 g)
Juice of half an orange (2 tbsp. juice)
½   tsp. dried basil
2   tbsp. teriyaki or soy sauce
1   tbsp. honey or maple syrup
1   tsp. Oriental sesame oil
1–2 cloves garlic, crushed
1–2 tsp. minced fresh ginger

1. Rinse chicken breasts; pat dry. Arrange in a single layer in an oblong casserole. Squeeze orange juice over chicken and sprinkle with basil. Add remaining ingredients and rub over chicken. Marinate for at least 30 minutes at room temperature, or cover and marinate for up to 24 hours in the refrigerator. Baste chicken once or twice with the marinade.

2. Preheat grill or broiler. If using the broiler, line the pan with foil. Remove chicken from marinade, reserving leftover marinade. Broil or grill chicken about 5 inches from the heat for 6 to 7 minutes, basting with a little marinade occasionally. Turn chicken over and cook 6 to 7 minutes longer, basting chicken as needed to prevent it from drying out. Cooking time will depend on the thickness of the chicken. Garnish chicken with orange slices, if desired.

Yield: 4 servings. Can be frozen.

181 calories per serving, 4.2 g fat (1 g saturated), 73 mg cholesterol, 27 g protein, 7 g carbohydrate, 409 mg sodium, 271 mg potassium, 1 mg iron, trace fiber, 22 mg calcium.

• Delicious with Oriental Rice (p. 214) and steamed broccoli.

Chicken Teriyaki Kabobs

Grilled Orange Teriyaki Chicken (above)
1   large red pepper, cut into 16 pieces
1   medium zucchini, sliced in 16 rounds
16 cherry tomatoes (or mushrooms)

1. Prepare chicken as directed, but cut each breast into 10 pieces before you marinate it. Soak 8 wooden skewers in cold water for 20 minutes. Remove chicken from marinade. Refrigerate any leftover marinade. Alternate veggies and chicken on skewers, starting and ending with red pepper. (Can be prepared in advance and refrigerated covered for several hours or overnight.)

2. Prepare broiler or grill. Brush chicken and vegetables with marinade. Broil or grill 5 inches from the heat for 8 to 10 minutes, turning skewers so chicken cooks evenly. Brush with marinade during cooking.

Yield: 8 kabobs. (Calculate 2 kabobs as 1 serving.) Do not freeze or vegetables will get soggy.

103 calories per kabob, 2.3 g fat (0.5 g saturated), 37 mg cholesterol, 14 g protein, 6 g carbohydrate, 208 mg sodium, 267 mg potassium, <1 mg iron, <1 g fiber, 16 mg calcium.

Hoisin Chicken Stir-Fry

Chicken & Marinade:
4   boneless, skinless chicken breasts, trimmed
2   cloves garlic, minced
2   tbsp. soy sauce
2   tbsp. orange juice
1   tbsp. lemon juice
1   tbsp. honey
2   tbsp. hoisin sauce
1   tbsp. fresh ginger, minced

Veggies & Sauce:
1   medium onion, sliced
1   red pepper, cut into strips
½   of a zucchini, sliced, if desired
2   additional cloves garlic, crushed
1–2 c. mushrooms, sliced
2   tsp. canola oil
2   tsp. cornstarch
¼   c. cold water, chicken or vegetable broth
1   tsp. Oriental sesame oil

1. Cut chicken into strips. Combine ingredients for marinade, add chicken and marinate for 30 minutes at room temperature, or cover and marinate overnight in the refrigerator.

2. Place onion, red pepper, zucchini, garlic and mushrooms in separate piles on a large plate. Remove chicken from marinade. Reserve marinade to use in the sauce.

3. Heat oil in a large skillet or wok. Add chicken and stir-fry on high heat for 2 or 3 minutes, until nearly cooked. (Add a bit of marinade if needed to prevent sticking.) Push chicken up the sides of the wok. Add onion to wok and stir-fry for 1 minute. Add red pepper, zucchini and garlic; stir-fry for 1 minute. Add mushrooms and stir-fry 30 seconds longer.

4. Combine reserved marinade with cornstarch and water or broth; mix well. Add marinade to wok and cook until thick and bubbling. Stir in sesame oil.

Yield: 4 servings. Reheats well in the microwave. Vegetables will get soggy if frozen.

243 calories per serving, 6.9 g fat (1.5 g saturated), 73 mg cholesterol, 28 g protein, 16 g carbohydrate, 653 mg sodium, 396 mg potassium, 2 mg iron, 1 g fiber, 31 mg calcium.

- **Variations and Serving Suggestions:** For variety, add or substitute any of the following: broccoli or cauliflower florets, sliced shiitake mushrooms, celery, red onions, bean sprouts and/or snow peas. If desired, add 1 to 2 teaspoons rice vinegar to cornstarch mixture in Step. 4. Serve over rice or pasta.
- **Vegetarian Stir-Fry:** Replace chicken with 1 pound firm tofu. Slice tofu ½-inch thick. Place on a plate between paper towels. Top with another

plate. Weigh down with cans and let stand for 20 minutes. Cut tofu in strips and marinate. Tofu needs only a minute or two of stir-frying in Step 3.
- **Hoisin Beef Stir-Fry:** Instead of chicken, use 1½ pound lean flank steak. Thinly slice meat across the grain into strips. Marinate and cook as directed above.

Orange Hoisin Chicken Stir-Fry with Oriental Vegetables

Bok choy (Chinese cabbage) is high in calcium. This is the "Choy of Cooking" in a wok!

6	boneless, skinless chicken breasts
	Orange Hoisin Marinade (p. 109)
2	carrots, peeled (or 1 c. baby carrots)
12	oz. bok choy or Chinese/Nappa cabbage
3	cloves garlic, minced
1	tbsp. fresh ginger, minced
2	stalks celery, in ½" diagonal slices
½	c. sliced green onions
2	red or green peppers, sliced
1	c. snow peas, trimmed
2	c. shiitake mushrooms, sliced
8	oz. can water chestnuts, drained, rinsed & sliced in half
1	tbsp. cornstarch dissolved in 2 tbsp. water
½–1	tsp. sesame oil

1. Trim excess fat from chicken. Cut chicken into strips. Marinate it for 30 minutes at room temperature or covered overnight in the refrigerator. Prepare marinade and set aside.

2. Place carrots in a saucepan and add water to cover. Bring to a boil and cook over medium heat for 4 to 5 minutes. Drain, rinse with cold water and

drain again. Cut diagonally in ½-inch slices. Separate bok choy leaves from stalks. Cut stems in 1-inch pieces. Tear leaves in bite-size pieces. Prepare remaining vegetables. Place in 5 separate piles on a large tray:

1) garlic/ginger
2) carrots/celery
3) green onions/bok choy stems/red peppers/snow peas/mushrooms
4) water chestnuts
5) bok choy leaves

3. Drain chicken, reserving marinade. Heat 1 tablespoon marinade on high heat in a wok or large non-stick skillet. Add chicken and stir-fry 2 to 3 minutes, until no longer pink. Transfer to a bowl; wipe pan dry.

4. Heat 2 tablespoons marinade in wok. Add garlic and ginger. Stir-fry for 20 seconds. Add carrots and celery and stir-fry 1 minute. Add green onions, bok choy stems, peppers, snow peas and mushrooms and cook 1 minute longer. (Add a bit of marinade if needed to prevent sticking.) Add water chestnuts and bok choy leaves; cook 30 seconds. Stir in remaining marinade and chicken; bring to a boil. Stir in cornstarch and sesame oil and cook until thickened. Serve over rice or noodles.

Yield: 6 to 8 servings. Vegetables will get soggy if frozen.

327 calories per serving, 6 g fat (1.3 g saturated), 73 mg cholesterol, 32 g protein, 38 g carbohydrate, 467 mg sodium, 852 mg potassium, 3 mg iron, 7 g fiber, 119 mg calcium.

• **Variations:** Blanched broccoli or cauliflower florets, red onions, enoki mushrooms, bean sprouts, or baby corn. You can substitute 2 pounds of London broil, thinly sliced across the grain, for boneless chicken breasts. Sprinkle stir-fry with toasted sesame seeds, if desired.

Oriental Chicken Breasts

Oriental Marinade:
- 3   cloves garlic, minced
- 1   slice ginger, about 2 tsp., minced
- ¼   c. lemon juice
- 2   tbsp. brown sugar, packed
- Freshly ground pepper
- ¼   c. soy or tamari sauce
- 1   tsp. Oriental sesame oil
- 5–6 drops Tabasco sauce, optional

Chicken & Sauce:
- 6   boneless, skinless chicken breasts, trimmed of fat (about 2 lb/1 kg)
- 1   tbsp. cornstarch
- ½   c. chicken broth, room temperature
- 1   red pepper, chopped
- 4   green onions, chopped

1. Combine marinade ingredients in a bowl. Marinate chicken for 30 minutes at room temperature, or cover and marinate up to 48 hours in the refrigerator, turning chicken over occasionally.

2. Preheat oven to 400°F. Spray a 10 x 15 x 1-inch baking sheet with nonstick spray. Remove chicken from bowl, reserving marinade. Arrange chicken in a single layer on baking sheet. Bake uncovered at 400°F for 20 minutes. Reserve any cooking juices from chicken.

3. Meanwhile, in a small saucepan, dissolve cornstarch in chicken broth. Stir in reserved marinade.

Add red pepper and green onions. Cook on medium heat until thickened and bubbling, stirring once or twice. (Or microwave 2 to 3 minutes on HIGH.) Stir in cooking juices from chicken and boil 1 minute longer. Arrange chicken on a serving platter; top with sauce.

Yield: 6 servings. Freezes and/or reheats well.

190 calories per serving, 3.9 g fat (1 g saturated), 73 mg cholesterol, 28 g protein, 9 g carbohydrate, 693 mg sodium, 317 mg potassium, 2 mg iron, <1 g fiber, 31 mg calcium.

- **Garlic and ginger** can be minced in a garlic press, or you can use your processor. A slice of ginger about the size of a quarter will yield about 2 teaspoons minced ginger.
- **Time Saving Tip:** In Step 1, combine chicken with marinade in an airtight storage container and freeze for up to 1 month. Defrost overnight in the fridge (or use the microwave).
- **Oven Stir-Fried Oriental Veggies:** Combine your favorite mix of veggies (e.g., sliced onions, peppers, mushrooms, zucchini, bok choy, sprouts and crushed garlic) with 3 tablespoons soy or teriyaki sauce (or use 3 tablespoons of your favorite bottled sauce or marinade). Place veggies on a sprayed baking pan. Preheat oven to 400°F oven. Bake veggies on top rack of oven for 20 minutes, stirring once or twice. Place chicken breasts on the bottom shelf to cook along with the veggies. Prepare sauce as directed. Everything will be ready at the same time, with no frying!
- **Oriental London Broil:** Marinate 2 pounds London Broil for 1 hour at room temperature or overnight in the fridge. Preheat grill or broiler. Reserve marinade. Grill meat for 10 minutes on the first side and 7 to 8 minutes on the second side, brushing often with marinade. Prepare sauce as directed in Step 3. Slice meat thinly across the grain, place on a platter and top with sauce.

Sesame Chicken Mandarin

Mexican and Oriental flavors blend perfectly in this high-fiber, low-fat dish. Nutrition with ease!

10	oz. can (284 ml) mandarin oranges
2	c. chunky salsa (mild or medium)
½	c. orange or 3-fruit marmalade
1	tsp. Dijon mustard
1	tbsp. teriyaki sauce
2	tbsp. rice vinegar or lemon juice
2–3	cloves garlic, crushed
6	boneless, skinless chicken breasts, trimmed & cut in 1" chunks
2	c. mushrooms, sliced
1	c. snow peas, trimmed & cut in 1" slices
3	tbsp. toasted sesame seeds

1. Drain oranges, reserving ¼ cup juice. In a large skillet, combine juice with all ingredients except snow peas and sesame seeds. Marinate for 30 minutes. Bring to a boil, reduce heat and simmer uncovered on medium for 25 minutes, stirring occasionally. Add drained mandarins and snow peas. Cook 5 minutes longer, until piping hot. Yummy over rice or noodles. Sprinkle with sesame seeds.

Yield: 6 servings. Reheats and/or freezes well.

290 calories per serving, 3.4 g fat (0.9 g saturated), 73 mg cholesterol, 29 g protein, 30 g carbohydrate, 442 mg sodium, 526 mg potassium, 9 mg iron, 3 g fiber, 82 mg calcium.

- **Sesame Apricot Chicken:** Instead of mandarins, use 1 cup canned apricots, drained and sliced.

Saucy Mexican Chicken

Fast and fabulous! My long-time friend, Phyllis Levy, makes this using fresh pineapple.

6   boneless, skinless chicken breasts, trimmed & cut in 1" chunks
2½ c. chunky salsa (mild, medium or hot)
14 oz (398 ml) can pineapple tidbits, drained
2   tsp. mustard
5–6 drops Tabasco sauce, if desired
2–3 cloves garlic, minced
3   tbsp. fresh lemon juice
Sweetener to equal 1 tbsp. sugar or honey
12 oz. can (341 ml) corn niblets, drained

1. Combine all ingredients except corn in a bowl; mix well. Cover and marinate in the refrigerator for 1 hour. Transfer to a large skillet and heat on medium, until bubbling. Reduce heat and simmer uncovered for 25 minutes, stirring occasionally, until sauce has reduced and is thickened. Add corn and cook 5 minutes longer, until piping hot. Serve over rice.

Yield: 6 servings. Reheats and/or freezes well.

241 calories per serving, 3.5 g fat (0.9 g saturated), 73 mg cholesterol, 30 g protein, 22 g carbohydrate, 553 mg sodium, 477 mg potassium, 2 mg iron, 4 g fiber, 78 mg calcium.

• **You can use 1 cup of apricot jam** instead of pineapple tidbits, but omit sweetener.
• Pasta Fasta Fiesta: Omit pineapple. Simmer a 19 ounce (540 ml) can of red kidney or black beans, drained and rinsed, with chicken/salsa mixture. Perfect with penne or fettucine.

Cajun Chicken Breasts

Add a little spice to your life. Simply fantastic, and so versatile!

4   boneless, skinless chicken breasts
½   tbsp. olive oil
2   tbsp. lemon juice
Salt & freshly ground pepper (to taste)
½   tsp. chili powder
½   tsp. paprika
½   tsp. cayenne
½   tsp. dried basil
2   cloves garlic, crushed

1. Rinse chicken and pat dry. Trim off excess fat. Combine oil, lemon juice, seasonings and garlic in a mixing bowl. Add chicken and marinate for an hour at room temperature, or up to 24 hours covered in the refrigerator. (Refer to "Fowl Play" in tips following this recipe.)

2. Preheat oven to 400°F. Remove chicken from marinade and arrange in a single layer on a foil-lined 10 x 15 x 1-inch baking sheet. Pour marinade over and around chicken. Bake uncovered for 20 minutes, turning chicken pieces over at half time. Baste occasionally with pan juices. When done, chicken will be springy when lightly touched. If overcooked, chicken will be tough.

Yield: 4 servings. Cooked chicken may be dry if frozen and reheated.

163 calories per breast, 4.9 g fat (1.1 g saturated), 73 mg cholesterol, 27 g protein, 2 g carbohydrate, 69 mg sodium, 257 mg potassium, 1 mg iron, trace fiber, 22 mg calcium.

• **Cajun Chicken** is great with Salsa Rice (p. 215) and steamed green beans.

- **Fowl Play:** Marinate a batch of chicken breasts, then freeze in meal-sized packages for up to a month. (Never do this with chicken that was previously frozen, then defrosted!) When needed, thaw chicken overnight in the refrigerator (or in the microwave), then cook as directed.
- **Leftovers?** Make Lighter Chicken Salad (p. 292). Chilled leftover chicken can also be thinly sliced across the grain and used in Cajun Chicken Breast Sandwiches (p. 120).
- **Cajun Chicken Tid-Bites:** These are yummy appetizers. Follow recipe for Cajun Chicken Breasts (above), but cut chicken into 1-inch pieces. (Each breast yields about 8 pieces.) Marinate and cook as directed, reducing cooking time to 15 minutes. Serve on toothpicks as hors d'oeuvres. Also great served on a bed of salad greens. Serve with salsa (bottled or homemade).
- **Crumby Cajun Chicken:** Marinate chicken as directed, then dip in seasoned cornflake crumbs. Arrange on a sprayed baking sheet and bake uncovered at 400°F. Allow 20 minutes for boneless chicken breasts and 12 to 15 minutes if chicken has been cut into small pieces or strips. Turn chicken over halfway through cooking.
- **Grilled Cajun Chicken Breasts:** Preheat grill or broiler. Marinate chicken as directed. Remove from marinade and pat dry. Grill or broil over medium to medium-high heat about 5 to 7 minutes on each side. Baste chicken frequently with marinade; don't overcook. Cooking time on the grill will be shorter than under the broiler because of the higher, direct heat.
- **BBQ Chip Tips!** For a gourmet touch, soak 3 or 4 handfuls of wood chips (mesquite, applewood, hickory) in water for at least half an hour. Toss the soaked chips on top of the hot coals just before placing chicken on the grill. Cook the chicken over heat, not flame, to prevent flare-ups.

Chicken Breasts with Colored Peppers

Simply delicious! This recipe is a winner with my students.

Vegetables:
1	tsp. olive oil
1	onion, sliced
1	green, 1 red and 1 yellow pepper, sliced
2	large cloves garlic, crushed
2–3	tbsp. water (as needed)
	Salt & pepper, to taste
$\frac{1}{2}$	tsp. dried basil (or 1 tbsp. fresh, minced)
$\frac{1}{2}$	tsp. dried thyme

Chicken:
4	skinless, boneless chicken breasts, trimmed of fat (about 1 lb./500 g)
	Freshly ground pepper
2	tsp. additional olive oil
2	green onions, minced
2	tbsp. flour
$\frac{1}{2}$	c. chicken broth
$\frac{1}{2}$	c. dry white wine
1	tsp. Dijon mustard (to taste)

1. Vegetables: Heat 1 teaspoon olive oil in a large non-stick skillet or wok. Add onion, peppers and garlic. Sauté on medium heat until tender, about 5 minutes, adding a little water if vegetables begin to stick. (Or microwave the vegetables covered on HIGH for 5 minutes, omitting water.) Sprinkle with salt, pepper, basil and thyme. Remove vegetables from skillet.

2. Chicken: Cut chicken breasts into strips or leave them whole. Sprinkle with pepper. Heat 2 teaspoons olive oil in wok. Stir-fry chicken breasts over medium-high heat for 2 to 3 minutes, until they turn white. Add green onions and cook 1 minute longer. Sprinkle flour over chicken. Cook about a minute longer to lightly brown the flour, scraping up any browned bits. Add broth, wine and mustard. Stir until mixture comes to a boil. Reduce heat and simmer uncovered for 3 or 4 minutes, basting chicken occasionally. Stir in vegetables. Cook 2 to 3 minutes longer, until vegetables are hot. Adjust seasonings to taste.

Yield: 4 servings. This dish reheats well. If frozen, peppers may develop a slightly bitter taste.

251 calories per serving, 6.7 g fat (1.4 g saturated), 73 mg cholesterol, 30 g protein, 13 g carbohydrate, 119 mg sodium, 438 mg potassium, 2 mg iron, 2 g fiber, 48 mg calcium.

- **Serve on a bed** of basmati rice or with boiled new potatoes.
- **Chicken Breasts with Mushrooms:** Use 2 cups sliced mushrooms instead of peppers. Freezes and reheats well.
- **Passover Version:** Substitute potato starch instead of flour. Substitute 1 tablespoon of fresh lemon juice for mustard.

Lemon Dill Chicken in a Pouch

This is a perfect dish for one person or for a crowd. For a large quantity, multiply all ingredients. Easy and versatile! Cold leftovers are delicious thinly sliced and served on a crusty roll or in a salad.

1 boneless, skinless chicken breast, trimmed of fat
   (^{1}/4 lb/125 g)
Salt, if desired
Freshly ground pepper, to taste
Paprika, to taste

1 tsp. fresh dill, minced (or ^{1}/2 tsp. dried)
^{1}/2 tsp. olive or canola oil
1–2 tbsp. fresh lemon juice

1. Place chicken in a bowl and sprinkle it with seasonings. Rub with dill, oil and lemon juice. Let marinate for 30 minutes at room temperature, or cover and refrigerate up to 24 hours.

2. Cut a large square of foil or parchment paper. Place chicken on the foil and drizzle lightly with marinade. Seal package by crimping edges closed. (If preparing several portions, make individual packages.) Place on a baking sheet and bake in a preheated 400°F oven for 20 to 25 minutes. (Use a toaster oven for 1 or 2 portions.) To serve, place pouch on a serving plate and cut open at the table.

Yield: 1 serving. Best served immediately, but if you make a large quantity, leftovers can be reheated. Cooked chicken might be too dry if frozen. (Read Time-Saving Secret.)

145 calories per serving, 4.9 g fat (1.1 g saturated), 63 mg cholesterol, 23 g protein, 1 g carbohydrate, 55 mg sodium, 209 mg potassium, <1 mg iron, trace fiber, 13 mg calcium.

- **Perfect with steamed rice** and broccoli florets or a garden salad.
- **Time-Saving Secret!** Combine chicken with seasonings, dill, oil and lemon juice in an airtight container. Freeze for up to 1 month. Thaw overnight in the fridge, or use the microwave. (One piece of chicken takes 2 to 3 minutes on DEFROST.) Cook immediately as directed in Step 2.
- **Forget-about-the-Pouch Version:** Place marinated breasts on a lightly greased baking sheet. Bake uncovered at 400°F for 20 minutes.

- **Grilled or Broiled Lemon Chicken:** Preheat grill or broiler. Prepare chicken as directed in Step 1. Remove chicken from marinade and pat dry. Grill or broil over medium-high heat, allowing 5 to 6 minutes per side. Baste often with marinade. Do not overcook or chicken will be dry.
- **Microwave Method:** In Step 2, wrap marinated chicken breasts in parchment paper. Cook 3 minutes on HIGH for 1 single breast, 4 to 4½ minutes for 2 single breasts, and 6 to 7 minutes for 4 single breasts (1 to 1¼ pounds). When done, chicken juices should run clear.
- **Chicken & Vegetables in a Pouch:** Prepare Lemon Dill Chicken as directed, but before sealing package(s), top chicken with one of the following veggie combinations: broccoli and/or cauliflower florets; chopped green, red and/or yellow peppers; julienned zucchini, carrots and/or green onions. Sprinkle with a little marinade or white wine. Bake or microwave as directed. If microwaving, add an extra minute or two for the veggies.
- **Salsa Chicken in a Pouch:** Prepare Lemon Dill Chicken as directed, topping each chicken breast with 2 or 3 tablespoons homemade or bottled salsa. Wrap in parchment; bake or microwave as directed.

Herbed Lemon Chicken Breasts with Mushrooms

Elegant and luscious, yet so easy!

4	boneless, skinless chicken breasts, trimmed
¼	c. fresh lemon juice
1	tsp. olive oil
	Salt & freshly ground pepper, to taste
1	tsp. dried rosemary
1	tsp. dried thyme
1	tbsp. additional olive oil
2	c. shiitake or cremini (brown) mushrooms, sliced
3	large cloves garlic, thinly sliced
3	tbsp. white wine or brandy
2	tbsp. fresh parsley, minced

1. Butterfly each chicken breast by cutting it almost in half, then open it like a book to make a large, thin piece. Place in a single layer in a glass casserole. Sprinkle with lemon juice, oil and seasonings. Marinate covered in the refrigerator for several hours or overnight.

2. Heat oil in a large nonstick frypan. Add mushrooms and garlic. Season lightly with salt and pepper and sauté on medium-high heat about 5 minutes, until browned. Remove pan from heat and transfer mushrooms to a bowl.

3. Return pan to the heat and pour in marinade from chicken. Add chicken breasts to hot marinade and brown on medium-high heat for 3 to 4 minutes per side, until cooked through. Remove chicken from pan. Stir in wine or brandy and scrape up any browned bits from bottom of the pan. Return chicken and mushrooms to pan and cook 2 or 3 minutes longer to heat through. Sprinkle with parsley. Serve immediately.

Yield: 4 servings. If reheating this dish, add a little chicken broth or water to create steam (about ¼ to ½ cup). This prevents it from drying out. Heat covered for a few minutes, just until piping hot.

241 calories per serving, 8 g fat (1.6 g saturated), 73 mg cholesterol, 28 g protein, 13 g carbohydrate, 69 mg sodium, 357 mg potassium, 2 mg iron, 2 g fiber, 34 mg calcium.

- **Serve with Company Stuffed Spuds** (p. 261) and Glazed Apricot Carrots with Peppers (p. 251).

Arlene's Chicken Latkas (Patties)

My friend Arlene Stein shared this quick and tasty recipe!

2   cloves garlic
1   medium onion, cut into chunks
2   carrots, cut into chunks
1   medium potato, peeled & cut into chunks
2   slices whole-wheat bread (or ½ c. matzo meal)
1   egg (or 2 egg whites)
1   lb. (500 g) lean ground chicken (ask your butcher to grind skinless, trimmed breasts)
¾   tsp. Cajun seasoning (or salt)
½   tsp. pepper
½   tsp. dried basil

1. Preheat oven to 425°F. Drop garlic through feed tube of processor while machine is running. Process until minced. Add onion, carrots and potato; process until finely minced. Empty into a large mixing bowl. Process bread until fine crumbs are formed; add to mixing bowl. Add remaining ingredients and mix gently to blend. Mixture will be quite soft.

2. Wet your hands and form mixture into 8 large patties. Arrange in a single layer on a lightly sprayed non-stick baking sheet. Bake at 425°F about 15 minutes, until browned on the bottom. Turn patties over and bake 10 minutes more, until nicely browned on both sides. Do not overbake.

Yield: 8 latkas. These reheat and/or freeze well. Serve hot or at room temperature. Great with salsa!

117 calories per latka, 2.4 g fat (0.7 g saturated), 58 mg cholesterol, 14 g protein, 10 g carbohydrate, 129 mg sodium, 243 mg potassium, 1 mg iron, 2 g fiber, 27 mg calcium.

- **Serve with mashed potatoes,** steamed carrots and a garden salad. Leftovers can be made into a sandwich the next day. Add mustard, lettuce, cucumber and tomato slices.
- **Turkey Latkas:** Prepare Chicken Latkas, but use minced boneless turkey breast. Each turkey latka contains 123 calories and 1.4 g fat (0.4 g saturated). (Turkey latkas contain slightly more calories than chicken latkas because there is less shrinkage during cooking. However, please note that turkey latkas are lower in fat.)
- **Tofu Latkas:** Prepare Chicken Latkas, but substitute tofu for chicken. Slice tofu 1-inch thick and place on a baking sheet lined with paper towels. Weigh tofu down with another baking sheet and let stand for 20 minutes. Process drained tofu until minced. Combine with remaining ingredients. Cook as directed above. Each tofu latka contains 139 calories, 6 g fat (1 g saturated), 27 mg cholesterol, 13 g carbohydrates and 137 mg calcium.
- **Miniature Latkas:** Prepare mixture as directed in Step 1. Shape into 24 small patties. Brown in a non-stick skillet on both sides until golden brown. Three minis equals 1 regular-sized latka. These are a great hors d'oeuvre served with salsa or plum sauce.
- **Variation:** Any of the above latkas can be browned in a little oil in a non-stick skillet. Cook 4 to 5 minutes per side. Transfer to a casserole; add ¼ cup water and 2 chopped onions. Cover and bake at 350°F for 20 to 30 minutes, until onions are tender.

Honey Garlic Meatballs

A favorite with my catering clients! Adding club soda to the meatball mixture produces a light-textured meatball. (Thanks to Julia Feldman, one of my residents at Manoir Montefiore in Montreal, for her delightful tip!) The meatball mixture is based on Julia's recipe. The sauce is mine.

Meat Mixture:
- 2 lb. lean ground turkey, chicken, beef or veal
- 1 egg (or 2 egg whites)
- Salt, to taste
- ¼ tsp. pepper
- ¼ tsp. paprika
- 2 cloves garlic, crushed
- ⅓ c. club soda or water (approximately)
- ½ c. bread crumbs (or matzo meal)

Sauce Mixture:
- 1½ c. Honey Garlic Sauce (homemade or bottled)
- 2 tbsp. cornstarch
- ½ c. orange juice
- ¼ tsp. red pepper flakes, optional
- 1 tsp. Oriental sesame oil, optional

1. Preheat oven to 400°F. Line a baking sheet with aluminum foil; spray with non-stick spray. Combine all ingredients for meat mixture and mix lightly. Wet your hands and shape mixture into small meatballs. Arrange them on the baking sheet; bake at 400°F for 20 minutes, until firm.

2. Heat sauce in a large pot. Dissolve cornstarch in orange juice; stir into simmering sauce. Add red pepper flakes and sesame oil, if using. When sauce is bubbling and thickened, add meatballs. Simmer partly covered for 10 to 15 minutes, stirring occasionally.

Yield: 10 servings (about 5 dozen meatballs). These freeze and/or reheat well.

190 calories per serving, 1.7 g fat (0.5 g saturated), 83 mg cholesterol, 24 g protein, 19 g carbohydrate, 563 mg sodium, 349 mg potassium, 2 mg iron, trace fiber, 46 mg calcium.

- **If using Kosher** ground beef or veal, do not add salt. These cuts of meat have been heavily salted during the Koshering process. If using turkey or chicken, add ½ teaspoon salt.
- **You can buy a bottled version** of Honey Garlic Sauce in most supermarkets. To make your own sauce, see recipe (p. 108). Make a double recipe and use 1½ cups for this recipe. Refrigerate the leftover sauce; it's yummy added to cooked rice.
- **Analysis is based** on lean ground turkey. If meatballs are made with extra-lean ground beef, one serving will contain 243 calories, 9 g fat (3.5 g saturated) and 54 mg cholesterol.
- **Serve with Vegetable Un-Fried Rice** (p. 211) and Teriyaki Asparagus (p. 246).
- **Tangy Sweet & Sour Meatballs:** Prepare meat mixture as directed in Step 1. (For Passover, use matzo meal instead of bread crumbs.) For the sauce mixture, combine 1 cup of ketchup, 2 cups ginger ale (diet or regular) and ½ teaspoon dried basil in a large saucepan. Add meatballs to simmering sauce. Cover partially and simmer for 1 to 1½ hours. If sauce becomes too thick, thin with a little ginger ale or water.

Secret Ingredient Sweet & Sour Meatballs

Ground chickpeas are the secret ingredient, and no one will know unless you tell! Chickpeas, carrots and oatmeal add soluble fiber. They also lower the fat content and cost. If you have trouble digesting chickpeas, substitute grated potato. You can double the meat mixture without doubling the sauce.

1   lb. (500 g) extra-lean ground beef, veal, minced turkey or chicken
1   c. canned chickpeas, drained & rinsed (or 1 large potato, peeled & cut in chunks)
2   cloves garlic
1   medium onion
1   large carrot
2   egg whites (or 1 whole egg)
½   tsp. salt, optional
¼   tsp. pepper
½   tsp. dried basil
⅔   c. quick-cooking oats or breadcrumbs
2   tbsp. ketchup, if desired

Sweet & Sour Sauce:
3   c. vegetarian spaghetti sauce (store-bought or homemade)
1   c. water
⅓   c. brown sugar, packed (to taste)
2   tbsp. lemon juice or vinegar
Pepper & basil, to taste

1. Place meat in a large mixing bowl. Process chickpeas (or potato), garlic, onion and carrot in the processor until fine, about 20 seconds. Blend in egg whites. Add to meat along with remaining ingredients for meat mixture. Mix lightly to blend. Shape into 1-inch balls, wetting your hands for easier handling. You will have about 60 balls.

2. Bake meatballs uncovered in a single layer on a lightly greased baking sheet at 350°F for 20 minutes (or microwave on HIGH for 5 to 7 minutes, shaking pan to mix meatballs at half time). Meatballs should be lightly cooked and fat will have drained out of the meat.

3. Combine sauce, water, brown sugar, lemon juice and spices in a large pot. Heat until simmering. Add drained meatballs, cover partially and simmer for 45 minutes, stirring occasionally.

Yield: Serves 10 as a main dish or 15 to 20 as hors d'oeuvres. Reheats and/or freezes well.

218 calories per serving, 7.6 g fat (2.1 g saturated), 17 mg cholesterol, 14 g protein, 25 g carbohydrate, 619 mg sodium, 575 mg potassium, 3 mg iron, 4 g fiber, 48 mg calcium.

- **Fat Saving Secrets!** Nutrients are calculated using extra-lean ground beef. Veal contains similar calories and fat. Ground chicken and turkey usually contain fat. Your leanest choice is skinless turkey or chicken breast. Grind it yourself, or have the butcher do it. One serving of turkey meatballs (about 6 meatballs) contains 195 calories and 4 g fat (0.6 g saturated).
- **Secret Ingredient Hamburgers:** Prepare meat mixture as directed in Step 1. Shape into 8 patties. Broil or grill burgers for 6 to 8 minutes per side, depending on thickness, until fully cooked.
- **Serve meatballs with pasta**, rice or bulgur. Peas and carrots add color and fiber.

New-Fashioned Cabbage Rolls in Cranberry Sauce

Lean minced chicken or turkey replaces fatty ground beef and cranberry sauce adds fabulous flavor to the sauce. You can also add a grated apple and a handful of raisins to the sauce.

Cranberry Sauce
1   medium cabbage (about 3 lb./1.4 kg)
14 oz. can (398 ml) jellied cranberry sauce
2   c. tomato sauce (preferably low-sodium)
1   c. water
⅓   c. brown or white sugar (to taste)

¹/₄ tsp. cinnamon
2 tbsp. lemon juice (to taste)

Cabbage Rolls

1¹/₂ lb. (750 g) ground chicken or turkey breast (remove skin and fat if grinding it yourself)
2 egg whites (or 1 egg)
4 green onions, minced
2 cloves garlic, minced
1 small carrot, grated
¹/₂ c. oatmeal, matzo meal or bread crumbs
¹/₂ tsp. salt
¹/₄ tsp. pepper
¹/₂ tsp. dried basil
¹/₂ c. uncooked rice
¹/₂ c. water
3–4 tbsp. ketchup

1. Remove 16 to 18 large leaves from cabbage. (Refer to Cabbage Without Damage!). Trim away the tough ribs; set aside. In a large pot, combine cranberry sauce, tomato sauce, water, sugar, cinnamon and lemon juice. Bring to a boil, stirring to break up cranberry sauce. Cut up leftover cabbage and add to the sauce. While sauce is simmering, prepare the cabbage rolls.

2. Combine ground poultry with remaining ingredients and mix lightly. Place a large spoonful of filling on each cabbage leaf. Roll up, folding in ends. Place cabbage rolls seam-side down in the pot of sauce. If sauce doesn't cover cabbage, add a little water. Cover and simmer slowly for 1¹/₂ to 2 hours, basting occasionally, until cabbage is tender.

Yield: 16 cabbage rolls. These reheat and/or freeze well.

Cabbage Without Damage!

- Large leaves are best for stuffing. Remove the core of cabbage with a sharp knife.
- Freezer Method: Place whole cabbage in a plastic bag in the freezer 2 days before. Remove cabbage from freezer the night before. Thaw overnight at room temperature. In the morning, the wilted leaves will separate easily.
- Boiling Method: Place the whole cabbage in a large pot of boiling water and simmer for 10 minutes, or until leaves are softened. When cool enough to handle, separate leaves.
- Microwave Method: Rinse cabbage but do not dry. Microwave covered on HIGH for 8 to 10 minutes, until outer leaves are pliable. Let stand covered for 3 or 4 minutes. Separate leaves. If cabbage is not flexible when you remove the last few leaves, microwave it 1 or 2 minutes longer.
- To roll cabbage leaves more easily, pare the thick rib portion with a sharp paring knife.

---

177 calories per cabbage roll, 1.7 g fat (0.4 g saturated), 24 mg cholesterol, 11 g protein, 30 g carbohydrate, 168 mg sodium, 343 mg potassium, 1 mg iron, 3 g fiber, 48 mg calcium.

- **Passover Cabbage Rolls or Meatballs in Cranberry Sauce:** Use white sugar instead of brown sugar in the sauce. Use matzo meal instead of oatmeal or bread crumbs in the chicken mixture. (You can even use matzo farfel; it will look like rice!) If making meatballs, omit cabbage and shape chicken mixture into small balls. Simmer meatballs for 1 to 1¹/₂ hours, until tender.
- **The sauce from** Secret Ingredient Sweet & Sour Meatballs (p. 175) can also be used for cabbage rolls.
- **Serve with Duchesse Potato Mounds with Mushrooms** (p. 399).

• **Vegetarian Cabbage Rolls:** Refer to recipe (p. 234).

Chicken or Turkey Meatloaf

Ask your butcher to grind skinless breast meat only, or do it in your processor. This way you can be sure that it isn't loaded with fat, skin and/or dark meat, which will increase the fat content substantially.

1½ lb. (750 g)	lean ground chicken or turkey breast (remove skin and fat if grinding it yourself)
2	cloves garlic
1	medium potato, peeled & cut in chunks
1	medium onion, cut in chunks
1	carrot, cut in chunks
2	egg whites (or 1 whole egg)
½ tsp.	salt
¼ tsp.	pepper
½ tsp.	dried basil
½ c.	bread crumbs (or matzo meal)
3 tbsp.	ketchup or BBQ sauce

1. Preheat oven to 350°F. Place ground poultry in a bowl. Process garlic, potato, onion and carrot in the processor until ground, about 20 seconds. Add egg whites; process until blended. Add to meat along with remaining ingredients. Mix lightly to blend. Spread in a sprayed loaf pan. Bake uncovered at 350°F for 50 to 60 minutes, until golden. Let stand for 5 minutes, then slice and serve.

Yield: 6 to 8 servings. Reheats and/or freezes well.

206 calories per serving, 3.2 g fat (0.9 g saturated), 63 mg cholesterol, 27 g protein, 17 g carbohydrate, 461 mg sodium, 411 mg potassium, 2 mg iron, 1 g fiber, 48 mg calcium.

• **Serve with mashed potatoes** and green peas.
• **Chicken or Turkey Burgers:** Follow recipe above, but shape mixture into 6 or 8 patties. Wet your hands for easier handling. Place patties in the freezer for about 20 to 30 minutes to firm them up before cooking. Meanwhile, preheat grill or broiler. Grill or broil patties for 7 to 8 minutes per side, depending on thickness, until fully cooked (or bake at 350°F for 20 to 25 minutes.)
• **New-Fashioned Shepherd's Pie:** Boil 6 potatoes until tender, about 20 minutes. Drain well, saving about ½ cup of the cooking water. Mash potatoes. Add some of the cooking liquid to moisten potatoes. Add salt and pepper to taste. Prepare chicken mixture as directed above. Spread evenly in a sprayed oblong Pyrex casserole. Top with drained corn, then with mashed potatoes; sprinkle with paprika. Bake at 375°F for 45 to 50 minutes. Serve with mixed greens.

Zelda's Meat Loaf

This should really be called "Used to be Zelda's Meat Loaf!" Marty Kaplan gave me his mother's recipe, which was a lot of work to prepare and fairly high in calories. I used my processor, did some "plastic surgery" on the recipe and made it with "the speed of light" for the new millennium.
Yummy!

2 lb. (1 kg)	ground turkey
1	onion
1 c.	mushrooms
½	of a green pepper
2	tomatoes
1	potato, peeled
1	large carrot
1–2	cloves garlic, crushed
½ c.	chicken broth

1   tsp. salt
¼   tsp. pepper
½   tsp. dried basil
¼   tsp. dried thyme
¼–⅓   c. bread crumbs
½   c. sun-dried tomatoes, cut in strips
½–¾   c. tomato or BBQ sauce

1. Preheat oven to 375°F. Place ground turkey in a large bowl. In the processor, chop onion, mushrooms and green pepper, using quick on/offs. Place in a microsafe bowl and microwave covered on HIGH for 5 minutes. Meanwhile, chop tomatoes and add to turkey. Grate potato and carrot. Add to turkey along with garlic, chicken broth, seasonings and bread crumbs. Add microwaved vegetables and mix lightly to blend.

2. Place meat mixture on a large sheet of plastic wrap and pat it into a rectangle about 1/2-inch thick. Place sun-dried tomatoes in 3 or 4 rows crosswise on the rectangle. Roll up the meat like a jelly roll. Discard plastic wrap. Transfer it to a sprayed loaf pan and drizzle tomato or BBQ sauce across the top. Bake uncovered at 375°F about 1 hour. Add a little extra sauce before the end of cooking if the top gets too dry. Drain off any excess fat, slice and serve.

Yield: 8 servings. Reheats and/or freezes well. Leftovers are great cold as a sandwich on a crusty roll the next day for lunch.

233 calories per serving, 9.9 g fat (2.8 g saturated), 90 mg cholesterol, 23 g protein, 14 g carbohydrate, 517 mg sodium, 659 mg potassium, 3 mg iron, 2 g fiber, 39 mg calcium.

- **You can substitute** extra-lean ground beef or half beef and half veal. Minced chicken breast can also be used. Minced turkey breast is the leanest choice.

- **If using oil-packed sun-dried tomatoes,** rinse well to remove excess oil; pat dry. You can substitute steamed asparagus or strips of roasted red pepper if you like.
- **Zelda didn't stuff** and roll her meat loaf, but I do. It makes a pretty pinwheel effect when sliced.
- **To keep turkey meat loaf** moist during cooking, I top it with a little sauce, but if using ground beef or veal, the sauce is a matter of personal preference.
- **Serve with baked or mashed potatoes** and steamed green beans sprinkled with toasted almonds.

Quick'n Spicy Turkey Meat Loaf

So simple! This sauce is also yummy with chicken, fish, burgers or meatballs, or serve it over rice.

14   oz. (398 ml) can jellied cranberry sauce
1¾   c. bottled salsa (440 ml jar)
3   tbsp. brown (or granulated) sugar
1   lb. (500 g) lean ground turkey breast
⅓   c. quick-cooking oats (or matzo meal)
Dash of salt & pepper

1. Preheat oven to 400°F. Melt cranberry sauce in a saucepan on medium heat. (Or microwave on HIGH for 3 minutes, until melted.) Stir well. Mix in salsa and brown sugar. Use half of sauce for this recipe. (Leftover sauce keeps for 10 days in the fridge or can be frozen.) In a bowl, combine ground turkey with ½ cup of sauce, oats and seasonings; mix lightly. Shape into a loaf and place in a sprayed oblong casserole or loaf pan. Pour 1 cup of sauce over the top of the loaf. Bake uncovered at 400°F for 45 minutes.

Yield: 4 to 5 servings. Reheats and/or freezes well.

Turkey Time!

- A 10- to 12-pound turkey (4.5 to 5.5 kg) will serve 10 to 12, plus leftovers for salads and sandwiches. You will have about 6 pounds of cooked turkey meat. Use the turkey carcass to make soup.
- A 4 oz. serving of roasted skinless turkey breast contains 153 calories, 0.8 g fat (0.3 saturated) and 94 mg cholesterol. The dark meat contains 212 calories and 8.2 g fat (2.7 g saturated)!
- If turkey is frozen, thaw it in its original plastic wrapper in the refrigerator. Allow 5 to 6 hours per pound (10 to 12 hours per kg). Defrost it on a tray to catch any drippings.
- To thaw turkey in cold water, immerse it completely, changing water from time to time. Allow 1 hour per pound/2 hours per kg.
- Rinse turkey thoroughly inside and out. Remove neck and giblets. Season turkey at least a day in advance for best flavor. Refrigerate covered until ready to cook.
- To roast a whole turkey, calculate 18–20 minutes per lb/500 g at 325°F. A 10–12-pound turkey takes about 3–3$\frac{1}{2}$ hours to cook. If turkey is stuffed, add 5 to 10 minutes more per pound.
- "Check the chick" by inserting a meat thermometer into thickest part of the thigh, not touching bone. When turkey is done, juices should run clear when turkey is pierced; the drumstick should move easily. A meat thermometer should read 180°F if turkey is stuffed, or 170°F if unstuffed. Stuffing temperature should be at least 165°F.
- Don't leave cooked turkey or stuffing at room temperature more than 2 hours. Chill that chick!

---

283 calories per serving, 1.4 g fat (0.3 g saturated), 82 mg cholesterol, 32 g protein, 36 g carbohydrate, 218 mg sodium, 450 mg potassium, 2 mg iron, 2 g fiber, 48 mg calcium.

- **Turkey mixture** can be made into patties or mini loaves. Baking time will be about 25 minutes.
- **Serve with rice or potatoes** and steamed broccoli.

Rozie's Freeze with Ease Turkey Chili

3 onions, chopped
2 tbsp. olive oil, divided
2 c. peppers, chopped (use a mixture of red, green & yellow peppers)
2 c. sliced mushrooms
3–4 cloves garlic, crushed
3 lb. minced turkey (preferably turkey breast)
19 oz. (540 ml) can red kidney beans
19 oz. (540 ml) can white beans
28 oz. can (796 ml) puréed Italian tomatoes
3 c. tomato sauce
2 5$\frac{1}{2}$ oz. cans (156 ml) tomato paste
19 oz. (540 ml) can tomato juice
Salt & pepper, to taste
2 tbsp. chili powder (or to taste)
1 tsp. each basil & oregano (or to taste)

1. Spray a large pot with non-stick spray. Heat 1 tablespoon oil on medium heat. Add onions and sauté for 5 to 7 minutes. Add peppers and mushrooms; sauté 5 minutes longer, until tender. Add a little water if veggies begin to stick or burn. Remove veggies from pot and set aside. Heat remaining oil. Add turkey and brown on medium high heat, stirring often. Rinse and drain beans. Add with remaining ingredients to pot. Simmer uncovered for 1 hour, stirring occasionally. Adjust seasonings to taste.

Yield: 15 servings. Reheats and/or freezes well. Freeze in meal-sized batches. Serve over pasta or rice.

285 calories per serving, 3.3 g fat (0.6 g saturated), 66 mg cholesterol, 32 g protein, 34 g carbohydrate, 474 mg sodium, 1164 mg potassium, 4 mg iron, 9 g fiber, 68 mg calcium.

• **If using cooked turkey**, add to chili during last 15 minutes of cooking.

Sweet & Sour Stuffed Peppers

Sheila Denton suggested adding honey and lemon juice to the sauce. A grated apple can be added.

6	peppers (green &/or red)
1½ lb. (750 g)	lean ground turkey breast
2	egg whites (or 1 egg)
1	onion, minced
½ tsp.	salt
¼ tsp.	pepper
½ tsp.	dried basil
½ c.	uncooked rice
2 c.	tomato sauce
¼ c.	honey
¼ c.	lemon juice
1	bay leaf

1. Cut tops off the peppers; carefully remove seeds and cores. Bring a large pot of water to a boil. Add peppers and simmer for 5 minutes, until softened. Drain well. Meanwhile, combine ground turkey with egg whites, onion, seasonings and rice.
2. Combine tomato sauce, honey, lemon juice and bay leaf in a large pot; bring to a boil. Add ½ cup of sauce to the turkey mixture. Stuff the peppers and place them in a single layer in the pot. Reduce heat and simmer covered for 1½ to 2 hours, basting occasionally. Discard bay leaf.

Yield: 6 servings. These reheat and/or freeze well.

291 calories per serving, 1.2 g fat (0.3 g saturated), 70 mg cholesterol, 32 g protein, 38 g carbohydrate, 784 mg sodium, 838 mg potassium, 3 mg iron, 3 g fiber, 44 mg calcium.

Glazed Roast Turkey

If you love stuffing but want to avoid the extra fat, bake it separately in a covered casserole to prevent it from absorbing the fatty drippings from the turkey.

Turkey:

10–12 lb. turkey (4.5 to 5.5 kg)	
3	oranges
Salt & pepper, to taste	
3	cloves garlic, crushed
2 tsp.	dried basil
2 tsp.	dried thyme

Glaze:

2 tsp.	olive oil
3 tbsp.	Dijon mustard
3 tbsp.	honey
3 tbsp.	apricot jam or glaze
2 tbsp.	orange liqueur (e.g. Sabra)

1. Remove giblets from turkey. Rinse turkey inside and out and pat dry. Squeeze juice from two of the oranges over turkey, both inside and out. Rub with garlic and sprinkle with seasonings. Slice the remaining orange and place slices under the turkey skin to keep turkey moist during cooking. (Turkey can be prepared in advance up to this point and refrigerated covered for up to 2 days.)

2. Preheat oven to 325°F. Place turkey breast side down on a rack in a roasting pan. Pour ½ cup of water into the pan. Cover turkey loosely with foil, leaving the ends open. Roast turkey for 3 hours. While turkey is roasting, prepare glaze. Heat oil, mustard, honey and jam in a small saucepan until hot. Remove from heat and stir in orange liqueur. Uncover turkey, turn it breast side up and brush with glaze. Roast uncovered about 30 to 60 minutes longer, until golden, basting with glaze occasionally. When done, a meat thermometer should register 170°F.

3. Transfer turkey to a cutting board or serving platter and cover with foil. Let stand for 20 minutes for easier carving. Remove skin and discard. Serve turkey with Homemade Cranberry Sauce (p. 110).

Yield: Ten 4-oz. servings, plus leftovers. Leftover turkey can be refrigerated or frozen.

253 calories per 4 oz. serving, 7 g fat (2 g saturated), 86 mg cholesterol, 34 g protein, 11 g carbohydrate, 196 mg sodium, 367 mg potassium, 3 mg iron, trace fiber, 48 mg calcium.

- **The Right Stuff:** Prepare stuffing in advance and refrigerate it separately. If you insist on cooking your turkey with stuffing (that's the chubby chick method!) stuff it just before cooking. Stuffing must be cooked until it reaches 165°F on a meat thermometer. To store leftovers, remove stuffing from turkey and wrap separately.
- **Serve turkey with High-Fiber Turkey Stuffing** (p. 182), Glazed Sweet Potatoes (p. 262) and Teriyaki Asparagus (p. 246), doubling the recipe for the sweet potatoes and asparagus.
- **Passover Tip!** Excellent with Company Stuffed Spuds (p. 261), Honey-Glazed Carrots (p. 403) and Passover Matzo Stuffing (p. 183). To glaze the turkey for Passover, substitute ketchup or salsa for mustard.

High-Fiber Turkey Stuffing

1–2 tbsp. olive oil
2   onions, chopped
3   stalks celery, chopped
2   c. mushrooms, sliced
3   carrots, grated
10 slices of rye or multi-grain bread
2   apples, cored, peeled & chopped
Salt & pepper, to taste
2   tbsp. fresh dill, chopped
2   tbsp. fresh basil, chopped (or 1 tsp. dried)
1   tbsp. fresh thyme (or 1 tsp. dried)
½–¾ c. chicken broth

1. Heat oil in a large, nonstick skillet. Sauté onions and celery until golden. Add mushrooms and carrots. Cook 5 minutes longer; remove from heat. Cut bread into cubes and add to skillet with remaining ingredients. Mix well. You will have enough for a 10- to 12-pound turkey. (Stuffing can be prepared up to 24 hours in advance and refrigerated, but don't add broth until just before cooking.) Remove excess fat from turkey neck and cavity. Stuff turkey loosely. Fold neck skin over and attach it with a skewer to the turkey. Cook turkey as per recipe directions, allowing 25 to 30 minutes per pound.

Yield: 10 servings. Reheats well. Freezing not recommended.

132 calories per serving, 2.6 g fat (0.7 g saturated), 0 mg cholesterol, 4 g protein, 24 g carbohydrate, 245 mg sodium, 182 mg potassium, 2 mg iron, 3 g fiber, 43 mg calcium.

- **Passover Matzo Stuffing:** Substitute 6 pieces soaked, drained matzo for the bread.
- **Skinnier Stuffing:** Bake stuffing separately in a covered greased casserole at 325°F for 1 hour.
- **Stuffin' Muffins:** Bake stuffing in sprayed muffin tins at 350°F for 25 minutes, until crispy.

Adele's Super Turkey Stuffing

1　large onion, chopped
2　stalks celery (about 1 c. chopped)
2　tsp. oil
2　cloves garlic, crushed (optional)
1　c. grated carrot
2　c. bread crumbs
1　c. rolled oats
1　c. cream of wheat
1　egg plus warm water to moisten mixture
Salt, pepper & paprika, to taste

1. Sauté onion, celery and garlic in oil until golden. Combine all ingredients in a mixing bowl, adding enough water to moisten the mixture without making it soggy. Use as a stuffing for turkey.

Yield: 10 servings. Leftover stuffing can be frozen.

208 calories per serving, 3.4 g fat (0.6 g saturated), 21 mg cholesterol, 7 g protein, 37 g carbohydrate, 206 mg sodium, 185 mg potassium, 7 mg iron, 3 g fiber, 90 mg calcium.

- **Belle's Chicken Stuffing:** Omit cream of wheat and add only ¼ cup bread crumbs and ½ cup rolled oats. Add ½ cup crushed cornflakes and 2 tablespoons matzo meal.

Oven-Roasted Turkey Breast

An excellent alternative when you don't need a whole turkey.

1　turkey breast, bone in (about 3–3½ lb/1.5 kg)
Salt, to taste
Freshly ground pepper
3　cloves garlic, crushed
1　tbsp. olive oil
1　tbsp. Dijon mustard (optional)
2　tbsp. balsamic vinegar or lemon juice
2　tbsp. brown sugar or honey
1　tsp. dried basil
1　tsp. paprika
2　onions, sliced
½　c. water

1. Loosen skin from turkey, but don't remove it. Trim off fat. Season turkey breast under the skin with a little salt and pepper. In a small bowl, combine garlic with remaining ingredients except onions and water. Rub mixture over turkey breast (under the skin).

2. Place onions and water in the bottom of a lightly sprayed casserole. Place turkey, bone-side down, over onions. Cover and marinate for an hour at room temperature or 24 hours in the refrigerator.

3. Preheat oven to 350°F. Roast turkey uncovered for 50 to 60 minutes, basting every 20 minutes. Calculcate 18–20 minutes per pound as your cooking time. After cooking, let turkey stand for 10 to 15 minutes for easier carving. Discard skin. Slice turkey meat on an angle off the bone.

Yield: 8 servings. Cooked turkey may become dry if frozen and reheated.

202 calories per serving, 2.7 g fat (0.5 g saturated), 97 mg cholesterol, 36 g protein, 7 g carbohydrate, 64 mg sodium, 410 mg potassium, 2 mg iron, <1 g fiber, 29 mg calcium.

- **Serve with Homemade Cranberry Sauce** (p. 110). Delicious with Carrot "Noodles" (p. 251) and Potatoes Boulangère (p. 259). Use leftover turkey in salads, sandwiches or stir-fries.
- **Fat-Saving Secrets!** Cooking turkey with the skin on does not add more calories or fat. If desired, place thin slices of orange just under the skin to help keep turkey moist during cooking. Discard turkey skin and orange slices after cooking. Place casserole with cooking juices in the freezer for a short time so the fat will rise to the top and congeal, making it easy to remove.
- **Oven-Roasted Chicken Breasts:** Follow recipe for turkey breast, using 8 skinless, boneless chicken breasts. Reduce water to ¼ cup. Preheat oven to 400°F. Roast chicken uncovered for 20 to 25 minutes, basting occasionally. One serving contains 186 calories, 4.8 g fat (1.1 g saturated) and 73 mg cholesterol.
- **The above seasoning mixture** is also excellent for a rolled boneless turkey roast.

Cholent

Cholent is a savory stew full of fiber and calcium! It is traditionally served for Saturday (Shabbat) lunch. Jewish law prohibits kindling a fire on the Sabbath, so Cholent must be partially cooked before candle lighting takes place. The Hebrew word for Cholent is Hamin (cha-meen).

1½ c. beans (navy, kidney &/or lima)
6 large potatoes, peeled & cut in chunks
4 carrots, cut into chunks (optional)
2 onions, cut into chunks
2 lb. (1 kg) lean veal or beef cubes
½ c. barley, rinsed
3–4 cloves garlic, crushed
Salt & pepper, to taste
1 tsp. paprika
3–4 tbsp. ketchup
Water, as needed

1. The night before, combine beans in a large bowl and cover them with triple the amount of cold water. Let soak overnight. Drain and rinse beans, discarding soaking water.

2. Place potatoes, carrots and onions in a large, heavy-bottomed pot. Add meat, barley, garlic and drained beans. Add seasonings and ketchup. Fill the pot ¾-full with water and bring to a boil. Remove any scum that comes to the surface. Reduce heat, cover and simmer for at least an hour. Meat should be halfway cooked at this point.

3. Shortly before Shabbat, place pot on a "blech" (see below) or place in a 200°F oven overnight, without stirring. Water should cover all ingredients by at least 1 inch and the pot must be tightly covered. Serve Cholent for lunch on Saturday for the Sabbath. Its consistency should be thick but not dry.

Yield: 8 servings.

424 calories per serving, 7.2 g fat (2.7 g saturated), 92 mg cholesterol, 32 g protein, 58 g carbohydrate, 341 mg sodium, 982 mg potassium, 4 mg iron, 19 g fiber, 101 mg calcium.

- **Chicken Cholent:** Instead of veal or beef, use 4 to 6 chicken quarters (legs and thighs). Remove and discard skin. Trim off excess fat from chicken. Chickpeas can replace part of the beans.
- **For a Middle-Eastern flavor**, add 1 to 2 teaspoons ground cumin. If you don't have high cholesterol, rinse 4 raw eggs and carefully push them into simmering cholent at the beginning of Step 3.
- **A "blech" is a metal sheet** which is placed over a low flame on top of the stove. Cholent can also be cooked in a slow cooker. Combine ingredients and cook on high for 5 to 6 hours, then set it on low for Shabbat. (Or cook it on the stove for about an hour, then transfer it to the slow cooker to complete its cooking.) Place some foil between the heating element and the crockery pot to serve as a "blech."
- **Winter cholent cooks longer** than summer cholent, so adjust the water level as needed. Depending on the season, a cholent can cook for 15 to 19 hours.
- **The word "cholent"** has 7 letters, ending on the 7th letter, and is eaten on the 7th day, Shabbat!

Italian Style Veal Stew

Easy and tasty. Enjoy!

1   large onion, chopped
3–4 tbsp. water
2   cloves garlic, minced
2   stalks celery, chopped
1   green pepper, chopped
1   red pepper, chopped
1–2 tbsp. olive oil
2   lb. (1 kg) lean veal stewing meat, in 1" cubes
1   c. dry white wine
3   tbsp. tomato paste

1   tsp. salt
Freshly ground pepper
$\frac{1}{2}$ tsp. dried basil
$\frac{1}{2}$ tsp. dried oregano
4   carrots, scraped, trimmed & cut in chunks
5–6 potatoes, peeled & cut into chunks

1. Spray the bottom of a large heavy-bottomed pot with non-stick spray. Heat pan briefly on medium heat. Add onions and water. Cook onions on medium heat for 5 minutes, adding water if necessary to prevent sticking. Stir in garlic, celery and peppers; cook 5 minutes longer. Remove from pot.

2. Add oil to pot and heat briefly. Add meat and sear quickly on all sides. Add cooked veggies back to pan. Stir in wine, tomato paste and seasonings; cover and simmer for 45 minutes. Stir occasionally. Add carrots and potatoes; simmer $\frac{1}{2}$ hour longer, until tender. Season to taste.

Yield: 6 servings. Leftovers taste terrific the next day. If freezing, omit potatoes.

388 calories per serving, 11.1 g fat (3.7 g saturated), 123 mg cholesterol, 32 g protein, 34 g carbohydrate, 579 mg sodium, 993 mg potassium, 2 mg iron, 5 g fiber, 74 mg calcium.

- **No wine?** No problem! Use chicken or vegetable broth plus 2 tablespoons lemon juice to make 1 cup.
- **Leftover Tomato Paste?** Combine with an equal amount of water and use instead of tomato sauce in another recipe! Or drop tomato paste by tablespoons onto a pan lined with wax paper, cover and freeze. Add frozen blobs of tomato paste to recipes that call for a couple of tablespoons.
- **Variation:** Omit potatoes. Add 3 zucchini, cut up, during the last 20 minutes of cooking. Serve over fettucine, penne or rice.

- **Vegetarian Version:** Omit veal. Add extra vegetables (e.g., mushrooms, squash, turnip, sweet potato and/or zucchini chunks) along with carrots and potatoes. If desired, add canned beans or chickpeas, well rinsed and drained, during the last 10 minutes of cooking.
- **Seitan (a meat analog made from wheat)** can be used instead of veal. See recipe for Homemade Seitan (p. 238). Cut it into 1-inch chunks and increase cooking time to 1½ hours. Prepared seitan is available in some natural food shops.
- **Beef Bourguignon:** Substitute lean stewing beef for veal. In Step 1, use 2 cups sliced mushrooms instead of peppers. In Step 2, use red wine instead of white (or use ½ cup red wine and ½ cup beef broth). Instead of basil and oregano, add 1 teaspoon dried thyme and 1 bay leaf. Simmer covered for 2 hours. Add carrots and potatoes and simmer ½ hour longer. One serving contains 403 calories, 13 g fat (4.3 g saturated) and 94 mg cholesterol.

Perfect Pasta-Bilities, Great Grains

Perfect Pasta-Bilities

- Pasta has become extremely popular because it is so quick to prepare, requires little fuss or muss, and can be made with just a few simple ingredients from your pantry or freezer.
- The main reason pasta has a bad reputation is due to portion size. Many people eat a heaping plate, thinking sky-high is the limit! Half a cup of cooked pasta is equivalent to 1 starchy choice, the same as a slice of bread. Most people eat 1½ to 2 cups pasta, equal to 3 or 4 slices of bread!
- Another reason many people gain weight from pasta is because of the fat that's added to the sauce! One tablespoon of oil (including olive oil) contains 14 grams of fat. Many recipes contain at least 2 or 3 tablespoons of oil (or more) per serving, while many pasta sauces are loaded with butter and cream (e.g. Alfredo sauce).
- Moderation is the key. Have a bowl of soup and side salad (using a guilt-free dressing) along with your pasta and enjoy your meal without the guilt trip.
- Good news! Research indicates that pasta has a significantly lower glycemic index on bread, thereby having less of an impact on blood sugar. People who are carb-sensitive can enjoy pasta in moderation, but should probably minimize their consumption of bread, especially white bread.
- Experiment with different pastas and sauces to experience a quick trip around the world, without leaving the comfort of your home.
- It's fun to use different shapes. Try shells, wagon wheels, bow ties, orzo, traditional or whole grain spaghetti, fettucine or angel hair pasta. Bulk stores have a wonderful selection, from spicy penne to spinach linguine, plus many pastas made from a variety of grains (e.g., Chinese cellophane noodles made from mung beans, soba noodles made from buckwheat, rice noodles, quinoa spirals, vegetable shells). Experiment and enjoy.

- Read labels before you buy. Choose enriched high-quality pasta made exclusively with hard (durum) wheat as it has more protein and less starch. Another excellent choice is whole wheat pasta made from durum whole wheat semolina as it is low in fat and high in fiber. If you can't find the shape called for in a recipe, use a similar type.
- To cook pasta, use a large pot and 4 to 5 quarts (liters) of water for each pound (500 g) of pasta. Don't add oil to the cooking water, but add a little salt if you are not on a salt-restricted diet. The glycemic index of pasta is lower when cooked al dente, so it is digested more slowly, preventing spikes in blood sugar.
- Noodles swell slightly when cooked; spaghetti and macaroni double in volume. Allow about 2 ounces of dried pasta as a side dish, 3 to 4 ounces as a main dish. It depends on what other ingredients are combined with the pasta, as well as the rest of your menu.
- I used to rinse cooked pasta, but don't any more, except for recipes like noodle kugel. Rinsing removes the starch that helps the sauce cling to the pasta.
- Save a little of the cooking water and mix it together with the pasta and sauce. It will act as a thickener, preventing the pasta from sitting in a puddle of water on the serving plate!
- In a hurry? A simple tomato sauce is always a great choice, either store-bought or homemade. For variety, add a handful of leftovers, such as cooked chicken, fish or vegetables. Other ideas are tofu, canned beans or chickpeas, herbs, garlic, onions, sun-dried tomatoes, frozen vegetables (e.g., broccoli, cauliflower, snow peas), sautéed mushrooms and/or onions.
- Add a little olive oil to tomato sauce for a healthy

helping of lycopene, which has anti-cancer properties. Lycopene is more readily available from cooked tomatoes, not raw, and needs fat to be absorbed. Top with a sprinkling of freshly grated Parmesan cheese for a simple, delicious meal.

- Cooked pasta reheats beautifully in the microwave. Allow 1 minute on HIGH per cup of pasta.

- Most pasta dishes freeze well, so why not double the recipe? Pack leftovers in individual containers, seal tightly, label and freeze. You'll have frozen dinners that taste better (and are better for you!) than expensive packaged meals in the supermarket freezer.

- Timesaving Secret! Cook extra pasta, rinse, drain and cool. Freeze portions in ziploc bags. When needed, remove pasta from bag, place in a strainer and rinse with hot water. Ready to serve with your favorite sauce! Thanks to my well-organized assistant Elaine Kaplan for the super tip!

- If you eat out frequently, make friends with the restaurant manager! Phone ahead and explain your needs. Most restaurants are glad to help. They need customers who will be around (not round!) for a long time.

- So wise up and you'll lighten up! Cut the fat, add some veggies and don't pass up the pasta.

Pasta Primavera Lite-Style

The microwave makes this family favorite quick and easy to prepare. It's delicious hot or cold!

12 oz. pkg. (340 g) spiral pasta
1 onion, cut into 1" chunks
1 green & 1 red pepper, cut into 1" chunks
2 c. broccoli florets
1 c. sliced carrots
3–4 cloves garlic, minced
1 c. snow peas, tails removed
1 c. sliced zucchini
Skinny Parmesan Sauce (below) or Cheese
   Sauce (p. 190)

1. Cook pasta according to package directions. Drain and rinse well. Combine veggies in a covered microsafe casserole. Sprinkle with 2 tablespoons water. Microwave covered on HIGH for 6 to 7 minutes, until tender-crisp, stirring at half time.

2. Prepare sauce. Mix together with pasta and vegetables. Place in a sprayed 3-quart casserole. If desired, thin with a little skim milk. (Can be made ahead and refrigerated.) Cover with waxed or parchment paper. Microwave on HIGH for 5 minutes (10 minutes if refrigerated), until piping hot. (Alternately, bake uncovered at 350°F for 25 minutes.) Adjust seasonings to taste.

Yield: 6 to 8 servings. Freezes well. Delicious cold as a pasta salad! Just thin with a little skim milk.

326 calories per serving, 6 g fat (3.1 g saturated), 18 mg cholesterol, 15 g protein, 53 g carbohydrate, 246 mg sodium, 466 mg potassium, 3 mg iron, 5 g fiber, 262 mg calcium.

- **Tortellini Primavera:** Substitute cheese or spinach tortellini for spiral pasta.
- **Modern Macaroni & Cheese:** Use elbow macaroni and Cheese Sauce (p. 190). Vegetables are optional!
- **Time-Saving Secret!** Substitute 4 cups of frozen California mixed vegetables for fresh vegetables.

Skinny Parmesan Sauce

*This is an excellent light sauce to use
with pasta, vegetables or fish.*

2 tsp. butter, margarine or oil
3 tbsp. flour
1½ c. skim milk or vegetable broth
1 bay leaf, if desired
½ c. grated Parmesan cheese
2 tbsp. minced fresh basil (or 1 tsp. dried)
Salt & pepper, to taste
¼ tsp. grated nutmeg

1. Combine butter and flour in a 4 cup glass measuring cup. Microwave on HIGH for 30 seconds. Gradually whisk in milk or broth. Add bay leaf. Microwave on HIGH 4 to 4½ minutes, until bubbling, whisking twice during cooking. Discard bay leaf. Stir in cheese and seasonings.

Yield: about 2 cups sauce (8 servings of ¼ cup).

71 calories per ¼ cup serving, 3.6 g fat (2.2 g saturated), 13 mg cholesterol, 5 g protein, 5 g carbohydrate, 164 mg sodium, 83 mg potassium, trace iron, trace fiber, 158 mg calcium.

- **Lactose-Free Skinny Sauce:** Prepare Skinny Parmesan Sauce (p. 191) as directed but use non-dairy margarine or oil instead of butter. Use vegetable broth, soy milk or lactose-free milk as your liquid. Eliminate Parmesan cheese. Add a dash of basil and oregano to sauce.
- **Cheese Sauce:** Prepare Skinny Parmesan Sauce (p. 191) but omit nutmeg and Parmesan cheese. Stir ⅓ cup grated low-fat Cheddar cheese and ½ teaspoon dried mustard into sauce.

Quick 'n Easy Tomato Sauce (Vegetarian Spaghetti Sauce)

This sauce is a quick and easy substitute for the bottled version! To make it fat-free, omit olive oil.

28 oz. can (796 ml) tomatoes (stewed, whole or crushed)
5½ oz. can (156 ml) tomato paste
1 tsp. olive oil (preferably extra-virgin)
3 cloves garlic, crushed
Salt & pepper, to taste
¼ tsp. cayenne or red pepper flakes
½ tsp. oregano
1 tbsp. fresh basil, minced (or ½ tsp. dried)
½ tsp. sugar
1–2 tbsp. red or white wine, optional

1. Combine all ingredients in a large saucepan or covered microsafe casserole, breaking up tomatoes if necessary. To microwave, cook covered on HIGH for 10 minutes, stirring at half time. To cook conventionally, bring sauce to a boil, reduce heat and simmer covered for 20 to 25 minutes, stirring occasionally. Adjust seasonings to taste.

Yield: approximately 4 cups sauce. Reheats and/or freezes well. Freeze in 1 cup portions.

43 calories per ½ cup serving, 0.8 g fat (0.1 g saturated), 0 mg cholesterol, 2 g protein, 9 g carbohydrate, 27 mg sodium, 413 mg potassium, 1 mg iron, 2 g fiber, 40 mg calcium.

- **If you are sodium-sensitive,** use canned tomatoes and tomato paste without added salt.
- **Sun-Dried Tomato Sauce:** Soak ½ cup sun-dried tomatoes (dry pack) in boiling water for 10 minutes, until soft. Drain well; chop coarsely. Add to sauce ingredients and cook as directed.

- **Light 'n Easy Meat Sauce:** Sauté 1 onion, 1 green pepper and 2 cloves crushed garlic in 2 tablespoons water until tender (or microwave on HIGH for 3 minutes). Add 1 pound lean ground turkey and cook until it loses its pink color, stirring occasionally (about 5 to 6 minutes in the microwave). Add remaining ingredients and simmer covered for about 1 hour (or 20 minutes on HIGH in the microwave). Stir occasionally. Adjust seasonings to taste. Makes about 6 cups of sauce. Half a cup of sauce contains about 91 calories and 3.7 g fat (1 g saturated).
- **Fiber Facts:** Add a finely grated carrot to the sauce for fiber and natural sweetness. For additional fiber and a "meaty" texture, add 2 to 3 tablespoons of quick-cooking oats to the sauce 5 minutes before the end of cooking. If the cooked sauce is too thick, thin it with a little water or wine.
- **Most pasta sauces freeze beautifully.** Pack in 1 cup containers for convenience, leaving about half an inch space at the top to allow for expansion. When you need some sauce, place the frozen container under running water briefly. Pop out the contents and transfer them to a microsafe bowl. Thaw on HIGH power. (DEFROST takes too long!) Stir several times. One cup of sauce takes about 5 minutes to thaw and heat.

Roasted Tomato, Garlic & Basil Sauce

Roasting brings out the flavor of the vegetables. This sauce is simply the best!

2   dozen Italian plum tomatoes (3 lb./1.4 kg)
2   onions, peeled
1   large red pepper, seeded
6–8 cloves garlic, peeled
1–2 tbsp. extra-virgin olive oil

¼–½ c. fresh basil, to taste
Salt & pepper, to taste

1. Preheat oven to 400°F. Core tomatoes and cut in half lengthwise. Cut onions and red pepper into chunks. Arrange in a single layer on a non-stick baking sheet along with garlic. Drizzle lightly with oil. Roast uncovered at 400°F for 45 to 50 minutes, or until vegetables are soft and lightly browned.

2. Combine roasted vegetables with basil in the processor. (You may have to do this in 2 batches.) Process until fairly smooth. Season to taste with salt and pepper.

Yield: about 4 cups sauce (8 servings of about ½ cup). Reheats and/or freezes well. (It's a great idea to make a double or triple batch!)

78 calories per ½ cup serving, 2.5 g fat (0.4 g saturated), 0 mg cholesterol, 2 g protein, 14 g carbohydrate, 21 mg sodium, 548 mg potassium, 1 mg iron, 3 g fiber, 23 mg calcium.

- **You can roast other vegetables** along with the tomatoes. Try zucchini, eggplant, mushrooms and/or green pepper. Cut vegetables in chunks before cooking. Process the cooked vegetables with basil using quick on/offs, until desired texture is reached.

Spaghetti with Roasted Tomato, Garlic & Basil Sauce

Roasted Tomato, Garlic & Basil Sauce (above)
1   lb. (500 g) enriched spaghetti
Grated Parmesan cheese, optional

1. Prepare sauce and keep it warm. Cook pasta according to package directions. Drain, reserving about ½ cup of the cooking water in the pot. Do not rinse pasta. Return pasta to the pot. Add just enough of the sauce to lightly coat the pasta; mix well. Place on serving plates. Serve with additional sauce. Sprinkle with a little grated Parmesan cheese, if desired.

Yield: 6 servings. Reheats and/or freezes well, providing sauce was not previously frozen.

321 calories per serving, 2.8 g fat (0.4 g saturated), 0 mg cholesterol, 16 g protein, 60 g carbohydrate, 28 mg sodium, 610 mg potassium, 2 mg iron, 6 g fiber, 38 mg calcium.

High-Fiber Vegetarian Pasta Sauce

Adding mashed kidney beans or lentils to the sauce will thicken it, as well as increase the fiber content. No one will know! This is an excellent sauce to serve over spiral pasta such as fusilli or rotini. I also love to use it as a sauce for chicken breasts or tofu.

1	tbsp. olive or vegetable oil
1	large onion, chopped
1	green pepper, chopped
1	red pepper, chopped
4	cloves garlic, crushed
3	medium zucchini, chopped (1 lb./500 g)
2	c. mushrooms, sliced
4	large fresh tomatoes, roughly chopped
2	5½ oz. (156 ml) cans tomato paste
2⅔ c. water	
Salt, to taste	
½	tsp. pepper
1	tsp. dried basil
1	tsp. sugar
19	oz. (540 ml) can red kidney beans or lentils, rinsed, drained & mashed

• **Conventional Method:** Heat oil in a large, heavy-bottomed pot. Sauté onion and peppers for 5 minutes on medium heat. Add garlic, zucchini and mushrooms and sauté 5 minutes longer. Add tomatoes and cook 3 minutes more. Add remaining ingredients and mix well. Bring to a boil. Simmer partly covered for 20 to 25 minutes, stirring occasionally.

• **Microwave Method:** Combine oil, onions and peppers in a 3-quart microsafe casserole. Microwave covered on HIGH for 3 minutes. Add garlic, zucchini and mushrooms. Microwave 3 minutes more. Add tomatoes and microwave 3 minutes. Stir in remaining ingredients. Cover and microwave on HIGH for 20 minutes, stirring once or twice.

Yield: about 8 cups (8 servings). Freezes well.

171 calories per serving, 2.7 g fat (0.3 g saturated), 0 mg cholesterol, 8 g protein, 32 g carbohydrate, 44 mg sodium, 777 mg potassium, 2 mg iron, 10 g fiber, 38 mg calcium.

• **If you substitute** 28 oz. (796 ml) canned tomatoes for fresh tomatoes, decrease water to 1⅓ cups.
• **If you have trouble digesting legumes**, omit them. Instead, thicken sauce with oats, a super source of soluble fiber. Stir ⅓ cup of quick-cooking oats into sauce during the last 5 minutes of cooking.
• **If desired, purée all or part** of the cooked sauce in batches in the food processor.

Broccoli Pasta Quicky

Broccoli, Mushroom & Pepper Sauté (p. 250)
3 c. cooked pasta (e.g. ruffles, rotini or shells)

1. Toss broccoli mixture together with pasta and serve immediately. Makes 4 to 6 servings.

202 calories per serving, 3.4 g fat (0.5 g saturated), 0 mg cholesterol, 8 g protein, 36 g carbohydrate, 23 mg sodium, 400 mg potassium, 3 mg iron, 4 g fiber, 51 mg calcium.

Cheater's Hi-Fiber Pasta Sauce

Great when you're in a hurry. Just combine a can of lentils, a jar of sauce and a splash of wine. Yum!

1   c. cooked lentils (or canned, rinsed & well-drained)
1   jar vegetarian spaghetti sauce (about 3 c.)
¼   c. water
1–2 tbsp. red or white wine, if desired

1. Process lentils in your food processor until puréed. Add spaghetti sauce and process until well-mixed, scraping down sides of bowl as needed. Combine puréed mixture with water and wine (if using) in a large saucepan. Bring to a boil and simmer partially covered for 10 minutes (or microwave uncovered on HIGH for 10 minutes), stirring occasionally.

Yield: about 4 cups sauce. Freezes and/or reheats well.

101 calories per ½ cup serving, 3.7 g fat (0.5 g saturated), 0 mg cholesterol, 4 g protein, 15 g carbohydrate, 499 mg sodium, 521 mg potassium, 2 mg iron, 4 g fiber, 29 mg calcium.

- **If using this sauce** in dishes which require further cooking, don't bother precooking the sauce.
- **To use sauce over spaghetti,** simmer the sauce while pasta is cooking. If desired, stir some frozen mixed vegetables into the sauce for extra nutrients. They'll defrost and cook with the sauce!
- **If you have time,** sauté some onions, peppers, mushrooms and/or zucchini in a little olive oil or vegetable broth. Combine veggies with sauce ingredients and simmer uncovered for 10 minutes.

Simple 'n Spicy Spirals

Simply wonderful when you're in a hurry!

Simple Salsa (p. 62) or 3 c. bottled salsa (mild or medium)
1   lb. (500 g) spirals (or bow tie pasta)
1   c. grated low-fat mozzarella cheese

1. Prepare salsa as directed and heat it until piping hot. Meanwhile, cook pasta according to package directions. Drain pasta but do not rinse. Return pasta to the pot. Mix pasta with some of the hot salsa to lightly coat pasta; mix well. Place on serving plates. Top with additional salsa; sprinkle lightly with cheese. It will melt from the heat of the pasta and salsa. (Or heat it in the microwave on HIGH for about a minute.) Serve immediately. Perfect with a large garden salad.

Yield: 6 servings. Reheats and/or freezes well.

351 calories per serving, 4.5 g fat (2.2 g saturated), 10 mg cholesterol, 16 g protein, 60 g carbohydrate, 566 mg sodium, 158 mg potassium, 4 mg iron, 4 g fiber, 190 mg calcium.

• **Greek-Style Pasta:** Use crumbled feta cheese instead of mozzarella. Prepare Simple Salsa but don't heat it. Combine cooked, drained pasta, salsa and feta cheese. Serve at room temperature.

Best-O Pesto

See photo (P-2). Best-O Pesto is ready "presto" with the help of your processor! My original recipe had 83 calories and over 8 grams of fat per tablespoon. This lighter version has a fraction of the fat!

2 tbsp. pine nuts (or walnuts)
2 c. tightly packed fresh basil leaves
$\frac{1}{2}$ c. fresh parsley
4 cloves garlic, peeled
2–3 tbsp. grated Parmesan cheese
2 tbsp. olive oil (extra-virgin is best)
$\frac{1}{4}$ c. tomato juice or vegetable broth
Salt & pepper, to taste

1. Place nuts in a small skillet and brown over medium heat for 2 to 3 minutes. Wash basil and parsley; dry thoroughly. Start the processor and drop garlic through feed tube. Process until minced. Add nuts, basil, parsley and Parmesan cheese. Process until fine, about 15 seconds. Drizzle oil and juice through the feed tube while the machine is running. Process until blended. Season to taste.

Yield: 1 cup. Pesto keeps for 4 or 5 days in the refrigerator, or can be frozen for 2 months.

27 calories per tbsp., 2.4 g fat (0.5 g saturated), <1 mg cholesterol, <1 g protein, <1 g carbohydrate, 30 mg sodium, 52 mg potassium, trace iron, trace fiber, 23 mg calcium.

• **When basil is expensive,** use a combination of fresh basil and fresh spinach. It works perfectly!
• **Freeze pesto in ice cube trays.** Transfer them to a plastic bag and store in the freezer. Each cube contains 2 tablespoon pesto. Add a cube or two to your favorite pasta sauce, soup or vegetarian stew.
• **A couple of spoonfuls** of pesto added to pasta salad or vinaigrette dressing will enhance the flavor.

Sun-Dried Tomato Pesto

$\frac{1}{2}$ c. sun-dried tomatoes (dry-pack)
$\frac{1}{3}$ c. tightly packed fresh basil leaves
$\frac{1}{2}$ c. parsley
4–5 large cloves garlic
2 tbsp. finely ground almonds
3 tbsp. grated Parmesan cheese
2 tbsp. olive oil (preferably extra-virgin)
$\frac{1}{2}$ c. tomato juice

1. Cover sun-dried tomatoes with boiling water. Let stand for 20 minutes, until rehydrated. Drain well. Rinse basil and parsley; dry well. Start the processor and drop garlic through feed tube. Process until minced. Add sun-dried tomatoes, basil, parsley, almonds and Parmesan cheese. Process until fine, about 15 to 20 seconds. Add olive oil and tomato juice and process until well blended, scraping down sides of bowl as necessary.

Yield: about 1$\frac{1}{2}$ cups. Pesto will keep for 4 or 5 days in the refrigerator, or can be frozen for up to 2 months.

31 calories per tbsp., 2.2 g fat (0.4 g saturated), <1 mg cholesterol, 1 g protein, 2 g carbohydrate, 99 mg sodium, 130 mg potassium, <1 mg iron, <1 g fiber, 23 mg calcium.

Penne with Roasted Peppers & Sun-Dried Tomatoes

The tomato sauce is used to moisten the pasta and give it a hint of color.

1   pkg. (1 lb./500 g) penne or other pasta
1   c. jarred roasted red peppers (or 2 Roasted Red Peppers, p. 57), cut in strips
1/2 c. sun-dried tomatoes
2   medium onions, chopped (or cut in strips)
1   tbsp. olive oil
1   zucchini, sliced (optional)
3   cloves garlic, minced
1/3 c. fresh basil, finely chopped
1/4 c. grated Parmesan cheese
1 1/2–2 c. tomato sauce
Salt & pepper, to taste

1. Set a large pot of water up to boil for the pasta. Meanwhile, roast peppers as directed. Cut them into strips. Soak sun-dried tomatoes in boiling water for 10 to 15 minutes, until rehydrated. Drain and dry well; cut into strips.

2. Sauté onions in olive oil on medium heat for 3 to 4 minutes. Add zucchini and garlic; cook 3 to 4 minutes longer. If necessary, add a little water to prevent burning. Cook pasta in boiling salted water for 10 to 12 minutes, until al dente. Drain well. Combine all ingredients and mix well. Delicious hot or at room temperature.

Yield: 6 servings. Reheats and freezes well. If necessary, add a little extra tomato sauce when reheating.

343 calories per serving, 5.2 g fat (1.4 g saturated), 3 mg cholesterol, 13 g protein, 62 g carbohydrate, 683 mg sodium, 509 mg potassium, 4 mg iron, 5 g fiber, 100 mg calcium.

- **If using roasted peppers** from the jar, drain and rinse them thoroughly to remove excess sodium.
- **Chef's Short-Cut!** Instead of soaking the sun-dried tomatoes, add them along with the pasta to the boiling water. They will rehydrate by the time the pasta has cooked!
- **Pasta with Mushrooms, Roasted Peppers & Sun-Dried Tomatoes:** Soak 1/4 to 1/3 cup of dried exotic mushrooms (e.g. porcini, shiitaki) in boiling water to cover. (Soak them separately from the sun-dried tomatoes. The soaking liquid from mushrooms can be added to your favorite vegetable broth to enhance the flavor.) Add drained mushrooms to the onions along with zucchini and garlic; sauté for 3 or 4 minutes.
- **Pasta with Pesto:** Omit tomato sauce and Parmesan cheese. Add Pesto Alfredo Sauce (p. 199) to pasta mixture. This is lovely with bow tie pasta.

Penne Al Pesto Jardinière

The starchy cooking liquid binds with the cheese to thicken the sauce. So pretty with 3-color pasta!

1   lb. penne (ziti, fusilli or rotini can be used)
1   onion, halved & cut in strips
4   peppers, (green, red, yellow &/or orange), halved, seeded & cut in strips
2   zucchini, cut in strips
3   cloves garlic, crushed
1 1/2 tbsp. olive oil
3–4 tbsp. balsamic vinegar or lemon juice
Salt & pepper, to taste
1/4 c. grated Parmesan cheese
1/2 c. fresh basil, finely chopped
1 1/2–2 c. tomato sauce (bottled or homemade)
1   chopped tomato, to garnish
Parmesan cheese, to garnish

1. Preheat oven to 425°F. Prepare vegetables and place on a sprayed (or non-stick) baking sheet. Add garlic, olive oil and vinegar. Sprinkle lightly with salt and pepper and mix well. Roast vegetables uncovered at 425°F for 20 minutes, until nicely browned.

2. Meanwhile, bring a large pot of salted water to a boil. Cook pasta according to package directions, about 10 minutes, until al dente. Ladle out a little of the cooking liquid just before draining pasta. Drain pasta but do not rinse.

3. Return pasta to saucepan. Add Parmesan, basil and about ¼ cup of reserved cooking liquid; mix well. Add tomato sauce and roasted vegetables. Adjust seasonings to taste. Cook briefly, just until heated through. Garnish with diced tomato and sprinkle with a light dusting of Parmesan cheese, if desired. Great hot or at room temperature.

Yield: 8 main dish servings. Reheats well. If frozen, vegetables may lose some of their texture.

267 calories per serving, 4.6 g fat (1.1 g saturated), 3 mg cholesterol, 9 g protein, 48 g carbohydrate, 342 mg sodium, 434 mg potassium, 3 mg iron, 4 g fiber, 77 mg calcium.

• **Penne with Roasted Vegetable Purée:** In Step 2, reserve about a cup of the cooking liquid from pasta. In Step 3, process 2 cups of the roasted vegetables until smooth. Add ½ cup of reserved cooking liquid to thin the mixture; process briefly. (If necessary, add a little more liquid.) Stir purée into pasta along with remaining ingredients. (This is a great way to get kids to eat their veggies!)

Rotini with Dried Mushrooms & Chunky Vegetables

5	quarts water
½	c. dried mushrooms plus 1 c. water for soaking
1	lb. (500 g) rotini (spirals)
1	tbsp. olive oil
2	onions, cut into chunks
1	red pepper, cut into strips
1	yellow or green pepper, cut into strips
2–3	cloves garlic, sliced
3–4	tbsp. dry white wine
28	oz. can (796 ml) canned tomatoes
1	tsp. dried basil
¼	tsp. dried thyme
	Salt & pepper, to taste
½	c. grated Parmesan cheese, to garnish

1. Put water for the pasta up to boil. Soak mushrooms in 1 cup of hot water for 20 to 30 minutes. Drain well, reserving the soaking water. Chop mushrooms into ½-inch pieces.

2. Heat oil in a large, non-stick skillet. Add onions and peppers. Sauté for 5 minutes on medium high heat. Add garlic and mushrooms and cook for 3 or 4 minutes more. Stir in wine and cook until wine evaporates, 2 to 3 minutes more. Add canned tomatoes, soaking water from the mushrooms and seasonings. Break up tomatoes, bring to a boil and reduce heat. Simmer uncovered for 10 to 15 minutes, stirring occasionally.

3. Meanwhile, cook pasta according to package directions. Drain pasta but do not rinse; reserve a little of the cooking water. Combine cooking water with pasta and sauce; mix well. Adjust seasonings to taste. Sprinkle with grated cheese.

Yield: 6 to 8 servings. Reheats well.

359 calories per serving, 6.3 g fat (2.2 g saturated), 7 mg cholesterol, 14 g protein, 61 g carbohydrate, 368 mg sodium, 457 mg potassium, 4 mg iron, 5 g fiber, 184 mg calcium.

• **Variation:** Put pasta and sauce in a lightly greased casserole. Instead of Parmesan cheese, sprinkle with 1 cup grated low-fat mozzarella cheese. Bake uncovered at 350°F for 20 to 25 minutes, until bubbling and cheese has melted.

Vegetarian Pad Thai

So yummy! It was very difficult to slash the fat from the original recipe. This version is much lower in fat, but if you don't watch your portion size, you'll be calling this dish "padded thighs!"

Fish Sauce (see directions following the recipe)
2   tsp. Worcestershire sauce
3   tbsp. sugar
¼   c. fresh lime juice (from 3 or 4 limes)
10   oz. pkg. extra-firm silken tofu, cut in 1″ cubes (1% fat)
12   oz. flat rice noodles (or fettucine)
1   tbsp. canola oil
2–3 cloves garlic, crushed
6   green onions, sliced
1   c. red pepper strips
¼   tsp. red pepper flakes
3–4 tbsp. chopped peanuts, divided
2   c. bean sprouts
¼   c. fresh coriander/cilantro, minced (to garnish)
1   red chili pepper, seeded & minced (to garnish)

1. Prepare fish sauce as directed. Combine with Worcestershire sauce, sugar and lime juice in a bowl. Add tofu cubes and marinate for 1 hour at room temperature or up to 8 hours in the refrigerator. Drain, reserving marinade.

2. If using rice noodles, soak in 6 cups of hot water until soft, about 1 hour. Discard water. If using fettucine, cook according to package directions. Drain well. Set aside.

3. Assembly: Use a large non-stick wok or skillet. Spray lightly with non-stick spray. Heat oil. Add garlic, green onions and red pepper strips. Sauté for 2 to 3 minutes on medium-high heat. Add red pepper flakes, drained tofu and 1 tablespoon of peanuts. Stir-fry 2 to 3 minutes longer. Add bean sprouts, reserved marinade and drained noodles. Stir-fry until heated through. Garnish with remaining peanuts, coriander and chiles. Serve immediately.

Yield: 4 to 6 servings. Do not freeze.

499 calories per serving, 9 g fat (1.5 g saturated), 5 mg cholesterol, 19 g protein, 87 g carbohydrate, 536 mg sodium, 461 mg potassium, 4 mg iron, 2 g fiber, 92 mg calcium.

• **Fish Sauce:** Commercial fish sauce is usually made from shrimp, salt and water. It can be found in Oriental groceries, but it is not Kosher. An acceptable Kosher substitute can be made from 6 anchovy fillets, well-rinsed and drained. Mash together with 1 clove of crushed garlic and 1 tablespoon soy sauce. It works beautifully in this recipe.

Hi-Fiber Vegetarian Lasagna

For smaller families, make several smaller lasagnas in loaf pans and freeze them. So handy! Boil some extra lasagna noodles and make Crisp Lasagna Chips (p. 71).

4 c. High-Fiber Vegetarian Pasta Sauce (p. 193) (or Cheater's Hi-Fiber Pasta Sauce, p. 194)
9 lasagna noodles, cooked, drained and laid flat on towels
2 c. low-fat Ricotta or dry cottage cheese
1½ to 2 c. grated low-fat Mozzarella cheese
6 tbsp. grated Parmesan cheese

1. Place about ⅓ of the sauce in the bottom of a lightly greased or sprayed 9 x 13-inch casserole. Arrange 3 lasagna noodles in a single layer over sauce. Top with half of the Ricotta, ⅓ of the mozzarella and half of the Parmesan. Repeat with sauce, noodles and cheese. Top with noodles, sauce and mozzarella cheese. (Can be made in advance up to this point and refrigerated or frozen. Thaw before cooking.) Bake uncovered in a preheated 375°F oven for 40 to 45 minutes. Let stand for 10 to 15 minutes for easier cutting.

Yield: 10 to 12 servings. Freezes and/or reheats well.

271 calories per serving, 9.3 g fat (5.2 g saturated), 27 mg cholesterol, 18 g protein, 30 g carbohydrate, 239 mg sodium, 408 mg potassium, 2 mg iron, 5 g fiber, 328 mg calcium.

- **Fresh lasagna noodles** or no-cook packaged noodles can be used. No need to precook them!
- **Dry cottage cheese** is more difficult to spread than ricotta, so thin it with a few drops of skim milk. If using creamed cottage cheese, purée it in the processor for 2 to 3 minutes, until smooth.
- **Don't fuss too much** about spreading the cheese evenly. Drop it by spoonfuls over the noodles. Don't worry if there are any spaces. The cheese will spread during baking.
- **Variation:** Instead of ricotta cheese, substitute So-Low Alfredo Sauce (see following recipe).

So-Low Alfredo Sauce

An excellent source of calcium.

2 tbsp. cornstarch
1¾ c. skim milk
3 cloves garlic, crushed
⅓ c. grated Parmesan cheese
3–4 tbsp. light cream cheese
Salt & pepper, to taste
2–3 tbsp. minced fresh basil (or 1 tsp. dried)
¼ tsp. nutmeg

1. Blend cornstarch with milk until smooth. Add garlic and microwave on HIGH for 4 to 5 minutes, until thick, stirring 2 or 3 times. Whisk in remaining ingredients until smooth. Makes 2 cups sauce.

56 calories per ¼ cup serving, 2.5 g fat (1.5 g saturated), 10 mg cholesterol, 4 g protein, 4 g carbohydrate, 117 mg sodium, 91 mg potassium, trace iron, trace fiber, 125 mg calcium.

- **Pesto Alfredo Sauce:** Add 3 tablespoons Best-O Pesto (p. 195). Great over fettucine.

Many Color Vegetable Lasagna

There are several steps to this excellent recipe, but it's really quite easy to make. It's a favorite of my catering clients. So many vegetables, so many vitamins! Packed with potassium, calcium and fiber.

4 c. tomato sauce (homemade or bottled)
So-Low Alfredo Sauce (p. 199)
9 lasagna noodles, cooked, drained & laid flat on towels
2 onions, sliced
3 or 4 cloves garlic, crushed
2 green & 2 red peppers, cut into strips

2   zucchini, sliced on an angle ½″ thick
2   c. mushrooms, sliced
3   c. frozen California mixed vegetables (or 1 cup each of fresh broccoli, cauliflower & carrots, cut up)
2   c. grated low-fat mozzarella cheese

1. Cook sauces as directed. (They can be prepared in advance and refrigerated for up to 2 days.) Prepare lasagna noodles.

2. In a large microwave casserole or glass bowl, combine onions, garlic and peppers. Cover and microwave on HIGH for 5 minutes, until tender-crisp. Add zucchini and mushrooms and microwave covered on HIGH 3 to 4 minutes longer. (Alternately, sauté onions, garlic and peppers in a little oil in a non-stick skillet until golden. Add zucchini and mushrooms and cook 5 minutes longer.)

3. In another microwave casserole or glass bowl, microwave frozen mixed vegetables covered on HIGH for 5 to 7 minutes, until tender crisp. (If using fresh vegetables, sprinkle them with a little water before microwaving. Alternately, cook veggies in a saucepan for 8 minutes.) Combine all the vegetables and mix gently.

4. Place ⅓ of the tomato sauce in the bottom of a lightly greased or sprayed 9 x 13-inch casserole. Arrange 3 lasagna noodles in a single layer over sauce. Top with half of the Alfredo Sauce. Arrange half the vegetables over the sauce. Sprinkle lightly with ⅔ cup of cheese. Repeat once more. Top with remaining noodles and tomato sauce. Sprinkle with cheese. (Can be made in advance up to this point and refrigerated.)

5. Bake uncovered in a preheated 375°F oven for 40 to 45 minutes. Let stand for 10 to 15 minutes for easier cutting.

Yield: 12 servings. Freezes and/or reheats well.

275 calories per serving, 7.3 g fat (4 g saturated), 21 mg cholesterol, 16 g protein, 39 g carbohydrate, 268 mg sodium, 727 mg potassium, 3 mg iron, 6 g fiber, 339 mg calcium.

• **Quick'n Easy Tomato Sauce** (p. 191) is delicious in this recipe!

Pasta Pinwheels

If you use large sheets of fresh lasagna (regular, spinach or whole-wheat), cook pasta for 5 minutes..

1   lb. lasagna noodles
2   slices whole-wheat bread
1   clove garlic, crushed
10 oz. pkg. (300 g) frozen spinach, cooked, drained & squeezed dry
1   lb. (500 g) part-skim ricotta or cottage cheese
½   c. grated Parmesan cheese
2   tbsp. fresh basil, minced (or 1 tsp. dried)
¼   c. skim milk
Dash of salt & pepper
2   c. vegetarian spaghetti sauce (bottled or homemade)
¾   c. grated low-fat mozzarella cheese

1. Cook lasagna noodles according to package directions. Drain and rinse well. Lay flat on clean towels and pat dry.

2. Meanwhile, prepare the filling. In the food processor, process bread until soft crumbs are formed, about 20 seconds. Add spinach, ricotta and Parmesan cheeses, basil, milk, salt and pepper. Mix well. Pour half of the spaghetti sauce into the bottom of a lightly sprayed 9 x 13-inch baking dish.

3. Cut noodles in half crosswise. (Omit this step if using large sheets of fresh pasta.) Spread a heaping tablespoon of filling in a thin layer on each noodle, spreading it right to the edges. Roll up tightly to make a pinwheel. Repeat with remaining noodles and filling. Arrange pinwheels cut-side up in baking dish. Pour remaining sauce over pinwheels. Sprinkle lightly with mozzarella cheese. (Can be prepared in advance and refrigerated for up to 24 hours. They can be frozen; defrost them overnight in the refrigerator before continuing with the recipe.)

4. Preheat oven to 375°F. Bake pasta for 25 to 30 minutes, until golden and bubbling.

Yield: 24 pinwheels. Allow 2 to 3 pinwheels per serving. Freezes and/or reheats well.

108 calories per pinwheel, 2.5 g fat (1.4 g saturated), 8 mg cholesterol, 6 g protein, 15 g carbohydrate, 83 mg sodium, 75 mg potassium, <1 mg iron, 1 g fiber, 100 mg calcium.

• **Stuffed Pasta Shells:** Cook 2 dozen jumbo pasta shells in boiling salted water until al dente. Drain and rinse well. Blot very dry with towels. Prepare stuffing as directed above and stuff the shells. Pour half of sauce in the bottom of a baking dish. Arrange shells in dish, top with sauce and sprinkle with cheese. Bake for 25 to 30 minutes at 375°F.

Cookie's Honey Mustard Chicken Pasta

My sister shared this quick and easy pasta dish that's sure to please! If company's coming, just add another chicken breast or two and a few more veggies. Eat it hot, eat it cold, even eat it two days old!

12 oz. (340 g) pkg. 3-color rotini or shells
1 red onion, sliced
2 c. cauliflower florets
2 c. broccoli florets
4 carrots, thinly sliced on the diagonal
1 red & 1 green pepper, cut in strips
2 c. mushrooms, sliced
2 skinless, boneless chicken breasts
2 tsp. canola oil
2–3 cloves garlic, crushed
½ c. bottled low-fat honey mustard salad dressing or Honey Mustard Dressing (p. 284)
2 tbsp. cornstarch
1½ c. chicken broth (at room temperature)
Salt & pepper, to taste
1 tsp. dried basil

1. Cook pasta according to package directions. Drain and rinse well. While pasta is cooking, prepare vegetables. In a large microsafe bowl, combine onion, cauliflower, broccoli, carrots, peppers and mushrooms. Sprinkle lightly with a little water. Microwave covered on HIGH for 5 to 6 minutes, until tender-crisp. Do not overcook.

2. Trim fat from chicken; cut into long strips. In a large non-stick skillet or wok, stir-fry chicken in oil on medium-high heat until no pink remains, about 2 to 3 minutes. Add garlic and stir-fry 30 seconds. Add microwaved vegetables and stir-fry 2 minutes longer. Add salad dressing and mix well.

Dissolve cornstarch in broth. Add broth to chicken and bring to a boil. Cook until thickened, stirring well. Add pasta and seasonings. Cook 2 or 3 minutes longer, until heated through.

Yield: 6 servings. Delicious hot or cold.

379 calories per serving, 7.3 g fat (1 g saturated), 24 mg cholesterol, 20 g protein, 60 g carbohydrate, 196 mg sodium, 471 mg potassium, 4 mg iron, 6 g fiber, 69 mg calcium.

- **Timesaving Tip:** Substitute 4 cups of frozen California mixed vegetables instead of cauliflower, broccoli and carrots. Microwave onion and peppers covered on HIGH for 3 minutes. Add frozen vegetables and microwave covered 4 or 5 minutes longer.

Peanut Butter Pasta with Chicken

I love to serve this chilled as part of a buffet! Four times the recipe will serve 24 people.

³/₄ c. Peanut Butter Sauce (p. 108)
2   boneless, skinless chicken breasts (¹/₂ lb./250 g)
1   clove garlic, minced
1   tbsp. soy sauce
2   tsp. lemon juice
1   lb. (454 g) fettucine or 3-color rotini
6   green onions, chopped
1   red pepper, chopped
¹/₂   of a green pepper, chopped
1   tsp. Oriental sesame oil, optional

1. Preheat oven to 450°F. Prepare Peanut Butter Sauce as directed; measure ³/₄ cup. Trim excess fat from chicken. Cut chicken into thin strips. Marinate it in garlic, soy sauce and lemon juice for

20 minutes. Spray a foil-lined baking sheet with non-stick spray. Arrange chicken in a single layer on baking sheet and bake at 450°F for 10 to 12 minutes, until no longer pink.

2. Meanwhile, cook pasta according to package directions. Reserve about ³/₄ cup of the cooking water. Drain pasta well but do not rinse. Combine reserved water with remaining ingredients and mix thoroughly. Delicious hot or cold. If desired, garnish with additional minced green onions and red peppers at serving time.

Yield: 6 servings. Do not freeze. Leftovers keep about 2 days in the refrigerator (if you have any)!

483 calories per serving, 8.3 g fat (1.8 g saturated), 24 mg cholesterol, 30 g protein, 72 g carbohydrate, 490 mg sodium, 332 mg potassium, 2 mg iron, 6 g fiber, 43 mg calcium.

Fasta Pasta

This is a great last-minute dish to make when you're rushed for time.

2   c. rotini or macaroni
1   onion, chopped
2   tsp. canola oil
1   lb. extra-lean ground turkey, chicken or beef
2¹/₂ c. bottled marinara/spaghetti sauce
¹/₂   c. water
3   c. frozen mixed vegetables
Salt, pepper & garlic powder, to taste

1. Cook pasta in boiling salted water according to package directions. Drain and rinse; set aside. Meanwhile, spray a large pot with non-stick spray. Sauté onion briefly in oil. Add meat and brown for

6 to 8 minutes, stirring often. Remove excess fat from browned meat mixture by placing it in a fine strainer and rinsing it quickly under running water. Return meat to pan along with tomato sauce, water and frozen vegetables. Cover and simmer for 15 minutes, stirring occasionally. Stir in pasta and cook 5 minutes longer, until heated through. Season to taste.

Yield: 6 servings. Leftovers will keep for a day or 2 in the refrigerator or can be frozen.

357 calories per serving, 7 g fat (0.9 g saturated), 55 mg cholesterol, 28 g protein, 48 g carbohydrate, 615 mg sodium, 877 mg potassium, 4 mg iron, 8 g fiber, 68 mg calcium.

Fettucine with Smoked Salmon

A little smoked salmon goes a long way when mixed with this luscious sauce. I love it with a mixture of green and white pasta. It's so pretty! Because it's high in calories, save this for special occasions.

So-Low Alfredo Sauce (p. 199)
1   lb. fettucine
¹/₂   lb. smoked salmon, cut into thin strips
2   tbsp. fresh dill, minced
2   tbsp. fresh basil, minced
Salt & freshly ground pepper, to taste
4   green onions, minced
Minced dill & green onions, to garnish

1. Prepare sauce as directed and keep it warm (or reheat it at serving time). Cook fettucine in boiling salted water until al dente. Drain but do not rinse. Combine pasta with remaining ingredients and mix gently. Season to taste and serve immediately. If desired, garnish with additional dill and onions.

Yield: 6 servings. Do not freeze. Serve with crusty bread and steamed broccoli or a garden salad.

456 calories per serving, 5.8 g fat (2.8 g saturated), 23 mg cholesterol, 31 g protein, 68 g carbohydrate, 942 mg sodium, 313 mg potassium, 2 mg iron, 4 g fiber, 219 mg calcium.

Homemade Cheese & Spinach Tortelloni

These are jumbo tortellini, alias Italian kreplach!

10   oz. pkg. (300 g) frozen chopped spinach, cooked, drained & squeezed dry
1   lb. (500 g) part-skim ricotta cheese
3   tbsp. grated Parmesan cheese
2   tbsp. fresh basil, minced (or 1 tsp. dried)
¹/₄   c. skim milk
Dash of salt & pepper
4   dozen wonton wrappers

1. Combine spinach, cheeses, basil, milk, salt and pepper. Mix well. Keep wonton wrappers covered to prevent them from drying out. Put a wonton wrapper on a work surface. Place a rounded spoonful of filling in the centre of each square. Moisten edges of dough with water. Fold in half and make a triangle. Seal completely by pinching edges together firmly. Join 2 points together to form a little "purse." Repeat with remaining dough and filling. (Can be prepared in advance and refrigerated covered for 24 hours, or frozen.)

2. Bring a large pot of salted water to a boil. Add tortelloni to pot, bring back to a boil and cook uncovered for 2 to 3 minutes (or 5 to 6 minutes if frozen). Remove with a slotted spoon and drain well. Serve with tomato sauce.

Yield: 4 dozen (about 8 servings). Freeze before or after cooking.

71 calories per tortelloni (without sauce), 0.4 g fat (0.1 g saturated), 3 mg cholesterol, 4 g protein, 13 g carbohydrate, 162 mg sodium, 38 mg potassium, <1 mg iron, <1 g fiber, 28 mg calcium.

Cheater's Pasta

This quick and easy recipe comes from Sharon Druker, a former student with a very busy lifestyle!

- 1 lb. (454 g) spaghetti or linguini
- 28 oz. can (796 mL) Italian chopped seasoned tomatoes
- 1 tsp. chopped garlic in oil
- $^1/_2$ tsp. dried basil (to taste)
- $^1/_2$ tsp. dried oregano (to taste)
- $6^1/_2$ oz. can (184 g) water-packed tuna, drained & flaked
- 1 to 2 tsp. capers
- $^1/_4$ to $^1/_2$ c. sliced black olives, optional

1. Cook pasta according to package directions. Drain but do not rinse. While pasta is cooking, put canned tomatoes, garlic and oil in a large pot. Add seasonings and heat to simmering. Add tuna and capers. Simmer just until heated through. Place pasta on serving plates and top with sauce. Garnish with olives if desired.

Yield: 6 servings. Do not freeze.

410 calories per serving, 0.7 g fat (0.1 g saturated), 9 mg cholesterol, 27 g protein, 71 g carbohydrate, 437 mg sodium, 159 mg potassium, 3 mg iron, 5 g fiber, 74 mg calcium.

Mexican Pasta with Beans

Full of fiber, full of beans, full of flavor!

- 2 tsp. olive oil
- 1 onion, chopped
- 2 cloves garlic, crushed
- 1 green or red pepper, chopped
- 1 jalapeño or chili pepper, seeded & minced
- 19 oz/540 mL can kidney or black beans, rinsed & drained
- 28 oz. can (796 mL) diced tomatoes
- Salt & pepper, to taste
- $^1/_2$ tsp. oregano
- 1 lb. spaghetti, penne or rotini
- $^1/_4$ c. chopped coriander (cilantro)
- $^1/_4$ c. chopped green onions, to garnish
- Grated low-fat cheddar cheese, optional

1. Heat oil in a non-stick skillet. Sauté onion, garlic and peppers for 5 minutes. Add beans, tomatoes, salt, pepper and oregano. Simmer uncovered for 10 to 15 minutes, stirring occasionally. Meanwhile, cook pasta according to package directions. Drain well but do not rinse, reserving $^1/_2$ to $^3/_4$ cup of the cooking water. Mix pasta with sauce and reserved cooking water. Serve on hot plates. Garnish with coriander and green onions. If desired, sprinkle lightly with grated cheese.

Yield: 6 servings. Sauce can be frozen.

456 calories per serving, 2.4 g fat (0.3 g saturated), 0 mg cholesterol, 24 g protein, 83 g carbohydrate, 12 mg sodium, 149 mg potassium, 2 mg iron, 12 g fiber, 31 mg calcium.

- **Wear rubber gloves** or put plastic bags on your hands when handling hot peppers. The smaller the pepper, the hotter it is. Don't rub your eyes or touch sensitive body parts after handling peppers.

Couscous & Mushroom Casserole

Many people think that couscous is a grain, but it is actually a pasta made from hard durum wheat. The bran and germ are stripped from the wheat berry, then the endosperm (semolina) is ground, steamed and dried to form tiny grains. There is also a delicious whole-wheat couscous available, with its natural bran layers intact.

1	c. couscous
2	c. water, chicken or vegetable broth
6	green onions, chopped
1	red &/or green pepper, chopped
3	cloves garlic, minced
2	tsp. olive or canola oil
1	c. mushrooms, sliced
1	c. canned chickpeas or black-eyed peas, drained & well-rinsed
1	medium carrot, grated
Salt & pepper, to taste
$\frac{1}{2}$	tsp. dried basil
2	tbsp. minced fresh dill (or 1 tsp. dried)

• **Microwave Method:** Combine couscous and water or broth in a 2-quart microsafe casserole and let stand. (Water will be absorbed by the couscous.) Combine green onions, peppers, garlic and oil in a microsafe bowl. Microwave uncovered on HIGH 3 to 4 minutes, until softened. Stir in mushrooms and cook 2 minutes longer. Add to couscous along with chickpeas, carrot and seasonings. Microwave covered on HIGH for 5 minutes, or until remaining liquid is absorbed. Fluff with a fork to separate the grains. Adjust seasonings to taste.

• **Conventional Method:** In a large saucepan or skillet, sauté green onions, peppers and garlic in oil until softened. Add mushrooms and sauté 3 to 4 minutes longer. Add water or broth and bring to a boil. Stir in couscous along with remaining ingredients. Bring back to a boil, cover and simmer until all the liquid is absorbed, about 5 to 10 minutes. Fluff with a fork to separate the grains. Adjust seasonings to taste. (If mixture seems dry, add a little extra liquid.)

Yield: 6 servings of approximately $\frac{3}{4}$ cup each. Freezes and/or reheats well.

196 calories per serving, 2.3 g fat (0.3 g saturated), 0 mg cholesterol, 7 g protein, 37 g carbohydrate, 155 mg sodium, 251 mg potassium, 2 mg iron, 5 g fiber, 42 mg calcium.

• **Couscous Middle-Eastern Style:** Omit basil and dill. Replace with $\frac{1}{2}$ teaspoon each of ground cumin, ginger and cinnamon. If desired, cook $\frac{1}{4}$ cup currants or raisins along with the couscous. For a delicious, crunchy texture, stir $\frac{1}{4}$ cup toasted pine nuts into couscous just before serving.

• **Couscous American-Style:** Cook $\frac{1}{3}$ cup dried cranberries (craisins) along with couscous. Stir $\frac{1}{4}$ cup toasted, chopped pecans into cooked couscous just before serving.

• **Couscous Italian-Style:** Add 1 cup diced zucchini and 1 cup canned diced tomatoes (with juice) to sautéed vegetables. Cook 5 minutes longer. Stir in couscous along with remaining ingredients. Omit dill and add 2 tablespoons fresh minced basil. (Chickpeas can be omitted, if desired.)

Oriental Orzo

Orzo is actually rice-shaped pasta. Your guests will try to guess what they're eating. So yummy!

2 c. orzo
2 tsp. canola oil
1 onion, diced
2 stalks celery, diced
2 cloves garlic, crushed
1 green & 1 red pepper, diced
1½ c. mushrooms, sliced
3 tbsp. teriyaki or soy sauce
¼ c. chicken or vegetable broth (or water)
1 tsp. brown sugar (to taste)
½ tsp. dried basil (or 1 tbsp. fresh)
1 tsp. Oriental sesame oil

1. Cook orzo in boiling salted water until al dente. Drain well; rinse with cold water and set aside. Heat oil in a large non-stick skillet or wok. Stir-fry vegetables on medium-high heat until tender-crisp, about 3 to 4 minutes. If vegetables begin to stick, add a little water. Stir in orzo along with remaining ingredients. Cook on low heat, stirring gently, just until heated through.

Yield: 6 servings. Reheats well (if there is any left)!

193 calories per serving, 3.1 g fat (0.3 g saturated), 0 mg cholesterol, 7 g protein, 35 g carbohydrate, 369 mg sodium, 247 mg potassium, 2 mg iron, 2 g fiber, 27 mg calcium.

Cream of Wheat Kasha with Shells

My grandmother, Baba Doba, used to make this nutritious dish for us. Once I took the whole serving bowl for myself. She exclaimed in Yiddish: "Nayn, dos eez for allemehn!" (No, this is for everybody!)

2 c. elbow macaroni or miniature bow ties
2 onions, chopped
1 tbsp. canola oil
1 c. cream of wheat cereal (not instant) or wheatlets
2 c. boiling water (approximately)
1 tsp. salt (or to taste)
½ tsp. pepper

1. Cook pasta in boiling salted water according to package directions. Drain and rinse well. Brown onions in oil in a heavy non-stick skillet. If necessary, add a little water or broth to prevent onions from burning or sticking. Remove onions from pan and set aside. Wash and dry skillet.

2. Place cream of wheat in dry skillet and brown on medium heat until it gives off a toasty aroma. Stir constantly and keep shaking the pan back and forth, being careful not to burn the cereal. It will take about 5 minutes for the cereal to become toasted. Remove pan from heat. Very slowly stir in boiling water, being careful to avoid spatters. Add salt and pepper. Cover and let stand for 5 minutes. Cool slightly, then break it up with a fork. Add onions and pasta. Season to taste.

Yield: 8 servings (or less!) Reheats and/or freezes well. Delicious with roast chicken.

194 calories per serving, 2.5 g fat (0.2 g saturated), 0 mg cholesterol, 6 g protein, 37 g carbohydrate, 294 mg sodium, 84 mg potassium, 7 mg iron, 2 g fiber, 38 mg calcium.

Kasha & Bow Ties with Mushrooms

See photo (P-6). Use gourmet mushrooms to bring this old-fashioned recipe to new heights. Kasha (buckwheat groats) is one of my favorite foods. It is rich in protein, particularly lysine, as well as iron, calcium and B vitamins. It's terrific to know that kasha is so good for me!

2   c. bow tie pasta (3-color or mini bow ties)
1   c. medium or coarse kasha
1   egg white
2   c. hot chicken or vegetable broth
Salt & pepper, to taste
1   tbsp. canola or olive oil
2   large onions, coarsely chopped
2   c. sliced mushrooms (portobello, shiitake, oyster or button mushrooms)
$^1/_2$ c. chopped red pepper, if desired
2–3 tbsp. minced fresh dill

1. Cook pasta in boiling salted water according to package directions. Drain and rinse well. In a large heavy-bottomed pot, mix kasha with egg white. Cook on medium heat, stirring constantly, until kasha is dry and toasted, about 5 minutes. Remove pan from heat and slowly add broth to kasha. Return pan to heat, cover and simmer for 10 to 12 minutes, until most of liquid is absorbed. Holes will appear on the surface and kasha should be tender. Remove from heat and let stand covered for a few minutes, until remaining liquid is absorbed. Fluff with a fork. Season with salt and pepper.

2. Heat oil in a large non-stick skillet. Add onions and sauté on medium-high heat for 7 to 8 minutes, until nicely browned. If necessary, add a little water or broth as needed to prevent sticking. Add mushrooms and red pepper. Cook a few minutes longer, until golden, stirring occasionally. Combine all ingredients and mix well. Adjust seasonings to taste.

Yield: 8 servings. Freezes and/or reheats well. Recipe can be doubled easily.

148 calories per serving, 2.4 g fat (0.2 g saturated), 0 mg cholesterol, 6 g protein, 26 g carbohydrate, 59 mg sodium, 150 mg potassium, 2 mg iron, 2 g fiber, 19 mg calcium.

- **For vegetarians who don't** eat eggs, use no-egg pasta. For those with celiac disease, gluten-free pasta is available in natural food shops. It's often made from quinoa, corn, rice or vegetables. Gluten is a protein found in wheat, rye and barley products.
- **For a light and fluffy texture,** use $^3/_4$ cup kasha and $^1/_4$ cup bulgur. Instead of mixing kasha with an egg white, brown it in 1 tablespoon additional oil. If cooked kasha seems dry, moisten it with additional broth before serving.
- **Kasha Pilaf with Squash:** Prepare kasha as directed above, but omit pasta. Pierce an acorn squash all over with the point of a sharp knife. Microwave on HIGH for 6 to 8 minutes, turning it over halfway through cooking. Let stand for 10 minutes. Test with a knife; it should pass through the squash easily. Cut squash in half, discard seeds and cut into $^1/_2$-inch cubes. Add to kasha along with sautéed onions, mushrooms and dill. Add salt and pepper to taste. Mmm, so good!

Barley & Mushroom Risotto

Pearl barley is more delicate in flavor than hulled (pot) barley, which is chewier and requires longer cooking. Barley is an excellent source of fiber. One cup of barley yields 3 cups cooked.

1   tbsp. olive or canola oil
1   large onion, chopped

1   red pepper, chopped
2–3 cloves garlic, crushed
1½ c. mushrooms, sliced
1½ c. pearl barley, rinsed & well drained
3½ c. hot chicken or vegetable broth
Salt & pepper, to taste
¼   c. fresh dill, minced

1. In a large non-stick skillet, heat oil. Sauté onion, red pepper, garlic and mushrooms until golden, 5 to 7 minutes. Stir in barley and cook until lightly toasted, about 5 minutes. Slowly stir in ½ cup of hot broth. Cook, stirring, until it evaporates. Stir in another ½ cup broth. Repeat until you have added about 2 cups of broth. Pour in the remaining broth, cover and simmer for 45 minutes, until tender. If necessary, add a little water or broth to prevent sticking. Add salt, pepper and dill.

Yield: 8 servings. Reheats well or can be frozen. Leftovers can be used as a filling for Vegetarian Stuffed Peppers (p. 233).

177 calories per serving, 2.2 g fat (0.3 g saturated), 0 mg cholesterol, 7 g protein, 33 g carbohydrate, 79 mg sodium, 199 mg potassium, 2 mg iron, 7 g fiber, 28 mg calcium.

No-Guilt Bulgur or Millet with Mushrooms

No added fat, no guilt! Bulgur comes from wheat berries. After the hull and bran are removed, the berries are steamed, dried and crushed. Medium grind is ideal as a side dish.

2   medium onions, chopped
2   cloves garlic, minced
2   c. mushrooms, sliced

3   tbsp. water, wine or vegetable broth
1   c. bulgur or millet, rinsed & well-drained
1   c. boiling water
1   c. vegetarian spaghetti or tomato sauce (store-bought or homemade)
Salt & pepper, to taste
1   tsp. dried basil

1. In a non-stick skillet, combine onions, garlic and mushrooms with 3 tablespoons liquid. Cook on medium-high heat for 5 to 7 minutes, until vegetables have softened and liquid has evaporated. (If necessary, add a little more liquid to prevent vegetables from sticking.) Stir in bulgur or millet. Cook uncovered 5 minutes longer, until toasted, stirring often. Remove pan from heat. Carefully add boiling water and sauce. Add seasonings. Cover and simmer for 20 minutes. Remove from heat and let stand covered for 10 minutes. Fluff with a fork.

Yield: 6 servings. Reheats and/or freezes well.

132 calories per serving, 2 g fat (0.3 g saturated), 0 mg cholesterol, 5 g protein, 27 g carbohydrate, 226 mg sodium, 409 mg potassium, 2 mg iron, 6 g fiber, 35 mg calcium.

Turkish Bulgur Pilaf

A gem of a recipe from Suzi Lipes of Montreal. She often prepares this colorful, nutrition-packed pilaf for dinner guests, hoping she'll have leftovers to enjoy the next morning for breakfast!

1½ c. Spanish onion, chopped
3   stalks celery, chopped
1   red pepper, chopped
1   tbsp. olive oil

½ c. fresh dill, minced
2 c. bulgur, rinsed & drained
2½ c. boiling chicken or vegetable stock
½ c. raisins or currants, rinsed & drained
1 c. dried apricots, rinsed & chopped
½ tsp. salt (to taste)
¼ c. chopped toasted nuts, if desired
½ c. fresh parsley, minced

1. In a large skillet, sauté onions, celery and red pepper in hot oil on medium-high heat for 5 to 7 minutes, until golden. Add dill and bulgur. Cook uncovered 4 or 5 minutes longer, stirring often.

2. Carefully pour in boiling liquid. Add raisins, apricots and salt. Cover and simmer for 20 minutes, until liquid is absorbed. Remove from heat and let stand for 5 minutes. Stir in nuts and parsley and fluff with a fork. Serve hot.

Yield: 10 to 12 servings. Reheats and/or freezes well. Leftovers keep for 4 or 5 days in the fridge.

175 calories per serving, 1.9 g fat (0.3 g saturated), 0 mg cholesterol, 6 g protein, 36 g carbohydrate, 180 mg sodium, 402 mg potassium, 2 mg iron, 7 g fiber, 38 mg calcium.

• **Slivered almonds, pecans** or pine nuts are delicious in this dish. Almonds are high in calcium. With almonds, one serving of pilaf contains 196 calories, 3.6 g fat (0.4 saturated) and 47 mg calcium.
• **Toasting brings out the full flavor** of nuts, so a little flavor goes a long way. Toast nuts uncovered for 8 to 10 minutes at 350°F. It's okay to enjoy a little decadence on special occasions!
• **You can also substitute** millet or quinoa instead of bulgur.
• **How to toast bulgur, millet and other grains:** Rinse and drain well. Place in a large heavy-bottomed skillet. Toast on medium heat for about 5 minutes, stirring constantly to prevent burning. (It's ready when it gives off a toasty aroma and makes a light popping sound.) Remove pan from heat. Add liquid slowly to prevent spattering. Add vegetables and seasonings. Cover and simmer until done, about 20 minutes. Remove from heat and let stand covered for 10 minutes.

Millet Pilaf

Millet is not just for the birds! This easy-to-digest grain is found in health food stores. It is high in protein, complex carbohydrates, phosphorus, potassium, iron, calcium and B vitamins. Millet triples in volume, so use a large pan. Pre-toasting eliminates bitterness and prevents mushy millet!

1 tbsp. olive or canola oil
2 medium onions, chopped
1 stalk celery, chopped
1 red pepper, chopped
1 green pepper, chopped
2 cloves garlic, minced
1 c. mushrooms, sliced
1 c. millet
2¼ c. water, chicken or vegetable broth
½ tsp. dried basil
½ tsp. dried thyme
Salt & freshly ground pepper, to taste
¼ c. chopped fresh parsley

1. Heat oil in a non-stick skillet. Add vegetables and sauté on medium-high heat until golden, about 5 to 7 minutes. If necessary, add a couple of tablespoons of water or broth if veggies begin to stick. (Or microwave veggies covered on HIGH for 5 minutes, omitting oil.)

2. Rinse and drain millet thoroughly. Place in a large heavy-bottomed frypan and toast it on medium heat for about 5 minutes, stirring constantly to prevent burning. It's ready when it gives off a toasty aroma similar to popcorn. Remove from heat and add broth slowly to prevent spattering. Add remaining ingredients except parsley. Cover and simmer for 20 to 25 minutes. Add parsley and let stand covered for 5 to 10 minutes. Fluff with a fork.

Yield: 6 servings. Reheats well. Leftovers keep 3 or 4 days in the fridge. (I usually don't have any!)

173 calories per serving, 3.9 g fat (0.6 g saturated), 0 mg cholesterol, 5 g protein, 31 g carbohydrate, 13 mg sodium, 230 mg potassium, 2 mg iron, 4 g fiber, 27 mg calcium.

- **If you cook veggies** without oil, 1 serving contains 153 calories and 1.6 g fat (0.3 g saturated).
- **Millet can be stored** in a tightly sealed container in the refrigerator or freezer for up to 4 months. Don't store it at room temperature for more than a couple of weeks, particularly in hot weather. If millet smells musty, throw it out.
- **Variations:** For added crunch, add 2 tablespoons toasted sesame seeds, pine nuts or slivered almonds to cooked millet mixture. Leftovers? Refer to variations of Fake & Bake Burgers (p. 402). Use 2 cups of cooked millet instead of mashed potatoes to make Grain Burgers.
- **Milletburgers:** Process leftover Millet Pilaf on the Steel Knife of your processor with either a little soy, tamari or teriyaki sauce until mixture holds together. (Millet should be somewhat moist and sticky for best results.) Combine with beaten egg (or egg whites) and some bread crumbs or matzo meal. Press firmly into patties. Brown on both sides in a little canola or olive oil in a non-stick skillet.

Basic Polenta (Cornmeal Mush)

Polenta is eaten as an alternative to rice or pasta in Northern Italy. European Jews love it topped with cottage cheese and sour cream or yogurt.

4 c. water
1 tsp. salt
1 c. yellow or white cornmeal

1. Combine water and salt in a large heavy saucepan and bring to a boil. Add cornmeal in a thin stream (like falling rain), stirring constantly. Reduce heat and cook over low heat for 20 minutes, stirring constantly with a long-handled spoon. Mixture will become a thick mass and pull away from the sides of the pan. For best results and lump-free polenta, don't stop stirring polenta until it is done.

Yield: 4 to 6 servings. Leftover polenta can be used to make Grilled Polenta Wedges (below).

110 calories per serving, 1.1 g fat (0.2 g saturated), 0 mg cholesterol, 3 g protein, 24 g carbohydrate, 592 mg sodium, 88 mg potassium, 1 mg iron, 2 g fiber, 2 mg calcium.

- **Grilled Polenta Wedges:** Spread polenta evenly in a sprayed 9-inch pie plate. Chill for at least 2 hours, or until firm. Cut into wedges. Broil or grill wedges for 2 to 3 minutes per side, until piping hot. Serve as appetizers.
- **Creamy Polenta:** Prepare polenta as directed. Stir in 1/2 cup of skim milk and 2 teaspoons of olive oil or tub margarine; mix well. If desired, top with a light dusting of grated Parmesan cheese.
- **Mamaliga:** Cook cornmeal as directed. Stir in 1/2 cup skim milk and 2 teaspoons olive oil or tub margarine. Top with a scoop of nonfat cottage cheese and yogurt or sour cream.

- **Variations:** Prepare polenta as directed. Spoon onto a serving plate and serve topped with salsa or tomato sauce (bottled or homemade). Polenta also makes an excellent vegetarian meal topped with Easy Vegetarian Chili (p. 225) or Simple & Good Ratatouille (p. 230). Try it topped with the mushroom mixture from Mushroom Crostini (p. 242).
- **Polenta Pizza:** Pour hot polenta into a sprayed 9- or 10-inch ovenproof skillet or casserole. Spread evenly. Top with sliced tomatoes, mushrooms, green peppers and garlic slivers. Drizzle lightly with olive oil and sprinkle with salt, pepper and basil. Top with ½ cup grated low-fat mozzarella cheese. Wrap the handle of of the skillet with aluminum foil to prevent it from becoming damaged. Bake uncovered in a preheated 350°F oven for 15 to 20 minutes. Cut in wedges to serve.

Basic Brown Rice

Brown rice has its bran layer intact. It's not polished like white rice, so it contains more nutrients, has a chewy texture and a nutty flavor. Short grain is stickier and chewier than long grain. Basmati brown rice has a mild flavor and is great for those who find regular brown rice too healthy-tasting!

2¼ c. water, vegetable or chicken broth
1   c. long-grain brown rice, rinsed & drained
½ tsp. salt
1   clove minced garlic, optional
½ tsp. each basil, oregano or thyme, optional

1. Place water or broth in a 2-quart heavy-bottomed saucepan. Cover and bring to a boil. Meanwhile, rinse rice; drain well. Add to boiling liquid along with desired seasonings. Bring back to a boil and simmer covered for 45 minutes. Remove from heat and let stand covered for 10 minutes, until liquid is absorbed. Fluff with a fork.

Yield: Six 3-cup servings). Reheats well. Do not freeze.

115 calories per ½ cup serving, 0.9 g fat (0.2 g saturated), 0 mg cholesterol, 3 g protein, 24 g carbohydrate, 199 mg sodium, 45 mg potassium, trace iron, 2 g fiber, 10 mg calcium.

- **Brown Rice in Half the Time!** Rinse and drain rice. Combine with water and salt in a saucepan. Soak at room temperature for several hours or overnight. (I do this in the morning, then cook it at mealtime.) Bring rice to a boil, reduce heat and simmer tightly covered for just 22 minutes! Turn off heat and let rice stand covered for 10 minutes.
- **Oven Method:** Combine boiling liquid, rice and desired seasonings in an ovenproof casserole. Cover tightly. Bake in a preheated 350°F oven for 50 to 60 minutes, until all liquid is absorbed.
- **Vegetable Un-Fried Rice:** Cook brown rice as directed. (Cooked white rice can be substituted.) Prepare 2 to 3 cups of any of the following: bean sprouts, snow peas, chopped celery, green onions, red pepper, mushrooms, broccoli florets. Add 1 tablespoon each of minced garlic and ginger to vegetables. Microwave covered on HIGH for 5 minutes, until tender-crisp. (No oil is needed, only a few drops of water to create steam.) Combine vegetables with cooked rice. Add 3 tablespoons soy sauce, 2 to 3 teaspoons Oriental sesame oil, salt and pepper to taste.
- **Brown Rice Pilaf:** Cook brown rice as directed, using vegetable or chicken broth. Prepare 2 cups of any of the following vegetables: chopped onions, peppers, celery, carrots, mushrooms, broccoli and/or cauliflower florets. Microwave covered on HIGH for 5 minutes. Add veggies to rice. Season with basil and thyme. Add salt and pepper to taste.

- **Chef's Cooking Secrets!** If cooked rice sticks to the bottom of the pot, place a heat diffuser or flame-tamer under the pot during cooking. If any liquid remains at the end of cooking, drain it off and place covered pot on low heat for a few minutes so that rice can dry out. If rice is too dry at the end of cooking, add a couple of spoonfuls of water, place pot on low heat and steam a few minutes longer.

Confetti Lemon Rice

3   c. vegetable broth
1¹/₂ c. basmati or long grain rice, rinsed & drained
Finely grated zest of a lemon
2   tbsp. fresh lemon juice
1   red pepper, chopped
2   medium carrots, chopped
4   green onions, chopped
3   cloves garlic, crushed
Salt & pepper, to taste
2   tbsp. fresh basil, minced
2   tbsp. fresh dill, minced

- **Conventional Method:** In a large saucepan, bring broth to a boil. Add remaining ingredients except basil and dill. Cover tightly and simmer for 20 minutes. Remove from heat and let stand covered for 10 minutes. If rice is too moist, drain off excess liquid. If too dry, add a little more broth. Add basil and dill. Fluff with a fork.

- **Microwave Method:** Combine all ingredients except basil and dill in a microsafe 3-quart casserole. Cover and microwave on HIGH for 6 to 7 minutes, until boiling. Reduce power to MEDIUM (50% power) and microwave 10 to 12 minutes longer. Let stand covered for 10 to 15 minutes, until liquid is absorbed. If rice is too moist,

microwave 3 or 4 minutes longer on HIGH. If too dry, add a little more broth. Add basil and dill. Fluff with a fork.

Yield: 8 servings. Reheats well. Do not freeze.

160 calories per serving, 0.9 g fat (0.2 g saturated), 0 mg cholesterol, 4 g protein, 35 g carbohydrate, 387 mg sodium, 84 mg potassium, <1 mg iron, 1 g fiber, 17 mg calcium.

Spinach Lemon Rice

So yummy! Leftovers make a delicious filling for Vegetarian Stuffed Peppers (p. 233).

Confetti Lemon Rice (above)
10 oz. pkg. (300 g) frozen chopped spinach, cooked & squeezed dry
1   additional tbsp. fresh lemon juice
2–3 tbsp. grated Parmesan cheese

1. Prepare rice as directed. Add spinach and additional lemon juice to rice along with basil and dill. Adjust seasonings to taste. Garnish each serving with a little Parmesan cheese. Delicious with fish.

174 calories per serving, 1.4 g fat (0.5 g saturated), 1 mg cholesterol, 6 g protein, 37 g carbohydrate, 437 mg sodium, 158 mg potassium, <1 mg iron, 2 g fiber, 73 mg calcium.

- **Time-Saving Secret!** Frozen spinach can be microwaved right in its package! Pierce the top of package in several places with a sharp knife. Place package on a microsafe plate. Cook on HIGH for 4 to 5 minutes. When cool, remove spinach from package and squeeze out excess moisture.

• **Omit Parmesan cheese** if serving this dish with poultry or meat, or if you are a vegan.

Rainbow Rice Pilaf

Pretty as a picture! See P-6. Colorful and vitamin-packed, this easy side dish also makes a fabulous filling for Vegetarian Stuffed Peppers (p. 233). Fresh vegetables can be used instead of frozen.

2   c. vegetable broth
1   c. long-grain or basmati rice, rinsed & drained
2   tsp. olive oil
1   large onion, finely chopped
2   cloves garlic, crushed
$^1/_2$ c. green pepper, finely chopped
$^1/_2$ c. red pepper, finely chopped
1   c. zucchini, finely chopped
$1^1/_2$ c. frozen mixed vegetables, thawed
Salt & pepper, to taste
$^1/_2$ tsp. dried basil

1. In a medium saucepan, bring broth to a boil. Add drained rice to saucepan, cover and simmer on low heat for 20 minutes. Remove from heat and let stand covered for 10 minutes. Meanwhile, heat oil in a non-stick skillet. Add onion and sauté for 5 minutes. Add garlic, peppers and zucchini. Sauté 4 or 5 minutes longer, until tender-crisp. If necessary, add a little broth or water to prevent sticking. Stir in mixed vegetables. Cover and let stand for 5 minutes to heat through. Combine veggie mixture with rice. Season to taste. Fluff with a fork.

Yield: 6 servings. Leftovers keep 2 days in the fridge and reheat well. Freezing is not recommended.

193 calories per serving, 2.3 g fat (0.3 g saturated), 0 mg cholesterol, 6 g protein, 39 g carbohydrate, 355 mg sodium, 238 mg potassium, 2 mg iron, 4 g fiber, 36 mg calcium.

Letcho

A Hungarian delight! This saucy, spicy rice dish is enhanced with lots of chunky vegetables.

1   c. long-grain rice
2   c. water
$^1/_4$ tsp. salt
2   onions, quartered & sliced
1   green & 1 red pepper, cut in strips
1   tbsp. olive or canola oil
2   cloves garlic, minced
1   medium zucchini, halved & sliced
2   c. tomato sauce (bottled or homemade)
Salt & pepper, to taste
1   tsp. chili powder, to taste
6   drops Tabasco sauce, to taste

1. Rinse rice and drain well. Bring 2 cups of water to a boil. Add salt and rice, cover and simmer for 20 minutes. Let stand covered for 10 minutes. Meanwhile, in a non-stick skillet, sauté onions and peppers in oil until golden. Add a little water if needed to prevent sticking. Add garlic and zucchini. Cook until softened, about 5 minutes. Add tomato sauce and seasonings and simmer for 10 minutes. Combine sauce mixture with rice and stir gently. Adjust seasonings to taste.

Yield: 6 servings. Reheats well. Freezing is not recommended.

229 calories per serving, 5.6 g fat (0.8 g saturated), 0 mg cholesterol, 5 g protein, 42 g carbohydrate, 632 mg sodium, 554 mg potassium, 2 mg iron, 2 g fiber, 52 mg calcium.

Oriental Rice

1   c. basmati or long-grain rice
2   c. water
1   clove garlic, minced
1   tsp. ginger, minced
2   tbsp. lemon juice
1   tbsp. brown sugar
2   tbsp. soy sauce
1/2   tsp. Oriental sesame oil
1/8   tsp. cayenne
1/2   tbsp. cornstarch
1/4   c. chicken broth, at room temperature
1/2   of a red pepper, chopped
1   c. mushrooms, sliced
2   green onions, chopped

1. Rinse rice in a strainer; drain well. Bring water to a boil. Add rice, cover and simmer for 18 to 20 minutes. Remove rice from heat and let stand 10 minutes. Meanwhile, combine garlic, ginger, lemon juice, brown sugar, soy sauce, sesame oil and cayenne in a 4-cup Pyrex measuring cup. Dissolve cornstarch in chicken broth; stir into sauce mixture. Add red pepper, mushrooms and onions. Microwave uncovered on HIGH for 3 to 4 minutes, until bubbling and thickened, stirring twice during cooking. Add to rice and mix well. Adjust seasonings to taste.

Yield: 6 servings. Reheats well. Do not freeze. Recipe can be doubled easily.

149 calories per serving, 0.7 g fat (0.1 g saturated), 0 mg cholesterol, 3.5 g protein, 32 g carbohydrate, 316 mg sodium, 111 mg potassium, 2 mg iron, 1 g fiber, 19 mg calcium.

Lentil & Rice Casserole (Medjaderah)

A Middle-Eastern favorite. Uli Zamir makes this vegetarian dish at least once a week.

1   c. brown lentils, rinsed & drained
6   c. water, divided
1   tbsp. canola oil
2   onions, chopped
3–4 cloves garlic, minced
Salt & pepper, to taste
1   tbsp. pareve soup mix (chicken flavor)
1   tsp. ground cumin (or to taste)
1 1/2 c. long-grain rice
1/4   c. coriander (cilantro), chopped

1. Bring lentils and 3 cups of water to a boil. Reduce heat and cook covered for 15 minutes, until partially cooked. Drain well. Meanwhile, heat oil in a non-stick skillet. Sauté onions and garlic in oil until golden, about 5 minutes. Add salt, pepper, soup mix and cumin. Cook until well browned, about 10 minutes, stirring often. Add rice, drained lentils and remaining 3 cups of water. Cover and simmer 20 to 25 minutes, until rice is tender. Add more water if necessary during cooking. Stir in coriander and adjust seasonings to taste. For a terrific vegetarian meal, serve with Israeli Salad (p. 280).

Yield: 10 servings. Reheats well. Freezing is not recommended.

198 calories per serving, 2.1 g fat (0.2 g saturated), trace cholesterol, 7 g protein, 37 g carbohydrate, 214 mg sodium, 266 mg potassium, 3 mg iron, 5 g fiber, 36 mg calcium.

Italian-Style Rice

1 large onion, chopped
2 cloves garlic, minced
½ of a green &/or red pepper, chopped
1–2 stalks celery, chopped
2 tsp. olive or canola oil
1¾ c. water
1–1½ c. tomato or pizza sauce
1 c. long-grain brown rice (e.g. basmati brown rice), rinsed and drained
Salt & pepper, to taste
½ tsp. each of dried basil & oregano (or 1 tbsp. fresh)

1. Sauté onion, garlic, peppers and celery in oil in a non-stick skillet (or microwave uncovered on HIGH for 5 minutes), until softened.

2. Bring water and 1 cup of tomato or pizza sauce to a boil. Add rice, vegetables and seasonings. Bring mixture to a boil once again and simmer covered for 45 minutes. Do not stir. Remove from heat and let stand covered for 10 minutes, until liquid is absorbed. Fluff with a fork. At this point, add an extra ½ cup of sauce if you prefer a saucier rice.

Yield: 4 to 6 servings. Reheats well. Do not freeze.

232 calories per serving, 3.9 g fat (0.6 g saturated), 0 mg cholesterol, 6 g protein, 45 g carbohydrate, 390 mg sodium, 410 mg potassium, 2 mg iron, 5 g fiber, 46 mg calcium.

- **If you want to use** white long-grain or basmati rice instead of brown rice, bring 1½ cups water and 1 cup of tomato or pizza sauce to a boil. Add sautéed veggies, rice and seasonings. Bring back to a boil, then simmer covered for 20 minutes. Let stand covered for 10 minutes. Then stir in an extra ½ cup of sauce.
- **Oven Method:** In Step 2 (above), combine boiling liquid with remaining ingredients in an oven-proof casserole. Cover tightly and bake in a pre-heated 350°F oven for 50 to 60 minutes, until all liquid is absorbed. Stir in an extra ½ cup sauce at the end of cooking.
- **Italian-Style Rice with Sun-Dried Tomatoes:** Soak 6 sun-dried tomatoes in boiling water to cover for 10 minutes. Drain and chop. Add to rice mixture and cook as directed in Step 2.
- **Salsa Rice:** Prepare as for Italian Style Rice (above), but use 1 to 1½ cups of bottled salsa instead of tomato or pizza sauce. If desired, add 1 cup of canned or cooked beans (black, pinto or red kidney beans) to cooked rice. Place rinsed, drained beans on top of rice, cover and let stand for 10 minutes to heat through. Mix gently to combine.
- **Leftovers?** Cooked rice keeps at least 2 or 3 days in the refrigerator. Reheat at 350°F for 15 to 20 minutes in covered casserole, or microwave covered on HIGH, allowing 1 minute for each cup of rice. I don't usually freeze rice because I find there is a change in texture. This recipe also makes a tasty filling for Vegetarian Stuffed Peppers (p. 233).

Mushroom Risotto With Sun-Dried Tomatoes

Simply wonderful! You need to stir the rice almost continuously during cooking, but it's fun to do. Besides, the steam from the cooking rice will moisturize your skin!

1	oz. dried exotic mushrooms, about 1 cup (e.g. porcini)
2	c. boiling water
2½–3	c. vegetable or chicken broth
1	tbsp. olive or canola oil
1	medium onion or 6 shallots, chopped
2	cloves garlic, minced
1½	c. Arborio rice
	Salt & pepper, to taste
¼	tsp. dried thyme
6	oil-packed sun-dried tomatoes, well rinsed & coarsely chopped

1. Pour boiling water over dried mushrooms. Soak for 20 minutes, until rehydrated. Drain mushrooms, reserving soaking liquid. Combine mushroom liquid with broth; heat liquid until piping hot. Coarsely chop the soaked mushrooms and set aside.

2. Heat oil in a non-stick skillet. Add onion and garlic; sauté for 3 minutes. If necessary, add a little water to prevent sticking or burning. Add chopped mushrooms and cook 2 to 3 minutes longer. Add rice and cook for 3 or 4 minutes, stirring to coat grains lightly with the oil. Reduce heat to medium and begin adding the hot broth ½ cup at a time. Continue to stir until you can pull a spoon along the bottom of the pot and almost no liquid remains. Add another ½ cup of stock. Continue adding broth in this way until the rice is nearly done, about 20 to 25 minutes, stirring often. Add seasonings and chopped sun-dried tomatoes. Cook 5 minutes longer.

Yield: 6 servings. This reheats beautifully in the microwave. Freezing is not recommended.

194 calories per serving, 3.2 g fat (0.4 g saturated), 0 mg cholesterol, 5 g protein, 37 g carbohydrate, 430 mg sodium, 130 mg potassium, 3 mg iron, 2 g fiber, 15 mg calcium.

- **If you don't have** dried mushrooms, substitute 2 cups sliced raw mushrooms in Step 1 and omit water. You'll need 4½ to 5 cups broth (or substitute ½ cup white wine for part of the broth).
- **Arborio rice is a short-grain,** starchy Italian rice. Don't rinse before cooking or you'll wash away the starch that helps create the thick, luscious sauce. I have made this recipe using long-grain rice and it is also very tasty, but the texture is firm, not creamy.
- **Sun-dried tomatoes** packed in oil need to be thoroughly rinsed to remove the oil. You could substitute dehydrated sun-dried tomatoes and soak them with the mushrooms in Step 1.
- **Risotto with Roasted Red Peppers:** For the last 5 minutes of cooking, add ½ cup of chopped roasted red peppers (homemade or from a jar) and 2 tablespoons minced basil along with the sun-dried tomatoes. If desired, stir in 2 to 3 tablespoons grated Parmesan cheese.
- **Risotto with Peas:** Add 1 cup of frozen (thawed) green peas along with sun-dried tomatoes during the last 5 minutes of cooking. Stir in 3 tablespoons each of minced fresh parsley and mint.
- **Asparagus Risotto:** Instead of mushrooms, ½ pound lightly steamed asparagus, cut on the diagonal into ½-inch slices, can be added with sun-dried tomatoes for the last 5 minutes of cooking. Stir in 2 teaspoons grated lemon rind, 2 to 3 tablespoons freshly squeezed lemon juice and 2 tablespoons minced parsley.

Wild About Rice

A great company dish! Wild rice is high in protein and a good source of B vitamins and iron.

1   c. wild rice
1   c. long-grain rice
1   stalk celery, chopped
6   green onions, chopped
1   red & 1 yellow pepper, chopped
2   cloves garlic, minced
1   tbsp. olive oil
½   c. dried cranberries or raisins, soaked in hot water for 15 minutes, then drained
Juice & rind of a large lemon
Salt & freshly ground pepper, to taste
¼   c. toasted pine nuts or slivered almonds

1. In a heavy saucepan, bring 2½ cups of lightly salted water to a boil. Add wild rice, cover and simmer 45 minutes, until the grains swell and burst. Remove from heat; let stand 10 minutes. Cook long grain rice in 2 cups boiling salted water for 20 minutes. Remove from heat; let stand 10 minutes. Sauté veggies in oil in a non-stick skillet until golden. Combine all ingredients and mix well.

Yield: 10 servings. Leftovers will keep 3 or 4 days in the fridge. Freezing is not recommended.

193 calories per serving, 3.6 g fat (0.5 g saturated), 0 mg cholesterol, 5 g protein, 36 g carbohydrate, 8 mg sodium, 151 mg potassium, 2 mg iron, 2 g fiber, 18 mg calcium.

Quinoa

Quinoa (keen-wah) was the staple food of the Incas for more than 5,000 years. An excellent source of iron, magnesium and potassium, it contains complex carbohydrates and high quality protein. Quinoa provides lysine, an amino acid missing from corn and wheat. Quinoa is very easy to digest. It's available at natural food shops. Store it in the fridge or freezer; it will keep for 3 to 4 months.

2   c. water, vegetable or chicken broth
1   c. quinoa
1   clove garlic
Pinch of salt

1. Bring water or broth to a boil. Place quinoa in a fine-meshed strainer. Rinse under running water to remove the bitter coating (saponin). Rinse until water runs clear; drain well. Add quinoa, garlic and salt to boiling liquid. Reduce heat and simmer covered for 15 minutes. Don't overcook. Remove from heat and let stand covered for 5 minutes. Fluff with a fork. If any liquid remains, drain in a strainer. Use quinoa instead of rice in pilafs, or in grain-based salads such as Quinoa Mandarin Salad (p. 289).

Yield: about 3 cups (6 servings).

107 calories per serving, 1.7 g fat (0.3 g saturated), 0 mg cholesterol, 4 g protein, 20 g carbohydrate, 57 mg sodium, 212 mg potassium, 3 mg iron, 2 g fiber, 20 mg calcium.

• **Crimson Quinoa:** Add 1 cup canned grated beets, well-drained, to hot quinoa. Mix well. Add 4 minced green onions, 2 tablespoons raspberry or balsamic vinegar, 1 tablespoon lemon juice and 2 tablespoons extra-virgin olive oil. Season with salt and pepper. Serve at room temperature.

Make It Meatless

Vegetarian Pleasures

- About 14 million North Americans consider themselves vegetarians. Of these, about one-third eliminate meat, fish and poultry from their diets. Some avoid red meat but include poultry or fish.
- There are many reasons for a vegetarian diet and lifestyle: health, environment, love of animals, concern for world hunger, belief in non-violence. Many Jews find it easier to keep Kosher. Some famous Jewish vegetarians include Albert Einstein, Franz Kafka and Isaac Bashevis Singer.
- A "real vegetarian" is someone who won't eat anything with either a face or a mother!
- Vegans don't eat any animal products, including meat, poultry, eggs and dairy products. Some won't eat honey. Many vegans won't use animal products such as leather or wool.
- Ovo-Lacto-Vegetarians eat both eggs and milk products. Lacto-Vegetarians eat milk products but no eggs. Ovo-Vegetarians include eggs but exclude milk products from their diet.
- Part-time or "almost" vegetarians eat small amounts of animal protein (mainly chicken and/or fish once or twice a week), lots of pasta, use skim-milk dairy products and egg whites. (That's me!) Traditional foods such as brisket are saved for special occasions like Rosh Hashonah or Passover.
- The key to a healthy vegetarian diet is the same as any other healthy diet. Eat a wide variety of foods including fruits, vegetables, legumes, whole grains and small amounts of nuts and seeds.
- A plant-based diet is cholesterol-free. It is also low in both total and saturated fats, except for nuts, seeds, oils and avocados.
- A mixture of proteins each day should provide enough essential amino acids. Most of us eat too much protein. You can get enough protein from plant foods by making healthful choices.
- Don't worry about eating enough protein. Each day, include some grains (barley, rice, kasha, couscous, pasta, bulgur, millet, quinoa) and some legumes (lima, white or black beans, lentils, chickpeas, black-eyed peas, split peas).They don't have to be eaten at the same time. Just eat them on the same day, within a few hours of each other (e.g., Healthier Hummous [p. 44] with a pita).
- Homemade Seitan (wheat meat) (p. 238) is a low-fat meat replacement that is great in stews. It's fun to make! There is a quick-mix which is sold in most natural food stores.
- Tofu (bean curd) and textured vegetable protein (TVP) are two other meat replacements. TVP is combined with water and used as a replacement for ground beef in recipes.
- Many people believe that starchy foods are fattening. Not true! Actually, carbohydrates are low in fat. It's the oil, butter, margarine or creamy sauces we add to them that are fattening. Portion distortion is also a big problem. If you eat too many calories, you'll end up with "thighs of regret"!
- "Lite" or low-fat margarine may contain gelatin, which is usually an animal-based product. Vegetarians and Kosher cooks should check labels carefully. Choose olive or canola oil instead of margarine whenever possible.
- Non-animal sources of iron include dried beans, lentils, leafy greens (spinach, Swiss chard, beet greens), bulgur, millet, almonds, blackstrap molasses, prunes, apricots, raisins and other dried fruit.
- To increase the amount of iron absorbed at a meal, include a food with vitamin C (e.g., oranges or other citrus fruits, strawberries, melons, tomatoes, peppers, broccoli). It's best to eat foods which are high in iron and calcium at different times to increase

iron absorption. Cooking food in cast iron cookware also adds to iron intake.

- For excellent information on calcium, see Calci-Yummy—Very Dairy Good (p. 35).
  - Vitamin B12 is important for proper nervous system function. It comes primarily from animal-derived foods. A diet containing some egg or dairy products provides adequate vitamin B12.
  - Fortified foods (e.g. cereals, pastas) are good non-animal sources of Vitamin B12. Check labels for products fortified with B12. You can also take a good multivitamin containing B12.

Using Your Bean!

- **Beans are a nutritional bargain** and they're inexpensive too! They're rich in B vitamins (niacin, riboflavin, thiamine and folic acid), calcium, iron, phosphorous, zinc and potassium.
- **One cup of cooked beans** or peas has just 200 to 300 calories. Beans contain no cholesterol or gluten. They are low in fat, except for soybeans which are high in unsaturated fat.
- **Bean there . . . ate that!** Beans are usually oval or kidney-shaped, peas are round, lentils are discs. They're so versatile! Add them to chili, soups, stews, casseroles, dips and spreads. Use them on their own, or add them to salads, pasta, rice or other grains. Combine them with veggies such as corn, eggplant, greens, squash, or tomatoes (either fresh or canned).
- **Dried beans and peas** are excellent sources of plant protein, containing about 7 grams in $1/2$ cup. This protein contains insufficient amounts of one or more essential amino acids, but you can complete the protein if you eat some rice, bread, pasta, grains or dairy products in the same day.
- **Beans are a great source of fiber.** A cup of cooked beans contains about 8 to 10 grams, almost half of your daily requirement. The fiber is mainly soluble, which may lower blood cholesterol. Beans, peas and lentils are excellent for diabetic and low-fat diets.
- **One pound of dried beans** (454 g) measures about $2^1/2$ cups. One cup yields 2 to $2^1/2$ cups cooked. Cooked beans will keep in the fridge for 3 or 4 days, or freeze them for up to 6 months.
- **Dried beans should be stored** in a cool, dark place. Try to use them within 6 months. The older the beans, the drier and harder they become, requiring longer cooking to make them tender.
- **To clean beans,** peas or lentils, pick them over, discarding any small stones or debris. Rinse thoroughly in a strainer under cold running water. Discard any that are shrivelled or discolored.
- **It's best to soak beans** before cooking. Lentils and green or yellow split peas don't require pre-soaking. Soaking and cooking dried beans is easy. It takes time but requires little work.
- **Presoaking beans shortens** cooking time and helps remove the indigestible sugars that cause gas! Many people who usually eat a low-fiber diet, then switch to a high-fiber diet, have a problem with flatulence. Their digestive tract doesn't have enough of the necessary enzymes to digest the bean sugars, so they pass undigested into the lower intestine where bacteria metabolize them and produce gas. Eventually your body will adjust and produce the necessary enzymes. Like many of life's problems, this too shall pass!
- **Overnight Soaking Method:** Place rinsed beans in a large bowl; cover with triple the amount of cold water. Soak overnight; drain and rinse. Cook in lots of fresh water. If your kitchen is very warm, beans can be soaked in the refrigerator for up to 2 days. At higher altitudes, longer soaking may be needed (up to 24 hours) to ensure tender beans.
- **Quick Soak Method:** Rinse beans; cover with triple the amount of cold water. Bring to a boil

Full of Beans Cooking Chart

Beans & Legumes (1 cup presoaked)	Cooking Times	Yield
Aduki beans	1 to 1½ hours	2 cups
Black (Turtle) beans	1½ to 2 hours	2 cups
Black-eyed peas	1 to 1½ hours	2¼ cups
Cannellini (white beans)	1 to 1½ hours	2 cups
Chickpeas (garbanzo beans)	2 to 3 hours	2½ cups
Cranberry (Romano) beans	1½ to 2 hours	2¼ cups
Fava beans	1½ to 2 hours	2 cups
Flageolets	1 to 1½ hours	2 cups
Great Northern beans	1 to 1½ hours	2¼ cups
Kidney beans	1½ to 2 hours	2 cups
Lentils (don't presoak)	30 to 45 minutes	2 cups
Lima beans (cook with salt to keep skins from slipping off, or beans will turn mushy!)	¾ to 1½ hours	2 cups
Navy or pea beans (white beans)	1½ to 2 hours	2 cups
Pinto beans	1½ to 2 hours	2¼ cups
Soybeans (beige)	3 to 4 hours	2¼ cups
Split Peas (green/yellow—don't presoak)	45 minutes	2 cups

and cook for 2 minutes. Remove from heat and let stand covered for 1 hour. Discard any that are floating. Drain and rinse well. Cook in fresh water.

- **Ready or not?** After soaking, cut a bean in half. The inside should be one color. If not, soak beans a little longer. Discard any loose skins before cooking.
- **Cooking Method:** Use 3 cups of cold water for each cup of beans. Bring beans to a boil, cover and simmer until tender. See chart for times. To reduce foaming, add a teaspoon of oil.
- **Chopped garlic** and a slice of fresh ginger (believed to reduce gas) can be added. A 3-inch piece of Kombu (sea kelp), available in health food stores, adds minerals, reduces gas and adds flavor.
- **Onions, carrots, celery, bay leaf** and your favorite dried herbs can be included (parsley, thyme or oregano). Don't add baking soda. It can destroy the B vitamin, thiamine.
- **Don't add salt or acidic ingredients** (lemon juice, vinegar, wine) until the end of cooking. They keep beans from softening. When beans are almost tender, add salt, lemon juice, etc. Cook 10 to 15 minutes longer so seasonings can permeate them. Lima beans are the exception. They should be cooked in salted water or they'll turn to mush!
- **Beans can be cooked successfully** in newer models of pressure cookers. Follow manufacturer's instructions. An excellent vegan cookbook is Lorna Sass' *Complete Vegetarian Kitchen* (Hearst Books). Her recipes include how to cook beans (and grains) in a pressure cooker.

- **If beans are very old** or dry, they can take much longer to cook, so always allow extra cooking time. If your water is very hard, cook beans in bottled water, or they'll be slow to soften.
- **Beans are ready when** you can crush them between your tongue and the roof of your mouth. If using beans for salads, cook just until firm, or they'll be mushy. Check for doneness after minimum cooking time. (See Full of Beans Cooking Chart on next page.)
- **Part-time vegetarians** can combine beans or legumes with some extra-lean ground beef or poultry for hearty casseroles. Add mashed chickpeas to ground meat to reduce the amount of meat needed when making burgers or meatballs. Use mashed beans to thicken pasta sauces.
- **Canned legumes** (beans, peas and lentils) are convenient, nutritious and ready to use. However, they are more expensive than dried and are generally higher in sodium. A quick trick is to rinse canned legumes well under cold running water to cut the amount of sodium in half.

Bean Cuisine—Fast from the Freezer Methods!

- **Method 1 (Soak & Freeze):** Soak dried beans in cold water overnight. Drain thoroughly but do not cook. Freeze in airtight containers for up to 6 months. When needed, empty frozen beans into a pot of boiling water, or add them to soups or casseroles. Most varieties cook in half the regular cooking time. Even soybeans and chickpeas will be ready to eat in about an hour. Most of the expansion takes place during soaking, so the cooked yield will be only slightly larger than the volume of frozen beans which you added to the pot.
- **Method 2 (Frozen Precooked Beans):** When you cook a batch of beans, make double or triple the amount. Freeze the cooked, drained beans in airtight containers for up to 6 months. When needed, empty the frozen beans right into your favorite soup, lasagna, chili or casserole recipe. There's no need to thaw them first. Cook until heated through.
- **Thaw frozen precooked beans** in the refrigerator overnight for recipes which do not require cooking or heating (e.g. salads). These are as convenient as canned beans, but without the added sodium. (P.S. They're virtually fat-free!)

Equivalents for Beans & Legumes

- 1 pound (500 g) of dried beans contains 2 to $2\frac{1}{2}$ cups of dried beans.
- A 14 oz. (398 ml) can of beans, drained equals $1\frac{1}{2}$ cups cooked beans.
- A 19 oz. (540 ml) can of beans, drained equals 2 cups cooked beans.
- $\frac{2}{3}$ cup of dried beans equals 2 cups of cooked beans.

Bev Bergman's Vegetarian Cholent

Bev's daughter Andrea is a vegetarian, so this recipe has become a favorite in the Bergman household. Broccoli and cauliflower develop a strong taste from long cooking, so you may prefer to omit them.

1	c. lima beans, rinsed
1	c. kidney beans, rinsed
1	tbsp. canola oil
1	large onion, diced
3–4	potatoes, peeled & diced
1	large sweet potato, peeled & cut in chunks
2	medium zucchini, cut in chunks

1 green & 1 red pepper, cut in chunks
1 c. broccoli, cut up (optional)
1 c. cauliflower, cut up (optional)
2–3 cloves garlic, crushed
1 c. barley, rinsed & drained
Salt, pepper & paprika to taste
1 tsp. garlic powder, optional
4 to 5 tsp. pareve instant soup mix plus water to cover ingredients completely

1. Soak beans overnight in cold water. Rinse and drain well. Spray a roasting pan with non-stick spray. Combine all ingredients in pan and mix well. (Barley absorbs salt and pepper, so season generously.) Cover tightly and place in a 275°F oven from late Friday afternoon until lunchtime Saturday.

Yield: 8 servings (or less if you have hungry teenagers!)

322 calories per serving, 2.9 g fat (0.3 g saturated), trace cholesterol, 13 g protein, 64 g carbohydrate, 522 mg sodium, 917 mg potassium, 4 mg iron, 13 g fiber, 58 mg calcium.

Easy Vegetarian Chili

See photo (P-3). You won't believe this delicious, high-fiber chili contains no meat! Don't be deterred by the long list of ingredients. They're mostly herbs and spices. This chili is quick to prepare and tastes better the next day! Cocoa is the secret ingredient. It deepens the color and rounds out the flavor.

1 tbsp. olive or canola oil
2 onions, chopped
2 green &/or red peppers, chopped
3 cloves garlic, crushed
2 c. mushrooms, sliced
2 c. cooked or canned red kidney beans
2 c. cooked or canned chickpeas
½ c. bulgur or couscous, rinsed
28 oz. (796 ml) can tomatoes (or 6 fresh tomatoes, chopped)
1 c. bottled salsa (mild or medium)
½ c. water
1 tsp. salt (or to taste)
1 tbsp. chili powder
1 tsp. dried basil
½ tsp. each pepper, oregano & cumin
¼ tsp. cayenne
1 tbsp. unsweetened cocoa powder
1 tsp. sugar
1 c. corn niblets, optional

• **Conventional Method:** Heat oil in a large pot. Sauté onions, peppers and garlic for 5 minutes on medium heat. Add mushrooms and sauté 4 or 5 minutes more. Add remaining ingredients except corn. Bring to a boil and simmer, covered, for 25 minutes, stirring occasionally. Stir in corn.

• **Microwave Method:** Combine oil, onions, peppers and garlic in a 3-quart microsafe pot. Microwave covered on HIGH for 5 minutes. Add mushrooms and microwave 2 minutes longer. Add remaining ingredients except corn. Cover and microwave on HIGH for 18 to 20 minutes, stirring once or twice. Add corn. Let stand covered for 10 minutes.

Yield: 10 servings of approximately 1 cup each. Freezes and/or reheats well.

179 calories per serving, 3 g fat (0.4 g saturated), 0 mg cholesterol, 9 g protein, 32 g carbohydrate, 431 mg sodium, 619 mg potassium, 4 mg iron, 9 g fiber, 81 mg calcium.

- **A 19 oz. (540 ml) can of beans** or chickpeas contains 2 cups. Rinse well to remove excess sodium.
- **Gluten-Free Chili:** If you are allergic to wheat, do not use bulgur or couscous. Instead, substitute 1 cup of quinoa or millet. Rinse thoroughly and drain well. (Millet requires pretoasting. Cook it on medium heat in a heavy-bottomed skillet about 5 minutes, stirring constantly to prevent burning. It's ready when it gives off a toasty aroma similar to popcorn.) Add to remaining ingredients and cook as directed.
- **Serve over rice, noodles or Basic Polenta (p. 210).** Great with Greek Salad (p. 280).

Black Bean & Corn Casserole

See photo (P-1). Picture perfect! Elegant enough for guests. Full of fiber, full of beans!

4   c. cooked or canned black beans
2   c. stewed tomatoes or tomato sauce
3   tbsp. maple syrup or brown sugar
2   medium onions, chopped
1   green pepper, chopped
1   red pepper, chopped
3/4 c. canned or frozen corn niblets
1   tsp. Dijon mustard
1/2 tsp. each cayenne pepper & chili powder
Freshly ground pepper, to taste

1. Spray a 2-quart ovenproof casserole with non-stick spray. Combine all ingredients and mix well. Bake covered at 350°F for 45 minutes, until bubbling hot and flavors are blended. (Or microwave in a covered microsafe casserole on HIGH for 15 to 18 minutes. Stir once or twice during cooking.)

Yield: 6 servings of about 1 cup each. Freezes and/or reheats well. Also delicious cold.

207 calories per cup, 1 g fat (0.2 g saturated), 0 mg cholesterol, 10 g protein, 42 g carbohydrate, 270 mg sodium, 577 mg potassium, 3 mg iron, 10 g fiber, 62 mg calcium.

- **Serve over rice or pasta** with Israeli Salad (p. 280), or use as a side dish.

Easy BBQ Chickpea Casserole

See photo (P-6). So delicious, so nutritious, so quick to prepare.

4   c. cooked or canned chickpeas (two 19-oz. cans, drained & rinsed)
2   c. canned stewed tomatoes
3–4 tbsp. maple syrup or honey
1   medium onion, chopped
1   green pepper, chopped
1   tsp. Dijon mustard
1/2 tsp. cayenne pepper
Freshly ground pepper, to taste

1. Spray a 2-quart ovenproof casserole with non-stick spray. Combine all ingredients and mix well. Cover and bake at 350°F for 1 hour.

Yield: 6 servings. Freezes and/or reheats well. Also excellent served cold.

242 calories per cup, 3.1 g fat (0.3 g saturated), 0 mg cholesterol, 11 g protein, 45 g carbohydrate, 218 mg sodium, 597 mg potassium, 4 mg iron, 10 g fiber, 95 mg calcium.

- **Variation:** Add 1 cup sliced mushrooms. Season with 1/2 teaspoon each dried basil and thyme.
- **Delicious with Vegetarian Stuffed Peppers** (p. 233), or Couscous & Mushroom Casserole (p.

205). Also good served over Quinoa (p. 217) or Basic Polenta (p. 210).

Lentil Spinach Paté

The food processor makes quick work out of this easy vegetarian paté. Slices make an excellent vegetarian sandwich filling, or serve hot with tomato sauce as a vegetarian alternative to meat loaf.

10	oz. pkg. (300 g) frozen chopped spinach
2	medium onions
1	stalk celery
2	cloves garlic, minced
1	tbsp. olive or canola oil
3–4	tbsp. water (as needed)
19	oz. can (540 ml) lentils, rinsed & drained
2	medium carrots, cut into chunks
1/2	c. fresh parsley
1	c. bread crumbs or matzo meal
1/2	tsp. salt (to taste)
1/2	tsp. pepper
1/2	tsp. each dried basil & dried thyme
2	eggs (or 1 egg plus 2 egg whites)

1. Preheat oven to 350°F. Thaw spinach; squeeze dry. Cut onions and celery in chunks. Process with quick on/offs, until coarsely chopped. Sauté onions, celery and garlic in oil until golden, about 5 minutes. If veggies begin to stick, add 1 to 2 tablespoons of water. Process lentils, carrots and parsley until minced, about 20 seconds. Add spinach with remaining ingredients and 2 tablespoons of water. Mix well.

2. Pour mixture into a sprayed 9 x 4-inch loaf pan. Bake uncovered at 350°F for about 45 minutes. A knife inserted into the center of the baked loaf should come out clean. Serve hot or cold.

Yield: 8 to 10 slices. Leftovers will keep for 3 or 4 days in the refrigerator or can be frozen.

177 calories per slice, 4.1 g fat (0.9 g saturated), 53 mg cholesterol, 9 g protein, 27 g carbohydrate, 317 mg sodium, 431 mg potassium, 4 mg iron, 7 g fiber, 105 mg calcium.

- **To serve as an appetizer,** let cool 15 minutes. Loosen with a flexible spatula or knife and invert carefully onto a serving plate; chill. Serve with sliced cucumbers, tomatoes and assorted breads.
- **Serve slices topped** with Quick'n Easy Tomato Sauce (p. 191). (It's like meat loaf, without the meat!) Perfect with baked potatoes and steamed broccoli.
- **Lentil Burgers:** Prepare mixture as directed in Step 1. In Step 2, heat a little oil in a non-stick skillet. Drop uncooked mixture from a spoon into skillet. (Use a teaspoon for miniatures, or a large spoon for regular-sized burgers.) Flatten slightly with the back of the spoon. Cook for 3 to 4 minutes on each side, or until golden. Pat with paper towels to remove excess fat. Serve miniatures in mini pitas or regular-sized burgers in hamburger buns. Top with salsa, lettuce, onions, etc. Recipe makes about 3 dozen miniatures or 8 to 10 large burgers.

Red Lentil Paté (I Can't Believe It's Not Chopped Liver!)

Savor the flavor of "almost-liver" without guilt or cholesterol. Thank you, Suzi Lipes.

2	c. red lentils, picked over and rinsed
4	c. vegetable broth or water
1	tbsp. olive oil
2	large onions, chopped

3–4 cloves garlic, minced
1 tsp. each dried basil, oregano & thyme
½ c. fresh parsley, minced
¼ c. seasoned bread crumbs (plus 2 tbsp. to coat the pan)
½ tsp. Kosher or sea salt (to taste)
Freshly ground pepper (to taste)
2 tsp. fresh lemon juice or balsamic vinegar
1 tsp. Oriental sesame oil

1. Cook lentils in broth or water until tender, about 25 minutes. Do not drain. Let cool, then mash. Heat oil in a large non-stick skillet. Add onions, garlic and dried herbs. Sauté on medium heat until brown, stirring often. Add to lentils along with remaining ingredients; mix well. Preheat oven to 350°F. Spray a 9 x 4-inch loaf pan with non-stick spray. Sprinkle pan with 2 tablespoons crumbs, lightly coating bottom and sides of pan. Spread lentil mixture in pan. Bake uncovered for 30 minutes, until set. When cool, unmold and refrigerate. Best served at room temperature.

Yield: 12 slices. Leftovers keep 3 to 4 days in the fridge. Freezing intensifies the flavor of the herbs.

144 calories per slice, 2.4 g fat (0.3 g saturated), trace cholesterol, 9 g protein, 23 g carbohydrate, 534 mg sodium, 379 mg potassium, 3 mg iron, 9 g fiber, 36 mg calcium.

Vegetarian Shepherd's Pie

Nutrient-packed! TVP is made from soy flour and is sold in natural food stores. You can top the "meat" mixture with mixed veggies. Garlic Mashed Potatoes (p. 257) also make a terrific topping.

Potato & Carrot Purée (p. 258)
1½ c. TVP (textured vegetable protein)
Water, as needed
1 onion, chopped
1 c. mushrooms, chopped
1–2 cloves garlic, minced
2 tsp. canola oil
1 tbsp. flour
2 tbsp. ketchup
Salt, pepper & basil, to taste

1. Prepare potato purée; set aside. Soak TVP in 2 cups of hot water for 10 minutes. In a non-stick skillet, sauté veggies and garlic in oil until golden. Add TVP and stir constantly for 5 minutes, until brown and crumbly. Stir in flour and cook 2 minutes longer. Add ketchup, ¼ cup water and seasonings. Place mixture in a sprayed deep 9-inch pie plate. Top with potato purée. Bake in a preheated 350°F oven for 15 minutes, until browned.

Yield: 6 servings. Reheats well. Can be frozen.

200 calories per serving, 2.5 g fat (0.5 g saturated), 2 mg cholesterol, 15 g protein, 35 g carbohydrate, 113 mg sodium, 1028 mg potassium, 3 mg iron, 7 g fiber, 135 mg calcium.

Fake 'n Bake Burgers

A wonderful way to use up mashed potatoes! Large patties make a super vegetarian main dish, minis make great hors d'oeuvres. These are also perfect for Passover. What a rainbow of color and flavor!

4 medium potatoes (or 3 sweet potatoes)
2 medium onions, chopped
1 green & 1 red pepper, chopped

2 cloves garlic, crushed
2 tsp. olive or vegetable oil
3 carrots, peeled & grated (about 1 c.)
2 unpeeled zucchini, grated (about 2 c.)
¼ c. minced dill &/or parsley
2 eggs (or 1 egg & 2 egg whites)
1 c. matzo meal (or bread crumbs)
Salt & pepper, to taste
1 tbsp. additional oil (approximately)

1. Peel potatoes and cut into chunks. Boil in salted water until tender, 15 to 20 minutes. Drain well and mash. You should have about 2 cups. While potatoes are cooking, prepare remaining veggies. (So quick in the processor!) In a large non-stick skillet (or microwave), cook onions, peppers and garlic in 2 teaspoons oil for 5 minutes, until softened. Add carrots and zucchini. Cook 3 or 4 minutes longer. Cool slightly. Add remaining ingredients except additional oil. Mix well.

2. Preheat oven to 375°F. Spray a foil-lined baking sheet with non-stick spray. Form mixture into patties. (An ice cream scoop or ¼ cup measure works well.) Oil your fingertips, then lightly oil the tops of patties, flattening them slightly. Bake uncovered at 375°F for 10 to 12 minutes. Turn patties over and bake 10 minutes longer.

Yield: about 18 patties. These reheat and/or freeze well.

76 calories per patty, 2 g fat (0.4 g saturated), 24 mg cholesterol, 2 g protein, 13 g carbohydrate, 17 mg sodium, 202 mg potassium, <1 mg iron, 2 g fiber, 15 mg calcium.

• **Variations:** Add a 10-ounce package (300 g) chopped cooked spinach, squeezed dry, to cooked vegetables. If desired, substitute chopped mushrooms for zucchini and add a dash of thyme. Be creative and try various vegetables. Leftover veggies are great!

• **Mini Burgers:** Prepare Fake 'n Bake Burger mixture and make small patties. Bake 15 to 20 minutes (or brown for 3 to 4 minutes per side in a little oil in a non-stick skillet.) You'll get about 60 minis, each one containing 23 calories and 0.6 g fat (0.1 g saturated).

• **Grain Burgers:** Follow recipe for Fake 'n Bake Burgers, but instead of potatoes, substitute 2 cups leftover cooked rice, bulgur, millet, couscous or quinoa. Cooked grain should be moist and sticky. Process on Steel Knife of processor until fine. Combine with remaining ingredients. Bake as directed, or sauté for 4 to 5 minutes per side in a little oil.

• **Vegetarian Burgers:** Follow recipe for Fake 'n Bake Burgers, but instead of potatoes, use 2 cups cooked or canned lentils, chickpeas or green peas. Rinse and drain well. Process until finely ground. Mix with remaining ingredients. Bake as directed, or sauté 4 to 5 minutes per side in a little oil.

Hearty Vegetable Stew (Givetch)

This satisfying stew is a winner with my students! Vary the vegetables according to what you have on hand. Baked beans give a wonderful flavor and also add fiber and protein. Enjoy without guilt!

1 tbsp. olive oil
2 onions, chopped
1 red or green pepper
2 stalks celery
1 medium eggplant (do not peel)
2 medium zucchini (do not peel)
3–4 cloves crushed garlic
2 potatoes, peeled
3 ripe tomatoes

3–4 carrots, peeled & trimmed
28 oz. can (796 ml) tomatoes
14 oz. can (398 ml) vegetarian baked beans (or
      canned vegetarian chili with beans)
Salt & pepper, to taste
2   tsp. dried basil (or 2 tbsp. fresh)

1. Heat oil on medium heat in a large, heavy-bottomed pot. Add onions and sauté for 5 minutes. Meanwhile, cut remaining vegetables into 1-inch chunks. Add red pepper and celery to onions. Reduce heat to low, cover and cook for 3 or 4 minutes. Add eggplant, zucchini and garlic. Cook covered for another 5 minutes.

2. Add remaining ingredients and mix well. Simmer covered 25 to 30 minutes longer, until vegetables are done, stirring occasionally.

Yield: 12 servings. Reheats and/or freezes well. Serve with rice, couscous, bulgur or polenta.

132 calories per serving, 1.8 g fat (0.3 g saturated), 0 mg cholesterol, 5 g protein, 28 g carbohydrate, 328 mg sodium, 736 mg potassium, 1 mg iron, 6 g fiber, 75 mg calcium.

• **Eggplant is available** all year round. Buy eggplant which is firm and heavy, with a smooth, glossy skin. Avoid those with rough, spongy spots and/or brown signs of decay. Small, slender eggplants have smaller seeds and are sweeter and more tender, but larger ones are more practical. For more information, see Eggplant Etcetera! (p. 59).
• **Instead of zucchini,** substitute 2 cups of butternut squash (peeled and cut into chunks).
• Replace potatoes with 8 to 10 new baby potatoes or 1 large sweet potato, peeled and cut in chunks.
• **Instead of fresh tomatoes,** substitute 1 cup sundried tomatoes. Substitute ½ teaspoon dried

rosemary and add ½ cup of chopped pitted black olives during the last few minutes of cooking.
• **Add 2 cups sliced mushrooms** along with the onions. (Tastes great with portobello mushrooms!)
• **Tofu that was frozen** works well in this recipe. Its texture will be slightly chewy. Thaw at room temperature for several hours, or soak in hot water and press well to express the liquid. Add with the remaining ingredients at the beginning of Step 2. Simmer covered for 25 to 30 minutes.

Simple & Good Ratatouille (Mediterranean Vegetable Stew)

2   medium eggplants (2½ lb./1.2 kg)
2   medium onions
1   green & 1 red pepper
1   medium zucchini
2   c. mushrooms
4   cloves garlic, minced
1–2 tbsp. olive oil
Salt & pepper, to taste
½   tsp. each dried basil & oregano
¼   c. balsamic or red wine vinegar
2   tbsp. brown sugar (to taste)
2   5½ oz. (156 ml) cans tomato paste
½   c. water

1. Spray a large, heavy-bottomed pot with non-stick spray. Dice vegetables (do not peel eggplant). Add oil to pot and heat on medium heat. Add vegetables and sauté for 10 to 15 minutes, stirring often. If necessary, add a little water to prevent sticking.

2. Add seasonings, vinegar, brown sugar, tomato paste and water. Simmer covered for 25 to 30 minutes, stirring occasionally. If mixture gets too thick, add a little water. Adjust seasonings to taste. Serve hot or cold.

Yield: 8 to 10 servings. Mixture keeps up to 10 days in the refrigerator or freezes well.

134 calories per serving, 2.4 g fat (0.4 g saturated), 0 mg cholesterol, 4 g protein, 28 g carbohydrate, 318 mg sodium, 906 mg potassium, 2 mg iron, 6 g fiber, 44 mg calcium.

- **Delicious over spaghetti squash**, rice, bulgur, couscous, polenta, millet or your favorite grain.
- **Ratatouille makes a great** vegetarian pasta sauce. Serve it hot over spiral pasta or penne and sprinkle with grated low-fat mozzarella or Parmesan cheese. Heat for 2 minutes in the microwave to melt the cheese.
- **Use Ratatouille instead of tomato sauce** in lasagna. It also makes a great filling for crêpes. Leftover Ratatouille makes a perfect pizza topping.
- **Serve a scoop** of chilled Ratatouille on a bed of salad greens as a starter or light main course.
- **Serve it cold** as an appetizer with Pita or Tortilla Chips (p. 72), crackers or assorted breads.
- **Easy Vegetarian Stew:** In Step 2, add any of the following cut-up vegetables: yellow squash, celery, carrots, potatoes or sweet potatoes, fresh or sun-dried tomatoes, green beans, asparagus. You can also add canned chickpeas, black beans and/or kidney beans, rinsed and drained. If desired, dice ½ pound (250 g) of tofu and add to stew mixture during the last 10 minutes of cooking. (Tofu that was frozen, then thawed, will have a meaty texture.) Serve over rice, bulgur, pasta, couscous or Basic Polenta (p. 210).

Belle's Chunky Ratatouille

*This is my mother's recipe for ratatouille.
It's addictive!*

2 onions, thinly sliced
1 tbsp. olive oil
3 cloves garlic, crushed
1 small eggplant (about 3/4 lb./340 g), cut in chunks
1 green pepper, cut in strips
2 red peppers, cut in strips
1 jalapeño pepper, finely chopped (optional)
2 medium zucchini, sliced
2 large ripe tomatoes, cut into chunks
8 oz. can (237 ml) tomato sauce
1 tbsp. balsamic vinegar
Salt & pepper, to taste
Pinch of chili flakes
⅛ tsp. chili powder
⅛ tsp. oregano
⅛ tsp. mixed Italian seasoning
⅛ tsp. cumin, optional
1 tsp. sugar
2 tbsp. fresh basil, chopped (or 1 tsp. dried)

1. Sauté onions in oil on medium heat for 3 or 4 minutes. Add garlic and saute briefly. Add eggplant. Sauté for 5 minutes longer, stirring occasionally. Add peppers and zucchini; saute for 5 minutes. Add remaining ingredients. Bring to a boil, reduce heat and simmer covered for 25 minutes longer, until vegetables are tender. Stir occasionally. Tastes even better when reheated.

Yield: 6 to 8 servings. This keeps 7 to 10 days in the refrigerator. Freezes well.

112 calories per serving, 3.1 g fat (0.5 g saturated), 0 mg cholesterol, 4 g protein, 21 g carbohydrate, 241 mg sodium, 801 mg potassium, 2 mg iron, 5 g fiber, 49 mg calcium.

Enchilada Lasagna

No-roll enchiladas are layered like lasagna.
Full of fiber and so calci-yummy!

2   tsp. olive oil
1   onion, chopped
1½ c. mushrooms, sliced
1   green pepper, chopped
2   cloves garlic, crushed
3   c. tomato sauce (low-sodium, if possible)
19 oz/540 ml can kidney beans (rinsed & drained)
½   tsp. chili powder (to taste)
7   corn or flour tortillas
¾   c. grated low-fat mozzarella cheese
¾   c. grated low-fat Swiss cheese

1. Preheat oven to 350°F. Heat oil in a non-stick skillet. Sauté veggies and garlic for 5 minutes. Add sauce, beans and chili powder. Simmer uncovered for 5 minutes. Spray a 2-quart casserole with non-stick spray. Layer 2 tortillas, ⅓ of sauce mixture and ⅓ of cheeses, until all ingredients are used, making 3 layers. Cut up the extra tortilla to fill in any empty spaces. Bake uncovered for 25 minutes.

Yield: 6 servings. Reheats and/or freezes well.

273 calories per serving, 5.8 g fat (2.2 g saturated), 13 mg cholesterol, 17 g protein, 41 g carbohydrate, 154 mg sodium, 617 mg potassium, 2 mg iron, 11 g fiber, 288 mg calcium.

Easy Enchiladas

1   onion, chopped
1   c. mushrooms, sliced
2   tsp. olive oil
2   cloves garlic, crushed
19 oz. (540 ml) can kidney beans
1   c. canned or frozen corn, drained
2   c. tomato sauce
¼   tsp. red pepper flakes
8   corn or flour tortillas
1   c. grated low-fat cheddar cheese

1. Preheat oven to 350°F. Sauté onion and mushrooms in oil for 5 minutes. Add garlic and cook 2 minutes longer. Rinse and drain beans thoroughly. Place beans in a bowl and mash slightly. Add to skillet along with corn. Add ½ cup of sauce and red pepper flakes; mix well.

2. Spray an oblong Pyrex casserole with non-stick spray. Soften tortillas by heating in the microwave on HIGH about 1 minute. Spread ½ cup sauce in bottom of casserole. Spoon some of bean/corn mixture on each tortilla in a strip across the middle. Roll up tightly and arrange seam side down in casserole. Top with remaining sauce. Cover and bake for 25 minutes. Uncover, sprinkle with cheese and bake uncovered 5 to 10 minutes longer, until cheese is melted.

Yield: 8 enchiladas. These reheat and/or freeze well.

199 calories per serving, 5 g fat (1.1 g saturated), 3 mg cholesterol, 11 g protein, 30 g carbohydrate, 508 mg sodium, 346 mg potassium, 1 mg iron, 5 g fiber, 105 mg calcium.

Eggplant Roll-Ups

Eggplant replaces pasta in this simple and delicious vegetarian dish. Great for brunch!

1   medium eggplant (do not peel)
10 oz. pkg. (300 g) frozen spinach, cooked, drained & squeezed dry
1   c. pressed dry non-fat cottage cheese
3   tbsp. grated Parmesan cheese
2   tbsp. fresh basil, minced (or 1 tsp. dried)
¼   c. skim milk
Salt, pepper & garlic powder, to taste
2   c. tomato sauce
¾   c. grated low-fat mozzarella cheese

1. Preheat oven to 350°F. Slice eggplant lengthwise into 12 slices, discarding the outer slices. Arrange on a sprayed baking sheet. Bake for 10 minutes, until soft and pliable. Meanwhile, process spinach, cheeses, basil, milk and seasonings. Mix well. Pour 1 cup of sauce into a sprayed 9 x 13-inch casserole. Spread filling in a thin layer on each slice of eggplant and roll up tightly. Place seam side down in casserole. Top with remaining sauce and sprinkle lightly with cheese. Bake uncovered for 25 to 30 minutes, until golden and bubbling. Perfect with a garden salad.

Yield: 8 rolls. Freezes and/or reheats well. Double the recipe if you have guests.

102 calories per roll, 2.7 g fat (1.6 g saturated), 11 mg cholesterol, 10 g protein, 11 g carbohydrate, 582 mg sodium, 480 mg potassium, 1 mg iron, 3 g fiber, 173 mg calcium.

Vegetarian Stuffed Peppers

See photo (P-6). Easy, delicious and colorful.

Rainbow Rice Pilaf (p. 213)
6   peppers (green, red, yellow &/or orange)
4   c. water
1½ c. tomato sauce (bottled or homemade)

1. Prepare Rainbow Rice Pilaf as directed, using vegetable broth. Cut peppers in half lengthwise through stem end. Carefully remove seeds and core. In a large saucepan, bring water to a boil. Add peppers and simmer for 3 or 4 minutes, until slightly softened. Drain well. Preheat oven to 350°F. Fill peppers with rice mixture. Spread 1 cup sauce on the bottom of a sprayed Pyrex oblong casserole. Arrange peppers in a single layer over sauce. Drizzle lightly with remaining sauce. Bake uncovered for 25 minutes (or microwave uncovered on HIGH for 12 to 15 minutes), until peppers are tender and heated through.

Yield: 6 servings as a main dish or 12 servings as a side dish. Reheats well. Do not freeze.

232 calories per main dish serving, 2.5 g fat (0.4 g saturated), 0 mg cholesterol, 7 g protein, 48 g carbohydrate, 727 mg sodium, 586 mg potassium, 3 mg iron, 5 g fiber, 52 mg calcium.

• **Variations:** Add ½ cup diced tofu to cooked rice for additional protein. For additional soluble fiber, add ½ cup canned red kidney beans or chickpeas, rinsed and drained. For additional calcium and protein, top each pepper with 2 tablespoons grated low-fat Swiss, Parmesan or mozzarella cheese during the last 10 minutes of baking (or last 5 minutes of microwaving).
• **Other Fillings:** Try Italian-Style Rice (p. 215), Confetti Lemon Rice (p. 212), Spinach Lemon

Rice (p. 212), Millet Pilaf (p. 209), Barley & Mushroom Risotto or No-Guilt Bulgur with Mushrooms (p. 208).

- **Stuffed Vegetables:** Any of the above fillings can be used to stuff Vegetarian Cabbage Rolls (p. 234). Other veggies which are lovely when stuffed are hollowed-out tomatoes, zucchini or yellow squash halves. Use your imagination!

Vegetarian Cabbage Rolls

Whether you call these Halishkes or Prakkes, they taste great!

Rainbow Rice Pilaf (p. 213)
1   medium cabbage (about 3 lb./1.2 kg)
Boiling water
19 oz. can (540 ml) tomatoes
5¹/₂ oz. can (156 ml) tomato paste
¹/₄ c. brown sugar, packed
2   tbsp. lemon juice
1   large onion, chopped

1. Prepare Rainbow Rice Pilaf as directed; let cool. Meanwhile, remove 12 of the large outer leaves from cabbage. Trim away tough ribs. Place cabbage leaves into a large pot of boiling water. Remove pot from heat, cover and let stand for 10 minutes. Drain cabbage thoroughly and set aside.

2. In the same pot, combine tomatoes, tomato paste, brown sugar and lemon juice. Break up tomatoes with a spoon. Remove ¹/₂ cup of sauce from pot and add it to rice mixture. Mix well.

3. Bring sauce mixture to a boil. Slice any leftover cabbage and add it to the sauce along with the chopped onion. Meanwhile, place a large spoonful of rice mixture on each cabbage leaf. Roll up, fold-

ing in ends. Carefully place cabbage rolls seam-side down in simmering sauce. Cook on low heat, partially covered, about 1 hour, until juice has thickened. Adjust seasonings to taste.

Yield: 12 cabbage rolls. These reheat well. Freezing is not recommended.

159 calories per cabbage roll, 1.7 g fat (0.2 g saturated), 0 mg cholesterol, 5 g protein, 34 g carbohydrate, 372 mg sodium, 479 mg potassium, 2 mg iron, 5 g fiber, 70 mg calcium.

- **For tricks on how** to prepare cabbage leaves, refer to Cabbage Without Damage! (p. 177).
- **Crushed or diced canned tomatoes** can be used. If you only have a very large can of tomatoes on hand, either freeze the leftovers or add them to your next vegetable soup or pasta sauce!
- **Veggie Variations:** If you have frozen tofu on hand, defrost and crumble it. You'll need about 1 cup. Combine crumbled tofu with rice mixture. Add salt, pepper and basil to taste. Stuff cabbage as directed. Another variation is to add 1 cup cooked or canned lentils or chickpeas.
- **For other ideas for fillings,** see notes following Vegetarian Stuffed Peppers (p. 233).
- **Serve with whole wheat bread** and Tomato, Onion & Pepper Salad (p. 281).

Baked Tofu in BBQ Sauce

Whenever I eat this tasty dish or the terrific variation below, I feel so healthy!

1   lb. firm tofu (500 g), sliced ¹/₂" thick
1¹/₂ c. bottled or homemade BBQ sauce
2   large onions, peeled & sliced
2   c. mushrooms, sliced

1. Preheat oven to 400°F. Place sliced tofu between layers of paper towels on a plate. Top with another plate. Weigh it down with cans and let drain for 20 minutes. Pour half of sauce into a sprayed oblong casserole. Add onions and mushrooms; mix well. Arrange sliced tofu over onion mixture. Top with remaining sauce. Bake uncovered at 400°F for 20 minutes. Turn tofu over with a spatula. Baste with sauce and spoon some of the onion mixture on top. Bake 10 minutes longer.

Yield: 6 servings. This reheats well, but freezing is not recommended. I like to serve it with brown basmati rice. Leftover baked tofu is delicious in sandwiches.

180 calories per serving, 7.9 g fat (1.2 g saturated), 0 mg cholesterol, 14 g protein, 17 g carbohydrate, 522 mg sodium, 420 mg potassium, 9 mg iron, 4 g fiber, 177 mg calcium.

- **Use tofu processed** with calcium sulphate for maximum calcium intake. This can also be made with light 1% fat extra-firm silken tofu. (This is softer than regular firm tofu.)
- **Terrific Baked Tofu:** Follow recipe above, but omit BBQ sauce. Substitute 1¼ cups tomato sauce and ¼ cup bottled Szechuan Spicy Duck Sauce or Chinese plum sauce. (If using plum sauce, add ¼ teaspoon red pepper flakes or a few drops of Tabasco sauce.)

Italian-Style Baked Tofu

1 lb. firm tofu (500 grams), sliced ½" thick (low-fat tofu can be used)
2 large onions, sliced
1 c. mushrooms, sliced
½ of a red pepper, chopped
½ of a green pepper, chopped
2½ c. vegetarian spaghetti sauce

1. Place sliced tofu between layers of paper towels on a plate. Top with another plate. Weigh it down with cans and let drain for 20 minutes. Preheat oven to 400°F. Spray a 9 x 13-inch casserole with non-stick spray. Place vegetables in the bottom of the dish. Add half of sauce and mix well. Place tofu on top of vegetable mixture. Top with remaining sauce. Bake uncovered for 40 to 45 minutes, basting once or twice during cooking.

Yield: 6 servings. Serve over pasta. Reheats well. Do not freeze.

213 calories per serving, 10.7 g fat (1.6 g saturated), 0 mg cholesterol, 15 g protein, 20 g carbohydrate, 560 mg sodium, 771 mg potassium, 10 mg iron, 5 g fiber, 192 mg calcium.

Baked Oriental Tofu

1 lb. (500 g) firm tofu, sliced ½" thick
½–¾ c. Garlic "Sparerib" Sauce (p. 108)
2 tbsp. sesame seeds
2 tbsp. sliced green onions

1. Press tofu (see above). Cut slices diagonally to make triangles. Marinate tofu in ½ cup sauce for 20 minutes. Preheat oven to 400°F. Spray an oblong casserole with nonstick spray. Remove tofu from marinade, reserving sauce. Arrange tofu in a single layer in casserole. Bake uncovered at 400°F for 12 to 15 minutes. Turn tofu over, baste with reserved sauce and sprinkle with sesame seeds. Bake 10 minutes longer. Top with a little additional sauce. Garnish with green onions.

Tofu Info!

- Tofu is often referred to as "meat without the bone." It is made by coagulating soy milk to create curds. The curds are drained and pressed into blocks. Tofu contains no cholesterol.
- Many Kosher brands are available. Tofu is pareve (i.e. contains no meat or dairy products).
- How to Buy Tofu: Check the expiration date and buy the freshest package you can. I use either firm or lite (1%) firm tofu for most of my recipes. Silken tofu is usually used for dips and spreads. Some manufacturers produce herb-flavored tofu.
- The main difference between brands is the amount of fat, calories and moisture contained. Regular tofu contains less calories and fat than firm tofu because regular tofu contains more water! Once tofu is pressed to remove the water, differences are negligible.
- Low-Fat ("Lite")Tofu: Mori-Nu makes a 1% fat Kosher silken tofu. According to nutritional information provided by the manufacturer, 3 oz. (84 grams) contain just 35 calories and 1 gram of fat. Check your health food store or supermarket for available low-fat brands in your area.
- Tofu processed with either calcium chloride or calcium sulphate is a non-dairy source of calcium. This is an excellent way for vegans and those with a lactose intolerance or milk allergy to increase their intake of calcium.
- Four ounces of tofu processed with calcium sulphate contain 170 mg of calcium, according to nutritional information provided by Vitasoy USA Inc., of South San Francisco, California.
- Storage: Once you've opened the package, place tofu in a container. Cover with cold water and refrigerate. Change the water every day. Before using, drain tofu well and pat it dry with paper towels. Once the original package has been opened, tofu will keep 5 or 6 days.
- To freeze tofu: Slice it $1/2$-inch thick. Wrap each slice in plastic wrap. Place packages in an airtight container. Tofu can be frozen for about 3 months. Defrost at room temperature.
- If you freeze tofu, its texture will change. Crumble defrosted tofu and use it as a meat substitute in recipes such as vegetarian lasagna, cabbage rolls, spaghetti sauce, chili or stew.

Tofu with Taste

- If you object to tofu's spongy texture and bland taste, try pressing it first. This removes excess liquid and helps the tofu absorb the flavor of the marinade or sauce in which it will be cooked.
- Pressed Tofu: Slice tofu. Place slices on a baking sheet between layers of paper towels. Top with a plate or baking sheet. Weigh down with heavy cans and let it stand at room temperature for 20 to 30 minutes (or refrigerate for up to 24 hours). Pat dry.
- What can you do with tofu? Cut pressed tofu into cubes or strips and use it in stir-fries, stews and casseroles instead of chicken or beef. Marinate cubes of tofu in bottled teriyaki sauce and make vegetarian kabobs. You can also use tofu in dips and spreads.
- Combine tofu with different vegetables and grains to make meatless main dishes. Change the flavor with different sauces or marinades.
- Sloppy Toe Topping: As a main dish, serve Sloppy Toes (p. 119) over rice or polenta.
- Grilled Tofu: Marinate slices of pressed tofu in your favorite Oriental marinade, teriyaki or soy sauce (or brush it with bottled BBQ or tomato sauce). Grill or broil until lightly browned.

To-Phooey?

- They won't say "phooey" to tofu any more! Although tofu tastes bland right out of the container, it takes on the flavor of the marinade or sauce in which it's cooked. Tasty choices are BBQ sauce, tomato sauce or salsa, Peanut Butter Sauce (p. 108) or Garlic "Sparerib" Sauce (p. 108).

- Tofu can replace part of the minced meat in your favorite meat loaf or burger recipe. Add 1/4 to 1/2 pound minced tofu to each pound (500 g) of lean ground beef or veal. (Mince tofu first in your food processor.) Prepare mixture according to your regular recipe. They won't know it's there!

- Tofu contains phytoestrogens (plant estrogen), which may help reduce hot flashes! Some studies have shown that diets high in tofu and soy products may help protect women against osteoporosis, and breast and ovarian cancers.

- Hey guys, this one's for you! The isoflavones in soy products may be linked to a lower rate of prostate cancer. Real men do eat tofu!

Yield: 6 servings. Do not freeze.

163 calories per serving, 8.2 g fat (1 g saturated), 0 mg cholesterol, 13 g protein, 12 g carbohydrate, 220 mg sodium, 247 mg potassium, 9 mg iron, 2 g fiber, 175 mg calcium.

- **Bottled sauce or Teriyaki Marinade** (p. 108) can be substituted. If using bottled sauce, check the label to make sure no fat has been added.
- **Serve with Vegetable Un-Fried Rice** (p. 211) and stir-fried vegetables.

Terrific Tofu Stir-Fry

See photo (P-4). This yummy, versatile dish is equally delicious with chicken or tofu! Calci-yummy!

Tofu & Marinade:
1 lb. firm tofu (500 g), sliced into 1/2" slices
1/4 c. vegetable or pareve chicken broth
3 tbsp. soy sauce
2 tbsp. rice or white wine vinegar
1 tsp. sugar

1 tbsp. grated ginger
2 cloves garlic, crushed

1. Place tofu between paper towels on a plate. Top with another plate, weigh down with cans and let stand for 20 minutes. Cut into 1/2-inch strips. Combine all marinade ingredients. Add tofu and marinate for 30 minutes, or refrigerate covered overnight, basting occasionally.

3 c. broccoli florets
2 tbsp. sesame seeds
1 tbsp. peanut or canola oil
2 red peppers, cut into strips
1 c. green onions, sliced
3 cloves garlic, crushed
1 tbsp. grated ginger
2 c. mushrooms, sliced
1/2 lb. fresh spinach, in bite-sized pieces
2 c. bean sprouts
2 tsp. Oriental sesame oil
1/4 tsp. red pepper flakes (crushed chilis)
1/2 tbsp. cornstarch dissolved in 1/4 c. orange juice or broth

2. Cook broccoli until bright green but still crunchy. (Microwave covered on HIGH for 2 minutes or boil for 2 or 3 minutes.) Rinse immediate-

ly in cold water; drain and set aside. In a wok, toast sesame seeds until golden, shaking pan to prevent burning. Remove from pan; set aside. Add oil to wok. Stir-fry peppers and green onions on high for 1 minute. Add garlic, ginger and mushrooms; stir-fry for 2 minutes.

3. Stir in tofu, marinade, broccoli, spinach and sprouts. Reduce heat to medium, cover and cook for 2 minutes, until heated through. Stir in sesame oil, red pepper flakes and cornstarch mixture. Bring to a boil and stir until thickened. Sprinkle with sesame seeds.

Yield: 8 servings. Serve over steamed rice or noodles. Do not freeze.

169 calories per serving, 9.3 g fat (1.3 g saturated), 0 mg cholesterol, 13 g protein, 12 g carbohydrate, 415 mg sodium, 510 mg potassium, 8 mg iron, 4 g fiber, 186 mg calcium.

- **Use leftover broccoli stems** in your favorite vegetable soup. Chinese greens, pea pods, sliced green peppers and/or partially cooked carrots can be added or substituted in the above recipe.
- **Chicken Stir-Fry:** Substitute 2 pounds boneless, skinless chicken breasts, cut in ¹/₂-inch strips. In Step 2, stir-fry chicken 2 to 3 minutes. Add peppers, ginger and green onions; complete recipe as directed. One serving contains 208 calories, 7 g fat (1.3 saturated) and 63 mg cholesterol.

Homemade Seitan

Seitan (wheat meat) is a chewy, high protein replacement for meat used in vegetarian dishes. Thanks to Joanne Moore for teaching me how simple it is to make!

Seitan:
- 6 c. whole-wheat flour (or high-gluten unbleached white flour)
- 3 c. or more of cold water (amount depends on gluten content of flour)
- Water for "washing" and cooking the dough

Tamari Broth:
- 3 quarts/ liters of water
- 6 tbsp. tamari (or soy sauce)
- 1" piece of fresh ginger, thinly sliced
- 1 piece kombu, 3" long (optional)

1. In a large bowl, combine flour and water. Mix together to make a fairly stiff dough. Knead for 10 minutes by hand. (Alternately, combine in processor and process until a ball forms, about 20 seconds. Then let machine run for 1 to 2 minutes, until dough is smooth and elastic.) Place dough in a large mixing bowl and cover completely with cold water. Let rest for 10 minutes.

2. Meanwhile, prepare broth. Bring 3 quarts of water to boil in a large pot. Add tamari sauce, ginger and kombu. Simmer for 15 to 20 minutes. Cool broth completely.

3. Discard soaking water from dough. Refill bowl with warm water. Knead dough by squeezing it with your fingers under water. Water will turn milky from the starch. Drain and repeat, continuing to knead the dough until water remains clear. For the final rinses, use cold water to firm up the gluten. (This takes 10 or 15 minutes and is easy exercise!) Dough will be brownish in color and elastic. Place it in a lightly sprayed bowl and let rest about 15 minutes to let it become more flexible.

4. There are 2 steps for cooking seitan. First, place the seitan in a large pot of boiling water and boil for 35 to 45 minutes, until it floats to the surface.

Drain well. Cut into slices ½-inch thick or 1-inch chunks.

5. Place cut-up seitan in cold tamari broth. Bring to a boil, reduce heat and simmer 1½ hours for slices or 45 minutes for chunks. When done, centre will be firm. Store in its broth in the refrigerator.

Yield: 8 servings. Seitan can be frozen either in or out of its broth for up to a month if well wrapped.

150 calories per serving, 1 g fat (0 g saturated), 0 mg cholesterol, 21 g protein, 14 g carbohydrate, 20 mg sodium, 65 mg potassium, 2 g fiber, negligible calcium.

- **Kombu is a sea vegetable** available in natural food shops. If you add kombu when cooking beans, it helps to reduce or prevent gas. It also adds flavor to vegetarian dishes.
- **Arrowhead Mills makes a quick-mix.** My nutritional analysis is based on their package information.
- **Seitan keeps for several months** if you bring it to a boil in its broth and boil for 10 minutes twice a week. Otherwise, it keeps about a week in the refrigerator if completely covered by broth.
- **Cooked seitan is an inexpensive** replacement for meat. Use it instead of meat or tofu in stews. Drain seitan before using. See Italian Style Stew (p. 185).

Pita Pizzas

So quick, so easy, so nutritious! Ideal as an appetizer, or perfect for kids as a quick meal. Pizzas can be topped with tuna, spinach, broccoli, cauliflower, zucchini, Parmesan cheese . . . have it your way!

2–4 whole-wheat or white pitas (6½")
½ c. tomato sauce
6 sun-dried tomatoes, rehydrated & cut into strips (or 4 fresh tomatoes, sliced)
½ c. sliced red or green pepper
½ c. sliced mushrooms
¼ c. sliced onion, optional
2 tbsp. fresh basil, minced (or ½ tsp. dried)
1 c. low-fat grated mozzarella cheese

1. If pitas are thick, split them in half. Place cut-side up on a foil-lined baking sheet. Spread each pita with 2 tablespoons sauce. Add toppings. Bake in a preheated 425°F oven for 10 minutes, or until cheese melts and pizzas are piping hot. As appetizers, cut into 24 wedges with scissors or a pizza wheel.

Yield: 4 pizzas as a main dish or 24 wedges as an appetizer. These freeze and/or reheat well.

189 calories per pizza, 5.9 g fat (3.2 g saturated), 15 mg cholesterol, 12 g protein, 24 g carbohydrate, 576 mg sodium, 372 mg potassium, 2 mg iron, 4 g fiber, 223 mg calcium.

- **To rehydrate sun-dried tomatoes:** (For homemade, see p. 264) Cover tomatoes with boiling water. Let stand for 10 minutes. (Or cover with cold water and microwave on HIGH for 1 minute. Soak for 5 minutes, until soft.) Drain well. Scissors work well to cut up sun-dried tomatoes.
- **As appetizers, each wedge contains** 32 calories, 1 g fat (0.5 g saturated) and 3 mg cholesterol.
- **Salsa Pita Pizzas:** Substitute salsa for tomato sauce. If desired, add 2 cloves of thinly sliced garlic. Monterey Jack can be used instead of mozzarella. Bake as directed. Cut into wedges.
- **Pesto Pita Pizzas:** Place pitas on a foil-lined pan.

Spread each pita with 1 or 2 tablespoons Best-O Pesto or Sun-Dried Tomato Pesto (p. 195). Top with Roasted Red Pepper strips (p. 57). Allow half of a pepper per pizza. Sprinkle each pita with ¼ cup grated low-fat mozzarella. Bake in a preheated 425°F oven for 10 minutes, until cheese melts. Cut into wedges.

- **Tortilla Pizzas:** In any of the above pizzas, substitute three 9-inch flour tortillas for pitas. Before adding toppings to tortillas, pierce in several places with a fork to prevent them from puffing up. Bake directly on the oven rack in a preheated 400°F oven about 5 minutes, until crisp. Transfer to a foil-lined baking sheet and top with desired toppings. Sprinkle with grated cheese. (Salsa and Monterey Jack cheese are great!) Place under the

---

Well-Dressed Pizzas!

You can make your own pizzas in about the same time it takes to run out and buy one! These are all low in fat. Just be light-handed with the cheese and choose low-fat or partly skimmed.

- **Cheese, Tomato & Fresh Basil:** Tomato sauce, fresh basil, grated mozzarella, sliced tomatoes and/or sun-dried tomatoes.
- **Roasted Vegetable:** Tomato sauce, oven-roasted or grilled vegetables (e.g. red peppers, roasted garlic, eggplant strips, sliced red onions, zucchini), grated Parmesan.
- **Mediterranean:** Sliced tomatoes, fresh or dried basil, crushed garlic, roasted red peppers, sliced black olives, grated Parmesan.
- **Sun-Dried Tomato:** Sun-dried tomatoes, fresh basil, garlic slivers, roasted red peppers, sliced green onions, tomatoes, grated Swiss or mozzarella.
- **Dream Team Favorite:** Tomato sauce, roasted red peppers, sun-dried tomatoes, sliced tomatoes, onions, sliced garlic, exotic mushrooms, fresh basil and grated mozzarella cheese.
- **Mushroom & Spinach:** Shiitake, porcini, portobello and/or cultivated mushrooms, chopped spinach, crushed garlic, roasted red peppers, red onions, grated mozzarella and/or Parmesan.
- **Greek:** Tomato sauce, sliced tomatoes, crumbled feta, chopped fresh spinach, black olives, green and red peppers, sliced onions, oregano, grated mozzarella.

- **Artichoke & Spinach:** Crushed garlic, olive oil, sliced artichoke hearts, chopped spinach, sliced mushrooms and tomatoes, grated mozzarella or cheddar.
- **Ratatouille:** Ratatouille (p. 230) and grated mozzarella or Swiss.
- **Mexican:** Salsa (homemade or bottled), sliced mushrooms, grated mozzarella or Monterey Jack.
- **Smoked Salmon Brunch Pizza:** Bake pizza crust at 425°F until golden, about 18 to 20 minutes. Blend 1 cup Firm Yogurt Cheese (p. 53) with 1 tablespoon minced dill and 1 teaspoon honey-style mustard. Spread over cooled crust. Top with smoked salmon, sliced tomato and red onion. Serve at room temperature. (Tastes like upscale bagels and lox!)
- **Chef's Secret!** Use Quick'n Easy Tomato Sauce (p. 191) or store-bought sauce. Buy low-sodium products if you're sodium-conscious (e.g., tomato or pizza sauce, tomato purée, tomato paste, canned tomatoes).
- Homemade "Sun-Dried" Tomatoes (p. 264) are wonderful on pizza, and simple to make! Prepare them in the fall, when tomatoes are plentiful, beautiful and inexpensive. (Rehydrate before using.)
- Sun-dried tomatoes packed in oil need to be rinsed very well before using to remove excess oil. Drain well and cut in strips with scissors.
- Roasted red peppers in a jar are very convenient to use, but they also need thorough rinsing to remove excess sodium. In the fall when peppers are in season, make your own! See recipe (p. 57).

broiler for a few minutes, until cheese melts. Cut into wedges.

Make & Bake Pizza with Herb Crust

The processor mixes up the dough in moments! Easy, healthy, delicious and versatile.

1	tsp. sugar
1/2	c. lukewarm water (110°F)
1	envelope dry yeast (regular or quick-rise)
1 1/3	c. all-purpose flour
1 1/2	c. whole-wheat flour
1 1/2	tbsp. sugar
3/4	tsp. salt
1/2	tsp. each dried basil & oregano
1	tbsp. plus 2 tsp. olive oil
3/4	c. lukewarm water
1	c. tomato or pizza sauce
1	c. sliced mushrooms
1	c. sliced green &/or red peppers
1 1/2	c. grated low-fat mozzarella cheese

1. Dissolve sugar in lukewarm water. Sprinkle yeast over water. Let stand 5 minutes, then stir to dissolve. Measure flours, sugar, salt and herbs into processor bowl. Process 10 seconds. Add yeast; process 10 seconds more. Combine 1 tablespoon oil with water. Add slowly through feed tube while machine is running. Process until dough gathers around the blades in a mass. Process 45 seconds longer. Dough should be slightly sticky. If machine slows down, add up to 1/4 cup more flour.

2. Place dough on a lightly floured surface. Knead for 2 minutes, until smooth and elastic. Divide in half and roll into two 12-inch circles (or 16 small circles or one 12 x 18-inch rectangle). Place on sprayed pan(s). Roll edges to make a rim. Let dough rise for 15 minutes. Meanwhile, prepare toppings. Preheat oven to 450°F.

3. Brush dough lightly with remaining 2 teaspoons oil and spread with sauce. Top with mushrooms, peppers and cheese. Bake on bottom oven rack at 450°F for 20 minutes, until crisp and golden.

Yield: 16 miniature pizzas, two 12-inch pizzas (16 wedges), or 16 to 24 squares. Freezes well.

132 calories per miniature pizza or wedge, 3.6 g fat (1.4 g saturated), 6 mg cholesterol, 6 g protein, 20 g carbohydrate, 259 mg sodium, 156 mg potassium, 1 mg iron, 2 g fiber, 88 mg calcium.

- **Prepare dough and toppings,** but don't assemble pizza until 1 hour before serving (or use a baked pizza shell!) When guests arrive, put pizza into a hot oven and bake.
- **Unbaked pizzas can be frozen.** Pop frozen pizza into a preheated oven and increase baking time by about 5 minutes. Baked pizzas also freeze well.
- **Suggested Toppings:** Shiitake, porcini or portobello mushrooms; yellow or red peppers; roasted peppers; artichoke hearts; hearts of palm; capers; salsa; tomato slices; sun-dried tomatoes; zucchini slices; herbs (basil, oregano, rosemary); sliced red onions; partly cooked eggplant slices; chopped spinach; slivered garlic; blanched broccoli, cauliflower or asparagus; grilled potato slices; sliced olives; anchovies; smoked salmon; grated low-fat cheese (Monterey Jack, Swiss, feta, Parmesan).

Mushroom Crostini

Both the mushroom topping and grilled bread (crostini) can be made several hours ahead of serving time. Reheat mushroom mixture gently before topping crostini. Also try the variations below.

1 loaf crusty bread (baguette, sourdough)
1 clove garlic, cut in half
2–3 tbsp. olive oil (approximately)
$\frac{1}{2}$ c. green onions, chopped
1 lb. (500 g) mushrooms (cultivated, shiitake or chanterelle), coarsely chopped
2–3 additional cloves garlic, crushed
Salt & pepper, to taste
$\frac{1}{2}$ tsp. dried thyme
$\frac{1}{4}$ tsp. dried rosemary
3–4 tbsp. white wine
2 tbsp. fresh lemon juice (to taste)
4 tbsp. chopped fresh parsley
1 c. grated low-fat Swiss cheese, optional

1. Grilled Bread: Cut bread on an angle into 16 slices, about $\frac{1}{2}$-inch thick. Preheat grill or broiler. Grill or broil slices just until brown around edges but still soft inside, about 2 to 3 minutes per side. Remove bread from heat and rub immediately with cut clove of garlic. Brush lightly with olive oil.

2. Mushroom Mixture: Heat 2 teaspoons of oil on medium heat in a large non-stick skillet. Add green onions and cook for 1 minute. Add mushrooms, crushed garlic and seasonings. Cook on medium-high heat for a minute or two, then add wine. Sauté 5 minutes longer, stirring often, until most of liquid has evaporated and mushrooms are tender and glazed. Stir in lemon juice along with 3 tablespoons of parsley. Remove pan from heat. (Can be made in advance. Reheat gently at serving time.)

3. Assembly: Mound a heaping spoonful of mushroom mixture on grilled bread slices. Garnish with remaining parsley. If desired, sprinkle with grated cheese and pop them under the broiler for 3 or 4 minutes, until cheese is melted. Serve immediately.

Yield: 16 crostini. Do not freeze.

103 calories per piece, 2.7 g fat (0.4 g saturated), 0 mg cholesterol, 3 g protein, 17 g carbohydrate, 174 mg sodium, 127 mg potassium, 1 mg iron, 2 g fiber, 28 mg calcium.

- **If you top each Crostini** with 1 tablespoon grated cheese, each one will contain 116 calories, 3 g fat (0.7 g saturated), 2 mg cholesterol and 96 mg calcium.
- **Variation:** Serve with Cauliflower Carrot Soup (p. 97), fresh garden salad and Strawberry Buttermilk Sherbet (p. 356). What a "deliteful" meatless meal!
- **Mushrooms in Toast Cups:** Eliminate Grilled Bread in Step 1. Prepare mushroom mixture as directed in Step 2. In Step 3, fill Toast Cups (p. 143) with hot mushroom mixture.
- **Creamy Polenta with Mushrooms:** Prepare mushroom mixture as directed in Step 2. Serve over Creamy Polenta (p. 210). Sprinkle with Parmesan cheese, if desired.
- **Mushroom Crêpes:** Prepare crêpes as directed (see p. 149). Fill with mushroom mixture and roll up. Bake covered at 400°F for 15 minutes. Sprinkle with 1 to 2 tablespoons cheese and bake uncovered 5 minutes longer, until cheese is melted.

Vegetables & Side Dishes

Vegetable Delights

- ACE those veggies! Vegetables are packed with vitamins, minerals, antioxidants and phytochemicals that help protect against disease. Many are rich in vitamins A, C, E, folate and other B vitamins. High in potassium and fiber, low in calories, they're a real nutritional bargain!

- Health experts recommend eating 5 to 10 servings of vegetables and fruits a day. Although it may seem like a lot, it's quite easy. Just include 1 or 2 vegetables or fruits with every meal and the only thing you'll have to count on will be good health!

- Eat 2 to 3 servings of veggies at dinner (e.g., a baked potato, broccoli, vegetable soup). Have a salad for lunch, or put some tomato and cucumber slices in your sandwich. Snack on baby carrots, zucchini or red pepper strips. Eat 2 servings of fresh or dried fruit as snacks each day. You'll soon be "on your weigh" to a healthier lifestyle!

- You can also increase your intake of vegetables by including them in other dishes. Add them to soups, casseroles, pasta dishes, grains, legumes, stir-fries, dips and spreads.

- What's a serving? Half a cup of most veggies, one cup of salad or one piece of fruit.

- Their nutrient value, color and texture will be affected by the cooking time and method.

- A chef's trick to brighten the color of green veggies like green beans and broccoli is to plunge them into boiling water for a minute, then immediately immerse them in ice cold water to stop the cooking process. The vegetables will still be raw, but their color will be beautiful and vibrant.

- Don't overcook vegetables. I have an old White House Cookbook from 1925 which recommends cooking cauliflower for one hour! No wonder people hated to eat vegetables.

- Try the French method of cooking veggies. Boil uncovered in a big pot of boiling salted water for 6 to 7 minutes. This helps keep green veggies green. If cooked longer, their color will change.

- The microwave is marvelous for cooking most vegetables, from asparagus to zucchini. Soak in cold water; shake dry. The soaking water clinging to them provides enough steam to cook them. Allow 5 to 7 minutes per pound/500 g. Stir or turn veggies over halfway through cooking.

- Veggies with a skin (e.g. potatoes, squash) should be pierced, then cooked on a microsafe rack.

- Steaming is another quick and excellent way to cook vegetables. Follow the 7 minute maxi-rule. To ensure that they will be properly cooked in this time, cut denser veggies in small pieces.

- Keep frozen vegetables handy in the freezer. If harvested and quick-frozen at their peak, they often have more vitamins than so-called fresh vegetables which have been in storage.

- Kids often don't like vegetables, but don't worry. When my son Doug was little, he only liked to eat white food (e.g., chicken, rice, potatoes and matzo balls). When I served him vegetables, he would say "Make them disappear, Mom. Put them in the food processor!" Today he is a chef, cooking all kinds of vegetables each day!

- To clean broccoli, trim and cut into bite-sized pieces. Place in a sinkful of cold water; add 1 to 2 tablespoons vinegar and a little salt. Soak 10 to 15 minutes. Rinse and drain, then cook as directed.

- Some Rabbis don't allow fresh broccoli to be used because there is a concern about the presence of microscopic bacteria. You can substitute two 10-oz. (300 g) packages of frozen broccoli florets.

- Don't store onions and potatoes together. Potatoes give off moisture and produce a gas which causes onions to deteriorate quickly. The gases produced by onions make potatoes spoil faster.

- Lycopene, a powerful antioxidant, can be found in tomatoes, watermelon, pink grapefruit and berries. The lycopene found in processed and cooked tomato products (e.g., tomato juice, tomato paste and sauce) may be more readily absorbed than that found in fresh tomatoes. It needs a little fat to be absorbed, so add a little olive oil.

Teriyaki Asparagus

1½ lb. (750 g) asparagus, trimmed & cut diagonally into 2" slices
2　tbsp. teriyaki sauce
1　tsp. minced fresh ginger
2　green onions, chopped
½–1 tsp. Oriental sesame oil
1　tbsp. honey
1　tbsp. fresh orange juice
½　tsp. Dijon mustard
2　tbsp. toasted sesame seeds

1. Soak asparagus in cold water; drain well. Place in a 1-quart casserole and drizzle with teriyaki sauce. Sprinkle with ginger and green onions. Microwave covered on HIGH for 6 to 7 minutes, until barely tender. Let stand covered for 3 minutes. Stir in sesame oil, honey, orange juice and mustard. Sprinkle with sesame seeds. Serve immediately (or reheat briefly in the microwave at serving time).

Yield: 4 to 6 servings. Do not freeze.

97 calories per serving, 3.2 g fat (0.2 g saturated), 0 mg cholesterol, 6 g protein, 14 g carbohydrate, 388 mg sodium, 304 mg potassium, 2 mg iron, 3 g fiber, 55 mg calcium.

- **Place sesame seeds** in a small pan and toast on medium heat for 3 to 4 minutes. Watch carefully to prevent burning. (I often use the sesame seeds from the bottom of the bag when I buy bagels!)

Simply Steamed Asparagus

1½ lb. (750 g) asparagus, trimmed & cut into 2" slices
Salt & pepper, to taste
1　tsp. fresh thyme leaves (or ¼ tsp. dried)
3　tbsp. fresh lemon, lime or orange juice
1　tsp. tub margarine (or 2 tsp. light tub margarine)

1. Soak asparagus in cold water; drain well. Steam for 3 to 4 minutes. Immediately transfer to a bowl of ice water to stop the cooking process. (To microwave asparagus, place it in an oval casserole and microwave covered on HIGH for 6 to 7 minutes, until tender-crisp. Let stand covered for 3 minutes.) Season with salt, pepper and thyme. Sprinkle with juice. Add margarine and mix well. At serving time, reheat for 2 or 3 minutes on HIGH in the microwave.

Yield: 4 to 6 servings. Do not freeze.

50 calories per serving, 1.5 g fat (0.3 g saturated), 0 mg cholesterol, 4 g protein, 8 g carbohydrate, 26 mg sodium, 269 mg potassium, 1 mg iron, 3 g fiber, 35 mg calcium.

- **Asparagus Vinaigrette:** Steam asparagus as directed. Omit lemon juice and margarine. Sprinkle asparagus with salt, pepper and thyme. Toss with non-fat or low-fat Italian salad dressing or Honey Mustard Dressing (p. 284).

Asparagus Tips for Success

- Choose asparagus with straight stalks, uniform green color and tight, pointed tips. Wrap unwashed spears in moistened paper towels, then in a plastic bag, and store in the refrigerator. You can also stand them upright in several inches of cold water like a bunch of flowers. Cover the tips with plastic wrap. Use within 2 to 3 days. One pound yields about 3 to 4 servings.
- Thick or thin? There is almost no difference in tenderness; just choose spears which are uniform in size. That way they'll all cook at the same time.
- Asparagus is a snap to prepare. Bend the asparagus at the point where it breaks off naturally; snap off the ends. (Don't discard the ends. They can be trimmed, peeled and used in soups.)
- If desired, peel stalks with a vegetable peeler, removing scales and stringy skin. Stop at least 1-inch from the tender tips. Soak asparagus thoroughly in cold water, adding a little salt and vinegar.
- Stalks take slightly longer to cook than tender tips. If microwaving asparagus, place thicker stalks towards the outer edge of the dish and thinner stalks towards the center. (Remember, thin ends in!) If asparagus is cut up, stir in the tips a minute after microwaving the stems.
- Cook asparagus just until tender-crisp. It should be bright, vivid green. The color becomes dull when it is overcooked. To test for doneness, take one spear and hold it by the base. If perfectly cooked, it should barely droop. If it hangs limply, it is overcooked!
- If asparagus seems to be overcooked, put it under cold running water to stop the cooking process. Don't discard if it's overcooked. Purée and use in soup.
- Asparagus is delicious when roasted. Arrange in a single layer on a sprayed baking pan, drizzle with olive oil and a little garlic; season with salt and pepper. Roast uncovered at 425°F for about 10 minutes. Yummy!

Mandarin Asparagus or Snow Peas

1	tsp. olive or canola oil
1	onion, chopped
$\frac{1}{2}$	of a red pepper, chopped
10	oz. can (284 ml) mandarin oranges
1	lb. asparagus (500 g) or snow peas, trimmed & cut diagonally into 2" slices
1	tsp. honey
1	tsp. cornstarch dissolved in 2 tbsp. water
$\frac{1}{8}$	tsp. pepper
1	tsp. Oriental sesame oil
2	tbsp. toasted sesame seeds or slivered almonds

1. Heat oil in a non-stick skillet. Add onion and red pepper; sauté 3 or 4 minutes. If necessary, add a little water to prevent sticking. Drain oranges, reserving juice. Add juice, asparagus or snow peas and honey to skillet. Cook for 3 or 4 minutes, stirring constantly, until tender-crisp. Stir in cornstarch mixture. Cook uncovered until thickened; stir often. Add oranges, pepper and sesame oil; simmer for 1 to 2 minutes. If too thick, thin mixture with a little water. Garnish with sesame seeds or almonds.

Yield: 4 servings. Do not freeze.

108 calories per serving, 4.7 g fat (0.4 g saturated), 0 mg cholesterol, 3 g protein, 15 g carbohydrate, 16 mg sodium, 246 mg potassium, <1 mg iron, 3 g fiber, 41 mg calcium.

- **Sesame Green Beans:** Substitute green beans and add 2 teaspoons soy sauce. Top with sesame seeds.

Beans & Carrots Amandine

Full of fiber and flavor. Yellow beans can be substituted. Almonds are a terrific source of calcium.

1   tsp. tub margarine, butter or olive oil
2   cloves garlic, crushed
¼   c. sliced almonds
2   c. green beans, cut in half crosswise
2   c. carrots, cut into matchsticks
½   c. water
¼   tsp. salt
½   tsp. dried basil (or 1 tbsp. fresh basil)
Salt & pepper, to taste
2   tbsp. grated Parmesan cheese, optional

1. Combine margarine and garlic in a 1 cup Pyrex measuring cup. Microwave uncovered on HIGH for 45 seconds. Stir in almonds. Microwave on HIGH for 3 to 4 minutes, until golden, stirring at half time. (Alternately, toast almonds with margarine and garlic in a non-stick skillet for 3 or 4 minutes.)

2. Combine green beans, carrots, water and salt in a 2-quart microsafe casserole. Microwave covered on HIGH for 7 to 8 minutes, stirring at half time. Let stand covered for 2 or 3 minutes. Veggies should be tender-crisp. Drain well. Combine vegetables with seasonings and almonds. Sprinkle with Parmesan cheese if desired.

Yield: 4 servings. Reheats well in the microwave.

120 calories per serving, 5.8 g fat (0.2 g saturated), 0 mg cholesterol, 4 g protein, 15 g carbohydrate, 207 mg sodium, 403 mg potassium, 2 mg iron, 6 g fiber, 79 mg calcium.

Homemade Baked Beans

Full of flavor, fiber, iron and calcium, yet low in fat. These are a nutritional bargain. No time to make beans? For a great shortcut, add 2 to 3 tablespoons maple syrup to a can of baked beans. Just heat and eat!

1   lb. (454 g) white beans (e.g. navy)
6   c. water
2   onions, chopped
¼   c. sugar (white or brown)
⅓   c. molasses
2   tbsp. red wine vinegar
1¾–2 c. tomato juice
1   tsp. dry mustard
¼   tsp. cayenne (to taste)
½   tsp. black pepper
Salt, to taste

1. Soak beans overnight; rinse and drain well. Cook in 6 cups unsalted water for 45 to 60 minutes, until tender. Reserve cooking water from beans; set aside. Preheat oven to 275°F. In an oven-proof dish, combine drained beans with remaining ingredients plus 1 cup of reserved cooking water. Bake covered until tender, about 5 hours. Add more water if needed to prevent mixture from drying out.

Yield: 10 servings. These taste even better a day or two later!

215 calories per serving, 0.8 g fat (0.2 g saturated), 0 mg cholesterol, 10 g protein, 44 g carbohydrate, 160 mg sodium, 674 mg potassium, 4 mg iron, 7 g fiber, 105 mg calcium.

Roasted Beets

2 lb. medium beets
1 tbsp. melted tub margarine or olive oil
Salt & pepper, to taste
1 tbsp. fresh dill, minced

1. Cut off beet greens, leaving 2 inches of stem. (To cook beet greens, refer to Great Greens on p. 254). Wrap beets in aluminum foil and bake in a preheated 350°F oven for 1 to 1½ hours, until tender. When cool, slip off the skins. Cut beets into slices. Add margarine, salt, pepper and dill. Mix well. Serve hot.

Yield: 6 servings.

78 calories per serving, 2.2 g fat (0.4 g saturated), 0 mg cholesterol, 2 g protein, 14 g carbohydrate, 123 mg sodium, 427 mg potassium, 1 mg iron, 3 g fiber, 23 mg calcium.

- **Boiled Beets:** Scrub beets but do not peel. Boil for 30 to 40 minutes, until tender. Rinse under cold running water while you press the skins off with your hands.
- **Pickled Beets:** Roast or boil beets. Peel and slice. Omit margarine and dill. Add ¼ cup balsamic or red wine vinegar, ¼ cup sugar, salt and pepper to taste. Mix well; chill until serving time.

Roasted Roots

Let's get back to our roots! Thanks to Hester Springer and my mom for this great recipe.

2 beets, peeled & sliced
2–3 potatoes, peeled & cut in wedges
2 large onions, quartered
2 sweet potatoes, peeled & cut in chunks
3–4 carrots, peeled & cut in chunks
2 parsnips, peeled & cut in chunks
1 medium turnip, peeled
2 tbsp. olive oil
2 tbsp. balsamic or red wine vinegar
3–4 cloves garlic, crushed
Salt & pepper, to taste
1 tsp. dried basil or thyme (or 1 tbsp. fresh)

1. Preheat oven to 400°F. Mix vegetables together with oil, vinegar, garlic and seasonings. Place in a single layer on a sprayed non-stick baking pan. Bake uncovered for 45 to 55 minutes, until tender and browned, stirring occasionally. Serve immediately.

Yield: 8 servings.

160 calories per serving, 3.7 g fat (0.5 g saturated), 0 mg cholesterol, 3 g protein, 30 g carbohydrate, 157 mg sodium, 580 mg potassium, 1 mg iron, 5 g fiber, 55 mg calcium.

- **My mom uses beets** but omits the sweet potatoes and parsnips. My friend Hester omits the beets but uses sweet potatoes, parsnips and turnips. You can use whichever vegetables you like!
- **Roasted Fennel with Onions:** Use 2 large onions and 2 fennel bulbs, cut in wedges. Mix together with 2 cloves crushed garlic, 1 tablespoon olive oil and 2 tablespoons balsamic vinegar. Add salt and pepper to taste. Cook as directed for Roasted Roots (above). Makes 4 servings.

Broccoli, Mushroom & Pepper Sauté

This is great over pasta! Don't overcook broccoli.
Heat destroys some of its protective antioxidants.

2   c. broccoli florets
4   c. cold water plus 1 tbsp. vinegar
2   tsp. olive oil
2   cloves garlic, crushed
2   c. mushrooms, sliced
$\frac{1}{2}$ c. red or yellow pepper, diced
Salt & pepper, to taste
1   tbsp. fresh basil, minced (or $\frac{1}{2}$ tsp. dried)

1. Soak broccoli in cold water and vinegar for 10 minutes. Drain and rinse well. Steam broccoli for 2 to 3 minutes (or microwave it). In a large non-stick skillet, heat oil. Add garlic, mushrooms and pepper; stir-fry for 2 minutes. Add broccoli and stir-fry 2 minutes more. Add seasonings and serve.

Yield: 4 to 6 servings.

54 calories per serving, 2.7 g fat (0.4 g saturated), 0 mg cholesterol, 3 g protein, 7 g carbohydrate, 22 mg sodium, 368 mg potassium, 1 mg iron, 3 g fiber, 44 mg calcium.

- **Cauliflower, Mushroom & Pepper Sauté:** Substitute cauliflower florets in the above recipe.
- **Quick Basil & Orange Broccoli:** Cover and microwave 3 cups cut-up broccoli on HIGH for 5 minutes. Add 2 tablespoons orange juice, 1 teaspoon margarine or olive oil, salt, pepper and a dash of basil. Yummy!

Sesame Broccoli

1   large bunch broccoli (1$\frac{1}{2}$ lb./750 g)
2   tbsp. sesame seeds
1   tsp. Oriental sesame oil
1   tbsp. fresh lemon juice
1   tbsp. brown sugar
Salt & pepper, to taste

1. Cut up broccoli, slicing stems thinly. Rinse well. Steam (or microwave covered on HIGH with 2 tablespoons water) for 5 to 7 minutes, until tender-crisp. Place sesame seeds in a small pan and toast on medium heat for 3 or 4 minutes. Watch carefully to prevent burning. Drain broccoli; combine with sesame oil, lemon juice, brown sugar and seasonings. Top with toasted sesame seeds.

Yield: 4 servings. Can be reheated briefly in the microwave.

97 calories per serving, 3.8 g fat (0.3 g saturated), 0 mg cholesterol, 6 g protein, 13 g carbohydrate, 56 mg sodium, 568 mg potassium, 2 mg iron, 6 g fiber, 99 mg calcium.

- **Sesame Green Beans:** Substitute one pound green beans. Steam (or microwave) for 6 to 7 minutes. Beans should be crisp and bright green. Drain and continue with recipe.
- **Quick Cauliflower Crown:** Trim leaves from cauliflower but leave it whole. Rinse and drain well. Place on a microsafe plate, cover it with an inverted glass bowl and microwave on HIGH for 7 to 8 minutes. Let stand covered for 3 minutes. Omit brown sugar. Season with salt, pepper and lemon juice. Top with sesame seeds. It's also yummy topped with Cheese Sauce (p. 191)!

Carrot "Noodles"

6   medium carrots, peeled & trimmed
Salt & pepper, to taste
½   tsp. dried basil &/or dill
1   tsp. olive oil or butter

1. With a carrot peeler, use long strokes to make thin parings that look like noodles. Boil carrots 3 to 4 minutes, until almost tender; drain well. Mix with seasonings and olive oil. Serve immediately.

Yield: 4 servings. Do not freeze.

55 calories per serving, 1.3 g fat (0.2 g saturated), 0 mg cholesterol, 1 g protein, 11 g carbohydrate, 66 mg sodium, 232 mg potassium, <1 mg iron, 3 g fiber, 35 mg calcium.

Glazed Apricot Carrots with Peppers

2   lb. carrots, peeled & sliced
1   red pepper, diced
1   onion, diced
¼   c. apricot jam (preferably low-sugar)
2   tbsp. fresh dill, minced
Salt & pepper, to taste

1. Slice carrots ½-inch thick. Cook in boiling salted water until nearly tender, about 10 to 12 minutes. Add red pepper and onion and simmer 4 or 5 minutes longer. Drain well and return to heat. Stir in jam and dill; mix well. Add salt and pepper to taste.

Yield: 6 servings.

100 calories per serving, 0.4 g fat (0.1 g saturated), 0 mg cholesterol, 2 g protein, 24 g carbohydrate, 96 mg sodium, 381 mg potassium, 1 mg iron, 5 g fiber, 50 mg calcium.

Easy Eggplant Parmesan

1   medium eggplant, sliced in ¼" rounds
Salt, to taste
¾   c. cornflake crumbs (or matzo meal)
3   tbsp. grated Parmesan cheese
Pepper & garlic powder, to taste
½   tsp. dried basil
2   egg whites (or 1 egg), lightly beaten
1   c. tomato sauce (bottled or homemade)
¾   c. grated low-fat mozzarella cheese

1. Preheat oven to 375°F. Sprinkle eggplant with salt and let stand for 20 minutes. Rinse well; pat dry with paper towels. Combine crumbs, Parmesan and seasonings. Dip eggplant in egg whites, then in crumbs. Place eggplant slices in a single layer on a sprayed non-stick baking sheet. Bake uncovered 15 minutes. Turn eggplant over, top with sauce and cheese and bake 10 minutes more, until golden.

Yield: 8 slices. If frozen, eggplant may be soggy.

114 calories per slice, 3.5 g fat (1.7 g saturated), 8 mg cholesterol, 6 g protein, 16 g carbohydrate, 426 mg sodium, 283 mg potassium, 1 mg iron, 2 g fiber, 113 mg calcium.

Stewed Cabbage or Brussel Sprouts with Noodles

Cabbage and brussel sprouts may help prevent certain cancers. They're also rich in vitamin C.

1	tbsp. olive or canola oil
2	onions, chopped
2	cloves garlic, crushed
3	c. finely sliced cabbage (or 1 lb. brussel sprouts, trimmed & cut in quarters)
1/2	of a red pepper, chopped
1	carrot, grated
3/4	c. chicken or vegetable broth
	Salt & pepper, to taste
2	c. cooked noodles (preferably yolk-free)

1. In a large non-stick skillet, heat oil. Add onions and sauté for 5 minutes. Add garlic, cabbage or sprouts, red pepper, carrot and broth. Cook uncovered for 6 to 7 minutes, stirring occasionally, until softened. Stir in seasonings and noodles. Cook just until heated through.

Yield: 6 to 8 servings.

171 calories per serving, 3.9 g fat (0.6 g saturated), trace cholesterol, 6 g protein, 29 g carbohydrate, 43 mg sodium, 204 mg potassium, 2 mg iron, 4 g fiber, 52 mg calcium.

Roasted Garlic

Did you know that an average head of garlic contains about 15 to 16 cloves?

2 large, fresh, plump heads of garlic

1. Preheat oven to 375°F. Cut a ¼-inch slice from the top of each head of garlic. Discard any loose, papery skins. Wrap each head of garlic in foil. Bake for 30 to 40 minutes, until very soft. (Garlic can also be baked in a toaster oven for 25 to 30 minutes, or cooked on the BBQ.) Cool slightly. Squeeze cloves out of the skin directly onto crackers or grilled bread and spread with a knife.

Yield: 2 or more servings. Do not freeze.

67 calories per head of roasted garlic, 0.2 g fat (0 g saturated), 0 mg cholesterol, 3 g protein, 15 g carbohydrate, 8 mg sodium, 181 mg potassium, <1 mg iron, 1 g fiber, 82 mg calcium.

- **Roasted garlic is so soft** that you can spread it on toasted bread like butter, so mild that you can eat it without risking killer garlic breath! Its mellow flavor enhances salad dressings, pastas, soups, sauces, dips, even mashed potatoes! Why not roast several heads? It tastes great hot or cold!
- **Leftovers can be stored** for 4 or 5 days in a tightly closed container in the fridge.
- **Roasted Garlic Bread:** Toast baguette slices at 375°F (or grill on the BBQ) until crisp and dry, about 10 minutes. Squeeze cloves of Roasted Garlic out of the skin and spread thickly on toasted baguette. Delicious hot or cold.

Garlic Spread

4 large, fresh, plump heads of garlic
½ c. chicken or vegetable broth (low-salt)

1. Place one of the garlic heads on a cutting board and cover it with a dish towel. (This keeps garlic from flying around like ammunition!) Bang the bottom of a heavy frypan or pot onto the cloth-covered garlic. Remove the cloth, separate the

The Goodness of Garlic

Since the beginning of civilization, garlic has been used as a miracle drug. Egyptian slaves who were building the Pyramids went on strike when deprived of their ration of garlic! Old-fashioned Jewish mothers often made their children wear a garlic necklace to keep away "the evil eye."

It is believed that garlic lowers blood pressure and cholesterol, discourages clotting, may reduce risk of heart attack and help prevent certain cancers. Garlic helps fight bacteria, viruses and colds, and boosts the immune system. It even acts as a decongestant! Crushed garlic in oil is handy, but must be refrigerated. I prefer to crush fresh garlic when I need it. Elephant garlic has large cloves but is mild-flavored. Garlic salt is mainly salt; I never use it. In a pinch, use a pinch of garlic powder!

Buying and storing garlic: Choose plump, firm heads. Store uncovered in the vegetable bin in the fridge. It can be stored uncovered at room temperature in a small basket or garlic keeper with air holes. It keeps for about a month. Elephant garlic spoils more quickly.

Peeling and mincing/crushing: To peel, place garlic clove(s) on a cutting board and smash with the flat side of a chef's knife. Discard the papery skins. Remove the green inner sprout which has a bitter taste. I usually crush garlic in my favorite garlic press (by Zyliss). However, if I'm using the processor for other vegetables, I also use it for garlic. Start the machine, then drop garlic through the feed tube while the machine is running. Process for about 10 seconds, until minced. If the processor bowl is dry, don't peel garlic first. Just pick out the skins with your fingertips. (Lemon juice removes the smell of garlic from your fingers, parsley removes it from your breath.)

Sautéeing garlic: Garlic burns easily when using very little oil. First, brown onions or other veggies on medium heat, then add garlic and cook 2 minutes more. If browning a large quantity of veggies at one time, add garlic at the beginning. The water released from the veggies during cooking protects garlic from burning. If garlic/veggie mixture begins to burn, add a little water or broth to the pan.

One final secret: To remove the smell of garlic from your hands, rub them on a stainless steel surface (e.g. a stainless steel sink.)

cloves and pick out any easily removed papery skins. Cover garlic again with the towel and hit it again a couple of times. Discard any remaining skins. Repeat with remaining heads of garlic.

2. Place peeled garlic and broth in a small saucepan and bring to a boil. Reduce heat, cover tightly and simmer gently until tender, about 20 minutes. If necessary, add 2 or 3 tablespoons more broth if most of it has evaporated. Spread garlic thickly on slices of toasted French bread, baguette or crackers.

Yield: 4 or more servings. Do not freeze.

71 calories per serving, 0.6 g fat (0.1 g saturated), 0 mg cholesterol, 3 g protein, 15 g carbohydrate, 133 mg sodium, 181 mg potassium, <1 mg iron, <1 g fiber, 82 mg calcium.

Simply Sautéed Greens

1   tbsp. olive oil
1   red pepper, chopped
2–3 cloves garlic, crushed
2   lb. greens, well-trimmed, washed & drained

1. In a wok or large skillet, sauté red pepper and garlic in oil for 2 minutes. Chop tender leaves into 1-inch pieces and add gradually to the pan. Reduce heat to medium, cover and cook until tender, stirring occasionally. (Beet greens and spinach take 2 to 3 minutes, Swiss chard and broccoli rabe take 3 to 4 minutes and kale takes 5 to 8 minutes.) Add a few tablespoons of water if mixture becomes dry. Season with salt and pepper. Remove greens from the pan with a slotted spoon.

Yield: 4 servings.

114 calories per serving (for kale), 4.4 g fat (0.6 saturated), 0 mg cholesterol, 5 g protein, 15 g carbohydrate, 54 mg sodium, 579 mg potassium, 2 mg iron, 3 g fiber, 176 mg calcium.

- **Kale or Spinach au Gratin:** Use 2 pounds of kale or spinach and sauté as directed above. Prepare Cheese Sauce (p. 191). Stir cooked greens into sauce; transfer to a sprayed casserole. Mix ½ cup bread crumbs with 1 teaspoon melted tub margarine or olive oil and 2 tablespoons grated Parmesan cheese. Sprinkle on top. Bake in a preheated 400°F oven 20 to 25 minutes, until golden. Makes 6 servings.

Great Greens!

- Green, light, go! Experts tell us we should "go for greens" because they're nutrient-packed, yet low in calories. Dark leafy greens contain vitamins C, E and beta carotene, which are antioxidants. In addition, they're packed with potassium, and many are a good source of absorbable calcium.
- How to choose greens: Buy crisp and tender greens; avoid those with yellowed leaves. Small young greens have the mildest flavor and are tender, whereas older greens can be tough and bitter. They wilt quite quickly, even if refrigerated, so cook them within a few days of purchase.
- How much? Allow one-half pound per person. When trimmed and cooked, one-half pound will yield 1 to 2 cups.
- How to clean greens: Cut away and discard any thick, tough stems and roots. Trim away limp or yellowed leaves. Soak greens in a sinkful of cold water for a few minutes, swishing them around gently to loosen dirt and sand. Lift them out of the water and drain in a colander.
- How to prepare and cook tender greens (e.g., spinach, Swiss chard, beet greens): Chop leaves in 1-inch pieces. Slice tender stems in ½-inch pieces. Use tough stems for vegetable stock. Beet greens are high in sodium. Swiss chard can replace spinach in many recipes. Spinach or Swiss chard can be steamed, sautéed or stir-fried briefly.
- For larger, less tender greens (kale, collards), remove the thick, tough ribs and stems. Chop or shred the leaves in ½-inch pieces. Steam kale for 4 or 5 minutes, then sauté quickly in a little olive oil and garlic. Season with balsamic vinegar, salt and pepper. For collards, boil them until tender, about 15 minutes. Drain well, then mix with a dash of balsamic vinegar, olive oil, salt and pepper.
- Bok Choy, Nappa/Chinese Cabbage: So delicious in stir-fries. Cook briefly to retain crunch.
- Kale: A member of the cabbage family, it's high in vitamin C, beta carotene, iron, fiber, potassium and calcium. It contains bioflavonoids and other substances which may help protect against cancer. Kale can be steamed, boiled, sautéed or used in stir-fries and soups. Since it shrinks tremendously when cooked, you'll need 3 cups of raw greens to make a 1 cup serving.

Marinated Mushrooms

Absolutely addictive! Serve warm or cold. These are excellent as an appetizer or a salad.

2   lb. mushrooms
1   tbsp. olive oil
½ of a small onion, finely chopped
4–5 large cloves garlic, minced
¾ c. dry white wine
Juice of half a lemon
¼ c. chicken or vegetable broth
¼ tsp. dried rosemary, crushed
¼ tsp. dried thyme
Salt & pepper, to taste
¼ c. fresh parsley, chopped
1   tbsp. minced fresh dill, if desired

1. Rinse mushrooms quickly and pat dry with paper towels. If mushrooms are large, cut them in half or in thick slices.

2. In a large non-stick skillet, heat olive oil on medium heat. Add onion and sauté for about 5 minutes, until tender. Add mushrooms and garlic. Sauté on medium heat until mushrooms begin to release their juices, about 6 to 8 minutes. Stir often. Add wine, lemon juice, broth, seasonings, parsley and dill. Bring to a boil and reduce heat. Simmer uncovered, stirring occasionally, for about 20 minutes, or until mushrooms are tender. Adjust seasonings to taste. If desired, garnish with additional parsley.

Yield: about 8 servings of ½ cup each. These keep for 2 or 3 days in the refrigerator. Do not freeze.

49 calories per serving, 1 g fat (trace saturated), 0 mg cholesterol, 2 g protein, 6 g carbohydrate, 51 mg sodium, 345 mg potassium, 2 mg iron, 2 g fiber, 15 mg calcium.

Be a Mushroom Maven!

To give your immune system a boost, try shiitake mushrooms. Medical research has indicated that they may help prevent and/or treat cancer, reduce high blood cholesterol and high blood pressure. However, no therapeutic benefits are known for the common button mushroom. Some experts claim they may have cancer-causing potential unless cooked. So even though a cup of raw mushrooms contains only about 20 calories, it's not a good idea to eat large quantities of raw mushrooms.

Should mushrooms be wiped or rinsed? According to expert Harold McGee, author of THE CURIOUS COOK (North Point Press), he prefers a quick rinse. They're already "90 percent water, so what difference could a few drops more make?" He's never noticed any difference in flavor. "And dry-wiping is the hard way to remove grit from a soft mushroom." As a test, he soaked 252 grams of mushrooms for 5 minutes, blotted them dry and reweighed them. He found that 23 mushrooms absorbed just a sixteenth of a teaspoon of water each! So, it's okay to rinse mushrooms before cooking. Just do it quickly, then wrap them in a towel to absorb excess moisture.

- **Chef's Trick!** An egg slicer is great for slicing mushrooms (and kiwis too)!
- **Choose mushrooms that are firm** and unblemished. Store unwashed in the fridge for up to 3 days.
- **Remove and discard** the stems of shiitake mushrooms since they are tough.

Roasted Onions

These are an excellent substitute for sautéed onions. So sweet, and no added fat! Roasted onions can be stored in the refrigerator for 2 or 3 days in a tightly closed container. I don't bother freezing them because they cook so quickly in the microwave. Onions are a natural decongestant. They may help lower blood pressure and cholesterol and may help decrease the ability of the blood to clot.

• **Micro-Roasted Onions:** (Ideal when you need only 1 or 2 sautéed onions.) Rinse onions, then pierce in several places with a sharp knife. Don't bother peeling them! Place on a plate and microwave on HIGH for 3 to 4 minutes for 1 onion, 6 to 7 minutes for 2 onions. To test for doneness, insert a sharp knife; onions should be very tender. Cooking time depends on size. When cool, peel and chop.

• **Oven-Roasted Onions:** (Ideal when you need a large amount of sautéed onions.) Rinse onions but do not peel. Pierce in several places with a sharp knife. Place on a sprayed baking sheet and bake in a preheated 400°F oven for 45 to 50 minutes, until tender. When cool, peel and chop.

57 calories per large onion, 0.2 g fat (0 g saturated), 0 mg cholesterol, 2 g protein, 13 g carbohydrate, 4 mg sodium, 213 mg potassium, trace iron, 2 g fiber, 28 mg calcium.

Oven-Baked Onion Rings

Be sure to use Vidalia onions when they're in season. They're sweet, mild and wonderful.

2	egg whites
2	tsp. olive or canola oil
2	large Vidalia or Spanish onions, peeled
1½	c. cornflake crumbs
½	tsp. no-salt seasoning (e.g. Mrs. Dash)
¾	tsp. chili powder
½	tsp. dried basil

1. Preheat oven to 375°F. Line a large baking sheet with aluminum foil and spray it with non-stick spray. In a large bowl, beat egg whites together with oil until foamy. Slice onions crosswise into ¼-inch thick slices. Separate into individual rings. Combine crumbs with seasonings in a plastic bag.

2. Add onion rings to egg white mixture and coat well. Drop a few onion rings at a time into crumb mixture and shake until completely coated. Place in a single layer on prepared baking sheet. Bake at 375°F for 15 minutes, until crispy outside and tender inside.

Yield: 8 servings. Do not freeze.

104 calories per serving, 1.2 g fat (0.2 g saturated), 0 mg cholesterol, 3 g protein, 22 g carbohydrate, 235 mg sodium, 272 mg potassium, 2 mg iron, 1 g fiber, 13 mg calcium.

• **Chef's Secrets!** Don't store onions under the sink or in areas of high humidity. They absorb moisture, making them spoil faster. Store in a cool, dry space with good air circulation. A hanging basket is ideal. Don't store onions and potatoes together; they cause each other to spoil quickly!

Black Bean & Corn Casserole (p. 226)

Pesto Pasta Salad (p. 288)
Best-O-Pesto (p. 195)

Easy Vegetarian Chili (p. 225)
Homemade Whole Wheat Bread (p. 301)

Terrific Tofu Stir-Fry (p. 237)

No-Fry Potato Latkas (p. 270)
Homemade Applesauce (p.360)

(Clockwise from top)
Easy BBQ Chickpea Casserole (p. 226)
Vegetarian Stuffed Peppers (p. 233)
Rainbow Rice Pilaf (p. 213)
Kasha & Bow Ties with Mushrooms (p. 207)

Herb Roasted Chicken (p. 156)
Rainbow Tabbouleh Salad (p. 283)

(Clockwise from top)
Noodle & Spinach Kugel (p. 272)
Glazed Apricot Mustard Chicken Breasts with Rosemary (p. 160)

Savory

Lemon Mint

Oregano

Chives

Sage

Tarragon

Rosemary

Chervil

Thyme

Marjoram

Basil

Hooray for Herbs! (p. 26)

Sweet Treats:
Less Sinful Cinnamon Twists (p. 373)
Fudgy-Wudgy Brownies (p. 366)
Hamentashen (p. 376)
Apricot Rogelach (p. 375)
Luscious Lemon Squares (p. 367)
Sugar Cookies (p. 375)

Purim Treats (Clockwise):
Apricot Rogelach (p. 375)
Phyllo Hamentashen (p. 377)
Dried Fruit Strudel (p. 378)
Hamentashen with Five-Fruit Filling (p. 376)

Blueberry Apple Phyllo Pie (p. 380)
Blueberry Apple Strudel (p. 379)

Double Chip Chocolate Cupcakes (p. 343)
Jumbleberry Crisp (p. 381)

Light 'n Luscious Strawberry Cheesecake Trifle (p. 352)

Strawberry Cheesecake with
Chocolate Mint Leaves (p. 348)

Honey & Spice & Everything
Nice Cake (p. 344)
Chocolate Chewies (p. 372)

Passover Chicken Muffins (p. 395)
Super Salsa (p. 61)

Festive Passover Meal:
Confetti Vegetable Kugel (p. 401)
Chicken Pepperonata (p. 396)
Duchesse Potato Mounds with Mushrooms (p. 399)
Fruit & Vegetable Tsimmis (p. 403)
Spaghetti Squash "Noodle" Pudding (p. 400)

Passover Vegetarian Pleasures
(Clockwise from top):
Israeli Salad (p. 280)
Vegetarian "Chicken" Broth (p. 81)
Herbed Passover Noodles (p. 404)
Spinach & Cheese Manicotti (p. 151)

My Mother's Passover Cake, Enlightened (p. 407)
Flourless Fudge Squares (p. 411)

Garlic Mashed Potatoes (Dairy)

Buttermilk adds a creamy, buttery flavor to these mashed spuds. Despite its deceptive name, a cup of buttermilk contains just 99 calories and 2 g fat.

4–5 large potatoes, peeled & cut in chunks
4   large, whole garlic cloves, peeled
Lightly salted water for cooking potatoes
³⁄₄ c. buttermilk or light sour cream
³⁄₄ tsp. salt (or to taste)
Freshly ground pepper, to taste

1. Place potatoes and garlic in a saucepan. Cover with water by at least an inch. Bring to a boil and simmer uncovered until potatoes are soft, about 20 minutes. Drain well. Return pot with potatoes to the heat and let them dry for a minute or two to evaporate excess moisture. Remove from heat. Mash potatoes with garlic. (Don't use the processor or potatoes will turn to glue!) Gradually beat in buttermilk a little at a time, until light and creamy. Season with salt and pepper. Serve immediately.

Yield: 4 servings. Do not freeze. These reheat well in the microwave.

168 calories per serving, 0.6 g fat (0.3 g saturated), 2 mg cholesterol, 5 g protein, 37 g carbohydrate, 57 mg sodium, 691 mg potassium, <1 mg iron, 2 g fiber, 67 mg calcium.

• **You can substitute** ¹⁄₂ cup skim milk and ¹⁄₄ cup non-fat yogurt for the buttermilk with excellent results. If desired, add a teaspoon of margarine, olive oil or Better Than Butter Spread (p. 125).
• **Parsnip & Potato Purée:** Use 3 potatoes and 3 parsnips, peeled and cut in chunks. Prepare as directed above. Add 1 tablespoon low-fat cream cheese and 2 teaspoons light margarine or olive oil along with buttermilk.

• **Chef's Secret!** When potatoes are exposed to sunlight, they develop a green layer under the skin called solanine which is poisonous. Cut away the green and discard any sprouts. End of problem!

Roasted Garlic Mashed Potatoes (Pareve)

Thanks to Gloria Schachter for this great recipe. Guaranteed to keep the vampires away!

1   head of Roasted Garlic (p. 252)
4–5 potatoes, peeled & cut into chunks
Lightly salted water
1–2 tsp. non-dairy tub margarine
³⁄₄ tsp. salt (to taste)
Freshly ground pepper, to taste

1. Roast garlic as directed. Cook potatoes in lightly salted water until soft, about 20 minutes. Drain off most of the water, reserving ¹⁄₂ cup. Return pot with potatoes to the heat and let them dry for a minute or two to evaporate excess moisture. Remove from heat. Mash potatoes with a potato masher or potato ricer. Squeeze the garlic cloves into potatoes and mash well. Gradually beat in the reserved cooking water a little at a time, until light and creamy. Add margarine, salt and pepper.

Yield: 4 servings. Do not freeze. These can be reheated in the microwave.

133 calories per serving, 1.1 g fat (0.2 g saturated), 0 mg cholesterol, 3 g protein, 29 g carbohydrate, 452 mg sodium, 467 mg potassium, <1 mg iron, 3 g fiber, 22 mg calcium.

Potato & Carrot Purée

Such a lovely pale, orange color. This yummy purée is full of flavor and vitamins, yet low in fat.

4   large potatoes (preferably Yukon Gold)
3   large carrots
3   cloves garlic, peeled
Salted water for cooking potatoes
¾ c. skim milk (or use rice or soy milk)
Salt & freshly ground pepper, to taste
½ tsp. dried basil (or 1 tbsp. fresh)
1   tsp. tub margarine or olive oil, optional

1. Peel potatoes and carrots and cut them into chunks. Place in a saucepan along with garlic. Cover with water and bring to a boil. Reduce heat and simmer covered about 20 minutes, until tender. Drain well. Return potatoes, carrots and garlic to the saucepan. Dry over medium heat for about a minute to evaporate any water. Meanwhile, heat milk (about 45 seconds on HIGH in the microwave).

2. Mash potatoes, carrots and garlic with a potato masher, or put them through a food mill. (Do not use a processor or your potatoes will be like glue!) Add hot milk and beat until light and creamy. Add salt, pepper, basil and margarine and mix well. Serve immediately.

Yield: 6 servings. These reheat beautifully in the microwave.

106 calories per serving, 0.2 g fat (0.1 g saturated), <1 mg cholesterol, 3 g protein, 24 g carbohydrate, 42 mg sodium, 432 mg potassium, <1 mg iron, 3 g fiber, 61 mg calcium.

• **Pareve Version:** Reserve ½ to ¾ cup of the cooking water from potato/carrot mixture. Add hot liquid to mashed potato mixture in Step 2.

• **Two Potato Purée:** Substitute 1 sweet potato for the carrots. Blend in 1 tablespoon light cream cheese.

Greek Potatoes

Shared with me by Elaine Stoller who got the original recipe from Ronni Pollock. Fabulous!

8–10 peeled potatoes, cut in half lengthwise, then in half again to make long, thick wedges
1½ c. water
2   tbsp. canola or corn oil
½ c. lemon juice (preferably fresh)
3   cloves garlic, chopped
2   tsp. salt (or to taste)
2   tsp. dried oregano
1   tsp. pepper

1. Preheat oven to 325°F. Line a 9 x 13-inch casserole with aluminum foil; spray with non-stick spray. Place potatoes in pan. Combine remaining ingredients and pour over potatoes. Bake uncovered for 2 hours at 325°F, turning potatoes a few times. Bake until liquid is gone.

Yield: 8 servings. Do not freeze.

182 calories per serving, 3.6 g fat (0.3 g saturated), 0 mg cholesterol, 3 g protein, 36 g carbohydrate, 590 mg sodium, 642 mg potassium, <1 mg iron, 3 g fiber, 18 mg calcium.

Oven Roasted Garlic Potatoes

Yummy, yet so easy.

4   large baking potatoes, cut into 8ths (peeled if
     desired)
Salt & pepper, to taste
1   tsp. dried rosemary, crushed
1   tsp. paprika (preferably Hungarian)
3–4 cloves garlic, crushed (to taste)
1   tbsp. olive oil

1. Preheat oven to 400°F. Spray a 2-quart oven-proof casserole with non-stick spray. Sprinkle potatoes with seasonings, garlic and olive oil. Rub mixture over potatoes to coat evenly. Cover casserole with foil. Bake at 400°F for 35 to 40 minutes. Remove foil and roast uncovered 30 minutes longer, stirring occasionally. Potatoes should be fork-tender, yet golden and crispy.

Yield: 4 to 5 servings. Do not freeze.

179 calories per serving, 3.6 g fat (0.5 g saturated), 0 mg cholesterol, 3 g protein, 35 g carbohydrate, 8 mg sodium, 621 mg potassium, <1 mg iron, 3 g fiber, 15 mg calcium.

Potatoes & Onions Boulangère

Simple is sometimes best! This recipe is great for a large crowd. Cooking time is long, but requires little attention. This is a great dish to serve with chicken.

3   large onions, peeled & thinly sliced
4–5 cloves garlic, crushed
10 potatoes, peeled & sliced
1   tbsp. olive oil

Salt & freshly ground pepper, to taste
1/2 tsp. dried thyme
4   c. chicken or vegetable broth
Paprika

1. Preheat oven to 375°F. Spray a 3-quart oval or oblong casserole with non-stick spray. Place a layer of onions in the bottom of the casserole. Add garlic and potatoes. Drizzle with oil and sprinkle with salt, pepper and thyme. Pour broth over potatoes and mix well. Sprinkle with paprika. Casserole dish will be quite full. Bake uncovered at 375°F for 1½ hours. Potatoes will be tender and well-browned.

Yield: 10 to 12 servings. Reheats well. Do not freeze.

159 calories per serving, 1.6 g fat (0.2 g saturated), 0 mg cholesterol, 5 g protein, 31 g carbohydrate, 76 mg sodium, 513 mg potassium, 1 mg iron, 3 g fiber, 31 mg calcium.

• **Chef's Secret!** I adjust the oven temperature for this recipe according to whatever else I am cooking for dinner. If my oven needs to be set at 350°F, I leave the potatoes in the oven a few minutes longer. If my oven needs to be set at 400°F, I leave them in a few minutes less.

No-Fry Fries

These are a favorite in my cooking classes. Adding an egg white to the oil reduces the amount of fat needed. If you are a vegan and don't use egg whites, use a little extra oil. You can make these with just salt and pepper, or season them with your favorite herbs and spices.

6 baking potatoes (e.g. Idaho, Russet)
1 tbsp. canola or olive oil
1 egg white
Salt & pepper, to taste
Basil, cayenne, paprika &/or garlic powder, to taste

1. Preheat oven to 400°F. Peel potatoes (or scrub very well). Cut into ¼-inch strips. (If you have time, first soak them in ice water for 20 to 30 minutes for crispier fries. Drain well; pat dry.) In a medium-size bowl, beat oil with egg white until frothy.

2. Coat potatoes with oil/egg white mixture. Spread in a single layer on a baking sheet which has been sprayed with non-stick spray. Sprinkle with seasonings. Bake in lower third of the oven at 400°F for 35 to 45 minutes, or until brown and crispy, stirring once or twice. Serve immediately.

Yield: 6 servings. Do not freeze.

115 calories per serving, 2.4 g fat (0.2 g saturated), 0 mg cholesterol, 3 g protein, 21 g carbohydrate, 16 mg sodium, 643 mg potassium, 1 mg iron, 2 g fiber, 9 mg calcium.

• **Crispy Coated No-Fries:** Combine seasonings with ½ cup bread crumbs or cornmeal and 1 teaspoon oil in a bowl or bag. Add potato strips and coat them with crumb mixture before baking.
• **Sweet Potato No-Fries:** Substitute 2 pounds sweet potatoes for the baking potatoes.
• **Two Potato No-Fries:** Use half baking potatoes and half sweet potatoes.
• **Time-Saving Secret!** Peel potatoes or scrub very well. Slice thinly into rounds. Combine all ingredients plus a few drops of water in a microsafe casserole; mix well. Cover and microwave on HIGH for 8 to 10 minutes, until tender. Stir once or twice during cooking. Potatoes will not be crisp when prepared this way, but they still taste great.

• **Potato Wedgies:** Scrub 6 large potatoes well but don't peel. Cut in half lengthwise, then crosswise. Cut into wedges and arrange on a sprayed, foil-lined pan. Drizzle with 1 to 2 tablespoons olive oil. Sprinkle with seasoning salt and cajun seasoning. Bake uncovered at 375°F for 45 minutes.
• **Chef's Secret!** If potatoes are refrigerated, they'll develop a sweet taste from the conversion of starch to sugar. It will disappear when the potatoes are brought back to room temperature. This is a good trick to know when making oven-fries. If you use potatoes that were refrigerated for at least 24 hours, the converted sugar will help the potatoes brown better in the oven!
• **The Power of Potatoes!** Potatoes are high in complex carbohydrates and fiber as well as being a good source of vitamins C and B6. They contain potassium, niacin, iron, magnesium and zinc. Most of the nutrients are just under the skin. If you scrub them well, peeling isn't necessary. One medium baked or boiled potato (4 oz.) contains about 100 calories and is virtually fat-free. The same amount of restaurant french fries contains 350 calories and 18 grams of fat!
• **For those of you** who are carbohydrate-sensitive, save potatoes for occasional use, as part of a mixed meal containing protein and fat. They are mostly composed of easily digested starch, so they are rapidly digested, causing a dramatic effect on blood sugar and insulin levels.

Skinny Potato Skins

4 large baking potatoes, 2 lb./1 kg
4 tsp. olive oil
1½ c. bottled salsa or tomato sauce
½ c. grated low-fat cheese (Swiss, Monterey Jack, mozzarella or Parmesan)

1. Scrub potatoes well. Pierce skin in several places with a fork. Bake in a preheated 400°F for about 1 hour, until tender. When cool enough to handle, cut potatoes in half lengthwise to make 8 halves. Scoop out pulp, leaving a ¼-inch-thick shell. Reserve potato pulp for another use.

2. Preheat broiler. Spray a foil-lined baking sheet with non-stick spray. Lightly brush insides of potato skins with oil. Cut in half to make 16 wedges. Arrange skin-side up on prepared baking sheet. Broil about 4 inches from heat for 2 minutes. Turn them over and broil 3 to 4 minutes longer. Spread a spoonful of salsa or tomato sauce on each wedge. Sprinkle with cheese. Broil just until cheese melts.

Yield: 16 pieces. To reheat, bake for 5 to 7 minutes at 450°F, just until heated through.

53 calories per piece, 1.3 g fat (0.3 g saturated), 1 mg cholesterol, 2 g protein, 8 g carbohydrate, 140 mg sodium, 87 mg potassium, 1 mg iron, 2 g fiber, 39 mg calcium.

Company Stuffed Spuds

My friend Peter loves these! They're a favorite at his family's Passover Seder, or any time of year.

8	large baking potatoes (preferably Idaho)
4	green onions, trimmed & chopped
1	red pepper, chopped
1	tbsp. olive oil
2	cloves garlic, crushed
½–¾	c. chicken or vegetable broth
2	tbsp. minced fresh dill
1	tsp. dried basil
Salt & pepper, to taste	

1. Scrub potatoes well. Pierce skin in several places with a fork. Bake 400°F for 1 hour, until tender. Cool slightly. In a non-stick skillet, sauté onions and red pepper in oil until golden. Add garlic and cook 2 minutes longer. Add a little water if veggies start to stick or burn. Cut a slice off the top of each potato. Scoop out pulp, leaving a wall about ¼-inch thick. Mash potatoes. Add remaining ingredients; mix well. Mixture should be moist, but not mushy! Restuff skins. (Can be prepared in advance, covered and refrigerated.) Bake uncovered at 375°F for 25 minutes, until golden.

Yield: 8 servings. These reheat well or may be frozen.

243 calories per serving, 1.9 g fat (0.3 g saturated), 0 mg cholesterol, 5 g protein, 52 g carbohydrate, 28 mg sodium, 886 mg potassium, 3 mg iron, 5 g fiber, 32 mg calcium.

• **Quicker Baked Potatoes:** Insert a metal skewer into each potato. Bake at 425°F for 30 to 40 minutes. Never bake potatoes wrapped in foil. They will steam and become soggy!

Stuffed Combo Potatoes

Even people who hate sweet potatoes will love these! Potassi-yummy!

3	baking potatoes (Idaho)
2	medium-size sweet potatoes
1	tbsp. margarine or olive oil
1	tbsp. apricot jam, marmalade or maple syrup
1	tbsp. brown sugar
¼	c. orange juice (or skim milk)
Salt, pepper and nutmeg, to taste	

1. Scrub potatoes and sweet potatoes well. Pierce the skins in several places with a fork. Bake in a preheated 400°F for 1 hour, until tender. Cool slightly. Cut in half and scoop out pulp, leaving a wall ¼-inch thick. Mash potato and sweet potato pulp. Add remaining ingredients; mix well. Stuff mixture into baking potato skins. Don't stuff the sweet potato skins. (Can be prepared in advance to this point, covered and refrigerated.) Bake uncovered at 350°F for 20 to 25 minutes, until golden.

Yield: 6 servings. These can be frozen.

189 calories per serving, 2.1 g fat (0.4 g saturated), 0 mg cholesterol, 3 g protein, 40 g carbohydrate, 29 mg sodium, 586 mg potassium, 2 mg iron, 4 g fiber, 25 mg calcium.

Glazed Sweet Potatoes

Sweet potatoes are virtually fat-free and provide nearly half the daily recommended nutrient intake of vitamin C. Most important of all, they're delicious!

2   onions, peeled & sliced
4   sweet potatoes, peeled & cut in 2" chunks
2   tsp. olive oil or melted margarine
2   tbsp. maple syrup or honey
Salt & pepper, to taste
¼   tsp. dried basil
¼   c. orange juice

1. Preheat oven to 375°F. Spray a 2-quart covered Pyrex casserole with non-stick spray. Arrange onions in the bottom of the casserole; add sweet potatoes. Drizzle with olive oil and maple syrup. Sprinkle with seasonings. Drizzle orange juice over

potatoes. Rub sweet potatoes well to coat them evenly with mixture. Cover and bake at 375°F for 45 minutes. Uncover and bake 15 minutes longer, stirring once or twice, until potatoes are tender and golden.

Yield: 6 servings. Reheats well, but do not freeze.

158 calories per serving, 1.9 g fat (0.3 g saturated), 0 mg cholesterol, 2 g protein, 34 g carbohydrate, 15 mg sodium, 278 mg potassium, <1 mg iron, 3 g fiber, 36 mg calcium.

• **Time-Saving Secret!** Microwave them covered on HIGH for 12 to 14 minutes, stirring once or twice. Potatoes will be partially cooked. Transfer casserole to a preheated 375°F oven. Bake uncovered 20 to 25 minutes, until tender, basting occasionally. If necessary, add a little more orange juice or water to casserole.

Minted Peas with Red Peppers

Green peas are more nutritious than green beans! They contain vitamins A and C and are high in fiber.

10   oz. pkg. (300 g) frozen green peas
2   tsp. tub margarine or olive oil
4   green onions (white part only), chopped
1   red pepper, chopped
1–2 tbsp. fresh mint, minced
Salt & freshly ground pepper, to taste
1   tbsp. fresh lime or lemon juice

1. Bring a saucepan of water to a boil. Add peas and simmer 3 to 4 minutes, until tender-crisp. Drain and rinse well under cold water to stop the cooking process. Set aside. Melt margarine in a non-stick skillet. Add onions and red pepper. Sauté for 4 or 5 minutes, until softened. Add peas and mint. Cook for 1 to 2 minutes, just until heated through. Add seasonings and lime juice. Serve immediately.

Yield: 3 to 4 servings.

104 calories per serving, 2.8 g fat (0.5 g saturated), 0 mg cholesterol, 5 g protein, 16 g carbohydrate, 99 mg sodium, 217 mg potassium, 2 mg iron, 5 g fiber, 29 mg calcium.

• **Rice Pea-laf with Peppers:** Prepare Minted Peas with Red Peppers as directed above. Combine with 3 cups of cooked white or brown basmati rice. Add salt and pepper to taste.

Squished Squash

Nutrient-packed, rich in beta-carotene and folic acid, this dish is potassi-yummy!

2   acorn squash or 1 butternut squash
1–2 tbsp. tub margarine or olive oil
Salt & pepper, to taste
¼   tsp. each of ground cinnamon & nutmeg

1. Preheat oven to 375°F. Cut squash in half crosswise. Place cut-side down on a sprayed non-stick baking pan. Bake uncovered until tender, about 50 to 60 minutes.

2. Cool slightly, then scoop out and discard seeds and stringy pulp from squash. Scoop out the flesh from squash into a bowl and mash together with margarine/olive oil and seasonings. Reheat before serving.

Yield: 4 servings. Do not freeze.

103 calories per serving, 3.1 g fat (0.6 g saturated), 0 mg cholesterol, 2 g protein, 20 g carbohydrate, 30 mg sodium, 601 mg potassium, 1 mg iron, 6 g fiber, 65 mg calcium.

• **To microwave squash,** pierce in several places with a sharp knife. Place on microsafe paper towels and microwave on HIGH, allowing 5 to 7 minutes per pound. Turn squash over halfway through cooking. Total cooking time will be 12 to 14 minutes. Complete as directed in Step 2.
• **Squash, anyone?** Winter varieties include acorn, buttercup, butternut, Hubbard, pumpkin, spaghetti and turban squash. They do not need refrigeration. Store at room temperature for about a month.

Upper Crust Tomatoes

Cooked tomatoes contain lycopene, a powerful antioxidant. Try this quick and delicious low-fat dish!

3   large, firm, ripe tomatoes, cut in half crosswise
Salt & pepper, to taste
3   tbsp. Honey Mustard Dressing (p. 284) or bottled low-fat Italian salad dressing
¾   c. seasoned croutons, crushed

1. Place tomatoes cut-side up on a sprayed non-stick baking pan. Sprinkle lightly with salt and pepper. Drizzle with salad dressing and sprinkle with crushed croutons. Broil 5 inches from heat for 4 to 5 minutes, until heated through. Serve immediately.

Yield: 6 servings. These are delicious hot or at room temperature. Great with fish!

66 calories per serving, 2.9 g fat (0.5 g saturated), trace cholesterol, 1 g protein, 10 g carbohydrate, 92 mg sodium, 186 mg potassium, <1 mg iron, 1 g fiber, 10 mg calcium.

Homemade "Sun-Dried" Tomatoes

Sun-dried tomatoes are great for salads, dressings, sauces, casseroles, dips, pizza, pasta, rice and other grains. Nutrient values were not available for homemade sun-dried tomatoes, so my analysis is for store-bought. These are fabulous!

1   dozen (or more) ripe Italian plum tomatoes
Salt, to taste

1. Preheat oven to 200°F. Rinse tomatoes. Either cut them in half or slice thinly. Pat dry with paper towels. Spread on foil-lined baking sheet(s) sprayed with non-stick spray. Sprinkle lightly with salt. Bake at 200°F until shrivelled, about 8 hours or overnight. Store in a tightly sealed container in the fridge. They'll keep several weeks. To rehydrate tomatoes, cover with boiling water. Soak for 10 minutes. Drain well.

35 calories per ¼ cup, 0.4 g fat (0.1 g saturated), 0 mg cholesterol, 2 g protein, 8 g carbohydrate, 283 mg sodium, 463 mg potassium, 1 mg iron, 2 g fiber, 15 mg calcium.

• **Small Italian plum tomatoes** (Roma) are ideal because of their low juice content.
• **Fat-Saving Secret!** Store-bought sun-dried tomatoes are often packed in oil. Rinse thoroughly with boiling water to remove the oil; pat dry. Oil left in the jar can be used for salad dressings, or instead of olive oil to sauté vegetables for pilafs and grain-based dishes.

Quick & Simple Zucchini

4   medium zucchini, sliced ¼" thick
Salt & pepper, to taste
1   tbsp. fresh lemon or lime juice
2   tbsp. fresh basil, chopped (or 1 tsp. dried)
2   tsp. soft margarine

1. Place zucchini slices in a round microwave-safe casserole. Sprinkle with seasonings and lemon juice. Cover and microwave on HIGH for 5 minutes, until tender crisp, stirring at half time. Let stand for 1 to 2 minutes. Stir in margarine. Serve immediately.

Yield: 4 servings. Reheats well in the microwave.

38 calories per serving, 2 g fat (0.3 g saturated), 0 mg cholesterol, <1 g protein, 5 g carbohydrate, 20 mg sodium, 322 mg potassium, <1 mg iron, 2 g fiber, 19 mg calcium.

• **Quick Stewed Zucchini:** Slice 2 pounds of zucchini. Heat 1 tablespoon olive oil in a non-stick skillet. Sauté zucchini in oil until golden, about 6 to 8 minutes, stirring often. Add 2 cloves of crushed garlic and cook 2 minutes longer. Add a 19-ounce can (540 ml) tomatoes (with juice), 1 teaspoon sugar and ½ teaspoon dried basil. Cover and simmer for 15 to 20 minutes, stirring occasionally. Makes 6 servings.

Vegetable Platter Primavera

2   c. broccoli florets
2   c. cauliflower florets
1   c. carrots, sliced on the bias
1   c. sliced zucchini or yellow squash
4   green onions (white part only), sliced

½ c. red pepper, diced
1 tbsp. olive oil (or melted margarine)
2 tbsp. lemon juice
1 tbsp. water
Salt & pepper, to taste
2 tbsp. minced fresh basil &/or dill

1. Soak broccoli, cauliflower and carrots in cold water for 10 minutes. Drain well but do not dry. Arrange broccoli and cauliflower florets in a ring around the outer edge of a large microwave-safe plate. Make an inner ring of carrots, then of zucchini. Place green onions and red pepper in the centre. Combine olive oil, lemon juice and water; drizzle over vegetables. Cover with an inverted Pyrex pie plate or a damp paper towel.

2. Microwave covered on HIGH for 6 to 8 minutes, until tender-crisp. Let stand covered for 2 minutes. Season with salt, pepper and herbs. Serve immediately.

Yield: 6 servings. Do not freeze.

62 calories per serving, 2.7 g fat (0.4 g saturated), 0 mg cholesterol, 3 g protein, 9 g carbohydrate, 111 mg sodium, 351 mg potassium, <1 mg iron, 4 g fiber, 45 mg calcium.

• **Vegetable Platter with Cheese Sauce:** Cook vegetables as directed, omitting oil. Melt 1 teaspoon tub margarine for 20 seconds on HIGH in the microwave. Stir in 2 tablespoons flour. Gradually whisk in 1 cup skim milk. Microwave uncovered on HIGH until steaming hot, about 2 minutes, whisking at half time. Blend in ½ cup grated low-fat cheddar cheese. Add salt, pepper and ½ teaspoon dried mustard. Stir well. Drizzle sauce over hot vegetables.

Vegetarian Harvest Oven Stir-Fry

So colorful, so healthy!

1 medium eggplant, unpeeled
1 red, 1 yellow & 1 green pepper
1 medium Spanish onion (about 2 c.)
2 medium zucchini, unpeeled
2 c. sliced mushrooms (try shiitake or portobello)
4 cloves garlic, crushed
1 tbsp. olive oil
2 tbsp. balsamic or red wine vinegar
Salt and pepper, to taste
2 tbsp. fresh chopped rosemary or basil (or 1 tsp. dried)

1. Preheat oven to 425°F. Cut eggplant, peppers, onion and zucchini into narrow strips. Combine all ingredients in a large bowl. (May be prepared in advance, covered and refrigerated for 3 or 4 hours.) Spread in a thin layer on a large foil-lined baking sheet which has been sprayed with non-stick spray.

2. Place baking sheet on top rack of oven. Bake uncovered for 25 to 30 minutes, until tender-crisp and lightly browned, stirring once or twice.

Yield: 6 servings. This dish reheats well either in the microwave or conventional oven. Veggies become soggy if frozen.

99 calories per serving, 3 g fat (0.4 g saturated), 0 mg cholesterol, 3 g protein, 18 g carbohydrate, 8 mg sodium, 532 mg potassium, 2 mg iron, 5 g fiber, 55 mg calcium.

Rozie's Vegetable Medley

1. Prepare vegetable mixture as directed in Step 1 of Vegetarian Harvest Oven Stir-Fry, omitting eggplant. Peel 2 sweet potatoes and cut them into chunks. Add 2 or 3 carrots, thickly sliced (or 2 cups baby carrots). Microwave sweet potatoes and carrots covered on HIGH for 4 to 5 minutes, until tender-crisp. Combine with remaining ingredients and mix well. If desired, add 1 cup of snow peas and/or canned baby corn, rinsed and drained.

2. Either cook veggies in the oven as described above, or place them in a sprayed grill basket or perforated wok designed for the BBQ. Grill until nicely browned and tender-crisp, about 20 to 30 minutes, stirring occasionally.

Oven Roasted Vegetables (Ratatouille-Style)

These vegetables are scrumptious served hot over pasta, at room temperature over salad greens, or at any temperature as a side dish. Any way you serve them, they're a winner!

1	medium eggplant, cut in strips or slices
1	tsp. salt
1	large red onion, halved and sliced
2	red peppers, cut in strips or slices
2	green peppers, cut in strips or slices
2	medium zucchini, cut in strips or slices
1	c. mushrooms, sliced
4	tomatoes, sliced
4	cloves garlic, crushed
2	tbsp. olive oil
2	tbsp. lemon juice or rice wine vinegar
2	tsp. dried basil (or 2 tbsp. fresh, minced)
1/2	tsp. dried thyme, if desired
	Salt & pepper, to taste

1. Sprinkle eggplant strips or slices with salt. Place in a colander or strainer over a bowl. Let stand 20 minutes. Press out excess liquid. Combine with remaining ingredients in a large mixing bowl and mix well. (May be prepared 3 or 4 hours in advance, covered and refrigerated until needed.) Spread in a single layer on a large baking sheet which has been sprayed with non-stick spray.

2. Preheat oven to 450°F. Bake uncovered on top rack of oven for 20 to 25 minutes, or until well browned and tender-crisp. Stir 2 or 3 times during cooking.

Yield: 8 servings. Reheats well, especially in the microwave. Do not freeze.

97 calories per serving, 4 g fat (0.6 g saturated), 0 mg cholesterol, 2 g protein, 16 g carbohydrate, 303 mg sodium, 562 mg potassium, 1 mg iron, 4 g fiber, 32 mg calcium.

- **Barbecued Vegetables:** Slice eggplant and onions 1/2-inch thick. Seed and core peppers; cut in quarters. Trim ends off zucchini, cut in half or thirds crosswise, then slice lengthwise. Use large mushrooms, but grill just the caps. (Portobellos are excellent.) Omit tomatoes. Preheat the grill. Rub vegetables with garlic, olive oil, lemon juice and seasonings. Place veggies in a sprayed perforated grill pan or basket. Grill for 6 to 8 minutes per side, until browned and tender-crisp. An alternative is to wrap veggies in heavy-duty foil packets (one per person), seal tightly and grill for 20 to 30 minutes.
- **Time- and Fat-Saving Secret!** Instead of rubbing the veggies with garlic, oil, lemon juice and sea-

sonings, substitute bottled fat-free Italian salad dressing, teriyaki sauce or your favorite bottled Oriental sauce.

• **Vegetarian Crêpes:** Prepare veggie mixture as directed and use as a filling for Crêpes (p. 149).

Ruthie's Oven-Grilled Veggies with Basil

Ruthie Dressler is an energetic, spiritual, beautiful lady who cooks the most tantalizing vegetarian dishes. The high oven temperature creates a scrumptious, grilled taste.

4   ripe, firm tomatoes
2   large sweet onions (e.g. Spanish)
3–4 colored peppers (red, green, yellow &/or orange)
3–4 zucchini (about 1 lb/500 g)
2   tbsp. olive oil
Coarse salt, to taste
¼   c. fresh basil, chopped

1. Preheat oven to 500°F. Cut tomatoes in wedges. Slice onions, peppers and zucchini into long strips. Place veggies on a foil-lined baking sheet. Drizzle with olive oil and sprinkle with coarse salt. Bake uncovered for 15 minutes, until slightly blackened and tender. Add basil and mix well. This tastes somewhat like a grilled ratatouille and is great hot or cold.

Yield: 6 to 8 servings. Do not freeze. Serve with pasta, rice, millet or bulgur.

119 calories per serving, 5.2 g fat (0.7 g saturated), 0 mg cholesterol, 3 g protein, 18 g carbohydrate, 16 mg sodium, 645 mg potassium, 1 mg iron, 4 g fiber, 37 mg calcium.

Grilled Skewered Vegetables

These are a great vegetable dish for your next BBQ. Miniature vegetables are a nice alternative. They are often available at specialty produce stores.

1   Japanese or small eggplant, cut in 1″ chunks
Salt, to taste
12 4″ wooden skewers
2   red peppers, cut in 1″ chunks
2   medium zucchini, sliced ½″ thick
2   green peppers, cut into 1″ chunks
1   large or 2 medium onions, cut into 1″ chunks
12 cherry tomatoes
½   c. bottled fat-free or low-calorie Italian salad dressing
2   tbsp. minced fresh basil &/or parsley

1. Sprinkle eggplant with salt. Place on a baking sheet and cover with another baking sheet. Weigh down with several cans; let drain 20 minutes. Rinse well; pat dry. Soak wooden skewers in cold water for 20 minutes. Arrange veggies alternately on skewers, starting with eggplant, then red pepper, zucchini, green pepper, onion and cherry tomato. Drizzle with salad dressing and marinate for 20 to 30 minutes. (Skewers can be prepared in advance up to this point and marinated for several hours.)

2. Preheat grill or broiler. Grill or broil vegetables about 4 inches from heat until nicely browned, about 3 to 4 minutes per side. Sprinkle with basil and/or parsley. Serve hot or at room temperature.

Yield: 12 kabobs. Allow 2 per person. Freezing is not recommended.

28 calories per kabob, 0.2 g fat (0 g saturated), 0 mg cholesterol, 1 g protein, 6 g carbohydrate, 100 mg sodium, 216 mg potassium, trace iron, 1 g fiber, 11 mg calcium.

Chinese Dumplings (Shao Mai)

8   dried mushrooms (e.g. shiitake)
Boiling water
10 oz. (300 g) pkg. fresh or frozen spinach
2–3 slices fresh ginger (1 tbsp. minced)
2   cloves garlic
2   green onions
1   carrot
½   of a red pepper
1   c. tofu (or cooked chicken)
1   tsp. Oriental sesame oil
1   tbsp. light soy sauce
½   tsp. Chinese chili sauce or paste
4   dozen thin wonton skins, preferably round (about 1 lb/500 g)

1. Break off mushroom stems and discard. Soak dried mushroom caps in boiling water for ½ hour. Drain well. If using fresh spinach, remove and discard stems; wash thoroughly. Place in a saucepan with just the water clinging to the leaves, cover and bring to a boil. Cook for 1 minute. Transfer to a colander and rinse under cold running water; squeeze dry. Frozen spinach should be thawed and squeezed dry.

2. In the processor, mince ginger and garlic. Add spinach and green onions; process with quick on/offs, until minced. Transfer to a bowl. Separately mince carrot, red pepper, tofu (or chicken) and mushrooms. Add to spinach. Add sesame oil, soy and chili sauce; mix well. Chill until needed.

3. If wonton skins are square, cut into rounds with a 2-inch round cookie cutter. Place 2 teaspoons filling in the center of each wonton. Moisten edges with water. Fold dough in half over filling to make crescents. Pinch edges together firmly. Place on a non-stick baking sheet. Flatten out bottoms of dumplings by tapping gently. Refrigerate uncovered until just before serving time.

4. Bring a large pot of water to a rolling boil. Add half the dumplings all at once and stir gently. In 3 to 4 minutes they will float to the surface and be done. Remove from pot with a slotted spoon and transfer to a colander. Shake colander to drain excess water. Transfer dumplings to a bowl or serving dish. Repeat with remaining dumplings. Serve hot (see following tips).

Yield: 4 dozen. Uncooked dumplings can be frozen. Boil frozen dumplings for 6 to 8 minutes.

37 calories per dumpling (without sauce), 0.5 g fat (0.1 g saturated), <1 mg cholesterol, 2 g protein, 7 g carbohydrate, 69 mg sodium, 52 mg potassium, <1 mg iron, <1 g fiber, 17 mg calcium.

- **Strain mushroom water** through a paper coffee filter. Freeze it, or add it to soups, stews or risotto for a terrific taste! If you don't have dried mushrooms, use ½ cup fresh, but don't soak them.
- **If Chinese chili sauce** or paste isn't available, use 1 tablespoon chili sauce or ketchup.
- **Dumplings with Peanut Butter Sauce:** Prepare Peanut Butter Sauce (p. 108). Heat gently. Thin with 3 to 4 tablespoons water. Gently mix hot dumplings with sauce. Top with minced chives.
- **Dumplings with Spicy Dipping Sauce:** Prepare Spicy Dipping Sauce (p. 109). Place in a pretty bowl. Arrange hot dumplings on a large serving plate with the sauce in the center.

Kreplach

This is the Jewish version of Chinese dumplings and Italian ravioli!

2   c. flour
¼   tsp. salt
1   egg plus 2 egg whites
¼   c. warm water
Chicken Filling (p. 269)
1–2 tsp. canola oil

1. In the processor, combine flour, salt, egg, egg whites and water. Process with the Steel Knife for 25 to 30 seconds, until dough forms a ball on the blades. Remove dough from bowl and wrap in foil for 20 minutes for easier handling. Meanwhile, prepare filling as directed.

2. Divide dough in four pieces. Shape 1 piece of dough into a square on a lightly floured surface. (Keep remaining dough covered.) Roll dough very thin into a rectangle. Cut into squares. Place 2 teaspoons of filling in the center of each square. Moisten edges of dough with water. Fold each square in half to make a triangle. Seal completely by pinching edges together firmly. Join 2 points together to form a little "purse." Repeat with remaining dough and filling. (May be made in advance up to this point and frozen on a baking sheet. When frozen, wrap well. Cook without thawing.)

3. Bring a large pot of salted water to a boil. Add kreplach to pot and cook uncovered for 15 minutes (or 20 minutes if frozen). They will rise to the top when done. Remove with a slotted spoon and drain well. Sprinkle lightly with oil to prevent sticking.

Yield: about 2½ to 3 dozen. Kreplach can be frozen before or after cooking.

60 calories each (with chicken filling), 1.6 g fat (0.4 g saturated), 22 mg cholesterol, 4 g protein, 7 g carbohydrate, 39 mg sodium, 46 mg potassium, <1 mg iron, trace fiber, 5 mg calcium.

- **Chicken Soup with Kreplach:** Fill dough with chicken filling. Prepare and cook as directed. Serve in Chicken Soup (p. 83). Kreplach are a traditional delicacy for Purim and Yom Kippur.
- **Easier Kreplach:** Use 3 dozen wonton wrappers instead of making your own dough.
- **Jewish Ravioli:** Serve Chicken Kreplach with Quick'n Easy Tomato Sauce (p. 191) as a main dish.
- **Cheese Kreplach:** Refer to recipe for Cheese Blintzes (p. 150). The cheese filling for blintzes is also excellent for kreplach. You will have enough filling to make 3 to 4 dozen. Prepare and cook as directed above. Serve with non-fat yogurt or sour cream and berries.
- **Potato Varenikas:** Prepare the potato mixture as directed in Step 1 of No-Dough Potato Knishes (p. 270). Prepare dough for kreplach as directed above. Use a 2-inch round cutter to cut dough into circles. Place a spoonful of potato mixture on each circle. Moisten edges and fold in half, pinching edges to seal completely. Cook varenikas as directed for kreplach in Step 3 (above).

Chicken Filling for Kreplach

1   onion, diced
2   tsp. canola oil
2   c. cooked chicken, cut into chunks
1   egg (or 2 egg whites)
Salt & pepper, to taste

1. In a non-stick skillet, sauté onion in oil until golden. Grind chicken in the processor, about 20 seconds. Add onion, egg and seasonings and process a few seconds longer. If mixture seems dry, add some chicken broth or water.

Yield: 2 cups of filling, enough for 3 dozen Kreplach.

24 calories per tbsp., 1.1 g fat (0.3 g saturated), 15 mg cholesterol, 3 g protein, trace carbohydrate, 10 mg sodium, 31 mg potassium, trace iron, trace fiber, 3 mg calcium.

No-Dough Potato Knishes

These are delicious with or without Chicken Filling. Perfect for Passover or any time of year.

6–8 large potatoes, peeled & cut up
Lightly salted water for cooking potatoes
3   large onions, chopped
1   tbsp. canola oil
2   egg whites (or 1 egg)
¼–½ c. hot chicken or vegetable broth (as needed)
Salt & pepper, to taste
½ c. seasoned bread crumbs (or matzo meal)
Chicken Filling (see previous recipe), optional

1. Cook potatoes in lightly salted water until tender, about 20 minutes. Drain well. Return saucepan to the heat for 1 or 2 minutes to evaporate excess moisture from potatoes. Mash potatoes well. Meanwhile, sauté onions in oil in a large non-stick skillet for 6 to 8 minutes, until well browned. Add a little water if necessary to prevent onions from sticking or burning. Mix onions and egg whites into mashed potatoes. Add enough broth to moisten; mix well. Add salt and pepper to taste.

2. Preheat oven to 375°F. Wet your hands and shape potato mixture into 12 patties. If desired, make a small indentation in each one and insert a spoonful of Chicken Filling. Cover filling with some potato mixture. Coat with bread crumbs. (For Passover, use matzo meal). Place on a lightly greased baking sheet and bake for 15 minutes. Turn them over and bake 10 to 15 minutes longer, until golden.

Yield: about 1 dozen. These reheat well. Freezing may change the texture of the potatoes.

115 calories per serving, 2.3 g fat (0.4 g saturated), 35 mg cholesterol, 4 g protein, 20 g carbohydrate, 154 mg sodium, 299 mg potassium, <1 mg iron, 1 g fiber, 22 mg calcium.

No-Fry Potato Latkas

See photo (P-5). My kids, Steven and Cheryl, love my latkas! These taste like the real thing, without the guilt! One no-fry latka contains just 1 gram of fat, compared to 2.7 grams for the fried version!

4   tsp. canola or olive oil, divided
4–5 medium Idaho potatoes (2 lb/1 kg)
1   medium onion
1   clove garlic, if desired
1   tbsp. fresh dill (or 1 tsp. dried dill)
1   egg & 2 egg whites (or 2 eggs), lightly beaten
¼   c. flour (white or whole-wheat)
½   tsp. baking powder
¾   tsp. salt
¼   tsp. pepper

1. Place oven racks on the lowest and middle positions in your oven. Preheat oven to 450°F. Line 2 baking sheets with aluminum foil. Spray each bak-

ing sheet lightly with non-stick spray, then brush each baking sheet with 1 teaspoon of oil. (This provides a crispy exterior to the latka.)

2. Peel potatoes or scrub them well if you don't want to peel them. Grate potatoes. (The processor does this quickly.) Transfer them to another bowl. Use the processor to finely mince onion, garlic and dill. Add potatoes, egg, egg whites and remaining 2 teaspoons of oil to the processor. Mix using quick on/off turns. Add remaining ingredients and mix briefly. If overprocessed, potatoes will be too fine.

3. Drop mixture by rounded spoonfuls onto prepared baking sheets. Flatten slightly with the back of the spoon to form latkas. Bake uncovered at 450°F for 10 minutes, or until bottoms are nicely browned and crispy. Turn latkas over. Transfer pan from the upper rack to the lower rack and vice versa. Bake about 8 to 10 minutes longer, or until brown. Best when served immediately.

Yield: 2 dozen medium latkas or 6 dozen minis. Serve with Homemade Applesauce (p. 360). Great with Tzadziki (p. 53), low-fat sour cream or yogurt topped with minced lox and chives! Latkas freeze well.

36 calories per medium latka, 1 g fat (0.1 g saturated), 9 mg cholesterol, 1 g protein, 6 g carbohydrate, 92 mg sodium, 143 mg potassium, trace iron, <1 g fiber, 10 mg calcium.

- **To fry latkas** instead of baking them, don't add oil to the latka mixture. Use a non-stick skillet and fry latkas in a little oil, about 2 teaspoons per batch. Drain on paper towels to absorb oil.
- **For latkas, my favorite choice** is russet potatoes (Idaho or P.E.I.) because of their higher starch content. Some people like Yukon Golds, others prefer red-skinned potatoes. The choice is yours!
- **Well-scrubbed potatoes** don't need peeling. (Most of the nutrients are just under the skin!)
- **Latkas may be made** a day in advance. When cool, cover and refrigerate. Reheat uncovered at 375°F for 10 minutes. To save oven space, stand them upright snugly in a loaf pan (like soldiers)!
- **Potato Apple Latkas:** Use 3 grated potatoes and 1 peeled and grated Granny Smith (green) apple. Add ½ teaspoon cinnamon; omit dill, garlic and pepper. Serve latkas with low-fat sour cream, yogurt or applesauce.
- **No-Fry Sweet Potato Latkas:** Prepare No-Fry Potato Latkas as directed above, but use 1 large sweet potato, 2 Idaho potatoes and 2 eggs plus 2 egg whites (or 3 eggs). One latka contains 50 calories, 1.3 g fat (0.2 g saturated) and 18 mg cholesterol.

No-Fry Potato & Spinach Latkas

Latkas (pancakes) are served at Chanukah to celebrate the miracle of a little bit of oil lasting for eight days. Traditional latkas are usually fried in at least 1/4 cup of oil, so one latka contains about 3 grams of fat. I don't know anyone who can stop at just one latka, so these "no-guilt" latkas are a terrific alternative. Each one contains just over a gram of fat—that's a miracle!

4	tsp. canola or olive oil, divided
3	medium Idaho potatoes
10	oz. pkg. frozen chopped spinach, thawed & squeezed dry
1	medium onion
1–2	carrots
2	tbsp. minced fresh dill (or 2 tsp. dried dill)
2	eggs plus 2 egg whites (or 3 eggs)
¼	c. flour (white or whole-wheat)
½	tsp. baking powder
¾	tsp. salt
¼	tsp. pepper

1. Place oven racks on the lowest and middle positions in your oven. Preheat oven to 450°F. Line 2 baking sheets with aluminum foil; spray with non-stick spray. Brush each pan with 1 teaspoon of oil. (Or use 2 non-stick baking sheets and brush each one lightly with oil.)

2. Peel potatoes or scrub well if you don't want to peel them. Using the grater of your processor, grate potatoes, using light pressure. Remove potatoes from processor. Insert Steel Knife and process spinach, onion, carrots and dill until fine. Add grated potatoes, egg, egg whites and remaining 2 teaspoons oil. Process with quick on/offs to mix. Quickly blend in remaining ingredients.

3. Drop mixture by rounded spoonfuls onto prepared baking sheets. Flatten slightly with back of the spoon to form latkas. Bake uncovered at 450°F for 10 minutes, or until bottoms are browned and crispy. Turn latkas over. Transfer pan on the upper rack to the lower rack and vice versa. Bake about 8 to 10 minutes longer, until brown. Serve immediately.

Yield: about 24 medium latkas or 6 dozen miniatures. (Three minis equal 1 medium latka.) Can be frozen. Serve with Super Salsa (p. 61), Tzadziki (p. 53), low-fat sour cream or yogurt.

42 calories per medium latka, 1.2 g fat (0.2 g saturated), 18 mg cholesterol, 2 g protein, 6 g carbohydrate, 97 mg sodium, 126 mg potassium, trace iron, <1 g fiber, 17 mg calcium.

- **Latkas may be made** a day in advance. When cool, cover and refrigerate.
- **To freeze latkas,** arrange in a single layer on a baking sheet. When frozen, wrap well.
- **To save space when freezing** or reheating latkas, stand them upright in a loaf pan. Reheat uncovered at 375°F for 8 to 10 minutes.

- **Instead of baking latkas,** brown them in a non-stick skillet. Instead of adding the oil to the latka mixture, use it for frying.
- **Tri-Color Latkas:** Omit spinach. Use 2 carrots and 2 medium zucchini, grated.

Noodle & Spinach Kugel

See photo (P-8). So colorful made with three-color noodles!

12 oz. pkg. (375 g) medium noodles
10 oz. pkg. (300 g) frozen chopped spinach
2 tsp. olive or canola oil
1 large onion, chopped
2 eggs & 4 egg whites (or 4 eggs)
1½ c. chicken or vegetable broth
Salt & pepper, to taste
½ tsp. dried basil

1. Preheat oven to 350°F. Cook noodles according to package directions. Drain and rinse well. Return noodles to pot; set aside. While noodles are cooking, thaw frozen spinach in the microwave. It will take 3 to 4 minutes on HIGH power. Cool slightly. Squeeze out any excess moisture.

2. Heat oil in a non-stick skillet. Add onion and sauté until golden. Combine all ingredients and mix well. Spread in a sprayed 9 x 13-inch casserole. Bake at 350°F for 50 to 60 minutes, until golden.

Yield: 12 servings. Freezes and/or reheats well.

146 calories per serving, 3 g fat (0.8 g saturated), 69 mg cholesterol, 8 g protein, 22 g carbohydrate, 88 mg sodium, 93 mg potassium, 2 mg iron, 2 g fiber, 42 mg calcium.

Broccoli Noodle Kugel

Mimi Brownstein gave me the idea for this luscious kugel. It's perfect for a buffet or dinner party!

12	oz. pkg. (375 g) medium noodles
1	bunch broccoli (about 1 lb/500 g)
2	tsp. canola oil
2	onions, chopped
1	red pepper, chopped
2	cloves garlic, crushed
1	c. mushrooms, sliced
3	eggs plus 4 egg whites (5 eggs or 1¼ c. egg substitute can be used)
2	c. chicken or vegetable broth

Salt & pepper, to taste

1. Preheat oven to 350°F. Cook noodles according to package directions. Drain and rinse well. Soak broccoli in cold water for 10 minutes. Drain well. Cut broccoli into florets; slice the stems. Steam or microwave the broccoli covered on HIGH for 5 minutes, until tender-crisp.

2. Heat oil in a non-stick skillet. Sauté onions, red pepper and garlic on medium-high heat until golden, about 5 minutes. (If needed, add a little water or broth to prevent sticking.) Add mushrooms and sauté 4 or 5 minutes longer. Combine all ingredients and mix well. Spread evenly in a sprayed 9 x 13-inch casserole. Bake at 350°F for 30 minutes. Cover with foil and bake 30 minutes longer. Cool for 10 minutes before slicing into squares.

Yield: 12 servings. Freezes and/or reheats well.

173 calories per serving, 3.6 g fat (0.9 g saturated), 87 mg cholesterol, 10 g protein, 26 g carbohydrate, 102 mg sodium, 262 mg potassium, 2 mg iron, 3 g fiber, 52 mg calcium.

SECTION 10

Salad Daze!

Salad Daze!

- There's more to salad than iceberg lettuce! Experiment with different varieties: use Boston, bibb or romaine lettuce, radicchio, endive, watercress, spinach or leafy field greens (mesclun). The darker the greens, the better. Buy crisp, fresh greens. Avoid those that are wilted or rotting.
- Bagged, prewashed salad greens are so handy and save on prep time.
- "Lettuce" forget about lettuce! You can make excellent salads with many other vegetables. Greek Salad (p. 280) and Rainbow Tabbouleh (p. 283) are sure to please.
- Cut tomatoes vertically instead of horizontally. This keeps the juices in the tomatoes, helping to prevent soggy sandwiches and salads.
- Let tomatoes ripen on the counter (or on a sunny window ledge). Don't refrigerate them because they'll lose flavor! Tomatoes that have been cut should be refrigerated. If you place the tomato cut-side down on a plate, you won't have to wrap it!
- Carotenes are responsible for many of the the colors found in fruits and vegetables (including red, orange, yellow and the dark green in leafy vegetables). They are among the antioxidants that protect against the effects of disease and aging.
- Bioflavonoids also have antioxidant properties. They are found in most fruits and vegetables (e.g., citrus fruits, cantaloupes, apricots, grapes, broccoli, green peppers, tomatoes). Add fruits to your vegetable salads and fruit juices to salad dressings to maximize both nutrition and flavor.
- Kitchen Sink Salad: Turn a salad into a complete meal by adding pasta, rice, bulgur, couscous or other cooked grains. Add canned black beans or kidney beans, lentils, chickpeas or corn niblets.
- Another option is to add a small portion of low-fat protein (e.g., chicken or turkey breast, tuna, salmon, etc.) to your vegetable salad.

- Did you know that commercial salad dressings can add up to 90 calories and 10 grams of fat per tablespoon? Use calorie-reduced or fat-free dressings to pare down those calories.
- Bottled low-fat or nonfat salad dressings are often made with a list of ingredients with names that are unpronounceable. The dressings are so full of chemicals that if you consume enough, you'll probably live forever because of the preservatives they contain!
- Most traditional recipes for homemade salad dressings are high in fat. Try the lighter dressings I've developed. Instead of the old formula of 3 parts oil to 1 part acid, use the following formula: $\frac{1}{3}$ olive or canola oil, $\frac{1}{3}$ lemon juice or vinegar, $\frac{1}{3}$ vegetable broth or defatted chicken broth. Add a pinch of sugar to lower the acidity. Increase the flavor with fresh or dried herbs. You'll lighten up your life and light up your taste buds!
- Do yourself a flavor! Use extra-virgin olive oil or Oriental sesame oil in dressings. Add Roasted Garlic (p. 252) to salad dressings to boost the flavor without added fat.
- For creamy-style dressings, add a little fat-free or light mayonnaise, or mayonnaise-type salad dressing. Yogurt or buttermilk are also excellent low-fat options.
- Leftover Tzadziki (p. 53) can be thinned down with a little milk and used as a salad dressing. Other dips which make great salad dressings are: Garden Vegetable Dip or Dressing (p. 51), Creamy Salsa Dip (p. 55), and Salsa Salad Dressing (p. 61).
- Salsa (homemade or bottled) makes a guiltless salad dressing. Combine it with equal parts of yogurt for a creamy dressing.
- Skinny Dipping! When eating salad in a restaurant, ask for the dressing on the side. First dip your fork into the dressing, then pick up some salad. Every bite of salad you take will have some dressing and you'll use only a fraction of the fat you'd usually use!

Red Cabbage Cole Slaw

The boiled dressing transforms the cabbage into a beautiful, brilliant magenta color.

1 medium red cabbage, cored & thinly sliced (about 8 cups)
4 green onions, thinly sliced
1 medium carrot, grated
2 tbsp. canola oil
1/4 c. red or white wine vinegar (also excellent with raspberry or balsamic vinegar)
2 tbsp. sugar
Salt & pepper, to taste

1. Combine vegetables in a large mixing bowl. In a medium saucepan, combine oil, vinegar and sugar. Bring to a boil. (Or combine in a 2-cup Pyrex measure and microwave uncovered for 45 seconds.) Pour hot dressing over vegetables. Mix well. Add salt and pepper to taste. Refrigerate to blend flavors.

Yield: 12 servings. Leftovers keep 3 to 4 days in the refrigerator.

45 calories per serving, 2.4 g fat (0.2 g saturated), 0 mg cholesterol, <1 g protein, 6 g carbohydrate, 8 mg sodium, 132 mg potassium, trace iron, 1 g fiber, 28 mg calcium.

Creamy 1,000 Island Cole Slaw

This super slaw is virtually fat-free and high in fiber and potassium. Enjoy without guilt!

1 medium green cabbage (about 8 c. shredded)
6 green onions, chopped
3 stalks celery, chopped

1 green & 1 red pepper, chopped
3 carrots, grated
1/2 c. nonfat yogurt
1/2 c. non-fat or low-fat mayonnaise
1/2 c. ketchup or salsa
2 tbsp. fresh chopped basil (or 1 tsp. dried)
2 tbsp. minced fresh dill
Salt & pepper, to taste

1. Prepare vegetables. (You can do this quickly in the processor.) Combine veggies in a large bowl. Add remaining ingredients; mix well. Chill to blend flavors.

Yield: 12 servings. Leftovers will keep for several days in the refrigerator.

50 calories per serving, 0.3 g fat (0 g saturated), trace cholesterol, 2 g protein, 11 g carbohydrate, 225 mg sodium, 326 mg potassium, <1 mg iron, 3 g fiber, 60 mg calcium.

• **Non-Dairy Version:** Omit yogurt, mayonnaise and ketchup. Substitute 1 1/2 cups bottled low-calorie 1,000 Island salad dressing. If desired, fold in 1 cup of drained pineapple tidbits.

Oriental Cole Slaw

Sesame oil and rice vinegar enhance the flavor of this non-traditional cole slaw. Addictive!

1 medium head green cabbage (8 c. shredded)
2–3 carrots, grated
3/4 c. thinly sliced red onion (or 6 green onions, sliced)
2–3 cloves garlic, crushed
1/3 c. canola oil
1/3 c. rice vinegar

¼ c. sugar
2 tsp. Oriental sesame oil
Salt & pepper, to taste

1. Combine cabbage, carrots, onions and garlic in a large mixing bowl. Combine canola oil and rice vinegar with sugar in a 2-cup Pyrex measure. Microwave uncovered on HIGH for 45 seconds, until almost boiling. Pour hot dressing over cabbage mixture. Add sesame oil and mix well. Season to taste.

Yield: 12 servings. Leftovers will keep about a week in the refrigerator.

98 calories per serving, 7 g fat (0.6 g saturated), 0 mg cholesterol, <1 g protein, 9 g carbohydrate, 13 mg sodium, 171 mg potassium, trace iron, 2 g fiber, 28 mg calcium.

Oriental Cucumber Salad

2 English cucumbers (unpeeled), thinly sliced
½ of a small red onion, thinly sliced
1 red pepper, thinly sliced
1 tsp. minced ginger
¼ c. rice vinegar
2 tsp. Oriental sesame oil
1 tbsp. sugar
1 tsp. salt (or to taste)
½ tsp. pepper

1. Combine all ingredients in a bowl and mix well. Adjust seasonings to taste.

Yield: 6 servings. Leftovers will keep for a day in the refrigerator.

30 calories per serving, 0.2 g fat (0 g saturated), 0 mg cholesterol, 1 g protein, 7 g carbohydrate, 391 mg sodium, 191 mg potassium, trace iron, 1 g fiber, 19 mg calcium.

- **Variation:** Add 2 tablespoons orange juice and 1 teaspoon soy sauce.
- **Old-Fashioned Cucumber Salad:** Omit ginger and sesame oil. Use white vinegar instead of rice vinegar and increase sugar to 2 tablespoons. Use Spanish onion instead of red onion, if desired.
- **The liquid at the bottom** of the bowl can be used as a yummy guilt-free dressing over salad greens!

Creamy Cucumber Salad

2 English cucumbers, thinly sliced
1 tsp. salt
4 green onions, sliced
2 cloves garlic, crushed
1 c. nonfat yogurt or low-fat sour cream
2 tbsp. vinegar
1 tbsp. sugar
Salt & pepper, to taste

1. Sprinkle cucumber slices with salt. Mix well; let stand for ½ hour. Press out excess liquid. Combine all ingredients in a bowl and mix gently, adding salt and pepper to taste. Serve chilled.

Yield: 6 servings. Leftovers will keep about a day in the refrigerator.

59 calories per serving, 0.2 g fat (0.1 g saturated), <1 mg cholesterol, 4 g protein, 12 g carbohydrate, 426 mg sodium, 276 mg potassium, <1 mg iron, 1 g fiber, 105 mg calcium.

- **One clove of garlic** contains 1 mg of calcium. If you eat 300 cloves, you'll get the same amount as in a glass of milk. You may have stronger bones, but probably will have less friends!
- **Your processor can turn** leftovers into Tzadziki in a flash. Process the mixture with quick on/offs, until desired texture is reached.

Greek Salad

I've reduced the fat content considerably for this marvelous Mediterranean salad, but not the flavor! It's perfect for a buffet. Double or triple the recipe for a large crowd since it disappears so quickly.

4   firm, ripe tomatoes
3   green peppers (or 1 green, 1 red, 1 yellow)
1   English cucumber, peeled
1/2 of a red or Spanish onion (about 1 c.)
1/4 c. pitted black olives
1/2 c. feta cheese, finely diced or grated
2   tbsp. olive oil (preferably extra-virgin)
Juice of a lemon (3 tbsp.)
Salt & pepper, to taste
1/2 tsp. each dried basil & oregano

1. Cut tomatoes, peppers, cucumber and onion into 1-inch chunks. Slice olives or cut them in half. Combine all ingredients in a large bowl and toss to mix. (Can be prepared several hours in advance and refrigerated.)

Yield: 6 servings of about 1 cup each. Leftovers keep for 1 or 2 days in the refrigerator.

136 calories per serving, 8.5 g fat (2.7 g saturated), 11 mg cholesterol, 4 g protein, 13 g carbohydrate, 202 mg sodium, 473 mg potassium, 1 mg iron, 3 g fiber, 93 mg calcium.

- **Lactose-Free Variation:** Substitute extra-firm tofu (preferably lite) for feta cheese. Slice tofu; place slices between 2 layers of paper towels. Cover with a baking sheet and top with several cans to press out excess liquid. Let stand 20 minutes. Dice tofu and add to salad. Add 2 to 3 tablespoons of Parmesan-flavored soy or rice cheese. Toss gently to mix.

Israeli Salad

See photo (P-19). I love to cook, but don't always have the patience to chop vegetables into the small cubes that make this salad so delicious. Bring a small taste of Israel to your table! This is a favorite at a buffet. Recipe can be halved, if desired.

1   head of Romaine or iceberg lettuce
4   green onions
1   medium onion
2   green peppers
1   red pepper
1   English cucumber, peeled
8   firm, ripe tomatoes (preferably Israeli)
4   tbsp. olive oil (preferably extra-virgin)
4   tbsp. fresh lemon juice
1   tsp. salt (or to taste)
Freshly ground pepper, optional

1. Wash and dry vegetables well. Dice them neatly into 1/2-inch pieces and combine in a large bowl. Sprinkle with olive oil and lemon juice. Add seasonings; mix again. Adjust seasonings to taste.

Yield: 8 servings. Salad tastes best eaten the same day it is made, but leftovers will keep for a day in the refrigerator. Drain off excess liquid in the bottom of the bowl before serving.

127 calories per serving, 7.7 g fat (1.1 g saturated), 0 mg cholesterol, 3 g protein, 14 g carbohydrate, 600 mg sodium, 637 mg potassium, 2 mg iron, 4 g fiber, 45 mg calcium.

• **Mediterranean Vegetable Salad:** Add ¹/₂ cup sliced black olives, ¹/₂ cup sliced radishes and ¹/₂ cup chopped fresh parsley or coriander/cilantro.

Tomato, Onion & Pepper Salad

3–4 firm, ripe tomatoes, in 8ths
1   c. thinly sliced Spanish or red onions
¹/₂ of a red pepper, sliced
¹/₂ of a green pepper, sliced
¹/₂ of a yellow pepper, sliced
2   tbsp. fresh basil, chopped (or 1 tsp. dried)
2   cloves garlic, crushed
2   tbsp. olive oil (preferably extra-virgin)
2   tbsp. fresh lemon juice or balsamic vinegar
Salt & freshly ground pepper
¹/₂ tsp. Dijon mustard, optional

1. Combine tomatoes, onions, peppers, basil and garlic in a large bowl. (Can be prepared a few hours in advance, covered and refrigerated.) Add remaining ingredients and toss gently. Serve immediately.

Yield: 6 servings. Leftovers will keep about a day in the refrigerator.

72 calories per serving, 4.9 g fat (0.7 g saturated), 0 mg cholesterol, 1 g protein, 7 g carbohydrate, 9 mg sodium, 281 mg potassium, <1 mg iron, 2 g fiber, 12 mg calcium.

Roasted Red Peppers Vinaigrette

*These are excellent as a garnish for salads
or in sandwiches.*

4   Roasted Red Peppers (p. 57)
2   cloves garlic, crushed
1–2 tbsp. olive oil (extra-virgin)
1–2 tbsp. lemon juice or balsamic vinegar
Salt & pepper, to taste
2   tbsp. chopped fresh basil (or 1 tsp. dried)

1. Slice roasted peppers into strips. Mix together with remaining ingredients and serve.

Yield: 6 to 8 servings. If you use lemon juice and fresh basil, the marinated peppers will keep in the refrigerator for 2 or 3 days. If you use balsamic vinegar and dried basil, they'll keep about 10 days.

36 calories per serving, 2.4 g fat (0.3 g saturated), 0 mg cholesterol, <1 g protein, 4 g carbohydrate, 1 mg sodium, 92 mg potassium, trace iron, <1 g fiber, 8 mg calcium.

• **Quick Trick:** Combine the roasted peppers with bottled low-calorie Italian salad dressing!

Blima's Marinated Red Peppers

2   dozen red peppers
Salt, to taste
3   c. vinegar
1   c. water
¹/₂ c. sugar
¹/₂ c. honey
¹/₄ c. corn syrup
1   tsp. additional salt
¹/₄ c. canola oil

1. Preheat grill. Grill peppers on all sides until blackened. Place in a large paper bag and sprinkle with salt. Let stand for 10 minutes. Empty peppers into the sink filled with cold water. Remove the blackened skins. In a gallon jar, mix together remaining ingredients except oil. Add peppers, then add oil on top. Cover jar and shake to mix ingredients. Let marinate at room temperature for 4 days; then refrigerate.

Yield: 2 dozen. These will keep at least 6 months in the refrigerator.

29 calories per pepper, 0.4 fat (0 g saturated), 0 mg cholesterol, <1 g protein, 7 g carbohydrate, 26 mg sodium, 127 mg potassium, trace iron, <1 g fiber, 7 mg calcium.

• **Abby's Marinated Peppers:** Abby Kleinberg-Bassel eliminates the sugar, honey and corn syrup in the above recipe and substitutes 36 g Splenda granulated sugar substitute. Perfect for diabetics!

Fattouche Salad

A fresh and lemony Middle-Eastern salad. Toasted pita is added just before serving. Yummy!

2 medium pitas
1 bunch flat-leaf or curly parsley
1 head iceberg or Romaine lettuce
2–3 ripe tomatoes, diced
$1/2$ of an English cucumber, diced
4 green onions (or 1 small onion, diced)

Dressing:
Juice of 1 lemon (3 tbsp.)
2 tbsp. fresh mint, finely chopped

3–4 tbsp. olive oil (preferably extra-virgin)
1 clove garlic, crushed (optional)
Salt & pepper, to taste

1. Split pitas in half and place on an ungreased baking sheet. Bake in a preheated 400°F oven until crisp, about 10 minutes. Break pitas into small pieces and set aside. Wash parsley and lettuce; dry well. Mince parsley leaves; tear lettuce in bite-sized pieces. In a large bowl, combine lettuce, parsley, tomatoes, cucumber and onions; chill. Combine dressing ingredients; set aside. Just before serving, combine all ingredients and mix well. Serve immediately.

Yield: 6 servings. Leftover salad will become soggy.

150 calories per serving, 7.7 g fat (1.1 g saturated), 0 mg cholesterol, 4 g protein, 18 g carbohydrate, 127 mg sodium, 386 mg potassium, 2 mg iron, 3 g fiber, 62 mg calcium.

Tofu Antipasto

Debbie Jeremias likes to serve this as one of several salads for Shabbat. "It goes like crazy!"

1 c. mushrooms, quartered
2 stalks celery, sliced
3 medium ripe tomatoes, diced
1 red pepper, diced
1 yellow pepper, diced
1 orange pepper, diced
2 green onions, sliced
2 cloves garlic, thinly sliced
$1/3$–$1/2$ c. pitted black olives, halved
$3/4$ lb. firm tofu, diced (about $1 1/2$ c.)
2 tbsp. balsamic vinegar
2 tbsp. olive oil (preferably extra-virgin)

1 tsp. dried oregano
1 tsp. dried basil
Sea salt & freshly ground pepper, to taste

1. Combine all ingredients in a large bowl and mix well. If you have time, let mixture stand for 20 to 30 minutes to develop the flavor. (Can be made several hours in advance and refrigerated.)

Yield: 8 servings. Leftovers will keep for 2 or 3 days in the refrigerator.

140 calories per serving, 8.2 g fat (1.2 g saturated), 0 mg cholesterol, 8 g protein, 12 g carbohydrate, 73 mg sodium, 454 mg potassium, 6 mg iron, 3 g fiber, 116 mg calcium.

• **To lower calories and fat,** use 1% silken extra-firm tofu. A 3-ounce (84 g) serving of tofu contains 35 calories and 1 g fat. Its texture is softer than regular firm tofu, but it works well in this recipe.

Rainbow Tabbouleh Salad

See photo (P-7). This colorful, vitamin-packed salad is guaranteed to be a winner on any buffet table! This is a wonderful way to use up fresh mint if you grow it in your garden.

¹/₃ c. bulgur or couscous
²/₃ c. boiling water
2 c. minced flat-leaf or curly parsley
1 c. mint leaves
1 green & 1 red pepper
4 firm, ripe tomatoes
4 green onions (scallions)
¹/₄ c. red onion
¹/₄ c. grated carrots

¹/₂ English cucumber, seeded & diced
¹/₄–¹/₃ c. olive oil (to taste)
¹/₄–¹/₃ c. fresh lemon juice (to taste)
Salt & pepper, to taste
1 tbsp. fresh basil, chopped (or 1 tsp. dried)
Fresh mint or basil leaves, to garnish

1. In a small bowl, combine bulgur or couscous with boiling water. Let stand for 20 minutes to soften. (Couscous will take only 10 minutes.) Meanwhile, soak parsley and mint in cold salted water for 15 to 20 minutes. Drain and dry well. Trim off tough parsley stems. Remove mint leaves from stems.

2. Mince parsley and mint leaves. Chop vegetables. (Do this in the processor in batches, using on/off turns to retain texture.) Combine parsley, mint and vegetables in a large mixing bowl. Add drained bulgur or couscous, olive oil and lemon juice. Mix well. Add salt, pepper and basil. Allow to stand for at least ¹/₂ hour for flavors to blend. Garnish with fresh mint or basil leaves.

Yield: 8 servings. Leftovers will keep for 2 or 3 days in the refrigerator.

121 calories per serving, 7.4 g fat (1 g saturated), 0 mg cholesterol, 3 g protein, 14 g carbohydrate, 22 mg sodium, 434 mg potassium, 2 mg iron, 4 g fiber, 47 mg calcium.

• **Store bulgur in an airtight container** in a cool dark place. It can be stored in the refrigerator for several months, or in the freezer for up to a year.
• **Reserve parsley stems** and use them when making chicken or vegetable broth.
• **Parsley should be well-dried** before chopping. Your processor makes quick work of this task. Measure parsley after chopping. You need

approximately twice as much before chopping to give you the required amount for this recipe.

- **If fresh mint is not available,** add 2 teaspoons dried mint. If you don't have dried mint, just leave it out. The salad will still have a delicious, garden-fresh flavor.
- **Variation:** Increase bulgur or couscous to 1 cup for a grain-based Tabbouleh. Soak the grain in double the amount of water.
- **Traditional Tabbouleh:** Omit red onion, carrots, cucumber and basil.
- **Quinoa Tabbouleh:** Use 1 cup of cooked quinoa (p. 217) instead of soaked bulgur or couscous.
- **Greek-Style Tabbouleh:** Crumble or grate ½ cup feta cheese over Tabbouleh. Add ⅓ cup sliced black olives. One serving contains 152 calories, 10 g fat (2.5 g saturated) and 98 mg calcium.

Spinach & Mushroom Salad with Honey Mustard Dressing

10	oz. pkg. (300 g) fresh spinach
½	c. mushrooms, thinly sliced
½	of a red onion, thinly sliced (about ½ c.)
1	small carrot, grated
½	c. Honey Mustard Dressing (below)

1. Trim tough stems from spinach leaves. Wash and dry thoroughly; tear into bite-size pieces. Combine all vegetables in a large bowl. Prepare salad dressing and set aside. (Vegetables and dressing can be prepared in advance and refrigerated separately for several hours.) At serving time, combine all ingredients and toss gently to mix. Serve immediately.

Yield: 6 servings. Leftover salad will become soggy.

91 calories per serving, 4.9 g fat (0.7 g saturated), 0 mg cholesterol, 2 g protein, 12 g carbohydrate, 95 mg sodium, 289 mg potassium, 1 mg iron, 2 g fiber, 43 mg calcium.

- **Fresh spinach** can be very sandy and gritty. Immerse trimmed spinach leaves in a sink full of cold water. Swish the leaves around, then let stand for a few minutes. Lift spinach from water, leaving sand and dirt behind in the bottom of the sink. Repeat until water is clean. Dry spinach thoroughly (in a salad spinner or by wrapping in a clean towel). Wrap spinach in paper towels and place in a sealed plastic storage bag. Refrigerate for up to 4 days.
- **Time-Saving Tip:** Washed baby spinach greens can be used instead of regular spinach. This saves time and clean-up!
- **Did you know** that spinach isn't an especially good source of calcium or iron? It contains oxalates, which reduce absorption of calcium, iron and other minerals.
- **Spinach, Mandarin & Almond Salad:** Omit mushrooms. Use 2 tablespoons rice vinegar and 2 tablespoons orange juice in the salad dressing. Combine spinach, onion and grated carrot in a bowl. Add ¾ cup canned mandarin oranges, drained and patted dry. You can also add ½ cup bean sprouts. Add dressing; toss gently to mix. Garnish with ¼ cup toasted slivered almonds or pine nuts.

Honey Mustard Dressing

Fabulous! Use as a dressing over salad greens or as a sauce for poached salmon for rave reviews!

¼	c. olive oil (preferably extra-virgin)
¼	c. white or rice wine vinegar (or 2 tbsp. orange juice and 2 tbsp. vinegar)

1/3 c. liquid honey
2 tbsp. Dijon or prepared mustard
1/4 c. water
Freshly ground pepper

1. Combine all ingredients in a jar, cover and shake well. Keeps in the refrigerator for up to a month.

Yield: about 1 cup.

42 calories per tbsp., 2.7 g fat (0.4 g saturated), 0 mg cholesterol, trace protein, 5 g carbohydrate, 36 mg sodium, 9 mg potassium, trace iron, 0 g fiber, 2 mg calcium.

Honey Mustard Carrot Salad

2 lb. carrots, peeled & grated
4 green onions, chopped
2 tbsp. chopped parsley &/or dill
3 tbsp. honey
1 tbsp. Dijon mustard (to taste)
1 tbsp. extra-virgin olive oil
1/3 c. raisins, rinsed & drained
1 tbsp. orange juice
1 tbsp. lemon juice
Salt & pepper, to taste

1. Combine all ingredients in a bowl and toss to mix. Adjust seasonings to taste. Serve chilled.

Yield: 6 servings.

115 calories per serving, 2.2 g fat (0.3 g saturated), 0 mg cholesterol, 2 g protein, 25 g carbohydrate, 90 mg sodium, 454 mg potassium, <1 mg iron, 4 g fiber, 43 mg calcium.

Fennel, Orange & Spinach Salad

Fennel, also known as finocchio, has a mild licorice flavor. The fronds (leaves) resemble fresh dill.

1 medium bulb fennel (about 1/2 lb.)
1/2 of a 10 oz. pkg. of fresh spinach
4 large seedless oranges
1 red pepper, halved, seeded & thinly sliced
1/2 c. chopped red onion (or 4 green onions)
2 tbsp. lemon juice or rice vinegar
1 clove garlic, crushed
1 tsp. honey-style mustard
2 tbsp. extra-virgin olive oil
Salt & pepper, to taste

1. Wash fennel; remove any stringy or brown outer stalks. Chop some of the fronds and reserve. Trim away root end. Slice fennel bulbs and stems into 1/4-inch slices and place in a serving bowl. Trim away tough stems from spinach. Wash spinach, dry well and tear into bite-size pieces. Peel oranges with a sharp knife, removing the white pith. Cut in half and slice thinly. Combine oranges in a bowl with fennel, spinach, red pepper and onion. Refrigerate until serving time. In a small bowl, combine lemon juice, garlic and mustard. Whisk in oil; refrigerate.

2. At serving time, pour dressing over fennel mixture and toss to coat with dressing. Season with salt and pepper. Garnish with fennel fronds.

Yield: 8 servings. So refreshing!

95 calories per serving, 3.7 g fat (0.5 g saturated), 0 mg cholesterol, 2 g protein, 16 g carbohydrate, 34 mg sodium, 398 mg potassium, <1 mg iron, 4 g fiber, 68 mg calcium.

- **To test fennel for freshness,** press the flesh lightly with your thumb. Avoid any bulbs that are soft.
- **Turkey, Fennel & Orange Salad:** Turn this salad into a main course by topping it with 2 cups of julienned smoked turkey (or chicken).

Doug's "Flower Power" Caesar Salad

This super salad is nutrient-packed. It's a specialty of my son Doug, the Salad King!

3   c. broccoli flowerets
3   c. cauliflower flowerets
1   c. sliced red cabbage
3   tbsp. grated Parmesan cheese
³/₄ c. Lighter Caesar Dressing (p. 295) or bottled low-fat Caesar dressing
¹/₂ tsp. freshly ground pepper

1. Wash vegetables well; drain thoroughly. Combine all ingredients in a glass bowl and mix well. (Optional: Steam the veggies for 3 or 4 minutes if you prefer them softer.) This salad keeps for 3 days in a glass (not metal) bowl in the refrigerator, if well-covered.

Yield: 6 servings.

68 calories per serving, 2.2 g fat (1.4 g saturated), 6 mg cholesterol, 6 g protein, 8 g carbohydrate, 401 mg sodium, 348 mg potassium, <1 mg iron, 3 g fiber, 148 mg calcium.

Greek-Style Black Bean Salad

So colorful, so good! Silken tofu can be substituted for the feta cheese for a non-dairy version.

2   19 oz. (540 ml) cans black beans, rinsed & drained (or 4 c. cooked black beans)
³/₄ c. chopped red onion
1   yellow pepper, chopped
1   red pepper, chopped
2–3 tbsp. extra-virgin olive oil
3   tbsp. fresh lemon juice
¹/₄ c. fresh mint leaves, minced
¹/₄ c. fresh parsley leaves, minced
Salt & freshly ground pepper, to taste
2   firm tomatoes, chopped
¹/₂ c. feta cheese, crumbled

1. Combine all ingredients except tomatoes and cheese; mix well. Marinate for at least 20 to 30 minutes. Adjust seasonings to taste and garnish with tomatoes and cheese just before serving.

Yield: 8 servings.

199 calories per serving, 6.9 g fat (1.9 g saturated), 8 mg cholesterol, 11 g protein, 26 g carbohydrate, 585 mg sodium, 185 mg potassium, 4 mg iron, 9 g fiber, 107 mg calcium.

Jodi's Famous Bean Salad

My daughter Jodi is always asked to bring this terrific bean salad to dinner parties and barbecues. Thank goodness it's so easy to make. My grandaughter Lauren loves it!

19 oz. (540 ml) can black beans
19 oz. (540 ml) can chickpeas
19 oz. (540 ml) can lentils
2   cloves garlic, crushed
1   green &/or red pepper, chopped
1   yellow pepper, chopped
¹/₂ c. red onion, chopped

¼ c. coriander/cilantro, minced
¼ c. extra-virgin olive oil
¼ c. balsamic vinegar
1 tsp. ground cumin (or to taste)
Salt & freshly ground black pepper

1. Rinse beans, chickpeas and lentils; drain well. Combine all ingredients in a large mixing bowl; mix well. Season to taste. Cover and refrigerate. This tastes even better the next day!

Yield: 12 servings. This salad will keep for up to 3 days in the refrigerator if tightly covered.

172 calories per serving, 6.1 g fat (0.7 g saturated), 0 mg cholesterol, 8 g protein, 23 g carbohydrate, 238 mg sodium, 190 mg potassium, 3 mg iron, 8 g fiber, 41 mg calcium.

Easy Lentil Salad

2 19 oz. (540 ml) cans lentils, rinsed & drained (or 4 c. cooked brown lentils)
2 cloves garlic, minced
1 red or yellow pepper, chopped
1 orange pepper, chopped
2 carrots, grated
6 green onions, chopped
¼ c. minced parsley
2 tbsp. extra-virgin olive oil
3 tbsp. lemon juice
Salt & pepper, to taste
½ tsp. each chili powder, dry mustard & cumin

1. Combine all ingredients in a large bowl and mix well. Season to taste. Cover and refrigerate.

Yield: 8 servings. This salad will keep in the refrigerator for up to 3 days if tightly covered.

Salad Quickies!

- **Quick Caesar Pasta Salad:** Cook a 12-ounce package of bow tie pasta according to package directions. Drain and rinse well. Mix with ½ to ¾ cup Lighter Caesar Salad Dressing (p. 295) or bottled low-cal Caesar dressing. Add ½ cup each chopped red pepper, green onion and basil. Season to taste.
- **Quick Potato Salad:** Combine 4 cooked, chopped potatoes with ½ cup each of chopped celery, red pepper, green pepper, grated carrots and green onions. Add 3 tablespoons low-fat mayonnaise, 3 tablespoons low-fat Italian dressing, 1 teaspoon mustard and 2 tablespoons minced dill. Add salt and pepper to taste.
- **New Potato Salad:** Steam 2 pounds of new potatoes until tender-firm. When cool, cut in half but do not peel. Toss with ½ to ¾ cup low-cal vinaigrette dressing or Ranch-Style Dressing (p. 278). Add ½ cup each of minced celery and green onions. Season to taste.

---

173 calories per serving, 4.1 g fat (0.6 g saturated), 0 mg cholesterol, 10 g protein, 26 g carbohydrate, 247 mg sodium, 551 mg potassium, 4 mg iron, 9 g fiber, 41 mg calcium.

- **Kidney Bean & Chickpea Salad:** Instead of lentils, substitute 1 can of red kidney beans and 1 can of chickpeas, rinsed and drained.
- **Quick Couscous Salad:** Omit lentils; substitute 2 cups of couscous. Add 4 cups of water or chicken broth. Let stand for 10 minutes to absorb liquid. Add remaining ingredients; mix well.
- **Variation:** Instead of chili powder, dry mustard and cumin, add 3 to 4 tablespoons minced basil. Add ½ cup chopped roasted red peppers and ½ cup chopped sun-dried tomatoes to either version of the above salad.

Pesto Pasta Salad

See photo (P-2). Excellent for a summer salad buffet, and so pretty. If you don't have pesto on hand, add 2 cloves of freshly crushed garlic and 3 tablespoons grated Parmesan cheese.

12 oz. pkg. (340 g) spiral pasta or 3-color rotini
2 c. frozen mixed vegetables (e.g. broccoli, cauliflower & carrots)
6 green onions, chopped
2 green peppers, chopped
1 red pepper, chopped
¼ c. parsley, minced
¼ c. fresh basil leaves, minced
3 tbsp. Best-O Pesto (p. 195), to taste
3 tbsp. extra-virgin olive oil
2 tbsp. lemon juice
⅓–½ cup nonfat yogurt or mayonnaise
Salt & pepper, to taste

1. Cook pasta according to package directions. Drain well. Cook vegetables according to package directions. Let cool. In a large bowl, combine all ingredients and mix well. Adjust seasonings to taste. Chill at least 2 or 3 hours or overnight to allow flavors to blend.

Yield: 10 servings. Leftovers will keep for 2 or 3 days in the refrigerator. Do not freeze.

209 calories per serving, 5.7 g fat (0.8 g saturated), trace cholesterol, 7 g protein, 34 g carbohydrate, 35 mg sodium, 256 mg potassium, 2 mg iron, 4 fiber, 59 mg calcium.

- **Variation:** Substitute bow tie pasta for 3-color pasta. As a vegetarian main dish, add 1 to 2 cups canned chickpeas, rinsed and drained. If needed, add a little extra yogurt or mayonnaise to moisten.

- **Pareve Pasta Salad:** Use low-fat mayo instead of yogurt. Omit Pesto; add 1 teaspoon Dijon mustard.
- **Salmon Pasta Salad:** Add 2 cups of cooked/canned salmon, in chunks. Dill can replace basil.

Barley Salad with Honey Mustard Dressing

Barley is high in soluble fiber. Store it in a sealed jar in the pantry for at least 6 months.

3 c. lightly salted water
1 c. pearl or pot barley (if using pot barley, soak it overnight)
1 red pepper, chopped
4 green onions, chopped
½ c. Honey Mustard Dressing (p. 284)
2–3 tbsp. fresh dill &/or basil, minced
2 tbsp. toasted sunflower seeds, optional

1. Bring water to a boil. Add barley and simmer covered for 45 to 60 minutes, until tender. (Pearl barley takes 45 minutes to cook; pot barley takes about an hour.) Drain if necessary. Barley can be cooked in advance and refrigerated up to 24 hours. Combine chilled barley with remaining ingredients and toss to mix.

Yield: 6 servings. Leftovers will keep in the fridge for 3 days. Add a little lemon juice to moisten.

179 calories per serving, 4 g fat (0.6 g saturated), 0 mg cholesterol, 4 g protein, 34 g carbohydrate, 53 mg sodium, 152 mg potassium, 1 mg iron, 6 g fiber, 20 mg calcium.

Indonesian Brown Rice Salad

This addictive rice salad was my favorite dish at a pot luck birthday party. Suzi Lipes generously shared this wonderful recipe with me, I reduced the fat and now share it with you. It's a winner!

1   c. brown rice
2   c. boiling water
¹/₂ c. raisins
2   c. green onions, chopped
1   c. fresh bean sprouts
1   red pepper, chopped
1   stalk celery, chopped
¹/₄ c. toasted sesame seeds
¹/₄ c. toasted pecans, chopped (optional)

Salad Dressing:
¹/₃ c. fresh orange juice
3–4 tbsp. canola or olive oil
1   tbsp. Oriental sesame oil
¹/₄ c. tamari or low-sodium soy sauce
2   tbsp. sherry
2   cloves garlic, finely minced (about 1 tsp.)
¹/₂" slice ginger, finely minced
Freshly ground pepper, to taste

1. Combine rice and boiling water in a saucepan. Cover, bring to a boil and simmer for 30 minutes. Remove from heat and let cool. Meanwhile, prepare remaining ingredients. Salad dressing can be prepared in the processor. In a large bowl, combine all ingredients except sesame seeds and pecans. Mix well. Cover and refrigerate for several hours or overnight to blend flavors. At serving time, add sesame seeds and pecans.

Yield: 8 servings as a side dish, or 10 to 12 servings as part of a buffet.

232 calories per serving, 9.7 g fat (1.1 g saturated), 0 mg cholesterol, 5 g protein, 33 g carbohydrate, 542 mg sodium, 302 mg potassium, 2 mg iron, 4 g fiber, 46 mg calcium.

Quinoa Mandarin Salad

This salad is also excellent made with cooked rice! For extra crunch, garnish it with toasted sesame seeds. The processor will help you prepare this salad quickly. Quinoa is also great in tabbouleh.

3   c. cooked, cooled quinoa (p. 217)
¹/₂ c. minced parsley
2   tbsp. minced fresh basil
2   slices of ginger, minced (1 tbsp.)
2   green onions, minced
¹/₂ of a red pepper, diced
10   oz. can mandarin oranges, drained
1   c. snow peas, trimmed & cut in ¹/₂" strips
2   tbsp. soy or tamari sauce
2   tbsp. rice vinegar
1   tbsp. Oriental sesame oil
Salt & pepper, to taste

1. Cook quinoa as directed; cool completely. Combine quinoa with remaining ingredients and mix gently. Adjust seasonings to taste. Chill before serving.

Yield: 6 servings. Leftovers will keep about 2 days in the refrigerator. Do not freeze.

160 calories per serving, 4.2 g fat (0.7 g saturated), 0 mg cholesterol, 5 g protein, 27 g carbohydrate, 368 mg sodium, 369 mg potassium, 4 mg iron, 3 g fiber, 40 mg calcium.

Curried Chicken, Red Pepper & Mango Salad

This salad is so pretty and it's packed with potassium! Some people are sensitive to mangoes and may develop a red, itchy rash when peeling them. If this applies to you, just wear rubber gloves!

Curried Chicken Salad (p. 292), or 4 cooked skinless chicken breasts, cut in strips
6   c. mixed salad greens
1   mango, peeled
2   red peppers, halved & thinly sliced
1   c. red onion, thinly sliced
1/2 c. grated carrots
12   cherry tomatoes, halved
2   tbsp. balsamic or rice vinegar
1 1/2 tbsp. olive oil
1/2 tbsp. sesame oil
2   tbsp. orange juice
1   tbsp. honey
1   clove garlic, minced
Salt & pepper, to taste
2   tbsp. toasted slivered almonds, optional

1. Prepare chicken salad (or chicken) as directed. Wash and dry salad greens; arrange on individual plates. Place chicken on greens. Slice mango from the outside through to the middle, saving any juices. Cut away the pit. Arrange sliced mangoes attractively around edge of plate. Garnish with sliced peppers, red onion, carrots and tomatoes. Cover and refrigerate until serving time.

2. Blend vinegar, olive and sesame oils, orange juice, reserved mango juice, honey and garlic. Season with salt and pepper. Drizzle over salad just before serving. Sprinkle with nuts.

Yield: 6 servings.

276 calories per serving, 8 g fat (1.5 g saturated), 64 mg cholesterol, 26 g protein, 26 g carbohydrate, 189 mg sodium, 753 mg potassium, 2 mg iron, 5 g fiber, 75 mg calcium.

Louisiana Chicken Salad

4   boneless, skinless chicken breasts
1/2 c. bottled fat-free Italian dressing
4   c. mixed salad greens or Boston lettuce
1   c. finely sliced red cabbage
1/2 c. grated carrots
1/2 c. chopped red onion
1/2 c. red pepper strips
1/2 c. Satay Salad Dressing (p. 108)

1. Marinate chicken in Italian salad dressing for at least 30 minutes (or cover and refrigerate for up to 24 hours). Remove from marinade and pat dry. Preheat grill or broiler. Grill or broil chicken 5 to 7 minutes per side. When cool, slice chicken in strips. Arrange salad greens on individual plates. Top with cabbage, carrots and red onion. Arrange chicken strips on top of salad. Garnish with red pepper strips and drizzle with Satay Salad Dressing.

Yield: 4 servings.

279 calories per serving, 9.7 g fat (2.3 g saturated), 73 mg cholesterol, 31 g protein, 17 g carbohydrate, 662 mg sodium, 660 mg potassium, 2 mg iron, 3 g fiber, 68 mg calcium.

Paul's Carolina Smoked Chicken Salad

My son-in-law Paul Sprackman is an excellent cook! This is one of his extra-special salads. Enjoy!

4   boneless, skinless chicken breasts
2   tsp. canola oil
¼   c. dry white wine
1   tsp. liquid smoke
8   sun-dried tomatoes (packed in oil), well-rinsed, patted dry & cut in strips
2   dozen seedless green grapes, halved
1   medium red onion, chopped
1   green &/or yellow pepper, chopped
¼–⅓ c. low-fat mayonnaise
4–6 drops additional liquid smoke
6–8 drops Tabasco sauce
2–3 tbsp. fresh basil, chopped
4   c. mixed salad greens (e.g., mesclun)
¼   c. pecans, coarsely chopped, optional

1. Marinate chicken in oil, white wine and liquid smoke. Cover and refrigerate overnight. Preheat the grill. Remove chicken from marinade and pat dry. Discard marinade.

2. Grill chicken about 5 to 7 minutes per side. When cool, cut into cubes. In a large bowl, combine chicken with remaining ingredients except salad greens and nuts. Toss gently. Arrange salad greens on individual serving plates. Top with chicken mixture. Sprinkle with pecans, if using.

Yield: 4 to 6 servings.

266 calories per serving, 9.5 g fat (1.7 g saturated), 77 mg cholesterol, 29 g protein, 15 g carbohydrate, 173 mg sodium, 640 mg potassium, 2 mg iron, 2 g fiber, 60 mg calcium.

Nancy's Chinese Chicken Salad

12   wonton wrappers (defrost if frozen)
Salt, to taste
1   c. rice vinegar
3   tbsp. sugar
1   tsp. onion powder
½   tsp. dried oregano
1   tbsp. soy sauce
1   tbsp. Oriental sesame oil
4–5 c. lettuce or salad greens
1   carrot, grated
1   c. poached or cooked chicken, diced
½   c. drained mandarin oranges

1. Preheat oven to 350°F. Spray a baking sheet with non-stick spray. Slice wonton wrappers into narrow strips. Sprinkle lightly with salt. Bake for 5 to 7 minutes, until crisp and golden. Bring vinegar to a boil. Add sugar and stir to dissolve. Add onion powder, oregano and simmer uncovered for 3 minutes. Add soy sauce and sesame oil. Set aside. (Can be made 24 hours in advance.) At serving time, combine all ingredients and toss together. Serve on chilled salad plates.

Yield: 4 servings.

234 calories per serving, 6.6 g fat (1.4 g saturated), 33 mg cholesterol, 14 g protein, 30 g carbohydrate, 412 mg sodium, 307 mg potassium, 2 mg iron, 2 g fiber, 41 mg calcium.

Lighter Chicken Salad

Nutritional analysis was done for skinless cooked chicken, using a mixture of light and dark meat. If made with only white meat, one serving will contain 1.3 g fat (0.4 g saturated).

2   c. cooked, diced or chopped chicken
¼   c. minced or grated carrots
2   tbsp. minced fresh dill &/or basil (or 1 tsp. dried)
2   stalks celery, chopped
4   green onions, chopped
½   of a red pepper, chopped
⅓   c. fat-free or light mayonnaise (approximately)
Salt & freshly ground pepper, to taste

1. Combine all ingredients and mix well. To prepare mixture in your processor, remove and discard skin and bones from chicken. Cut chicken and vegetables into large chunks. First, mince carrots and dill using the Steel Knife. Add celery, green onions and red pepper. Process until chopped. Add chicken and process with quick on/offs, until desired texture is reached. Blend in mayonnaise. Season to taste.

Yield: about 3 cups. Do not freeze.

67 calories per ¼ cup, 2.3 g fat (0.6 g saturated), 27 mg cholesterol, 9 g protein, 2 g carbohydrate, 82 mg sodium, 137 mg potassium, <1 mg iron, <1 g fiber, 14 mg calcium.

• **Curried Chicken Salad:** Omit dill and/or basil. One apple, peeled, cored and diced, can be added to the chicken mixture for additional fiber. Season with curry powder to taste.
• **Chutney Chicken Salad:** Omit dill and/or basil. Add 2 to 3 tablespoons chutney. Add curry powder to taste.
• **Oriental Chicken Salad:** Omit dill and/or basil.

Add ½ cup each drained, chopped water chestnuts, green pepper and/or pineapple tidbits to chicken salad. Blend in 1 to 2 teaspoons soy sauce and a few drops of Oriental sesame oil.
• **Honey Mustard Chicken Salad:** Blend 2 teaspoons Dijon mustard and 2 teaspoons honey into mayonnaise. Instead of dill or basil, use 1 teaspoon dried thyme or tarragon.

Lighter Turkey Salad

1. Substitute cooked turkey breast (or a mixture of white and dark meat) in Lighter Chicken Salad (above) or any of its variations. (Nutritional analysis is calculated using cooked turkey breast.)

52 calories per ¼ cup, 0.4 g fat (0.1 g saturated), 26 mg cholesterol, 10 g protein, 2 g carbohydrate, 72 mg sodium, 147 mg potassium, <1 mg iron, <1 fiber, 14 mg calcium.

Balsamic Salad Splash

An almost fat-free dressing. Perfect over salad greens.

¼   c. balsamic vinegar
¼   c. water
¼   c. honey
¼   tsp. garlic powder
3–4 drops Tabasco sauce (to taste)
2   tsp. olive or canola oil

1. Combine all ingredients in a jar; shake well. Refrigerate until needed. Shake well before serving.

Yield: about ¾ cup. Dressing can be stored in the refrigerator for up to a month.

28 calories per tbsp., 0.6 g fat (0.1 g saturated), 0 mg cholesterol, 0 g protein, 6 g carbohydrate, 2 mg sodium, 4 mg potassium, trace iron, 0 g fiber, 1 mg calcium.

Simply Basic Vinaigrette

A light and luscious vinaigrette salad dressing.

¼ c. olive or canola oil
¼ c. rice, balsamic or red wine vinegar
¼ c. chicken or vegetable broth
1 tsp. Dijon mustard
1 tbsp. honey or maple syrup
Freshly ground pepper
½ tsp. dried basil (or 1 tbsp. fresh minced)
1 clove garlic, crushed
Salt & pepper, to taste

1. Combine all ingredients and mix well. Drizzle over your favorite salad greens and toss to mix.

Yield: about ¾ cup dressing. Leftovers can be refrigerated for 2 or 3 days.

43 calories per tbsp., 4.1 g fat (0.6 g saturated), 0 mg cholesterol, trace protein, 1 g carbohydrate, 12 mg sodium, 4 mg potassium, trace iron, 0 g fiber, 3 mg calcium.

- **If dressing is refrigerated,** olive oil will congeal. Just let dressing stand at room temperature for a few minutes before serving; shake well.
- **Orange Vinaigrette:** Use ¼ cup of orange juice instead of chicken or vegetable broth. Dressing will keep for 2 weeks.
- **Poppy Seed Dressing:** Combine ¼ cup canola oil, ¼ cup rice vinegar, 2 tablespoons orange juice, 2 tablespoons lemon juice and ¼ cup sugar in a saucepan. Bring to a boil. Add 1 teaspoon poppy seeds, ¾ teaspoon Dijon mustard and a dash of salt. When cool, store in a jar in the refrigerator. Shake well to blend before serving. One tablespoon of dressing contains 47 calories, 3.7 g fat (0.2 g saturated) and 4 g carbohydrate.

Orange Balsamic Vinaigrette

Wonderful on mixed salad greens. It also makes a yummy marinade for boneless chicken breasts.

¼ c. olive or canola oil
6 tbsp. orange juice
¼ c. balsamic vinegar
1–2 cloves garlic, crushed
2 tbsp. minced fresh basil (or ½ tsp. dried)
1 tbsp. sugar
Salt & pepper, to taste

1. Combine all ingredients and mix well. Dressing will keep in the refrigerator about 2 weeks.

Yield: about ¾ cup.

43 calories per tbsp. 3.7 g fat (0.5 g saturated), 0 mg cholesterol, trace protein, 2 g carbohydrate, 1 mg sodium, 15 mg potassium, trace iron, 0 g fiber, 2 mg calcium.

Be a Mayonnaise Maven!

- Look for brands made with soybean oil, canola oil or olive oil. Most major brands are made with soybean oil.
- Read mayonnaise labels carefully to check the amount of fat per serving. Reduced-fat mayonnaise contains 5 grams fat and 50 calories per tablespoon.
- Regular mayonnaise contains approximately 100 calories and 11 to 12 g fat per tablespoon!
- Choose fat-free (10 to 12 calories per tablespoon) or ultra low-fat mayonnaise-type dressing to reduce your fat intake.
- Miracle Whip "ultra low fat" salad dressing has only 0.4 g of fat, but contains some cholesterol as well as dairy ingredients. Light mayonnaise has 3.1 g fat, regular mayonnaise has 6.9 g fat.
- For a super substitute for mayonnaise, blend equal parts of Creamy Yogurt Cheese (p. 53) and fat-free or low-fat mayo. Add a little Dijon mustard and a pinch of sugar to round out flavor.

Shake It Up Salad Dressing

You'll twist and shout about this salad dressing. It contains less than a gram of fat per tablespoon! So simple, so guilt-free. It can also be used as a marinade for chicken or fish.

$^3/_4$ c. tomato or vegetable juice
3   tbsp. balsamic or red wine vinegar
1   tbsp. olive oil (preferably extra-virgin)
1–2 cloves garlic, crushed
1   tsp. sugar (to taste)
$^1/_2$ tsp. Worcestershire sauce (to taste)
$^1/_2$ tsp. dry mustard
$^1/_2$ tsp. dried basil

1. Measure all ingredients into a jar. Cover and shake well to blend. Refrigerate dressing. Shake well before serving. Serve over your favorite greens.

Yield: about 1 cup. Dressing keeps for 2 or 3 weeks in the refrigerator.

14 calories per tbsp., 0.9 g fat (0.1 g saturated), 0 mg cholesterol, trace protein, 1 g carbohydrate, 41 mg sodium, 27 mg potassium, trace iron, trace fiber, 3 mg calcium.

Ranch-Style Dressing

$^3/_4$ c. nonfat yogurt
$^1/_4$ c. fat-free mayonnaise
1   tbsp. white or cider vinegar
$^1/_2$ tsp. sugar
2   tsp. Dijon mustard
1   green onion, finely minced
1   clove garlic, crushed
$^1/_4$ tsp. dried thyme
Freshly ground pepper

1. Measure all ingredients into a small bowl. Mix well and refrigerate. Serve chilled. Stir before using.

Yield: about 1 cup. Dressing will keep about 4 or 5 days in the refrigerator.

9 calories per tbsp. 0.1 g fat (0 g saturated), trace cholesterol, <1 g protein, 1 g carbohydrate, 42 mg sodium, 29 mg potassium, trace iron, 0 g fiber, 21 mg calcium.

Thousand Island Dressing (or Dip)

½ c. nonfat yogurt
½ c. nonfat or low-fat mayonnaise
⅓ c. chili sauce or ketchup
3 tbsp. relish
2 tbsp. minced onion
1 tsp. lemon juice (to taste)
Salt & pepper, to taste

1. Combine all ingredients and mix well. Cover and refrigerate.

Yield: about 1½ cups. Dressing will keep 4 or 5 days in the refrigerator.

11 calories per tbsp. 0 g fat (0 g saturated), trace cholesterol, trace protein, 2 g carbohydrate, 92 mg sodium, 27 mg potassium, 0 mg iron, trace fiber, 10 mg calcium.

Lighter Caesar Salad Dressing

Creamy and delicious. You won't miss the fat!

½ c. nonfat yogurt
¼ c. fat-free or low-fat mayonnaise
1 clove garlic, crushed
¼ c. grated Parmesan cheese
½ tsp. Worcestershire sauce
2 tbsp. lemon juice (to taste)
¾ tsp. salt (to taste)
Freshly ground pepper, to taste

1. Combine all ingredients and mix well; chill. Delicious over Romaine lettuce or spinach.

Yield: about 1 cup. Dressing will keep 4 or 5 days in the refrigerator.

15 calories per tbsp., 0.6 g fat (0.4 g saturated), 2 mg cholesterol, 1 g protein, 2 g carbohydrate, 168 mg sodium, 27 mg potassium, 0 mg iron, 0 g fiber, 37 mg calcium.

SECTION 11

Breads & Muffins

Breads Made Easy—How to Be Well-Bread!

- With a processor, heavy-duty mixer or bread machine, you can prepare bread dough in just minutes. You can even make bread using a large bowl, a wooden spoon and your hands! You need a few simple ingredients: yeast, flour, water, salt and a bit of sugar. Some recipes call for milk instead of water. Oil and eggs (or egg whites) may be added for flavor and tenderness. That's it!

- A bread machine makes bread automatically from start to finish, or you can knead, proof and rise the dough in the machine, then take it out, shape it by hand and bake it in a regular oven. See Loafing Around with Bread Machines (p. 313) for more information.

- Bread made with water is delicious the day it's made, but it dries out more quickly than bread made with milk. When you use water, crust will be thicker and crispier. Bread made with milk has a finer grain, more tender crust and stays fresher longer. Milk adds calcium and flavor. You can use water and add some powdered milk (2 to 3 tablespoons per loaf) along with the dry ingredients for additional calcium and tenderness.

- Many older recipes called for milk to be scalded (heated just below the boiling point), then cooled until lukewarm. This is no longer necessary. Just heat the milk slightly warmer than body temperature. Dip your finger into the milk—it should feel like a child with a bit of fever!

- Fresh yeast is perishable. Store it in the refrigerator and use it within a week or two. It can also be frozen; use immediately after defrosting. Buy fresh yeast at a commercial bakery.

- Active dry yeast is sold in envelopes ($1/4$ ounce/8 grams), or in bulk. One 8 gram envelope equals $2^1/4$ teaspoon dry yeast or $1/2$ ounce of fresh yeast.

- Active dry yeast is available in several forms. Traditional (regular) and quick-rise (instant/rapid rise) yeast are interchangeable in most recipes, but add sugar to water used to dissolve yeast. Also check expiration date before using. Questions? Call Fleischmann's at 1-800-777-4959.

- To proof yeast (i.e., test if it is good), combine 1 teaspoon sugar with a small amount of the warm liquid called for in the recipe. Add yeast and let stand for 5 to 10 minutes. It should begin to swell and foam. If nothing happens, use new yeast.

- The temperature of the liquid used to dissolve the yeast is important. If the temperature is too hot, it kills the yeast. If it is too cool, it slows down its growth. Liquid should be 105 to 115°F (43°C), like a hot bath. An instant-read thermometer (found in kitchen shops) is helpful.

- Breads made with quick-rise (instant) yeast are ready to bake 50 percent faster than those made with traditional yeast. See Quick-Rise Method which follows.

- Quick-Rise Method: Instead of dissolving quick-rise (instant) yeast in liquid, mix undissolved yeast with half of the flour and the other dry ingredients. Heat the total amount of liquid called for in the recipe to 120 to 130°F (50 to 55°C). Mix hot liquid with yeast/flour mixture. Add remaining flour and ingredients. Knead until smooth and elastic, cover and let rise just 15 minutes. Shape dough, place it on greased pan and cover. Let shaped bread rise $1^1/2$ to 2 hours, until doubled. Bake as directed in the recipe.

- Yeast should be stored in a cool place, or in your fridge or freezer. Yeast becomes active when mixed with warm liquid. To mix yeast with dry ingredients, bring it to room temperature. Eggs add flavor, color and nutrients to bread. You can use 2 egg whites for one whole egg.

- Most bread recipes include some fat for tenderness. Fat helps keep bread fresh longer. Canola oil is a healthier choice than butter or shortening. Add oil to dough along with liquid ingredients. Usually, you don't need to add more than 1 to 2 tablespoons of oil for each loaf of bread.

- All-purpose flour is available either bleached or unbleached. Unbleached flour has not been bleached by chemicals. They can be used interchangeably in bread baking. The choice is yours.

- Bread flour is a specially formulated flour which contains about 14 grams of protein per cup. It is available in bulk food stores and some supermarkets. It produces a hearty, well-shaped loaf.

- Canadian flour is milled from harder wheats. It is similar in protein content to bread flour; they can be used interchangeably. American all-purpose flour has a lower protein content. For best results, Americans should use bread flour for bread recipes from my book.

- Whole-wheat flour is beige colored with a more assertive flavor. It contains the bran, more fiber and nutrients than white flour. Its fat content is slightly higher than all-purpose or bread flour because it contains the germ. I like to use some whole-wheat flour in many of my recipes.

- King Arthur Flour makes an excellent multipurpose white wheat flour. It is an unbleached 100 percent whole-wheat flour with the nutrition of whole-wheat flour and a taste similar to white flour. Contact: King Arthur Flour, Dept. WWW, Box 1010, Norwich, Vermont 05055.

- Soy flour adds calcium to breads. For each cup of regular flour, remove 2 tablespoons flour and add 2 tablespoons soy flour. (Thanks to cookbook author Jan Main for the terrific tip!)

- Store flour in an airtight container. All-purpose flour can be kept at room temperature for about 6 months. Whole-wheat flour can turn rancid quickly because of the oil in the germ, so buy small amounts. Store it in a plastic bag in the refrigerator for 6 months, or freeze it for up to a year. Bring flour to room temperature before using.

- When working with yeast doughs, add just enough flour to make a dough that is slightly sticky. (It isn't necessary to sift the flour.) This produces a moister loaf.

- The amount of flour needed varies according to weather and humidity. Hot, humid weather requires more flour. For more nutritious bread, add 2 tablespoons wheat germ and/or flax seeds for each cup of flour.

- If dough has been kneaded enough, the surface will be rough and blistery. To test it, poke your finger into kneaded dough. The hole should fill in if dough has been kneaded long enough.

- If you're busy, make the yeast dough, then put it in the refrigerator at any point during the rising or shaping process for a few hours (or even for a few days)! Remove from the fridge and bring it back to room temperature before continuing with the recipe.

- MicroWays! You can rise bread dough in your microwave in just 30 minutes. (See p. 306.)

- If your kitchen is cool, turn oven on to 200°F for 1 minute to warm it slightly, then turn it off. Put bowl of dough in oven along with a large bowl of hot water. This produces a warm, steamy, draft-free environment, much like the proofers used in commercial bakeries.

- A good test to see if dough has doubled in bulk is to do another finger test. Poke your finger fairly deep into the dough. If the hole remains, the dough is ready.

- Once dough has been shaped and placed in (or on) the pan, it takes about an hour or two to double in bulk. It is then ready to bake.

- Spray a little water on the oven floor before closing the door. (A plant mister works well.) Repeat once or twice during baking. This creates steam, producing breads with a crisp crust.

- Bake bread in the lower third of the oven. It's done if it sounds hollow when tapped with your fingertips. Remove from pan to avoid condensation; cool on a rack. Slice with a serrated knife.

- Breads made without fat get stale faster than those made with fat. Freeze what you can't use within 48 hours. Bread can be frozen for at least a month if wrapped airtight. Stale bread can be made into toast, croutons or breadcrumbs. Now, let's make some dough!

Homemade Whole-Wheat Bread (Processor Method)

See photo (P-3). Wholesome and hearty.

1   tsp. sugar
½   c. warm water (about 110°F)
1   pkg. yeast (regular or quick-rise)
¾   c. skim milk (or lukewarm water)
1⅓ c. all-purpose flour
1½ c. whole-wheat flour (about)
¼   c. wheat germ, optional
1½ tbsp. sugar or honey
1   tsp. salt
1   tbsp. canola oil

1. Dissolve sugar in warm water. Sprinkle yeast over water and let stand 8 to 10 minutes. Stir to dissolve. Heat milk until lukewarm (about 40 seconds on HIGH in the microwave). Measure flours into processor bowl. Add wheat germ, sugar, salt and oil. Process 10 seconds. Add dissolved yeast; process 10 seconds more. Add milk slowly through feed tube while machine is running. Process until dough gathers around the blades in a mass. Process 45 seconds longer. Dough should be slightly sticky. If machine slows down, add 3 or 4 tablespoons more flour.

2. Turn dough out onto a lightly floured surface. Knead for 2 minutes, until smooth and elastic. Shape into a ball and place in a large lightly greased bowl. Cover bowl with plastic wrap and let dough rise in a warm place until doubled, about 1½ to 2 hours. Punch down.

3. Roll or pat dough on a lightly floured board into a 9 x 12-inch rectangle. Roll up jelly roll-style from the short side. Seal ends by pressing down with the edge of your hand. Place seam-side down in a sprayed 9 x 5-inch loaf pan or on a sprayed baking sheet. Cover with a towel and let rise until double, about 1 hour. Bake in a preheated 425°F oven for 25 to 30 minutes. Remove from pan; let cool.

Yield: 1 loaf (16 slices). Freezes well.

94 calories per slice, 1.2 g fat (0.1 saturated), trace cholesterol, 3 g protein, 18 g carbohydrate, 153 mg sodium, 85 mg potassium, 1 mg iron, 2 g fiber, 20 mg calcium.

- **Homemade White Bread:** Substitute all-purpose flour for whole-wheat flour.
- **Rolls:** In Step 3, shape dough into 12 balls. Place on a sprayed or non-stick cookie sheet, cover and let rise until doubled. Bake at 375°F for 20 minutes, until golden.
- **Herb Bread:** In Step 1, add ½ teaspoon each of dried basil, dill, thyme, oregano and/or rosemary to flour. Add remaining ingredients, mix, shape and bake as directed.
- **Herbed Cheese Bread:** In Step 3, roll dough into a rectangle. Spread with 2 teaspoons olive oil, 2 cloves minced garlic, ⅓ cup grated Parmesan and 2 tablespoons minced onion. (You can add 2 tablespoons minced fresh basil, ¼ cup minced sun-dried tomatoes and/or red peppers). Roll up and seal ends. Brush with an egg yolk mixed with 1 tablespoon water. Sprinkle with sesame seeds. Place on a sprayed baking sheet, cover and let rise until double. Bake at 425°F 25 to 30 minutes.
- **Cinnamon Babka:** In Step 3, sprinkle dough with ½ cup cinnamon-sugar and ½ cup raisins. Roll up and slice in 1-inch pieces. Place in a sprayed 10-inch spring form pan, with buns barely touching. Brush with melted apricot jam. Cover and let rise until double. Bake at 375°F for 30 minutes.

Fred's Fat-Free Country Bread

Fred Hansen of Montreal named this "country bread" because you can make it even if you live in the country with very few ingredients or utensils available! Fred worked for many years at a major Canadian flour mill. He's now retired and bakes this wonderful bread every week.

Starter:
- 1 c. warm water (about 110°F)
- 1/8 tsp. sugar
- 1 1/4 oz. fresh cake yeast (or 1 1/4 tbsp. active dry yeast)
- 1 c. all-purpose or bread flour

Additional Ingredients for Dough:
- 1 liter (4 1/2 c.) liquid (use part water and part skim milk)
- 4 tsp. salt
- 5 c. whole-wheat flour (or multi-grain flour)
- 5 c. all-purpose flour
- 3 to 4 c. additional all-purpose flour
- Cornmeal to dust pans, if desired

1. Yeast Starter: Whisk together water, sugar, yeast and flour in a 10 to 12 cup mixing bowl. When smoothly blended, scrape down sides of bowl with a rubber spatula. Cover bowl with plastic wrap, set in a warm place and leave for several hours, or preferably overnight.

2. Dough: Stir the yeast mixture. Then add the liter of liquid and salt; mix well. Transfer to a large mixing bowl. Add 5 cups whole-wheat flour and 5 cups white flour. Mix with a wooden spoon or with your hands until well blended, usually 2 or 3 minutes. This can be done in a heavy duty electric mixer, if available. The dough will be sticky.

3. Place remaining all-purpose flour on a clean work surface. Transfer dough to floured surface and knead well for 15 minutes, adding flour as needed to avoid sticking. You will use 3 to 4 cups. Place dough in a lightly greased large bowl. Cover with a damp towel and let rise about an hour, until doubled. Punch down and let rise a second time, until tripled, about 2 hours. Punch down again. (If you are busy, dough can be refrigerated for several hours, or even overnight.)

4. Divide dough into 5 equal portions. Shape into loaves. Place on lightly greased baking sheets (or in loaf pans) which have been sprinkled with a little cornmeal. Cover and let rise once again until double in size, about an hour. Make 3 or 4 slashes across the top of each loaf with a sharp knife. Dust with a little flour.

5. Preheat oven to 375°F. Bake loaves in the lower third of the oven for 40 minutes, until golden brown. Dough should sound hollow when tapped with your fingers. Remove from pans and cool completely on racks before placing them in plastic bags. Loaves can be frozen and used as needed.

Yield: 5 loaves (about 16 slices per loaf). Freezes well. Stale bread makes great toast or crumbs!

80 calories per slice, 0.3 g fat (0.1 g saturated), trace cholesterol, 3 g protein, 17 g carbohydrate, 121 mg sodium, 80 mg potassium, 1 mg iron, 1 g fiber, 14 mg calcium.

Dill-icious Cottage Cheese Bread

This excellent bread is adapted from a recipe shared with me by my dear friend and computer expert, Rosie Krakower, of Ottawa. So quick and easy to make with the help of your processor.

2¼ c. flour (half whole-wheat, if desired)
2 tbsp. sugar
2 tsp. dehydrated onion flakes
2 tsp. dried dill (or 2 tbsp. minced fresh dill)
1 tsp. salt
¼ tsp. baking soda
1 pkg. yeast (regular or quick-rise)
1 tbsp. canola or olive oil
1 c. low-fat (1%) creamed cottage cheese
¼ c. hot water
2 egg whites (or 1 egg)
1 tbsp. skim milk, optional
Coarse salt, optional

1. Combine flour, sugar, onion flakes, dill, salt, baking soda, yeast and oil in processor bowl. Process for 10 seconds. Add cottage cheese and process 15 seconds longer. With the machine running, add hot water and egg (or egg whites) through the feed tube. Process for 45 seconds, until dough forms a sticky mass around the blades. (Have an extra ¼ cup of flour ready in case the processor slows down; dump in through the feed tube if necessary. The amount of flour depends on the water content of cottage cheese.)

2. Turn out onto a lightly floured surface. Knead for 2 minutes, until smooth and elastic, adding just enough flour to prevent dough from sticking. Transfer dough to a large greased bowl. Cover and let rise in a warm place until light and double in bulk, about 1 hour. Punch down.

3. Shape dough into 1 large or 12 small balls. Place on a lightly greased or non-stick baking sheet. Cover and let rise until double in bulk, about ¾ hour. Preheat oven to 375°F. (If desired, brush the top of loaf lightly with milk and sprinkle with coarse salt.) Bake loaf for 30 to 35 minutes, or rolls for about 20 minutes, until golden.

Yield: 1 loaf (12 slices) or 12 rolls. Freezes well.

123 calories per slice, 1.6 g fat (0.2 g saturated), <1 mg cholesterol, 6 g protein, 21 g carbohydrate, 307 mg sodium, 70 mg potassium, 1 mg iron, <1 g fiber, 20 mg calcium.

- **Howard Krakower's Bread Machine Version:** See recipe for Dill Onion Bread (p. 314), which is a variation of the above recipe, except Howard adjusted it to make a 2-pound loaf. This is an excellent example of how to convert a regular recipe into a bread machine recipe.
- **Howard Krakower,** Maurice Borts and Elaine Kaplan shared terrific tips and techniques on how to make yeast doughs and bake beautiful breads using a bread machine. See "Loafing Around with Bread Machines" (p. 313).

Whole-Wheat Processor Challah

A healthier, quicker version of traditional challah for today's cook.

1 tsp. sugar
¾ c. warm water (about 110°F)
1 pkg. active dry yeast
2 c. all-purpose flour (approximately)
1 c. whole-wheat flour
1 tsp. salt
2–3 tbsp. canola oil
3 tbsp. honey
1 egg plus 2 egg whites (or 2 eggs)
1 additional egg white mixed with 1 tsp. water (to glaze Challah)
2–3 tbsp. sesame or poppy seeds

1. Dissolve sugar in warm water. Sprinkle yeast over water and let stand for 8 to 10 minutes, until

foamy. Stir to dissolve. Combine flours and salt in processor bowl. Add yeast mixture and process for 10 to 12 seconds. Add oil, honey, 1 egg plus 2 egg whites (or 2 eggs). Process until dough gathers and forms a mass around the blades. Process 45 seconds longer, until dough is smooth and elastic, but still somewhat sticky. (In case the processor slows down and begins to stall, add a little extra flour through feed tube to let the processor return to normal speed.)

2. Turn dough out onto a lightly floured surface. Knead 1 to 2 minutes by hand, until smooth and elastic. Place in a large, greased bowl. Cover bowl and let rise in a warm place until dough is double in bulk, about 1½ to 2 hours. Punch down. If you have time, let dough rise once again, about ¾ to 1 hour, or shape it at this point.

3. Divide dough into 4 equal portions. Shape 3 portions of dough into long ropes, flouring your hands for easier handling. Place them on a greased baking sheet and form them into a large braid, tucking ends under. Divide the 4th portion of dough into 3 smaller ropes and form a small braid. Place it on top of the larger braid. Pinch dough in several places to join the two braids together.

4. Cover with a towel and let rise until doubled, about 2 hours. Brush with egg white and sprinkle with sesame seeds. Preheat oven to 400°F. Bake loaf in the lower third of your oven for 30 to 35 minutes, until golden brown. Loaf should sound hollow when tapped with your fingers.

Yield: 1 large loaf (16 slices). Freezes well.

126 calories per slice, 3 g fat (0.4 g saturated), 13 mg cholesterol, 4 g protein, 21 g carbohydrate, 171 mg sodium, 75 mg potassium, 1 mg iron, 2 g fiber, 9 mg calcium.

- **Whole-Wheat Holiday Round Raisin Challah (Feigel):** Follow instructions for Whole-Wheat Challah, adding ¾ cup of Sultana raisins at the end of Step 1. After dough has doubled, place it on a lightly floured board. Flour your hands and form dough into a long thin rope, tapering one end. Place it on a sprayed, foil-lined baking sheet. Starting with the thick end, coil dough up like a snail. Tuck the tapered end under. Cover and let rise until doubled. Brush with beaten egg white and sprinkle with sesame seeds. Bake in a preheated 400°F oven for 30 to 35 minutes, until golden brown. Loaf should sound hollow when tapped with your fingers.
- **Challah Rolls (Knippes):** Instead of braiding Challah, divide dough into 12 equal portions (or 24 portions for miniatures). Roll each piece between your palms into a rope, then tie in a knot. Place on a greased baking sheet, cover and let rise until doubled. Brush with beaten egg white or yolk and sprinkle with sesame seeds. Bake at 400°F for 15 to 18 minutes, until golden.
- **Malka's No-Braid Round Challah:** Make your favorite Challah dough. Instead of braiding it, divide dough into 12 equal portions. Roll each piece into a rope, then tie each rope into a knot. Arrange knots in a greased large round Pyrex bowl or springform pan, barely touching. Cover and let rise. When doubled, they will join together to make a round "braided" loaf. Brush with egg glaze; sprinkle with poppy seeds. Bake at 400°F for 30 to 35 minutes, until golden.
- **Nancy Weisbrod's Braided Holiday Challah Ring with Honey:** Make your favorite Challah dough. Divide dough into 3 equal pieces and shape into long ropes. Make a long braid; join ends together to make a large ring. Place ring on a greased baking sheet. Remove paper from an empty can. Place the can in the center of the ring to help keep its shape. Cover with a towel and let rise until doubled. Brush with egg glaze; sprinkle

with poppy seeds. Bake at 400°F about 30 minutes. Remove can. Place a bowl filled with honey in the center of the ring. So pretty!

Whole-Wheat Pitas

For hors d'oeuvres, make miniature pitas.
Baking time will be 5 to 6 minutes.

1 tsp. sugar
¼ c. warm water (about 110°F)
1 pkg. active dry yeast
1½ c. all-purpose flour
1½ c. whole-wheat flour (approximately)
1 tsp. salt
2 tsp. additional sugar
1 c. lukewarm water
1 tsp. canola oil

1. Dissolve sugar in warm water. Sprinkle yeast over water and let stand for 8 to 10 minutes, until foamy. Stir to dissolve. Combine flours, salt, additional sugar and yeast mixture in processor. Process for 8 to 10 seconds. Pour lukewarm water and oil through feed tube while machine is running. Process until dough is well-kneaded and gathers in a mass around the blades, about 1 minute. If machine begins to slow down, add 2 or 3 tablespoons additional whole-wheat flour.

2. Transfer dough to a lightly floured surface. Knead dough for 2 minutes by hand, until smooth. Divide dough into 16 balls. Roll each ball into a circle about ¼ inch thick. Cover with a towel and let rise for ½ hour. Roll out thinly once again and let rise ½ hour longer.

3. Preheat oven to 500°F. Place pitas on a lightly greased or sprayed baking sheet. Bake about 6 to 8 minutes, or until puffed up and golden. Insides of pita will be hollow. Cool on a rack. To fill, make a slit along one edge of pita and stuff as desired.

Yield: 16 pitas. These freeze very well.

88 calories per pita, 0.6 g fat (0.1 g saturated), 0 mg cholesterol, 3 g protein, 18 g carbohydrate, 147 mg sodium, 67 mg potassium, 1 mg iron, 2 g fiber, 6 mg calcium.

Herbed Focaccia

Here is a wonderful recipe to make your own Focaccia for sandwiches or appetizers. Fabulous!

Dough:
1 tsp. sugar
½ c. warm water (about 110°F)
1 pkg. active dry yeast
1½ c. all-purpose flour
1½ c. whole-wheat flour
1 tsp. salt
½ tsp. each dried dill weed, basil and rosemary
1 tbsp. olive oil
¾ c. additional water

Topping:
1 tbsp. olive oil
2 to 3 cloves garlic, crushed
Fresh or dried basil and rosemary, to taste
Coarse salt, optional
2 tbsp. sesame seeds

1. Dissolve sugar in warm water. Sprinkle yeast over water and let stand for 8 to 10 minutes, until foamy. Stir to dissolve. Combine flours, salt and herbs in a food processor or large mixing bowl. Mix in yeast mixture. Add oil. Slowly blend in additional water. Mix to form a soft dough. Knead dough on a lightly floured surface about 5 minutes, until smooth and elastic. Place in a large greased bowl. Cover bowl and let dough rise until doubled, about 2 hours, or refrigerate dough overnight if you don't have time. (Alternately, see MicroWays, below.) Punch down.

2. Lightly spray a large baking sheet with non-stick spray. Transfer dough to baking sheet and pat it into a large rectangle or 8 smaller ovals about ½ inch thick. Let rise for 45 minutes, or until doubled in bulk. Preheat oven to 375°F. Poke your fingers into the surface of the dough to give it a dimpled appearance. Brush top of dough lightly with olive oil, then sprinkle it with remaining topping ingredients. Bake for 25 to 35 minutes, or until crisp and golden.

Yield: 8 servings. Freezes very well.

211 calories per serving, 5.2 g fat (0.7 g saturated), 0 mg cholesterol, 6 g protein, 36 g carbohydrate, 294 mg sodium, 153 mg potassium, 3 mg iron, 4 g fiber, 40 mg calcium.

- **If desired, omit whole-wheat flour** and increase all-purpose flour to 3 cups.
- **Focaccia Appetizers:** Prepare dough as directed above. Pat it into a large rectangle and place on baking sheet. Brush dough with oil and sprinkle it with herbs. (Sesame seeds are optional.) Top with thinly sliced zucchini, red peppers and/or red onions. Sprinkle lightly with grated Parmesan cheese. Bake as directed above. Cut into small squares to serve. Addictive!
- **MicroWays!** You can rise yeast dough in your microwave in 30 minutes. You need a power level of LOW (60 to 80 watts). After mixing, place dough in a large microsafe glass bowl. Cover with a microsafe plate (or moisten a piece of baking

parchment and mold it around the bowl). Place bowl of dough into a larger glass bowl. Pour 3 cups warm water into the outer bowl to make a water bath. Microwave covered on 10% (LOW) for 15 minutes. Don't let dough get too warm. Let stand 15 minutes. Dough will double in bulk. Shape and complete as directed in recipe.

Montreal-Style Bagels

Montreal is famous for its bagels, which are dense, chewy and slightly sweet. Many a suitcase leaves Montreal bulging with bags full of bagels! Cities throughout Canada have opened up Montreal-style bagel bakeries. They can even be found as far away as Florida. Now you can make your own at home.

1	tsp. sugar
½	c. warm water (about 110°F)
1	pkg. active dry yeast
4½–5	c. all-purpose or bread flour
1	tsp. salt
2	tbsp. sugar
2	tbsp. honey
¾	c. lukewarm water
2	tbsp. canola oil
1	egg
6	c. water (for boiling the bagels)
3	tbsp. additional honey
⅓–½	c. sesame and/or poppy seeds

1. Dissolve sugar in warm water. Sprinkle yeast over water. Let stand for 8 to 10 minutes. Stir to dissolve. Reserve about 1 cup of flour and sprinkle it on the countertop. In a large mixing bowl (or in your processor), combine 3½ cups of the flour, salt, sugar, honey and dissolved yeast mixture. Add ¾ cup lukewarm water, oil and egg. Mix well to make a soft dough (about 1 minute in the processor or 5 minutes by hand). If dough is sticky and machine slows down, add a little extra flour as needed.

2. Turn dough out onto floured surface. Knead until smooth and blistered, gradually adding flour as necessary to prevent dough from sticking (about 5 minutes if dough was mixed in the processor, 10 minutes if dough was mixed by hand). Cover dough with a towel and let it rest for 10 minutes.

3. Divide dough into 15 pieces. Roll each piece into a long rope. Shape each one into a bagel by joining ends to form a ring. Pinch well to seal. Cover and let rise for 20 minutes. Meanwhile, preheat oven to 450°F. Line 2 baking sheets with cooking parchment and set aside. In a large pot, bring water to a rolling boil. Stir in honey. Reduce heat slightly so water is boiling gently.

4. Drop 3 to 4 bagels at a time into the water. Cook for 45 seconds; flip bagels over and cook 45 seconds longer. Remove from water with a slotted spoon and place them on a clean dishtowel to drain. Sprinkle with sesame and/or poppy seeds. Transfer to prepared baking sheets.

5. Place pans in the oven and immediately reduce heat to 425°F. Bake for 12 to 14 minutes on 1 side. Turn bagels over and bake them 5 minutes longer, until golden and crisp. Let cool.

Yield: 15 bagels. These freeze very well.

195 calories per serving, 4.4 g fat (0.5 g saturated), 14 mg cholesterol, 5 g protein, 33 g carbohydrate, 162 mg sodium, 69 mg potassium, 2 mg iron, 2 g fiber, 13 mg calcium.

• **Montreal's best bagels** are baked in a wood-fired oven, usually on long wooden boards! You can bake your own directly on a preheated baking or pizza stone (available at kitchenware shops).

Oatmeal Wheat Germ Bread

1	c. rolled oats (quick-cooking or regular)
2	c. boiling water
1	tsp. sugar
½	c. lukewarm water (about 110°F)
1	pkg. active dry yeast
¼	c. molasses
¼	c. maple syrup
2	tsp. salt
2	tsp. canola oil
3	c. all-purpose or bread flour
1½	c. whole-wheat flour
½	c. wheat germ
1	egg white beaten with 1 tbsp. cold water

1. Place oats in a large mixing bowl. Pour boiling water over oats and let stand for 20 minutes. Dissolve sugar in ½ cup lukewarm water. Add yeast and let stand for 10 minutes. Stir to dissolve. Add yeast mixture to oats along with molasses, maple syrup, salt and oil. Slowly stir in flours and wheat germ; mix well. Transfer dough to a floured surface and knead for 3 or 4 minutes.

2. Place in a lightly greased large bowl, cover and let rise in a warm place for 1½ hours. Punch down. Shape into 2 loaves; place in sprayed loaf pans. Cover and let rise until doubled, about 1 hour. Brush with egg white mixture. Preheat oven to 375°F. Bake for 40 to 45 minutes, until golden. When done, loaves will pull away from sides of pans. Remove from pans and cool on racks.

Yield: 2 loaves (32 slices). These freeze well.

93 calories per slice (1/16 loaf), 0.8 g fat (0.1 g saturated), 0 mg cholesterol, 3 g protein, 19 g carbohydrate, 150 mg sodium, 103 mg potassium, 1 mg iron, 2 g fiber, 13 mg calcium.

Simple Spelt Bread

Linda Winter of Winter-peg gave me this unique recipe! Spelt flour is found in natural food shops.

3¹/₂	c. spelt flour
1¹/₂	tsp. salt
1	tbsp. active dry yeast
1	tsp. sugar
1¹/₈	c. lukewarm water (105 to 110°F)
2	tbsp. canola oil

1. Combine flour, salt, yeast and sugar into a large bowl. Add water and oil. Beat until combined, then knead the dough until smooth, about 5 minutes. Cover and let rise for 45 minutes, until doubled. Punch down and shape into a loaf. Place in a sprayed loaf pan. Cover and let rise for 30 minutes.

2. Preheat oven to 400°F. Place 1 cup of water in the oven with the bread. Bake at 400°F for 30 minutes, until done. Brush top lightly with water. Remove from pan and cool on a rack.

Yield: 1 loaf (16 slices). Wrap leftovers well to prevent bread from drying out. Bread freezes well.

124 calories per serving, 2.1 g fat (0.2 g saturated), 0 mg cholesterol, 4 g protein, 20 g carbohydrate, 224 mg sodium, 15 mg potassium, trace iron, 1 g fiber, 3 mg calcium.

Pumpernickel Bread

This tasty bread has a dense texture.

1	tsp. sugar
1¹/₄	c. warm water (110°F)
1	pkg. active dry yeast
1	c. rye flour
2	c. all-purpose or bread flour
2	tsp. salt
1	tbsp. brown sugar
2	tbsp. molasses
2	tsp. unsweetened cocoa
1	tsp. instant coffee granules
1	tbsp. boiling water
1	tsp. canola oil
1–2	tbsp. caraway seeds
2	tbsp. onion flakes

1. Dissolve sugar in warm water. Sprinkle yeast over water. Let stand for 8 to 10 minutes. Stir to dissolve. In a large mixing bowl (or in a processor), combine flours, salt, brown sugar, molasses, cocoa and dissolved yeast mixture. Dissolve instant coffee in boiling water. Add coffee, oil, caraway seeds and onion flakes to bowl. Mix well to make a soft dough (about 1 minute in the processor or 5 minutes by hand). If dough seems sticky, add a little extra flour as needed.

2. Turn dough out onto a lightly floured surface. Knead until smooth and blistered (about 2 to 3 minutes if dough was mixed in the processor, 10 minutes if it was mixed by hand). Add flour as needed to prevent dough from sticking.

3. Shape dough into a ball and place it in a lightly greased large bowl. Cover bowl with a towel and let dough rise in a warm place for 1¹/₂ to 2 hours, or until doubled. Punch down. Shape dough into a round loaf and place it on a baking sheet which has been sprayed with non-stick spray. Cover and let rise until doubled. Preheat oven to 400°F. Bake for 40 to 45 minutes, until bread sounds hollow when tapped with your fingertips. Remove from oven and let cool.

Yield: 1 loaf (16 slices). Freezes well.

101 calories per serving, 0.8 g fat (0.1 g saturated), 0 mg cholesterol, 3 g protein, 21 g carbohydrate, 293 mg sodium, 145 mg potassium, 2 mg iron, 3 g fiber, 18 mg calcium.

Sourdough Starter

1   pkg. active dry yeast (1 tbsp.)
2   c. lukewarm water (110°F)
2   c. all-purpose flour

1. In a large glass bowl or non-metal container, dissolve yeast in water. Add flour and stir thoroughly. Cover loosely and let stand at room temperature for 3 days. The first day, starter will bubble up and quadruple in volume, then deflate. After 3 days, stir well. Cover and refrigerate until ready to use.

Yield: about 3 cups starter. Can be frozen (see below).

289 calories per cup, 0.9 g fat (0.1 g saturated), 0 mg cholesterol, 9 g protein, 60 g carbohydrate, 7 mg sodium, 127 mg potassium, 4 mg iron, 3 g fiber, 16 mg calcium.

Fat-Free Sourdough Bread

Guilt-free and fabulous!

1   pkg. active dry yeast
1½ c. lukewarm water (110°F)
1   c. Sourdough Starter at room temperature (p. 309)
5½–6 c. all purpose flour
2   tsp. salt
1   tbsp. sugar
½   tsp. baking soda

1. In a large bowl, sprinkle yeast over water. Let stand for 5 minutes, then stir to dissolve. Add Sourdough Starter, 2 cups flour, salt and sugar. Stir well. In another bowl, mix 3 cups flour with baking soda. Add to flour/yeast mixture along with enough of the remaining flour to make a stiff dough. Turn dough out onto a lightly floured surface. Knead until smooth and elastic, about 5 to 7 minutes. Add more flour as needed to prevent dough from sticking.

2. Shape dough into a ball and place it in a lightly greased bowl. Cover and let rise in a warm place for 1 to 1½ hours, until doubled. Punch down and divide in half. Cover and let rest for 10 minutes.

3. Shape dough into 2 round or baguette-shaped loaves and place them several inches apart on a lightly greased large baking sheet. With a sharp knife, make several diagonal slashes across the top of each loaf. (Round breads also look terrific if you make a tic-tac-toe design.) Cover and let rise until doubled, about 1 to 1½ hours. Dust tops lightly with a little flour, if desired.

4. Preheat oven to 375°F. Bake loaves for 35 to 40 minutes, or until bread sounds hollow when tapped with your fingertips. If desired, brush tops of breads with a little water 5 minutes before the end of baking. (This makes a crisp crust.) Remove bread from oven and cool completely.

Yield: 2 loaves (16 slices per loaf). These freeze well.

89 calories per slice, 0.2 g fat (0 g saturated), 0 mg cholesterol, 3 g protein, 19 g carbohydrate, 166 mg sodium, 31 mg potassium, 1 mg iron, <1 g fiber, 4 mg calcium.

• **Whole-Wheat Sourdough Bread:** Replace 2 cups of all-purpose flour with whole-wheat flour in above recipe. Add 2 tablespoons molasses and 2 teaspoons canola oil to yeast mixture along with starter.

Sourdough Rye Bread

1   pkg. active dry yeast
1½ c. lukewarm water (110°F)
1   c. Sourdough Starter at room temperature (p. 309)
2   c. rye flour
2   tsp. salt
2   tbsp. sugar
2   tsp. canola oil
1   tbsp. molasses
1   tbsp. caraway seeds
3   c. bread flour (approximately)
½ tsp. baking soda
2–3 tbsp. cornmeal
1   egg white, lightly beaten

1. In a large bowl, sprinkle yeast over water. Let stand for 5 minutes, then stir to dissolve. Add Sourdough Starter, rye flour, salt, sugar, oil and molasses. Stir well. Mix 2 cups of bread flour (or all-purpose flour) with baking soda. Add to flour/yeast mixture along with enough of the remaining flour to make a stiff dough. Turn dough out onto a lightly floured surface. Knead until smooth and elastic, about 6 to 8 minutes. Add additional flour as needed to prevent dough from sticking.

2. Shape dough into a ball and place it in a lightly

Getting "Startered"!

• To keep the starter going: Each time you use a cup of the starter to make bread, add 1 cup of lukewarm water, 1 cup flour and 1 teaspoon sugar to remaining starter. (If you need a larger amount of starter, you can add 2 cups each of water and flour.) Mix until blended with a whisk. Any lumps will dissolve as the mixture ferments. Let stand at room temperature until bubbly, usually overnight or up to 24 hours. The starter is then ready to be used again, or can be refrigerated until needed.

• The starter must be "fed" once a week with more flour, water and sugar to keep it active. Stir at least weekly to invigorate the yeast and expel some of the alcohol.

• You can freeze the starter if you will be away or cannot use it frequently. Place the starter in two sterilized, airtight containers and freeze. (This way you have a backup if anything happens to one of them! Starter can be frozen for 6 months.) Thaw a container of starter 2 days before you need to use it. Transfer to a sterilized, non-metal storage container. Add 1 cup each of water and flour. Cover and let it stand at room temperature for 12 hours or overnight. It's then ready to use.

• About once a month, remove starter from storage container and sterilize the container with boiling water.

greased bowl. Cover and let rise in a warm place for 1 to 1½ hours, until doubled. Punch down. (If you have time, let dough rise once again, until doubled.) Divide dough in half. Cover and let rest for 10 minutes.

3. Shape dough into 2 long loaves and place them a few inches apart on a lightly greased large baking sheet which has been sprinkled with cornmeal. With a sharp knife, make 4 or 5 diagonal slashes across the top of each loaf. Cover and let rise until doubled, about 1 to 1½ hours. Brush loaves lightly with egg white.

4. Preheat oven to 375°F. Bake for 35 to 40 minutes, or until breads sound hollow when tapped with your fingertips. Remove from oven and cool completely.

Yield: 2 loaves (16 slices per loaf). These freeze well.

84 calories per slice, 0.6 g fat (0.1 g saturated), 0 mg cholesterol, 3 g protein, 17 g carbohydrate, 168 mg sodium, 44 mg potassium, <1 mg iron, 1 g fiber, 8 mg calcium.

• **Chef's Secret!** If you use all-purpose flour instead of bread flour, your loaf may spread and flatten. That's because bread flour is higher in gluten than all-purpose flour and produces a better shaped loaf. My bread expert Fred Hansen said if you don't have bread flour, use 1½ cup rye flour and 3½ cups all-purpose flour to make your dough. You will end up with a lighter rye bread than the one above, but it will still be tasty. See recipe for Fred's Country Bread (p. 302).

Vampire Bread

Plump cloves of garlic throughout the loaf are sure to keep those vampires away! The garlic will have a mild, sweet flavor, but won't be visible to the eye once it has been baked inside the bread. Thanks to my sister Rhonda Matias for inspiring this recipe.

1	head garlic
½	tsp. water
2¼	c. all-purpose flour (approximately)
1	c. whole-wheat flour
2	tsp. sugar
1	tsp. salt
1	pkg. quick-rise instant yeast (2¼ tsp.)
1	tsp. dried basil
1⅓	c. hot water (120 to 130°F)
1	tbsp. olive oil

1. Cut the top off the head of garlic with a sharp knife, exposing the cut cloves. Place ½ teaspoon water in a small microsafe dish. Place garlic cut-side up in dish. Microwave uncovered on HIGH for 30 to 40 seconds. Turn garlic over and microwave 30 seconds longer. Let stand 1 minute. Separate into cloves. Hold clove from the uncut end and squeeze gently; the garlic will pop out. Set aside.

2. Measure flours into processor bowl. Add sugar, salt, yeast and basil. Process for 10 seconds. Add water and oil slowly through the feed tube while machine is running. Process until dough gathers around the blades in a mass. Process 45 seconds longer. Dough should be slightly sticky. If machine slows down, add an extra 2 or 3 tablespoons flour. (Alternately, dough can be mixed by hand in a large mixing bowl. Mixing and kneading time will be about 10 minutes by hand.)

3. Turn dough out onto a lightly floured surface. Knead for 2 or 3 minutes, until smooth and elastic. Cover dough and let it rest for 15 minutes. Flatten it into an oblong and arrange garlic cloves on dough. Roll up dough into a cylinder. Lengthen and thin the cylinder into a long loaf about 16 inches long by 3 inches wide by rolling it back and forth with your hands. Place on a lightly sprayed foil-lined baking sheet. Cover loaf with a towel and let rise until doubled, about 1 to 1½ hours.

4. Preheat oven to 400°F. Carefully make several V-shaped slashes across the top of loaf with a sharp knife. (V is for vampire!) Sprinkle with a little flour. Bake in the lower third of the oven for 25 to 30 minutes, until done. Dough should sound hollow when tapped with your fingers.

Yield: 1 large loaf (24 slices). Freezes well.

127 calories per slice, 0.9 g fat (0.1 saturated), 0 cholesterol, 4 g protein, 26 g carbohydrate, 97 mg sodium, 65 mg potassium, 1 mg iron, 2 g fiber, 11 mg calcium.

- **Instead of microwaving the garlic** with water in Step 1, Roasted Garlic (p. 252) can be substituted. If you really love garlic, you can use 2 heads in this recipe!
- **If you don't have whole-wheat flour,** substitute all-purpose flour.
- **Variation:** In Step 3, sprinkle 3 to 4 tablespoons grated Parmesan cheese over the flattened dough along with the garlic. Strips of Roasted Red Peppers (p. 57) can also be added. Continue as directed.

Breadsticks

Easy and delicious! My mom got me hooked on these.

1	tbsp. sugar
¼	c. warm water (about 110°F)
1	pkg. active dry yeast (1 tbsp.)
3	c. all-purpose flour
1	c. whole-wheat flour
1	tsp. salt
1¼	c. lukewarm water (approximately)
1	tbsp. olive or canola oil
1	egg white, lightly beaten

Optional Toppings: poppy seeds, sesame seeds, caraway seeds, coarse salt, dried basil and/or onion flakes

1. Dissolve sugar in warm water. Sprinkle yeast over and let stand for 8 to 10 minutes. Stir to dissolve. Place flours and salt in the food processor. Add dissolved yeast, lukewarm water and oil. Process for about a minute, or until dough gathers around the blades in a mass. If the dough is too dry, add a little more water. Process 45 seconds longer. Dough should be slightly sticky. If machine begins to slow down, add a couple of tablespoons of flour.

2. Turn dough out onto a lightly floured board and knead for a minute or two by hand, until smooth and elastic. Shape into a ball and place in a large, lightly greased bowl. Cover and let rise until doubled, about 1 to 1½ hours. Punch down.

3. Preheat oven to 400°F. Line 2 baking sheets with aluminum foil. Spray with non-stick spray. Divide dough in half. On a lightly floured board, roll each half into a large rectangle. Cut dough into ½-inch strips. (You should have about 3 dozen in total.) Stretch the strips into long ropes by taking one end

Loafing Around with Bread Machines

- A bread machine can make bread automatically, from start to finish. It acts as a mixer, kneader, proofer and oven. You can also prepare dough in the machine, take it out and form it by hand, then bake it in your regular oven. It's great for pizza dough, focaccia, pita bread, Challah and rolls.
- To convert any bread recipe to a bread machine recipe, adjust amount of flour to the capacity of your machine. If you have a 1½-pound or 2-pound machine, use 3 or 4 cups of flour respectively; then adjust the other ingredients accordingly.
- The bread machine has a non-stick metal baking pan placed inside a chamber heated by a heating element. A mixing paddle protrudes into the pan to knead the dough.
- Place the machine at least 2 inches away from walls or cabinets to allow steam from vents to escape. Unplug machine before starting. Also make sure you read the manufacturer's manual!
- Always fill baking pan out of the machine. Keep the machine's lid closed to prevent spilling ingredients into the chamber accidentally. (Thanks to Howard Krakower for this terrific tip!)
- Measure ingredients into pan. Add liquid first (including eggs), then oil, sugar, salt and flour. Yeast is added last. The main thing is to keep yeast and liquid separated.
- Measure meticulously! For dry ingredients, use dry measuring cups and spoons. Use the straight edge of a knife to level off ingredients. For liquids, use a glass measuring cup; check measurements at eye level.
- Bread machine yeast is called for in some recipes. If the recipe calls for 2 teaspoons bread machine yeast, you can use 2¼ teaspoons (1 pkg.) active dry yeast (not rapid rise). Check expiration date.
- In the U.S., use bread flour for best results. In Canada, use Canadian all-purpose or bread flour.
- Liquid should be at room temperature (not cold). If liquid is hotter than 115°F, it can kill the yeast. Also, if ingredients are too cool or too hot, some machines won't start.
- Insert baking pan into the oven chamber as directed in your manual, then close the lid.
- Select desired cycle. The basic bread cycle is for breads made with white flour. Use the whole-grain cycle for breads made with heavier flours (e.g., rye, whole wheat). The dough cycle is for breads which will be completed by hand. Many machines have a rapid cycle. If using the delayed baking cycle, don't use perishable ingredients such as fresh eggs, milk or cheese.
- Check consistency of dough during the first few minutes of the kneading cycle. If too wet, add some flour. If too dry, add some liquid to make a soft dough. (It should feel like a baby's bottom!)
- When baking bread in the machine, don't open lid during baking cycle to avoid underbaking.
- To prevent a soggy crust, remove the bread immediately after baking. Unplug the machine and lift the hot pan by its handle, using potholders to avoid burns.
- Remove bread from pan carefully. Invert pan and shake the loaf out. Remove paddle from bread. Don't use metal utensils or you might scratch the non-stick coating on the pan and paddle.
- Cool the bread on a rack for 20 to 30 minutes. Slice with a serrated bread knife.
- Clean your machine! Immediately after removing bread, partially fill the pan with lukewarm water and let it soak to facilitate removal of the paddle from the shaft. Don't use harsh cleaners or you may damage the nonstick coating. The pan and paddle can be expensive to replace!
- Power failure? If the bread hasn't started to bake, transfer dough to a large bowl, cover and place in a cool place until power is restored. Then return dough to machine and start at the beginning.
- Check out the bread machine cookbooks written by Laura Brody (e.g., BREAD MACHINE BAKING— PERFECT EVERY TIME) published by William Morrow & Company.

in each hand and gently pulling. Arrange them about 1 inch apart on baking sheets. Lightly brush the tops of breadsticks with beaten egg white. Sprinkle with desired toppings.

4. Bake at 400°F for 18 to 20 minutes, until nicely browned. Cool on wire racks.

Yield: about 3 dozen. Store in an airtight container. Delicious with soups, salads or dips.

55 calories per breadstick, 0.5 g fat (0.1 g saturated), 0 mg cholesterol, 2 g protein, 11 g carbohydrate, 67 mg sodium, 30 mg potassium, <1 mg iron, <1 g fiber, 3 mg calcium.

- **Whole-wheat flour** can be omitted but increase all-purpose flour to 4 cups.
- **Grissini (Thin Crisp Breadsticks):** Prepare dough and let rise as directed. In Step 3, divide dough into 4 pieces. Roll out dough very thin to make a 12-inch square. Use a fluted pastry wheel or pizza cutter and cut dough into 12 strips. Repeat with remaining dough. Arrange them 1 inch apart on prepared baking pans. Brush with egg white (or a little olive oil), then sprinkle with coarse salt and other desired toppings. Bake at 400°F until golden brown, about 5 to 7 minutes. Cool on wire racks. Store them at room temperature. Recipe makes about 4 dozen.

Dill Onion Bread (Bread Machine Method)

Thanks to my friend Howard Krakower for this recipe. It's a winner! Let's get "doughing!"

1	c. water (at room temperature)
1	egg (or 2 egg whites)

⅝	c. low-fat (1%) cottage cheese
4	c. bread flour or all-purpose flour
1½	tsp. dried dill
2	tsp. salt
3	tbsp. sugar
2	tbsp. canola oil
1¼	tsp. active dry yeast
½	c. chopped onions

1. Place all the ingredients (except chopped onions) in baking pan of the bread machine in the order given. Select the basic bread cycle. Add the onions 5 minutes before the end of the kneading cycle, (generally when the machine beeps to add additional ingredients such as raisins). Using oven mitts, remove bread immediately after the bake cycle is finished to prevent crust from getting soggy. Remove bread from pan; cool on a rack. Fill pan with lukewarm water and soak for easier cleanup. (*Note:* This bread rises very high, particularly if you decide to use more onions.)

Yield: one 2-pound loaf (16 or less servings). Bread freezes well.

162 calories per slice, 2.8 g fat (0.4 g saturated), 16 mg cholesterol, 6 g protein, 28 g carbohydrate, 333 mg sodium, 61 mg potassium, 2 mg iron, <1 g fiber, 15 mg calcium.

- **The amount of yeast is correct.** Howard buys his yeast in bulk because it is more economical. (He bakes bread almost every day!) Store yeast in the fridge; bring to room temperature before using.
- **For more information and tips,** refer to Loafing Around with Bread Machines (p. 313).

Howard's Raisin Cinnamon Bread (Bread Machine Method)

Howard Krakower says this tastes better than any supermarket premium raisin bread around!

1½ c. skim or 1% milk
4 c. bread flour or all-purpose flour
1 tsp. salt
3 tbsp. sugar
2 tbsp. canola oil
1½ tsp. cinnamon
1½ tsp. active dry yeast
⅔ c. raisins

1. Place all the ingredients (except raisins) in baking pan of the bread machine in the order given. Select the basic bread cycle. Add raisins 5 minutes before the end of the kneading cycle, (generally when the machine beeps to add additional ingredients). Using oven mitts, remove bread immediately after the bake cycle is finished to prevent crust from getting soggy. Cool bread on a rack. Fill pan immediately with lukewarm water and let soak for easier cleanup.

Yield: one 2-pound loaf (16 or less servings). This is addictive. Bread freezes well if there is any left!

176 calories per slice, 2.4 g fat (0.2 g saturated), trace cholesterol, 5 g protein, 33 g carbohydrate, 159 mg sodium, 126 mg potassium, 2 mg iron, 1 g fiber, 40 mg calcium.

Maurice's Cranberry Bread (Bread Machine Method)

My friend Maurice Borts is an expert bread machine baker who enjoys creating unusual breads.

1 c. water (room temperature)
2 tbsp. canola oil
2 tbsp. honey or sugar
¾ tsp. salt
½ c. rolled oats
½ c. whole-wheat flour
2 c. bread flour
1½ tsp. bread machine yeast
½–¾ c. dried cranberries (to taste)

1. Place all the ingredients (except cranberries) in baking pan of the bread machine in the order given. Select the whole-grain cycle or basic bread cycle. Add cranberries 5 minutes before the end of the kneading cycle (generally when the machine beeps to add additional ingredients). Using oven mitts, remove bread immediately after the bake cycle is finished to prevent crust from getting soggy. Cool bread on a rack. Fill pan immediately with lukewarm water and let soak for easier cleanup.

Yield: 1½-pound loaf (12 or less servings). This is addictive. Bread freezes well if there is any left!

160 calories per slice, 3 g fat (0.3 g saturated), 0 mg cholesterol, 4 g protein, 29 g carbohydrate, 147 mg sodium, 69 mg potassium, 2 mg iron, 2 g fiber, 8 mg calcium.

Myra's Banana Nut Bread
(Bread Machine Method)

Milk and almonds add calcium to this delicious and unusual yeasted banana bread.

3/4 c. skim milk (at room temperature)
2 tbsp. canola oil
3 tbsp. honey
1/2 tsp. ground nutmeg
1 tsp. salt
3/4 c. very ripe mashed bananas
1/2 c. whole-wheat flour
2 1/2 c. bread flour
1 1/2 tsp. bread machine yeast
1/4 c. chopped almonds or walnuts

1. Place all the ingredients (except nuts) in baking pan of the bread machine in the order given. Select either the whole-grain cycle or basic bread cycle. Add nuts 5 minutes before the end of the kneading cycle (generally when the machine beeps to add additional ingredients). Using oven mitts, remove bread immediately after the bake cycle is finished to prevent crust from getting soggy. Cool bread on a rack. Fill pan immediately with lukewarm water and let soak for easier cleanup.

Yield: 1 1/2-pound loaf (12 or less servings). Bread freezes well.

192 calories per slice, 4.4 g fat (0.5 g saturated), trace cholesterol, 6 g protein, 34 g carbohydrate, 203 mg sodium, 163 mg potassium, 2 mg iron, 2 g fiber, 34 mg calcium.

Maggie's Favorite Onion Rye Bread
(Bread Machine Method)

Maggie is Maurice and Myra Borts' English Springer Spaniel. Oh, to be a dog in a Jewish home!

3/4 c. water (at room temperature)
1 tbsp. canola oil
1 tbsp. honey
3/4 tsp. salt
2 c. bread flour
1 c. rye flour
1 tbsp. caraway seeds, if desired
1 1/2 tsp. bread machine yeast
1/2 c. chopped onions

1. Place all the ingredients (except onions) in baking pan of the bread machine in the order given. Select either the whole-grain cycle or basic bread cycle. Add the onions 5 minutes before the end of kneading cycle (generally when the machine beeps to add additional ingredients). Using oven mitts, remove bread immediately after the bake cycle is finished to prevent crust from getting soggy. Cool bread on a rack. Fill pan immediately with lukewarm water and let soak for easier cleanup.

Yield: 1 1/2-pound loaf (12 or less servings). Bread freezes well.

142 calories per slice, 1.7 g fat (0.2 g saturated), 0 mg cholesterol, 4 g protein, 25 g carbohydrate, 147 mg sodium, 60 mg potassium, 1 mg iron, 2 g fiber, 7 mg calcium.

Elaine's Lemon Poppy Seed Braid

This recipe was inspired by a yummy lemon loaf that "my friendly assistant" Elaine Kaplan makes in her bread machine. She serves it with non-fat lemon yogurt. The combination is fabulous! I modified her recipe so it could be made in the processor, to the delight of my students. It's like eating cake.

1   tsp. sugar
1/2   c. lukewarm water (105 to 110°F)
1   pkg. active dry yeast
1   c. skim milk
4   c. bread or all-purpose flour
3   tbsp. additional sugar

1 1/2   tsp. salt
2   tsp. fresh lemon juice
1 1/2   tsp. grated lemon rind
2   tbsp. poppy seeds
2   tbsp. canola oil

Topping:
1   tbsp. skim milk to glaze loaf
1   tbsp. poppy seeds to sprinkle on top

1. Dissolve sugar in lukewarm water. Sprinkle yeast over water and let stand 10 minutes. Stir to dissolve. Heat milk until lukewarm (about 1 minute on HIGH in the microwave). Measure flour into the processor bowl. Add sugar, salt, lemon juice,

More Bread Machine Secrets!

- If you reduce the oil in Maurice's Cranberry Bread to 1 tablespoon, one serving will contain 150 calories and 1.9 g fat (0.2 saturated). Just replace the oil with a tablespoon of water.
- Because breads made in a bread machine come in various shapes, it's difficult to determine how many slices a loaf yields. Most machines make bread in the shape of a tall, square column with a rounded top. Some machines make bread that more closely resembles the traditional rectangular loaf. The 2-pound machine makes larger slices than the 1 1/2-pound. machine.
- My bread-baking friends (mostly men with big appetites!) say that a loaf of homemade bread usually disappears within hours of baking. Remember, if you overindulge, you will bulge!
- If your whole-grain breads are low in volume, try a double cycle. Place ingredients in the machine, program the dough cycle and press Start. At the end of the final kneading, reprogram the machine for either the bread or whole-wheat cycle. The extra kneading

should result in a higher loaf.
- Sweeteners such as honey or sugar add flavor and enhance the browning process. If you prefer a sugar substitute, bread results may vary with the type and amount of sugar substitute used.
- Buttermilk can replace water or milk in your favorite breads for a slightly tangy flavor.
- Soy milk can replace milk if you are lactose-intolerant.
- Some bread machines have a viewing window in the lid that lets you watch. Do not clean the window with a commercial glass cleaner. Don't wash any of the parts in the dishwasher.
- If the mixing paddle gets baked into the bread, carefully use a toothpick to pull out the paddle. If the hole in the paddle gets clogged, clean it with a toothpick or soft brush.
- If the paddle gets stuck on its shaft, fill pan with hot water and soak for 1/2 hour, or until it loosens and can be removed.
- The non-stick coating on the pan and paddle is very fragile, so clean with care!

rind, poppy seeds and oil. Process for 10 seconds. Add dissolved yeast; process 10 seconds more. Add milk slowly through the feed tube while the machine is running. Process until dough gathers around the blades in a mass. Process 45 seconds longer. Dough should be slightly sticky. If machine slows down, add 3 or 4 tablespoons additional flour.

2. Turn dough out onto a lightly floured surface. Knead for 2 minutes, until smooth and elastic. Shape into a ball and place in a large lightly greased bowl. Cover bowl with plastic wrap and let dough rise in a warm place until doubled, about 1½ to 2 hours. Punch down.

3. Divide dough into 3 equal portions. Shape dough into long ropes, flouring your hands for easier handling. Place them on a greased baking sheet and form them into a large braid, tucking ends under. Cover with a towel and let rise until doubled, about 2 hours. Brush lightly with 1 table-spoon milk; sprinkle with 1 tablespoon poppy seeds. Preheat oven to 400°F. Bake loaf in the lower third of the oven for 30 to 35 minutes, until golden brown. Loaf should sound hollow when tapped with your fingertips.

Yield: 1 large loaf (18 slices). Freezes well (if it doesn't disappear in a flash!)

147 calories per slice, 2.7 g fat (0.3 g saturated), trace cholesterol, 5 g protein, 26 g carbohydrate, 202 mg sodium, 74 mg potassium, 2 mg iron, 1 g fiber, 44 mg calcium.

• **Bread Machine Method:** Use only ⅓ cup water. Liquids should be at room temperature. Measure ingredients. Add them in the following order to the baking pan of the bread machine: water, milk, oil, sugar, salt, lemon juice, rind, flour, poppy seeds and yeast. Select the dough setting. At the end of the final kneading cycle, remove dough and place it on a lightly floured surface. Continue as directed in Step 3. (Elaine mixes and bakes this bread completely in her bread machine on the rapid bake cycle. If possible, remove bread immediately after the bake cycle is finished to prevent a soggy crust. Cool on a rack. Recipe makes a 2-pound loaf.)

No-Knead Cinnamon Babka

This is a reduced-fat version of my Mother's easy-to-prepare Babka. No need to knead or punch down the dough. The only rising necessary is done right in the baking pan. What could be easier?

1	tsp. sugar
¼	c. warm water (110°F)
1	pkg. active dry yeast
1	c. skim milk
3	tbsp. canola oil
3	c. all-purpose flour
½	c. sugar
½	tsp. salt
2	eggs (or 4 egg whites)
¾	c. raisins or chopped dried apricots, rinsed & drained
2	tsp. cinnamon
⅓	c. brown sugar, packed
1	tbsp. unsweetened cocoa

1. Dissolve sugar in warm water. Add yeast and let stand until foamy, about 8 to 10 minutes. Stir to dissolve. Meanwhile, heat milk until hot. (Microwave it about 1 minute on HIGH.) Add oil to milk. Place flour, sugar and salt in processor bowl. While machine is running, add eggs, dissolved yeast mixture, milk and oil through the feed tube. Process for 1½ minutes, stopping machine once or twice to scrape down the sides of bowl. Batter will be very sticky and will drop in a sheet from a rubber spatula. Add raisins or apricots and process 10 seconds longer.

2. Spray a 10-inch Bundt or springform pan with non-stick spray. Spread half of batter in pan. Combine cinnamon, brown sugar and cocoa. Sprinkle half over batter. Drop remaining batter by spoonfuls to cover the cinnamon mixture. Sprinkle with remaining cinnamon mixture. Cover with a towel and let rise until doubled, about 2 hours. Babka should reach the top of the pan.

3. Preheat oven to 350°F. Bake for 45 to 50 minutes, until golden. Let cool for 20 minutes, then remove from pan. Cool completely.

Yield: 16 servings. Freezes well.

191 calories per serving, 3.5 g fat (0.5 g saturated), 27 mg cholesterol, 4 g protein, 36 g carbohydrate, 92 mg sodium, 147 mg potassium, 2 mg iron, 1 g fiber, 38 mg calcium.

- **MicroWays!** To bring refrigerated eggs to room temperature quickly, break eggs into a microsafe bowl. Microwave uncovered on HIGH for 10 seconds. (As a general guideline, allow 4 seconds for every egg (or every two egg whites.)
- **Optional:** Blend ½ cup of sifted icing sugar with 1 tablespoon milk until smooth. Drizzle over the top of the cooled Babka. Each serving will contain 206 calories and 3.6 grams of fat.

Belle's Flatbread (Lavasch)

These are a great alternative to packaged crackers. Luscious with soups, salads, dips & spreads.

1	c. flour
½	c. rolled oats (regular or quick-cooking)
¼	tsp. salt
1	tbsp. onion flakes
2	tbsp. sesame seeds
¼	tsp. garlic powder
2	tbsp. canola oil
6	tbsp. water

Optional Toppings: sesame seeds, coarse salt, dill weed, dried basil and/or dehydrated onion flakes

1. Preheat oven to 475°F. Line 2 baking sheets with aluminum foil and spray with non-stick spray. Combine flour, rolled oats, seasonings and oil in the processor. Process until mixed. Slowly add water through the feed tube and process until mixture gathers together into a crumbly mass. Remove dough from processor and press it together to form a ball. Divide into 18 smaller balls.

2. On a floured surface, roll out each piece of dough as thin as possible into long strips. During the rolling process, sprinkle dough with desired toppings, pressing the toppings into the dough with the rolling pin. (Alternately, use a pasta machine to roll out dough.) Bake at 475°F for 5 to 6 minutes, until crisp and golden.

Yield: 18 pieces. Store in an airtight container.

54 calories per piece, 2.2 g fat (0.1 g saturated), 0 mg cholesterol, 1 g protein, 7 g carbohydrate, 35 mg sodium, 19 mg potassium, <1 mg iron, <1 g fiber, 6 mg calcium.

Bran & Date Muffins

Moist, low in fat, high in flavor, these are guaranteed to be a regular at your house! Originally, I was making these marvelous muffins with ¼ cup of oil, but discovered that they tasted even more delicious when I substituted Prune Purée (p. 334) for part of the fat.

1½ c. natural bran or All-Bran cereal
2   tbsp. canola oil
¾–1 c. dates, cut-up
¾   c. raisins, rinsed & drained
½   c. hot water
2   tbsp. Prune Purée (p. 334) or applesauce
2   egg whites (or 1 egg)
1   c. buttermilk or sour milk
2   tbsp. molasses or honey
1¼ c. flour (whole-wheat or all-purpose)
⅓   c. sugar (brown or white)
1   tsp. baking soda
½   tsp. baking powder

1. Combine bran, oil, dates and raisins in a large mixing bowl. Pour hot water over mixture; let cool slightly. Stir in purée, egg whites, buttermilk and molasses. Add remaining ingredients and stir just enough to moisten dry ingredients. If you have time, let mixture stand for 20 to 30 minutes. (I usually do this while the oven is heating and I'm cleaning up.)

2. Preheat oven to 400°F. Line muffin pans with paper liners. Fill ¾-full with batter. Bake for 20 to 25 minutes, until nicely browned.

Yield: 1 dozen. These freeze well.

193 calories per muffin, 3.2 g fat (0.4 g saturated), <1 mg cholesterol, 5 g protein, 42 g carbohydrate, 227 mg sodium, 424 mg potassium, 2 mg iron, 5 g fiber, 67 mg calcium.

- **Fiber Facts!** Bran is available in two forms, unprocessed and processed. Just compare: ½ cup unprocessed natural wheat bran (e.g., Quaker brand) contains 14 grams of dietary fiber, ½ cup of All-Bran contains 10 grams, but ½ cup of processed bran flakes has only 3 grams of fiber.
- **To cut up dates easily,** dip scissors in flour first. This prevents sticking. (For variety, make one batch of muffins with raisins or dried apricots, make another batch with dates.)
- **My first choice** is to use Prune Purée in these muffins. It takes just moments to make, adds fiber and flavor, and keeps perfectly in the fridge for at least 3 months. Do try it! You can substitute unsweetened applesauce if it's more convenient. Either one is excellent.
- **To make sour milk,** mix 1 tablespoon lemon juice or vinegar plus skim milk to equal 1 cup. For dairy-free recipes, substitute soy or rice milk plus lemon juice or vinegar.
- **An alternative to sour milk** or buttermilk in muffin and cake recipes is to mix ½ cup of non-fat yogurt with ½ cup of water.
- **For even-sized muffins,** scoop out batter with an ice cream scoop, or use a ½ cup dry measure.
- **Lee's Ever-Ready Muffin Mixture:** Lee Stillinger, one of my enthusiastic students, loves this recipe so much, she makes four times the original recipe and stores the batter in the refrigerator in an airtight container. (It keeps for about 3 weeks.) That way, she can have fresh muffins whenever she's in the mood. (If you're not quite as enthusiastic, just double the recipe!)

Muffinformation!

- Homemade muffins contain less fat and calories than most commercial mega-muffins. A muffin can be a little cake in disguise and may contain more than 500 calories, with 30 to 35 grams of fat!
- Substitute unsweetened applesauce or Prune Purée (p. 334) for half the fat in your favorite muffins.
- If you store an open box of baking soda in the fridge to absorb odors, don't use it for baking.
- Batters made only with baking soda have to be baked right away because they release all their leavening when mixed with liquid. Baking soda should be mixed together with dry ingredients.
- Muffin batters made with baking powder can be stored tightly covered in the refrigerator for 2 or 3 days before baking. This is because baking powder releases part of its leavening when it comes in contact with liquid, then releases the remainder when exposed to oven heat.
- To test if baking powder is still active, stir 1 teaspoon baking powder into ½ cup hot water. If it fizzes, it's good. Baking powder keeps about a year stored in a dry place in a tightly closed container.
- For variety, add dried cherries, cranberries, blueberries or strawberries to muffin batters.
- Overmixing makes muffins heavy and full of tunnels. If using a processor, use quick on/offs to mix the dry and wet ingredients together. If mixing by hand, 15 to 20 strokes is usually enough, just until flour disappears. Mixture will be lumpy rather than smooth.
- Lining muffin pans with paper liners makes for easy removal and cleanup. Muffins made with little or no fat may stick to the paper liners, so you may prefer to use non-stick spray.
- Muffin compartments should be filled ¾-full before baking. A half-cup measure or ice cream scoop can be used for measuring batter into compartments of muffin pan.
- Overfilling causes batter to spill onto top of the pan, producing muffins with overhanging tops. Muffins will be harder to remove, plus the pan will require scrubbing.
- Muffins should be baked in a preheated oven at 375°F to 400°F on the center rack.
- When done, tops of muffins will be golden brown and will spring back when lightly touched. A cake tester inserted into the center of the muffin should come out clean.
- Miniatures: Bake 12 to 15 minutes at 375°F. Three minis equal one regular muffin.
- Jumbos: Bake 25 to 30 minutes at 375°F. One jumbo muffin equals 1½ regular muffins.
- Mushroom Cap Muffins: These are baked in a special pan with an extra rim around the edge of each compartment to handle the extra batter. (Pans are available in bakery supply houses or specialty kitchen boutiques.) Fill each compartment of sprayed or greased pans just to the top, but don't let batter overflow into the rims. As the batter rises, it will flow into the rims.
- Muffin Tops: These are baked in special pans with shallow, round compartments. You end up with crusty muffin tops, the favorite part of the muffin for many people!
- Muffin Loaf: Instead of using a muffin pan, line a 9 x 5-inch loaf pan with aluminum foil and spray with non-stick spray. Pour muffin batter into prepared pan. Bake loaf in a preheated 350°F oven for 45 to 55 minutes, or until a cake tester inserted comes out clean. Thanks to Carolyn Melmed for the terrific idea! (While the loaf bakes, I try to go out for a brisk walk!)
- Muffin batter can also be baked in a cake pan. This is easier than trying to divide the batter evenly among the compartments of your muffin pan, and also saves on cleaning up those inevitable spills around the edges! The batter for 12 muffins can be baked in a 7 x 11-inch cake pan. Your baking time will be 35 to 45 minutes at 350°F. When cooled, cut into squares to serve.
- One regular-size muffin takes 20 to 25 seconds on HIGH to defrost in the microwave.

Apple Streusel Oatmeal Muffins

One day I was rushed for time and baked my cake in muffin pans. These were the result!

1. Prepare batter for Apple Streusel Oatmeal Cake as directed (see p. 339). Place batter in paper-lined muffin pans. Bake at 375°F for 25 minutes.

Yield: 15 muffins.

195 calories per muffin, 4.6 g fat (0.6 g saturated), 14 mg cholesterol, 4 g protein, 36 g carbohydrate, 92 mg sodium, 172 mg potassium, 1 mg iron, 2 g fiber, 53 mg calcium.

Cathy's Ever-Ready Honey Bran Muffins

Cathy Ternan, my exercise partner, special friend and proofreader, shared this excellent do-ahead muffin recipe with me. I replaced part of the honey with molasses and used applesauce to replace part of the fat in these tender, tasty muffins. They're not too sweet and are packed with fiber and flavor.

6	c. natural bran, divided
1³/₄	c. boiling water
¹/₂	c. canola oil
1³/₄	c. honey
¹/₄	c. molasses
¹/₂	c. unsweetened applesauce
4	eggs (or 2 eggs plus 4 egg whites)
4	c. buttermilk
5	c. whole-wheat flour
5	tsp. baking soda
1	tsp. salt
1	tbsp. cinnamon
2	c. raisins, rinsed & drained

1. Place 2 cups of bran in a very large mixing bowl or storage container. Pour boiling water over bran, stir well to moisten and let mixture stand for about 5 minutes.

2. Add oil, honey, molasses, applesauce, eggs, buttermilk and remaining bran to bowl. Stir to combine. Sift in flour, baking soda and salt. Mix in cinnamon and raisins. Batter will keep for up to 6 weeks in the refrigerator. Bake as many muffins as needed.

3. Preheat oven to 375°F. Fill paper-lined muffin cups ³/₄-full with batter. Bake for 20 to 25 minutes, until nicely browned.

Yield: about 4 dozen. These freeze well.

164 calories per muffin, 3.6 g fat (0.5 g saturated), 18 mg cholesterol, 4 g protein, 33 g carbohydrate, 266 mg sodium, 275 mg potassium, 2 mg iron, 4 g fiber, 45 mg calcium.

- **Quaker Oats** makes natural wheat bran (in a green box), or you can buy it in bulk. Substitute all or part All-Bran cereal if you are short of natural bran.
- **Optional at baking time:** Add chopped dates, apples, chocolate chips, nuts, etc. to batter.
- **Oatmeal Bran Muffins:** Follow recipe above, but use 4 cups of wheat bran and 2 cups of oats (quick-cooking or regular). Replace the honey with 2 cups of firmly packed brown sugar.

Wheat Germ Bran Muffins

Wheat germ should be stored in the refrigerator to prevent it from becoming rancid.

3	tbsp. tub margarine or canola oil
¹/₂	c. brown sugar, packed

¼ c. molasses
2 eggs (or 1 egg plus 2 egg whites)
1 c. skim milk
1½ c. natural bran
¼ c. wheat germ
½ c. all-pupose flour
½ c. whole-wheat flour
1½ tsp. baking powder
½ tsp. baking soda
¾ c. raisins, rinsed & drained (or chopped dates)
1 tbsp. grated orange zest

1. Preheat oven to 400°F. Beat margarine with brown sugar, molasses and eggs until well blended, about 2 or 3 minutes. Add milk and bran; blend well. Add wheat germ, flours, baking powder and soda. Mix just until smooth. Stir in raisins and orange zest. Spoon the batter into paper-lined muffin cups, filling them about ¾-full. Bake at 400°F for 20 to 25 minutes, until golden brown.

Yield: 12 muffins. These freeze well.

197 calories per muffin, 4.6 g fat (1 g saturated), 36 mg cholesterol, 5 g protein, 38 g carbohydrate, 223 mg sodium, 407 mg potassium, 3 mg iron, 4 g fiber, 101 mg calcium.

• **Bran & Prune Muffins:** Follow recipe for Wheat Germ Bran Muffins (above), but substitute 1 cup of cut-up pitted prunes for raisins. (Dip your scissors in flour first to cut prunes.)

Rozie's Magical Carrot Muffins

These versatile muffins will disappear like magic!

1½ c. whole-wheat flour (all-purpose flour can replace part of the flour)

⅛ tsp. salt
1½ tsp. baking soda
1 tsp. cinnamon
¾ c. wheat bran
¾ c. oat bran
1 c. grated carrots (about 3 medium)
1 egg plus 2 egg whites (or 2 eggs)
3 tbsp. canola oil
1½ c. orange juice, skim milk or yogurt
2 tbsp. lemon juice
⅔ c. maple syrup or honey
¾ c. raisins or cut-up prunes (or ½ c. mini chocolate chips)

1. Preheat oven to 375°F. Combine dry ingredients and blend well. Add carrots, egg, egg whites and oil. Mix until blended. Add orange juice, lemon juice, maple syrup and raisins (or chocolate chips). Mix just until blended. Line muffin cups with paper liners. Fill ¾-full with batter. Bake at 375°F for 20 to 25 minutes, until golden brown.

Yield: 18 muffins. These freeze well.

145 calories per muffin, 3.3 g fat (0.4 g saturated), 14 mg cholesterol, 4 g protein, 29 g carbohydrate, 166 mg sodium, 251 mg potassium, 1 mg iron, 3 g fiber, 28 mg calcium.

Mary's Best Bran-ana Bread

Low in fat, high in flavor! I reduced the fat by half from Mary Goldwater's yummy recipe. I'm glad she shared it because it's become one of my absolute favorites. Also refer to Going Bananas (p. 329).

2 tbsp. canola oil
1 c. sugar
1 egg plus 2 egg whites (or 2 eggs)

1   tsp. vanilla
1   c. All-Bran cereal
2   tbsp. water or skim milk
3   very ripe bananas (1½ c. mashed)
1½   c. flour (part whole-wheat can be used)
⅛   tsp. salt
2   tsp. baking powder
½   tsp. baking soda

1. Preheat oven to 350°F. Spray a 9 x 5-inch loaf pan. In the processor or a large bowl, beat oil, sugar, egg, egg whites and vanilla. Add bran; mix well. Add bananas and water and beat until smooth. Add dry ingredients and mix just until blended. Pour batter into prepared pan and bake at 350°F for 1 hour. A cake tester should come out dry.

Yield: 1 loaf (12 slices). Freezes well.

196 calories per slice, 3.1 g fat (0.4 g saturated), 18 mg cholesterol, 4 g protein, 41 g carbohydrate, 263 mg sodium, 230 mg potassium, 2 mg iron, 4 g fiber, 58 mg calcium.

Chocolate Chip Bran-ana Muffins

You won't taste the bran in these yummy muffins. What a great way to sneak in some extra fiber! Fruit, cereal and milk all come together in one healthy handful. Do try the variations listed.

1   c. All-Bran or natural bran cereal
1   c. buttermilk or sour milk
1   c. mashed ripe bananas (about 2 large)
2   egg whites (or 1 egg)
2   tbsp. canola oil
2   tbsp. unsweetened applesauce
½   c. sugar (brown or white)
1   c. all-purpose flour
½   c. whole-wheat flour
1   tsp. baking powder
1   tsp. baking soda
1   tsp. cinnamon
¼–½ c. miniature chocolate chips
2   tbsp. wheat germ, optional

1. Preheat oven to 375°F. Combine cereal with buttermilk in a large bowl. Let stand 3 or 4 minutes to

Chef's Secrets for Dairy-Free, Lower-Fat Baking!

- If you want to make muffins and cakes dairy-free, just substitute soy milk or rice milk for regular milk. Although they are higher in fat than skim milk, you can always dilute them with a little water.
- For a dairy-free replacement for buttermilk or sour milk, place 1 tablespoon vinegar or lemon juice in a measuring cup. Add enough soy milk or rice milk to measure 1 cup of liquid.
- Orange juice, apple juice or water can be used to replace milk in most baking recipes.
- Non-dairy (pareve) margarine can be used as a substitute for butter. The calories and fat content are the same

(100 calories per tablespoon), but tub margarine is lower in saturated fat than butter. Many margarines contain trans fatty acids, which are similar to saturated fat.
- Canola or vegetable oil can replace butter or margarine, but you may notice a slight difference in texture of baked items. Oil is probably a healthier choice.
- Oil is slightly higher in calories than butter or margarine. One tablespoon of oil contains 120 calories. However, its fat is mainly unsaturated.
- Light oils are not lower in calories. They are lighter in color or in flavor.
- Read "Say 'Hooray' for Prune Purée!" (p. 333).

soften. Add bananas, egg whites, oil and applesauce to bran mixture; blend well. Add remaining ingredients and stir just until blended. Do not overmix. Spoon batter into paper-lined muffin cups, filling them ³/₄-full. Bake at 375°F for 20 to 25 minutes, until golden brown.

Yield: 12 muffins. These freeze very well.

174 calories per muffin, 3.9 g fat (1 g saturated), <1 mg cholesterol, 4 g protein, 34 g carbohydrate, 270 mg sodium, 280 mg potassium, 2 mg iron, 4 g fiber, 68 mg calcium.

- **To make sour milk**, mix 1 tablespoon lemon juice or vinegar with enough skim milk to equal 1 cup.
- **You can replace the chocolate chips** with ¹/₂ cup raisins or chopped dates. Chopped walnuts or almonds are another healthy option.
- **Fat-Free Bran-ana Muffins:** Substitute ¹/₄ cup Prune Purée (p. 334) for oil and applesauce. Omit chocolate chips. (If desired, add ¹/₂ cup raisins or chopped dates.) Spray muffin pans with non-stick cooking spray. If you use paper liners, they should be sprayed before filling; otherwise muffins may stick because of the lack of fat in the batter.
- **A-B-C Muffins (Applesauce, Apricot, Bran & Chocolate Chips):** Substitute applesauce for mashed bananas. Add ¹/₂ cup chopped dried apricots to batter.
- **A-B-C-D Muffins (Applesauce, Bran, Chocolate Chips & Dates):** Substitute applesauce for mashed bananas. Add ¹/₂ cup chopped dates to batter.
- **C-B-A Muffins (Cranberry, Bran & Applesauce):** Substitute applesauce for mashed bananas. Soak ¹/₂ cup of dried cranberries in hot water for 5 to 10 minutes, then drain well before adding them to the batter. (To use fresh or frozen cranberries, mix 1 cup of berries with 1 tablespoon flour and 2 tablespoons sugar. Gently mix into batter.)
- **Mini-Muffins:** Prepare desired batter (above). Pour into paper lined mini-muffin tins. Bake at 375°F for 15 to 18 minutes. Recipe makes 3 dozen minis. Three minis equal 1 regular muffin.

Best Blueberry Orange Muffins

Scrumptious!

1	egg plus 2 egg whites (or 2 eggs)
1	c. sugar
3	tbsp. canola oil
¹/₂	c. orange juice (or concentrate)
1¹/₂	c. flour (you can use part whole-wheat)
1¹/₂	tsp. baking powder
¹/₈	tsp. salt
1	tsp. grated orange rind, optional
1	tsp. vanilla
2	c. blueberries (fresh or frozen)
1	tbsp. flour
2	tbsp. sugar

1. Preheat oven to 375°F. Beat egg, egg whites, sugar and oil until light. Add juice and mix well. Add flour, baking powder, salt, orange rind and vanilla. Mix just until flour disappears. In a small bowl, combine blueberries with 1 tablespoon flour and 2 tablespoons sugar. Gently stir blueberry mixture into batter.

2. Line muffin pan with paper liners. Fill ³/₄-full with batter. Bake at 375°F for 22 to 25 minutes, until golden brown.

Yield: 12 muffins. These freeze beautifully, if they don't disappear in a flash!

190 calories per muffin, 4.1 g fat (0.4 g saturated), 18 mg cholesterol, 3 g protein, 36 g carbohydrate, 110 mg sodium, 73 mg potassium, <1 mg iron, 1 g fiber, 41 mg calcium.

Nancy's Blueberry Streusel Muffins

I've lightened these up from Nancy Gordon's original recipe, which contained ³/₄ cup of fat!

1   tbsp. tub margarine or oil
¹/₄ c. brown sugar, firmly packed
³/₄ tsp. cinnamon
¹/₄ c. flour
    Best Blueberry Orange Muffin batter (see previous recipe)

1. To make the topping, mix together margarine, brown sugar, cinnamon and flour until crumbly. Set aside. Prepare muffin batter as directed. Fill paper-lined muffin pans ³/₄ full with batter. Sprinkle with topping. Bake at 375°F for 22 to 25 minutes, until golden.

Yield: 12 muffins. These freeze well.

226 calories per muffin, 5.1 g fat (0.6 g saturated), 18 mg cholesterol, 3 g protein, 43 g carbohydrate, 120 mg sodium, 93 mg potassium, 1 mg iron, 1 g fiber, 48 mg calcium.

• **Blueberry Streusel Coffee Cake:** Prepare batter and topping as directed above. Pour batter into a sprayed 8-inch square baking pan. Sprinkle with topping. Bake at 350°F for 45 to 50 minutes.

Carrot Muffins

1. Prepare Moist'n Luscious Carrot Cake (p. 341) as directed. Pour batter into sprayed muffin pans and bake at 375°F for 20 to 25 minutes.

Yield: 18 muffins.

193 calories per muffin, 3 g fat (0.3 g saturated), 12 mg cholesterol, 3 g protein, 40 g carbohydrate, 180 mg sodium, 173 mg potassium, 1 mg iron, 2 g fiber, 19 mg calcium.

Belle's Best Cornmeal Muffins

My Mom's cornmeal muffins are moist and tender, yet very low in fat. For "berry good" muffins, make any of the variations below.

1   c. all-purpose flour
1   c. cornmeal (medium or fine grind)
3   tbsp. sugar
1¹/₂ tsp. baking powder
¹/₂   tsp. baking soda
¹/₈   tsp. salt
1¹/₂ c. buttermilk (or 4 tsp. lemon juice plus enough skim or soy milk to make 1¹/₂ cups)
2   tbsp. canola oil
2   eggs (or 1 egg plus 2 egg whites)

1. Preheat oven to 375°F. Spray compartments of muffin pan with non-stick spray. Combine dry ingredients in a large mixing bowl and mix until blended. Add buttermilk, oil and eggs. Stir lightly, just until smooth. Fill each muffin compartment with ¹/₂ cup batter.

2. Bake at 375°F for 20 to 25 minutes, until golden brown. Cool slightly and remove from pan.

Yield: 12 muffins. These freeze well.

145 calories per muffin, 3.5 g fat (0.6 g saturated), 36 mg cholesterol, 4 g protein, 24 g carbohydrate, 180 mg sodium, 68 mg potassium, 1 mg iron, <1 g fiber, 75 mg calcium.

- **Blueberry Cornmeal Muffins:** Place a few blueberries (about 6 to 8 berries) on each muffin. Press gently into batter so berries are barely covered. (Placing the berries in this way prevents the batter from becoming streaked and stained with purple from the berries.) Bake as directed above.
- **Raspberry Cornmeal Muffins:** Place a few fresh or frozen raspberries on each muffin. Press gently so berries are barely covered with batter. Bake as directed above.
- **Cranberry Cornmeal Muffins:** Place a few frozen cranberries on each muffin. Press gently so berries are just covered with batter. (Alternately, fold ½ cup dried cranberries into muffin batter.) Bake as directed above.
- **Easy Cornbread:** Prepare batter as directed above. Line a 9 x 5-inch loaf pan completely with aluminum foil. Spray with non-stick spray. Spread batter evenly in pan. Bake in a preheated 350°F oven for 45 to 55 minutes. (You can also make cornbread with ½ to ¾ cup of blueberries, raspberries or cranberries folded into the batter.)

Zucchini Pineapple Chocolate Chip Muffins

2	medium unpeeled zucchini (2 c. grated)
2	large eggs (or 1 egg & 2 egg whites)
¼	c. canola oil
¾	c. sugar
1	c. brown sugar, firmly packed
½	c. unsweetened applesauce
2	tsp. vanilla
½	c. crushed pineapple, well drained
1	tbsp. cinnamon
1½	c. all-purpose flour
1¼	c. whole-wheat flour
1½	tsp. baking powder
1½	tsp. baking soda
½	c. chocolate chips

1. Preheat oven to 350°F. Spray 24 muffin compartments with non-stick spray. Grate zucchini; measure and set aside. Beat eggs, oil, sugars, applesauce and vanilla until light, about 2 minutes. Add grated zucchini, drained pineapple and cinnamon. Mix briefly. Add flour, baking powder and baking soda. Mix briefly, just until flour disappears. Stir in chocolate chips. Pour batter into prepared muffin tins. Bake at 350°F for 20 to 25 minutes. A toothpick inserted into the center of a muffin should come out with no batter clinging to it.

Yield: 24 muffins. Freezes well.

157 calories per muffin, 3.8 g fat (0.8 g saturated), 18 mg cholesterol, 3 g protein, 30 g carbohydrate, 103 mg sodium, 132 mg potassium, 1 mg iron, 2 g fiber, 19 mg calcium.

Love That Lemon Loaf!

1	tbsp. grated lemon rind
1¾	c. flour
1½	tsp. baking powder
½	tsp. baking soda
2	eggs (or 1 egg plus 2 egg whites)
⅔	c. sugar
3	tbsp. soft tub margarine or canola oil
½	c. unsweetened applesauce

¼ c. fresh lemon juice
½ c. non-fat yogurt

Lemon Syrup:
¼ c. additional fresh lemon juice
¼ c. additional sugar

1. Preheat oven to 350°F. In a bowl, combine rind, flour, baking powder and baking soda. In the processor, combine eggs, sugar, margarine and applesauce; beat until light, 2 to 3 minutes. Add dry ingredients, lemon juice and yogurt. Mix together with quick on/offs, just until flour disappears. Spread batter in a sprayed 9 x 5-inch loaf pan. Bake at 350°F for 40 to 45 minutes. Loaf will have a crack down the center.

2. Meanwhile, combine ingredients for syrup and heat until piping hot; stir well. Poke holes all over the top of the loaf with a wooden skewer or toothpick. Slowly drizzle hot syrup all over the top of the loaf, letting it soak up the liquid. When cooled, remove from pan.

Yield: 12 luscious servings. This tastes even better the next day. Freezes well.

177 calories per serving, 3.9 g fat (0.8 g saturated), 36 mg cholesterol, 4 g protein, 32 g carbohydrate, 124 mg sodium, 94 mg potassium, 1 mg iron, <1 g fiber, 30 mg calcium.

• **Lemon Cranberry Bread:** Follow basic recipe for Love that Lemon Loaf, but combine ¾ cup fresh or frozen cranberries with 1 tablespoon flour; mix well. Fold into batter and bake as directed. Recipe can also be made with dried cranberries (craisins), dried blueberries, strawberries, raspberries or cherries. (These can be found in specialty food shops or bulk food stores.)

• **Lemon Poppy Loaf:** Follow basic recipe for Love that Lemon Loaf, but fold 3 tablespoons poppy seeds into batter.
• **Lemon Muffins:** Make any of the versions of Love that Lemon Loaf. Spray a muffin tin with non-stick spray. Pour batter into pan. (You'll have enough batter for 9 or 10 muffins. Fill empty compartments of pan with water to prevent pan from burning.) Bake at 375°F about 20 minutes. Poke holes in tops of muffins. Slowly drizzle hot syrup over muffins, letting them soak up syrup.

Carolyn's Thin Muffin Loaf

Carolyn Melmed walked side by side with me on the treadmill most mornings in our quest for thinness and health! She shared her delicious recipe for bran muffins, which she bakes as a loaf. I revised it slightly, reducing fat and sugar without a loss in flavor or moistness. Enjoy without the guilt trip!

2   c. All-Bran or natural bran cereal
1¾ c. skim milk
½ c. orange juice
2   eggs (or 1 egg plus 2 egg whites)
¼ c. canola oil
½ c. unsweetened applesauce (or Prune Purée, p. 334)
2   tsp. vanilla
1   c. flour plus 1 c. whole-wheat flour (or 2 c. all-purpose flour)
2   tsp. baking powder
2   tsp. baking soda
1   c. brown sugar, packed
1   c. raisins, rinsed & drained

1. Preheat oven to 350°F. Line two 9 x 5 x 3-inch loaf pans completely with aluminum foil. Spray with non-stick spray. Measure bran into a large

Going Bananas?

- Banana Muffins: Follow recipe for Banana Bread above, but bake batter in muffin pans. You will get 16 muffins. (Fill the empty muffin compartments with water.) Bake at 375°F for 20 to 25 minutes. One muffin contains 170 calories, 4.1 g fat (0.4 g saturated), 14 mg cholesterol and 31 g carbohydrate.
- Banana Blueberry Muffins: 1½ cups of fresh or frozen blueberries (do not thaw if frozen) can be added to the batter. Place batter in paper-lined or sprayed muffin tins. Place 6 or 8 blueberries on top of each muffin and press gently into batter. (This method prevents streaking.) Bake muffins at 375°F for 20 to 25 minutes. Blueberries are a great source of fiber! (One muffin contains 178 calories and 2 g fiber.)
- If you have a lot of ripe bananas and don't have time to bake, don't bother peeling and mashing them. Just put the bananas in a plastic freezer bag and freeze them until needed. When you have time to bake, thaw them slightly (about 10 minutes at room temperature). Peel and cut into chunks. Process bananas with the Steel Knife of the processor until smooth.
- If you're in a hurry, put frozen banana under hot water for 30 seconds, or defrost for 20 seconds on HIGH in the microwave. Cut away the peel with a sharp paring knife. What a cool idea!
- Another suggestion for using up ripe bananas is to peel them, then mash and freeze them in containers holding the exact amount you need for your favorite recipe. Thaw before using.
- When bananas are on sale, buy a bunch and freeze them, using any of the methods above.
- Make some Banana Smoothies (p. 105) or Strawberry & Banana Frozen Yogurt (p. 355)!

bowl. Add milk, orange juice, eggs, oil, applesauce and vanilla. Let stand for 5 minutes. Add remaining ingredients to bran mixture. Mix just until blended. Do not overmix.

2. Pour mixture into prepared pans. Bake at 350°F for 50 to 55 minutes, or until a cake tester inserted into the center of the loaf comes out clean. Cool 10 minutes. Remove from pans.

Yield: 2 loaves (24 slices). These loaves freeze beautifully. If well-wrapped, they'll stay fresh for 3 or 4 days at room temperature.

145 calories per slice, 3.1 g fat (0.4 g saturated), 18 mg cholesterol, 4 g protein, 29 g carbohydrate, 246 mg sodium, 240 mg potassium, 2 mg iron, 4 g fiber, 66 mg calcium.

- **Lighter Bake,** which is a fat replacer made from fruit purée, works beautifully in this recipe. It is not currently available to consumers in Canada, so I buy several jars when I go to the States.
- **When I was in the middle** of preparing to move to Toronto, I packed most of my baking pans. All that was left in my kitchen was one lonely 9 x 13-inch rectangular pan. Not to worry! I just made one big muffin cake! (Baking time is about 5 minutes less if you bake the batter in a cake pan.)

Yogurt Banana Bread

Low in fat, full of flavor!

3	large, very ripe bananas
¼	c. canola oil or tub margarine
1	c. sugar
1	egg plus 2 whites
1	tsp. vanilla

³/₄ c. non-fat yogurt
1   tsp. baking soda
1   tsp. baking powder
1   c. whole-wheat flour
1   c. all-purpose flour

1. Process bananas with the Steel Knife of the processor until smooth, about 20 seconds. Measure 1¹/₃ cups purée. Freeze any leftovers for another time.

2. Beat oil, sugar, egg, egg whites and vanilla until light, about 3 or 4 minutes. Add yogurt and process for 3 or 4 seconds. Add banana purée, baking soda, baking powder and flours. Process with several quick on/offs, just until flour disappears.

3. Preheat oven to 325°F. Spray a 9 x 5-inch loaf pan with non-stick spray. Spread batter evenly in pan. Bake at 325°F for 50 to 60 minutes, until golden brown. Batter should not cling to your knife or cake tester when inserted to check for doneness. Freezes well.

Yield: 1 loaf (12 slices).

227 calories per slice, 5.5 g fat (0.6 g saturated), 18 mg cholesterol, 5 g protein, 41 g carbohydrate, 160 mg sodium, 249 mg potassium, 1 mg iron, 2 g fiber, 40 mg calcium.

Cakes & Desserts

Baking the Low-Fat Way

- For baking, because of health concerns, I've made the switch from butter to canola oil or tub margarine. I use either Fleishmann's tub margarine, which is dairy-free (pareve), or Becel tub margarine, which contains dairy. When I want the flavor of butter, I do indulge occasionally and use butter, but in very small amounts.
- Margarine is not less fattening than butter! It's just lower in saturated fats and cholesterol. Margarine and butter contain the same number of calories, about 100 calories per tablespoon.
- Reduced fat/low-calorie brands of margarine and butter are fine as spreads, but don't use them for baking. They contain 50 percent water, so they won't work properly in most baking recipes. However, I have used "lite" margarine in fruit crisp toppings with excellent results.
- In your traditional favorite baking recipes, you can reduce the fat by at least half by using fruit purées such as unsweetened applesauce or prunes (see Say "Hooray" for Prune Purée!)
- Cakes made with butter or margarine get some of their volume from the air that is incorporated into the batter when you cream fat with sugar. If you eliminate all the fat from the recipe, your baked goods will be more compact. Start by replacing only half the fat in your recipe. Check out the results and if satisfactory, next time reduce the fat a little more.
- How low can you go? Use $1/3$ of the amount of fat called for in the original recipe, and replace the remainder with fruit purée (e.g. instead of 1 cup of oil, use $1/3$ cup oil and $2/3$ cup unsweetened applesauce or Prune Purée.)
- When should you add the fat substitute? In most recipes, beat it together with the oil or margarine, sugar and flavoring. Baked goods may be slightly more dense than those made with the full amount of fat, but flavor and moistness are fine.

- To retain moistness when baking fat-free and fat-reduced items, I often reduce the oven temperature by 25 degrees to prevent overbaking. Test with a wooden skewer or toothpick. It should come out clean when inserted into the center.
- Quick Fixes: Dust cakes with a combination of cocoa and icing sugar. Place a doily, stencil or small cookie cutters on top of cake before sprinkling it with cocoa/sugar mixture.
- Sugar-free pudding (any flavor) makes a delicious icing for cakes!

Say "Hooray" For Prune Purée!

- Mention the word "prunes" and the usual associations that come to mind are prune juice, stewed prunes, hamentashen—and digestive systems in need of a little boost for regularity! Whenever I see prunes, I'm reminded of a song my sister and I used to sing as children: "No matter how young a prune may be, he's always full of wrinkles. A baby prune's just like his dad, but he's not wrinkled quite so bad! We have wrinkles on our face, a prune has wrinkles every place!"
- Well, that wrinkled old prune has become a boon to low-fat bakers. Invest just 5 minutes of your time and whip up an excellent fat replacement to use in most of your baking recipes. Prune Purée is high in pectin, a soluble fiber, which helps hold in the air bubbles, and also helps keep baked goods moist. It works well in your favorite chocolate cake, brownies, banana bread, carrot or zucchini muffins. Go ahead, experiment! Baked goods will have a slightly fruity taste, but no one will be able to guess that you've substituted prunes for fat.
- Add a little fiber to your diet by adding Prune Purée to home-baked goodies. One cup contains 12 grams of fiber! (What better excuse do you need to indulge in a brownie or two?)

- For light-colored cakes, Prune Purée can be combined with unsweetened applesauce.
- For best results, be sure to use some fat in your low-fat baking recipes. Don't be tempted to replace all of the fat with fruit purée. Otherwise, the tops of baked goods usually end up being somewhat sticky and the texture can be a bit rubbery.
- You can purchase "lekvar," a commercially prepared prune butter. It usually contains corn syrup, water, sugar, pectin and citric acid. It's much sweeter and more expensive than homemade purée. Baby food puréed prunes are usually too watery to use as a fat alternative.
- A fat-free product called "Lighter Bake" is an excellent fat replacement for butter, margarine, oil and shortening. It can be used in moist, soft and chewy baking recipes or mixes. It's made from prunes, apples and pectin. It is used as a fat replacement in the same way you use prune purée or applesauce. It is manufactured by Sunsweet, 501 N. Walton Avenue, Yuba City, CA 95993. Call 1-800-417-2253 between 9 a.m. and 6 p.m. (Pacific time) for information or recipes. From Canada, call their Consumer Relations Dept. at 209-467-6260.
- Homemade Prune Purée makes a delicious filling for Hamentashen. If desired, add a teaspoon of grated orange or lemon rind (zest). It also makes a delicious fat-free spread on bread or toast instead of jam. So the plump little plum, even when it reaches old age, has found a new purpose in life. After all, what's a wrinkle or two between friends?
- Dare To Compare! One cup of Prune Purée contains 304 calories and less than 1 gram of fat. One cup of butter contains 1,628 calories and 184 grams of fat. One cup of oil contains 1,927 calories and 218 grams of fat!

Prune Purée

This is a fabulous fat substitute to use in baking! It's quick and easy to make, plus it's much cheaper than the commercial version. Prune Purée is packed with potassium and fiber.

2   c. pitted prunes (about 36)
1   c. hot water

1. Combine prunes and hot water in a bowl. Cover and let stand for 5 minutes, until plump. In a processor or blender, process prunes with water until smooth, about 1 minute. Scrape down sides of bowl several times.

Yield: about 2 cups. Store tightly covered in the fridge for up to 3 months, or freeze for 6 months.

20 calories per tbsp., 0 g fat (0 g saturated), 0 mg cholesterol, trace protein, 5 g carbohydrate, <1 mg sodium, 63 mg potassium, trace iron, <1 g fiber, 4 mg calcium.

304 calories per cup, 0.7 g fat (0.1 g saturated), 0 mg cholesterol, 3 g protein, 80 g carbohydrate, 8 mg sodium, 948 mg potassium, 3 mg iron, 12 g fiber, 67 mg calcium.

Angel Food Cake

Fat-free, cholesterol-free, guilt-free! Read Egg White Wisdom (p. 335).

3/4 c. flour
1/2 c. icing sugar

Egg White Wisdom

- Start with egg whites at room temperature. Make sure no yolk gets into the whites or they won't whip properly. Separate each egg white into a small bowl before adding it to the other whites. That way, if a drop of yolk gets into the white, it can be removed easily with a piece of egg shell!
- Use a glass, stainless or copper bowl. Egg whites won't whip properly in a plastic bowl. Beaters must be clean and grease-free. Even a trace of grease will keep whites from whipping properly.
- If using a copper bowl, clean it with a little lemon juice and salt just before you use it.
- Cream of tartar helps egg whites reach maximum volume. Use ¼ teaspoon of cream of tartar for every 4 whites. Omit cream of tartar when whipping egg whites in a copper bowl. For Passover recipes (or if you have no cream of tartar), substitute 1 teaspoon lemon juice for ¼ teaspoon cream of tartar.
- Beat egg whites with cream of tartar (or lemon juice) until foamy. Gradually add sugar, about 2 tablespoons at a time. Properly beaten whites will be stiff but not dry. They should look glossy, and you should be able to turn the bowl upside down without the whites falling out!
- No-guilt egg whites: Buy liquid egg whites in a carton. They're found in the refrigerated section at the supermarket. So convenient, and you don't have to feel bad about throwing out the yolks!
- One egg white measures 2 tablespoons liquid. For 1 whole egg, substitute ¼ cup liquid egg whites.

¼ tsp. salt
¾ c. granulated sugar
1½ c. egg whites (about 12), at room temperature
1 tsp. cream of tartar
1 tsp. vanilla

1. Preheat oven to 325°F. Sift flour, icing sugar and salt into a bowl. In the processor, process granulated sugar until fine, about 20 seconds. In a large mixing bowl, beat egg whites with cream of tartar until soft peaks form. Gradually add finely ground sugar a little at a time, beating at high speed until whites are stiff but not dry. Blend in vanilla. Using a rubber spatula, gently fold in flour mixture about ¼ cup at a time, just until blended.

2. Pour batter into an ungreased 10-inch tube pan and smooth the top. Use a knife to gently cut through batter to remove any large air bubbles. Bake on the middle rack at 325°F for about 45 minutes, until golden. Immediately invert cake pan onto its raised feet (or hang it upside down over the neck of a bottle). Let cake hang until completely cool.

3. To remove cake from pan, slide a thin-bladed knife or flexible spatula between pan and sides of the cake. Push up the bottom of the pan; remove sides. Loosen around the center tube and the bottom of the pan. Carefully invert cake onto a large round serving platter. Cut with a serrated knife.

Yield: 12 servings. Cake can be frozen for 2 or 3 weeks if well wrapped.

111 calories per serving, 0.1 g fat (0 g saturated), 0 mg cholesterol, 4 g protein, 23 g carbohydrate, 155 mg sodium, 98 mg potassium, trace iron, trace fiber, 3 mg calcium.

Substitutions & Alternatives in Low-Fat, Low-Cholesterol Baking

FOR:	USE:
1 tbsp. butter	1 tbsp. tub margarine, canola or walnut oil. (Light margarine can be used for streusel toppings, but not regular baking. Some light brands contain gelatin, an animal-based product, and may not be Kosher.)
$\frac{1}{2}$ c. butter, oil or margarine	3 tbsp. canola oil or tub margarine plus $\frac{1}{3}$ c. unsweetened applesauce, Prune Purée (p. 334) or fruit purée fat replacer (e.g. Lighter Bake, sold in the U.S.A.)
1 c. butter, oil or margarine	$\frac{1}{3}$ c. canola oil or tub margarine plus $\frac{2}{3}$ c. unsweetened applesauce or fruit purée fat replacer
1 c. whole or 2% milk	1 c. skim milk or lactose-reduced milk/lactaid. (For dairy-free baking, use orange or apple juice, water, coffee, soy milk or rice milk.)
1 c. buttermilk or yogurt	1 tbsp. lemon juice or vinegar plus skim milk to equal 1 c.
1 c. sour cream	1 c. non-fat or low-fat sour cream or yogurt (or buttermilk).
1 c. cream cheese	1 c. dry cottage cheese (pressed or smooth texture) or ricotta cheese (non-fat/low-fat), Firm Yogurt Cheese (p. 53), Homemade Cottage Cheese (p. 145) or low-fat cream cheese
2 c. whipped cream	2 c. lightly sweetened Creamy Yogurt Cheese (p. 53). Or: Combine $\frac{1}{3}$ c. ice water, 2 tsp. lemon juice and $\frac{1}{2}$ tsp. vanilla in a deep bowl. Blend in $\frac{1}{3}$ c. skim milk powder plus 2 tbsp. sugar. Whip 5 to 10 minutes, until stiff.
1 c. sugar	$\frac{1}{2}$ c. sugar plus $\frac{1}{2}$ c. granulated substitute (e.g. Splenda) for reduced-sugar baking. (Baked goods may be drier or lower in volume.) Or: Reduce liquid in recipe by $\frac{1}{4}$ cup. Use $\frac{3}{4}$ c. honey, $\frac{3}{4}$ c. maple syrup, 1 c. corn syrup or $1\frac{1}{4}$ c. molasses. Or: $\frac{2}{3}$ cup fructose (fruit sugar).
1 c. brown sugar, packed	1 c. granulated sugar plus 2 tbsp. molasses.

Substitutions & Alternatives in Low-Fat, Low-Cholesterol Baking (continued)

FOR:	USE:
1 c. all-purpose or unbleached flour	$1/2$ cup whole-wheat flour plus $1/2$ cup all-purpose flour. (If you use only whole-wheat flour, texture will be heavier.) Or: 2 tbsp. wheat germ or soy flour plus all-purpose flour to equal 1 cup. Or: 1 c. sifted whole-wheat (or white) cake and pastry flour.
1 c. cake and pastry flour	2 tbsp. cornstarch plus all-purpose flour to equal 1 cup.
2 tbsp. flour (for thickening)	1 tbsp. cornstarch or potato starch.
1 square unsweetened chocolate	3 tbsp. unsweetened cocoa plus $1/2$ tbsp. canola oil.
1 egg (in baking or cooking)	2 egg whites or $1/4$ cup egg whites or egg substitute (or use omega-3/reduced-cholesterol eggs).
1 egg (in baking) (Vegan alternative)	$1/4$ c. mashed banana, tofu or low-fat sour cream. (Baked goods may be more dense and heavy than those with eggs.)
1 egg (in baking) (Vegan alternative)	Grind flax seed in a coffee grinder or spice mill (or buy flax seed already ground). For 1 egg, combine 1 tbsp. ground flax seed with 3 tbsp. water in a small bowl. Let stand until thick, about 2 or 3 minutes. Store flax seed in the freezer to avoid rancidity. It is high in essential omega-3 fatty acids.
Juice of a lemon	3 to 4 tbsp. lemon juice (fresh or bottled).
Juice of a orange	$1/4$ to $1/3$ c. orange juice.
Juice of a lime	2 tbsp. lime juice.
1 tsp. vanilla extract	1 tsp. orange, coffee or almond flavored liqueur.
1 tsp. baking powder	$1/2$ tsp. cream of tartar plus $1/4$ tsp. baking soda.
$1/2$ c. nuts	$1/4$ c. finely chopped nuts. (Toast nuts at 350°F for 5 to 10 minutes before chopping to enhance flavor.) Supplement with $1/4$ c. crunchy cereal (e.g. Grape Nuts).
$1/2$ c. raisins	$1/2$ c. dried cherries, blueberries, cranberries, strawberries, chopped dates, apricots, prunes (for muffins/baked goods).

- **Heavenly Chocolate Orange Cake:** At the end of Step 2, fold 2 teaspoons of freshly grated orange rind and 2 squares grated semi-sweet chocolate into batter. One serving of cake will contain just 134 calories, 2 g fat (1.1 g saturated) and 25 mg carbohydrate. Wow!
- **Chocolate Cherry Angel Cake:** Fold 2 squares of grated semi-sweet chocolate and ½ cup well-drained chopped maraschino cherries into cake batter. If desired, pour Decadent Chocolate Glaze (p. 366) over top of cake. Spread glaze over the top, allowing some to drizzle unevenly down the sides of the cake.
- **Frozen Heaven!** Slice Angel Cake in 3 layers. Spread your favorite flavor of slightly softened frozen yogurt between layers. Prepare dessert topping mix as per package directions. Frost outside of cake. Freeze until firm; then wrap well. For easier slicing, remove cake from freezer 15 minutes before serving.
- **Have some heavenly trifle** without flushing your diet down the drain! Angel Food Cake is excellent in Guilt-Free Chocolate Trifle (p. 352), or in the variation of Light'n Luscious Strawberry Cheesecake Trifle (p. 352). Experience true decadence without the guilt trip!

Apple Coffee Cake

Topping:
- ¾ c. brown sugar, firmly packed
- ¼ c. pecans or walnuts, finely chopped
- 1½ tsp. cinnamon

Batter:
- 3–4 apples, peeled & cored
- 1 c. sugar
- ½ c. brown sugar, firmly packed
- ¼ c. tub margarine or canola oil
- 2 eggs (or 1 egg plus 2 egg whites)
- ¼ c. unsweetened applesauce
- 1 tsp. vanilla
- 3 c. flour (you can use part whole-wheat)
- 1 tsp. baking soda
- 2 tsp. baking powder
- 1 tsp. cinnamon
- 1 c. non-fat yogurt (or drained whey from Yogurt Cheese, p. 53)

1. Preheat oven to 350°F. Spray a 9 x 13-inch pan with non-stick spray. Combine ingredients for topping. Mix until crumbly; set aside. Grate the apples (can be done in the processor). Set aside.

2. Combine sugars, margarine, eggs, applesauce and vanilla. Beat until light and fluffy, about 3 or 4 minutes. Combine dry ingredients. Add to the batter alternately with yogurt and mix just until blended. Gently mix in apples. Spread batter in pan. Sprinkle reserved topping evenly over batter. Bake at 350°F for 50 to 55 minutes, until cake tests done when a toothpick is inserted.

Yield: 24 servings. May be frozen.

183 calories per serving, 3.4 g fat (0.6 g saturated), 18 mg cholesterol, 3 g protein, 36 g carbohydrate, 106 mg sodium, 126 mg potassium, 1 mg iron, 1 g fiber, 40 mg calcium.

Fabulous Low-Fat Apple Cake (Pareve)

Applesauce replaces the oil in this scrumptious cake. The only fat is found in the yolk(s). The cake will be moister the next day. For a large family, double the recipe and bake it in a 9 x 13-inch pan.

2	eggs (or 1 egg plus 2 egg whites)
1	c. sugar
1	tsp. vanilla
1/2	c. unsweetened applesauce
2	tbsp. water
1 1/2	c. flour (you can use half whole-wheat)
2	tsp. baking powder
1/2	tsp. cinnamon
6	apples, peeled & thinly sliced
1/4	c. brown sugar, firmly packed
2	tsp. additional cinnamon

1. Preheat oven to 350°F. Beat eggs, sugar and vanilla until light. Add applesauce and mix well. Add water, flour, baking powder and 1/2 teaspoon cinnamon. Mix just until flour disappears. In another bowl, mix apples with brown sugar and cinnamon. Spray a 7 x 11-inch Pyrex pan with non-stick spray.

2. Spread half of batter in pan. Spread apples evenly over batter. Top with remaining batter and spread evenly. (If you wet your spatula, the batter will be easier to spread.) Bake at 350°F for 45 to 55 minutes, until golden brown.

Yield: 12 servings. If frozen, cake will become more moist. Just reheat it for 10 minutes at 350°F.

198 calories per serving, 1.4 g fat (0.3 g saturated), 35 mg cholesterol, 3 g protein, 45 g carbohydrate, 52 mg sodium, 139 mg potassium, 1 mg iron, 3 g fiber, 20 mg calcium.

• **Blueberry Apple Cake:** Replace 3 of the apples with 2 cups of blueberries.

Apple Streusel Flan

Thanks to Gloria Goodman for inspiring this luscious variation of the above recipe. Great for brunch!

1. Prepare batter for Apple Cake as directed above, but don't mix the apples with cinnamon and sugar. Spread half of batter in a thin layer in a sprayed 10-inch springform pan. Arrange half of apple slices over cake batter. Top with remaining batter. Arrange remaining apples on top. Mix together 1/3 cup brown sugar and 1 teaspoon cinnamon; sprinkle evenly over apples. Bake at 350°F about 45 minutes, until cake tests done. If desired, make a glaze by combining 1/4 cup of icing sugar with 1 teaspoon water and 1/4 teaspoon vanilla. Drizzle glaze over top of cooled cake.

Apple Streusel Oatmeal Cake

A delicious oatmeal and apple cake, topped with a mixture like those used on fruit crisps. Perfect with coffee. Pleasure without guilt!

Topping:

1/4	c. flour
1/2	c. oats (quick-cooking or regular)
1	tsp. cinnamon
1	tbsp. tub margarine or canola oil
1	tbsp. water
1/4	c. brown sugar, packed

Batter:
- 1   c. oats (quick-cooking or regular)
- ³/₄ c. non-fat yogurt
- ¹/₄ c. unsweetened applesauce
- 2   large apples, peeled & cored
- 1   egg plus 1 egg white
- 1   c. brown sugar, firmly packed
- 3   tbsp. canola oil
- 1   c. flour
- 1   tsp. baking powder
- ¹/₂ tsp. baking soda
- 1   tsp. cinnamon

1. Preheat oven to 350°F. Spray a 7 x 11-inch oblong pan with non-stick spray. In a bowl, mix topping ingredients together until crumbly. Set aside.

2. In another bowl, combine oats, yogurt and applesauce; mix well. Let stand until softened, about 3 or 4 minutes. Grate or chop apples; set aside. In the processor, combine egg, egg white, brown sugar and 3 tablespoons oil and beat until well mixed, about 2 to 3 minutes. Add oats/yogurt mixture and mix just until blended. Add flour, baking powder, soda and cinnamon. Mix briefly, just enough to moisten the flour mixture. Gently mix in apples.

3. Pour batter into pan. Sprinkle evenly with crumb topping. Bake at 350°F for 45 to 50 minutes. A toothpick inserted into the center of the loaf should come out without any batter clinging to it.

Yield: 15 servings. Freezes well.

195 calories per serving, 4.6 g fat (0.6 g saturated), 14 mg cholesterol, 4 g protein, 36 g carbohydrate, 92 mg sodium, 172 mg potassium, 1 mg iron, 2 g fiber, 53 mg calcium.

• **Apple Streusel Oatmeal Muffins:** Place batter in paper-lined muffin pans. Bake at 375°F for 25 minutes. Recipe makes 15 muffins.

Banana Cake

- 3   large, very ripe bananas
- ¹/₄ c. canola oil
- 1   c. sugar
- 1   egg plus 2 egg whites (or 2 eggs)
- 1   tsp. vanilla
- ³/₄ c. non-fat yogurt
- 1   tsp. baking soda
- 1   tsp. baking powder
- 1   c. whole-wheat flour
- 1   c. all-purpose flour

1. Preheat oven to 325°F. Spray a 7 x 11-inch Pyrex baking dish with non-stick spray. Purée bananas in the processor until smooth. Measure 1¹/₃ cups purée. Beat oil, sugar, egg, egg whites and vanilla until light, about 3 or 4 minutes. Blend in bananas. Add yogurt and process for 5 seconds. Add baking soda, baking powder and flour. Process with quick on/off turns, until flour disappears. Spread batter evenly in prepared pan. Bake at 325°F for 45 to 55 minutes, until golden brown. Insert a cake tester into the center of cake. No batter should cling to it when done.

Yield: 15 servings. Freezes well.

177 calories per serving, 4.3 g fat (0.5 g saturated), 14 mg cholesterol, 4 g protein, 32 g carbohydrate, 128 mg sodium, 181 mg potassium, <1 mg iron, 2 g fiber, 32 mg calcium.

• **When you have lots of ripe bananas,** purée them in the processor or mash with a potato masher.

Measure 1⅓ cups purée into each container and freeze. Freezing makes bananas taste sweeter.

Pareve Banana Cake

Use ripe bananas that are almost black for maximum flavor. Batter can also be baked as muffins.

3	large, very ripe bananas (1½ c. mashed)
¼	c. pareve tub margarine
1	c. sugar
1	egg plus 2 egg whites (or 2 eggs)
1	tsp. vanilla
1	tsp. baking soda
1	tsp. baking powder
1	c. whole-wheat flour
1	c. all-purpose flour
½	c. orange juice
½	c. chocolate chips, optional

1. Preheat oven to 350°F. Spray a 7 x 11-inch Pyrex baking dish with non-stick spray. Purée bananas in processor until smooth, about 20 seconds. Measure 1½ cups purée. Beat margarine, sugar, egg, egg whites and vanilla until light, about 3 or 4 minutes. Blend in bananas. Add baking soda, baking powder and flour. Drizzle orange juice over flour mixture. Process with several quick on/off turns, just until blended. Stir in chocolate chips, if using. Spread batter evenly in prepared pan. Bake at 350°F for 45 to 50 minutes, until golden brown and cake tests done.

Yield: 15 servings. Freezes well.

169 calories per serving, 3.8 g fat (0.7 g saturated), 14 mg cholesterol, 3 g protein, 32 g carbohydrate, 144 mg sodium, 167 mg potassium, <1 mg iron, 2 g fiber, 9 mg calcium.

Moist'n Luscious Carrot Cake

Dave Horan's favorite! You won't believe it's low-fat. Most low-fat carrot cakes include buttermilk or yogurt, but I was determined to create a dairy-free cake. My testers loved the results. If you must have icing on your cake, use Light Cream Cheese Frosting (see following recipe). Guiltless pleasure!

3	c. grated carrots (6–8 carrots)
1	egg plus 2 egg whites (or 2 eggs)
3	tbsp. canola oil
1¾	c. sugar
2	tsp. vanilla
¾	c. unsweetened applesauce
2½	c. flour (I use half whole-wheat flour)
1½	tsp. baking powder
1½	tsp. baking soda
1	tbsp. cinnamon
¼	tsp. salt
2	tbsp. wheat germ
½	c. raisins or mini chocolate chips
	Light Cream Cheese Frosting, if desired

1. Preheat oven to 350°F. Spray a 9 x 13-inch baking pan with non-stick spray. Grate carrots, measure 3 cups and set aside. Beat egg, egg whites, oil, sugar, vanilla and applesauce. Beat until light, about 2 to 3 minutes. Add grated carrots and mix well. Combine flour, baking powder, baking soda, cinnamon, salt and wheat germ. Add to batter and mix just until flour disappears. Stir in raisins or chocolate chips. Pour batter into prepared pan. Bake at 350°F for 45 to 50 minutes, or until a toothpick inserted into the center of the cake comes out with no batter clinging to it.

Yield: 24 servings. Freezes well.

144 calories per serving (without frosting), 2.2 g fat (0.2 g saturated), 9 mg cholesterol, 3 g protein, 30 g carbohydrate, 135 mg sodium, 130 mg potassium, <1 mg iron, 2 g fiber, 14 mg calcium.

Light Cream Cheese Frosting

½ c. (4 oz/125 g) light cream cheese
2½ c. icing sugar
2–3 tsp. lemon juice (preferably fresh)
½ tsp. grated lemon zest, optional

1. Combine all ingredients in the processor and blend until smooth.

60 calories per serving (1/24th of a recipe), 0.9 g fat (0.6 g saturated), 3 mg cholesterol, <1 g protein, 13 g carbohydrate, 15 mg sodium, 9 mg potassium, trace iron, 0 g fiber, 6 mg calcium.

Guilt-Free Pareve Chocolate Cake

A deep, dark secret from a light kitchen! This is a low-fat version of the pareve chocolate cake that's a family favorite from my cookbook The Food Processor Bible. *I reduced the fat from 1¼ cups to just ¼ cup. If you don't divulge the secret ingredient, I won't!*

⅔ c. cocoa
2¼ c. flour
2 c. sugar
1½ tsp. baking powder
1½ tsp. baking soda
¼ tsp. salt
¾ c. coffee

¾ c. orange juice
2 eggs plus 2 egg whites (or 3 eggs)
¾ c. unsweetened applesauce or Prune Purée (p. 334)
¼ c. canola oil

1. Preheat oven to 350°F. Combine all dry ingredients in the processor bowl. Process until blended, about 10 seconds. Add coffee, orange juice, eggs, egg whites and applesauce. Start processor and add oil through the feed tube while the machine is running. Process batter for 45 seconds. Do not insert pusher in feed tube and do not overprocess.

2. Pour batter into a sprayed 12-cup Bundt pan. Bake at 350°F for 55 to 60 minutes, until cake tests done. Cool for 20 minutes before removing cake from pan.

Yield: 18 servings. Freezes well.

222 calories per serving, 4.7 g fat (0.8 g saturated), 27 mg cholesterol, 4 g protein, 43 g carbohydrate, 314 mg sodium, 125 mg potassium, 2 mg iron, 2 g fiber, 89 mg calcium.

- **If you don't have brewed coffee** on hand, use 1½ teaspoons instant coffee granules and 1½ cups orange juice or water.
- **Skinnier Version:** If you use 1 egg and 4 egg whites, one serving will contain 219 calories, 4.4 g fat and 13 mg cholesterol.
- **Chocolate Raspberry Torte:** Line a 10 x 15 x 2-inch jelly roll pan with baking parchment. (If you don't have parchment, use aluminum foil. Spray foil to prevent sticking.) Pour in batter and spread evenly. Bake at 350°F about 20 minutes, until cake tests done. When cool, cut cake in half to make 2 rectangles each measuring 10 x 7½ inches. Spread one half with good quality raspberry jam. (You'll need 1 to 1¼ cups.) Top with

the second cake layer. Glaze with Decadent Chocolate Glaze (p. 366) and garnish with fresh raspberries.

No-Egg Double Chocolate Cupcakes

See photo (P-13). These chocolate cupcakes make great guilt-free treats for chocoholics! I've replaced part of the fat in my original recipe with fruit purée. With my savings, I added chocolate chips!

1½ c. flour (part whole-wheat can be used)
1   c. sugar
⅓   c. unsweetened cocoa
1   tsp. baking soda
¼   tsp. salt
3   tbsp. canola oil
2   tbsp. Prune Purée (p. 334) or applesauce
1   tbsp. white vinegar
1   tsp. vanilla
½   c. orange juice
½   c. coffee or water
¼   c. mini or regular chocolate chips
Icing sugar, if desired

1. Preheat oven to 350°F. Spray a muffin tin with non-stick spray. Combine dry ingredients in a large bowl or processor. Mix well. Add remaining ingredients except chocolate chips. Mix just until smooth and blended. Stir in chocolate chips. Do not overmix batter or cupcakes will be tough.

2. Pour batter into muffin tins. Bake at 350°F for 20 to 25 minutes, until done. Cool completely. If desired, sprinkle lightly with icing sugar.

Yield: 12 cupcakes. Recipe can be doubled easily. These freeze very well.

183 calories per cupcake (with chocolate chips), 5 g fat (1.1 g saturated), 0 mg cholesterol, 2 g protein, 34 g carbohydrate, 155 mg sodium, 103 mg potassium, 1 mg iron, 2 g fiber, 9 mg calcium.

- **If you eliminate** the chocolate chips, each cupcake will contain 166 calories, 3.9 g fat (0.5 g saturated) and 32 g carbohydrate.
- **No-Egg Double Chocolate Cake:** Spread batter evenly in an 8-inch square baking pan which has been sprayed with non-stick spray. Bake at 350°F for 30 minutes.
- **Miniature Double Chocolate Cupcakes:** Spoon batter into miniature muffin tins which have been sprayed with non-stick spray. Miniatures take about 15 to 18 minutes to bake. Recipe makes 2 dozen mini cupcakes. Each miniature cupcake (with chocolate chips) contains 83 calories, 2 g fat (0.2 g saturated) and 16 g carbohydrate.
- **Miniature Black Bottom Cupcakes:** Prepare batter without chocolate chips. Pour into sprayed mini muffin tins. Combine ½ cup dry cottage cheese with ¼ cup sugar and 1 egg white. Beat until smooth and creamy. Stir in ¼ cup mini chocolate chips. Drop a small blob of cheese mixture from a spoon onto the center of each cupcake. Bake at 350°F for 15 to 18 minutes. Store cupcakes in the refrigerator. Recipe makes 2 dozen miniature cupcakes. Each one contains 104 calories, 2.5 g fat (0.5 g saturated) and 19 g carbohydrate.

Honey & Spice & Everything Nice Cake (Pareve)

See photo (P-16). A wonderful way to welcome in a sweet New Year for the Jewish High Holidays.

3 eggs plus 2 egg whites (or 4 eggs)
1 c. brown sugar, packed
1/3 c. canola oil
1¼ c. liquid honey
3 c. flour (you can use part whole-wheat)
2 tsp. baking powder
1 tsp. baking soda
2 tsp. cinnamon
¼ tsp. ground ginger
¼ tsp. allspice
3/4 c. cold tea or coffee
¼ c. brandy, whiskey or orange juice
½ c. raisins, rinsed & well-drained
½ c. dried apricots, cut up

1. Preheat oven to 325°F. Spray a 10-inch Bundt pan with non-stick spray. In the processor, beat eggs, egg whites, sugar and oil until light. Add honey; mix well. Combine dry ingredients and spices. Add to batter, alternating with tea and brandy. Mix just until blended. Stir in raisins and apricots. Pour batter into pan. Bake at 325°F for 1 hour and 15 minutes, or until cake tests done. A wooden skewer inserted into the center should come out dry. Remove from oven and let cool for 20 minutes. Loosen cake from pan with a flexible spatula. Carefully invert onto a serving plate.

Yield: 20 servings. Freezes well. (Not recommended for diabetics because of its high sugar content.)

247 calories per serving, 4.7 g fat (0.5 g saturated), 32 mg cholesterol, 4 g protein, 48 g carbohydrate, 113 mg sodium, 176 mg potassium, 2 mg iron, 1 g fiber, 24 mg calcium.

Devastatingly Delicious Three-Yolk Sponge Cake

8 egg whites (at room temperature)
½ tsp. cream of tartar
3/4 c. sugar
3 egg yolks
½ c. additional sugar
2 tbsp. each lemon and orange juice
1 tsp. vanilla
1¼ c. all-purpose flour
1 tsp. baking powder
¼ c. water

1. Preheat oven to 325°F. Place a 10-inch tube pan in the oven for at least 5 minutes to heat. In a large bowl, beat egg whites with an electric mixer until foamy. Blend in cream of tartar. Add 3/4 cup sugar a little at a time, beating until stiff peaks form. In another bowl, beat yolks for 3 minutes. Gradually add ½ cup sugar and beat until pale yellow. Blend in juices and vanilla. Add dry ingredients alternately with water; mix well. Stir a little of the beaten whites into the mixture. Gently fold in remaining whites. Pour batter into preheated pan (do not grease). Bake at 325°F for 1 hour. Invert pan immediately; cool completely. To remove from pan, see method for Angel Food Cake (p. 334).

Yield: 12 servings. Cake can be frozen if carefully wrapped.

157 calories per serving, 1.4 g fat (0.4 g saturated), 53 g cholesterol, 4 g protein, 32 g carbohydrate, 99 mg sodium, 90 mg potassium, <1 mg iron, trace fiber, 10 mg calcium.

Almost Goldie's Marble Cake (Pareve)

Goldie Levitsky was my friend Rozie Brown's mother. She was a wonderful source of information when Second Helpings Please! *was written in the 1960s! Her measurements were sometimes vague, but we kept testing until we finally got things right. This light, luscious, low-fat version of her marvelous Marble Cake contains less than half the fat of the original. Perhaps Goldie would approve!*

4	eggs, separated
2	c. sugar
2	tsp. vanilla
¼	c. canola oil
½	c. unsweetened applesauce
2	c. flour (you can use part whole-wheat)
3	tsp. baking powder
⅛	tsp. salt
1	c. orange juice
¼	c. cocoa, sifted

1. Preheat oven to 350°F. Spray a 10-inch tube or Bundt pan with non-stick spray. Beat egg whites until stiff. Set aside. Combine egg yolks, sugar, vanilla, oil and applesauce. Beat until light, about 5 minutes. Combine flour, baking powder and salt; add to batter alternately with orange juice. Mix just until blended.

2. Gently fold in beaten egg whites. Divide batter in half. Gently mix cocoa into half of batter.

Alternately pour chocolate and white batters into pan. Cut through batter with a knife in 5 or 6 places to make a swirled design.

3. Bake at 350°F for 1 hour and 10 minutes. A cake tester inserted should come out clean with no batter clinging to it. Let cool for 20 minutes. Invert cake onto a platter and remove from pan.

Yield: 18 servings. Cake freezes well. If desired, drizzle with Decadent Chocolate Glaze (p. 366).

194 calories per serving, 4.5 g fat (0.7 g saturated), 47 mg cholesterol, 3 g protein, 36 g carbohydrate, 70 mg sodium, 101 mg potassium, 1 mg iron, <1 g fiber, 11 mg calcium.

• **This cake was also tested** with 1¾ cups sugar, but my tasters preferred the sweeter version. The choice is yours!

Streusel Poppy Seed Bundt Cake (Dairy)

Blima Posluns convinced me to slim down this recipe, and I'm so glad I did. The original recipe called for one cup of butter, but you'll never miss the fat in this enlightened version. Excellent!

⅓	c. sugar (white or brown)
2	tsp. cinnamon
2	tsp. cocoa
⅓	c. poppy seeds
1	c. buttermilk (or 1 tbsp. lemon juice plus enough milk to make 1 cup)
⅓	c. tub margarine
4	eggs, separated
⅔	c. unsweetened applesauce or fruit purée (e.g. Lighter Bake)

2   tsp. vanilla
1½ c. sugar, divided
2½ c. flour (you can use part whole-wheat)
2   tsp. baking powder
1   tsp. baking soda

1. In a small bowl, combine ⅓ cup sugar with cinnamon and cocoa. Add poppy seeds to buttermilk and let soak for 15 minutes. Preheat oven to 350°F. Spray a 10-inch Bundt pan with non-stick spray.

2. In the large bowl of an electric mixer, combine margarine, egg yolks, applesauce and vanilla with 1 cup of sugar. Beat until light and fluffy, about 5 minutes. Combine flour, baking powder and baking soda. Add to batter alternately with buttermilk/poppy seed mixture.

3. Using clean, dry beaters, beat egg whites in a glass or stainless bowl until soft peaks form. Gradually add remaining ½ cup sugar; beat until stiff but not dry. Gently fold egg whites into batter.

4. Pour half of batter into prepared pan. Sprinkle with cinnamon mixture. Top with remaining batter. Bake at 350°F for 50 to 55 minutes. A cake tester inserted near the center should come out clean. Cool cake for 15 to 20 minutes before removing from pan.

Yield: 18 servings. Can be frozen.

218 calories per serving, 6 g fat (1.3 g saturated), 55 mg cholesterol, 4 g protein, 37 g carbohydrate, 156 mg sodium, 101 mg potassium, 1 mg iron, 1 g fiber, 68 mg calcium.

Lemon Poppy Seed Cake (Pareve)

Moist and lemony with a slight crunch from poppy seeds, this sin-free cake is a winner! You need two large, juicy lemons for this recipe, one for the cake, the other for the syrup. I used 3/4 cup of liquid egg whites from the carton to make the cake, but you can substitute fresh eggs if you prefer.

1   tbsp. fresh lemon rind
½ c. fresh lemon juice, divided
¾ c. orange juice
⅓ c. poppy seeds
6   egg whites (or 3 eggs)
⅓ c. tub margarine or canola oil
⅔ c. unsweetened applesauce
1¼ c. sugar
2½ c. flour
2   tsp. baking powder
1   tsp. baking soda
6   additional tbsp. sugar

1. Grate rind from one large lemon and measure 1 tablespoon rind. Squeeze juice from 2 lemons. You should have ½ cup juice. Reserve ¼ cup lemon juice for glaze. Combine remaining ¼ cup lemon juice with orange juice. Add poppy seeds and let soak for 15 minutes. Preheat oven to 350°F. Spray a 10-inch Bundt pan with non-stick spray.

2. In the processor or an electric mixer, combine egg whites, margarine, applesauce and 1¼ cups sugar. Beat until light, about 3 minutes. Combine flour with baking powder and baking soda. Add to batter along with lemon rind. Pour poppy seed mixture over flour mixture. Mixture will bubble and fizz, but that's okay! Process with quick on/offs, just until flour disappears.

3. Pour batter into prepared pan. Bake at 350°F for 50 to 60 minutes. A cake tester inserted near the center should come out clean. Just before cake is done, prepare lemon syrup. Combine remaining 6 tablespoons sugar with the reserved ¼ cup lemon juice and heat gently, stirring to dissolve sugar.

4. Remove cake from oven. Poke holes into the top of hot cake with a metal skewer. Use a brush and slowly brush half of the lemon syrup over the hot cake. It will take about 5 minutes. Let cake cool in pan for 15 to 20 minutes. Then invert cake onto a large piece of foil and remove pan. Poke holes into the rest of the cake and slowly brush with remaining syrup. When completely cool, wrap cake in foil and let stand at least 12 hours before serving so that cake will absorb the lemon syrup.

Yield: 18 servings. Cake can be frozen.

194 calories per serving, 4.6 g fat (0.6 g saturated), 0 mg cholesterol, 4 g protein, 35 g carbohydrate, 161 mg sodium, 86 mg potassium, 1 mg iron, 1 g fiber, 45 mg calcium.

Blueberry Streusel Coffee Cake

1. Prepare batter and topping as directed for Nancy's Blueberry Streusel Muffins (p. 326). Pour into a sprayed 8-inch square baking pan. Sprinkle with topping. Bake at 350°F for 45 to 50 minutes.

Yield: 12 servings. Freezes well.

226 calories per serving, 5.1 g fat (0.6 g saturated), 18 mg cholesterol, 3 g protein, 43 g carbohydrate, 120 mg sodium, 93 mg potassium, 1 mg iron, 1 g fiber, 48 mg calcium.

Used-to-Be Sour Cream Coffee Cake

This is still a wonderful tasting cake, with no sacrifice in flavor! Sour cream has been replaced by skim milk plus lemon juice, the fat in the original cake has been reduced from ¾ cup to ⅓ cup and the nuts have been decreased from 1 cup to ¼ cup.

Filling:
- ¼ c. pecans or walnuts
- ½ c. brown sugar, packed
- 2 tsp. cinnamon
- 1 tbsp. unsweetened cocoa
- 3 tbsp. wheat germ, optional

Batter:
- 1 tbsp. lemon juice plus skim milk to equal 1½ cups
- ¼ c. tub margarine
- ½ c. unsweetened applesauce
- 1½ c. granulated sugar
- 2 eggs plus 2 egg whites (or 3 eggs)
- 2 tsp. vanilla
- 3 c. flour (you can use part whole wheat)
- 1½ tsp. baking powder
- 1½ tsp. baking soda

1. Combine filling ingredients in the processor and process with quick on/off turns to start, then let machine run about 20 to 25 seconds, until nuts are coarsely ground. Empty and rinse processor bowl.

2. Combine lemon juice with milk and set aside. Beat margarine with applesauce, sugar, eggs, egg whites and vanilla until well mixed, about 3 to 4 minutes. Add half of milk mixture and half of dry ingredients. Process just until blended, about 10 seconds. Add remaining milk and dry ingredients and process a few seconds longer.

3. Spray a 10-inch Bundt pan with non-stick spray.

Pour in $\frac{1}{3}$ of the batter. Sprinkle with $\frac{1}{3}$ of the filling. Repeat twice more, ending with filling. Bake in a preheated 350°F oven for 50 to 55 minutes, until cake tests done. Let cool 15 minutes before inverting cake to remove it from pan. If desired, turn cake over so that filling is on top.

Yield: 20 servings. Freezes well.

198 calories per serving, 4.1 g fat (0.7 g saturated), 22 mg cholesterol, 4 g protein, 37 g carbohydrate, 160 mg sodium, 107 mg potassium, 1 mg iron, <1 g fiber, 37 mg calcium.

- **Decadent Variation:** Add $\frac{1}{4}$ to $\frac{1}{3}$ cup semi-sweet chocolate chips to filling. Sprinkle over the filling between two of the layers, but not on top of cake. Bake as directed. One serving contains 212 calories, 4.9 g fat (1.2 g saturated) and 39 g carbohydrate.
- **You can substitute** $1\frac{1}{2}$ cups buttermilk, non-fat or low-fat sour cream or yogurt for the lemon juice/skim milk mixture.
- **Lactose-Free Variation:** Substitute 1 tablespoon lemon juice plus enough soy milk to equal $1\frac{1}{2}$ cups.

Chocolate Mint Leaves

See photo (P-15). Unlike most other chocolate leaves, these are unique because the leaf is eaten together with the chocolate coating! Mint leaves are edible. Have a little folacin with your chocolate!

3   oz. bittersweet or semisweet chocolate
18   large, fresh mint leaves

1. Melt chocolate on low heat in a double boiler (or microwave chocolate on MEDIUM power for 2 minutes; stir. Then microwave on MEDIUM 1 minute longer, until barely melted.) Let cool to just below body temperature, stirring occasionally.

2. Meanwhile, wash mint leaves thoroughly. Dry very well with paper towels. Line a cookie sheet with aluminum foil. Dip mint leaf completely in melted chocolate. Both sides of the leaf should be coated. Let excess chocolate drip back into the bowl. Place leaves on foil-lined tray and refrigerate until set. Use to decorate the top of cheesecake and around edges of serving plate.

Yield: 18 leaves. These will keep in the refrigerator up to 2 days.

20 calories per leaf, 1.7 g fat (0.9 g saturated), 0 mg cholesterol, trace protein, 2 g carbohydrate, trace sodium, 26 mg potassium, trace iron, trace fiber, 3 mg calcium.

Strawberry Cheesecake With Chocolate Mint Leaves

See photo (P-15). Absolutely sensational!

$1\frac{1}{4}$ c. graham cracker crumbs
3   tbsp. melted tub margarine, canola oil or butter
$\frac{1}{2}$ tsp. cinnamon
2   tbsp. orange juice
2   tbsp. sugar
1   lb. (500 g) light cream cheese
1   lb. (500 g) dry cottage cheese (non-fat)
$1\frac{1}{4}$ c. sugar
2   eggs plus 4 egg whites (or 4 eggs)
1   tbsp. lemon juice (or 1 tsp. vanilla)
4   c. strawberries, washed, hulled & dried
$\frac{1}{2}$ c. apricot preserves (reduced-sugar)
1   tbsp. orange-flavored liqueur
Chocolate Mint Leaves (p. 348), optional

1. Preheat oven to 350°F. On the lower oven rack, place a baking pan partly filled with water. Spray a 10-inch springform pan with non-stick spray. In a medium bowl, combine crumbs, margarine, cinnamon, orange juice and 2 tablespoons sugar. Press evenly into the bottom of prepared pan.

2. In the processor or electric mixer, beat cream cheese, cottage cheese and 1¼ cups sugar until smooth and blended. Add eggs and egg whites. Beat just until well mixed, scraping down sides of bowl once or twice. (If you overbeat after adding the eggs, cheesecake will rise during baking, then fall back and crack.) Blend in lemon juice. Pour mixture over crust.

3. Place cheesecake on middle rack of oven and bake for 45 to 55 minutes at 350°F. (The pan of water helps prevent cheesecake from cracking during baking.) When done, edges will be golden and set, but the center will be slightly jiggly. Turn off oven, open door partially and allow cheesecake to cool in the oven for an hour. Cheesecake will firm up as it stands. Let cool. Cover and refrigerate. (Cheesecake can be made up to 2 days in advance before topping it with strawberries.)

4. Using a flexible metal spatula or knife, carefully loosen cheesecake from sides of springform pan. Remove sides of pan, but do not remove the metal base. Place on a flat serving plate. Wash, hull and dry strawberries; set aside. Heat apricot preserves with orange liqueur just until melted, about 45 seconds on HIGH in the microwave. Strain if nec-

De-Lightful Desserts!

- In your desserts, substitute lightly sweetened Firm Yogurt Cheese (p. 53) for whipped cream.
- Frozen yogurt, sherbet, gelato or fat-reduced ice cream can replace higher-fat ice cream.
- Fruit-flavored yogurts usually contain a lot of sugar. It's better to add your own fresh fruit to unflavored non-fat yogurt (e.g., sliced apples, bananas, strawberries, mango, melon, etc.).
- Flavors with the illusion of sweetness are pure vanilla, almond extract, nutmeg and cinnamon.
- Substitute orange or lime rind instead of lemon rind for an interesting flavor.
- A little bit of chocolate goes a long way to making you feel better when you feel depressed. Chocolate contains phenylethylamine, the same chemical produced by humans when they are in love. That's the reason many people binge on chocolate when suffering from a broken heart!
- Cocoa heals a hurting heart the same way as pure chocolate, without the damage or fat. My favorite snack when I'm blue is a cup of cocoa. It calms me down and feels like a big warm hug! Fat-Free Chocolate Pudding (p. 353) is another comforting delight.
- To remove the sulphates used as a preservative in packaged dried fruits (e.g., apricots, raisins), pour boiling water over the fruit and let soak for at least half an hour. Drain and rinse thoroughly.
- Quick Fruit Compote: Combine 3 cups of mixed dried fruits (e.g. prunes, apricots, raisins) in a microsafe glass bowl. Add either water, apple or cranberry juice to cover the top of fruit by at least 1 inch. Microwave covered on HIGH for 10 to 12 minutes, stirring once or twice. When cool, refrigerate. Liquid becomes sweeter the longer it stands.
- Quick Granola Baked Apples: Core 4 large apples and place them in a microsafe baking dish. Fill each one with 2 to 3 tablespoons low-fat granola. Microwave uncovered on HIGH for 6 to 8 minutes.

essary. Brush top of chilled cheesecake with a very thin layer of apricot glaze. Arrange berries in an attractive design on top of cheesecake. Brush with remaining glaze. Garnish with Chocolate Mint Leaves. Refrigerate several hours before serving. Cut with a sharp, serrated knife.

Yield: 18 servings. Do not freeze.

230 calories per serving (without garnish), 7.9 g fat (3.5 g saturated), 40 mg cholesterol, 8 g protein, 33 g carbohydrate, 241 mg sodium, 152 mg potassium, 1 mg iron, 1 g fiber, 54 mg calcium.

- **To reduce the carbs,** omit crust. Dust bottom of pan with 2 to 3 tablespoons of graham cracker crumbs in step 1.
- **For diabetics,** substitute 1¼ cups granular Splenda for the sugar in step 2.

Mini Cheesecakes

These mini cheesecakes are so versatile. They're smooth and decadent tasting, yet low in fat. I like to make them with Yogurt Cheese, which is fat-free and provides a wonderful creamy texture.

¼	c. non-fat sour cream (or 1½ c. non-fat yogurt)
1	lb. (500 g) dry cottage cheese (non-fat)
¾	c. granulated sugar
2	eggs (or 1 egg plus 2 egg whites)
1	tbsp. lemon juice
2	tsp. cornstarch
½	c. reduced-sugar jam (or 1 c. fresh berries)

1. If using yogurt, place it in a strainer lined with a paper coffee filter. Place over a bowl and let drain for 3 to 4 hours. You will have ¼ cup of Yogurt Cheese.

2. Preheat oven to 350°F. Beat cottage cheese with sugar until smooth and creamy, about 1 to 2 minutes. Add sour cream or Yogurt Cheese, eggs, lemon juice and cornstarch. Mix just until blended.

3. Line 12 muffin tins with paper baking cups. Fill 3/4-full with cheese mixture. Place muffin pan into a larger pan. Pour hot water into the larger pan to come halfway up the sides of the muffin pan. Bake at 350°F for 30 minutes, just until set. Cool to room temperature. Cover and chill for several hours or overnight. Top each cheesecake with a spoonful of your favorite jam. You could also use fresh blueberries, sliced strawberries or raspberries.

Yield: 12 mini cheesecakes. Do not freeze. These will keep for 2 or 3 days in the refrigerator.

117 calories per serving (with 2 tsp. jam), 1 g fat (0.3 g saturated), 38 mg cholesterol, 6 g protein, 21 g carbohydrate, 132 mg sodium, 54 mg potassium, trace iron, trace fiber, 30 mg calcium.

- **Praline Cheesecakes:** Use firmly packed brown sugar instead of granulated sugar. Use 1 teaspoon vanilla instead of lemon juice. When cool, garnish each one with a pecan half.
- **Passover Mini Cheesecakes:** Substitute potato starch for cornstarch.
- **Diabetic Mini Cheesecakes:** Substitue Splenda for sugar.

Blima's Light & Luscious Cherry Cheesecake

1	c. graham cracker crumbs
2	tbsp. sugar

2 tbsp. canola oil
²/₃ c. sugar
¹/₃ c. flour
1 tbsp. cornstarch
1 tsp. vanilla
1 c. dry cottage cheese (non-fat)
8 oz. (250 ml) light cream cheese
2 eggs
¹/₂ c. skim milk
¹/₃ c. non-fat yogurt
3 egg whites
¹/₄ c. sugar
19 oz. can (540 ml) light cherry pie filling (or any fruit topping you like)

1. Preheat oven to 300°F. Spray a 9-inch spring-form pan with non-stick spray. Combine crumbs, 2 tablespoons sugar and oil. Press firmly into the bottom of pan. Combine ²/₃ cup sugar, flour, cornstarch, vanilla, cheeses and eggs. Beat until smooth. Add milk and yogurt. Beat egg whites until they form soft peaks. Gradually add remaining ¹/₄ cup of sugar and beat until stiff. Fold egg whites into cheesecake batter. Pour batter into pan.

2. Bake at 300°F for 55 minutes, or until almost set. Let cool. Cover and chill for at least 8 hours. Top with pie filling.

Yield: 16 servings. Do not freeze.

202 calories per serving, 6 g fat (2.2 g saturated), 36 mg cholesterol, 7 g protein, 31 g carbohydrate, 173 mg sodium, 119 mg potassium, <1 mg iron, <1 g fiber, 52 mg calcium.

Easy Graham Cracker Dessert

¹/₂ c. sugar
6 tbsp. cornstarch
4 c. skim milk
2 tsp. vanilla
36 single graham crackers
12 large ripe strawberries, to garnish

1. Combine sugar and cornstarch in a saucepan or large microsafe bowl. Slowly whisk in milk. Cook on medium heat, stirring often, until boiling and thickened. (Or microwave uncovered on HIGH for 8 to 10 minutes, stirring every 2 to 3 minutes.) Remove from heat and blend in vanilla.

2. Place 8 graham crackers in the bottom of a sprayed 6 x 10-inch oblong Pyrex casserole. Spread with 1 cup of pudding. Repeat to make 3 more layers. Crush the 4 remaining crackers and sprinkle on top of pudding. Chill overnight. Cut into squares. Garnish each one with a strawberry.

Yield: 12 servings. Do not freeze.

173 calories per serving, 2.5 g fat (0.1 g saturated), 2 mg cholesterol, 4 g protein, 34 g carbohydrate, 208 mg sodium, 188 mg potassium, <1 mg iron, <1 g fiber, 103 mg calcium.

Light 'n Luscious Strawberry Cheesecake Trifle (No-Bake)

See photo (P-14). So elegant and yummy, it's hard to believe it's low-fat! You need to plan ahead in order to make the Yogurt Cheese, but otherwise, this trifle is very quick and easy to make.

4	c. non-fat yogurt (or 2 c. Yogurt Cheese)
½	lb. (250 g) light cream cheese
½	lb. (250 g) dry cottage cheese (non-fat)
1	c. icing sugar
1	tbsp. lemon juice
5	Chocolate Cupcakes (p. 343)
3	c. strawberries, sliced (reserve a few whole berries for garnishing)
2	tbsp. grated semi-sweet chocolate, optional

1. To make Yogurt Cheese, line a strainer or sieve with cheesecloth, paper toweling or a large paper coffee filter. Place the strainer over a bowl. Spoon yogurt into the strainer. Cover and refrigerate for 3 hours. You will have about 2 cups of Yogurt Cheese. (The whey that drips into the bowl can be used to replace yogurt or buttermilk in baking, or add it to your bath water for a luxurious milk bath!)

2. In a processor or electric mixer, combine cream cheese with cottage cheese. Beat until smooth. Add icing sugar and lemon juice. Mix until thoroughly blended. Add Yogurt Cheese and mix just until smooth. Do not overbeat. Cut cupcakes into 1-inch cubes.

3. In the bottom of a pretty glass serving bowl, spread ⅓ of the cheese mixture. Arrange half of the cake cubes in a layer over cheese. Top with a layer of sliced strawberries. Repeat once again with cheese mixture, cake and strawberries. Top with remaining cheese mixture, forming peaks with the back of a spoon. Garnish with whole berries. If desired, sprinkle lightly with grated chocolate. Chill several hours or overnight before serving.

Yield: 16 servings. Do not freeze.

168 calories per serving, 4.3 g fat (2 g saturated), 10 mg cholesterol, 7 g protein, 26 g carbohydrate, 168 mg sodium, 188 mg potassium, <1 mg iron, 1 g fiber, 88 mg calcium.

- **If you prefer,** use half of an angel food cake (homemade or store-bought) instead of chocolate cupcakes. One serving of trifle will have 156 calories and 2.8 g fat (1.6 g saturated).
- **Strawberry Cheesecake Parfaits:** Prepare ingredients as directed above in Steps 1 and 2. Spoon a layer of cheese mixture into 8 or 10 parfait glasses. Top with cake cubes. Place strawberry slices so they stand upright around the edges of each glass. Top with remaining cheese mixture. Garnish with a strawberry and sprinkle with grated chocolate. Chill before serving.
- **Variation:** Other fruits can be substituted. Sliced kiwis, raspberries, blackberries or mandarin oranges will add fiber, flavor and decadence to this luscious dessert!

Guilt-Free Chocolate Trifle

Oh, this trifle is so de-lightful! The name tells it all.

	Fat-Free Chocolate Pudding (see following recipe)
4	c. low-calorie whipped topping mix (made with skim milk)
1	angel food cake (bought or homemade)
2	tbsp. coffee or chocolate-flavored liqueur

1. Prepare pudding as directed. Place a sheet of waxed paper directly on its surface to prevent a skin from forming. Cool completely. Prepare topping as directed on package. Set aside 1½ cups to decorate trifle. Combine remaining whipped topping with chilled pudding and mix well.

2. Cut cake into 1-inch chunks. Arrange ½ of cake in the bottom of a large glass serving bowl. Sprinkle lightly with liqueur. Pour in half of pudding mixture. Repeat with remaining cake chunks and pudding. Garnish with topping. Chill overnight.

Yield: 16 servings. Trifle can be made up to 2 days in advance.

169 calories per serving, 1.5 g fat (1.3 g saturated), <1 mg cholesterol, 5 g protein, 37 g carbohydrate, 130 mg sodium, 170 mg potassium, <1 mg iron, <1 g fiber, 47 mg calcium.

- **To cool the pudding** in half the time, transfer it to a shallow pan and cover with waxed paper.
- **For a decadent version** of this trifle, you could sprinkle some Skor toffee bits between the layers!

Fat-Free Chocolate Pudding

½ c. sugar
¼ c. unsweetened cocoa
3 tbsp. cornstarch or potato starch
⅛ tsp. salt
2¼ c. skim milk
1 tsp. vanilla (or 1 tbsp. coffee or chocolate-flavored liqueur)

1. Combine sugar, cocoa, cornstarch and salt in a saucepan (or large microsafe bowl). Slowly whisk

in milk. Cook on medium heat until boiling and thickened, stirring often to prevent sticking (or microwave uncovered on HIGH for 6 to 7 minutes, stirring every 2 to 3 minutes.) Stir in flavoring. Pour into individual dessert dishes and chill for several hours.

Yield: 4 servings. Makes enough to fill a 9-inch Cookie Crumb Crust (p. 383).

183 calories per serving, 1 g fat (0.6 g saturated), 3 mg cholesterol, 6 g protein, 40 g carbohydrate, 146 mg sodium, 313 mg potassium, <1 mg iron, 2 g fiber, 177 mg calcium.

- **If using artificial sweetener,** add it after cooking to prevent a bitter flavor. (Splenda can be added at the beginning of cooking.) One serving of pudding will contain 108 calories and 20 grams of carbohydrate.
- **If using potato starch,** be sure to stir the mixture often during cooking to prevent lumps.

Mom's Rice Pudding

It's best to use short-grain rice for this dessert for a creamy texture. Now that's comfort food!

1 c. water
½ c. short-grain rice
2 c. milk (skim or 1%)
3–4 tbsp. sugar
⅓ c. raisins, rinsed & drained
1 tsp. vanilla extract
½ tsp. cinnamon

1. Combine water and rice in a large, heavy-bottomed saucepan and bring to a boil. Cook uncovered for 20 minutes, until almost all of the water is

absorbed. Stir milk and sugar into rice. Heat slowly until mixture begins to bubble. Simmer uncovered for 30 to 40 minutes, stirring occasionally, until milk is mostly absorbed and mixture is thick and creamy. Remove from heat; stir in raisins and vanilla. Place in dessert dishes and sprinkle with cinnamon. It will thicken as it stands. Delicious hot or cold.

Yield: 5 to 6 servings. Leftovers will keep about 2 days in the refrigerator if well covered.

147 calories per serving, 0.3 g fat (0.2 g saturated), 2 mg cholesterol, 5 g protein, 32 g carbohydrate, 52 mg sodium, 247 mg potassium, <1 mg iron, <1 g fiber, 129 mg calcium.

• **Lactose-Free Variation:** Substitute rice milk or soy milk.

Quick'n Simple Rice Pudding

This recipe is ideal when you're short on time but are craving that old-fashioned taste.

6   serving size pkg. (170 g) vanilla pudding mix (not the "instant" kind)
3   c. skim or 1% milk
1¹/₂ c. cooked rice
¹/₂ c. raisins, rinsed & drained
³/₄ tsp. cinnamon
³/₄ tsp. vanilla extract

1. In a large microsafe glass bowl, combine pudding mix, milk and rice. Microwave uncovered on HIGH for 9 to 10 minutes, until boiling, stirring 2 or 3 times. Stir in raisins and cinnamon. Cover and let stand for 10 minutes. Stir in vanilla. Place in dessert dishes and refrigerate.

Yield: 8 servings. Do not freeze. Leftovers keep for 2 or 3 days in the refrigerator if well covered.

181 calories per serving, 0.4 g fat (0.2 g saturated), 2 mg cholesterol, 4 g protein, 41 g carbohydrate, 210 mg sodium, 248 mg potassium, <1 mg iron, <1 g fiber, 130 mg calcium.

• **Chocolate Rice Pudding:** Use chocolate pudding mix in the above recipe and omit the raisins.

Strawberry Surprise

One cup of strawberries contains 85 mg of vitamin C, more than an orange! Strawberries are packed with antioxidants and contain virtually no fat. One cup of berries contains 46 calories and more than 3 grams of fiber. Now that's very berry good news, and so are the desserts that follow!

3   c. non-fat natural yogurt (without gelatin or stabilizers)
4   c. ripe strawberries, hulled & sliced
2–3 tbsp. orange liqueur (e.g., Sabra)
3   tbsp. maple syrup or honey (to taste)

1. Line a strainer with a paper coffee filter, paper towelling or a cheesecloth. Place strainer over a large glass measuring cup or bowl. Spoon yogurt into strainer and let drain for 1 hour, or until yogurt has reduced to 2 cups. (Drained whey can be used instead of buttermilk or yogurt in baking.)

2. Sprinkle strawberries with liqueur and marinate for 30 minutes; drain. Fold half of berries into thickened yogurt. Sweeten to taste. Layer remaining berries and yogurt mixture in 6 parfait or wine glasses, starting and ending with berries. Chill before serving.

Yield: 6 servings. Leftovers can be refrigerated for up to 2 days if well-covered.

131 calories per serving, 0.6 g fat (0.1 g saturated), 2 mg cholesterol, 7 g protein, 24 g carbohydrate, 60 mg sodium, 382 mg potassium, trace iron, 2 g fiber, 171 mg calcium.

- **Variations:** If you don't have any orange liqueur on hand, substitute 2 tablespoons of white wine and 1 tablespoon orange juice. If desired, arrange a layer of peeled, sliced kiwis as the middle layer.
- **Strawberry Pudding Parfaits:** Instead of yogurt, substitute 1 pkg. (6 serving size) vanilla pudding mix. Cook according to package directions, using skim milk. Stir 1 tablespoon of orange liqueur into cooked pudding. Cover to prevent a skin from forming; chill. Layer marinated strawberries and pudding in parfait glasses. Chill before serving.
- **Strawberry & Ice Cream Parfaits:** Instead of drained yogurt, substitute low-fat ice cream (strawberry or vanilla) or frozen yogurt. Layer marinated strawberries and ice cream in parfait glasses. Serve immediately. (This is also scrumptious if you prepare the yogurt/berry mixture as directed in the main recipe and use it as a topping over the ice cream and strawberries!)

Strawberry & Banana Frozen Yogurt

For maximum flavor, use very ripe fruit for this recipe.

1	pint very ripe strawberries, hulled (or 2 cups unsweetened frozen berries)
3	very ripe medium bananas, peeled
½	c. non-fat yogurt
1	to 2 tbsp. honey (to taste)

1. Cut fruit into 1-inch pieces. Arrange in a single layer on a baking sheet and freeze for 2 or 3 hours, until firm. (Fruit can be frozen for several weeks in plastic storage bags.)

2. Place the processor bowl and Steel Knife into the freezer for 15 to 20 minutes. Combine all ingredients in chilled processor bowl. Process with quick on/offs to start, then let machine run until mixture is smooth. (If you have a small processor, do this in 2 batches.) Serve immediately, or transfer mixture to a serving bowl and freeze for up to ½ hour before serving.

Yield: 6 servings.

91 calories per serving, 0.5 g fat (0.1 g saturated), trace cholesterol, 2 g protein, 22 g carbohydrate, 17 mg sodium, 371 mg potassium, trace iron, 3 g fiber, 52 mg calcium.

Mock Banana Soft Ice Cream

2	large ripe bananas, sliced
½	c. non-fat cottage cheese, Firm Yogurt Cheese (p. 53) or part-skim ricotta cheese
½	tsp. vanilla
4	tsp. sugar

1. Arrange banana slices in a single layer on a waxed-paper lined plate. Cover and freeze until firm. Frozen slices can be frozen in a tightly sealed container for up to a month. (I've also frozen whole bananas in their skins, then removed them from the freezer at serving time and placed them under running water for 30 seconds. Peel with a sharp knife and cut into chunks.) At serving time, combine ingredients in the processor and process until smooth. Serve immediately.

Yield: 4 servings.

102 calories per serving, 0.3 g fat (0.1 g saturated), 3 mg cholesterol, 5 g protein, 22 g carbohydrate, 93 mg sodium, 300 mg potassium, trace iron, 2 g fiber, 19 mg calcium.

- **Mock Banana-Strawberry Soft Ice Cream:** Follow the recipe above, using 1 banana and 1½ cups ripe strawberries. One serving contains 82 calories and 16 g carbohydrate.
- **Easiest Frozen Banana Mousse:** Peel and slice 4 ripe bananas. Arrange in a single layer on a plate and cover tightly to prevent them from absorbing any odors. Freeze completely. When needed, thaw for 5 minutes, then process with 1 teaspoon of lemon juice in the processor until smooth. Serve immediately. Makes 4 servings.

Strawberry Buttermilk Sherbet

So pretty, so delicious! Leftover buttermilk can be used in muffin or cake recipes.

1½–2 c. frozen strawberries
¼ c. sugar or honey
¼–⅓ c. buttermilk
1 tsp. lemon juice

1. Process berries with sugar until the texture of snow. Gradually add buttermilk and lemon juice through the feed tube. Process until well mixed and the texture of sherbet. Serve immediately.

Yield: 3 to 4 servings. Recipe can be doubled easily.

99 calories per serving, 0.3 g fat (0.1 g saturated), <1 mg cholesterol, 1 g protein, 25 g carbohydrate, 23 mg sodium, 144 mg potassium, <1 mg iron, 2 g fiber, 36 mg calcium.

- **Either use 1 package** of frozen unsweetened strawberries (about 1½ cups), or freeze 2 cups of very ripe strawberries for this recipe. The more berries you use, the more buttermilk you need to add.
- **Raspberries can be used** instead of strawberries. No-fat yogurt can be used instead of buttermilk.

Pineapple Sherbet

Easy, light and refreshing, this quick sherbet is scrumptious.

1. Open a 14 oz. can (398 ml) of pineapple (crushed or tidbits) packed in natural juice. Spoon pineapple and juice into an ice cube tray. Freeze until nearly frozen, about 2 to 3 hours (or even overnight). Any canned fruit in its own juice can be substituted (e.g., peaches, apricots).

2. Just before serving time, process pineapple "ice cubes" in processor until the texture of sherbet. Scrape down sides of bowl 2 or 3 times. Serve immediately. If desired, garnish with fresh berries or mint leaves. (If you are not worried about raw egg whites, blend 1 egg white into pineapple slush.)

Yield: 3 servings. To double the recipe, process in two batches.

88 calories per serving, 0.1 g fat (0 g saturated), 0 mg cholesterol, <1 g protein, 23 g carbohydrate, 2 mg sodium, 178 mg potassium, trace iron, 1 g fiber, 20 mg calcium.

- **A large, very ripe fresh pineapple** can be substituted. Cut it into quarters. Cut away the skin and hard core. Slice thinly and freeze for several hours or overnight in a tightly sealed container. Process pineapple slices until the texture of sherbet, scraping down sides of bowl as needed. Sweeten with a little honey or maple syrup. Serve immediately.
- **Other frozen fruits** can be processed with the pineapple (e.g., ripe bananas or strawberries).

Mango Meringue Shells

No, this isn't a dance, although your guests will probably jump for joy when you serve this delectable dessert! Other flavors of frozen low-fat yogurt can be used, so you'll really have something to dance about!

4	egg whites (at room temperature)
½ tsp.	cream of tartar
½ tsp.	vanilla
1 c.	granulated or superfine sugar
4–5 c.	(1 liter) mango frozen low-fat yogurt (Haagen Daaz makes a luscious frozen yogurt)
	Strawberry or Raspberry Purée (p. 359)
1	large mango, peeled, pitted & sliced

1. Preheat oven to 250°F. Line a baking sheet with parchment paper or aluminum foil. Spray lightly with non-stick spray. In an electric mixer, beat egg whites until frothy. Add cream of tartar and vanilla; beat at high speed until soft peaks form. Gradually add sugar a tablespoon or two at a time, beating until stiff peaks are formed. Mixture will look like marshmallow.

2. Spoon meringue onto the prepared baking sheet to make 8 mounds. Use the back of a spoon to build up the sides and shape each mound into a 3-inch shell. Bake at 250°F for 1 hour, until crisp and dry. Turn off oven, keep door closed and let shells dry in the oven for an hour. Cool completely.

3. A few minutes before serving time, remove frozen yogurt from the freezer. Let stand at room temperature for a few minutes to soften (or microwave on HIGH for 20 seconds). Place meringue shells on individual serving plates. Fill each shell with a scoop of frozen yogurt. Drizzle with purée and garnish with mango slices.

Yield: 8 servings.

253 calories per serving, 1.5 g fat (0.9 g saturated), 5 mg cholesterol, 7 g protein, 55 g carbohydrate, 88 mg sodium, 364 mg potassium, trace iron, 1 g fiber, 163 mg calcium.

- **Use 1 teaspoon lemon juice** instead of cream of tartar. Perfect for Passover Meringue Shells (see next page).
- **Superfine sugar** dissolves more quickly than granulated sugar when making meringues. To make your own superfine sugar (also known as fruit sugar), process granulated sugar in the processor for 30 to 40 seconds.
- **Meringues can be** prepared in advance and frozen for a month, or stored at room temperature in a tightly closed container for a week or so. Fill shells at serving time. Each meringue shell contains 106 calories, 25 g carbohydrate, 0 g fat, 0 g cholesterol. Guilt-free pleasure!
- **For a "de-light-ful" dessert,** fill meringue shells with your favorite flavor of frozen yogurt or sorbet. Serve lemon sorbet with sliced kiwis or raspberries, orange sorbet with mandarin orange slices, strawberry or raspberry frozen yogurt with berries, or coffee yogurt with fat-free chocolate syrup.

- **Passover Meringue Shells:** Use Strawberry Surprise (p. 354) as the filling, but sweeten with honey instead of maple syrup for Passover. Fresh fruit salad also makes an refreshing filling.
- **Read Egg White Wisdom** (p. 335).

Blima Posluns' Lemon Mousse

They'll surely ask you for the recipe for this one! It's a winner. Blima always keeps a can of evaporated milk in the refrigerator so she can prepare this dessert at a moment's notice.

Graham Cracker Crust:
- 1½ c. graham cracker crumbs
- 3 tbsp. tub margarine, melted (or canola oil)
- 3 tbsp. orange juice
- 2 tbsp. sugar

Mousse Mixture:
- 12 oz. can (384 ml) 2% evaporated milk, chilled for 24 hours
- 3 oz. pkg. (85 g) lemon-flavored gelatin
- 1¼ c. boiling water
- ½ c. sugar
- Juice of 2 lemons

1. Preheat oven to 350°F. Spray a 9 x 13-inch Pyrex casserole or 10-inch spring form pan with non-stick spray. Combine ingredients for crust and mix well. Reserve ⅓ cup of mixture for topping. Press remainder into the bottom of pan and bake at 350°F for 5 to 7 minutes. Let cool. (Can be prepared in advance.)

2. Place can of milk in the refrigerator 24 hours in advance. Mix gelatin, boiling water and sugar with the juice of one lemon. Refrigerate until thick but not set, about 35 to 45 minutes.

3. In a large mixing bowl, beat chilled milk with juice of a lemon until soft peaks form, about 5 minutes. Combine with gelatin mixture and mix on medium speed of electric mixer until blended. Pour over crumb base. Sprinkle with reserved crumbs. Refrigerate for 6 to 8 hours before serving.

Yield: 18 servings. Freezing is not recommended.

125 calories per serving, 3.3 g fat (0.8 g saturated), 2 mg cholesterol, 3 g protein, 22 g carbohydrate, 117 mg sodium, 94 mg potassium, trace iron, trace fiber, 64 mg calcium.

- **If soft peaks** don't form when you whip the milk in Step 3, put the bowl and the milk in the freezer for a few minutes, until ice crystals form around the edges of the bowl.
- **Strawberry Mousse:** Substitute strawberry gelatin. Fold 2 cups of hulled, cut-up berries into mousse mixture. Assemble as directed. To garnish, arrange strawberry slices (or several whole raspberries) in a flower design on top of mousse. One serving contains 130 calories and 3.4 g fat.
- **Pineapple Lime Mousse:** Substitute lime gelatin. Fold 1½ cups of well-drained pineapple tidbits into mousse mixture. Nutrients are similar.
- **Sugar-free (diet) jello** and sugar substitute can be used in this recipe.

Strawberries with Balsamic Vinegar or Red Wine

The natural sugars in the berries and vinegar make a yummy syrup. Always rinse berries before you remove the stems. Otherwise, berries will become waterlogged.

2 pints strawberries
1 tbsp. orange juice or Grand Marnier
3 tbsp. balsamic vinegar or red wine
3 tbsp. brown sugar (or to taste)

1. Rinse, hull and slice berries. Mix gently with remaining ingredients. Refrigerate covered for at least ½ hour. (The longer they stand, the more delicious they become.)

Yield: 4 to 6 servings.

94 calories per serving, 0.6 g fat (0 g saturated), 0 mg cholesterol, 1 g protein, 23 g carbohydrate, 8 mg sodium, 283 mg potassium, <1 mg iron, 3 g fiber, 31 mg calcium.

Melons & Berries in Wine

A light and refreshing dessert, loaded with potassium and fiber.

1½ c. medium white wine
2 tbsp. honey or sugar
2–3 slices ginger root
½ of a medium cantaloupe, halved & seeded
½ of a honeydew, seeded
½ of a Casaba or Crenshaw melon, seeded
2 c. fresh strawberries, hulled & halved
1–2 c. fresh blueberries

1. In a saucepan, combine wine with honey and ginger. Bring to a boil, reduce heat and simmer uncovered for 5 minutes. Remove from heat and let cool to room temperaure. Discard ginger.

2. Use a melon baller to scoop out balls from the melons. Place in a large bowl along with the strawberries and blueberries. Pour the cooled wine over fruit and mix gently. Refrigerate for 1 to 2 hours to blend the flavors. Spoon fruit into chilled serving dishes. Drizzle wine over fruit.

Yield: 8 servings.

162 calories per serving, 0.6 g fat (0.1 g saturated), 0 mg cholesterol, 3 g protein, 33 g carbohydrate, 40 mg sodium, 876 mg potassium, 1 mg iron, 4 g fiber, 30 mg calcium.

- **Half a cantaloupe supplies** nearly double the daily recommended intake of vitamin C. It will provide as much vitamin C as 1½ oranges. Cantaloupe is also a great source of beta carotene. So save the other half of the cantaloupe for a mega-healthy breakfast. The vitamin C in the melon enhances iron absorption from your bowl of cereal.
- **Super Smoothie:** Combine the flesh of ½ canteloupe, ½ melon, 1 banana, 8 strawberries and a few ice cubes in the blender or processor. Makes 2 servings.

Strawberry or Raspberry Purée

Perfect over pancakes, blintzes, waffles, frozen yogurt, fresh fruit or cake.

2 c. ripe strawberries or raspberries
2–3 tbsp. honey or sugar
1 tsp. Grand Marnier, optional

1. Purée berries until smooth. Sweeten with honey or sugar. (Raspberries should be strained through a sieve to remove seeds.) If desired, blend in Grand Marnier.

Yield: about 1½ cups. Can be frozen.

9 calories per tbsp., 0 g fat (0 g saturated), 0 mg cholesterol, trace protein, 2 g carbohydrate, trace sodium, 23 mg potassium, trace iron, trace fiber, 2 mg calcium.

Homemade Applesauce

See photo (P-8). Applesauce makes a wonderful accompaniment to potato latkas, or is a simple, delicious dessert on its own. My Baba Masha always added a ripe pear. Her applesauce was the best!

8   medium apples
1   Bartlett pear, optional
¼   c. water or apple juice
3–4 tbsp. sugar (or equivalent sweetener)
1   tsp. cinnamon

1. Peel and core the apples and pear. Cut them into chunks. Combine all ingredients (except artificial sweetener, if using) in a large saucepan. Bring to a boil, reduce heat to simmer and cook partially covered for 20 to 25 minutes, until tender. (To microwave, cook covered on HIGH power for 6 to 8 minutes, or until tender. Stir once or twice during cooking.) Break up applesauce with a spoon, or serve it chunky.

Yield: 6 servings. Freezes well.

124 calories per serving, 0.8 g fat (0.1 g saturated), 0 mg cholesterol, <1 g protein, 32 g carbohydrate, 2 mg sodium, 166 mg potassium, trace iron, 5 g fiber, 14 mg calcium.

• **If you have a food mill,** cook apples without peeling; wash well before cooking and discard stems. After cooking, put mixture through a food mill. Applesauce will be rosy pink.
• **If using apple juice,** use minimum amount of sugar or sweetener. If you want apples to keep their shape, add sugar after cooking, not before. If using sweetener, add after cooking.
• **Applesauce with Mixed Fruits Compote:** Use your favorite combination of fruits (e.g., apples, pears, blueberries, strawberries, rhubarb, peaches, plums, nectarines) for a delicious dessert.
• **Rella's Blueberry Apple Sauce:** Add 2 cups of blueberries 5 minutes before end of cooking time.
• **Pat Richman's Easiest Pink Apple Sauce:** Add a 16 oz. (425 gram) package thawed sliced strawberries (or raspberries) in syrup to a 28 oz. (796 ml) jar of applesauce. Serve in sherbet glasses. Pretty luscious! (Thanks to Devah Wine for sharing a "taste memory.")

Barbecue Fruit'n Cream

Easy and decadent. Calci-yummy!

3   tbsp. maple syrup
2   c. sliced fresh peaches, nectarines and/or pears
2   c. vanilla frozen low-fat yogurt

1. Drizzle maple syrup over fruit. Wrap in heavy-duty aluminum foil, seal well to make a package and heat for 20 minutes on the dying embers of your BBQ. Serve piping hot over frozen yogurt.

Yield: 4 servings. Leftover fruit can be refrigerated for a day or two and reheated in the microwave.

236 calories per serving, 2.6 g fat (1.5 g saturated), 45 mg cholesterol, 9 g protein, 46 g carbohydrate, 56 mg sodium, 198 mg potassium, trace iron, 2 g fiber, 308 mg calcium.

Simply Ambrosia

10 oz. (285 ml) can pineapple tidbits, drained
3 large seedless oranges, peeled & cut in ½" chunks
1 c. seedless grapes
2 c. strawberries, halved
3 c. miniature marshmallows
3 c. low-fat lemon yogurt
6 chocolate cookies, crushed

1. Pat fruit dry. Combine fruit, marshmallows and yogurt in a bowl; mix gently. Transfer to a glass serving bowl and sprinkle with cookie crumbs. Cover and chill overnight.

Yield: 12 servings.

149 calories per serving, 1.5 g fat (0.6 g saturated), 3 mg cholesterol, 5 g protein, 32 g carbohydrate, 64 mg sodium, 327 mg potassium, <1 mg iron, 2 g fiber, 134 mg calcium.

Citrus or Melon Baskets

- **Basket without Handle:** Trim top and bottom of citrus fruit or melon to form a stable base at both ends. Cut in half with a V-shaped knife (or make uniform zigzag cuts with a sharp knife), cutting all the way through to the center. Adjust the last cut to meet the first cut. Separate the halves. Use a melon baller to hollow out melon. Pulp from citrus fruit can be removed with a sharp paring knife or grapefruit knife. Fill grapefruit, orange or melon baskets with colorful fresh fruit salad.
- **Basket with Handle:** Trim bottom of fruit to form a stable base. Cut away two wedges from the top side so you are left with a handle in the middle of the basket. Make uniform zigzag cuts around basket and handle with a V-shaped or sharp knife, adjusting the last cut to meet the first cut. (Don't cut through the handle!) Cut away pulp under the handle with a sharp knife. Remove pulp, leaving a shell that is firm enough to hold the filling. Use a small ice cream scoop for watermelon, a melon baller for smaller melons and a grapefruit knife for citrus fruit. A few hours in advance, fill as desired. Trim the handle with overlapping citrus slices anchored with toothpicks. Top each toothpick with a grape or strawberry. Refrigerate until serving time.

Sweet Endings: Squares, Cookies & Pastries

Sweet Delights

- Life is short, so eat dessert first! Yes, there's still room in our lives for a little decadence! If you're faced with temptation, your best choice is a dessert based on fresh fruits. Limit rich desserts, but if you must indulge, eat a small portion, very, very slowly! Savor every mouthful.
- The average North American consumes 1½ pounds of sugar a week. How sweet life is! Sugar is a simple carbohydrate which is hidden in many prepared foods. It has little in the way of nutrients.
- Decrease the sugar called for in your favorite recipes. Start with a 25 percent reduction, then taste to see if flavor and texture have been compromised. Sometimes sugar can be reduced by up to 50 percent.
- Sugar substitutes (artificial sweeteners) can be used in many recipes, but I prefer to use some sugar. When I use a sugar substitute in baking, my guideline is to use ½ cup sugar plus ½ cup of sweetener for each cup of granulated sugar. See How Sweet It Is! (p. 36).
- Sugar creates moisture and volume in baking recipes. Sugar substitutes are often starch-based, resulting in lower-volumed items. Finished baked goods may be drier, so you might have to increase the amount of liquid. It's often a matter of trial and error!
- Saccharin-based sweeteners become bitter when heated. Sweeteners based on aspartame (Equal/Nutrasweet) often lose their sweetening power during baking.
- When using sugar substitutes, I usually use the ones that look and pour like sugar (e.g. Splenda). One teaspoon sweetener equals 1 teaspoon sugar. When using individual packets, read label for sweetening equivalents. Some are equal to 1 teaspoon sugar while others are equal to 2 teaspoons sugar.
- Substitute liquid sugar substitute for liquid sugar (e.g. honey, maple syrup, molasses). Substitute powdered sugar substitute for sugar or brown sugar.
- Fructose is a sweetener derived from the natural sugars in fruit, honey and invert sugar. It's 1½ times sweeter than sugar and is metabolized more slowly. Fructose is found in natural food stores.
- Fruit purées like unsweetened applesauce and Prune Purée (p. 334) will lower the fat by at least half. As a bonus, Prune Purée is loaded with fiber!
- Health experts recommend 20 to 35 grams of fiber a day. Add oat bran, wheat bran and wheat germ to muffins, quickbreads, cookies and toppings for fruit crisps.
- To increase the fiber and tenderness in baked goods, replace half of the flour with whole-wheat flour. Another way to make baked goods more nutritious is to remove 2 tablespoons all-purpose flour from each cup called for in the recipe and replace with soy flour or wheat germ.
- Decrease the fat in your favorite recipes. Use non-fat or low-fat products wherever possible.
- Buttermilk, yogurt and low-fat sour cream can be substituted for each other in baking.
- Buttermilk is similar in fat content to skim milk, despite its high fat name!
- Substitute skim or 1% milk (or evaporated skim milk) for whole milk for baking and desserts.
- Instead of rich, fat-laden pie crusts, use Cookie Crumb Crust (p. 383).
- Better than Butter (p. 125) replaces butter to make an excellent reduced-fat pastry dough. The New Cream Cheese Pastry (p. 374) is an example.
- Use non-stick vegetable spray to coat baking pans. However, sprays are made mainly from vegetable oils. A one-third second spray contains over ¼ gram of fat, so spray lightly, my friend!
- Non-stick baking pans are great for low-fat baking and easy cleaning. If using dark or glass baking pans, lower oven temperature called for in the recipe by 25°F.
- Read Baking the Low-Fat Way (p. 333) and Substitutions & Alternatives in Low-Fat, Low-Cholesterol Baking (p. 336) for more ideas on low-fat baking techniques.

Fudgy-Wudgy Brownies

See photo (P-10). These brownies are decadent and delectable, even without icing. For very special occasions, ice them with Decadent Chocolate Glaze. Enjoy!

¾ c. flour
½ c. plus 2 tsp. unsweetened cocoa
⅛ tsp. salt
½ tsp. instant coffee granules
¾ tsp. baking powder
2 tbsp. tub margarine or butter, melted
3 tbsp. unsweetened applesauce or Prune Purée (p. 334)
¾ c. granulated sugar
½ c. brown sugar, firmly packed
1 egg plus 2 egg whites (or 2 eggs)
1 tsp. coffee liqueur or vanilla

1. Preheat oven to 325°F. Combine flour, cocoa, salt, instant coffee and baking powder. Mix well. Add remaining ingredients and blend well, about 1 to 2 minutes. Spread batter evenly in a sprayed 8-inch square Pyrex baking pan. Bake at 325°F for about 25 minutes. The top should be set when touched with your fingertips, and if you insert a toothpick in the center, it will come out slightly moist. Do not overbake or brownies will be dry.

Yield: 25 brownies. Freezes well.

72 calories per brownie (without glaze), 1.4 g fat (0.4 g saturated), 9 mg cholesterol, 1 g protein, 15 g carbohydrate, 40 mg sodium, 61 mg potassium, <1 mg iron, <1 g fiber, 8 mg calcium.

• **Optional:** Glaze the cooled brownies with Decadent Chocolate Glaze (below). Cut into squares. (Freeze them first for 45 minutes so they'll be easier to cut.) If glazed, each brownie contains 86 calories, 2.3 g fat (0.9 g saturated), 9 g cholesterol and 16 g carbohydrate.

• **Variation:** Sprinkle 3 tablespoons chopped almonds or pecans over the top of brownies before baking.

Decadent Chocolate Glaze

Although no fat is added, chocolate naturally contains some. A little glaze goes a long way! An excellent glaze for Brownies (above), or to drizzle over your favorite chocolate cake or Bundt cake.

2 squares bittersweet or semi sweet chocolate (2 oz/ 56 g)
1 tbsp. honey or corn syrup
1½ tbsp. hot water or coffee
½ tsp. vanilla or coffee liqueur

1. Melt chocolate over low heat, or microwave on MEDIUM (50 percent power) for about 2 minutes, stirring once or twice. Blend in remaining ingredients. Mixture will be quite liquid. Pour over brownies, tipping pan so they are completely glazed. Freeze for about 45 minutes for easier slicing.

Yield: Makes enough glaze for an 8-inch square pan of brownies to serve 25.

14 calories per serving, 0.9 g fat (0.5 g saturated), 0 mg cholesterol, trace protein, 2 g carbohydrate, trace sodium, 15 mg potassium, trace iron, trace fiber, 1 mg calcium.

Apricot Almond Squares

Crust:
- 1¼ c. all-purpose flour
- ¼ c. cornstarch
- ⅓ c. tub margarine or butter, cut up
- ⅓ c. sugar
- 3 tbsp. non-fat or low-fat yogurt

Filling:
- 1½ c. apricot preserves (sugar-reduced or all-fruit preserves)
- ¼ c. lemon juice
- ¼ c. sliced almonds

1. Preheat oven to 350°F. In the processor, mix flour, cornstarch, margarine and sugar until fine. Add yogurt; process with quick on/off pulses, just until mixture is crumbly. Reserve ½ cup crumbs. Press the remainder firmly into the bottom of a sprayed 9 x 13-inch baking pan. Bake at 350°F for 18 to 20 minutes, until golden.

2. Combine filling ingredients and mix well. Spread evenly over baked crust. Sprinkle with reserved crumb mixture. Bake 15 minutes longer, until set. Cool completely. Cut into squares.

Yield: 48 squares. These freeze very well.

53 calories per square, 1.6 g fat (0.3 g saturated), 0 mg cholesterol, <1 g protein, 9 g carbohydrate, 14 mg sodium, 18 mg potassium, trace iron, trace fiber, 5 mg calcium.

Luscious Lemon Squares

See photo (P-10). This lighter version of fat-laden Lemon Squares is tart, lemony and yummy!

Crust:
- 1¼ c. all-purpose flour
- ¼ c. cornstarch
- ⅓ c. tub margarine or unsalted butter, cut in chunks
- ⅓ c. sugar
- 3 tbsp. non-fat or low-fat yogurt

Filling:
- 4 eggs (or 3 eggs plus 2 egg whites)
- 2 c. granulated sugar
- ¼–⅓ c. lemon juice
- ¼ c. all-purpose flour
- 1 tsp. baking powder

1. Preheat oven to 350°F. In the processor, mix flour, cornstarch, margarine and sugar until fine. Add yogurt. Process with quick on/off pulses, just until mixture is crumbly. Press firmly into the bottom of a sprayed 9 x 13-inch baking pan. Bake at 350°F for 18 to 20 minutes, until golden. Process ingredients for filling until blended. Pour over baked crust. Bake 25 to 30 minutes longer, until golden and set. When cool, cut into squares.

Yield: 48 squares. These freeze very well.

73 calories per square, 1.8 g fat (0.4 g saturated), 18 mg cholesterol, 1 g protein, 14 g carbohydrate, 22 mg sodium, 17 mg potassium, trace iron, trace fiber, 5 mg calcium.

Slimmer Hello Dollies

My dear daughter, Jodi Sprackman, adores these! I've reduced the fat substantially from the original recipe, but "Dolly" didn't say "Goodbye" to all the fat, so save them for special occasions. Low-fat sweetened condensed milk has half the fat of regular condensed milk, but almost the same calories!

- ⅓ c. tub margarine or butter
- 1⅓ c. graham cracker crumbs
- 1 c. flaked or shredded coconut
- ⅔ c. semi-sweet chocolate chips
- ½ c. pecans or almonds
- 14 oz. can (1⅓ cups/300 ml) sweetened condensed skim milk (low-fat)

1. Preheat oven to 350°F. Spray a 9 x 13-inch pan with non-stick spray. Put margarine in pan and place in the oven to melt. Mix in crumbs and spread evenly in pan. Sprinkle with coconut. Coarsely chop chocolate chips and pecans in processor. Sprinkle over coconut. Drizzle condensed milk evenly over the top. Bake at 350°F for 25 minutes, until golden. Cool completely. Cut into squares.

Yield: 4 dozen. Freeze leftovers, but seal your mouth with masking tape until they're packed away!

81 calories per square, 4.5 g fat (1.9 g saturated), 1 mg cholesterol, 1 g protein, 10 g carbohydrate, 40 mg sodium, 57 mg potassium, trace iron, <1 g fiber, 26 mg calcium.

Sweet Nothings (Sesame Kichel)

A family favorite from Winnipeg, with the fat reduced. Addictive!

- 3 eggs plus 2 egg whites
- ⅓ c. canola oil
- 3 tbsp. sugar (or use artificial sweetener)
- 1⅔ c. plus 2 tbsp. flour
- ¾ c. sesame seeds mixed with 3 tbsp. sugar (poppy seeds can be substituted)

1. Preheat oven to 500°F. Line 1 or 2 baking sheets with foil; spray with non-stick spray. Beat eggs, egg whites and sugar in processor for 30 seconds. Pour oil through feed tube while machine is running; process 1 minute longer. Add flour by heaping spoonfuls through feed tube while machine is running. Process 40 seconds more. Dough will be very sticky and machine will begin to slow down. Drop blobs of dough by scant teaspoonfuls into sesame seed/sugar mixture, pushing dough from tip of spoon with another spoon or rubber spatula. Coat with sesame seeds. (If desired, gently stretch and twist dough into finger-shapes; coat again with seeds.) Place 2 inches apart on prepared baking sheets.

2. Place cookies on middle rack of oven. Immediately reduce temperature to 400°F. Bake for 8 minutes, or until golden. Reduce heat to 300°F; bake 10 minutes more, until the color of coffee with cream. Shut off heat and let dry in oven 20 minutes. They will be puffed, light and crispy.

Yield: 48 kichel (cookies). These freeze very well (if you're quick!) or store them in cookie tins.

53 calories per cookie, 2.9 g fat (0.4 g saturated), 13 mg cholesterol, 1 g protein, 6 g carbohydrate, 9 mg sodium, 19 mg potassium, trace iron, <1 g fiber, 5 mg calcium.

Tayglach

These honeyed treats are traditionally served for Rosh Hashonah. Tayglach can be cut into diamonds, rolled into clusters or served in syrup (see Variation below). They are very sweet, so eat with caution!

3 eggs (or 2 eggs plus 2 egg whites)
2 tbsp. canola oil
1½ c. flour
Pinch of salt
¼ tsp. baking powder
¼ tsp. ground ginger
1 c. liquid honey
1 c. sugar
¼ tsp. additional ground ginger
½ c. walnuts, coarsely chopped
Unsweetened coconut, optional

1. Preheat oven to 350°F. Line a large cookie sheet with aluminum foil. Spray with non-stick spray. Combine eggs and oil in a mixing bowl or food processor. Mix well. Add flour, salt, baking powder and ¼ teaspoon ginger. Mix to make a soft dough.

2. Turn out onto a floured board and knead briefly, until smooth and not sticky. Break off pieces of dough and roll into pencil-thin ropes. Cut into ½-inch marble-sized pieces. Place dough pieces on cookie sheet, not touching each other. You should have 80 to 90 pieces, depending upon size. Bake at 350°F for 12 to 15 minutes, until bottoms are lightly browned.

3. While tayglach are baking, combine honey, sugar and remaining ginger in a large pot. Cook on low heat, stirring occasionally, until boiling. Reduce heat and simmer uncovered until sugar is dissolved, stirring occasionally, about 5 minutes.

4. Carefully add a few baked tayglach at a time to hot syrup. Simmer for 5 minutes. Add nuts and cook 10 minutes longer, stirring often. When done, tayglach should be golden brown and crisp.

5. Spoon tayglach and syrup onto a wet cutting board. Flatten into a single layer. Let cool until syrup begins to hold together and mixture is cool enough to handle. Either cut into 1-inch diamonds or roll into 3-inch balls. Roll in coconut, if desired. Serve in candy paper cups.

Yield: Makes about 30 diamonds or 3-inch balls. Store in a single layer to keep them from sticking together. Do not freeze.

112 calories per diamond, 2.7 g fat (0.4 g saturated), 21 mg cholesterol, 2 g protein, 21 g carbohydrate, 19 mg sodium, 30 mg potassium, <1 mg iron, trace fiber, 6 mg calcium.

• **Variation:** Omit nuts and coconut. At the end of Step 4, add ¼ cup of hot water immediately to saucepan; mix well. Cool completely. Omit step 5. Spoon tayglach pieces into a storage container. Pour syrup over tayglach. Each piece contains 37 calories, 0.6 g fat (0.1 g saturated), 8 mg cholesterol and 8 g carbohydrates.

Chocolate Almond Meringues

One of my students, Monique Rousseau, shared this delicious cookie recipe with me which I altered slightly to produce several different variations. These are truly guilt-free!

½ c. sugar, divided
¼ c. ground almonds
1 tbsp. cocoa

1   tsp. cornstarch
2   egg whites
⅛   tsp. cream of tartar
½   tsp. vanilla (or ¼ tsp. almond extract)

1. Preheat oven to 250°F. Spray a foil-lined baking sheet with non-stick spray. In a small bowl, mix 2 tablespoons of the sugar with almonds, cocoa and cornstarch. In a stainless or glass bowl, beat whites with an electric mixer until frothy. Add cream of tartar and beat on high speed until soft peaks form. Gradually add flavoring and remaining sugar. Beat until stiff and shiny. Gently fold cocoa mixture into meringue.

2. Drop cookie mixture from a teaspoon onto the baking sheet to form small mounds. Leave about 2 inches between each mound. (Mixture could also be piped through a large pastry bag fitted with a large star tube.) Bake at 250°F for 40 minutes. Cookies should be dry and slightly browned. Cool completely. Store in a tightly covered container.

Yield: about 2½ dozen. These can be frozen.

18 calories per cookie, 0.3 g fat (0 g saturated), 0 mg cholesterol, trace protein, 4 g carbohydrate, 7 mg sodium, 12 mg potassium, 0 mg iron, trace fiber, 2 mg calcium.

• **Chewy Meringue Cookies (Forgotten Cookies):** Preheat oven to 375°F. Prepare cookies as directed. Place pan of cookies in oven and turn off heat immediately. Forget about the cookies for 6 hours (or overnight). Do not open the oven door once cookies are in the oven.
• **Chocolate Chip Nut Meringues:** Follow recipe for Chocolate Almond Meringues, but use ¼ cup coarsely chopped filberts. Coarsely chop ½ cup chocolate chips in the processor; fold them gently into meringue. For dry, crisp cookies, bake at 250°F for 40 minutes. For chewy cookies, place in a preheated 375°F oven, turn off heat and forget about the cookies for 6 hours (or overnight). One cookie contains 34 calories, 1.5 g fat (0.6 g saturated) and 6 g carbohydrate.
• **Passover Chocolate Meringue Cookies:** Omit cornstarch; substitute ½ teaspoon lemon juice instead of cream of tartar. (These are delicious with chocolate chips added!)

Lemon Meringue Clouds

1. See recipe (p. 410). Instead of lemon juice, ¼ teaspoon cream of tartar can be substituted.

14 calories per cookie, 0 g fat (0 g saturated), 0 mg cholesterol, trace protein, 3 g carbohydrate, 13 mg sodium, 7 mg potassium, 0 mg iron, 0 g fiber, <1 mg calcium.

Melba Mandel Bread

The only fat in this recipe is the natural fat contained in the almonds! I usually make 4 times the recipe, then freeze the baked loaves. When I need something special, I defrost a loaf, slice it as thin as possible, then toast the slices in the oven. These are addictive!

2   eggs plus 4 egg whites (or 4 eggs)
¾   c. sugar
1   tsp. vanilla
1½   c. flour
½   tsp. baking powder
¾–1 c. whole almonds
2   tsp. cinnamon mixed with ¼ c. sugar

1. Preheat oven to 350°F. Beat eggs and egg whites until light. Gradually add sugar and vanilla; beat well. Mix in flour and baking powder. Stir in almonds. Line a 9 x 5-inch loaf pan with heavy-duty aluminum foil, leaving enough foil extending over the edges so you can wrap the loaf airtight after baking. Spray foil lightly with non-stick spray. Spread mixture evenly in pan. Bake at 350°F for 50 to 60 minutes, until golden. Cool for 10 minutes. Wrap the hot loaf tightly in foil and refrigerate it for 2 or 3 days. (Loaf can also be frozen for up to a month. Defrost either in the refrigerator or at room temperature without unwrapping.)

2. Unwrap loaf. Slice it as thin as possible with a sharp serrated knife. Arrange slices in a single layer on foil-lined cookie sheets. Sprinkle lightly with cinnamon-sugar mixture. Bake at 300°F for about 30 to 40 minutes, until crisp and toasted.

Yield: about 4 dozen slices. These freeze well.

49 calories per slice, 1.4 g fat (0.2 g saturated), 9 mg cholesterol, 1 g protein, 8 g carbohydrate, 14 mg sodium, 29 mg potassium, trace iron, trace fiber, 9 mg calcium.

• **Sheila's Curled Mandel Slices:** In Step 2, crumple the foil that was used to wrap the loaf. Form the foil into a log-shaped roll. Use additional foil and make several more log-shaped rolls. Place foil "logs" on baking sheets. Slice mandel bread and drape each slice over the foil "logs," pressing lightly so that slices become curved. Sprinkle with cinnamon-sugar. Dry at 300°F for 30 to 40 minutes, until crisp and toasted. Serve in a pretty bowl, with a border of curled mandel slices draped over the rim. So pretty!

Special K Mandel Bread (Jewish Biscotti)

In my family, we're addicted to this marvelous mandel bread. I've cut the fat in half, so now we only feel half as guilty when we indulge . . . except when I double the recipe and we eat twice as much! This cookie is very similar to biscotti and is perfect with tea or coffee.

3 eggs (or 2 eggs plus 2 whites)
3/4 c. sugar
1/2 c. canola oil
2 c. flour
2 c. Special K, rice krispies or corn flakes
2 tsp. baking powder
3/4 tsp. cinnamon
1/2–3/4 c. sliced almonds
1/2–3/4 c. chocolate sprinkles, optional
2 tsp. cinnamon mixed with 1/3 c. sugar

1. Spray a large baking sheet with non-stick spray. In a large bowl, beat eggs with sugar and oil until well mixed. Add flour, cereal, baking powder, cinnamon, almonds and chocolate. Mix well.

2. Chill mixture in refrigerator for 15 to 20 minutes. Preheat oven to 350°F. Divide the dough evenly into 4 long, narrow rolls directly on the baking sheet. Flour your hands for easier handling. Leave at least 3 inches between the rolls because they'll spread during baking. Dough will be somewhat sticky. Smooth the tops and make the edges neat with a rubber spatula.

3. Bake at 350°F for 25 minutes, until pale golden in color. Remove pan from oven and cool slightly. Reduce oven temperature to 250°F.

4. Using a sharp knife, cut rolls on a slight angle

into ½-inch-thick slices. Lay cut-side up on baking sheet. Sprinkle with cinnamon-sugar mixture. Bake at 250°F about 45 minutes, until dry and crisp.

Yield: about 4½ dozen slices. These freeze well, if you can hide them fast enough!

64 calories per slice, 2.8 g fat (0.3 g saturated), 12 mg cholesterol, 1 g protein, 9 g carbohydrate, 22 mg sodium, 22 mg potassium, <1 mg iron, trace fiber, 6 mg calcium.

- **When using certain brands** of sprinkles, the color may "bleed" into the mandel bread. My mother substitutes 2 squares of grated bitter-sweet or semi-sweet chocolate for the sprinkles. (Each square [1 oz./28 grams] yields ¼ cup when grated.) One slice of mandel bread made with grated chocolate contains 69 calories, 3.2 g fat (0.5 g saturated), 12 mg cholesterol and 9 g carbohydrate.
- **Shaping Tip!** My friend Barb Sotolov of Winnipeg liked to use 3 metal ice cube trays (sprayed with non-stick spray) to bake her mandel bread. This keeps rolls uniform in width and prevents spreading. (Trays may be difficult to find. Check at new or used appliance stores, or in Grandma's cupboard!)

Chocolate Chewies

See photo (P-16). Pretty as a picture! These are a chocoholic's delight. For a lower calorie version, make Rice Krispie Chewies (below).

½ c. unsweetened cocoa
2   c. icing sugar
2   tbsp. flour
3   egg whites
½   tsp. vanilla
1¾ c. low-fat granola cereal
¼   c. finely chopped almonds or walnuts

1. Preheat oven to 350°F. Line 2 baking sheets with aluminum foil and spray with non-stick spray. In the large bowl of an electric mixer, combine cocoa, icing sugar and flour. Blend in egg whites on low speed. Increase to high speed and beat 1 to 2 minutes longer. Stir in vanilla, cereal and nuts.

2. Drop mixture by rounded teaspoonfuls on baking sheets, leaving about 2 inches between cookies. Press tops slightly with the bottom of a small glass to flatten. Bake on middle rack at 350°F for about 15 minutes, until set and crispy. Cool completely. Store in an airtight container.

Yield: about 4 dozen. Can be frozen.

41 calories per cookie, 0.7 g fat (0.1 g saturated), 0 mg cholesterol, <1 g protein, 9 g carbohydrate, 14 mg sodium, 33 mg potassium, trace iron, < 1 g fiber, 3 mg calcium.

- **Rice Krispie Chewies:** Substitute 2 cups of rice krispie cereal for granola. Each cookie contains 32 calories, 7 g carbohydrate and 0.5 g fat (0.1 g saturated).

Less Sinful Cinnamon Twists

See photo (P-10). A slimmed-down treasure from my late Baba (grandmother), Doba Rykiss. This recipe has been handed down from generation to generation and evokes marvellous taste memories.

3	eggs (or 2 eggs plus 2 whites)
1	c. sugar
$\frac{1}{2}$	c. canola oil
3	c. flour
2	tsp. baking powder
2	tsp. cinnamon mixed with $\frac{1}{3}$ c. sugar

1. Preheat oven to 350°F. Combine eggs, sugar and oil; mix well. Add flour and baking powder. Mix just until flour disappears. Use a scant tablespoon of dough for each cookie. Roll dough between your palms to make pencil-shaped rolls about 5 inches long. Shape into half-twists (like half of a figure 8). These can also be made into crescents or letters of the alphabet! Roll in cinnamon-sugar. Place on foil-lined cookie sheets sprayed with non-stick spray. Bake at 350°F for 15 minutes, until golden and crisp.

Yield: 4 dozen. These are yummy right from the freezer, so hide them from the cookie monster!

74 calories per cookie, 2.6 g fat (0.2 g saturated), 9 mg cholesterol, 1 g protein, 12 g carbohydrate, 15 mg sodium, 19 mg potassium, trace iron, trace fiber, 4 mg calcium.

Oatmeal Cookies

1	c. flour
1	c. rolled oats (regular or quick-cooking)
$\frac{1}{2}$	c. sugar (white or brown)
$\frac{1}{2}$	tsp. baking powder
$\frac{1}{2}$	tsp. baking soda
$\frac{1}{4}$	tsp. salt
1	tsp. cinnamon
2	egg whites
$\frac{1}{4}$	c. canola oil
$\frac{1}{3}$	c. corn syrup
1	tsp. vanilla
$\frac{2}{3}$	c. raisins or dried cranberries, rinsed & drained

1. Preheat oven to 375°F. Line a large baking sheet with foil and spray with non-stick spray. In a large mixing bowl, combine flour, oats, sugar, baking powder, soda, salt and cinnamon. Add remaining ingredients and stir until well mixed. Drop from a teaspoon 2 inches apart onto prepared pan. Press slightly to flatten. Bake on middle rack of oven at 375°F about 10 minutes, until set and golden. Remove pan from oven and let cool. Cookies will become crisp upon standing.

Yield: about $3\frac{1}{2}$ dozen cookies. These freeze well.

55 calories per cookie, 1.5 g fat (0.1 g saturated), 0 mg cholesterol, <1 g protein, 10 g carbohydrate, 40 mg sodium, 34 mg potassium, trace iron, trace fiber, 4 mg calcium.

- **Oatmeal Chocolate Chip Cookies:** Substitute chocolate chips for the raisins. Yummy! Each cookie contains 60 calories, 10 g carbohydrate and 2.2 g fat (0.6 saturated).

Square Moon Cookies (Poppy Seed Cookies)

½ c. sugar
3 egg whites
⅓ c. canola oil
1 tbsp. lemon or orange juice
1 tsp. grated lemon or orange zest
¼ c. poppy seeds
2 c. flour
1 tsp. baking powder
⅛ tsp. baking soda

Topping:
1 additional egg white
¼ c. additional sugar

1. Beat sugar, egg whites and oil until light. Add remaining ingredients except those for the topping. Mix to make a soft dough. Divide into 3 balls. Refrigerate at least ½ hour. Preheat oven to 350°F. Spray the back of a cookie sheet with non-stick spray. Flour dough lightly. Roll out dough very thin into a rectangle on the back of the cookie sheet. Trim edges. Prick dough with a fork. Brush with egg white; sprinkle with sugar. Cut with a pastry wheel or pizza cutter into 2-inch squares. Bake at 350°F for 8 to 10 minutes. When cool, separate cookies on the lines you made with the pastry wheel.

Yield: about 4 dozen cookies. Dough can be frozen and baked when needed. Cookies freeze well.

50 calories per cookie, 1.9 g fat (0.2 g saturated), 0 mg cholesterol, 1 g protein, 7 g carbohydrate, 17 mg sodium, 18 mg potassium, trace iron, trace fiber, 12 mg calcium.

The New "Cream Cheese" Pastry

Whenever I need dough that is fail-proof, this is the recipe I use. Both versions are excellent.

Variation #1:
½ c. "Better Than Butter" (p. 125), chilled
½ c. pressed non-fat cottage cheese (or low-fat or non-fat cream cheese)
1 c. flour

Variation #2:
½ c. tub margarine, chilled
½ c. pressed non-fat cottage cheese (or low-fat cream cheese)
1 c. flour

1. Cut "butter" and cheese into 1-inch pieces. Combine with flour in the processor. Process with quick on/off pulses to start, then let the machine run until mixture forms a ball, about 20 seconds. If dough seems soft, add an extra tablespoon of flour. Chill dough for 20 to 30 minutes before using.

Yield: two 9-inch circles of dough. This dough freezes beautifully. Recipe can be doubled easily.

Variation #1: 1,190 calories per recipe, 72.8 g fat (24.9 g saturated), 107 mg cholesterol, 31 g protein, 103 g carbohydrate, 768 mg sodium, 323 mg potassium, 6 mg iron, 3 g fiber, 169 mg calcium.

Variation #2: 1,348 calories per recipe, 92.6 g fat (16.2 g saturated), 10 mg cholesterol, 29 g protein, 100 g carbohydrate, 1,144 mg sodium, 252 mg potassium, 6 mg iron, 3 g fiber, 109 mg calcium.

- **Use this dough** for your favorite fruit pie, Hamentashen (p. 376), Apricot Rogelach (p. 375) or Sugar Cookies (below). Variation #1 has the taste of butter and contains less calories and total fat (but more saturated fat and cholesterol) than Variation #2. The choice is yours.

- **Please note my analyses** have been done for a full recipe of dough to show the difference in nutrients between each variation. A full recipe makes 24 cookies, so don't panic!
- **Just compare!** The traditional recipe for Cream Cheese Pastry made with butter and cream cheese contains 1,674 calories per recipe, 133.8 g fat (81.9 g saturated) and 370 mg cholesterol. Wow!

Sugar Cookies

See photo (P-10). Kids of all ages love these!

The New "Cream Cheese Pastry" (see previous recipe)
2   egg whites, lightly beaten
2   tbsp. sugar

1. Prepare dough as directed. Preheat oven to 350°F. Roll out dough on a lightly floured surface 1/8 inch thick. Using assorted cookie cutters, cut dough into shapes. Brush lightly with beaten egg white and sprinkle with sugar. Place on a sprayed foil-lined cookie sheet. Bake at 350°F for 10 minutes.

Yield: about 2 dozen cookies. These freeze very well.

55 calories per cookie, 3 g fat (1 g saturated), 5 mg cholesterol, 2 g protein, 5 g carbohydrate, 41 mg sodium, 17 mg potassium, trace iron, trace fiber, 7 mg calcium.

Apricot Rogelach

See photos (P-10, P-11). Rogelach are usually topped with finely ground nuts, cinnamon and sugar. In this updated version, low-fat granola cereal makes an excellent substitution for nuts, and apricot jam provides a wonderful flavor. Raspberry preserves are also delicious!

The New "Cream Cheese Pastry" (p. 374)
1/2 c. low-fat granola cereal
1/2 c. apricot preserves (reduced sugar)
Icing sugar, if desired

1. Line a cookie sheet with foil. Spray with non-stick spray. Preheat oven to 375°F. Prepare dough as directed. Divide dough into 2 balls. Flour each piece of dough lightly. Roll out on a lightly floured surface into a circle about 1/16 inch thick. Crush or grind cereal to make fine crumbs.

2. Spread each circle of dough with 1/4 cup jam. Sprinkle with half of the crushed granola. Cut each piece of dough into 12 triangles. Roll up from the outside edge toward the center. Place on prepared cookie sheet. Bake at 375°F for 18 to 20 minutes, until lightly browned. If desired, sprinkle with icing sugar when completely cool.

Yield: 2 dozen. Recipe can be doubled easily. These freeze very well.

69 calories per cookie, 3.2 g fat (1 g saturated), 5 mg cholesterol, 2 g protein, 9 g carbohydrate, 37 mg sodium, 23 mg potassium, trace iron, <1 g fiber, 7 mg calcium.

- **Analysis was done** using Variation #1 of Cream Cheese Pastry. With Variation #2 of the dough, each cookie contains 76 calories, 4 g fat (0.7 saturated) and trace cholesterol.

• **If desired, brush unbaked** Rogelach with lightly beaten egg white before baking, but don't sprinkle them with icing sugar after baking.

Date-Apricot Filling (for Hamentashen)

2   c. pitted dates
1½ c. dried apricots
½   c. sultana raisins
2   tsp. grated lemon rind, if desired
3   tbsp. almonds, coarsely chopped

1. Combine all ingredients in the processor and process until minced, about 20 seconds. Scrape down sides of the bowl as necessary.

Yield: about 3 cups filling. One cup of filling is enough to fill about 12 to 16 hamentashen, depending on size. You can also use this mixture in Dried Fruit Strudel (p. 378). Mixture can be prepared in advance and refrigerated for several days, or frozen.

43 calories per tbsp., 0.3 g fat (0 g saturated), 0 mg cholesterol, <1 g protein, 10 g carbohydrate, <1 mg sodium, 133 mg potassium, trace iron, 1 g fiber, 7 mg calcium.

Five-Fruit Filling (for Hamentashen)

1   medium seedless orange (thin-skinned)
1   c. raisins
1   c. pitted dates
1   c. pitted prunes
1   c. dried apricots

1. Cut orange into chunks, but do not peel. Cut away both the navel and the stem end. In the processor, process orange until finely ground, about 20 seconds. Add remaining ingredients and process until finely ground, about 15 to 20 seconds. Scrape down sides of bowl as necessary.

Yield: about 3 cups filling. One cup of filling is enough to fill 12 to 16 hamentashen, depending on size. Mixture can be prepared in advance and refrigerated for several days, or frozen.

36 calories per tbsp., 0.1 g fat (0 g saturated), 0 mg cholesterol, trace protein, 10 g carbohydrate, <1 mg sodium, 120 mg potassium, trace iron, 1 g fiber, 7 mg calcium.

Hamentashen

See photos (P-10, P-11). They're so quick to make in the processor, it's easy to make a large batch.

The New "Cream Cheese Pastry," double recipe (p. 374)
Five Fruit Filling (above)
1   egg plus 1 egg white, lightly beaten

1. Line a cookie sheet with aluminum foil and spray with non-stick spray. Prepare dough as directed and chill it until needed. Prepare filling. Preheat oven to 375°F. Divide dough into 4 pieces. Flour each piece of dough lightly. Roll out dough thinly on a floured surface. Cut into 3-inch circles. Place a rounded spoonful of filling in the center of each circle.

2. Bring three edges of dough upwards so that they meet in the center just above the filling. Pinch edges together to seal, leaving a small opening in the center about the size of a nail-head, just so the

Fun With Phyllo

- Phyllo (filo) dough is virtually fat-free. It usually comes in 12 x 16-inch sheets. One pound of phyllo dough contains about 30 to 40 sheets, depending on the thickness.
- If possible, buy refrigerated dough that has not been frozen. Some brands of frozen dough become dry and crumbly when defrosted. Defrost overnight in the refrigerator (not at room temperature).
- Since the leaves dry out quickly when exposed to air, take out just what you need and keep the rest covered with plastic wrap. (I used to cover the dough with a damp cloth, but if the cloth is too wet, the dough will get soggy.) Store dough tightly wrapped in the fridge for 2 to 3 weeks.

- Because phyllo dough is so thin, sometimes the filling leaks out during baking. For easy cleanups, line baking sheet with aluminum foil and spray with non-stick spray.
- Fat Saving Secret! Traditional recipes call for brushing phyllo with melted butter. To replace 1/2 cup of melted butter or margarine, blend 3 or 4 egg whites with 1/2 of an egg yolk. Brush dough lightly and evenly with egg white mixture. (If you are not as concerned about the fat content, brush each layer of phyllo dough very lightly with canola oil.) Some chefs spray phyllo dough with non-stick spray. However, dough sprayed with non-stick spray may shatter if you freeze it.

filling shows through. Arrange hamentashen on prepared baking sheet. Repeat with remaining dough and filling. Brush with egg glaze. Bake at 375°F for 18 to 20 minutes, until golden.

Yield: about 3 dozen, depending on size. These freeze well.

120 calories per hamentash, 4.3 g fat (1.4 g saturated), 12 mg cholesterol, 3 g protein, 19 g carbohydrate, 47 mg sodium, 191 mg potassium, <1 mg iron, 2 g fiber, 20 mg calcium.

- **Prune Hamentashen:** Use 3 cups of Prune Purée (p. 334) for the filling.
- **Date Apricot Hamentashen:** Use Date-Apricot Filling (p. 376).

Phyllo Hamentashen

See photo (P-11). Phyllo dough makes an excellent guilt-free alternative to cookie dough.

    4   egg whites
    1/2 of an egg yolk
    12 sheets of phyllo dough
    Five-Fruit Filling (p. 376) or Date-Apricot Filling (p. 376)
    Icing sugar, optional

1. Line a cookie sheet with aluminum foil and spray it with non-stick spray. In a mixing bowl, blend egg whites with egg yolk. Place one sheet of phyllo dough on a dry work surface so that longer edge of dough is parallel to edge of counter. Brush lightly with egg glaze. Cover with a second sheet of dough and brush with egg glaze. (Keep remaining dough covered with plastic wrap to prevent it from drying out.) Cut dough into 6 strips. Place a rounded spoonful of filling 1 inch from the bottom of each strip. Fold dough upwards once so that filling is covered.

2. Fold the dough as you would a flag. First, bring the right bottom corner of dough upwards diagonally to meet the left edge, making a triangle. Continue folding upwards and from side to side, until the strip is completely folded. Place triangles seam-side-down on prepared baking sheet. Brush lightly with egg glaze. Repeat with remaining dough and filling. (Hamentashen may be either baked or frozen at this point. Cover tightly and freeze. They do not need to be thawed before baking.) Bake in a preheated oven at 375°F for about 18 to 20 minutes, or until golden.

Yield: 3 dozen. When completely cool, sprinkle lightly with icing sugar, if desired. These freeze well.

73 calories per hamentash, 0.5 g fat (0.1 g saturated), 3 mg cholesterol, 1 g protein, 17 g carbohydrate, 44 mg sodium, 180 mg potassium, <1 mg iron, 2 g fiber, 11 mg calcium.

Dried Fruit Strudel

See photo (P-11). When you're tired of shaping hamentashen, make this strudel. It's much faster!

6   sheets of phyllo dough
3   egg whites
½ of an egg yolk
Five-Fruit Filling (p. 376)

1. Spray a foil-lined baking sheet with non-stick spray. In a bowl, blend egg whites with yolk. Place a sheet of phyllo on a dry work surface; brush lightly with egg glaze. Repeat to make 3 layers of dough. Place a narrow band of filling 1-inch from bottom edge; roll up into a long cylinder. Fold in sides of

dough so filling won't leak out. Place seam-side-down on baking sheet. Brush with egg glaze. Make cuts 1-inch apart through the top of dough, but don't cut completely through. (Cuts provide steam vents and make the baked roll easier to slice.) Repeat with remaining dough and filling.

2. Bake in a preheated 350°F oven for 25 to 30 minutes, until golden. Cool completely. If desired, sprinkle lightly with icing sugar. Cut into slices.

Yield: about 2 dozen slices. Freezes well.

94 calories per slice, 0.5 g fat (0.1 g saturated), 4 mg cholesterol, 2 g protein, 23 g carbohydrate, 39 mg sodium, 265 mg potassium, <1 mg iron, 2 g fiber, 16 mg calcium.

Apple Turnovers

If you are not concerned with the fat content, brush each sheet of phyllo dough very lightly with canola oil instead of the egg mixture.

6   large apples, peeled, cored & sliced
2   tsp. cinnamon
3–4 tbsp. brown sugar
1   tbsp. lemon juice
2   egg whites
½ of an egg yolk
8   sheets phyllo dough
3   tbsp. graham cracker or bread crumbs

1. Cook apples, cinnamon and brown sugar in a saucepan until soft, about 6 to 8 minutes. Stir in lemon juice. In a small bowl, blend egg whites with yolk. Preheat oven to 400°F. Spray a foil-lined baking sheet with non-stick spray. Place a sheet of phyllo on a dry work surface. Brush lightly with egg. Top with another sheet of dough; sprinkle lightly with crumbs. Cut into 3 long strips.

2. Place a spoonful of drained apple filling 1 inch from the bottom of each strip. Fold dough upwards to cover filling. Then fold right bottom corner of dough upwards diagonally to meet left edge, making a triangle. Continue folding from side to side until folded. Repeat with remaining dough and filling. Place triangles seam-side-down on baking sheet. Brush lightly with egg mixture. Bake at 400°F for 18 to 20 minutes, until golden. (To reheat, bake uncovered at 350°F for 10 minutes.)

Yield: 12 servings. If frozen, the dough will not be as crisp.

105 calories per serving, 1.5 g fat (0.3 g saturated), 9 mg cholesterol, 2 g protein, 22 g carbohydrate, 94 mg sodium, 101 mg potassium, <1 mg iron, 3 g fiber, 14 mg calcium.

Apple Strudel

Oodles of apple strudel without the guilt trip! Isn't that ap-peeling?

6	large baking apples, peeled, cored & sliced (about 6 c. sliced)
2	tsp. cinnamon
3–4	tbsp. brown sugar (to taste)
1	tbsp. lemon juice
3	tbsp. whole-wheat or all-purpose flour
2	egg whites
1/2	of an egg yolk
8	sheets phyllo dough
1/3	c. graham cracker or bread crumbs
2	tsp. sugar

1. Combine apples, cinnamon, brown sugar, lemon juice and flour in a bowl. Mix well. In another bowl, blend egg whites and yolk. Preheat oven to 375°F. Spray a foil-lined baking sheet with non-stick spray. Place a sheet of phyllo dough on a dry work surface. Brush lightly with egg mixture; sprinkle lightly with crumbs. Repeat until you have 4 layers of dough. Spoon half of the filling along one long edge of dough, leaving a 1 1/2-inch border at bottom and sides. Fold sides inwards and roll up dough. Place seam-side-down on baking sheet. Repeat with remaining dough and filling. Brush tops and sides of strudel with egg mixture; sprinkle with sugar.

2. Bake at 375°F about 30 minutes, or until golden. Fruit should be tender when strudel is pierced with a knife. Best served warm. (To reheat, bake uncovered at 350°F for 15 minutes.)

Yield: 12 servings. If frozen, the dough will not be as crisp.

120 calories per serving, 1.7 g fat (0.3 g saturated), 9 mg cholesterol, 2 g protein, 25 g carbohydrate, 103 mg sodium, 111 mg potassium, 1 mg iron, 3 g fiber, 15 mg calcium.

- **Blueberry-Apple Strudel:** See photo (P-12). Follow recipe for Apple Strudel (above), but use 3 apples and add 2 cups of blueberries. (If using frozen blueberries, thaw and drain them.) Increase brown sugar to 1/3 cup. One serving contains 124 calories, 1.6 g fat and 26 g carbohydrate.
- **Peachy-Blueberry Strudel:** Follow recipe for Apple Strudel (above), but use 3 cups of peeled, sliced peaches and 2 cups of blueberries. Use 1/4 cup sugar. One serving contains 117 calories, 1.5 g fat and 24 g carbohydrate. (Nectarines can be substituted for peaches.)

• **Chef's Serving Suggestions:** Spoon ¼ cup Strawberry or Raspberry Purée (p. 359) onto each dessert plate. Fill a plastic squeeze bottle with lightly sweetened non-fat yogurt; drizzle yogurt in a swirl or zigzag design on Purée. Slice strudel carefully with a sharp serrated knife. Place sliced strudel on Purée. Garnish with a few berries. Apple Turnovers (p. 378) are also lovely served this way for guests. Simply elegant!

Blueberry Apple Phyllo Pie

See photo (P-12). This is fabulous and so easy! What a lovely, lighter alternative to fat-laden pie.

2	c. fresh blueberries (or frozen blueberries, thawed & drained)
3	large baking apples, peeled, cored & sliced
3	tbsp. whole-wheat or all-purpose flour
⅓	c. brown or granulated sugar
1	tsp. cinnamon
1	tbsp. lemon juice
2	egg whites
½	of an egg yolk
5	sheets phyllo dough
¼	c. graham cracker or bread crumbs
1	tsp. sugar

1. Preheat oven to 375°F. In a bowl, combine berries, apples, flour, sugar, cinnamon and lemon juice. In another bowl, blend egg whites with yolk. Spray a 10-inch quiche dish with non-stick spray. Place a sheet of phyllo dough in dish, letting ends of dough hang over sides. Brush with egg; sprinkle with crumbs. Repeat until you have 4 layers of dough. Overlap each one slightly like the petals of a flower. Ends of pastry will hang over sides of pan. Reserve the last sheet of dough.

2. Spoon filling into pastry. Fold edges of pastry inwards to cover filling completely. Top with last sheet of phyllo dough, tucking ends of dough between dish and edge of pie. Brush top of pie with egg; sprinkle with sugar. Cut several slits in top of pie so steam can escape. Bake at 375°F about 45 minutes, until golden. Fruit should be tender when pie is pierced with a sharp knife. Serve warm. If desired, sprinkle with a light dusting of icing sugar.

Yield: 8 to 10 servings. If frozen, dough will not be as crisp.

156 calories per serving, 1.8 g fat (0.4 g saturated), 13 mg cholesterol, 3 g protein, 34 g carbohydrate, 115 mg sodium, 155 mg potassium, 1 mg iron, 3 g fiber, 21 mg calcium.

Madeleine's Fruit Clafouti

My lighter version of her French pudding-like dessert made with peaches, plums, pears or berries.

3	c. fresh fruit of your choice (e.g. peaches)
2	tbsp. plus ¼ c. sugar
1	c. skim milk
1	c. non-fat yogurt
2	eggs plus 2 egg whites (or 3 eggs)
½	c. flour
⅛	tsp. salt
1	tsp. vanilla

1. Preheat oven to 375°F. Spray a 2-quart baking dish with non-stick spray. Arrange sliced, peeled fruit in dish; sprinkle with 2 tablespoons sugar. Combine remaining ingredients in processor. Process for 45 seconds, until smooth. Pour batter over fruit and bake for 45 to 50 minutes, until browned.

Yield: 8 servings. Delicious served warm or at room temperature. Dust with icing sugar, if desired.

145 calories per serving, 1.6 g fat (0.5 g saturated), 54 mg cholesterol, 7 g protein, 27 g carbohydrate, 118 mg sodium, 292 mg potassium, <1 mg iron, 2 g fiber, 110 mg calcium.

Jumbleberry Crisp

See photo (P-13). My cousin Nancy Gordon of Toronto gave me the idea for this fast and fabulous crisp based on her yummy Bumbleberry Pie. I combined various berries, eliminated the crust, and this delectable dessert is the result. If you're missing one kind of berry, just use more of another. If using frozen berries, don't bother defrosting them. If you don't have apples, add extra berries!

Filling:
- 1½ c. strawberries, hulled & sliced
- 2 c. blueberries
- 1½ c. cranberries &/or raspberries
- 2 large apples, peeled, cored & sliced
- ⅓ c. flour (whole-wheat or all-purpose)
- ⅓ c. sugar (white or brown)
- 1 tsp. cinnamon

Topping:
- ⅓ c. brown sugar, packed
- ½ c. flour (whole-wheat or all-purpose)
- ¾ c. quick-cooking oats
- 1 tsp. cinnamon
- ¼ c. canola oil

1. Combine filling ingredients; mix well. Spray a 10-inch glass pie plate or ceramic quiche dish lightly with non-stick spray. Spread filling ingredients evenly in dish.

2. Combine topping ingredients (can be done quickly in the processor). Carefully spread topping over filling and press down slightly. Either bake at 375°F for 35 to 45 minutes until golden, or microwave uncovered on HIGH for 12 to 14 minutes, turning dish at half time. Serve hot or at room temperature. Delicious topped with a small scoop of low-fat frozen yogurt!

Yield: 10 servings. Freezes well.

202 calories per serving, 6.3 g fat (0.5 g saturated), 0 mg cholesterol, 3 g protein, 36 g carbohydrate, 6 mg sodium, 186 mg potassium, 1 mg iron, 4 g fiber, 25 mg calcium.

- **Topping can be** prepared ahead and frozen. No need to thaw before using!
- **Prepare crisp as directed,** but use 6 to 7 cups of assorted frozen berries and omit apples. Assemble in an aluminum pie plate, wrap well and freeze it unbaked. When you need a quick dessert, unwrap the frozen crisp and bake it without defrosting at 375°F about 45 minutes.
- **If you are making** this dessert in the microwave, place a large microsafe plate or a sheet of waxed paper under the cooking dish to catch any spills!
- **Skinny Version:** Reduce oil to 2 tablespoons and add 2 tablespoons water or apple juice to the topping mixture. One serving will contain 178 calories and 3.6 g fat (0.3 g saturated).
- **Skinniest Version:** Substitute 3 tablespoons "lite" margarine instead of ¼ cup of oil in the topping mixture. One serving will contain 168 calories and 2.6 g fat (0.4 g saturated).
- **Fruit Crisp:** Substitute 6 to 7 cups of assorted sliced fresh (or frozen) fruits &/or berries (peaches, pears, nectarines, blackberries, etc.).

Peachy Crumb Crisp

Filling:
- 6 c. peeled, sliced peaches (or a combination of peaches, nectarines and plums)
- 1 tbsp. lemon juice
- ¼ c. brown sugar, packed
- ¼ c. flour (whole-wheat or all-purpose)
- 1 tsp. cinnamon

Topping:
- ¼ c. brown sugar, packed
- ½ c. flour (whole-wheat or all-purpose)
- ¾ c. quick-cooking oats
- 1 tsp. cinnamon
- 2 tbsp. tub margarine or canola oil
- 2 tbsp. orange juice

1. Combine filling ingredients and place in a sprayed 10-inch ceramic quiche dish. Combine topping ingredients and mix until crumbly. Sprinkle over fruit. Bake at 400°F for 45 minutes. If necessary, cover loosely with foil to prevent over-browning.

Yield: 10 servings. Freezes well.

162 calories per serving, 2.9 g fat (0.5 g saturated), 0 mg cholesterol, 3 g protein, 33 g carbohydrate, 24 mg sodium, 308 mg potassium, 1 mg iron, 4 g fiber, 27 mg calcium.

- **Blueberry Peach Crisp:** Use 4 cups sliced peaches and 2 cups blueberries in the filling. Add 1 teaspoon grated orange zest.
- **Blueberry Nectarine Crisp:** Use 4 cups sliced nectarines and 2 cups blueberries in the filling.
- **Apple Crisp:** Instead of peaches, use 6 cups sliced apples. Add ½ teaspoon nutmeg.
- **Strawberry Rhubarb Crisp:** Instead of peaches, use 2 cups sliced strawberries and 4 cups fresh or frozen (thawed) rhubarb, cut in ½-inch pieces. Increase sugar in filling to ⅔ cup. Add 1 teaspoon grated orange zest.

Bottomless Jumbleberry Pie

To save calories and fat, make this without a bottom crust! Use any fruit combination you like.

Pareve Pastry (p. 383)
Filling for Jumbleberry Crisp (p. 381)
- 2 tbsp. skim milk (or water)
- 1 tbsp. sugar, if desired

1. Prepare pastry and filling as directed. Preheat oven to 400°F. Lightly spray a deep 9-inch pie pan with non-stick spray. Place filling in pan. Roll out dough on a floured board into a circle slightly larger than pan. Cut several slits in dough and carefully place it over filling. Fold edges of dough under to make a smooth edge; press with a fork so pastry adheres to the pie pan. Brush pastry lightly with milk and sprinkle with sugar. Bake at 400°F for 40 to 45 minutes, until golden.

Yield: 10 servings. Can be frozen.

217 calories per serving, 7.8 g fat (1.1 g saturated), trace cholesterol, 3 g protein, 35 g carbohydrate, 72 mg sodium, 143 mg potassium, 1 mg iron, 3 g fiber, 19 mg calcium.

Pareve Pastry

*This reduced-fat pastry can be used
for pies, tarts or quiches.*

¼ c. tub margarine, frozen
1½ c. flour
⅛ tsp. salt
2 tbsp. canola oil
3 tbsp. cold water
1 tbsp. lemon juice

1. Combine margarine, flour and salt in processor. Process with quick on/offs, until crumbly. Add oil, water and lemon juice. Process with on/offs, just until dough begins to gather together. Press dough together to form a ball. Wrap in plastic wrap and chill for 20 minutes. Roll out dough between 2 sheets of plastic wrap into a large circle about ⅛ inch thick. Place in an ungreased 9-inch pie plate. Turn edges under to make a fluted edge, or press with a fork.

2. Prick bottom of pastry all over with a fork. Refrigerate for 20 minutes. Preheat oven to 425°F. Bake about 10 minutes, until golden.

Yield: one 9-inch pie shell (10 servings). Dough freezes well before or after baking.

133 calories per serving, 7.5 g fat (1 g saturated), 0 mg cholesterol, 2 g protein, 15 g carbohydrate, 68 mg sodium, 24 mg potassium, <1 mg iron, <1 g fiber, 4 mg calcium.

Cookie Crumb Crust

1¼ c. graham cracker crumbs
3 tbsp. melted tub margarine or butter
2 tbsp. orange juice
2 tbsp. sugar (white or brown)
½ tsp. cinnamon

1. Preheat oven to 350°F. Spray a 10-inch springform pan or 9-inch pie plate with non-stick spray. In a bowl or food processor, combine crumbs, margarine, orange juice, sugar and cinnamon. Press evenly into the bottom of prepared pan. Bake at 350°F for 7 to 8 minutes. Cool completely.

Yield: 10 servings. Can be frozen.

105 calories per serving, 4.9 g fat (1 g saturated), 0 mg cholesterol, 1 g protein, 15 g carbohydrate, 120 mg sodium, 29 mg potassium, <1 mg iron, <1 g fiber, 7 mg calcium.

Festive Holiday Tables, Passover Pleasures

Festive Holiday Tables

As summer comes to an end, we look forward to the High Holidays, a time to gather with families and friends around the festive holiday table, a time for new beginnings. Once again we resolve to eat healthier, but it's difficult to keep focused with so many wonderful aromas coming from the kitchen! Our "taste memories" are easily awakened, and it is very difficult to resist the special dishes associated with the holidays. Don't despair! You can enjoy your old (and soon-to-be new) festive favorites without guilt. If you have vegetarians at your table, there are many options available for them as well.

On ROSH HASHONAH, the Jewish New Year, it is customary to serve round Challah dipped in honey, expressing the wish for a good, sweet year. It is traditional to dip apple slices in honey. Pomegranates can be served to symbolize the wish that our merits be increased like its numerous seeds.

Throughout the year, we try to make healthy, lower-fat choices. For the High Holidays, most Jewish homemakers like to serve traditional roast brisket, veal and other higher-fat meats as a special treat. Kosher cuts of beef are higher in fat than non-Kosher cuts. Sweet'n Sour BBQ Brisket (p. 398) is delicious. Cook in advance and refrigerate overnight. Trim off excess fat; slice thinly. Discard hardened fat from gravy and eat moderate portions. Remember, 3½ oz. (100 g) brisket contains 16 grams of fat, compared to skinless chicken breast with 3 grams!

Fruit & Vegetable Tsimmis (p. 403) is low in fat and includes dried fruits for fiber and flavor. Your guests will savor Blueberry Apple Phyllo Pie (p. 380), which is far lighter than customary pie with its fattening pastry. Berries add a healthy helping of fiber and vitamins, plus a splash of color! Honey & Spice & Everything Nice Cake (p. 344) contains just ⅓ cup of oil instead of a cupful!

YOM KIPPUR (The Day of Atonement) is the holiest day of the year. It is a day of fasting and prayer. Every Yom Kippur, traditional foods such as Challah dipped in honey, chicken soup with kreplach and boiled chicken are served. Kreplach (p. 269) are filled with ground chicken instead of beef to reduce calories and fat. In order to avoid thirst during the fast, one should not eat very spicy or salty foods. Eat small amounts of protein and include foods that are high in complex carbohydrates. Drink adequate liquids before fasting to help prevent dehydration.

We break the fast with a festive meal. Many people prefer to eat dairy foods instead of meat because they feel dairy is easier to digest. A selection of salads, assorted breads, poached or gefilte fish, pasta dishes or kugels often fill the buffet table.

SUKKOT is known as the Festival of Booths or Tabernacles. It commemorates the final gathering of the harvest before the winter. During the seven days of Sukkot, we rejoice at the holiday table inside the Sukkah, an outdoor structure with a roof partly open to the sky. The roof is usually made of branches. The Sukkah symbolizes the frail and makeshift huts which our ancestors lived in during their 40 years in the desert. Often, several families share one large Sukkah, creating an atmosphere of harmony, togetherness and sharing. The special mitzvah of lulav (date palm) and etrog (a citron fruit that looks like a lemon, but with a fabulous fragrance) is performed on all seven days of Sukkot.

SHEMINI ATZERET AND SIMCHAT TORAH are the culmination of the High Holy Days. On Shemini Atzeret, the 8th day of Sukkot, it is customary to eat in the Sukkah. On Simchat Torah, we resume eating our meals indoors. Cabbage Rolls in Cranberry Sauce (p. 176) are lovely for Simchat Torah. Enjoy the harvest of healthy recipes I've created. Have a happy and healthier New Year.

The Festival of Lights—Light Delights for Chanukah!

The Festival of Chanukah (Hanukkah) is celebrated in December to celebrate the miracle that took place over 2,000 years ago. A small band of Jews led by Judah Maccabee revolted against their enemies, the Syrians, who tried to force them to give up their religious faith and to worship Greek gods. The Jews forced the Syrian armies from Jerusalem and reclaimed their temple.

During the rededication of the Holy Temple, when the Maccabees searched for pure oil with which to light the menorah, only one small jar was found. Miraculously, this jar of olive oil, enough to burn only for one day, burned for eight. The story of Chanukah is the story of light, and it brings light and inspiration to Jews all over the world at the darkest time of the year, when night descends early.

Chanukah is celebrated for eight days. The Chanukiah (Menorah) has eight branches, and a ninth holder for the shammes (servant candle). The candles are lit by the flame of the shammes. On the first night, we light one candle. Each night, an additional candle is lit. On the eighth night, all the flames burn brightly.

We spin dreidels (four-sided tops) and give the children token gifts or "Chanukah gelt" (money). Families and friends gather to eat festive meals. Traditionally, in honor of the miracle which occurred with a small jar of oil, we eat foods fried in oil. Potato latkas (pancakes) are traditionally served by those with Ashkenazi roots. Sufganiyot (deep-fried jelly donuts) are traditionally served in Israel. (If you indulge too freely, perhaps your belly will shake like jelly!)

With so many people concerned with healthier cooking, it's definitely time for a lighter latka. What a culinary challenge to make a little bit of oil go a long way. There are many kinds of latkas, including spinach, zucchini, sweet potato, carrots or cheese. Try my No-Fry Potato Latkas (p. 270). Latkas can be served as an appetizer, main course or as a side dish. So let's celebrate Chanukah in a new "lite weigh" and enjoy the pleasures of healthy eating.

Light Purim Delights Fit for a King . . . or Queen!

Purim (which means "lots") is celebrated in late February or early March. It refers to the lots that Haman, the evil Prime Minister to King Achashverosh of Persia, drew to determine the day on which to carry out his plans to annihilate the Jews. The Megillah tells the story of how Queen Esther and Mordechai saved the Jews. Whenever Haman's name is mentioned, the children twirl noisemakers.

What would Purim be without Hamentashen, those delectable three-cornered pastries which come in an assortment of sizes, depending on who makes them! Some families serve triangular-shaped foods, such as Kreplach (p. 269), or Challah shaped like a giant hamentash, sprinkled with poppy seeds.

Hamentashen are stuffed with sweet fillings, including poppy seeds, prune purée or other dried fruits. Do try Five-Fruit Hamentashen (p. 376), made with New "Cream Cheese" Pastry (p. 374) or phyllo dough. My recipes contain no added sugar and fat is kept to a minimum.

It is traditional to send shalach monos (food gifts) to friends and family. It is a mitzvah to send food gifts to the elderly and needy. The custom of wearing masks and disguises on Purim is illustrated in my dessert recipes. They give the appearance of being rich and decadent, but actually are lighter versions of some of my favorites. Fudgy-Wudgy

Brownies (p. 366) are moist and yummy, Luscious Lemon Squares (p. 367) live up to their name. Light, sweet delights—now that's a miracle!

Shavuot—A Dairy Good Holiday!

Shavuot is the Hebrew word for "weeks." Shavuot takes place seven weeks after Passover, on the fiftieth day, in late May or early June. During these seven weeks, no festivities are permitted. Shavuot is the Festival of the First Fruits (Chag Ha-Bikkurim). It also commemorates the giving of the Torah to the Jewish people at Mount Sinai. On the first day of Shavuot, the Ten Commandments are read from the Torah. They are considered the most authoritative moral code in existence.

The synagogue and home are decorated with flowers, plants and fruits. Dairy foods are customarily served. An example is Cheese Blintzes (p. 150), which represent the shape of the Torah. Cottage Cheese Pancakes (p. 148) or Johnny Cake (p. 152) are also great choices. Milk and honey symbolize the land of Israel. Fruits and vegetables commemorate the spring harvest. For dessert, serve Strawberry Buttermilk Sherbet (p. 356), Strawberry Cheesecake with Chocolate Mint Leaves (p. 348) or Moist'n Luscious Carrot Cake with Light Cream Cheese Frosting (p. 342). So say "Cheese Please!" and enjoy!

The Sabbath (Shabbat)

The Sabbath is considered the most important of all holy days. Shabbat begins at sundown on Friday evening and ends after sundown on Saturday. Women and girls usher in Shabbat by reciting the blessing over the candles prior to sunset. The head of the household or any male over thirteen recites Kiddush (the blessing that sanctifies the Sabbath) over the wine. The two Challahs are blessed. The Sabbath meal follows and often there are guests at the table. The meal is social and leisurely.

The finest foods and delicacies are reserved for the Friday night meal. Do try my Gefilte Fish Ring (p. 131)! Glazed Apricot Mustard Chicken (p. 160) and Dracula Chicken (p. 158) are delicious. Vegetarians love Mushroom Mock Chopped Liver (p. 65) and Black Bean & Corn Casserole (p. 226). For dessert, enjoy Three Yolk Sponge Cake (p. 344) or Almost Goldie's Marble Cake (p. 345).

Cooking is prohibited on Shabbat, but foods can be kept warm by covering the heating element with a thin sheet of aluminum called a blech. Foods kept on the blech for more than an hour must remain hot, not warm, to prevent spoilage. For Shabbat lunch enjoy a hearty Cholent (p. 184) or Vegetarian Cholent (p. 224). Shabbat Shalom, Good Shabbos!

The Pleasures of a Healthy, Low-Fat Passover!

Passover is the eight-day spring festival commemorating the exodus of Jews from Egyptian slavery more than 3,000 years ago. All over the world, Jewish families gather around the table on the first two nights of Passover to participate in the Seders. In Israel, the Seder takes place only on the first night. We read the Haggadah, drink four cups of wine and symbolic foods are eaten.

During the eight days of Passover, it is forbidden to eat chametz (leavened products) which contain wheat, barley, oats, rye or spelt. Ashkenazi (European) Jews will not eat kitniyot (beans, peas, lentils, corn, rice or soy products). Many Sephardic

Jews eat legumes and rice. Fresh fruits, herbs and most vegetables are Kosher for Passover. Some Jews won't eat fruits and vegetables which can't be peeled.

In their haste to escape from Egypt, the Jews did not have time to let their dough rise. The resulting unleavened bread became the first matzos. During Passover, Jews are not allowed to eat leavened bread or wheat flour. Matzo is made from special wheat flour, but it must be prepared and baked in less than eighteen minutes, under strict supervision. This prevents the flour and water mixture from absorbing wild yeast cells from the air and fermenting (the sourdough principle of bread baking). Shmurah matzo, which is handmade and round, is baked from grains which have been carefully guarded from the time of harvest to keep them from coming in contact with water.

Many Jews will not eat gebrocks, which eliminates foods containing matzo and its derivatives (cake meal, matzo meal, farfel) that are combined with liquid. In this way they will not eat foods that could possibly ferment. Some Jews eat these foods only on the eighth day of Passover. Other Jews will eat matzo products which are combined with fruit juice but not with water. Consult your Rabbi for guidelines.

In today's health-conscious world, people eat less red meat and more chicken, fish, vegetables and fruit. Vegetarian food is "in." Nearly 14 million North Americans consider themselves vegetarians and will not eat meat, poultry or fish. Vegans also eliminate eggs and dairy products and won't use animal by-products. A wonderful way to celebrate the coming of spring is to include lots of fresh fruits and vegetables when planning your Passover menus, whether or not you are feeding vegetarians.

The fat-conscious cook can lighten up traditional Passover meals by preparing more vegetable-based dishes. Sauté vegetables in water, chicken or vegetable broth. Experiment with fish, chicken and turkey recipes, preferably those using white meat. Experts agree that it makes very little difference whether you remove the skin from poultry before or after cooking. If you refrigerate the gravy or pan juices after cooking, the congealed fat can be removed easily.

Many traditional Passover recipes are based on eggs. One large egg yolk contains 5 g fat (1.6 g saturated) and 213 mg cholesterol. There is no cholesterol in the white of an egg. To reduce the number of yolks in a recipe, substitute 2 egg whites for each egg. I generally replace 2 eggs with 1 egg plus 2 egg whites. If a recipe calls for 3 eggs, use 2 eggs plus 2 whites.

In baking, potato starch replaces flour or cake meal. Ground almonds can also replace flour. As a thickener when converting chametz recipes, substitute 1 tablespoon potato starch for 1 tablespoon cornstarch or 2 tablespoons flour. In baking, substitute $5/8$ cup potato starch for 1 cup of flour, or use $1/2$ cup cake meal and $1/4$ to $1/3$ cup potato starch instead of 1 cup of flour.

Try to choose non-fat and low-fat dairy products. As the demand increases, more products will become available. Do your best to prepare "delight-ful" dishes for a happy, healthy Passover!

The Ceremonial Seder Plate

Zeroah: A roasted shankbone, chicken neck or wing represents the Paschal lamb eaten on the eve of the exodus from Egypt. (Vegetarians can use a broiled beet, as suggested in the Talmud. A mushroom, with its fleshy texture, is another alternative.)

Beitzah: A hard-boiled egg represents the holiday offering brought to the Temple. (Many vegans use either a potato or an avocado pit.)

Maror: Bitter herbs represent the bitterness of

slavery that our forefathers in Egypt endured. Grated fresh horseradish is usually used. Endives or Romaine lettuce leaves are sometimes used.

Charoset: A mixture of apples or dried fruits, nuts, wine and cinnamon resembles the mortar and bricks made by the Jews when they were slaves under Pharaoh.

Karpas: A green vegetable, usually a sprig of parsley or a piece of celery, represents Spring. A slice of onion or potato may be used.

Chazeret: This is another form of bitter herbs, usually endive, watercress or Romaine lettuce.

Setting the Seder Table

The Ceremonial Seder Plate: This contains the six symbolic Seder foods (above).

Three Matzos: There are three ceremonial matzos placed on top of each other in a special matzo cover or in a napkin. These represent the Kohens (priests), Levis (assistants in the Temple) and Israelites (the people of Israel). The middle matzo becomes the Afikoman or dessert following the Seder meal. Additional matzos are placed on a separate plate to be eaten during the main meal.

Wine Decanter and Glasses: You need enough wine for Four Cups of Redemption for each person.

Elijah's Cup: A special cup is filled with wine and put on the table to welcome Elijah (Eliyahu Hanavi), the prophet who heralds freedom and redemption.

Charoset: Although there is Charoset on the Seder plate, extra is often served as part of the meal.

Dish of Salt Water: The Karpas (parsley or celery) is dipped into salt water and eaten to remind us of the tears of the Jewish people while they were in slavery.

Candlesticks: The blessing over the candles is recited before the Seder begins.

Haggadahs: You should have one book for each person. This book includes the story of Passover, including prayers, songs and rituals that comprise the Seder.

Pillows: Pillows are placed on the Seder leader's chair to represent the symbol of freedom from slavery.

The Seder Meal

After eating the ritual foods including matzo, bitter herbs and charoset, after drinking wine and reading the story of the exodus from Egypt, the Passover meal is finally served! The harried hostess needs all the help she can get to prepare a meal for the larger-than-usual, hungry Passover crowd. Proper planning is the key. Do as much as possible in advance. Set the table, make the desserts, choose dishes that can be cooked ahead and that will reheat well. Co-op cooking is a wonderful way to cope when large families gather together. Each cook has their own specialty, creating a rich culinary experience for those partaking in the Seder meals.

The traditional festive meal begins with a hard-boiled egg and/or potato dipped in salt water. (Just the egg white can be eaten by those with cholesterol concerns.) Gefilte fish or chopped liver and chicken soup with matzo balls are then served. It's time to establish new, healthier traditions! Gefilte Fish Ring (p. 131), Passover Chicken Muffins (p. 395), Mushroom Mock Chopped Liver (p. 65), Low-Fat Matzo Balls (p. 394) and Vegetarian "Chicken" Broth (p. 81) are healthy alternatives to start off your Seder meal.

The main part of the meal may include chicken, turkey or roast brisket. A three ounce serving of brisket contains 16 grams of fat, but a roasted skin-less chicken breast has just 3 grams of fat and 2 ounces of skinless turkey breast has only 1 gram of fat! Chicken Pepperonata (p. 396), Saucy Szechuan Pineapple Chicken (p. 158) and Herbed Lemon Chicken Breasts with Mushrooms (p. 173) are all fabulous and guilt-free. Passover Cabbage Rolls (or Meatballs) in Cranberry Sauce (p. 177) are lighter than those made from fatty ground beef.

If you do decide to indulge and serve brisket, try my Coke Brisket (p. 398). The following tips will help trim away excess fat. Cook brisket a day ahead and refrigerate it. Lift off the hardened fat from the gravy and discard it. Trim fat from brisket and slice meat very thin. Less will seem like more!

It has become more common to have some veg-etarians at the Seder table, so why not prepare sev-eral vegetarian choices? Although grains and legumes are not allowed, prepare colorful salads, vegetable kugels, latkas and steamed or stir-fried vegetables. If you prepare Fake'n Bake Burgers (p. 228), Confetti Vegetable Kugel (p. 401), Israeli Salad (p. 280) and Duchesse Potato Mounds with Mushrooms (p. 399), you will delight both vege-tarian and non-vegetarian guests!

Dessert is usually fruit compote, poached pears or fruit salad, cookies and sponge cake (formerly laden with egg yolks). You must try My Mother's Passover Cake, Enlightened (p. 407). Tasting is believing! Ilene Gilbert's Lemon Meringue Dessert (p. 409) is another winner. The delicious recipes included in this chapter and throughout the book provide wonderful, lighter alternatives to tradi-tional fat-laden, "cholester-full" Passover dishes.

Eat small portions of food which are higher in fat. Fill up on soup, vegetables and salads. Choose a fruit dessert or have a smaller slice of cake to avoid indulging. Eat slowly and chew your food well. Use these suggestions to enjoy a healthier, slimmer Passover!

Kosher for Passover Foods

To commemorate our ancestors' flight from Egypt, Jews do not eat foods containing leavening (chametz) during Passover. The following foods are not allowed:

- Barley, bulgur, corn, kasha, legumes (beans, lentils, peas), millet, mustard, oats, rice, rye, spelt, wheat, or their by-products (soy sauce, peanut butter).
- Leavened breads, cakes, cookies, crackers and cereals.
- Products made with flavoring from grain alcohol (vanilla extract, brandy, beer or liquor).

Several categories of foods are allowed for Passover:

- Foods with a label certified Kosher for Passover by a proper Rabbinical authority.
- Foods that don't require a Kosher for Passover label if purchased in unopened packages or con-tainers, or in a natural state.
- Some products are labeled Kosher for Passover for Those Who Eat Kitniyot (legumes). Also, there are different regional customs. For example, Israelis use sesame seeds and Sephardim eat rice and legumes. Manufacturers add or delete items each year, so availability of products will vary. Check with your Rabbi for further guidance.

Foods requiring a Kosher for Passover label are:

- Beverages (juices, soft drinks, wines and liquors).
- Baking supplies (chocolate chips, cocoa, Passover baking powder).
- Candies, chocolates, cookies, cakes, marshmal-lows.
- Canned, bottled and packaged foods (cereals, soups, sauces, salads, salad dressings, fruits, veg-

etables, ketchup, pickles, gefilte fish, horseradish, mayonnaise, herring, sardines, salmon, tuna, puddings, gelatin).
- Cheese, cream, butter, margarine, yogurt.
- Confectioners' sugar (regular confectioners' sugar contains cornstarch).
- Dried fruits (raisins, prunes, apricots).
- Dried herbs and spices.
- Jams and jellies.
- Matzos, matzo meal, cake meal, matzo farfel, matzo cereal, potato starch.
- Shortening, oils (olive, vegetable), vinegar.
- Passover noodles, egg barley.

Foods that don't need a Kosher for Passover label if purchased in unopened packages or containers, or in a natural state are:

- Coffee, tea, granulated sugar, salt, pepper.
- Eggs.
- Fresh herbs, fruits and vegetables (except beans, peas and corn).
- Frozen fruits and vegetables normally permitted for Passover use, as long as they have not been cooked or processed.
- Nuts (but not peanuts, which are legumes).

Date & Apple Charoset

This version of Charoset blends Sephardic and Ashkenazic flavors! It makes a delicious jam-like spread for matzos for breakfast!

3	tbsp. almonds or walnuts
2	apples, peeled & cored
3/4	c. pitted dates
1	tsp. grated lemon zest, optional
2	to 3 tbsp. honey or sugar

3	to 4 tbsp. sweet red wine (to taste)
1	tsp. cinnamon
1/4	tsp. ground ginger, optional

1. Toast nuts at 350°F for 10 minutes. Cool slightly. In the processor, chop nuts coarsely with quick on/off turns. Add remaining ingredients and pulse several times, until coarsely chopped. Serve with matzos at the Seder.

Yield: about 2 cups. (Recipe can be doubled easily.)

26 calories per tbsp., 0.4 g fat (0 g saturated), 0 mg cholesterol, trace protein, 5 g carbohydrate, trace sodium, 37 mg potassium, trace iron, <1 g fiber, 3 mg calcium.

Matzo Farfel Salad (Passover Fattoush Salad)

Salad:

2	c. matzo farfel
6	c. lettuce, coarsely chopped
1	red & 1 green pepper, chopped
1	English cucumber, chopped
1	c. parsley, finely chopped
6	green onions, thinly sliced
5	ripe tomatoes, chopped (reserve juices)

Dressing:

	Reserved juices from chopped tomatoes
1/4	c. extra-virgin olive oil
1/4	c. fresh lemon juice
2–3	cloves garlic, crushed
1	tsp. dried oregano
2	tbsp. fresh mint, chopped
	Salt & pepper, to taste

1. Preheat oven to 350°F. Place farfel on a baking pan and toast for 15 minutes. Let cool. Meanwhile, prepare vegetables and combine them in a large salad bowl. Chill until needed. About 10 minutes before serving, combine salad with ingredients for dressing; mix well. At the last minute, stir in the toasted farfel.

Yield: 10 to 12 servings.

127 calories per serving, 6.2 g fat (0.9 g saturated), 0 mg cholesterol, 3 g protein, 17 g carbohydrate, 14 mg sodium, 326 mg potassium, 1 mg iron, 3 g fiber, 33 mg calcium.

• **During the year,** omit matzo farfel. Use 3 pitas, toasted and broken into small pieces.
• **This refreshing salad** can be turned into a main dish by topping it with a scoop of tuna salad or diced cooked chicken.

Low-Fat Matzo Balls from a Mix

The package instructions call for 2 eggs plus 2 tablespoons of oil. One matzo ball from the packaged mix contains 46 calories, 35 g cholesterol and 3.2 g fat (0.4 g saturated). My version lowers the fat and cholesterol without sacrificing flavor or texture.

1   egg plus 2 egg whites
1   tbsp. oil
1   tbsp. water, chicken broth or club soda
1   packet Matzo Ball Mix
2½ quarts (liters) salted water

1. In a small bowl, blend egg, egg whites, oil and liquid with a fork. Add matzo ball mix and mix well. Cover and chill for at least 20 minutes.

2. In a large pot, bring salted water to a boil. Wet your hands and shape mixture into 1-inch balls. Drop matzo balls into boiling water, cover very tightly and simmer for 20 minutes. Remove from water with a slotted spoon and transfer to chicken soup or vegetable broth.

Yield: 12 matzo balls. These may be frozen in soup.

• **Chef's Secret!** My Mom freezes matzo balls on a cookie sheet, then transfers them to a plastic freezer bag. She reheats the frozen matzo ball(s) right in the soup!

32 calories per matzo ball, 1.6 g fat (0.2 g saturated), 18 mg cholesterol, 2 g protein, 3 g carbohydrate, 119 mg sodium, 19 mg potassium, trace iron, trace fiber, 4 mg calcium.

Low-Fat Matzo Balls

Club soda is the secret ingredient to make these knaidlach (matzo balls) light and fluffy! This recipe can be doubled easily, but be sure to use a large pot and don't peek during cooking!

½   c. matzo meal
½   tsp. salt
⅛   tsp. pepper
⅛   tsp. garlic powder
1   egg plus 2 egg whites
2   tbsp. club soda (or ginger ale)
1   tsp. vegetable oil
1   tbsp. minced dill
2½ quarts (liters) salted water

1. Combine matzo meal, salt, pepper and garlic powder in a bowl. Add egg, egg whites, club soda, oil and dill; mix well. Cover and refrigerate for 30 minutes.

2. In a large pot, bring salted water to a boil. Wet your hands and shape mixture into 1-inch balls. Drop matzo balls into boiling water, cover tightly and simmer for 45 to 50 minutes. Remove from water with a slotted spoon and transfer to chicken soup or vegetable broth.

Yield: 12 matzo balls. These may be frozen in soup, or refer to my Mom's trick (see "Chef's Secret!" in prevous recipe).

25 calories per matzo ball, 0.9 g fat (0.2 g saturated), 18 mg cholesterol, 2 g protein, 3 g carbohydrate, 120 mg sodium, 19 mg potassium, trace iron, trace fiber, 4 mg calcium.

Passover Chicken Muffins

See photo (P-17). During testing, I wanted to try using potato starch instead of matzo meal in my chicken mixture, but the combined ingredients were too sticky to handle. My assistant Doris Fink suggested baking the mixture in muffin tins, and this recipe was the result! Regular-sized muffins make a great starter, minis make a perfect hors d'oeuvre.

2	cloves garlic
2	medium onions
2	carrots
6	boneless, skinless chicken breasts
2	eggs plus 2 egg whites (or 3 eggs)
$1/3$	c. potato starch (or $1/2$ c. matzo meal)
$3/4$	tsp. salt
$1/8$	tsp. pepper
$1/2$	tsp. sugar

1. Drop garlic through feed tube of processor while machine is running. Process until minced.

Cut onions, carrot and chicken in chunks. Process in batches in your processor until finely minced, about 30 seconds. Combine all ingredients and mix well. Spoon into 12 sprayed or greased muffin cups. Smooth the top of each muffin with a spatula. Bake at 350°F for 25 minutes, until golden.

Yield: 12 servings. These reheat and/or freeze well. Serve hot or at room temperature. Serve with Super Salsa (p. 61).

102 calories per serving, 2.3 g fat (0.7 g saturated), 67 mg cholesterol, 13 grams protein, 6 g carbohydrate, 209 mg sodium, 166 mg potassium, <1 mg iron, <1 g fiber, 18 mg calcium.

- **Fat Saving Secrets!** You can substitute 2 pounds (1 kg) of lean ground chicken. However, if you grind the chicken yourself, you can control the fat content to ensure that no fatty skin is added. Turkey can be used instead of chicken to reduce the fat content even more.
- **Mini Chicken Muffins:** Bake mixture in greased miniature muffin tins for 15 to 18 minutes. They're perfect as hors d'oeuvres, or to put in the kids' lunch boxes.

New-Fashioned Cabbage Rolls in Cranberry Sauce

Refer to recipe (p. 176), but prepare the Passover variation for cabbage rolls or meatballs. These make an excellent appetizer or main dish for Passover.

Quick'n Spicy Turkey Meat Loaf

Refer to recipe (p. 179). Prepare as directed, using granulated sugar instead of brown sugar, and matzo meal instead of quick-cooking oats. This mixture is also excellent for meatballs or patties.

Herbed Lemon Chicken Breasts with Mushrooms

Luscious! See recipe (p. 173). Prepare chicken as directed, using white wine, fresh rosemary and thyme.

Chicken Pepperonata

See photo (P-18). A wonderful main dish for your Seder or all year 'round! This scrumptious dish certainly doesn't taste like the usual Passover chicken! It's sure to become a new family favorite.

12 boneless, skinless chicken breasts, trimmed of fat
Pepper & paprika, to taste
2 tbsp. olive or vegetable oil
3 tbsp. lemon juice (juice of a lemon)
4 green peppers, cut into strips
2 red peppers, cut into strips
4 onions, sliced
28 oz. can (796 ml) tomatoes, drained & chopped
5½ oz. can (156 ml) tomato paste
½ c. Passover sweet or dry red wine
3–4 cloves garlic, minced
2 tbsp. sugar or honey (to taste)
1 tbsp. additional lemon juice (to taste)
½ c. raisins, rinsed & drained (optional)

1. Place chicken breasts in a large bowl. Sprinkle lightly with seasonings. Add oil and lemon juice. Rub into chicken. Marinate chicken at least ½ hour at room temperature, or up to 24 hours in the refrigerator. (You can freeze the chicken at this point if it wasn't previously frozen. Defrost overnight in the refrigerator when needed.)

2. Preheat oven to 400°F. Spray 2 foil-lined baking sheets with non-stick spray. Arrange chicken in a single layer on one pan. Combine any leftover marinade with peppers and onions and spread them on the other pan. (If you're short of marinade, add a little more lemon juice to the vegetables.) Bake uncovered at 400°F for 15 to 18 minutes, until chicken is just baked through and vegetables are softened, but still bright in color. Transfer chicken to a large shallow baking dish. Reserve vegetables.

3. Meanwhile, prepare sauce. Combine drained tomatoes, paste, wine, garlic, sugar and remaining lemon juice in a skillet. Simmer uncovered for 10 minutes; stir occasionally. Add raisins and simmer sauce 3 or 4 minutes longer.

4. Pour sauce over chicken. Reduce oven heat to 350°F. Bake covered for 15 minutes. Uncover, add vegetables and mix well. Bake covered 10 to 15 minutes longer.

Yield: 12 servings. Reheats and/or freezes well, but vegetables will be softer if frozen.

237 calories per serving, 5.6 g fat (1.2 g saturated), 73 mg cholesterol, 29 g protein, 16 g carbohydrate, 288 mg sodium, 646 mg potassium, 2 mg iron, 2 g fiber, 52 mg calcium.

• **If desired,** cut chicken into chunks or strips. This makes it easy to serve if you've made several main dishes. Your guests can taste a little bit of each dish without waste or guilt!

- **For variety,** add sliced zucchini and mushrooms to vegetable mixture in Step 2.
- **Serve with Honey-Glazed Carrots** (p. 403) and Duchesse Potato Mounds with Mushrooms (p. 399). The recipe can be doubled easily for a large crowd.

Zesty Garlic Chicken

The garlic becomes mild and sweet after long, slow cooking. So good!

3   onions, sliced
3½ lb. (1.6 kg) chicken, cut up
15 cloves garlic (about 1 head), peeled
Pepper, paprika & basil to taste
11 oz. can (312 g) Passover tomato mushroom sauce
    (or 1¼ c. tomato sauce)
½   c. Szechuan-style duck sauce

1. Preheat oven to 350°F. Spray a large roasting pan with non-stick spray. Place onions in bottom of pan. Remove skin and excess fat from chicken. Place chicken in roasting pan. Crush 3 of the garlic cloves and rub them over the chicken. Season with pepper, paprika and basil. Pour tomato sauce and duck sauce over chicken. Scatter remaining garlic around chicken. Cover pan tightly with foil.

2. Bake chicken at 350°F covered for 1½ hours. Uncover and bake ½ hour longer, basting occasionally with pan juices.

Yield: 6 servings. Reheats and/or freezes well. Recipe can be doubled for a large crowd.

269 calories per serving, 7.6 g fat (2.1 g saturated), 84 mg cholesterol, 30 g protein, 20 g carbohydrate, 406 mg sodium, 577 mg potassium, 2 mg iron, 2 g fiber, 45 mg calcium.

- **Perfect with Spinach Vegetable Kugel** (p. 400) and steamed cauliflower garnished with diced red pepper.

Chicken à la Doris

This quick and easy recipe is an old favorite which I've lightened up. A complete meal in one pan!

2   chickens, cut up
8–10 large potatoes, peeled & quartered
6   carrots, cut in chunks
Salt, pepper & garlic powder, to taste
3   onions, sliced
1   tbsp. oil
½   c. ketchup
½   c. water

1. Spray a large roasting pan with non-stick spray. Remove skin and excess fat from chicken. Arrange chicken in a single layer in roasting pan. Add potatoes and carrots. Sprinkle with seasonings on all sides. In a non-stick skillet, brown onions in oil until golden. If necessary, add a little water to prevent sticking or burning. Combine ketchup and water. Add to chicken along with onions.

2. Cover with aluminum foil and bake in a preheated 350°F oven for 1½ hours, until very tender. Remove foil and bake 15 to 20 minutes longer, until nicely browned, basting occasionally.

Yield: 10 servings. Chicken freezes well, but omit potatoes as they don't freeze well.

376 calories per serving, 10.5 g fat (2.6 g saturated), 100 mg cholesterol, 37 g protein, 33 g carbohydrate, 279 mg sodium, 875 mg potassium, 2 mg iron, 4 g fiber, 48 mg calcium.

Coke Brisket

Brisket is quite high in fat, so serve it on special occasions. Cola makes the meat very tender.

3   onions, sliced
4¹/₂–5 lb. beef brisket, well-trimmed
4   cloves garlic, crushed
Salt & pepper, to taste
1   tsp. dried basil
1   tbsp. paprika
¹/₄ c. apricot jam
2   tbsp. lemon juice
1   c. diet cola

1. Spray a large roasting pan with non-stick spray. Place onions in pan; place brisket on top of onions. Rub meat on all sides with garlic, seasonings, jam and lemon juice. Pour cola over and around brisket. Marinate for an hour at room temperature or overnight in the refrigerator.

2. Preheat oven to 325°F. Cook covered. Allow 45 minutes per pound as the cooking time, until meat is fork tender. Uncover meat for the last hour and baste it occasionally. Remove from oven and cool completely. Refrigerate overnight, if possible. Discard hardened fat which congeals on the surface. Slice brisket thinly across the grain, trimming away any fat. Reheat slices in the defatted pan juices.

Yield: 12 servings. Reheats and/or freezes well.

293 calories per serving, 14.3 g fat (6.4 g saturated), 103 mg cholesterol, 33 g protein, 6 g carbohydrate, 84 mg sodium, 385 mg potassium, 3 mg iron, <1 g fiber, 19 mg calcium.

Sweet & Sour BBQ Brisket

3   onions, sliced
4¹/₂–5 lb. beef brisket, well-trimmed
3   cloves garlic, crushed
1   tsp. paprika
1   c. salsa
3   tbsp. honey
2   tbsp. lemon juice

1. Spray a large roasting pan with non-stick spray. Place onions in pan. Place brisket on top of onions and rub with garlic and paprika. Combine remaining ingredients and spread mixture over brisket. Marinate brisket for 1 hour at room temperature or overnight in the refrigerator.

2. Preheat oven to 325°F. Cook covered for 45 minutes per pound, until meat is fork tender. Uncover meat for the last hour and baste occasionally. Cool completely. Refrigerate overnight, if possible. Discard congealed fat. Slice brisket thinly across the grain, trimming away fat. Reheat slices in the defatted pan juices.

Yield: 12 servings. Reheats and/or freezes well.

300 calories per serving, 14.3 g fat (6.4 g saturated), 103 mg cholesterol, 33 g protein, 8 g carbohydrate, 137 mg sodium, 410 mg potassium, 3 mg iron, <1 g fiber, 24 mg calcium

Duchesse Potato Mounds with Mushrooms

See photo (P-18). These are sure to be a hit at your Seder table! My friend Roz Brown shared the original recipe with me many years ago. I've lightened it up for you and your guests to enjoy. Why not use several types of exotic mushrooms, such as shiitake or portobello? Delightful!

10–12 large potatoes, peeled & cut up (about 4 lb./2 kg)
2   eggs plus 2 egg whites
½ c. chicken or vegetable broth (about)
2   tbsp. pareve tub margarine or olive oil, divided
Salt & pepper, to taste

Mushroom Filling:
3   c. mushrooms, coarsely chopped
2   onions, coarsely chopped
½ tsp. dried thyme
Paprika, to garnish

1. Cook potatoes in lightly salted water until tender, about 15 to 20 minutes. Drain well. Place pan with drained potatoes over high heat for a minute to evaporate excess moisture. Mash potatoes until smooth. Add eggs, egg whites and just enough broth to moisten. Beat well. Add 1 tablespoon margarine/oil and season with salt and pepper. Mixture should be firm enough to pipe through a pastry bag. Amount of broth used will depend on the size of potatoes and how dry they are when you mash them.

2. In a non-stick skillet, sauté mushrooms and onions in remaining margarine/oil on medium-high heat until nicely browned. If necessary, add a little broth. Season with salt, pepper and thyme.

3. Line a baking sheet with foil and spray with non-stick spray. Place potato mixture in a large pastry bag fitted with a large star tube. Pipe potatoes into mounds onto prepared baking sheet, leaving a small opening in the center of each mound. Spoon in some of the mushroom filling. Sprinkle lightly with paprika. (Can be prepared ahead of time.) Bake uncovered at 400°F for 20 minutes, until golden.

Yield: 12 servings. Reheats well. Do not freeze.

159 calories per serving, 3 g fat (0.7 g saturated), 35 mg cholesterol, 5 g protein, 29 g carbohydrate, 59 mg sodium, 530 mg potassium, <1 mg iron, 3 g fiber, 22 mg calcium.

- **Potato Surprise:** Spread half of potato mixture in the bottom of a sprayed oblong casserole. Spread mushroom filling evenly over potatoes. Top with remaining potato mixture. Sprinkle with paprika and ¼ cup lightly seasoned matzo meal. Bake at 400°F for 30 minutes, until golden.
- **Duchesse Potatoes with Almonds:** Follow recipe above, but omit mushroom filling. Pipe potatoes into mounds on prepared baking sheet. Insert a few sliced or slivered almonds partway into each mound. Sprinkle lightly with paprika. Bake at 400°F for 20 minutes. Lovely for guests!

Spaghetti Squash "Noodle" Pudding

See photo (P-18). Spaghetti squash pulls into strands like spaghetti noodles, yet it has its own unique flavor. This recipe will have your guests guessing as to what the mysterious ingredient is!

3	lb. (1.2 kg) spaghetti squash (approximately)
2	onions, chopped
2	cloves garlic, crushed
1	tbsp. olive oil
1	medium zucchini, finely grated
2	medium carrots, finely grated
2	eggs plus 4 egg whites (or 4 eggs)
1/2	c. matzo meal
2	tbsp. chopped fresh basil (or 1 tsp. dried)

Salt & pepper, to taste

1. Cut squash in half. Place cut-side down on a sprayed foil-lined pan. Bake at 350°F about 45 minutes, until tender. (Alternately, do not cut squash in half. Pierce it in several places with a fork. Microwave on HIGH until tender, 15 to 18 minutes, turning it over at half time. Let stand 15 minutes. Cut in half and let cool.)

2. Preheat oven to 375°F. In a non-stick skillet, sauté onions and garlic in oil for 5 minutes. Add zucchini and carrots and cook on medium heat until tender-crisp, about 5 minutes longer, stirring often. If necessary, add a little water to prevent burning or sticking. Cool slightly.

3. Discard squash seeds. Use a fork to pull out strands of squash. In a large mixing bowl, combine squash with remaining ingredients; season to taste. Transfer mixture to a sprayed 2-quart rectangular or oval casserole. Bake at 375°F for 50 to 60 minutes, until golden.

Yield: 10 to 12 servings. Reheats well.

101 calories per serving, 2.8 g fat (0.6 g saturated), 42 mg cholesterol, 5 g protein, 15 g carbohydrate, 87 mg sodium, 269 mg potassium, <1 mg iron, 3 g fiber, 43 mg calcium.

- **This recipe can be baked** in sprayed individual ramekins or muffin pans. Bake at 375°F for 25 to 30 minutes, until golden.
- **Delicious served** as a dairy dish with non-fat yogurt.
- **Cooked spaghetti squash** is excellent served as an alternative to pasta during Passover. Top the strands of spaghetti squash with your favorite recipe of ratatouille or tomato sauce.

Spinach Vegetable Kugel

The vegetables for this colorful, vitamin-packed kugel can be prepared quickly in the food processor. Double the recipe for a large crowd. It's a winner! Use frozen spinach instead of fresh if you prefer.

10	oz. pkg. (300 g) fresh spinach
2	onions, chopped
1	stalk celery, chopped
1	red pepper, chopped
3	carrots, grated
1	c. mushrooms, chopped
1	tbsp. olive oil
2	eggs plus 2 whites (or 3 eggs)
3/4	tsp. salt
1/4	tsp. each pepper & garlic powder
1/2	tsp. dried basil
1/4	c. matzo meal

1. Preheat oven to 350°F. Wash spinach thoroughly. Remove and discard tough stems. Cook spinach in a covered saucepan until wilted, about 3 minutes (or microwave on HIGH for 4 minutes).

Don't add any water. The water clinging to the leaves will provide enough steam to cook it. Cool and squeeze dry.

2. Heat oil in a non-stick skillet on medium heat. Sauté onions, celery, red pepper and carrots for 5 minutes, until golden. Add mushrooms and cook 5 minutes longer. (Or cook vegetables uncovered in the microwave for 6 to 8 minutes on HIGH.)

3. Chop spinach coarsely. Combine with remaining ingredients and mix well. Pour into a sprayed 7 x 11-inch Pyrex casserole. Bake uncovered at 350°F for 45 to 50 minutes, until firm. Cut in squares to serve.

Yield: 10 to 12 servings. Reheats well or may be frozen.

81 calories per serving, 2.7 g fat (0.5 g saturated), 42 mg cholesterol, 4 g protein, 11 g carbohydrate, 241 mg sodium, 257 mg potassium, 2 mg iron, 2 g fiber, 52 mg calcium.

• **Spinach Muffins:** Follow recipe above, but spoon batter into 12 sprayed muffin cups. Bake at 350°F for about 25 minutes, until golden. Serve as a side dish with meat, poultry or fish. Great for the lunch box!

Passover Noodle Kugel

Refer to recipe for Noodle & Spinach Kugel (p. 272), but use Passover noodles and cook them according to package directions. Fresh spinach can be substituted for frozen, if desired. Use Passover olive or vegetable oil.

Confetti Vegetable Kugel

See photo (P-18). So colorful, so delicious! Excellent for vegetarians and non-vegetarians.

3	medium zucchini, unpeeled (1 lb./500 g)
3	carrots, peeled
2	sweet potatoes or 3 large potatoes, peeled (about 1 lb./500 g)
2	medium onions
2	cloves garlic
1/2	c. parsley leaves
3–4	tbsp. chopped fresh basil (or 1 tsp. dried)
4	eggs plus 4 egg whites (or 6 eggs)
1/2	c. potato starch or matzo meal
1 1/4	tsp. salt (to taste)
1/2	tsp. pepper (to taste)
2	tsp. olive oil

1. Preheat oven to 375°F. Grate zucchini, carrots and sweet potatoes. (Can be done in the food processor.) Finely mince onions, garlic, parsley and basil. Combine all ingredients in a large mixing bowl and mix well. Spray a 3-quart rectangular or oval casserole with non-stick spray. Add vegetable mixture and spread evenly. Bake at 375°F for 1 hour and 10 minutes, or until golden brown and firm.

Yield: 12 servings. Freezes and/or reheats well.

101 calories per serving, 2.7 g fat (0.7 g saturated), 71 mg cholesterol, 4 g protein, 15 g carbohydrate, 315 mg sodium, 280 mg potassium, <1 mg iron, 2 g fiber, 35 mg calcium.

• **Mixture can be baked** in sprayed muffin tins at 375°F for 25 to 30 minutes, until golden brown.
• **Recipe may be halved.** Bake in a 1 1/2-quart greased casserole for 45 to 55 minutes.

Apple & Apricot Kugel

"Out of this world!" according to Joy Bucknoff, who shared her yummy recipe with me.

6   eggs, beaten (or 4 eggs plus 4 whites)
½   c. sugar
6   apples, peeled & grated
½   c. matzo meal
Juice of 1 lemon (3 tbsp.)
1   c. dried apricots, cut up
2   tbsp. sugar mixed with ½ tsp. cinnamon

1. Preheat oven to 350°F. In a large mixing bowl, combine eggs with sugar; mix well. Add apples, matzo meal and lemon juice. Mix until smooth. Soak apricots in hot water for 5 minutes; drain well. Spray a 7 x 11-inch Pyrex casserole with non-stick spray. Spread half of mixture in pan. Arrange apricots in a single layer over batter. Top with remaining batter; spread evenly. Sprinkle with cinnamon-sugar. Bake at 350°F about 1 hour, until golden.

Yield: 10 servings. Reheats well. Can be frozen.

190 calories per serving, 3.6 g fat (1 g saturated), 127 mg cholesterol, 5 g protein, 37 g carbohydrate, 40 mg sodium, 308 mg potassium, 1 mg iron, 4 g fiber, 28 mg calcium.

Farfel Vegetable Kugel

3   c. matzo farfel
2½ c. hot water or chicken broth
2   tsp. oil
1   onion, chopped
1   green & 1 red pepper, chopped
1   c. mushrooms, sliced
2   eggs plus 2 whites (or 3 eggs)
Salt & pepper, to taste
½   tsp. each dried basil & thyme

1. Preheat oven to 375°F. Place farfel in a large mixing bowl. Add hot water or broth and let stand for 5 minutes to soften. Drain excess liquid. Meanwhile, heat oil in a non-stick skillet. Add onion and peppers. Sauté on medium heat for 5 minutes, until softened. Add mushrooms and cook 5 minutes longer. Cool slightly. Combine all ingredients and mix well.

2. Spread mixture evenly in a sprayed 7 x 11-inch Pyrex casserole. Bake at 375°F for 45 minutes, or until golden and firm.

Yield: 10 servings. Recipe may be doubled for a large crowd. Reheats and/or freezes well.

103 calories per serving, 2.3 g fat (0.4 g saturated), 42 mg cholesterol, 4 g protein, 18 g carbohydrate, 36 mg sodium, 83 mg potassium, trace iron, 1 g fiber, 13 mg calcium.

• **Farfel Muffins:** In Step 2, bake mixture in sprayed muffin pans for 25 minutes at 375°F.

Fake'n Bake Burgers

See recipe (p. 228), but use matzo meal in the vegetable mixture. The variation which includes spinach is also delicious for Passover. However, the variations of this recipe for Grain Burgers and Vegetarian Burgers are not for Passover use.

No-Dough Potato Knishes

See recipe (p. 270), but use Passover olive or vegetable oil instead of canola oil. Use matzo meal instead of seasoned bread crumbs in the potato mixture. These are an excellent side dish for Passover!

Honey-Glazed Carrots

This fat-free recipe makes a large quantity, perfect for a Seder. For a smaller family, make half the amount. Leftovers reheat beautifully. During the year, substitute cornstarch for potato starch.

4   lb. carrots, peeled & sliced
2   tbsp. potato starch
1   c. orange juice
$^{1}/_{2}$ to $^{3}/_{4}$ c. liquid honey (to taste)
$^{1}/_{4}$ c. orange marmalade or apricot preserves
3   tbsp. lemon juice
Salt & pepper, to taste

1. Cook carrots in boiling salted water to cover until tender, about 15 minutes. Drain off most of the water, leaving about 1 inch in the bottom of the pot. Dissolve potato starch in orange juice. Add to carrots. Stir in honey, marmalade and lemon juice. Season to taste with salt and pepper.

2. Bring mixture to a boil, stirring gently. Transfer to a sprayed ovenproof or microsafe casserole. (Can be prepared up to this point, covered and refrigerated.) Bake uncovered in a preheated 350°F oven for 25 minutes (or microwave covered on HIGH for 10 minutes), stirring once or twice.

Yield: 12 servings. Freezes and/or reheats well.

137 calories per serving, 0.3 g fat (0.1 g saturated), 0 mg cholesterol, 2 g protein, 34 g carbohydrate, 96 mg sodium, 372 mg potassium, 1 mg iron, 5 g fiber, 49 mg calcium.

Fruit & Vegetable Tsimmis

See photo (P-18). In Yiddish, a tsimmis means much ado about nothing. This colorful, vitamin-packed tsimmis is really something! It's not only full of fiber, beta carotene and potassium, it tastes terrific.

$^{3}/_{4}$ c. pitted prunes
$^{3}/_{4}$ c. dried apricots
$^{1}/_{3}$–$^{1}/_{2}$ c. raisins
2   lb. (1 kg) carrots, peeled & sliced
1   sweet potato, peeled, quartered & sliced
$^{1}/_{2}$ c. honey (to taste)
14 oz. (398 ml) can pineapple chunks, drained (reserve $^{1}/_{2}$ c. juice)
$^{1}/_{2}$ c. orange juice
Salt & pepper, to taste
2   tsp. pareve tub margarine
1   tsp. cinnamon

1. Soak prunes, apricots and raisins in boiling water to cover for $^{1}/_{2}$ hour, until plump. Drain well. Meanwhile, cook carrots and sweet potato in boiling water until tender but firm, about 15 minutes. Drain well. Combine reserved pineapple juice with remaining ingredients except pineapple chunks; mix gently. Place mixture in a sprayed 3-quart casserole. Bake covered in a preheated 350°F oven for 35 minutes. Stir in pineapple chunks and bake uncovered 15 minutes more, basting once or twice.

Yield: 10 servings. Freezes and/or reheats well.

195 calories per serving, 1.1 g fat (0.2 g saturated), 0 mg cholesterol, 2 g protein, 48 g carbohydrate, 66 mg sodium, 581 mg potassium, 2 mg iron, 6 g fiber, 52 mg calcium.

Passover Herb Blintzes (Crêpes)

These are used for blintzes or manicotti, or cut into strips for soup noodles. See photo (P-19).

½ c. potato starch
⅛ tsp. salt
1 egg plus 2 egg whites (or 2 eggs)
1 c. water
1 tbsp. vegetable oil
¼ tsp. dried basil

1. Combine potato starch, salt, egg and egg whites. Whisk together until no lumps remain. Gradually whisk in water, oil and basil; mix until smooth. (Can be done in a processor.) Let batter stand for 15 minutes. Batter can be refrigerated up to 24 hours in advance.

2. Use a crêpe pan or non-stick skillet. Grease pan lightly for the first blintz, or spray pan with non-stick spray. Stir mixture well. Pour about 3 tablespoons batter (just enough to cover the bottom of the pan) into the skillet. Cook about 1 minute, until edges are brown and top surface is dry. Flip the blintz onto its second side and cook 10 seconds longer. Turn out onto a clean tea towel. Repeat with remaining batter, stirring occasionally to prevent potato starch from settling to the bottom. If blintzes begin to stick to the pan, grease pan with a little oil on a paper towel.

Yield: 12 crêpes/blintzes. These freeze well.

37 calories per crêpe, 1.6 g fat (0.2 g saturated), 18 mg cholesterol, 1 g protein, 5 g carbohydrate, 48 mg sodium, 14 mg potassium, trace iron, 0 g fiber, 4 mg calcium.

• **Freezing and Heating Directions:** Blintzes can be frozen either filled or unfilled for up to 1 month. Place a double layer of waxed paper between unfilled blintz leaves to make it easy to separate them. For filled blintzes, arrange in a single layer on a cookie sheet, not touching. Wrap well and freeze. When needed, thaw overnight in the refrigerator. Arrange filled blintzes in a lightly greased casserole; brush tops lightly with oil. Bake uncovered at 400°F about 20 minutes, until golden.
• **Suggested Fillings:** Ratatouille (p. 230); Potato, Mushroom & Onion Filling (p. 150). To minimize fat, "sauté" onions in a non-stick skillet in a little vegetable broth.
• **Passover Cheese Blintzes:** Make the filling for regular Cheese Blintzes (p. 150), but use the above recipe to make the blintz leaves, omitting basil.
• **Herbed Passover Noodles:** Follow recipe for Passover Herb Blintzes (above), but substitute 1 teaspoon freshly minced dill for basil. Fry thin pancakes as if making blintzes. Roll each pancake up like a jelly roll and cut into ¼-inch strips. At serving time, add to hot soup. Makes enough for 8 to 10 servings.

Eggplant Roll-Ups

See recipe (p. 233). These are made using eggplant slices instead of blintz leaves. What a delicious dairy dish for Passover! If Parmesan cheese is not available, omit it. Fresh spinach can be used if frozen is not available. Wash it well, drain and cook covered for 2 to 3 minutes. Drain and squeeze dry.

Passover Spinach & Cheese Manicotti

See photo (P-19). You won't believe these are for Passover! During the year, use regular crêpes.

Passover Herb Blintzes (p. 404)
2 c. bottled marinara or tomato sauce
1½–2 c. grated low-fat cheese (Swiss or mozzarella)
10 oz. pkg. (300 g) spinach, cooked & squeezed dry
1 egg (or 2 egg whites)
1 lb. (500 g) dry cottage cheese
Salt & pepper, to taste
½ tsp. dried basil
1 tbsp. fresh dill, minced

1. Prepare blintz leaves as directed. Spread 1 cup of sauce in a sprayed 9 x 13-inch casserole. Combine half of grated cheese with spinach, egg, cottage cheese and seasonings. Mix well. Place 3 tablespoons filling at the lower end of each blintz. Roll up into a cylinder, leaving ends open. Arrange seam-side down in a single layer over the sauce. Top with remaining sauce. Sprinkle with remaining cheese. (Can be prepared in advance and refrigerated or frozen until needed. If frozen, thaw before baking.)

2. Bake uncovered in a preheated 375°F oven for 25 minutes, until bubbling and golden.

Yield: 12 manicotti (6 servings). These reheat well. They can be frozen either before or after baking.

131 calories per manicotti, 4.3 g fat (1.1 g saturated), 44 mg cholesterol, 12 g protein, 11 g carbohydrate, 485 mg sodium, 325 mg potassium, 1 mg iron, <1 g fiber, 217 mg calcium.

• **Serve with Israeli Salad** (p. 280). Fruit salad makes a refreshing dessert.

Passover Pizza

Make sure to allow for second helpings!

3 c. matzo farfel
2½ c. hot water
2 eggs plus 2 whites (or 3 eggs), lightly beaten
½ tsp. salt
¼ tsp. pepper
½ c. matzo meal
11 oz. can (312 g) Passover tomato mushroom sauce
2 c. mushrooms, sliced
1 green & 1 red pepper, chopped
½ lb. (250 g) part-skim mozzarella cheese (2 c. grated)

1. Preheat oven to 375°F. Place farfel in a large mixing bowl. Add hot water and let stand for 5 minutes to soften. Drain off any excess liquid. Add eggs, egg whites, salt and pepper; mix well. Use a 10 x 15-inch baking pan with 1-inch sides; spray it with non-stick spray. Sprinkle with matzo meal. Spread farfel mixture evenly over bottom of pan. Bake uncovered at 375°F for 20 to 25 minutes, until golden and firm. Remove from oven.

2. Cool slightly; spread with sauce. Top with mushrooms and peppers. Sprinkle cheese evenly over vegetables. Return pizza to oven and bake until cheese is golden and bubbly, about 12 to 15 minutes.

Yield: 12 slices. Reheats well. Can be frozen.

147 calories per slice, 4.3 g fat (2.2 g saturated), 46 mg cholesterol, 9 g protein, 20 g carbohydrate, 342 mg sodium, 197 mg potassium, <1 mg iron, 1 g fiber, 134 mg calcium.

• **Substitute 1¼ cups bottled** or homemade tomato sauce or salsa, if desired.
• **Optional Toppings:** Sliced tomatoes, olives, zucchini and red onion.

Quick Matzo Pizza

Quantities are for one pizza. Just multiply the ingredients by the number of pizzas you need.

1   matzo (preferably whole wheat)
2–3 tbsp. tomato sauce
3   tbsp. grated low-fat mozzarella cheese
2   tbsp. chopped red &/or green pepper
2   mushrooms, sliced
4   tomato slices
Salt, pepper & dried basil, to taste

1. Preheat oven to 375°F. Line a baking sheet with foil; spray with non-stick spray. Spread matzo with sauce. Sprinkle with cheese, peppers and mushrooms. Top with tomato slices; sprinkle with seasonings. Bake for 10 minutes (or microwave on MEDIUM for 2 minutes), until cheese melts.

Yield: 1 serving.

193 calories per pizza, 4.3 g fat (2.3 g saturated), 12 mg cholesterol, 11 g protein, 32 g carbohydrate, 293 mg sodium, 549 mg potassium, 3 mg iron, 6 g fiber, 155 mg calcium.

Passover "Sandwiches"

Thanks to Blima Posluns for the terrific idea! An excellent alternative to high-fat Passover rolls. To improve the nutrient content, use 4 whole wheat matzos, broken up, instead of matzo farfel.

1. Prepare the base for Passover Pizza (above) as directed in Step 1, but increase baking time to 25 to 30 minutes at 375°F. When cool, cut it into 12 pieces. Use as a substitute for bread to make sandwiches for Passover!

Yield: 12 pieces. Can be frozen, but be sure to wrap well.

84 calories per piece, 1.2 g fat (0.3 g saturated), 35 mg cholesterol, 4 g protein, 16 g carbohydrate, 127 mg sodium, 24 mg potassium, trace iron, <1 g fiber, 6 mg calcium.

Rozie's Hot Cheese Cake, Passover Style

Roz Brown is known as "Rozie Stewart, the sister of Martha" because of her culinary talents!

Topping:
  ¼ c. matzo meal or mandlen crumbs
  ½ tsp. cinnamon
  1   tbsp. sugar

Base:
  1½ c. cake meal
  ⅓ c. tub margarine, cut in chunks
  ⅓ c. sugar
  ½ tsp. cinnamon
  ¼ c. non-fat yogurt

Filling:
  2   lb. low-fat dry (pressed) cottage cheese
2–3 tbsp. lemon juice
  4   eggs (or 2 eggs plus 4 egg whites)
  1   c. sugar
Dash of salt
  2   tbsp. potato starch dissolved in 1 c. skim milk

1. Preheat oven to 350°F. Combine topping ingredients; set aside. Process cake meal, margarine, sugar and cinnamon until fine. Add yogurt and process with quick on/off pulses, just until crum-

bly. Press base firmly into a sprayed 9 x 13-inch Pyrex casserole.

2. Combine all ingredients for filling and blend well, about 30 seconds. Pour filling over base. Sprinkle with reserved topping. Bake at 350°F for 1 hour, until golden brown. Serve hot. Delicious with sliced strawberries and a dollop of low-fat yogurt sweetened with a little sugar.

Yield: 16 large or 24 small servings. Freezes well.

203 calories per serving, 5.3 g fat (1.1 g saturated), 58 mg cholesterol, 11 g protein, 29 g carbohydrate, 249 mg sodium, 105 mg potassium, <1 mg iron, <1 g fiber, 66 mg calcium.

Passover Cheese Latkas

1	c. dry cottage cheese (non-fat or low-fat)
2	eggs plus 2 egg whites
2	tbsp. sugar
2	tsp. melted tub margarine
1/4	c. non-fat yogurt
1/2	c. matzo meal
1/8	tsp. salt
1/4	tsp. ground cinnamon

1. In the processor, process all ingredients until smooth and blended, about 30 seconds. Spray a large non-stick skillet with non-stick spray. Heat on medium heat. Spoon the batter by rounded spoonfuls onto the hot pan. Brown on medium heat on both sides until golden. Serve with yogurt and berries.

Yield: about 12 latkas.

50 calories per serving, 1.6 g fat (0.4 g saturated), 37 mg cholesterol, 5 g protein, 4 g carbohydrate, 123 mg sodium, 50 mg potassium, trace iron, trace fiber, 26 mg calcium.

My Mother's Passover Cake, Enlightened

See photo (P-20). This is a reduced cholesterol version of her recipe which calls for 9 eggs. I used only 2 egg yolks plus 7 egg whites to reduce the fat and cholesterol. Potato starch is used instead of cake meal. Orange juice and Sabra liqueur provide flavor. So yummy, yet low in fat and calories.

2	oz. bittersweet Passover chocolate
7	egg whites
2	egg yolks
1	c. sugar, divided
1/4	c. orange juice
1	tsp. vanilla or Sabra liqueur
1	tsp. lemon juice
1	c. potato starch (potato flour)
1/4	tsp. salt

1. Preheat oven to 350°F. Grate chocolate and set aside. Place egg whites in a large, grease-free stainless or glass bowl and bring them to room temperature. In another mixing bowl, beat egg yolks for 2 or 3 minutes. Gradually add 1/2 cup sugar and beat 3 to 4 minutes longer, until light and lemon-colored. Gradually add orange juice and flavoring; beat 2 to 3 minutes longer.

2. Wash beaters and dry well. Beat egg whites until foamy. Beat in lemon juice. Gradually beat in remaining 1/2 cup sugar. Beat until whites are stiff and glossy, but not dry.

3. Sift potato starch and salt into egg yolk mixture. Gently fold in whites and chocolate. Don't worry if some white streaks remain. Gently pour batter into an ungreased 10-inch tube pan. Smooth the top with a spatula. Bake cake on center rack of oven at 350°F for 1 hour. Top of cake should be golden and will spring back when lightly touched and a cake tester should come out clean. Invert pan immediately and cool completely, about 1½ hours. (If your pan doesn't have little feet, invert cake over the neck of a bottle or on a rack.)

4. To remove cooled cake from pan, slide a thin-bladed knife between pan and sides of cake. Push up the bottom of the pan; remove sides. Carefully loosen around the center tube and the bottom of the pan. Turn cake over onto a large round serving platter.

Yield: 12 servings. This cake is delicate, so pack it carefully to prevent crushing if you are going to freeze it.

146 calories per serving (without glaze), 2.7 g fat (1.3 g saturated), 35 mg cholesterol, 3 g protein, 29 g carbohydrate, 116 mg sodium, 71 mg potassium, <1 mg iron, trace fiber, 10 mg calcium.

- **Low-Fat Passover Sponge Cake:** Omit the chocolate from above recipe. One serving contains 123 calories, 0.9 g fat (0.3 g saturated) and 35 mg cholesterol.
- **If desired, pour Pareve Chocolate Glaze** (p. 411) over the top of the cake, allowing some of the glaze to drizzle down the sides. Refrigerate briefly to set glaze. Garnish with fresh orange segments. If you want to freeze this cake, glaze and garnish it after thawing.
- **For special guests,** prepare Strawberry Purée (p. 359). Raspberries are not in season during Passover! Instead of Grand Marnier, use Sabra liqueur. Serve purée over slices of cake.

Low-Fat Chocolate Passover Cake

Guilt-free pleasure! The only fat comes from the 3 egg yolks (most Passover cakes contain 6 to 9 eggs)! Separate 8 eggs, but discard 5 of the yolks (or mix with water and feed them to your plants!)

```
3   egg yolks
1¼  c. sugar, divided
⅓   c. brewed coffee (at room temperature) or orange
    juice
¼   c. potato starch
½   c. cake meal
⅓   c. unsweetened cocoa
8   egg whites
```

1. Preheat oven to 350°F. Beat egg yolks on high speed with an electric mixer until light. Gradually add ¾ cup of the sugar and beat 3 to 4 minutes longer. Slowly pour in coffee and beat 3 or 4 minutes more. Combine potato starch, cake meal and cocoa in a strainer. Add gradually to yolk mixture, folding it in gently. Beat whites until foamy. Add remaining ½ cup sugar a little at a time, beating on high speed. Beat until stiff, but not dry. Mix about ¼ of the meringue into yolk mixture to lighten it. Carefully fold in remaining meringue. Pour batter evenly into an ungreased 10-inch tube pan.

2. Bake at 350°F for 1 hour. Remove cake from oven and immediately invert cake pan onto a rack. Let hang until completely cool. Loosen cake from pan with a flexible spatula and carefully transfer to a serving plate. If desired, serve with fresh strawberries.

Yield: 12 servings. Can be frozen, but package the cake carefully to prevent it from being crushed.

134 calories per serving, 1.7 g fat (0.6 g saturated), 53 mg cholesterol, 4 g protein, 27 g carbohydrate, 61 mg sodium, 81 mg potassium, <1 mg iron, <1 g fiber, 12 mg calcium.

Passover Pie Crust

1   c. matzo meal
¼   c. sugar
1   tsp. cinnamon
¼   c. tub margarine or vegetable oil
2   tbsp. orange juice

1. Combine ingredients in the processor and mix until blended, about 20 seconds. Press into the bottom of a lightly sprayed 10-inch spring form pan (or into the bottom and up the sides of a 9-inch pie plate). Bake at 375°F for 15 minutes, until golden.

Yield: 1 pie crust (10 to 12 servings). May be frozen.

92 calories per serving, 4.7 g fat (0.8 g saturated), 0 mg cholesterol, 1 g protein, 12 g carbohydrate, 39 mg sodium, 22 mg potassium, <1 mg iron, <1 g fiber, 6 mg calcium.

Ilene Gilbert's Lemon Meringue Dessert

My friend and dietician, Ilene Gilbert, shared this winner with me. Prepare and freeze it in advance. To reduce fat and calories, omit the crust. You need 6 eggs plus 6 egg whites for this recipe, but one serving contains just half a yolk. This yummy dessert will disappear in a flash at your Seder meal!

Passover Pie Crust (p. 409)
3   whole eggs
3   egg yolks (reserve the 3 egg whites)
½   c. fresh or bottled lemon juice
Zest of ½ a lemon
1¼ c. sugar
3   tbsp. additional sugar

Meringue:
6   additional egg whites
1   tbsp. additional sugar

1. Crust: Prepare pie crust mixture as directed. Press into the bottom of a sprayed 9 or 10-inch springform pan. Bake in a preheated 375°F oven for 15 minutes.

2. Filling: Combine eggs, egg yolks, lemon juice, lemon zest and 1¼ cups sugar in the top of a double boiler over simmering water. Heat until thick, stirring constantly. Let cool. Beat the reserved 3 egg whites until foamy. Gradually beat in 3 tablespoons additional sugar. Beat until stiff. Fold into cooled lemon mixture. Pour over crust. Wrap with foil. Freeze at least 4 hours or overnight.

3. Meringue: Beat 6 egg whites until foamy. Gradually add 1 tablespoon sugar and beat until stiff. Spread on frozen dessert. Broil until meringue is light brown. Return to freezer.

Yield: 12 servings. This freezes well. Remove dessert from freezer 15 minutes before serving.

224 calories per serving, 6.5 g fat (1.5 g saturated), 106 mg cholesterol, 6 g protein, 37 g carbohydrate, 117 mg sodium, 87 mg potassium, <1 mg iron, trace fiber, 20 mg calcium.

• **Variations:** Omit crust. Line sides of springform pan with Passover ladyfingers, placing the rounded sides outwards. (Cut off tips from bottom end so they'll stand upright!) At serving time, garnish dessert with long strips of lemon rind.

• **In Step 1, omit Passover Pie Crust.** Crush ½ pound packaged Passover mandelbroit cookies. Combine with 3 tablespoons melted margarine and mix well. Press into the bottom of a sprayed springform pan, but do not bake. Complete recipe as directed above.

Lemon Meringue Clouds

These guilt-free treats taste a lot like lemon meringue pie! They're easy to make, and fat-free.

3	egg whites, at room temperature
1	tsp. lemon juice
6	tbsp. sugar
1	tbsp. grated lemon zest

1. Preheat oven to 250°F. Spray a foil-lined baking sheet with non-stick spray. In a large glass or stainless mixing bowl, beat egg whites with an electric mixer until foamy. Drizzle in lemon juice and beat until soft peaks form. Gradually beat in sugar 1 tablespoon at a time. Continue beating until stiff and shiny. Fold in lemon zest. Drop cookie mixture from a tablespoon onto baking sheet in small mounds.

2. Bake at 250°F for 1 hour. Turn off heat but don't open the oven door. Leave cookies in the oven 1 hour longer. Remove cookies from oven and cool completely.

Yield: about 2 dozen cookies. These can be frozen or store them in a tightly covered container.

14 calories per cookie, 0 g fat (0 g saturated), 0 mg cholesterol, trace protein, 3 g carbohydrate, 13 mg sodium, 7 mg potassium, 0 mg iron, 0 g fiber, <1 mg calcium.

Passover Lemon Squares

A Passover version of my enlightened Luscious Lemon Squares (p. 367).

Crust:
1½	c. cake meal
⅓	c. tub margarine, cut in chunks
⅓	c. sugar
¼	c. non-fat or low-fat yogurt

Filling:
4	eggs (or 2 eggs plus 4 egg whites)
2	c. granulated sugar
¼	c. lemon juice
3	tbsp. potato starch
1	tsp. Passover baking powder, optional

1. Preheat oven to 350°F. In the processor, mix cake meal, margarine and sugar until fine. Add yogurt and process with quick on/off pulses, just until crumbly. Press firmly into the bottom of a sprayed 9 x 13-inch baking pan. Bake at 350°F for 18 to 20 minutes, until golden.

2. Mix together ingredients for filling. Pour over baked crust. Bake 25 to 30 minutes longer, until golden and set. Cool completely. Cut into squares.

Yield: 48 squares. These freeze very well.

68 calories per square, 1.7 g fat (0.4 g saturated), 18 mg cholesterol, <1 g protein, 13 g carbohydrate, 17 mg sodium, 15 mg potassium, trace iron, trace fiber, 6 mg calcium.

Flourless Fudge Squares

See photo, (P-20). Yummy and decadent.
Cereal replaces part of the nuts to allow
for small indulgences!

¼ c. tub margarine
6 oz. semi-sweet or bittersweet chocolate
½ c. granulated sugar
1 egg plus 2 egg whites (or 2 eggs)
1 tsp. vanilla or Sabra liqueur
½ c. almonds or filberts, finely ground
¾ c. Passover cereal (Crispy-O's or frosted flake-style cereal), finely crushed

1. Preheat oven to 325°F. Melt margarine and chocolate together on low heat; stir until smooth. (You can microwave them together on MEDIUM for 2 to 2½ minutes, stirring twice, just until melted.) Cool slightly. Blend chocolate together with sugar, egg, egg whites and flavoring. Add nuts and cereal; mix well. Spread evenly in a sprayed 8-inch square Pyrex dish.

2. Bake at 325°F for 30 to 35 minutes, until top is dry to the touch. When cool, chill until firm. Cut into squares. Serve at room temperature.

Yield: 25 squares. These freeze well.

88 calories per serving, 5.4 g fat (1.7 g saturated), 9 mg cholesterol, 2 g protein, 9 g carbohydrate, 30 mg sodium, 55 mg potassium, trace iron, 1 g fiber, 9 mg calcium.

- **Complete nutritional data** was not available for Passover cereal. The analysis was done using regular Cheerios, which has a similar nutritional profile.
- **If desired,** glaze Fudge Squares with Pareve Chocolate Glaze (below).
- **For special guests,** prepare Strawberry Purée (p. 359). Raspberries are not in season during Passover! Instead of Grand Marnier, use Sabra liqueur. Spoon a little purée on individual serving plates. Top with a Fudge Square. Mmm . . . decadent!

Pareve Chocolate Glaze

This makes a great glaze for My Mother's
Passover Cake, Enlightened (p. 407).

2 oz. semi-sweet or bittersweet chocolate
2 tbsp. hot water
½ tsp. tub margarine
1 tsp. honey

1. Melt chocolate with hot water and margarine. This takes 1 to 1½ minutes in the microwave on MEDIUM power. Stir well. Add honey and mix well. Cool slightly. Drizzle glaze over the top of your favorite cake, allowing some of the glaze to drip down the sides. Makes enough to glaze a large cake.

26 calories per serving, 2 g fat (1.1 g saturated), 0 mg cholesterol, trace protein, 3 g carbohydrate, 2 mg sodium, 29 mg potassium, trace iron, trace fiber, 3 mg calcium.

METRIC CONVERSIONS

VOLUME – APPROXIMATE REPLACEMENTS

G tsp.	=	1	ml		N cup	=	75	ml
H tsp.	=	2	ml		H cup	=	125	ml
1 tsp.	=	5	ml		1 cup	=	250	ml
1 tbsp.	=	15	ml		4 cups (1 qt.) =		1	liter
G cup.	=	50	ml					

WEIGHTS – APPROXIMATE REPLACEMENTS

1 oz.	=	28.5	grams	kilograms	x	2.2	=	lb.
3.5 oz.	=	100	grams	grams	x	0.035	=	ounces
8 oz.	=	225	grams	lb.	x	0.45	=	kilograms
1 lb.	=	454	grams	ounces	x	28	=	grams
2.2 lb.	=	1	kilogram					

APPROXIMATE METRIC SIZES FOR CASSEROLES & DISHES

8" square pan x 2" deep	=	20 cm x 5 cm
7" x 11" x 2" oblong casserole	=	30 x 20 x 5 cm (2 litres)
9" x 13" x 2" oblong casserole	=	22 x 33 x 5 cm (3 litres)
9" pie plate	=	22 cm
10" quiche dish	=	25 cm
1 quart casserole	=	1 litre casserole
2 quart casserole	=	2 litre casserole
3 quart casserole	=	3 litre casserole

2.5 centimetres = 1 inch   30 centimetres = 12 inches

TEMPERATURE – APPROXIMATE CONVERSION

32°F	=	0°C		350°F	=	180°C
65°F	=	18°C		375°F	=	190°C
100°F	=	38°C		400°F	=	200°C
212°F	=	100°C		425°F	=	220°C
275°F	=	140°C		450°F	=	230°C
300°F	=	150°C		475°F	=	240°C
325°F	=	160°C		500°F	=	260°C

To convert from °F to °C: (°F -32) divided by 1.8 = °C
To convert from °C to °F: (1.8 x °C) plus 32 = °F

Index

-Z-